1987

THE ESSENTIAL ARTICLES SERIES

Volumes Available

ESSENTIAL ARTICLES FOR THE STUDY OF
ENGLISH AUGUSTAN BACKGROUND
Edited by Bernard N. Schilling

ESSENTIAL ARTICLES FOR THE STUDY OF JOHN DRYDEN
Edited by H. T. Swedenberg, Jr.

ESSENTIAL ARTICLES FOR THE STUDY OF OLD ENGLISH POETRY
Edited by Jess Bessinger and Stanley J. Kahrl

ESSENTIAL ARTICLES FOR THE STUDY OF FRANCIS BACON
Edited by Brian Vickers

ESSENTIAL ARTICLES FOR THE STUDY OF EDMUND SPENSER
Edited by A. C. Hamilton

ESSENTIAL ARTICLES FOR THE STUDY OF JOHN DONNE'S POETRY
Edited by John R. Roberts

ESSENTIAL ARTICLES FOR THE STUDY OF THOMAS MORE
Edited by Richard S. Sylvester and Germain Marc'hadour

ESSENTIAL ARTICLES FOR THE STUDY OF
GEORGE HERBERT'S POETRY
Edited by John R. Roberts

Also Available

POPE: RECENT ESSAYS BY SEVERAL HANDS
Edited by Maynard Mack and James Anderson Winn

Essential Articles

for the study of
George Herbert's Poetry

Edited by
JOHN R. ROBERTS
University of Missouri
Columbia

Archon Books   Hamden, Connecticut   1979

Library of Congress Cataloging in Publication Data
Main entry under title:

Essential articles for the study of George Herbert's
poetry.

(The Essential articles series)
Bibliography: p.
1. Herbert, George, 1593-1633 — Criticism and interpretation — Addresses, essays,
lectures. I. Roberts, John Richard.
PR3508.E8   1979   821'.3   79-14033
ISBN 0-208-01770-4

© 1979 John R. Roberts
First published in 1979 as an Archon Book,
an imprint of The Shoe String Press, Inc.
Hamden, Connecticut 06514

CONTENTS

VI. INDIVIDUAL POEMS

VII. LATIN POETRY

PREFACE

During the past several decades George Herbert's poetry has engaged some of the best critical minds of the scholarly world. Primarily because of the quantity and quality of their efforts, Herbert is no longer seen as merely one of the many talented disciples of John Donne or as a simple, pious Anglican versifier, but has now been firmly established not only as a major metaphysical poet of the seventeenth century but also as one of the best poets in the English language. Today most serious students of English literature would readily agree with Joseph H. Summers, who has called Herbert "the author of the best extended collection of religious lyrics in English, a man whose art is as unquestionable as is his spiritual authenticity" (*George Herbert: Selected Poetry* [1978], p. ix).

Although Herbert has been revered and admired by certain critics and readers since his own day, his reputation at the turn of this century was by no means established and assured. In a review of George Herbert Palmer's eccentric, yet monumental, three-volume edition of *The English Works of George Herbert* (1905), Frances Duncan, writing in *The Critic,* called Herbert "a comparatively unimportant poet" (p. 183), an opinion shared by a number of her contemporaries, and warned that American readers, in particular, "with our scanty supply of artistic instinct, our journalistic despatch, our matter-of-fact literalness" (p. 185), might find little appeal in the poetry of this curious Anglican versifier. In 1906, Herbert J. C. Grierson, who was later an admirer of Donne and the metaphysical poets, evidenced a decidedly cool attitude toward Herbert's poetry, and characterized it as didactic and rhetorically quaint; two years later George Saintsbury, though grudgingly admitting that Herbert's poetry is "scarcely ever bad," argued that it "has not the rarest touch of his fellow-disciples, Crashaw and Vaughan." Most early twentieth-century critics, while admiring Herbert the man, the near saint, and respecting his subject matter, the detailed, inner workings of a genuinely Christian soul, felt more than a little uneasiness about his style, his use of elaborate conceits, and his inventiveness in stanzaic forms. Carl Holliday, for instance, in 1910 concluded his critical evaluation of Herbert by charitably acknowledging that "soul-earnestness goes a long way in art and will cover a multitude of technical sins."

Perhaps better than anyone else, Walter S. Hinchman, in an appreciative essay published in *Haverford Essays: Studies in Modern Literature* (1909), summarized the basic conflict that permeated Herbert criticism of his time. After presenting a rhapsodic tourist's impression of Salisbury and Bemerton and offering a hagiographical sketch of Herbert's life and personality, Hinchman concluded that "much of Herbert's verse ... is of a not very high order" and suggested that its "quaintness often renders it dull to anyone who is not particularly interested in seventeenth century lyrics" (p. 82). Hinchman concluded his essay by posing a question that informed much Herbert criticism of the early twentieth century: "We find it hard, under these old trees, to answer the searching question: which is it that you really like — Bemerton, or Herbert, or his verse?" (p. 86). In 1911, F. E. Hutchinson, who was to become, thirty years later, Herbert's major twentieth-century editor, frankly admitted in his essay in *The Cambridge History of English Literature* that the fascination of Herbert "is due as much to his character as his writings" (p. 30).

Yet even during the first two decades of this century, Herbert had his champions, critics like George Herbert Palmer, for instance, who kept insisting on the quality of Herbert's highly conscious art; or A. Clutton-Brock, who in a brief essay in *TLS* (April 1, 1920), cautioned that "It is never safe to reject a poem of Herbert as a failure; the failure may be in you, and with another attempt you may discover a secret beauty which seems all the more beautiful for having lain hid so long" (p. 206); or William Stebbing, who, in *Five Centuries of Verse* (1910), called Herbert "the model, the exemplar, the prince, of sacred poets" (p. 79) and compared him favorably with Sidney. In fact, some of Herbert's most devoted admirers during this period were, in some respects, unwittingly his worst enemies. More often inspired by their own Christian zeal and enthusiasm than by serious critical thought and reflection, they praised Herbert's "elegant sanctity" and piety, calling his poems "sweet roses of undying fragrance from the garden of his soul," and proclaiming that "only to a sensitive and suffering soul will they yield their meaning." Fortunately, however, few of Herbert's most dedicated commentators sank to the sentimental depths of Mary Virginia (Hawes) Teyhune, who, writing in 1910 under the pseudonym Marion Harland, assured her readers that Herbert's "sacred lyrics have been for long, long years songs in the house of my pilgrimage, coming readily to my lips in moments of sudden joy or sorrow, staying my soul under the stress of homely toils and carking, belittling cares as are known, in all their meanness and weariness, to women only" (p. 251). Such endorsements of Herbert's life and poetry, although surely well-intentioned and sincere, contributed to a climate of opinion that most later critics of Herbert, sometimes quite defensively, felt called upon to challenge and refute.

With the publication of Herbert J. C. Grierson's *Metaphysical Lyrics & Poems* in 1921 and T. S. Eliot's review of this important anthology in the same year, Herbert criticism entered a new phase. Most critics would agree that the so-called metaphysical revival of the twentieth century was first of all a Donne revival. Once Donne's poetry became widely known and appreciated not only by critics but also by practicing poets of the day, it was natural that readers would turn to the other metaphysical poets — Herbert, Vaughan, Crashaw, Marvell, Traherne — in the hope that they would find in these so-called disciples of Donne the witty intellectuality, the elaborate uses of metaphor and conceit, and the intense passion and colloquial directness that they admired in the master. Grierson's anthology was one of the first major modern critical statements about the nature of metaphysical poetry, one of the most articulate and convincing descriptions of those elements that early twentieth-century critics came to appreciate most about Donne and his followers. Grierson made it very clear that Donne is "the great master of English poetry in the seventeenth century" (p. xvi), and the other poets considered in his introduction, including Herbert, were primarily contrasted with or compared to Donne. By his introduction and the choice of poems included in his collection, Grierson, in effect, defined for his age the metaphysical school, although he cautioned against an indiscriminate use of the term.

Perhaps as important as Grierson's anthology itself, however, was T. S. Eliot's review of it in *TLS,* in which he announced in its most rudimentary form his theory of dissociation of sensibility, a notion which for thirty years thereafter shaped much of the critical evaluation of all the metaphysical poets. Although Eliot's theory contains a number of inconsistencies and is, by any standards, derivative and undeveloped in his own critical writings, it provided scholars and critics with a ready-made scheme not only for viewing the metaphysical poets of the seventeenth century but also for charting the course of the development of English poetry thereafter. The theory of dissociation of sensibility also appealed because it was a doctrine that could be used to canonize the tastes and preferences of a number of practicing poets and critics of the '20s and '30s. Eliot himself in his later years was somewhat baffled that his phrase had been taken so uncritically and so completely as a valid diagnosis of the development of English poetry. Commenting in *To Criticize the Critic and Other Writings* (1965) on his role in the modern revival of interest in metaphysical poets, he said: "I think that if

I wrote well about the metaphysical poets, it was because they were poets who had inspired me. And if I can be said to have had an influence whatever in promoting a wider interest in them, it was simply because no previous poet who had praised these poets had been so deeply influenced by them as I had been" (p. 22). He added: "As the taste for my own poetry spread, so did the taste for the poets to whom I owed the greatest debt and about whom I had written. Their poetry, and mine, were congenial to that age" (p. 22). What Eliot seemed not to recognize fully perhaps is that much of his critical commentary on metaphysical poetry and on individual metaphysical poets was often little more than an account of his own poetical development at that time; in other words, he found in certain poets of the seventeenth century some of the elements that he most prized in his own poetry. But once the famous poet and literary critic announced his tastes to an admiring world, any number of critics and poets eagerly incorporated his dicta into their own critical thinking. Even today, some twenty-five years after the theory of dissociation of sensibility has been generally discredited, the old notion rears its head in many studies of seventeenth-century poetry. Nevertheless, in spite of the limitations of Eliot's theory, it can never be denied that he, more than any other critic of our time, was largely responsible for the modern revival of interest in metaphysical poetry. It is worth noting that the longest essay that Eliot wrote on a single metaphysical poet was his study of Herbert for the British Council's Writers and Their Works Series (1962) and that as late as 1965, Igor Stravinsky reported in an *Esquire* interview that Eliot told him that "Herbert is a great poet . . . and of the few I can read again and again" (p. 92).

During the twenties and thirties, a number of critical essays appeared that attempted to delineate more precisely the nature of metaphysical poetry and to define more accurately how Herbert fitted into the school of Donne. Many of these studies were simply expansions or refinements of the basic ideas of Grierson and Eliot. Less interested in individual poems of Herbert, the critics seemed insistent on demonstrating how the poetry of Herbert, considered as a whole, met the categories and assumptions that by that time had become generally accepted as facts of literary history. In 1930, George Williamson, for instance, published *The Donne Tradition: A Study in English Poetry from Donne to the Death of Cowley,* in which he intended to compliment Herbert by asserting that "Of all the Metaphysicals, Herbert is in some ways most like Donne" (p. 99). He challenged George Herbert Palmer's claim that Herbert "devised the religious love-lyric" and "introduced structure into the short poem" (p. 103) by maintaining that "rather than give Herbert the emphasis of a pioneer, it is more exact to say that Herbert simply carried on the sacred side of the Donne tradition and developed it in certain ways" (p. 110). While most critics of the time warned against overemphasizing the influence of Donne or stressing too uncritically that likenesses between Donne and Herbert, they often at least implied that the most honorific title that could be bestowed on Herbert was to call him a "true metaphysical poet," which, more often than not from their perspectives, meant most like Donne.

In the mid-thirties three major pioneering books on metaphysical poetry appeared: Joan Bennett's *Four Metaphysical Poets* (1934), later revised and entitled *Five Metaphysical Poets;* J. B. Leishman's *The Metaphysical Poets: Donne, Herbert, Vaughan, Traherne* (1934); and Helen C. White's *The Metaphysical Poets (1936)*. These were to shape the course of critical discussion on Herbert during the next twenty years. Much of the criticism that followed on metaphysical poetry in general and on the individual poets themselves was either an elaboration or a development of certain ideas presented in these three works or, in many instances, was refutation or quibble arising from some comment in them. Bennett made the case that the word *metaphysical* referred primarily to the style of the poets, not to their subject matter, but she also was quick to point out that "style reflects an attitude to experience" (p. 3). She praised Herbert's individual talent: his uses of dialectic structure, concrete imagery, sound patterns that imitate the rhythms of speech, and his metrical ingenuity and experimentation. Like Bennett, Leishman, whose book is essentially an anthology with a running commentary, called attention to some of Herbert's most appealing features: his common sense and humor, his technical excellence and originality, and his masterful control of forms and rhythms. White, unlike the other two, focused her attention primarily on the religious sensibilities and attitudes in Herbert's poetry: the nature of his faith, his concept of God, the note of personal intimacy in his poetry, and his spirit of quiet confidence. While attempting to come to terms with the particular qualities of Herbert's poetry, all three compared and contrasted Herbert to Donne, as well as to the other metaphysical poets; yet often they found certain strengths and qualities in Herbert's poetry that are noticeably lacking in Donne's. Thus ever so slowly, Herbert began to emerge as a major poet in his own right and not as merely one of the better disciples of Donne.

The most significant literary event for Herbert scholarship in the 1940s was the publication of F. E. Hutchinson's *The Works of George Herbert,* which not only provided critics with an important text that was free from the biographical fallacy of Palmer's edition, but which also by its detailed notes and commentary contributed many rich insights into

Herbert's art. Although a number of recent textual critics have pointed out certain inadequacies in Hutchinson's edition, it has remained the standard text since it first appeared in 1941. Also Samuel and Dorothy Tannenbaum's *George Herbert: A Concise Bibliography* (1947) provided scholars with a helpful research tool, even though it is unannotated, incomplete, and sometimes inaccurate. Throughout the decade of the 1940s several still valuable critical studies on Herbert appeared; especially noteworthy are Leicester Bradner's essay on Herbert's Latin poetry that appeared in *Musae Anglicanae: A History of Anglo-Latin Poetry, 1500-1925* (1940); L. C. Knights's "George Herbert" in *Scrutiny* (1944); and, of course, Douglas Bush's survey of Herbert's poetry in *English Literature in the Earlier Seventeenth Century, 1600-1660* (1945). Although neither was centrally concerned with Herbert's poetry, both Rosemond Tuve's *Elizabethan and Metaphysical Imagery: Renaissance Poetic and Twentieth-Century Critics* (1947) and Rosemary Freeman's *English Emblem Books* (1948) made important contributions in rescuing all the metaphysical poets from the excesses of certain of the New Critics by demonstrating that metaphysical poetry was fully informed by large and consistent rhetorical, literary, philosophical, and religious traditions that preceded it and was, therefore, much less radically innovative than these New Critics suggested. A few years later, Louis Martz in *The Poetry of Meditation: A Study in English Religious Literature of the Seventeenth Century* (1954) argued that Herbert and the other religious poets of the period should no longer be viewed as disciples in a Donne tradition, but rather as highly individual participants in a meditative tradition that found its first notable example not in Donne but in the Jesuit, Robert Southwell. In different ways and to varying degrees, all three — Tuve, Freeman, and Martz — contended that by seeing Herbert and the others in the light of seventeenth-century traditions the modern reader is better able to appreciate the genuine originality and the subtle complexities of their art.

The early 1950s marked a definite high point in the history of modern Herbert criticism. In quick succession, three major books appeared, the first full-length critical studies in this century devoted exclusively to Herbert. In 1952 in *A Reading of George Herbert,* Rosemond Tuve, continuing her argument against the New Critics, especially William Empson, maintained that a poem "is most beautiful and most meaningful to us when it is read in terms of the tradition that gave it birth" (p. 22); therefore, she set out to demonstrate that unless the modern reader familiarizes himself with the complex cultural, linguistic, and religious traditions of the seventeenth century, especially the liturgical, allegorical, and iconographical contexts of Herbert's poetry, he cannot arrive at a genuine understanding and appreciation of it. Margaret Bottrall in *George Herbert* (1954) presented a general survey of Herbert's life, personality, and art, commenting with much critical intelligence on the many influences that informed his poetry, the sources of his imagery, and his architectonic skill in creating original meters, forms, and structures. However useful Bottrall's book may be, it was superseded, in most respects, in the same year that it appeared by Joseph H. Summer's *George Herbert: His Religion and Art* (1954), a full-scale study of Herbert's religion as it is reflected in his poetry and a critically engaging interpretation of the poetry in the light of Herbert's convictions and sensibilities. This study, which still remains the best and most balanced overall critical evaluation of Herbert's art, is divided into three major sections: in the first three chapters, Summers explores Herbert's poetic reputation, his life, and his religious thought; in the next two he discusses brilliantly Herbert's theories of form and language; and in the last section, he applies these concepts to the poems themselves. Summers allowed himself only two broad assumptions: (1) that Herbert's art is intimately connected with his particular religious tradition and experience, and (2) that Herbert is "one of the best lyric poets who has written in the English language" (p. 7). Free from the thesis-ridden mentality and the limited historical and/or critical perspectives of many earlier, and later, Herbert critics, Summers admirably supports both of his assumptions.

During the past two decades, nearly four hundred critical essays and books have been written on Herbert, nearly as many as were published on him during the preceding fifty years. Also, several important textual studies and editions of both the English and Latin poems as well as several excellent biographical and bibliographical studies have appeared since 1954. I have listed the more significant ones in the selective bibliography at the end of this collection. Obviously, it is impossible to summarize fairly or to outline comprehensively in this brief preface the wide range of interests and approaches that this vast body of criticism represents. Kenneth Burke, however, in an essay unfortunately entitled "On Covery, Re- and Dis-," which appeared in *Accent,* 13 (1953), 218-26, pinpointed, perhaps more succinctly than anyone else, the major conflict and creative tension that have run through most Herbert scholarship and criticism during the past twenty years. In an assessment of Tuve's argument with the New Critics, Burke contrasted her insistence on "re-covery" of the past with the tendency of many modern critics to engage in what he called "dis-covery," that is, the attempts of modern critics to find "new things about the workings of Herbert's mind by applying modern terms quite alien to his thinking" (p. 218). Burke, while applauding Tuve's fine scholarship, suggested that her approach and her conception of art were perhaps too restrictive and that if modern readers accepted her position too rigidly many of the most productive and rewarding ways of viewing Herbert's art would be closed to them. The debate, of course, cannot be resolved in this introduction, nor is it my purpose to engage in it. I would suggest, however, that if one surveys the vast amount of criticism written on Herbert in the past two decades, one will find the most critics chose either to "re-cover" some seventeenth-century aspect of Herbert's art for the present age or chose to "dis-cover" facets of his mind and art that only a modern critic would be capable of discussing. As one might expect, those who endorse the position represented by Tuve often regard much modern critical writing on Herbert as superficial, uninformed, and misleading, while those critics who attempt to find "new things about the workings of Herbert's mind by applying modern terms," be those linguistic, Freudian, affective stylistic, or what have you, often view the labors of traditional scholars as sheer pedantry or harmless drudgery. In the selection of essays that I present in this collection, I have tried to represent both points of view.

Since there is such an overabundance of first-rate modern criticism on Herbert, I recognized from the very beginning of this project that I would need to impose certain severe, even arbitrary, limitations on my selections. First of all, in a volume of this size it seemed impractical to include essays on both Herbert's poetry and prose; therefore, I decided to include only articles on the poetry, although I recognize that some excellent work has been done recently on Herbert's prose. Also, since the editors of this series suggested that only articles in learned journals or complete essays in volumes by various hands be included, I have excluded possible selections from book-length studies, although several times I have bent this rule somewhat by including a few essays which, though originally published as articles, were later incorporated into book-length studies. In every instance but one, I have reprinted the article as it first appeared; the exception is Florence Sandler's essay in which, following the suggestions of the author, I have made some minor corrections. From the remaining plethora of riches, I have chosen thirty-four essays that seem to me to be both critically interesting in and for themselves and that also reflect in some way several of the major concerns of modern Herbert criticism. In selecting articles that should or could be included in a volume such as this, no two editors could possibly agree on all points. One is confronted with so many good pieces that all limitations and guidelines finally seem curiously subjective and perhaps quixotic. Also, I should mention that I would feel more comfortable if this collection were simply entitled "critical essays on

Herbert's poetry," for the word *essential* may erroneously imply to the reader either that only these essays are important or that one cannot possbily understand the genius of Herbert's poetry unless he reads these specific pieces. Clearly I intend neither implication.

I wish to thank the Research Council of the University of Missouri-Columbia for a grant that made this book possible. I should also like to express my appreciation to Professors Heather Asals, Amy M. Charles, Stanley E. Fish, Louis L. Martz, Jerry Leath Mills, Virginia Mollenkott, C. A. Patrides, Mary Ellen Rickey, Arnold Stein, Joseph H. Summers, Humphrey Tonkin, Helen Vendler, and Frank Warnke, each of whom gave me useful suggestions and much encouragement. My primary debt, of course, is to the authors, who generously allowed me to reprint the essays and thus gave me the privilege of sharing the fruits of their research and critical intelligence with others.

John R. Roberts
Columbia, Missouri
December, 1978

I. GENERAL STUDIES

GEORGE HERBERT AND THE RELIGIOUS LYRIC

Robert Ellrodt

If we leave out some impersonal hymns and meditations — and among them Milton's 'Nativity Ode' — the best religious lyrics of the seventeenth century were written in 'the Donne tradition'. Their authors were all amateur poets who never attempted longer compositions in the nobler 'kinds'. They were all born within the pale of the Church of England, and, though Marvell strayed into the Puritan camp and Crashaw found full bliss in the bosom of the Roman Church, something of the Anglican spirit shines in all. All of them lived for a time in a sheltered social world, provincial and pastoral, homely and aristocratic. In the minds of all, the 'Elizabethan world picture' must have lingered: the sense of order and degree, form and design, sympathy and corre- spondence. Some of them, however, moved through a shattered world of civil war, cosmic change and cultural revolution into the Restoration world of infinite space, Hobbesian materialism or Cartesian dualism, and reasonable Christianity. The earlier poets — Herbert and Crashaw — wrote in the liturgical tradition of the Church: they lived in a sacramental world. Later poets — Vaughan and Traherne — chose to raise a freer world of spiritual meditation, Hermetic or Platonic, in Nature. Let them possess these worlds: 'each hath one, and is one'. They owe much to their age, but individual modes of apprehension, thought and feeling command their allegiance to the various doctrines and philosophies, their response to experience and their poetic utterance. A strong flavour of individuality is the distinguishing mark and excellence of the religious lyric in seventeenth-century England, as compared with earlier devotional verse or with the Baroque lyric of the Continent. This originality may be due to the example, though not to the influence, of Donne. Accordingly, rather than trace currents of thought or patterns

Reprinted from *English Poetry and Prose, 1540-1674,* ed. Christopher Ricks (London: Barrie & Jenkins, 1970), pp. 173-205, by permission of the author and the publisher.

of style and verse, this chapter will concentrate on 'the private world of imagination' (a phrase which has been used for Vaughan but applies to all), on the individual intuition of time and space and the personal modes of religious sensibility.

George Herbert (1593-1633) had a Welsh ancestry and a poetic lineage: his cousin, William Herbert, Earl of Pembroke, was the nephew of Sir Philip Sidney. 'If a literary genealogy must be traced for Herbert', Margaret Bottrall claimed, 'there is much to be said for affiliating him to Wyatt and Sidney as well as to Donne'. With Donne, however, Magdalen Herbert's younger son was intimately acquainted. Urged by an intelligent mother, the Cambridge student entered into a successful career. Public Orator from 1620, befriended by Bacon, he knew 'the ways of learning': scientific imagery, from 'the fleet Astronomer' and 'subtil Chymic' to medicine, metallurgy or navigation, is not absent in his poetry, though less obtrusive, more allusive than Donne's. But his youth and spirit 'also took/The way that takes the town' ('Affliction I'). Enjoying powerful connections at Court and the King's favour, he could look for some 'great place'. Whether all hope of a public career did die with his 'friends' at Court and King James himself, or whether his youthful intention of dedicating his life to the service of God reasserted itself decisively after the death of an ambitious and domineering mother, he resigned the Public Oratorship in 1626 and took Orders as deacon. His hopes of serving God were defeated for three years by ill health — a setback recorded in 'The Crosse' and other poems. In 1629, however, he married, was ordained and settled at Bemerton to lead the humble and active life Walton delightfully described and he himself suggested in his prose treatise, *A Priest to the Temple or, The Country Parson*. This halo of rustic piety, however, should not prove misleading. Though his translation of 'Outlandish Proverbs' shows a genuine taste for popular wisdom, reflected in his gnomic poetry, the chaplain of Lady Pembroke, the friend of Nicholas Ferrar, the divine who appended 'Brief Notes on Valesso's Considerations', was a gentleman and a scholar. Homeliness and sophistication meet in his poems, enriched by his worldly experience. Besides, the English poet had served an apprenticeship to the Latin Muse in his polemical 'Musae Responsoriae,' a defence of Anglican rite, and in his heart-felt elegies 'Memoriae Matris Sacrum.' He had courted wit and learned conciseness in the epigrams of 'Lucus' and 'Passio Discerpta.' Of the book of poems, 'which now bears the name of *The Temple* ... Mr. Farrer would say, "There was in it the picture of a divine soul in every page"' (Walton), but it also bore the mark of a conscious artist.

The Temple, however, can hardly be described as a fully organized whole, controlled by a dominant intention. Some kind of unity is no doubt conferred on the sequence by the architectonics of the Church, the liturgical year and Christian eschatology. From 'The Church-Porch' we proceed to 'The Altar' or leap to 'The Windows'; from 'Good Friday' we move to 'Easter', 'Whitsunday' and 'Trinity'; after 'Death', 'Doomsday' and 'Judgment', the reception of the soul in Heaven is beautifully dramatized in 'Love (III)'. One may agree that *The Temple* is at once 'The British Church', double-moated by God's grace, and a symbol for 'the life of man within that Church'; or even a hieroglyph for the body of the Christian as the living temple of the Holy Spirit, and yet fail to discover in the arrangement of the poems as clear a 'principle of organization' as J. H. Summers claimed. Others have argued that the Hebraic or even the classical temple for pagan worship were in the poet's mind, that he meant to suggest the substitution of the Covenant of Grace for the Covenant of Works (J. D. Walker), or to underline 'the contrast between the life of grace offered by the Church and the natural value of the ancients' (Mary Rickey). One may assent to the symbolic implications and reject the assumption of persistent or even consistent design.

To trace a clear spiritual pattern and progression in the sequence is no less hazardous, though ingenious minds may delight in reading the poems as an illustration of the three ways of the spiritual life or as a hieroglyph of time's passage: 'the soul moves in time from an earlier state of unpreparedness to a later one of preparedness'. Palmer's biographical heresy is revived when the poems are hypothetically rearranged to suggest a spiritual pilgrimage from affliction to joy in the acceptance of God's will and love.[1]

The subtitle still offers the safest description: 'Private Ejaculations'. Herbert's sense of form is obvious, but it is mainly displayed in the shapeliness of the isolated poem. His intuition of time is vivid but not expressed through continuance and progress.

With Herbert, as with Donne, 'Onelie the present is thy part and fee' ('The Discharge'). The moment of experience is recorded with dramatic immediacy in prayer, meditation or apostrophe. Brusque openings let us into particular situations:

Busie enquiring heart, what wouldst thou know? ('The Discharge')
What is this strange and uncouth thing? ('The Crosse')

Herbert's 'present', however, is more spacious than Donne's instant. It can espouse the continuity of music:

Now I in you without a bodie move,

> Rising and falling with your wings:
> ('Church-musick')

In a poem by Donne the present leaps into being and may even rob the past of all reality, as in 'The Good-morrow'. In *The Temple* the moment gone may be the subject of the poem and a source of pathos, like a presence in absence:

> It cannot be. Where is that mightie joy
> Which just now took up all my heart?
> ('Temper II')

The Christian is eager to treasure or recapture gleams of spiritual joy: their very intermittence invites a brooding over the vanishing moment: 'Thou cam'st but now; wilt thou so soon depart ... ?' ('The Glimpse'). Herbert is the poet of return and rebirth in a different way from Vaughan's; not into a previous state but into the present:

> And now in age I bud again,
> After so many deaths I live and write;
> I once more smell the dew and rain,
> And relish versing: O my onely light,
>   It cannot be
>   That I am He
> On whom thy tempests fell all night.

His true bent is not retrospection, but recapitulation. A poem which opens as narrative will lead up to a present climax: 'I made a posie, while the day ran by ... Farewell deare flowers, sweetly your time ye spent ... I follow straight ...' ('Life'). The self-enclosed narrative may also blur the distinction between the present and the future, which is apprehended as completion rather than grasped in anticipation (as in Donne's outcry: 'What if this present were the worlds last night?'). At the end of 'The Pilgrimage' the poet has firmly placed himself — that is, placed us — in present death — his own death: 'After so foul a journey death is fair,/ And but a chair.' In his imagination past and future are rolled up into a ball — one of his favourite images. Distance, whether historical or eschatological, disappears: Christ is 'dying daily' ('Affliction III'). The drama of Redemption is told in the preterite as an apologue, but the words spoken on the Cross are intensely present:

> there I him espied,
> Who straight, *Your suit is granted*, said, & died.

Herbert's intuition of time, his mode of devotion and his sense of form are interrelated. A mind which takes in more than the present moment is capable of the concentration on religious experience which was denied to Donne's dispersed or pin-pointed attention. 'All the day' may be filled with the ever-welling call of the loving heart: *'My joy, my life, my crown'* ('A true Hymne'). The poetry of ejaculation shows him at his most lyrical. Instantaneity and repetition are combined in a space of time: 'this day' is a frequent phrase. More frequent still is the building up of the poem to an unexpected close, artfully contrived. Donne's agile mind could spring such surprises on us, but it tacked about from one argument to another. Through his piled-up statements or questionings, Herbert moves steadily towards a conclusion, which at once unifies and reverses the meaning:

> Then for thy passion — I will do for that —
> Alas, my God, I know not what.

or

> But as I rav'd and grew more fierce and wilde
> at every word,
> Me thoughts I heard one calling, *Child!*
> And I reply'd, *My Lord.*

This premeditated composition turns the dramatic monologue into a single conceit instead of a succession of witty flashes. It is the triumph of form within the recorded moment of experience, within the self-enclosed lyric.

Emphasis on public worship rather than private devotion may be misleading. The reaction against romantic interpretations, though wholesome, has been carried too far by recent critics. In the age of Herbert, Summers reminds us, 'the expression of individual experience was valued not for the sake of self-expression but for its didactic effectiveness; not because of its uniqueness but because of its universal applicability'. This approach may account for the composition of obviously didactic poetry, like 'The Church-Porch', or even for the faint effort at thrusting the lyrics into some sort of logical or theological order. It cannot account for the creative impulse. Self-expression need not be 'Romantic'. The religious lyric of the Middle Ages often was an Augustinian 'Soliloquy' — a colloquy between the soul and God as well as a self-communing. To Puttenham in his *Arte of English Poesie* (I.xxii-xxvii), to Sidney in his *Defence of Poesie*, to Donne in 'The Triple Foole', lyrical poetry was an outlet for human emotions. Though

Walton's relation may not record Herbert's actual words, *The Temple* is, indeed, 'a picture of the many spiritual conflicts that have passed betwixt God and [the poet's] soul'.

Some of the pieces are even more clearly autobiographical than any of Donne's self-dramatizations, which only revealed or recreated a single experience. Not utterly fascinated by the present (which only joins the particular and the universal), Herbert can survey his whole life, enclose it in narrative ('Affliction I') or in drama ('The Collar'), gather in one past and present ('The Flower', 'The Glance'), retrace his steps to a distant point: 'And now, me thinks, I am where I began/ Sev'n years ago' ('The Bunch of Grapes'). The poet, no doubt, is conscious of his sacerdotal office: unlike Donne, he does not confine his attention to his 'naked thinking heart'. The emphasis, however, is unchanged. The priest meditates on the perfection expected from Christ's minister, but he meditates in privacy: the poem comes to a close when the invitation is spoken: 'Come people; Aaron's drest' ('Aaron'). 'Miserie' defines the wearisome condition of humanity and the hero is Everyman. Yet, when the sick-tossed vessel is dashed on 'his own shelf', the personal meaning is flashed: 'My God, I mean my self'.

The common ideal of self-knowledge may be expressed in the Christian mode ('Church-porch', 'The H. Scripture', 'Even-song') or in Stoic phrase, as in the close of 'Content'. In his self-examination, however, Herbert hardly practises on his own heart, nerves and brain as keen a vivisection as Donne's. We miss the note of perplexity for his desire is not to seek himself but 'to seek God only' (as the Dean of St. Paul's professed to do). His poetry is talk; and God, silent or speaking, is the poet's constant interlocutor. Donne only gave an illusion of dialogue: 'For Godsake hold your tongue, and let me [talk]' might have been spoken to his mistress. There is no give and take, even when he meets objections raised by his own mind. In his religious poetry the true centre of interest is the poet's self. Emotions of fear and love, acts of worship, egotistic petitions are directed to God as an object. The action of a Divine subject is never felt, with the single exception of a thrilling invocation: 'Heare thy selfe now, for thou in us dost pray' ('A litanie', xxiii). Only through his own prayer is Donne able to *realize* the Divine presence and the circle runs from self to self. Herbert's God will speak to his 'Child' ('Dialogue', 'The Collar', 'Artillerie'). Open dialogue is infrequent, but there is no interruption in the soul's intercourse with the divine lover, constantly addressed as 'my God', 'my Lord', 'my Master'.

Though his poetry is not always self-centred, Herbert discloses a

modern subjectivity of feeling and expression in such poems as 'Affliction (I)'. At other times self-examination may be veiled in allegory or
personification; it may thicken into emblem or metaphor. Yet through
such metaphors introspection will search the closets of the heart and
disclose an open breast, fit to challenge the clearest diamond ('Confession'). This mode of self-awareness may be responsible for flashes of
irony or humour, unknown to the religious poetry of Crashaw and
Vaughan. The note of burlesque in 'Dooms-day' or 'Conscience' could
be a simple illustration of holy mirth. But the playful insight into the
ruse of the human heart in 'Gratefulnesse' or 'Time' discloses a subtler
form of irony directed at oneself. There is sadness but also a touch of
humorous acceptance in the quiet admission of man's essential foolish-
ness ('Miserie'). When a passionate outburst in 'The Thanksgiving',
'Affliction (I)' or 'The Collar' ends in the sudden recognition of its
futility, one feels the very surge of emotion was controlled from the
beginning by the poet's critical self-awareness.

This ironical detachment may account for Herbert's delight in
understatement. The constant expression of sacred truth in homely
language does not merely proceed from an ideal of Christian simplicity.
Such familiarity is not ingenuous but artful. This poetry works like the
glass described in 'The Elixir':

> A man that looks on glasse
> On it may stay his eye;
> Or if he pleaseth, through it passe,
> And then the heav'n espie.

A deeper complexity is achieved through the subdued expression of
feeling. When Herbert resorts to hyperbole, as in the superficially
Donne-like 'Church-monuments', he is least original. His distinctive art
and ambiguity are revealed in 'Death'. The poet's apparently naïve gaze
does not shrink from 'the uncouth hideous thing', but there is a quiet
irony and no horror in the contemplation: 'Thy mouth was open; but
thou couldst not sing'. The Christian knows that 'all [these] bones with
beautie shall be clad'. There is no shudder and no rapture, for the
simultaneous awareness of the stark reality of death and the glory of
eternity tempers both fear and exultation. The last stanza takes up the
well-worn comparison of death with sleep. Yet the sober assertion of
immortality through the stillness of sleep in an 'honest grave' rests on the
fearless acceptance of the gruesome image. Dissonance lurks under a
deceptive simplicity. The mention of the body as 'Half that we have'

reminds us with Herbertian restraint that 'gluttonous death will instantly unjoynt' body and soul, as in Donne's sonnet 'This is my playes last scene ...' The final balance between the symbols of downy sleep and dreadful dissolution expresses the poet's composure in front of life and death.

The colloquiality of language and rhythm, the even tone, the deliberate understatement are the stylistic expression of an intellectual control, all the more severe since Herbert was not even-tempered. There is a conscious avoidance of rude and strident emotion. It is through this self-consciousness and reticence that Herbert's poetry achieves obliquity or ambiguity. Empson's analysis of 'Hope' and 'The Pilgrimage' in *Seven Types* cannot be surpassed, but it should be related to the poet's cast of mind, which may give him a better title to 'metaphysical poetry' than many critics have acknowledged. 'His wit', Margaret Bottrall confessed, 'is one of his foremost qualities. But since this wit does not depend for its effect upon far-fetched conceits, recondite allusions or reasoned arguments, there seems to be no good reason for describing it as metaphysical, or for connecting it inseparably with the wit of Donne'. Yet, in Miss Rickey's words, there is no intimation that 'writing from the heart necessitates writing without the head'. The concentration and intellectual ingenuity of 'metaphysical poetry' is achieved by Herbert. It often lurks in his supposedly quaint titles: they all effect 'some special communication, either an enriching ambiguity, or the suggestion of a motif which qualifies the materials of the text itself' (Rickey).

It has been claimed that Herbert's wit was fired by the paradoxes of the Christian tradition rather than the example of Donne. Conceits based on the paradoxical nature of man's individual experience are bound to be fewer in *The Temple* than in the *Songs and Sonets*, but they are hardly less striking when they arise. 'Let me not love thee, if I love thee not' ('Affliction I'): man's love for God may be forgetful but its roots are so deep that the worst affliction that might be inflicted on the poet for this intermittence would be to root out his love altogether. Besides, even a traditional paradox can be modulated into something new, rich and strange. Thus, in 'The Reprisall', Herbert declares himself ready to die for Christ, yet owns his defeat: 'For by thy death I die for thee'. The paradox of 'Redemption' is refined when the Christian discovers that he only finds the strength of dying through the death of Christ.

In 'The Sacrifice', one of the longest and least personal poems, 'Metaphysical' ambiguity and richness have been traced to the liturgical tradition by Rosemond Tuve in *A Reading of George Herbert*. Without disclaiming the lineage one could show that neither the liturgy nor the Mediaeval lyrics offer the same intellectual density, nor the same subtlety in dramatic irony.[2] One striking instance is this quiet proclamation of the awe-inspiring *Deus absconditus:*

> My face they cover, though it be divine.
> As *Moses* face was vailed, so is mine,
> Lest on their double-dark souls either shine.

Throughout the poem, indeed, attention is focused not on the sufferings of Christ nor even on the mystery of Redemption, but on man's blindness as discerned by the dreadful, yet loving omniscience of God. The sources of irony are more subjective here than in Greek tragedy: self-deceit, not deceitful fate, is exposed. Among innumerable poems on the Redemption, Herbert's 'Sacrifice' does not owe its distinctive excellence only to epigrammatic art, or dramatic vividness; its strength arises from the exclusion of easy pathos, from the intellectual control and terrifying lucidity.

A further distinction between a passive allegiance to some religious or literary tradition and the spontaneous workings of the individual imagination can be traced in the poet's awareness of the two natures in Christ or of man's amphibious nature. With Herbert as with Donne, the Incarnation is more than the centre of christian faith: it commands their vision of the world and their inspiration as if it were a structure of their minds. In 'Affliction (IV)' the poet describes himself as 'A wonder tortur'd in the space/Betwixt this world and that of grace', but he always seeks to bring both worlds together and find the incarnation of spiritual reality in the grosser world, as in 'Sunday': 'The fruit of this; the next world's bud'. He delights in 'the bridall of the earth and skie' ('Vertue'). Man's middle nature between angel and beast is a Renaissance commonplace, but Herbert, unlike the Platonists or the satirists, is never tempted to consider either of them in isolation. In his intuition of the complexities of mire or blood, his soul will clap its hands and sing, for

> Whether I flie with angels, fall with dust,
> Thy hands made both, and I am there.
>
> ('Temper I')

Human experience is an experience of duality and union. As a Christian Herbert cannot but believe in the Real Presence: the sacrament must be more than a figure of a purely spiritual reality. Yet the Anglican poet argued against transubstantiation with surprising scholastic acrimony in the MS poem on 'The H. Communion' excluded from

The Temple. Though the ecstatic tone in 'The Invitation' and 'The Banquet' reveals a sacramental sensibility almost as keen as Crashaw's, the printed version of 'The H. Communion' still insists on 'the wall that parts/Our souls and fleshy hearts'. Yet it proclaims at the same time the influence of the Eucharist on the 'rebel-flesh', and the privilege of Grace, which alone can open 'the souls most subtile rooms' while the elements 'to spirits refin'd, at doore attend/Dispatches from their friend'. This description of the Eucharist is more reminiscent of Donne's conception of love in 'The Exstasie' than of any theological doctrine. Both poets maintain between sense and soul a barrier which even the blood-begotten spirits cannot wholly overcome, yet they assert their close conjunction. Neither of them is satisfied by a merely spiritual ecstasy. In his rapture Herbert cries out: 'Give me my captive soul, or take/My bodie also thither'.

Through this sacramental approach one may trace a mode of thought and sensibility. More space than is available would be required to show how Herbert's mind apprehends the concomitance of two actions in divided or distinguished worlds; how his imagination grasps in a single flash the opposition and conjunction of two natures or realities, sensible and spiritual. Catholic doctrine, which the sensuous imagination of Crashaw will espouse of its own accord, blurs the distinction and relies on metamorphosis. Calvinistic and even Anglican doctrine asserted the simultaneity of a spiritual and a physical action, but their conjunction seemed gratuitous since the spiritual alone had efficacy and meaning. Herbert's mode of apprehension is truly original.

This mode governs his poetic inspiration as well as his religious emotions. His most deeply-felt paradoxes bring together but never confuse contrary notions, indissolubly connected in human experience: the finite and the infinite, time and eternity, life and death. Puritan writers, when they express spiritual truth, either keep the contrasting notions well apart or abolish the contrast in Neoplatonic idealism. With Catholics like Crashaw the sensible and the spiritual interfuse on the pattern of transubstantiation, and contraries, like pain and pleasure, melt into one another.

The same type of relationship obtains in Herbert's handling of the abstract and the concrete. Yet he seldom offers palpable abstractions, like Donne's 'dull privation and leane emptinesse'. He avoids scholastic quiddities. His mind seems to move in a purely material universe, clotted with objects. The contemporary vogue of emblems no doubt influenced his poetic inspiration, as Rosemary Freeman and others have shown. As Jean Hagstrum tersely points out in *The Sister Arts*: 'Herbert's poetry is not descriptive but emblematic . . . The iconic poetry of Drayton, like the tapestries it describes, contents the eye; Herbert's contents the mind'. However, one should make a further distinction. In the emblems of Quarles, image and idea are distinctly perceived. Many of Herbert's images are metaphors so condensed that the mind hardly forms a sensuous image in the quick apprehension of meaning:

> Thy clothes being fast, but thy soul loose about thee
> ('Church-porch')

> This is but tuning of my breast,
> To make the music better.
> ('Temper I')

When human dust and bones are described as 'The shells of fledge souls left behinde' ('Death'), this beautiful evocation should not call up a visual image of broken eggs and feathered souls, which would be even more grotesque than the winged hearts of the emblematists. The imagination is deeply stirred because the full significance is grasped through the lingering image of the actual bones, a faint and almost abstract impression of white brittleness and dereliction, together with the elation of a breaking out, a sense of flight and freedom.

Some poems, no doubt, call attention to an emblematic image, but one may wonder why 'Love Unknown' leaves us unmoved, whereas 'The Churche-floor' can evoke a poetic thrill. The heart's progress from font to cauldron or thorns is an unreal apologue, a mere fabrication. The 'square speckled stone' *is* an actual slab in the church-floor and *means* intensely ('is' and 'means' are interchangeable when we hear that the stone *'Is Patience'*). However this is not symbolism, for the sign and the thing signified are not truly one. Such images differ at once from symbols and from conventional emblems in the same way as Herbert's conception of the Eucharist differs from both Catholic and Calvinistic doctrine. In each case the poet's originality lies in a simultaneous apprehension. The stones are at once an object for the eye and for the mind.

Though the topics of *The Temple* 'can be accurately styled *metaphysical*', Miss Rickey observes, Herbert speaks of Heaven 'in terms remarkable only for their earthliness'. Yet, at his most sensual, he will 'thrust' his mind into each experience, into the very sweetness and odour of the words *My Master*: 'This broth of smells, that feeds and fats my *minde*' ('The Odour'). We do not breathe the freer air of Vaughan's or Traherne's spacious worlds of philosophic meditation. Herbert's world of devotion is a little stuffy, but intellect is ever watchful and never allows materiality to melt into mindlessness as in many of Crashaw's conceits.

This is not the poet of perspective and expansion. His imagination is circumscribed in space as in time. Its apprehension of the world is organic and kinesthetic. Images of muscular violence and contraction abound to suggest the inner wrestlings of the soul: 'Stretch or contract me, thy poor debter: /This is but tuning of my breast,/To make the musick better' ('Temper I'). Sin is a 'press and vice' ('Agonie'), thoughts are 'a case of knives' ('Affliction IV'). Nor does the poet ever paint an effortless ascension, a smooth flight to Heaven: he will be 'toss'd from earth' ('Sunday'), tossed to God's breast ('The Pulley').

Herbert's imagination may call for circumscription out of a yearning for security: 'O let me, when thy roof my soul hath hid,/ O let me roost and nestle there' ('Temper I'). Space, distance, infinity only give pain and terror: 'O rack me not to such a vast extent;/Those distances belong to thee' ('Temper I'). The only world the poet gladly inhabits must be solid and full, like the boxes and chests, the cabinets 'packt' with sweets on which he dwells lovingly. He knows 'the soul doth span the world', but *his* will only 'hang content/From either pole unto the centre' when Heaven shrinks to a local habitation: 'Where in each room of the well-furnisht tent/He lies warm, and without adventure' ('Content'). This substitution of spiritual loneliness for cosmic amplitude or metaphysical profundity implies a limitation in imaginative range, a loss in poetic intensity. However, the dialectics of the finite and the infinite, immanence and transcendence, is ever present, though unobtrusive:

> Thy will such a strange distance is,
>   As that to it
> East and West touch, the poles do kisse,
>   And parallels meet.
>   ('The Search')

No poet had a finer sense of the Divine presence and 'nearenesse', 'Making two one' ('The Search'). And the God that will '[Him] selfe immure and close/In some one corner of a feeble heart' ('Decay') brings with Him infinite riches in a little room. When all differences are told, Herbert and Donne still have one common characteristic: their apprehension of the eternal and the infinite in a single point of space and time. 'Shine here to us, and thou art every where', the lover said to the 'Sunne Rising'. Herbert has the same metaphysical confidence when addressing his Sun and Son:

> Thy power and love, my love and trust
> Make one place ev'ry where.

('Temper')

Not with the Metaphysicals, but with the Baroque poets of the Continent is the inspiration of Richard Crashaw commonly linked. Born in London in 1612, the son of a Puritan Preacher and polemicist, he died at Loretto, a Roman convert, in 1649. The conversion, however, had been no sudden change for the Charterhouse and Cambridge student who modelled his early verse on the Jesuit epigrammatists, for the fellow of Peterhouse, a hotbed of Laudian High Churchmanship, for the visitor at Little Gidding and the spiritual son of Mary Collet, for the exile in Leyden and Paris, the protégé of the Countess of Denby and Queen Henrietta Maria, the friend of Joseph Beaumont and Thomas Car, the flaming heart who yearned, when yet among the Protestants, for the mystical death of Saint Teresa.

Donne's devotion was self-centred. Herbert's attention centred on the intercourse between God and his own soul. Crashaw's ecstatic piety aims at self-annihilation. 'Leave nothing of my SELF in me', he cries out to the Foundress of the Carmelites: 'Let me so read thy life, that I / Unto all life of mine may dy' ('The Flaming Heart'). Lyrical, intensely emotional, his poetry nevertheless proves impersonal. He is lost in the contemplation of some outer object: Christ, the Virgin or a Saint. Whereas the inner presence of God in the soul invited Herbert's self-questionings, Crashaw's faith and imagination are centrifugal: 'Goe, Soul out of thy Self ...' ('To the Name Above Every Name').

An insight into the human heart can hardly be expected from such a poet, but he himself is a case for the psychologist. Ambiguity is displaced by the ambivalence that characterized Crashaw's sensibility long before he became acquainted with the Spanish mystics. In countless poems the same sharp confusion of pain and pleasure attends an ecstatic death, erotic in an 'Epithalamium', mystical in the Teresa hymns.

> O how oft shall thou complain
> Of a sweet & subtle PAIN.
> Of intolerable JOYES;
> of a DEATH, in which who dyes
> Loves his death, and dyes again.
> And would for ever so be slain.

And lives, & dyes; and knowes not why
To live, But that he thus may never leave to DY.
('A Hymn to the Name and Honor of the Admirable
                                    Sainte Teresa')

The metaphysical shudder, the anguish of the grave, therefore will be absent. The death of the body is but the ultimate ecstacy, 'When These thy DEATHS, so numerous,/Shall all at last dy into one,/And melt thy Soul's sweet mansion' (Teresa 'Hymn').

The influence of the erotic mysticism of the Counter-Reformation is undeniable, but Crashaw's own sensuality was revealed in his early poems, only published in 1646 as *The Delights of the Muses*. No chaster Muse can be found than 'That not impossible She' addressed in his 'Wishes to his (Supposed) Mistresse', yet more than sensuousness is betrayed by the Marlovian fascination for the 'crimson streame' of blood 'warme in its violet channel' (elegies on Mr Stanninow, on Lady Parker, 'On ye Gunpowder-Treason'). However, a merely erotic or a purely spiritual interpretation of the poet's sacred language should be rejected alike. An unconscious perversity may have been the starting-point, but a genuine sublimation was achieved. The *Epigrammata Sacra* and the other poems written before 1637 are filled with the imagery of blood and milk, wounds and breasts, and the psychoanalyst may gloat over the lines 'Hee'l have his Teat e're long (a bloody one)./The mother then must suck the Son'. The thirst for martyrdom is still morbid, not mystic. With the 'Nativity' and 'Assumption Hymns' or the lines 'On a prayer booke', we move away from blood to clearer themes, 'soft exhalations/Of soule; deare, and divine annihilations', but the 'rarifyed delights' called up in verse of Shelleyan lightness are not free from a cloying sweetness reminiscent of Salesian devotion.

'Lov's manly flame' first burned in the poems inspired by Saint Teresa, 'A Woman for Angelical height of speculation, for Masculine courage of performance more than a woman'. The poet himself for the first time struck the note of supreme intensity: 'Love thou art absolute, sole Lord/Of life and death'. He too, had now in him all the eagle and all the dove, and quaffed 'large draughts of intellectual day'. The word 'intellectual', as Ruth Wallerstein observed, recurs in the poems from 1643 to 1652. Crashaw's insistent use does not denote a rejection of concreteness but the poet's images seem to lose their sensuous gloss. They are symbols used in ritualistic drama or discourse:

O costly intercourse
Of deaths, & worse,

> Divided loves. While son & mother
> Discourse alternate wounds to one another.
>
> ('Sancta Maria')

In the 'Stabat Mater' the wounds of Christ are no longer roses and rubies, or lips to be sensually kissed: their spiritual significance is uppermost. The influence of the mediaeval liturgy on the poetic imagination of the convert is suggested by his own free translation of St. Thomas's 'Adoro Te':

> Down down, proud sense! Discourses dy.
> Keep close, my soul's inquiring ey!
> Nor touch nor tast must look for more
> But each sitt still in his own Dore.

Crashaw had proclaimed himself Herbert's disciple in *Steps to the Temple,* but those steps were mostly laid before 1634 and *The Temple* was published in 1633. 'On Mr. G. HERBERTS book ... sent to a Gentlewoman' was written in a key of devout gallantry and mystical mawkishness alien to the spirt of Herbert. The influence of *The Temple* is first felt in the second edition of 1648 and best traceable in 'Charitas Nimia. Or the Dear Bargain':

> Lord, what is man? why should he coste thee
> So dear? what had his ruin lost thee?
> Lord what is man? that thou hast overbought
> So much a thing of nought?
>
> Love is too kind, I see; & can
> Make but a simple merchant man.

One may choose to think that Crashaw changed his style as he turned away from the Latin amorists, the Jesuit epigrammatists and Marino to imitate George Herbert, translate the mediaeval liturgy or read the Spanish mystics. The progress, however, is not merely stylistic. Crashaw's taste matured and his sensibility was purified. That the change proceeded from a spiritual evolution rather than literary influence is confirmed by the very limitations of this poetic development. The Teresian 'dowr of LIGHTS & FIRES' burned away the sensual dross of the early poems, yet the fundamental ambivalence persisted to the last. The poet may 'vow to make brave way/ Upwards, & presse on for the pure intelligentiall Prey' ('Epiphanie'), but his own splendid evocation of the 'mystic night' of the Areopagite reveals the persistence and power of a visionary imagination. It is felt even in the semi-abstract splendour of his celebration of the 'frugall negative light':

> Now by abased liddes shall learn to be
> Eagles; and shutt our eyes that we may see.

The 'Epiphanie' Hymn is not an isolated poem in Crashaw's work, as Warren and Watkin differently claimed. It shows the utmost bound Crashaw's imagination could reach in one direction. The true bent of his mind reasserts itself in the close, through the sensuous and emblematic images of the visible Sun:

> Somthing a brighter SHADOW (sweet) of thee.
> Or on heavn's azure forhead high to stand
> Thy golden index; . . . .

However, the hard clarity and materiality of the emblem is unsuited to the lyrical and musical inspiration of Crashaw. Donne's and Herbert's imagination moved among fixities; their paradoxes and ambiguities oppose or associate definite notions and emotions. In the sensibility of Crashaw 'kind contrarietyes' ('The Weeper') melt into each other and the result is transmutation rather than paradox, confusion rather than complexity:

> No where but here did ever meet
> Sweetnesse so sad, sadnesse so sweet.
>
> ('The Weeper')

The characteristic ambivalence emerges when he calls to the 'soft ministers of sweet sad mirth' ('To the Name Above Every Name'), yearns for 'all those stings/Of love, sweet bitter things' ('Sancta Maria') or cries 'Welcome, my Griefe, my Joy' (Divine Epigrams). Though its literary or liturgical descent is obvious, this rhetoric of contraries has a personal significance. Joy and grief, day and night, fire and water, were apprehended in static opposition by the Petrarchans; they are now suggestive of change or exchange: 'A commerce of contrary powres' ('Epiphanie'). We have entered a world of movement and fluidity.

Donne's and Herbert's worlds of imagination, though dynamic, were solid and dense; Crashaw's is a 'general flood'. Substances like gold and silver, pearl and crystal only lend their lustre: their hardness is dissolved in 'Thawing crystall', 'Warm sylver shoures' ('Weeper') or 'The water of a *Diamond*' ('Teare'). The prevailing liquidity is not unlinked with the dominant thirst for feminine tenderness, for the maternal milk. 'Sitiens laboro' (in the epigram 'Spes Diva') is the leit-motiv for 'this dry soul' who would be 'drunk of the dear wounds' ('Adoro Te', 'Sancta Maria'). Streams and seas are hyperboles for the outflow of milk or blood or tears, or the 'strong wine of love': fluids of human source. The deeper longings of poets and mystics are expressed in their imagery. Traherne's illuminations are conveyed in radiant symbols; Vaughan's yearning for revelation and regeneration is expressed through gleaming light and living waters. With other mystics fire is dominant. Crashaw's sacred ebriety calls for 'brim-fill'd Bowles' and a 'draught of liquid fire' ('Flaming heart'). Such fire will be 'moist spark' ('Teare'), a flame 'quench't in a flood' (Epigram, 'Luc. 7'). Nor fire nor water attract the poet's imagination by themselves but only as they meet in 'sister-Seas of virgins Milke', in a woman's breast, 'the noblest nest/Both of love's fires and flouds'.

This watery and organic world is without space and perspective. Everything is in motion, but the sense of direction is lost. There is no Donne-like 'progress', no bullet-like trajectory: *vagus* is a favourite epithet in the Latin poems, but the wandering is felt from inside, not related to outer objects. Motion is a vagrancy or tremulousness at the heart of things—tears and stars and bubbles—or a streaming from nowhere, a swelling into a sea. When tears 'melt the yeare/Into a weeping motion' ('Weeper'), the conceit conveys an intuition of the very essence of time and movement, which finds its expression in liquidity.

Music is experienced and expressed in the same way. The soul will bathe 'in streames of liquid Melodie'—not in the airy sounds of an Ariel or Shelley. The 'sleeke' and 'lubricke' throat of the nightingale is an 'ever-bubling' spring: 'She opes the floodgate, and lets loose a Tide/Of streaming sweetnesse'. Following 'those little rills', the listener 'sinkes into a Sea of *Helicon*' ('Musicks Duell'). Liquidity once more has a milky substance: the 'creame of Morning *Helicon*' with which sweet-lipp'd Angell-Imps ... swill their throats' ('Musicks Duell').

So unlike Herbert's moment, so like the poet's own description of the ever-renewed death of rapture, Crashaw's flowing and heaving time is a stream and swell of sensations, 'In many a sweet rise, many as sweet a fall' till 'A full-mouth *Diapason* swallowes all' ('Musicks Duell'). Each sensation spurts, climbs to the pitch of ecstasy and dies. Each musical resolution is a mystic dissolution. 'Young *Time* is taster to Eternity' but 'in the lap of Loves full noone/It falls, and dyes: oh no, it melts away/As doth the dawne into the day' ('On Hope'). Between the temporal and the eternal there is no discontinuity for the poet only seeks the endless extension of the pleasure felt in the very moment of death: erotic, musical or mystic. No intuition of transcendence is required when eternity is 'the long/ And everlasting series of a deathless SONG' ('Name of Jesus').

These modes of imagination command the poet's apprehension of the Christian mysteries. Herbert's wonder, like Donne's, was truly metaphysical, nearer perplexity than admiration. Not because his Church distrusted miracles, but because of his concentration on spiritual experience the author of *The Temple,* though fascinated by the Incarnation and Passion, was never attracted to the miraculous. Crashaw was still in the fold of the Anglican Church when he wrote endless variations on the miracles of Christ. Even at his barest, in the Epiphany hymn, he still chooses to describe the eclipse of the sun with such precision that the symbolic significance is nearly lost in admiration of this 'new prodigious might'. The emphasis on the marvellous blurs the greater mysteries. The Nativity hymn seeks to unite 'all WONDERS in one sight' with no sense of the difference between the accidental—Summer in Winter, Day in Night—and the central paradox: 'aeternity shutt in a span . . . Heaven in earth, & GOD in MAN'.

As the poet lived in a world of metamorphosis where tears turn into milk and dew, pearl and crystal, gold and silver, the Christian will incline of his own accord to the doctine of transubstantiation. Herbert's interpretation of the Real Presence required a mysterious harmony between the world of nature and the world of grace. The mystery is explained away by post-Tridentine theology, but this explanation again implies a disruption of the natural order, a miracle. In the same way, Crashaw's central experience, the inversion of pain and pleasure, brings contradictory terms together in an oxymoron. But since there is a transfer of value and meaning, since pain *is* pleasure, transmutation again prevails over paradox. Even the death of ecstacy—a death 'in which who dyes/ Loves his death, and dyes again—is nothing but a succession of 'intollerable joys': pain in the mode of pleasure.

That is why Crashaw's conceits or paradoxes are pointless or superficial when you seek to grasp their meaning. But this intellectual approach is wrong. In *The Temple*, as in Donne's sacred poetry, attention was focused on the significance of the Christian mysteries and it was explored through the individual experience of the believer in some particular dramatic situation: 'For by thy death, I die for thee'. Crashaw does not explore or meditate. He contemplates scenes of the Passion of the Nativity (disregarded by Herbert) and, like a Baroque painter, seeks to excite our affections and his own through a violent display of images. The Ignatian technique known as the application of the senses becomes here a free surrender to the suggestiveness of each sensation. One feels that Crashaw might have been a greater poet if his imaginative association had been dictated only by his deeper feelings and the major symbols. He often succumbed to an intellectual irritability which, in the literary atmosphere of the age, bubbled up in superfluous conceits. His true excellence lies in the lyrical afflatus, and the highest intensity is reached in strains of straightforward assertion and simple imagery. In such moments the figurative fancy displayed in 'The Weeper' no longer calls up visual images. Metaphors are 'felt': they spring from the poet's emotion and only bring us the same flush and glow. In the close of 'The Flaming Heart' lights and fires, the eagle and the dove, the thirsts and deaths of love and the soul's final kiss proceed from the symbolic imagination:

> O thou undanted daughter of desires!
> By all thy dowr of LIGHTS & FIRES;
> By all the eagle in thee, all the dove;
> By all thy lives & deaths of love;
> By thy larg draughts of intellectuall day,
> And by thy thirsts of love more large than they;
> By all thy brim-fill'd Bowles of feirce desire
> By thy last Morning's draught of liquid fire;
> By the full kingdome of that finall kisse
> That seiz'd thy parting Soul, & seal'd thee his ...

Crashaw may be contrasted with Herbert for his reliance on the sheer emotional value rather than the meaning of such symbols. But with Vaughan and Traherne, as Louis Martz pointed out, we move away from 'the liturgical and eucharistic symbols' of both Herbert and Crashaw towards three 'dominant fields of reference': 'the Bible, external Nature, and the interior motions of the Self' (*The Paradise Within*). One might be tempted to say, with due diffidence in the precision of literary terms, that we pass from the Metaphysical and the Baroque to the Pre-Romantic, or rather to the 17th century Hermetic and Platonic Prelude of a later Romanticism.

Silurist and 'Swan of Usk', Henry Vaughan (1622-95) and his twin brother, the Hermetist Thomas, were born in Breconshire 'above the voiceful windings of a river'. Henry left Oxford without a degree to study law in London, but he took to literature among the wits, wrote his first poems and translated the 'Tenth Satyre' of Juvenal with his mind on Strafford. Always a staunch Royalist and a Churchman, he may have fought in the Civil War though he claimed he never shed innocent blood.

His courtship and marriage inspired a trickle of love poems — the 1646 volume. A hardly thinner collection of commendatory and meditative verse, with translations from Ovid, Boethius and Casimire, appeared in 1651, though collectd by 1647. 'To Amoret Walking in a Starry Evening' and 'Upon the Priorie Grove, His usual Retyrement' were already clear revelations of his poetic personality. More youthful verse and secular (though never profane) poetry made up a later collection, *Thalia Rediviva* (1678). But only with the two parts of *Silex Scintillans* (1650, 1655) will his name flow on for ever

> Through pastures of the spirit washed with dew
> And starlit with eternities unknown.
> (Siegfried Sassoon, 'At the Grave of Henry Vaughan')

Whether inspired by the gloom of defeat in a Puritan commonwealth, or grief at the death of a dearly loved younger brother, by the influence of George Herbert — acknowledged in the Preface — or a keener interest in the spiritual alchemy of Thomas Vaughan, a sense of conversion pervades the first part of *Silex Scintillans*. It is a record of private experience: secretive self-communings. The best poetry of Vaughan is subjective: 'A sweet *self-privacy* in a right soul' ('Rules and Lessons'). He addresses God — 'Thou that know'st for whom I mourne' — not the reader who will only discover incidentally that the loved one is now a brother, now a wife. The elegiac, *In Memoriam* note is insistent and 'unseen tears' blend with the theme of retirement and solitude — a retreat 'from the Sun into the *shade*' (advocated in the prose treatise *Flores Solitudinis*), a refuge in the Circle of the Cell ('Misery') or a deeper seclusion, the life 'hid above with Christ in God' or the 'Dear, secret Greenness' of the Seed growing secretly, 'unseen and dumb'.

Vaughan only meets himself in solitude, not in dialogue with a Mistress or his Master. His self-awareness is a self-expression in reverie and sympathy. Donne and Herbert focussed their attention on a centre. Vaughan may long for the 'Centre and mid-day' but he can only 'see through a long night/Thy edges, and thy bordering light!' ('Childe-hood'). His diffusive imagination will 'Rove in that mighty, and eternall light' ('Resurrection and Immortality') or seek 'that night! where I in him/ Might live invisible and dim!' ('Night').

Another expression of his subjectivity is his belief in Hermetic *sympathies*, proclaimed with a personal intensity of emotion in 'Sure, there's a tye of Bodyes'. The mysterious attraction which was still scientific truth to the seventeenth century mind is much more than a source of conceits or intellectual perplexity to Vaughan: it is the nostalgic apprehension of a bond with 'Absents', an animistic experience of 'the strange resentment after death' of the 'Timber', wasting 'all senseless, cold and dark',

> Where not so much as dreams of light may shine,
> Nor any thought of greenness, leaf or bark.

Vaughan's intercourse with Nature has been aptly described by Elizabeth Holmes as 'a kind of interpenetration of himself with a spirit which his special philosophy taught him to find in the objects of Nature'. But, as the same critic pointed out, 'he not only believed with the Hermetists in the 'tye of bodies', but he felt the tie; and the expression of his sense of kinship with the creatures of Nature leaves a curious impression in the reader's mind of a tie as strong as the physical or even the uterine link'.

In such projections, or in the dispersion of reverie, Vaughan, unlike Herbert, first goes out of himself; but, unlike Crashaw, he returns to himself. In his self-diffusing he remains self-centred, but without a keen interest in his states of mind, without the feverish self-obsession of Donne or the self-probings of Herbert. He is apt to generalize his experience: 'Such is man's life, and such is mine' ('Miserie'). This oscillation from the universal to the individual occurred in *The Temple*, but the dramatic impact of personality was not so often diluted in impersonal reflection. Many of Vaughan's poems centre on a natural object ('The Waterfall', 'The Showre') or on a Biblical episode, a verse from Scripture, as if his meditation was provoked by some occasion from outside, whereas Donne's and Herbert's poems mostly sprang from the sudden awareness of an inner experience, a state of mind. Accordingly there will be little psychological complexity in *Silex Scintillans*. Similes do not aim at defining but intensifying the emotion, as in 'Unprofitableness':

> 'Twas but just now my bleak leaves hopeless hung
> Sullyed wih dust and mud;
> Each snarling blast shot through me, and did share
> Their Youth, and beauty, Cold showres nipt, and wrung
> Their spiciness, and bloud ...

Self-examination, when attempted, is conducted through allegory and the search is not ultimately directed to self-discovery. In 'Vanity of Spirit', an epitome of his mystic quest and favourite symbolism, the poet leaving his 'Cell' by 'dawn' lingered by a 'spring' (of living waters) and 'gron'd to know' the Author of Nature. The alchemist in vain 'summon'd nature' and rifled her 'wombe'. He 'came at last/To search [him] selfe'. Yet not after the manner of Donne seeking 'the *Ego*, the particular, the individual, I' (*Eighty Sermons*, xxxiv, p. 338). The 'traces' and 'Hyero-gliphicks' he discovers in a 'nook' of his own soul, like the 'Ecchoes beaten from the eternall hills', are intimations of a Divine mystery and only build up another fantastic world of 'weake beames' and 'Moone-shine night'. Thus the poet's thought first turns to Nature, then from the contemplation of Nature moves to self-exploration, but with no Augus-tinian sense of opposition. In his comparison of Vaughan's quest with the questioning of Nature by Augustine in book X of the *Confessions*, Martz slurs over the movement of recoil, because it cannot be found in the poem: 'Interrogavi terram et dixit non sum'. Unlike Augustine, or Herbert at that, Vaughan leaves no clear boundary between the world of objects and the subjective experience; unlike Traherne he does not enclose the outer world in the sphere of soul. His longing for a fuller revelation in death, unlike Donne's, is not a search for his own identity but a yearning for the discovery of the Divine, were it 'but one half glaunce', through the rending of 'these veyls' ('Vanity of Spirit') or 'mists' ('They are all gone into the world of light') in either Nature or the soul. This is closer to the Hermetic approach than to Augustine's close analysis of memory in his journey of the mind towards God as a reality 'interior intimo meo'.

What Vaughan has in common with many Christian mystics is a yearning to recapture something lost. It may be connected with his particular intuition of time. Not for him the 'here and now' of Traherne, or, with a difference, Herbert. The present is always filled with the remembrance of things past or the expectation of future things. When momentary, the 'moment' is integrated to 'time's silent stealth' like the 'lingring' of the 'Waterfall'. The present is emotion recollected in tranquillity. Compare Donne's 'What if this present were the worlds last night?' and Vaughan's 'I saw Eternity the other night'. A sense of distance is forced upon us: 'Silence and stealth of dayes! 'tis now/Since thou art gone,/Twelve hundred hours...' There is no instant projection: the imagination seems to move up a continuous stream, and full awareness of duration: 'So o'er fled minutes I retreat / Unto that hour...' Indeed, 'The Retreate' and 'Looking back' are intimations of this fundamental mode which unifies the poet's essential longings for childhood, Eden and the Biblical ages.

Yet Vaughan does not 'long to travell back' merely to revive the past. Retrospection is inseparable from expectation, and the 'backward steps' towards Eden only supply an assurance that the 'forward motion' will ultimately take us to 'That shady City of Palme trees'. The distinctive note is the sense of delay and resistance: 'Tyme now/Is old and slow'. Therefore the intuition of the eternal cannot be a present apprehension:

eternity is *beyond* time and *above* the World, as 'The Evening-watch', 'The Agreement' and 'The World' show. To Donne and Herbert eternity was a mode of being and a metaphysical concept. To Vaughan, as in the more naïve interpretations of Plato, it is the 'country beyond the stars', a world of light, calm and insubstantiality. The 'great Ring' gathers into itself all the impressions dear to the poet: 'Joys/Active as light, and calm without all noise' ('Mount of Olives').

'Beauteous shapes, we know not why,/Command and guide the eye' ('The Starre'). A feeling for sensuous beauty does command Vaughan's allegiance to Christian Platonism and his preference for natural theology. The aesthetic emotion in spiritual natures becomes an intuition of transcendence. The light of Creation is but the shadow of God, *umbra Dei*. The aesthetic contemplation of the created world only feeds the poet's dreams of Eden, his nostalgia for a diviner world, meditating 'what transcendent beauty shall be given to all things in that eternall World, seeing this transitory one is so full of Majesty and freshnesse' (*The World Contemned*). Hence the 'gazing soul' will dwell on 'the living works' of God

> And in those weaker glories spy
> Some shadows of eternity.
>
> ('The Retreate')

The mystic naturalism of the 17th century Hermetists suited this poet's sensibility. It implied an unbroken continuity in the material and spiritual world, not the abstract relation of form and matter in the contemplations of Marvell. 'Spirit' is the key-word. It is more than 'that subtle knot, which makes us man', effecting the conjunction of body and soul as in Donne's 'Exstasie' or Herbert's 'The H. Communion'. It is the 'fire-spirit of life', the 'preserving spirit ... Which doth resolve, produce, and ripen all' ('Resurrection') in the natural cycle, but is none other than 'the knowing, glorious spirit' ('The Book'), the Divine Intelligence 'whose spirit feeds/All things with life' ('The Stone'). The spirit that passes untainted through Nature still quickens, 'refines' and transmutes matter, raising it to immateriality, 'Till all becomes [God's] cloudless glass,/ ... Fixt by [His] spirit to a state/For evermore immaculate' ('L'Envoy').

Vaughan, like the Hermetists, spurns the grossness of matter, yet obscures the distinction between 'spirit' as refined matter and the immaterial soul or mind. Accordingly his response to Christian dogma will be different from Donne's and Herbert's. He almost explains away the Resurrection when he discovers '*prolusions* and strong *proofs* of our *restoration* laid out in *Nature*, besides the promise of the *God* of nature'

(*The Mount of Olives*; compare 'Resurrection and Immortality'). On the other hand, his exclamation 'O that I were all Soul!' contrasts with Donne's conviction that 'the body is not the man, nor the soul is not the man, but the union of these two make up the man'. He has therefore little interest in the paradox of the Incarnation as the meeting of two natures in Christ. The presence of the Redeemer in 'the fields of *Bethani* which shine/All now as fresh as *Eden*' ('Ascension-day') or his roaming at night 'where *trees* and *herbs* did watch and peep/And wonder' ('The Night') move him deeply through these associations with Nature and Paradise. His attention and hopes are not focused on the historical fulfilment of the Atonement, but on the 'mystic birth' of the Lord of Life in the individual soul ('Christ's Nativity'), on the process or regeneration described in the symbolism of the 'spiritual alchemists' ('Regeneration').

The religious poet at times imitates the conceited style of his predecessors, but a personal intensity is only felt in the mystical paradoxes that enlarge the imagination rather than perplex the mind:

> Most blest believer he!
> Who in that land of darkness and blinde eyes ...
> Did at mid-night speak with the Sun! ...
>   There is in God (some say)
> A deep but dazling darkness
>
>   ('The Night')

The peculiar reverberation of Vaughan's poetry, when contrasted with Herbert's, its emotional impact and stronger appeal, at least for the Romantically inclined, proceed from a closer connection between his natural symbolism and the deeper layers of the archetypal imagination. From such hidden sources spring his dreams of Eden and Paradise, his yearning for a far-off 'country' or 'home' (a frequent word in *Silex*), his constant quest or 'search', ascent or 'Ascension', and the recurrent image of the archetypal Mount, the holy Hill and 'those *clear heights* which above tempests shine' ('Joy'). His light imagery is insistent and individual through the perception of light as substance — the 'firie-liquid light' of heaven ('Midnight') — as life or soul — the 'Sunnie seed' ('Cock-crowing') or Hermetic star-soul in each creature — and through the poet's sensitiveness to dawn as a new birth: 'mornings, new creations are' ('Day-spring'; compare 'Rules and Lessons'). The frequent association of light with silence or the starry heavens rather than the radiance of noon is remarkable. Hence the poet's ability to strike the deeper chords in his celebration of 'Night'.

The pervasive water-symbolism suggests a longing for purity and lustration, but is related to the feeling for life and growth expressed in the symbols of vegetation. The reader of Vaughan 'shall feel/That God is true, as herbs unseen/Put on their youth and green' ('Starre'). The analogical imagination alone was at work in the Biblical parable which suggested 'The Seed growing secretly', but the poem achieves the perfect fusion of the sensible and the spiritual through the emotion awakened in the poet's soul by the actual life of the seed underground: 'Dear, secret *Greenness*! nurst below/Tempests and windes, and winter-nights ...' Fancy plays with outward form. Imagination here pierces at once to the heart of matter and the heart of life: life, '*a quickness which my God hath kist*' ('Quickness'). This realism of the symbolic imagination extends to all the recurrent images and lends substance to spiritual emotions. Since 'not a wind can stir' but straight the poet thinks of God ('Come, come ...'), the sensuous reality of breath and wind may be given to the Spirit who first moved upon the face of the waters ('Midnight', 'Water-fall').

Neither the modes of sensibility nor the symbolic imagination invite ambiguity or ambivalence in the poetry of Vaughan. His 'sad delight' has nothing in common with Crashaw's. A unity of tone and feeling prevails. Emotions freely mingle in a nostalgic pensiveness without sharp contrasts or changes. Vaughan is the poet of osmosis rather than transubstantiation. His debased use of 'mystical' in 'The Water-fall' has been criticized by Empson, but it is the only apt word to convey this emotional halo about things, this sense of their spiritual depth, at once intense and vague, though more precise than the later Romantic emotions because of its associations with a definite theology or philosophy.

Therefore, Vaughan's greater moments are moments of balance between mystery and clarity, symbolic suggestion and precise allusion:

> God's silent, searching flight:
> When my Lords head is fill'd with dew, and all
> His locks are wet with the clear drops of night;
> His still, soft call;
> His knocking time; The souls dumb watch,
> When Spirits their fair kinred catch.
>
> ('The Night')

With a few exceptions isolated lines rather than poems have this haunting power, for the author of *Silex Scintillans* has neither the unerring artistry of Herbert nor the sustained intensity of Donne. Emotion cools and the style flags when vision or intuition fade into moral meditation. Despite a feeling for aural beauty — 'How shril are silent tears?' ('Admission') — the music of the verse is uneven. In the association of colloquiality and imaginative vision, Vaughan may reach heights unattained by the more conceited 'metaphysicals': 'I saw Eternity the other night' ('The World'). However, the lack of wit is felt when his plain utterance — in description or meditation — is no longer the language of the imagination. His literal conception of poetic sincerity, unlike the sophisticated simplicity of Herbert, looks towards the Romantic ideal; 'O! 'tis an easie thing/To write and sing;/But to write true, unfeigned verse/Is very hard!' ('Anguish').

Yet this is how Thomas Traherne (1637-1674), parson, poet, and mystic, wrote with ease among Restoration gentlemen:

> A simple Light, Transparent Words, a Strain
> That lowly creeps, yet maketh Mountains plain,
> Brings down the highest Mysteries to sense
> And Keeps them there, that is Our Excellence:
> At that we aim....
> ('The Author to the Critical Peruser')

The true importance of Traherne, however, is not in the history of poetry, but in the history of thought and religious sensibility. Alone among the 'metaphysicals' he expounds a philosophy and delivers a message. Though influenced by the Hermetic writings, Plato and the long line of Platonists, from Alexandria to Florence and Cambridge, though well-read in the moralists of antiquity and probably acquainted with the more daring sects of the Puritan age, he only borrowed what responded to the needs of his mind and sensibility. He modified and made his own such ideas as entered into his Gospel of Felicity — including the Biblical texts he turned to his own ends.

His originality proceeds from a conjunction of self-centredness and expansiveness. The solipsistic absorption of the newborn child was the image of his own consciousness:

> Unfelt, unseen let those things be
> Which to thy Spirit were unknown,
> When to thy Blessed Infancy
> The World, thy Self, thy God was shewn.
> ('The Instruction')

Then indeed, 'The World was more in me, than I in it' ('Silence'). The child and the mystic, both inflamed 'With restlesse longing Heavenly Avarice' ('Desire') discover that 'self LOV is the Basis of all Lov' (*Centuries of Meditation*, iv. 55). But since the poet is 'a lover of company, a delighter in equals' whose Soul 'hateth Solitude' ('A

Thanksgiving and Prayer for the Nation') — almost a Whitman figure — self-love overflows in a love directed to all men. A love still egocentric, for Traherne looks on his 'lovely companions' as his 'peculiar treasures' and seeks society in order that others may glorify him as he glorifies God.

Out of this intense awareness of his individual existence springs the poet's 'Insatiableness' (a revealing title): 'There's not a Man but covets and desires/A Kingdom, yea a World; nay, he aspires/To all the Regions he can see/Beyond the Hev'ns Infinity' ('Misapprehension'). However, man's desire is infinitely satisfied: 'all is yours', as Saint Paul and Seneca had proclaimed, for the world is seated in your soul. Distance is illusion; perception is spiritual possession since every object 'Was present in the Apple of my Eye' and 'in my Soul a Thought/Begot, or was' ('My Spirit'). Traherne anticipates Berkeley's theory of vision and the celebrated *esse est percipi*.

The poet, however, does not really call in question the reality of the outer world. His main point is that 'not to appear is not to be'. Thus his subjectivism supports the Christian and Hermetic notion that the prime function of man is to contemplate the Creation and glorify the Creator. But the mystic presses his claim further. A 'Mind exerted, will *see* infinity' ('My Spirit'), for 'We first by Nature all things boundless see' ('The City'). Though the astronomical discoveries and the theory of endless space fired his imagination, like Henry More's, Traherne's passion for the unbounded really proceeds from the dilation of an 'enlarged Soul', his vivid sense of the unlimited 'capacity' of the mind and his quenchless thirst for infinite treasures. The same instinct directs the contemplation of eternity by the soul 'whose Glory it is that it can see before and after its Existence into Endless Spaces' (*Centuries*, i. 55). At other times, however, Eternity is a more mystical experience, a vision of the world in glory, of the works of God in their changeless essence and beauty:

> 'The Corn was Orient and Immortal Wheat, which never should be reaped, nor was ever sown. I thought it had stood from everlasting to everlasting ...'
>
> (*Centuries*, iii. 3)

In the illumination of 'Innocence' (primal or recaptured) 'the ancient Light of *Eden*' shines over the present world and in the poet's soul. Paradise is here and now, not a distant dream. Even when the themes are alike, Traherne and Vaughan speak from a different point of view. Both poets herald the Romantic glorification of childhood, though Traherne's

message alone is consistently based on the illumination of infancy and
the conviction of original innocence. To both, however, childhood is
essentially a symbol of a spiritual state. But Vaughan only longs to travel
back: Traherne lives in a Paradise regained.

Religious contemplation in the Gospel of Felicity becomes a contemplation of the universe. Despite the idealistic transmutation of things
into thoughts, attention is focused on what sense and the imagination
can reach and apprehend. Though free from sensuality, the celebration
of the senses in the 'Thanksgiving for the Body' strikes a note as yet
unheard. The Christian mysteries are still an occasion for wonder, but
the significance of the Redemption has suffered a sea-change when
Christ is presented as the 'Heir of the whole world' who taught us 'how to
possess all the things in Heaven and Earth after His similitude': 'To this
poor Bleeding Naked Man did all the Corn and Wine and Oyl, and Gold
and Silver in the World minister in an Invisible Manner, even as he was
exposed Lying and Dying upon the Cross' (*Centuries*, i. 60).

In his absence of sin-consciousness, in his faith in the natural instincts,
in his reliance on Reason and his conviction that 'Things pure and true
are Obvious unto Sence' ('Ease') and irresistibly taught by Nature as
long as it is uncorrupted by Custom, Traherne departs from the
Christian tradition of Herbert, Crashaw and Vaughan. Despite his
confidence in intuition (or because of it) he stands on the threshold of
the age of *Christianity not Mysterious* and already looks in the direction
of eighteenth-century primitivism. In his sense of wonder and illuminated vision he stands alone.

'Amazement was my Bliss' cried the mystic in 'Wonder', and the poet
claimed, with Theophilus Gale, that 'Affections are the greatest Wits'.[3]
The purity of impression will shine through the transparency of the
style:

> How like an Angel came I down!
>
> ('Wonder')
>
> Order the Beauty even of Beauty is
> ('The Vision')

Lyrical ejaculation, though fitfully Blake-like in 'The Rapture', is
usually artless to the point of formlessness. Rhapsodical accumulation,
of Whitman-like amplitude in the 'Thanksgivings', proves wearisome in
the shorter lyrics. Only the prose of the *Centuries of Meditation* reaches
a higher excellence when it beats with rapture and burns with beauty, as
in the record of the child's intimations of immortality.

The diversity disclosed by the divine poems of Herbert and Crashaw,

Vaughan and Traherne shows that the distinguishing mark of the main 'metaphysical' poets is the individuality of their inspiration and style. It also suggests a historical evolution of wider significance in the modes of thought and sensibility and the forms of poetic expression. The literary historian could find confirmation of it in the lyrics of the minor poets though the various trends overlap chronologically.

One could speak perhaps with more propriety of a 'school of Herbert' than a 'school of Donne'. In tone and temper, sweetness and strength, subdued emphasis and deliberate understatement, in the homeliness of diction and imagery and their counterpointed rhythm, the religious lyrics of Thomas Beedome and Ralph Knevet, Edmund Elys and Nathaniel Wanley are obviously modelled on *The Temple*. The superiority of Herbert's approach and style in devotional poetry appears when the occasional felicity of these uninspired imitations is contrasted with the relative failure of a greater poet, Robert Herrick, when he affects a rustic yet elegant simplicity in his 'Thanksgiving to God, for his Home.' On the theme of Crucifixion the difference in intensity and thoughtfulness between the Vicar of Dean Prior and the parson of Bemerton is obvious. The baroque flame and luxuriance of Crashaw are trimmed and tempered in the poems on the Babe who lies 'the Lillie-banks among'. The vision of 'Eternitie' and 'The white Island: or place of the Blest' combines in a simple, 'romantic' mood Vaughan-like imagery and classical terseness.

While the strains of Donne and Herbert meet and mingle in the divine poems of John Collop and Thomas Philipott, William Strode and Patrick Carey are closer to Herrick and look forward to the Restoration. Saintsbury was attracted by Carey's absence of 'pose', but the 'Crashaw-like "Crucifixion"' is Crashaw diluted and sentimentalized, and 'the fine "Crux via Caelorum"' is no doubt fine, but with the straightforward, rhetorical impulse of Dryden's lyrics.

With the beautiful 'Nox nocti indicat Scientiam' of William Habington another trend had appeared: an already Vaughan-like contemplativeness in Nature, a philosophic meditativeness smoothly ranging from the personal to the great commonplaces. The line extends through John Hall and William Hammond to the lyrics of Thomas Flatman, who praised solitude and melancholy, exalted 'Thoughts' and the pleasures of the imagination in pre-Romantic fashion without the mysticism of Traherne. Eclecticism, however, prevailed before the Restoration. John Hall achieved a happy balance between the nearness of Herbert and the naïvety of Traherne in 'A Pastoral Hymn'. Hammond sweetly imitated 'The Forerunners' in 'Grey Hairs', yet he reminds us of Marvell and his urbane wit when he combines human and divine love, pastoralism and the Bible, an hedonistic awareness of the power of 'sense' and platonic philosophy, in 'A Dialogue upon Death' between Phillis and Damon. His obsession with the stars, his sense of secrecy and philosophic musings, recall the themes and inspiration of Vaughan in 'The World'. Yet his obtrusive scientific imagery and his abruptness are reminiscent of Donne in other poems. Douglas Bush declared Hammond's *Poems* (1647) 'not distinctive'. The critic may accept the aesthetic judgement but to the historian of literary taste there are few poets more 'characteristic' of their age. He offers in a few pieces a full though feeble illustration of the cross-currents in the religious lyric of the seventeenth century.

THEME, TONE, AND TRADITION
IN GEORGE HERBERT'S POETRY

A. L. Clements

Although scholarship on George Herbert has contributed significantly to our knowledge of the religious elements in the poetry of *The
Temple*, various critics are divided on the vexed matter of Herbert's
mysticism.[1] Some, like George H. Palmer and Margaret Bottrall, assert
that he was not a mystic. Others, like Helen White and Itrat Husain,
argue that he was. Still others, like Joseph Summers, hold that he was
not a mystic in the sense of one who practices the "negative way" to
union with God, but that he might be considered a mystic of the *via
positiva*.[2]

In *The Poetry of Meditation*, Louis Martz has given us a valuable new
perspective on Renaissance literature, and we are indebted to him for
our understanding of the meditative structure and its role in seventeenth-
century poetry. Because meditation leads to and easily blends into
contemplation (the mystic state), and because devotional writers
frequently have recourse to mystical terminology as a source of
powerful metaphor, Martz properly cautions against hasty and inaccurate labeling of meditative writers as mystical. He is of course aware of
the presence of mystical elemens in Donne, Herbert, Crashaw, Vaughan,
and Traherne; but he believes that "the term 'meditative' seems ... more
accurate than 'mystical' when applied to English religious poetry of the
seventeenth century."[3]

Although "meditative" seems more accurate than the term "mystical"
when applied *in general* to English poetry of the seventeenth century,
there remain two important questions: (1) which term is more accurate
when applied to *particular* poems and to a *particular* seventeenth-
century poet; (2) to what extent did "medieval" contemplative literature
in addition to sixteenth-century meditative literature "influence"

Reprinted from *English Literary Renaissance,* 3 (1973), 264-83, © 1973. *English Literary
Renaissance,* by permission of the author and the publisher.

seventeenth-century English religious poetry? Undoubtedly, as Martz
has shown, Herbert was conversant with meditative patterns of writing
and ways of thinking as found in such meditative writers as St. Francis
de Sales and Lorenzo Scupoli. But to what extent did Herbert also avail
himself, as Vaughan and Traherne did,[4] of contemplative modes of
writing and thinking as found in such contemplatives as Meister
Eckhart, Walter Hilton, and Julian of Norwich? I believe that we may
come to a fuller and more exact understanding of Herbert's poetry by
studying it, especially neglected aspects of it, against the background of
the complex contemplative tradition, and that the division of the critics
on Herbert's mysticism necessitates re-thinking and re-evaluation along
these lines. As a contribution toward these ends, this essay shall first
present a reading of a seldom-noticed poem of Herbert's, "Artillerie,"
and then attempt to relate this and other Herbert poems to the curiously
well integrated and great speculative tradition of late medieval Christian
mysticism.

I

Given the title, theme, and major imagery of "Artillerie," a special
pertinence to this representative poem obtains in the famous description
of *The Temple* which Herbert himself, according to Izaak Walton, is
said to have written when he sent his book to Nicholas Ferrar: "a picture
of the many Spiritual Conflicts that have past betwixt God and my Soul,
before I could subject mine to the will of Jesus my Master: in whose
service I have now found perfect freedom." "Artillerie" is a picture of
one of the many spiritual conflicts between God and Herbert's soul; and
it ends on that dominant theme in Herbert's poetry: submission of his
will to God's. Like Donne, Herbert is often "at war" with God in his
religious poetry, but unlike Donne, who seems usually to remain at the
battlement demanding still that God batter his heart, Herbert, in
"Artillerie," as in many of his poems, finally lays down his weapons,
crosses over into God's camp, and surrenders unconditionally. An
overview of "Artillerie" indicates that its dialectical structure under-
scores the unqualified completeness of the submission of Herbert's will:
the first stanza establishes the conflict of wills; the second achieves a
temporary, incomplete submission; the third ironically qualifies this
surrender, which in effect continues the conflict; the fourth resolves the
tension of wills through Herbert's absolute submission. This dialectical
structure not only reflects Herbert's description of *The Temple*, as we
might expect, but also is a structure that Herbert re-employs with or

without modification in a number of other poems. The final submission is not a disillusioned resignation, but a thoroughly deliberated acceptance of his limitations in the face of God, and, paradoxically, through this acceptance a greater enhancement and awareness of his own true value. The poem's rest and serenity, those high desiderata in Herbert, result not from any easy optimism but from a courageous and complete acceptance or, rather, affirmation of God's will. The tension of contrary wills is resolved and peace follows.

The first two lines of "Artillerie" have a striking and arresting quality often observed in the opening lines of "metaphysical" poets: "As I one ev'ning sat before my cell,/ Me thoughts a starre did shoot into my lap."[5] It seems to the speaker of the poem that as he sat, no doubt meditatively, before his chamber in a state of apparent restfulness a star shot into his lap, "lap" here having, as later lines confirm, the seventeenth-century generalized meaning of "breast" (*OED*). This is an extraordinary and fantastic occurrence, yet the tone is calm, composed, almost casual and complacent. From the beginning of the poem, Herbert establishes an esentially assured, quiet, nearly playful tone that reflects an attitude underlying and pervading the whole poem; with his turning to God in the third line of stanza two, Herbert will permit his reasoning intellect also to operate, though never solemnly, and with the intellect's collapse, so to speak, into the final paradox of stanza four the reader will see there has never been a real contest or battle. It is as if the poet uses logic to confute and destroy logic itself and thereby lead us to overwhelming paradox. Herbert's common sense, his logic, dictates his shaking the flaming star away from his clothes, an action which is immediately practical but ultimately misguided. "I rose, and shook my clothes, as knowing well,/ That from small fires comes oft no small mishap." The simple rising, rather than anxious jumping or leaping up, to shake off the fire and the studied understatement of the last quoted line (l. 4) indicate equanimity and good-humored irony, as indeed does the subsequent sudden advice:

> When suddenly I heard one say,
> *Do as thou usest, disobey,*
> *Expell good motions from thy breast,*
> *Which have the face of fire, but end in rest. (ll. 5-8)*

This advice of lines 6-8 apparently is spoken by an inner voice in a dialogue of self or by some heavenly voice. (The poem's conclusion suggests that the inner self may finally be one with the divine self.) Ironically, the advice is intended to have an effect opposite to what it states: do *not*, as is your habit, expel good motions (that is, shooting stars, impulses, workings of God or his ministers in your soul) from your heart, for they will purify you so that you will finally rest with God. Acceptance of one's sufferings, purification by fire, is the way that leads to rest with God. By pointing to customary or habitual opposition and by describing a particular instance of it, the first stanza, then, presents the conflict between Herbert's will and God's will.

The second stanza arrives at an initial but incomplete and temporary submission:

> I, who had heard of musick in the spheres,
> But not of speech in starres, began to muse:
> But turning to my God, whose ministers
> The starres and all things are; If I refuse,
>   Dread Lord, said I, so oft my good;
>   Then I refuse not ev'n with bloud
>   To wash away my stubborn thought:
> For I will do or suffer what I ought. (ll. 9-16)

In lines 9-10, a personal tone of jestful conversation obtains; Herbert humorously makes a slight joke. The phrase "But turning to my God" marks the somewhat more serious turn which the poem now takes for the remainder of this stanza. Herbert knows there can be no genuine war between his will and God's, for the line "whose ministers/The starres and all things are" implies the orderliness of the universe, implies at least one central aspect of the Renaissance concept of the great chain of being.[6] All things, properly ordered and functioning, including stars, are God's ministers, that is, not only his agents or representatives, but also his attendants and servants; all things are subordinate to God, "who maketh his angels spirits; his ministers a flaming fire" (Ps. 104.4). Herbert would have a particular consciousness of his own special humble place as ordained minister and servant to the "Dread Lord."

The fuller meanings of *star*, a key word in the poem, now become clearer. All created things testify to God, but stars traditionally have assumed distinct roles in Christian belief. Literally guiding lights for sailors, they are in Christian thought beacons which lead to God. The pagan belief that the souls of illustrious persons after death appear as new stars finds its Christian parallel in the idea of the stars as God's saints, most notably in the well-known verses of Daniel 12.3: "And they that be wise shall shine as the brightness of the firmament; and they that turn many to righteousness as the stars for ever and ever." In "Joy of my life," a poem thought to be written in memory of his first wife, Henry Vaughan tells us that "Stars are of mighty use," for "God's Saints are shining lights." Thus the astrological notion, widely held during the Renaissance, that the stars influence human affairs, sway destinies, and mold temperaments undergoes, in Herbert's poem, as in Vaughan's, its Christian transformation: the enlightened holy ones, shining like stars in the sky, set the example and provide guidance for those who are lost and wandering in search of divine truth. Herbert's flaming, speaking star inevitably suggests Acts 2.3: "And there appeared unto them cloven tongues like as of fire," enabling the apostles to preach the truth to all men. Revelation 8 and 9 are also germane: after the third and fifth angels sound their trumpets a star falls from heaven and great affliction upon mankind follows, all of which will be finally concluded by Christ's ultimate triumph. One of the signs of Christ's coming is that ". . . the stars shall fall from heaven . . ." (Matt. 24.29). In "Artillerie" there is the coming, the acceptance of Christ, preceded and "effected" by a falling star, into the heart of a specific individual.

With the full significance of lines 11-12 evident to him, Herbert cannot ignore the central message of the New Testament: "For this is my blood of the new testament, which is shed for many for the remission of sins" (Matt. 26.28). He cannot refuse to wash away his stubborn thought with Christ's blood. Since Christ made a total sacrifice of himself, Herbert must accept the ironic advice of the first stanza, which, in effect, he does in the conclusive line, "For I will do or suffer what I ought." He submits his will and yields to the dangerous and disturbing motions which eventually end in rest; he follows the example of Christ and the saints in accepting redemptive suffering. Thus stanza two ends in Herbert's submission.[7]

This acquiescence, however, is only temporary, for stanza three, employing reversal strategy, a device favored by Donne also, qualifies it and hence continues the conflict of wills; if the divine advice of stanza one is ironic, then indeed so may Herbert's response be playfully ironic.

> But I have also starres and shooters too,
> Born where thy servants both artilleries use.
> My tears and prayers night and day do wooe,
> And work up to thee; yet thou dost refuse.
>> Not but I am (I must say still)
>> Much more oblig'd to do thy will,
>> Then thou to grant mine: but because
> Thy promise now hath ev'n set thee thy laws. (ll. 17-24)

The effect of such qualification will be to make possible a profounder and more permanent submission — that of stanza four. For the brief time being, however, Herbert, by parodying several traditions or conventions, further exploits the dominant martial metaphor and expands the love metaphor that has been adumbrated by the tone of familiar conversation between lovers. We shall subsequently discuss sixteenth-century spiritual exercises, particularly Lorenzo Scupoli's *Spiritual Combat.* A second, parodied convention is the Petrarchan. Throughout his poetry, Herbert boldly borrowed Petrarchan imagery, especially the complicated imagery of the heart. In stanza three of "Artillerie," he parodies the courtly lover unsuccessfully wooing his lady. Whereas Donne inverts the Petrarchan convention in some of his secular poems, Herbert uses it to woo God.

The stars and shooters born in Herbert's heart are his tears and prayers; these are his artilleries, his arrows,[8] which "night and day do wooe, / And work up to thee." The emblem tradition which itself exploits courtly and Petrarchan conventions and biblical tradition, particularly the Psalms, underlies this idea. In Francis Quarles' *Emblems* there is a print of a devout suppliant kneeling, with an arrow from his breast pointing upward; above him arrows bearing banners of prayers and sighs ascend upward to God's eye and ears; beneath him is a reference to Psalm 38.9 and the words: "On Thee, O Lord, is fixed my whole Desire To Thee my Groans ascend, my Prayers aspire." The accompanying poem in its most relevant lines reads:

> ... In prayer and patience, find Him out again:
> Make Heav'n thy mistress; let no change remove
> Thy loyal heart, — be fond, be sick of love:
> What if he stop his ear, or knit his brow?
> At length he'll be as fond, as sick as thou:
> Dart up thy soul in groans; ...
> Shoot up the bosom shafts of thy desire,
> Feather'd with faith, and double-fork'd with fire;
> And they will hit: fear not, where Heaven bids come;
> Heav'n's never deaf, but when man's heart is dumb.[9]

Like many of Herbert's titles, the title of our poem is emblematic; "Artillerie" is the poetic equivalent of an emblem, symbolizing the spiritual combat between God and Herbert. Herbert, however, deviates from the emblem and Petrarchan "traditions" in that his God still refuses him, as the God addressed in emblem poetry will not, indeed seemingly cannot refuse, and in that Herbert's language is playful and bantering (note the parenthetical "I must say still"), whereas the traditions he draws upon and parodies tend to be more solemn. True, the final consequence is the same in all cases: complete capitulation to God, and ultimate joy. But though and because Herbert knows all the time that "I am ... / Much more oblig'd to do thy will, / Then thou to grant mine," he can ironically insist in his own contrary way that God is bound to obey His own promise, for hasn't He promised to wash away all man's sins and sufferings with His own blood? Herbert the poet, as distinguished from the speaker, has known all along that "There is no articling with thee (l. 31)"; there is no need for it. He can be casual and playful in tone precisely because he sees so clearly that ultimately there is no possibility of deviating from the will of God. His casualness is an aspect of the nature of children — innocent, spontaneous, unself-conscious inheritors of Eden who, as Henry Vaughan writes in "Childe-hood," "by meer playing go to Heaven." Ironic qualification (a mode of playfulness) of his compliance to God's will renders possible and more meaningful and vividly emphasizes the utter submission of stanza four.

> Then we are shooters both, and thou dost deigne
> To enter combate with us, and contest
> With thine own clay. But I would parley fain:
> Shunne not my arrows, and behold my breast.
> > Yet if thou shunnest, I am thine:
> > I must be so, if I am mine.
> > There is no articling with thee:
> > I am but finite, yet thine infinitely. (ll. 25-32)

This last stanza, a "fireworks" of reflexive phrases and lines wherein the metaphors of war and love merge, as in Donne's Holy Sonnet 14, summarizes and resolves the preceding three stanzas. On the basis of what Herbert has said in stanzas one and three he can conclude in line 25, "Then we are shooters both." And his constant awareness of God's supremacy enables him to recognize and write of God's condescension when "thou dost deigne / To enter combate with us, and contest / With thine own clay." Knowing he is no match for his divine opponent, Herbert seeks a truce and mutual surrender. The "arrows," which he asks God not to shun, are both weapons against the Almighty and darts of love; the merging of war and love metaphors unites the conventions Herbert has been parodying, and, like the Psalmist, emblemist, and the courtly lover, Herbert pleads "behold my breast." The last four lines, using both military language and the language of lovers, emphatically reaffirm the conclusion of stanza two and assert with earned finality the paradox that Herbert's true being lies in giving up his finite ego in infinite submission to God.

II

I have previously alluded to Scupoli's *Spiritual Combat*, a book which, considering Herbert's use of the term "Spiritual Conflicts" in his own description of *The Temple,* is perhaps of some direct significance especially in that one English edition of Scupoli's book was entitled *Spiritual Conflict.* I wish now briefly to consider Scupoli's work in relation to Herbert, and then, while affirming the pertinence of sixteenth-century spiritual exercises as one of several "traditions" Herbert drew upon, to go on to suggest the relevance of late medieval contemplative tradition, and particularly its basic doctrine or idea of the two selves, to Herbert's "Artillerie" and other poems.

Spiritual Combat, according to Louis Martz, is "the second great landmark in the development of spiritual exercises during the sixteenth century ... a book which may hold some significance for English literature of the seventeenth century and especially for ... Herbert...."[10] The martial metaphor implied in the title of the book is pervasive in the book itself, and it is quite possible that "Artillerie" and similar poems, allowing for the transformation effected by Herbert's originality, were influenced and nourished by the book's major metaphor. "The center of the book is self-analysis, the prime weapon in the spiritual combat":

> ... you must wage continual warfare against yourself and employ your entire strength in demolishing each vicious inclination, however trivial....

> The first thing to do when you awake is to open the windows of your soul. Consider yourself as on the field of battle, facing the enemy and bound by the iron-clad law — either fight or die....

> Begin to fight immediately in the name of the Lord, armed with distrust of yourself, with confidence in God, [with] prayer, and with the correct use of the faculties of your soul. With these weapons, attack the enemy....[11]

There can hardly be any question that Herbert was very aware of and knowledgeable about the central ideas and imagery of *Spiritual Combat,* if not the book itself. In his prose work *A Priest to the Temple, or, the Countrey Parson,* Herbert discusses the "double state of a Christian even in this Life, the one military, the other peaceable."

> The military is, when we are assaulted with temptations either from within or from without. The Peaceable is, when the Devill for a time leaves us, as he did our Saviour, and the Angels minister to us their owne food, even joy, and peace; and comfort in the holy

Ghost. These two states were in our Saviour, not only in the
beginning of his preaching, but afterwards also, as *Mat.* 22, 35. He
was tempted: And *Luke* 10. 21. He rejoyced in Spirit: And they
must be likewise in all that are his. (p. 280)

The military state here described (similar in language, tone, and other
qualities to *Spiritual Combat*) doubtlessly derives ultimately from the
basic and well-known idea of St. Paul that the Christian life is like a
battle and the Christian like a soldier. St. Paul describes the discipline to
which the Christian is subject, his armor and his weapons of offense, and
the enemies, internal and external, against whom he has to fight.

As Rosemond Tuve and other critics have shown, Herbert characteristically employs in his poetry a traditional central invention; he
explores and labors within it to discover new veins of meaning and
nuance. What is for our purposes especially remarkable is the significant
difference in tone between "Artillerie" and the typical passages quoted
from Scupoli. Although the imagery of both is martial and derivative
from that most important companion volume to the reading of Herbert's
poetry, the Bible, the deadly serious tone of *Spiritual Combat* is quite
unlike the familiarity and playfulness of "Artillerie." The difference in
tone between Scupoli's and Herbert's work signalizes the spiritual
distance or progress between the early or meditative stages of the
religious life and Herbert's own attainment of more advanced or
contemplative stages as evidenced in "Artillerie" and a number of his
other poems. Considering Herbert's use of other conventions and
traditions in the poem, "Artillerie," in tone at least, would seem to be a
particular result of one of Herbert's poetic practices, a kind of gentle
parody of *Spiritual Combat.*[12] Herbert the poet, as distinguished from
the speaker, appears to be in fuller control. He seems to know in this
poem what the conclusion, both in and outside the poem, is going to be,
and thus he can adopt a less sombre and more assured tone than that of
Spiritual Combat. Indeed, the merging of the metaphors of war and love
in the last stanza suggests that the poem is not the intense, passionate
"warfare" of the spiritual exercises but rather, simply a lovers' quarrel, a
quarrel between the two "selves" of the poem. To help account for the
differences, particularly the differences in tone and theme, between
Herbert and Scupoli, one should look more closely at the conception of
the two selves found in *The Temple.* Since this conception itself develops
out of biblical, contemplative tradition about which Herbert, the
country parson, was knowledgeable, one should, in other words, look to
the tradition constituted by the Bible and "the Fathers also, and the
Schoolmen, and the later Writers, or a good proportion of all."[13]

The contemplative tradition's fundamental conception of man's twofold self derives, naturally enough, from the Bible. The Old Testament provides important scriptural authority in well-known verses such as "So God created man in his own image, in the image of God created he him" (Gen. 1.27). The New Testament sometimes expresses the idea of man's dichotomous nature directly, as in "The first man Adam was made a living soul; the last Adam was made a quickening spirit" (1 Cor. 15.45), and in "though our outward man perish, yet the inward man is renewed day by day" (2 Cor. 4.16; see also Heb. 4.12, Rom. 7.22, Eph. 3.16, Col. 3.9). Sometimes the twofold distinction is embodied in the crucial paradox of gain through loss or of life through death: "Except a corn of wheat fall into the ground and die, it abideth alone; but if it die, it bringeth forth much fruit. He that loveth his life shall lose it; and he that hateth his life in this world shall keep it unto life eternal" (John 12.24-25; see also Luke 9.24-25). All these and many other biblical passages pertain to the central conversion experience of hating and giving up the corrupt egoistic life of the old Adam or outward man to realize the life of the true Spirit, inward man, or last Adam.

The contemplatives, that is a good proportion of "the Fathers . . . and the Schoolmen, and the later Writers," variously articulate the idea that man is made in God's image, that when the fallen outward man is purged away the real Self in the depth of the particular individual may be seen as identical with or at least like unto the Divinity. Largely under the influence of Augustine, "image theology" made its way to late-medieval writers who expressed the essential spiritual unity of man and God in such terms as the apex of the soul, the ground, the spark, anima, the interior castle, the two Adams, created and uncreated nature, and so on. Julian of Norwich, an English mystic with a religious sensibility not unlike Herbert's, writes that "the good Lord showed his own Son and Adam as one man," and "by *Adam* I always understand *Everyman*." Still another English mystic, Walter Hilton, who freely translated the very popular medieval spiritual classic *Stimulus Amoris*, declares that "yet mickle more wonder and more delightable and without comparison, more ought to be coveted the gracious turning and the glorious changing [of a man] into God. . . . This turning is here, in his life through grace." Lastly, writing on "the fundamental dogma of mystical psychology," Abbe Bremond further clarifies "the distinction between the two selves: *Animus*, the *surface self; Anima*, the *deep self; Animus*, rational knowledge; and *Anima*, mystical or poetic knowledge . . . the I, who feeds on notions and words and enchants himself by doing so; the Me, who is united to realities."[14]

The basic contemplative doctrine, then, is that man has two selves: the phenomenal or finite ego, of which he is mainly conscious and which he tends mistakenly to regard as his true self, and an infinite and hence not wholly definable self, the inward man or image of divinity in him, which is in reality his true Self. It is important to emphasize that this idea does not mean that "therefore, I am God Almighty!" For the "I" or ego is one's conception of himself, the known created object, not the knowing creative actuality. It is a prideful sense of separate and independent existence, the role one assumes and is assigned to play, a somewhat abstract and conventional self. In order to know God fully and be united to Him, man's will and entire being must come into full accord with God's will and being. The isolated and isolating ego, the fallen Adam, must itself die so that a process of infinite expansion may occur, so that inner unity may be attained.

The Temple may very well be regarded as a various record of many spiritual conflicts, griefs, and joys, coordinated and made more coherent by the central theme of submission to God's will, particularly if this submission is understood as the major means for effecting the glorious changing of the fallen Adam into the Son of God. Indeed, this transformation of a man and this submission to divine will are but two ways of speaking of the same event, as, for example, "The Crosse" makes perfectly clear. Throughout *The Temple*, Herbert frequently voices the idea of the two selves in each man through the distinction expressed in the words *mine* and *thine*, the most crucial words in the last stanza of "Artillerie." "The Altar," at the beginning of "The Church," concludes with this petition:

> That, if I chance to hold my peace,
> These stones to praise thee may not cease.
> O let thy blessed SACRIFICE be mine,
> And sanctifie this ALTAR to be thine.

If the speaker comes to peace and silence, rather than being enchanted by notions and words, his poems paradoxically will endlessly praise God (for Herbert believed that only certain appropriate spiritual states and attitudes could produce immortal divine poetry). In the last two lines, the speaker prays to become Christ-like, to have the altar which is his heart ("A broken ALTAR, Lord, thy servant reares, / Made of a heart") become Christ's own. The word *Sacrifice* in the penultimate line is picked up in the title of the next poem, "The Sacrifice," which treats Christ's Passion in the first person voice of Christ and which contains the refrain "Was ever grief like mine?" The record throughout *The Temple* of Herbert's own afflictions, sufferings, and many spiritual conflicts is, then, a way of indicating the speaker's movement toward

Christ-likeness, a movement which is completed in "Love" (III), the last poem in "The Church." A eucharistic feast at the allegorical level, "Love" (III) is, anagogically, a description of the soul's perfection in union with Christ.[15] The first and last Adams, the served, the servant, and the host become one in communion, that is, in the bloodless re-enactment of Christ's sacrifice and in final union: "My deare, then I will serve./ You must sit down, sayes Love, and taste my meat: / So I did sit and eat."

Some of the more important recurrences of the *mine-thine* distinction which appears between "The Altar" and "Love" (III) confirm the centrality of the contemplative conception of the two selves in Herbert's poetry. An obvious and prominent example is "Clasping of hands," a poem that is a constant, quite serious playing upon the repeated *mine* and *thine*. At least one and often both of these words occur in eighteen of the poem's twenty lines. The metaphysical convolutions or shifts in meaning and identity consequent upon the poem's playful variations may be difficult to follow closely, but the conclusion is plainly a prayer for union:

> LORD, thou art mine, and I am thine,
> If mine I am: and thine much more,
> Then I or ought, or can be mine,
> Yet to be thine, doth me restore;
> So that again I now am mine,
> And with advantage mine the more,
> Since this being mine, brings with it thine,
> And thou with me dost thee restore.
>   If I without thee would be mine,
>   I neither should be mine nor thine.
>
> Lord, I am thine, and thou art mine:
> So mine thou art, that something more
> I may presume thee mine, then thine.
> For thou didst suffer to restore
> Nor thee, but me, and to be mine,
> And with advantage mine the more,
> Since thou in death wast none of thine,
> Yet then as mine didst me restore.
>   O be mine still! still make me thine!
>   Or rather make no Thine and Mine!

The second stanza of "Clasping of hands" shows that the "Lord" being addressed is the Second Person of the Trinity, the Son of God or Christ.

It is usually, but not always, the case in *The Temple* that Herbert employs the terms *mine* and *thine* to designate specifically the first and last Adams.

"Judgment," which appears near the end of *The Temple* and appropriately has an eschatological theme, similarly involves the last Adam whose sacrifice included the bearing of blame for man's sins. The speaker of the poem considers that time when each man's book of his life shall be called for to be examined, and he concludes:

> But I resolve, when thou shalt call for mine,
>   That to decline,
> And thrust a Testament into thy hand:
>   Let that be scann'd.
> There thou shalt finde my faults are thine.

On the other hand, "The Quip," a poem in the allegorical mode, does not make distinctions clearly with respect to divine Person. In successive stanzas, Beautie, Money, Glory, Wit, and Conversation are presented with their respective temptations, and each stanza ends with the refrain "But thou shalt answer, Lord, for me." The final stanza reads:

> Yet when the houre of thy designe
> To answer these fine things shall come!
> Speak not at large; say, I am thine:
> And then they will have their answer home.

The interesting point about the penultimate line is its ambiguity. That is, not only may it mean, in indirect quotation, that the speaker's being is the Lord's, but it may also be understood in direct quotation that the Lord's being is the speaker's, that the Lord is to say "I am thine."[16] Taken in the second sense, the speaker's own answer is the best answer or quip because it is the shortest possible answer. It is no answer of his own. He has chanced to hold his peace, as "The Altar" petitions, and the end result is, so the speaker hopes, that the Lord shall answer for him and shall answer in terms which suggest the ultimate identity or union of the individual suppliant with God. The recurrent uses of *mine* and *thine*, then, point significantly to the centrality in and pervasiveness throughout *The Temple* of the contemplative tradition's basic idea of the two selves which are to be one, temporarily in illumination and permanently in final union.

The critically widely-noted alternation in state of mood, mind, and soul in *The Temple*, sometimes from poem to poem and at other times even within the same poem, not only parallels the stanzaic alternation (in poems such as "Artillerie" and "Dialogue") between conflict and accord but also, more importantly, reflects the self within the speaker (or Herbert) which is predominant at any one time. These alternating states of affliction and joy, of spiritual conflict and perfect freedom, that obtain throughout Herbert's work find a correspondence in the fifteenth chapter of Dame Julian's *Revelations of Divine Love*. This chapter concerns "the recurring experience of delight and depression." Like Herbert, Julian writes "then I felt the pain again; then the joy and pleasure; now it was one, and now the other, many times." She understands, as Herbert comes to understand, "that it was for their own good that some souls should have this sort of experience: sometimes to be consoled; sometimes to be bereft and left to themselves. The will of God is that we should know he keeps us safely, alike 'in weal or woe'.... Both are equally his love."[17] While many of Herbert's poems might here be cited, "The Temper" (I) best expresses and embodies the ideas in Julian's fifteenth chapter:

> How should I praise thee, Lord! how should my rymes
>   Gladly engrave thy love in steel,
> If what my soul doth feel sometimes,
>   My soul might ever feel!
>
> Although there were some fourtie heav'ns, or more,
>   Sometimes I peere above them all;
> Sometimes I hardly reach a score,
>   Sometimes to hell I fall.
>
> O rack me not to such a vast extent;
>   Those distances belong to thee:
> The world's too little for thy tent,
>   A grave too big for me.
>
> Wilt thou meet arms with men, that thou dost stretch
>   A crumme of dust from heav'n to hell?
> Will great God measure with a wretch?
>   Shall he thy stature spell?
>
> O let me, when thy roof my soul hath hid,
>   O let me roost and nestle there:
> Then of a sinner thou art rid,
>   And I of hope and fear.
>
> Yet take thy way; for sure thy way is best:
>   Stretch or contract me, thy poore debter:

> This is but tuning of my breast,
> To make the musick better.

> Whether I flie with angels, fall with dust,
> Thy hands made both, and I am there:
> Thy power and love, my love and trust
> Make one place ev'ry where.

Presumably, it is the "Immortal Heat" of God, addressed in "Love"
(II), immediately preceding "The Temper" (I), which will purge, refine,
and temper the steel-like, stony-hard heart of the old Adam by means of
alternate stretching and contracting from heaven to hell, thereby
initiating his transformation into the new Adam. The poem works
subtly. The speaker's plea in stanza three, though understandable
enough, is at a deeper level a contesting of God's will and ways, and
hence it is a form of egoistic willfulness. In asking not to be racked, the
speaker is in effect, if unwittingly, refusing to follow Christ and the
model he provides through his own racking, his willing self-sacrifice and
suffering in the crucifixion. The fourth stanza, in terms not unlike
"Artillerie," spells out the battle of wills between God and man. The
questions asked are: will God meet arms with man, as in a duel, a
meeting of swords, or will God measure with, that is compete with or try
his strength against (*OED*) wretched man? (Of course, as indicated by
l.16, "measure" may also retain its usual meaning, and "meet" may be a
pun on "mete.") In stanzas six and seven, again as in "Artillerie," there is
finally a turning toward and affirmation of God's will. The stretching
and contracting, the alternate joy and affliction or rising to heaven and
falling to hell, are at last seen as a tempering or tuning of the heart. Both
weal and woe, delight and depression, ascent and descent, are equally
God's love. In other words, through God's power and love and man's
love and trust, the way down and the way up are one and the same; man's
willingness to affirm God's will and even to accept the burden of
suffering, "for sure thy way is best," makes him Christ-like and
consequently ultimately gives him joy. Notably, if we take *The Temple*
as a body of poems which are in some sense sequential, the opening lines
of "The Temper" (II), following immediately after (I), reveal that the joy
just attained is soon lost, and affliction and conflict return:

> It cannot be. Where is that mightie joy,
> Which just now took up all my heart?
> Lord, if thou must needs use thy dart,
> Save that, and me; or sin for both destroy.

A pattern similar to the alternate grief and joy, or spiritual darkness and illumination, of "The Temper" poems is observable in the four-poem sequence of "The Search," "Grief," "The Crosse," and "The Flower." These four poems suggest, however, that the narrator is past the purgative and illuminative stages and is experiencing the dark night of the soul. They represent a steady progression of the soul, which by descending ascends. The speaker's "shrivel'd heart . . . was gone / Quite under ground" ("The Flower"). Although the speaker has a sense of sin, at least of past sins (see, for example, "The Search," 1.28 and "The Flower," 1.28), he has not abandoned God but feels, mistakenly, that God has abandoned him: "Whither, O, whither art thou fled, / My Lord, my Love," "The Search" begins. He is plunged deeper into the depths of grief, a repeated word throughout the four poems, by the sense that he has relapsed to a lower spiritual level after having attained illuminative joys and even that he is now farther away than when he first undertook his ascent to the Divine Center. All that the speaker feels — the absence of God, the sense of sin, the loss of the self's former peace and joy, the profound depths of grief and suffering, the apparent relapse to a lower spiritual level — are characteristics, according to Evelyn Underhill, of the dark night of the soul.[18]

The speaker's griefs, as the poet knows, have the redemptive value of teaching him on his pulses the utter futility of the old Adam's willfulness, even when the will is bent toward a good end but presumes or acts "as if heav'n were mine own" ("The Flower"). This difficult lesson seems to necessitate much anguish in the learning. Indeed, the speaker's grief as recorded throughout *The Temple* and particularly in "The Search," "Grief," and "The Crosse" is cumulatively equivalent to the grief of the speaker of "The Sacrifice" and constitutes an affirmative response to Christ's refrain "Was ever grief like mine?" as the brilliant last stanza of "The Crosse" indicates:

> Ah my deare Father, ease my smart!
> These contarieties crush me: these crosse actions
> Doe winde a rope about, and cut my heart:
> And yet since these thy contradictions
> Are properly a crosse felt by thy Sonne,
> With but foure words, my words, *Thy will be done.*

As in "Artillerie," when after stanzaic alternations between conflict and submission Herbert finally concedes "there is no articling with thee," and as in "The Temper" (I), when after averring that "sure thy way is best," Herbert begins to understand that both grief and joy are somehow paradoxically equally God's love, so in "The Crosse," after affirming

God's will Herbert experiences a spiritual renewal, confirmed in "The Flower." The ambiguity and wordplay of the last stanza of "The Crosse" are similar to the double sense of "I am thine" in "The Quip." The grievous "Crosse actions" felt by Herbert are indeed "properly a crosse felt by thy Sonne." By following Christ's example and making his words "*Thy will be done*" "my words," Herbert spiritually and actually realizes with Dame Julian in serious playfulness that God's Son and Adam, who is Everyman, are one man. By these means, the first Adam becomes the last Adam. Herbert could say with Walter Hilton that "it is a wonderful changing of a sinful wretch to be God's son made, through the right hand of him that is highest."[19]

The third stanza of the much-discussed and deservedly-praised "The Flower," a poem revelatory of the correspondence between natural cyclical life and human spiritual life, is especially notable after the last stanza of "The Crosse":

> These are thy wonders, Lord of power,
> Killing and quickning, bringing down to hell
> And up to heaven in an houre;
> Making a chiming of a passing-bell.
> We say amisse,
> This or that is:
> Thy word is all, if we could spell.

While the first half of the stanza echoes "The Temper" (I), the last three lines, as profound a mystical statement as one might find, have more than a single meaning. First, like Milton's Christ in *Paradise Regained*, whose preference for Hebraic over classical literature has critically been regarded as springing from a hierarchy of values which embodies an intense thirst for the beatific vision, Herbert believes that if one could read and comprehend by study God's word, the Bible, or scan and consider it intently (all various meanings of *spell* according to the *OED*, which cites Herbert's "Shall he thy stature spell?") that would suffice for spiritual knowledge or "true wisdom." Secondly, the mystical sense seems to be that God's word as he is described in John 1, the Word that in the beginning was God, made all things, and was the true light and life of men, is all, at least to those who, truly understanding, receive him and become sons of God (John 1.11). When rightly apprehended, all else ("this or that") is egoistic illusion, and God's word, as sacred words (including especially *Thy will be done*) and as the Son of God, is all that really is.

In "The Flower," Herbert is not "Fast in thy Paradise, where no flower can wither"; he is not "past changing" in final union. Although he has not reached the tenth and last rung in the ladder of love described by St. John of the Cross, he has perhaps reached the eighth rung, which is characterized by knowing God at intervals and at least for short and intense periods. Even so, this should be recognized as a considerable achievement. Some of the critical confusion on Herbert's mysticism is owing to the failure to make sufficient and clear distinctions between process and result, between meditation and achieved (if temporarily) contemplation, between "the many Spiritual Conflicts" and the attained "perfect freedom." "The Flower," like a number of other poems in *The Temple*, points to such attainment:

> And now in age I bud again,
> After so many deaths I live and write;
>   I once more smell the dew and rain,
> And relish versing: O my onely light,
>   It cannot be
>   That I am he
> On whom thy tempests fell all night.
> These are thy wonders, Lord of love,
> To make us see we are but flowers that glide:
>   Which when we once can finde and prove,
> Thou hast a garden for us, where to bide.
>   Who would be more,
>   Swelling through store,
> Forfeit their Paradise by their pride.

Just as the corn of wheat that falls into the ground and dies brings forth much fruit, so the poet who undergoes "many deaths" blooms again in Paradise. Seeing that "we are but flowers that glide" is essentially equivalent to not clinging to the prideful life of the outward man and so finding life eternal as the Son of God. Typically, in Herbert's poems the self is to be at once obliterated and exalted; that is, the willful, combative, self-seeking, fallen Adam must die, and the new Adam must arise reborn, atoned, and united to God. After many griefs, Herbert sees the absurdity of opposing, even in presumably good causes, the finite, illusory ego against the infinite real Self; he knows he has free will in order to will his self-will out of existence and so eventually come to live continuously in a state of "at-one-ment." He thinks of the incarnation as a constantly renewed fact of experience. As the three Magi were led, historically, by a star to the place of the incarnation, so Herbert in "Artillerie" is led, imaginatively, by a star to an understanding of the incarnation in its full sacramental meaning, to the paradoxical and profound realization of his being in God or God's being in him. In

Meister Eckhart's words, "God's being is my life, but if it is so, then what is God's must be mine and what is mine God's. God's is-ness [*istigkeit*] is my is-ness, and neither more nor less."[20] Herbert's mode of articulating this central contemplative idea is less abstract and philosophical but no less precise. "I am thine." "I am but finite, yet thine infinitely." "Thy word is all." "So I did sit and eat." For in God's "Providence," "all things have their will, yet none but thine." On his characteristic final note of holding his peace and totally affirming divine will, Herbert's infinitely enhanced true Self may "end in rest."

GEORGE HERBERT AND THE INCARNATION

Richard E. Hughes

George Herbert (1593-1633), one of the brightest ornaments of the 17th century English church, defined the principal articles of his faith in the poem "Ungratefulnesse": "Thou hast but two rare cabinets full of treasure,/ The *Trinitie*, and *Incarnation*."[1] But in the same poem, he indicated to what extent he, as both priest and poet, could comprehend and expand on these articles:

> The statlier cabinet is the *Trinitie*,
>> Whose sparkling light accesse denies:
>>> Therefore thou dost not show
>>> This fully to us, till death blow
>>> The dust into our eyes:
>
> For by that powder thou wilt make us see.
>
> But all thy sweets are packt up in the other;
>> Thy mercies thither flock and flow:
>>> That as the first affrights,
>>> This may allure us with delights;
>>> Because this box we know;
>
> For we have all of us just such another.

Herbert's natural reticence to expound on the Trinity has, of course, been shared by all conservative theologians; and Herbert's poetry attests to that reticence. God is rarely addressed in familiar terms: the feudal appellations of *Lord* and *King* dominate. Allusions to the persons of the Trinity are exceptionally sparse: he mentions the Son, as specifically of the Trinity, in the poems "Even-song," "Home," "Grieve not the Holy Spirit," "The Crosse," and "The Sonne." The Holy Ghost appears in "Whitsunday," "Grace," "Grieve not the Holy Spirit," and in the first of the early sonnets he wrote to his mother (printed in Izaac Walton's *Life of George Herbert*, 1670). The Trinity *qua* Trinity appears in only two of

Reprinted from *Cithara*, 4 (1964), 22-32, by permission of the author and St. Bonaventure University.

his poems, "L'Envoy" and "Trinitie Sunday" (in the latter, in the title only). In the whole canon of the more than 170 English poems that are definitely Herbert's, these are obviously minimal. We may accept Herbert's protestation in "Ungratefulnesse" that he will not, and can not, dilate on the doctrine of the Trinity in his poetry.

We should expect, since the poetry fulfills the first half of the doctrinal program as Herbert implied it in "Ungratefulnesse," that his poetic works would be a constant development and praise of the doctrine of the Incarnation. But at first glance, we are disappointed, and tempted to under-value Herbert's insistence that "This may allure us with delights." The Incarnation is mentioned explicitly only once, in the poem "An Offering." However, the church demonstrates the doctrine of the Incarnation in two ways, the first historically in the *Vita Christi*, the second sacramentally in the Eucharist; and this is, up to a point, Herbert's way. He has seven poems which celebrate the Eucharist: two versions of "H. Communion" (one appearing in the early printed editions of Herbert's poetry, the second in the Williams manuscript), "Peace," "The Bunch of Grapes," "The Invitation," "The Banquet," and "Love (III)." The life, ministry and death of Christ are, of course, the historic and graphic illustrations of the Incarnation. Herbert emphasizes the Passion and Death, minimizing the early years and ministry of Christ. In "Faith" and "Christmas" alone does he recount the birth of Christ; in but one poem, "Marie Magdalene," does he present an episode in the ministry of Christ; and there are but two references to Mary and the Virgin Birth, one in "Ana (Mary) Army gram," the other in "To all Angels and Saints." Events at the end of the life of Christ, however, bulk largely in Herbert's poetry: the Resurrection provides either subject or symbol in "Easter" and "Easter-wings." The Passion and Death of Christ (obviously, for Herbert, the central activity of the redemptive process) is legion in his poetry: in no less than twenty-four poems the events of Passion Week are Herbert's subject ... "The Church-Porch," "Sacrifice," "Thanksgiving," "Reprisall," "Agonie," "Good Friday," "Redemption," "Sepulchre," "H. Baptism (I)," "Prayer," "Affliction," "Affliction (II)," "Unkindnesse," "Conscience," "Dawning," "Businesse," "Church-rents and schismes," "The Pilgrimage," "Longing," "The Bag," "The Crosse," "Death," "The Church Militant," and "L'Envoy." Clearly, we are to accept Herbert's implication that he is the poet of the Incarnation even if not of the Trinity.

But to have noted that the Incarnation is frequently Herbert's subject is only the first step in understanding his work. What Herbert felt about the Incarnation is, without question, the central issue of his poetry; and

we cannot really understand his poetry until we understand the role the
Incarnation played in his writing. Briefly, Herbert did not merely write
about the Incarnation: he saw poetry itself as a miniature version of the
Incarnation; and each divine poem as a microcosm of the Incarnation.
The doctrine provided Herbert, not only with subject, but with form,
technique and meaning.

Involved in the doctrine of the Incarnation is one of the great
archetypal dichotomies of the imagination, the war between chaos and
order, fragmentation and harmony. While the Incarnation is an historical and ontological act, the birth of Christ whereby the God-head is
clothed in flesh, it is also a symbolic act, involving psychological,
ethical, and moral implications. The literal incarnation of Christ is
conceived to be the *typos* of all human affairs, *theandrism*, the
involvement of the divine in all temporal activity, the elevation of the
human to the divine. The voice of God in the void, bringing order out of
chaos, is one analogue of the Incarnation, as is every individual
regeneration whereby incomplete human experience is sanctified by
union with divinity. Meaninglessness brought to order, on any plane,
reflects the Incarnation; and Herbert's instinctive love of ritual, liturgy
and the English church, wherein gesture is translated into meaningful
symbol and objects become sacramentals, is a fact necessary to our
understanding of his poetry. For all liturgy is a prolongation of the
Incarnation,[2] inasmuch as human actions and temporal objects (the
voice, the body, the altar, church artifacts) become divinized by their
participation in religious activity. It was fortunate that Herbert died
before the establishment of the Protectorate when the iconoclastic
Puritan regime destroyed the high altars and the stained glass, and
interdicted the traditional form of Anglican worship, for he could never
have understood and would have been dismayed by the denial of the
sacramental sense. Church music and church furniture and the decencies of Anglican ritual were venerated by Herbert, not for their own
sake, but for the fact that they were all made meaningful by their
association with divinity and since by their very artfulness they could
preach that triumph of order over chaos which is one lesson of the
Incarnation.

Herbert's delight in, and reverence for, the orderly decencies of his
church are paramount in his work. In "The British Church" he wrote:

> I joy, deare Mother, when I view
> > Thy perfect lineaments and hue
> > > Both sweet and bright.
> Beautie in thee takes up her place.   (p. 109)

He has poems which praise "Church-monuments" and "Church-musick." The poem "The Windowes" most adequately expresses the faith he had in the sacramentals of his church:

> Lord, how can man preach thy eternall word?
> He is a brittle crazie glasse:
> Yet in thy temple thou dost him afford
> This glorious and transcendent place,
> To be a window, through thy grace.   (p. 67)

Prof. Joseph H. Summers has spoken of "Theological conceptions with inevitable aesthetic corollaries"[3] in Herbert's poetry; it is a corollary that works both ways, in that aesthetic attitudes possess, for Herbert, theological meanings. Orderliness implied sanctification and ultimately incarnation; God's presence in the world of the flesh and of material is announced by the triumph of order. The transforming power of music, for instance, is not aesthetic only, but theological as well. In "The Thanksgiving" God is identified with music, as He is in "Deniall." God is the supreme artist in "The Temper (II)." The decree that music and poetry must be turned, not to profane uses but to sacred ends and thus to embody the belief that God in entering the world brought harmony to cacophony, is insistent throughout Herbert's canon: it is an idea to be found in the poems "Providence," "Sinnes round," "Jordan," "Deniall," "Grieve not the Holy Spirit," and in the first sonnets to his mother. And throughout his poetry there are images and symbols drawn from music.

To emphasize the element of music at the expense of the whole poem would, however, be a mistake. Herbert not only refers to music, he is one of the most musical of English poets, and each single poem is a piece of music. (The honored place many of his poems hold in Anglican hymnals attests to this.) Herbert celebrates the presence of God in the world through the whole poem, not through isolated symbol or metaphor. The poem is the unit of order; and in the creation of a poem, Herbert re-enacts the whole drama of the Incarnation. Expression itself, ordered, musical and sacred, is the symbol of the Incarnation. Herbert values the *word* in the same way and to the same extent that it was valued by the early Church Fathers and their philosophic predecessors.

To recognize the value we must place on the uttered word, the basic unit of the poet's craft and the way above all others which Herbert chose to demonstrate his faith, we ought to recognize that there was a venerable tradition of seeing the *word* as the prime symbol of the Incarnation upon which Herbert could draw. That is the tradition of the "Logos doctrine," which identified the incarnate Christ with the word of God, and which saw the *word* as the link between the beginning of time and the end of time, and the *word* as the intermediary between God and man.

The concept of Divine Mind, single, eternal and immutable, out of which all single things flow and to which they will all return, is not, of course, a monopoly of Christian philosophy. While it is demonstrably a natural defence against the spectre of chaos and total heterogeneity in the world, the belief in the One Mind, or Logos, is also a sophisticated philosophic doctrine. "Logos is a phrase of the Hellenic schools. It has a long history, and had already [before the time of Philo Judaeus, first century] gathered round itself many associations, that fitted it for the new part it was now to assume. It denotes with equal facility the uttered word, the reasoning mind, or again a plan, scheme, system. It is the Platonic Idea of Good, the Stoic World-Spirit, or Reason of God, immanent in creation which it fosters and sustains."[4] Logos doctrines appear in the Jewish Cabbalah, in the writings of Valentinus, the second century Gnostic, in the works of the Ionian philosopher Heraclitus of the fifth century B.C. It is strongly implied in the *Corpus Hermeticum*, particularly in the doctrine of the Aeon: "God then is the source of all things; the Aeon is the power of God; and the work of the Aeon is the Kosmos, which never came into being, but is ever coming into being by the action of the Aeon ... That which holds this universe together is the Aeon."[5]

In whatever body of philosophy the Logos or Word appears, it is always the principle of order. It was left to the Church Fathers, most especially Origen and Clement, to emphasize the Johannine identification of the Logos with Christ and thus with the Incarnation. Once this was accomplished, it was possible to perceive the Word-Incarnation-Order equation which underlies Herbert's poetry.

What initiated the patristic identification of the Logos with the Incarnation is problematic, but there are two possible explanations not necessarily exclusive of each other. The first may have been the recognition of similar phraseology in Genesis and John: "In the beginning God created the heaven and the earth. And the earth was without form, and void; and darkness was upon the face of the deep. And the Spirit of God moved upon the face of the waters. And God said, Let there be light: and there was light" and "In the beginning was the Word, and the Word was with God, and the Word was God. The same was in the beginning with God. All things were made by him; and without him was not any thing that was made. In him was life; and the life was the light of men." It is noteworthy that both St. Augustine in the *De Civitate Dei* and Martin Luther in his commentary on Genesis connect the two texts, and see the one as defining the other. The Logos or Word of Genesis thus becomes the Christ of St. John.[6]

The second possible explanation lies in the peculiar task of both the evangelists and the early Christian apologists, who had not only to shake the people's faith in the old paganism, but provide a substantial intellectual basis for the new teaching; and the use of an already-accepted classical concept to demonstrate a Christian concept may have been thought a brilliant propaedeutic device. Whatever the explanation, the early apologists emphasized the Incarnation in terms of the Logos or Word. Justin Martyr in the second century argued that the incarnate Christ was the fulfillment of the Logos of the old law; Athanasius in the fourth century and Maximus Confessor in the seventh defined Christ in terms of the Greek Logos.[7] But of all the Fathers, it was Clement of Alexandria and Origen who, in the second century, did most to enunciate the Logos-Incarnation-Order triad.

Logos, as it was understood before the evangelists and before the Fathers, was the antidote to anarchy and disorder, the Force or Spirit of cohesion and harmony which prevented a return to primal night. It was the identification of this cosmic principle of order that was accomplished first by St. John and then, in greater detail, by the Fathers. Professor Wolfson has made clear the points of connection between the Logos and Christ:

> [John's] description of the Logos is modeled upon Paul's description of the preëxistent Christ, Philo's description of the preëxistent Logos, and the Wisdom of Solomon's description of the preëxistent wisdom. Like Paul, who speaks of the preëxistent Christ as God's 'own son' and the 'firstborn' and like Philo, who speaks of the preëxistent Logos as the 'firstborn son of God,' and like the Wisdom of Solomon which speaks of the 'understanding spirit' in the preëxistent wisdom, which is identical with the preëxistent wisdom itself, as the 'only begotten,' John describes the Logos as the 'only begotten Son of God.' Then, like Paul who speaks of the preëxistent Christ as he by whom 'all things were created,' and like Philo who speaks of the preëxistent Logos as that 'through which the world was framed,' and like the Wisdom of Solomon which speaks of the preëxistent wisdom as 'the artificer of all things,' John says concerning the Logos, 'All things were made through him.' Then, again, like Paul who says concerning the preëxistent Christ that, after the creation of the world, 'in him all things hold together,' and like Philo who says that after the creation of the world God implanted the Logos within it so that

'extending himself from the midst to its utmost bounds and from its extremities to the midst again, keeps up through all its length nature's unvanquished course,' and like the Wisdom of Solomon which speaks of wisdom as that which 'pervades and penetrates all things,' John says concerning the Logos that, after the creation of the world, 'he was in the world.' Then, applying to the Logos the traditional conceptions of the hidden Messiah and the hidden wisdom, already made use of by Paul, he says of the Logos, 'The world knew him not.' Finally, reflecting Paul's description of the birth of the preëxistent Messiah as 'being made in the likeness of men' or 'in the likeness of sinful flesh,' he says 'And the Logos became flesh.'[8]

For Origen, "the Logos sets the world in order."[9] God's Reason projected into the void brought harmony and meaning into the world. That same projection of intelligibility continues by the presence of Christ in the affairs of men; and Origen represents the Eucharist as the chief symbol of the operative Logos. Logos is Incarnate Christ: "*Verbe*, λογος, désignant alors sans hésitation possible la personne du Fils"[10] and Logos is also "essentiellement, pour Origène, l'intelligence divine."[11] The second look at Origen's *De Principiis* develops his doctrine of the Logos as Intelligence, while his *De Oratione* identifies the Eucharist as immanent Logos. The triumph of order over disorder, the Incarnation, and the Eucharist are welded into one doctrine by Origen.

Even more thorough was Clement of Alexandria, who "made [the Logos] into the highest principle for the religious explanation of the world. The Logos is the creator of the universe. He is the one who manifested God in the Law of the Old Testament, in the philosophy of the Greeks and finally in the fullness of time in His incarnation ... The Logos is, as divine reason, essentially the teacher of the world and the lawgiver of mankind."[12] In his *Exhortation to the Greeks*, Clement apostrophized Christ-Logos as "the new song": "it is this which composed the entire creation into melodious order, and tuned into concert the discord of the elements, that the whole universe might be in harmony with it."[13]

The Incarnate Christ is Logos, Word, Order, Music, Intelligibility: this is the tradition lying behind Herbert's celebration of the Incarnations, the doctrine into which "all thy sweets are packt up." He refers not only to the historic demonstrations of the Incarnation, the Life of Christ (for, as chronicler of that life, Herbert is markedly incomplete, as we have seen), nor to the sacramental demonstration of the Incarnation (seven poems do not constitute a major portion of his work). Herbert's sense of the Incarnation cannot be limited to the few poems whose *subject* is the Incarnation. Rather, his sense of the Incarnation pervades nearly every poem he wrote, and each poem is a further celebration of the Incarnation.

For the Incarnation, as we have seen it defined, envisions a series of conflicts and triumphs: form overcoming inchoate matter, reason overcoming incomprehensibility. In such terms as these, the Incarnation is both a theological and an artistic concern. What Incarnate Christ as Logos has done, so too the poet must do, bring order out of disorder, and bestow divinity on raw matter. Herbert's poetry was not a diversion, something different from his taking Anglican orders or his ministry at the small parish church in Bemerton or his attendance at worship in Salisbury cathedral or his devotion to the sacraments and ritual of his faith. They are all the same thing, the search for divine meaning in the disorder of the world, and the transformation of discord into music. This defines his religion and it defines his poetry, and both religion and poetry are analogues of the Incarnation.

It is this which accounts for the unique quality of his poetry, through which he sees the world "as a web of significances, not as a collection of phenomena which we may either endow with significance or leave unendowed. He writes not of events and facts, but of meanings and values, and he uncovers rather than creates these meanings."[14] It is Herbert's refusal to become involved with the simple "factness" of objects and experiences which distinguishes him from his contemporary and other great representative of metaphysical poetry, John Donne. Whereas Donne often gives the impression of being ensnared by all the complexities of the single, the temporal and the confusing, Herbert ignores the individual and drives for the transcendent.[15] The poem becomes a re-enactment of the Incarnation. Thus, the majority of Herbert's poems are intensely abstract and anti-empirical. Historical personages shed their individuality and become allegories of a divine truth, as Melchisidec becomes a prototype of Christ in "Peace," as does "Aaron." Events become not experienced acts but symbols, as when graphic details in the "Easter" and "Christmas" poems are omitted so that the sacred meaning of both feasts may be presented. Objects disappear to be replaced by abstract inferences, as when "Joseph's coat" never appears as an object in the poem but becomes an image of Christ in Passion Week and the grace-bedecked Christian. The confrontation of a mystery and the sudden resolution of the mystery through Christ is a recurrent subject, as in the poems "Justice" and "Death." Poems are left deliberately incomplete or quizzical up to a point, and are "finished" and made cogent only by the entrance of divinity, as in "Prayer" or "The Quip." Metres are disturbed in part of a poem, and made melodic as soon as allusion to the Lord is made, as in "The Collar." None of these poems is *about* the Incarnation, but each is a miniature version of the Incarnation as sanctified order.

To demonstrate in some detail how Herbert fashions his poetry so that the entire poetic process becomes incarnative, we might consider the last of his poems on the Eucharist, "Love."

> Love bade me welcome: yet my soul drew back,
>   Guiltie of dust and sinne.
> But quick-ey'd Love, observing me grow slack
>   From my first entrance in,
> Drew nearer to me, sweetly questioning,
>   If I lack'd anything.
> A guest, I answer'd, worthy to be here:
>   Love said, you shall be he.
> I the unkinde, ungratefull? Ah my deare,
>   I cannot look on thee.
> Love took my hand, and smiling did reply,
>   Who made the eyes but I?
>
> Truth Lord, but I have marr'd them: let my shame
>   Go where it doth deserve.
> And know you not, sayes Love, who bore the blame?
>   My deare, then I will serve.
> You must sit down, sayes Love, and taste my meat:
>   So I did sit and eat.   (pp. 188-189)

In the first stanza Herbert presents the defining term (the temporal fact) and the defined term (the spiritual idea) as co-existing in easy harmony. Each term makes good sense in its own sphere. Thus, the temporal figure of the begrimed traveller, stopping at the inn, somewhat reluctant to foul the house because of his road-stained condition, greeted by the hospitable inn-keeper chanting the traditional appeal of his class ... all this makes perfectly good sense on the literal, visual and temporal level. The same must be said of the transcendent, abstract and spiritual level: the dejected soul, despairing of its redemption, willingly embraced by the Lord, is cogent. In the first stanza of "Love," Herbert maintains the conservative one-for-one relationship expected of rudimentary allegory.

The second stanza is quite another matter. The abstraction continues to be entirely coherent: the soul, wrapped in its dark night, sees its own reprobation as the veil separating it from the Beatific Vision, while the Divine Mercy offers itself to the sinner. But the temporal details go violently awry, and the literal figures of the inn-keeper and traveller shimmer and break. It is impossible to equate the language and actions of the second stanza with the empirical *dramatis personae* of the poem. In this second stanza, that troublesome point of all allegory at which the one-for-one correspondence cannot be sustained, has been reached. At such a point the poet must elect one of two alternatives, to keep intact either the temporal or the transcendent. There is no question as to which Herbert elects.

This bifurcation of the literal-abstract, temporal-spiritual in Herbert's poem might very well be owing to the *genus* of allegory, and to see anything significant in Herbert's allowing the bifurcation to happen might be opposed by the question "Can a poet be said to *allow* something which must inevitably happen?" But Herbert's artistic voli-tion is still at work; although he may not be causing the literal to break away from the abstract, he uses this breaking away as part of an especially brilliant strategy and converts what might have been a failure in poetic structure into a successful symbolic statement.

He accomplishes this in the last stanza. As there is a sharp division between stanzas one and two (the first stanza keeping the temporal and spiritual views in balance, the second stanza "allowing" them to separate, with its accompanying disparagement of temporal meaning), so there is a striking dichotomy here. The first three lines continue to be absurd from the literal point of view (the remarks of the host are ludicrous in the literal context of inn-host-traveller), but meaningful from the transcendent point of view. The second three lines re-unify the temporal and spiritual, bringing together what had been sundered. "Then I will serve" is a credible statement for the host of the inn to make, since that is one of his literal functions. It is also a credible description of the Atonement undertaken by the Host who is celebrated in the communion service, Christ. "You must sit down . . . and taste my meat" is both the host of the inn speaking, and also Christ at the Last Supper, "Take, eat; this is my body" (Matthew, 26:26). "So I did sit and eat" describes equally well the temporal and literal traveller at his meal, and the reception of the Eucharist. The last three lines of the poem re-unite the temporal and spiritual, even as the doctrine of the Real Presence in the Eucharist re-unites the two. The structure of the poem — union, disruption, re-union — embodies and reflects the universal repair of the Fall through sacramental regeneration.

Herbert, in brief then, rejects the validity of temporal detail in the second stanza. He sanctifies the temporal in re-admitting its validity in the final stanza. That validating can be understood as a miniature incarnative process in which the temporal is once again allowed to be a participant in the sacred realities. The Incarnation is recalled in the Eucharist; the final stanza of the poem describes and becomes the Eucharist; structure and sacrament define one another.

To reiterate an earlier remark: the Incarnation is the central issue of Herbert's poetry. His poetry is an assault on the incomplete and the meaningless, and a clarifying and sanctifying of chaos through Christ as Divine Word. His poetry is not simply about the Incarnation, it is a constant imitation of the Incarnation. "This box we know," he said in "Ungratefulnesse," "for we have all of us just such another." Each comely service, each grace-full life, and each poem is a further testament to the Incarnation.[16]

"SETTING FOOT INTO DIVINITY" GEORGE HERBERT AND THE ENGLISH REFORMATION

Ilona Bell

Most critics of *The Temple* have taken George Herbert's Anglicanism for granted because he announces his allegiance so lovingly and clearly in "The British Church":

> I joy, deare Mother, when I view
> Thy perfect lineaments and hue
>   Both sweet and bright.
>   (1-3)[1]

Herbert's "British Church," standing independently between Rome and Genevá, acknowledges none of the difficult theological choices which troubled Donne's poems and precipitated so many seventeenth-century treatises and sermons. Instead, Herbert's "Divinitie" mocks the perpetrators of "curious questions and divisions" and asserts that "all the doctrine, which he taught and gave,/Was cleare as heav'n, from whence it came" (12-14). Accordingly, critics have depicted the religious conflicts of *The Temple* as personal, paradoxical, conventional, humanistic, spiritual — as anything but theological. Formal critics like Helen Vendler have removed Herbert's poems from their historical context; religious critics have claimed their universal Christian significance; historical critics like Louis Martz and Rosemond Tuve have confidently produced medieval and Catholic models.[2] Supported by Walton's biography, which connected Herbert with Laud, Charles I, and Anglo-Catholicism, critics directed their attention toward "the regulations, the forms the accumulations and customs of the Church" rather than its doctrines.[3] Even Joseph Summers, who illuminated the Puritan association and Protestant convictions in Herbert's life, concluded that "most of Herbert's lyrics are hardly 'religious' at all ... if we think of the

Reprinted from *MLQ*, 38 (1977), 219-44, by permission of the author and the publisher.

religious as immediately concerned with abstract theological definitions or controversies."[4]

Although Herbert shunned the "curious questions and divisions" which preoccupied so many of his contemporaries, he lived in a period of extraordinary religious publication and agitation, between a recent Reformation and a forthcoming Civil War. It is easy for us to disregard the theological turmoil which provoked, or at lease justified, all this political turmoil, but it was almost impossible for seventeenth-century poets to protect their religion from controversy. Herrick, Vaughan, and Milton, for example, who were alive fifteen years after Herbert's death, found their talents completely displaced by the war. Herbert withdrew from public life in 1627, probably before he wrote the "sacred poems and private ejaculations" of *The Temple,* so his political and religious allegiances remained relatively quiescent. Yet just after he died in 1633, Laud's strict regimentation and censorship solidified religious divisions, and Herbert's poems quickly became the object of partisan designs. Royalists like Christopher Harvey adopted Herbert and adapted his poems to "Make curs'd confusion and contention cease," to make "The Church" more "Anglican," more polemical, ceremonious, and hier-archical.[5] In 1650, when Henry Vaughan published *Silex Scintillans,* another volume of "sacred poems and private ejaculation," the relative calm of Herbert's "British Church" was beyond salvation: in Vaughan's version, "The Souldiers ... dare divide and stain."[6]

Despite the bitter, religious divisions of the war, the Royalists had no monopoly on Herbert's "Church". Everyone seemed to love Herbert's poetry, and many claimed him as a posthumous ally. Herbert was no less an inspiration for the Puritan expatriate Edward Taylor than for the Anglican Henry Vaughan, and many devout English Puritans embraced him. When Richard Baxter praised *The Temple* in the preface of the *Poetical Fragments* (1681), he admired "Heart-work and Heaven-work," spiritual inwardness, not ceremonial richness. Because of Walton's genius and the restoration of the Church of England, the high Anglican worship of *The Temple* has generally prevailed. Nevertheless, I believe this has been less than faithful to the original spirit of Herbert's poetry, and apparently Laud's censors were equally wary of Herbert's sympathies.

When Nicholas Ferrar first attemped to publish *The Temple,* the Cambridge censor demurred, fearing its subversive effects. Herbert's prophecy for "The Church Militant" — "Religion stands on tip-toe in our land, / Readie to passe to the *American* strand" (235-36) — looked disturbingly separatist. Moreover, Herbert's own *Country Parson* was never published during Laud's rule, and when it was finally "exposed to publick light" in 1652, its editor, Barnabas Oley, extolled Herbert as a valiant soldier of the Protestant Reformation: "And he that reads Mr. Herbert's Poems attendingly, shall finde not onely the excellencies of Scripture Divinitie, and choice passages of the Fathers bound up in Meetre; but the Doctrine of Rome also finely and strongly confuted."[7] While modern critics have studiously protected Herbert's "Church" from the religious disputes of the seventeenth century, his contemporaries could not and did not. His "private ejaculations" immediately became embroiled in public "definitions or controversies."

Herbert's own immersion in theology began long before he became a published poet or a country parson. On March 18, 1617/18, he wrote from Cambridge to his stepfather, Sir John Danvers: "You know Sir, how I am now setting foot into Divinity, to lay the platform of my future life . . ." (p. 364). He goes on to ask for money to purchase "those infinite Volumes of Divinity, which yet every day swell, and grow bigger" (p. 365). His interest in these swelling and growing volumes suggest that he was anxiously keeping up with the burgeoning arguments of Calvinists, Puritans, and Anglo-Catholics, all substantial and vocal parties in the pre-Laudian Church of England. In writing the Latin poems *Musae Responsoriae,* Herbert even entered the fray for a short time. He was intellectually sophisticated, theologically curious, and politically ambitious; given the religious turmoil of the early seventeenth century in England, it seems plausible that he could have envisioned the "British Church" as peacefully or unquestioningly as we have assumed. Therefore, I think we should try, difficult as it now is, to read Herbert's poems as he and his contemporaries did: we should consider the theological disputes about the development of the British Church, so that we can recognize their imaginative and dramatic effects on Herbert's "Church" — on his style, imagery, wit and point of view.

Theological and stylistic questions are most closely intertwined in the poems which have seemed most conventional in recent years, the poems about Christ's sacrifice which imitate medieval poetry and Catholic mediation.[8] These poems can be divided into four groups: a coherent sequence of Latin poems entitled *Passio Discerpta;* a few similar Latin poems in *Lucas;* a sequence of poems at the beginning of "The Church" including "The Sacrifice" and "The Thanksgiving"; a few recollections of the sacrifice scattered throughout *The Temple.* The meditation on Christ's sacrifice, conventional and successful in the Latin poems, becomes self-conscious, introspective, uncertain, and finally unproductive in *The Temple,* where we can see Herbert maturing in his commitment to the doctrines of the English Reformation, trying out and turning away from a traditional Catholic vision to create a more Protestant poetic voice and style.

When we reconsider Herbert's attitudes toward Catholic meditation, we will see that his English poetry is as rebellious, witty, and innovative as Sidney's or Donne's. In *The Temple* Herbert finds, as Sidney did at the beginning of *Astrophel and Stella,* that conventional attitudes can no longer express personal conviction, that "others feet still seemed but strangers in my way." As he becomes more committed to the Reformation and Protestantism, to reform and protest, Herbert discovers that religous poetry will be more fruitful if it is fresh and unconventional. But he also finds that old conventions can be an extremely useful base for a protesting poet. So, much as Sidney and Donne raided and exploded the Petrarchan conventions, Herbert used and doomed the familiar images, postures, and goals of Catholic meditation.

Herbert's attitude toward these meditative traditions has been difficult to recognize for two reasons. First, the traditions themselves are known to most of us, if at all, at several removes. Second, Herbert's debt to Catholic conventions is obvious in the Latin poems and "The Sacrifice," but his subsequent withdrawal is less obvious, arising as it does from specific theological issues which Herbert never explicitly identifies. As long as the poems remained "private ejaculations" addressed to God or personal friends, Herbert had no reason to explain his theological assumptions; and if he later intended the poems for posthumous publication, he had an even better reason not to spell out their controversial implications: the religious censors could prove ornery, as Ferrar later discovered.

Since Herbert's religious assumptions are so allusive, and since the genre of religious meditation is so unfamiliar, it may be helpful to glance first at some contemporary poems which defend Catholic meditation and explain its relationship to the Reformation. The best English examples are the sonnets of William Alabaster, Herbert's notorious predecessor at Westminster School and Trinity College, Cambridge.[9]

Although Alabaster grew up in a devout Puritan family, he was powerfully attracted to the conventions of medieval poetry and Catholic meditation. His second sonnet sequence, *Upon the Ensigns of Christ's Crucifying*, seeks a direct, personal experience of Christ's sacrifice, using an "application of the senses" as taught by Catholic meditational manuals like Loyola's *Spiritual Exercises*. Alabaster's method, like Loyola's, is at once meditative and sensory; his goal is also a feeling of mental, emotional, and physical communion with Christ: the petition "ought to be according to the subject-matter, i.e., if the contemplation is on the Resurrection, to ask for joy with Christ in His joy; if it be on the Passion, to beg for sorrow, tears, and fellowship with Christ in His sufferings."[10] Alabaster's "Upon the Crucifix (1)" is a fine example of the traditional meditative petition to participate in Christ's suffering:

> Before thy Cross, O Christ, I do present
> My soul and body into love distilled.
> . . . .
> Wound all my thoughts to think on thy disdain,
> And let my mouth savour of thy distaste,
> And love flow from my breast since thine did stream,
> And learn my body with thy grief to waste,
> And in thy Cross mine honour to esteem.

The speaker asks for nothing less than a complete intermingling of his own thoughts and senses with Christ's, for a delicious savoring of mutual, loving pain. As Alabaster presents himself before Christ's Cross, he follows the famous first prelude of the *Spiritual Exercises*, the composition of place: "to see with the eye of the imagination the corporeal place where the object I wish to contemplate is found" (p. 45). Alabaster strives to maintain this meditative presence throughout his sequence, as even the participial form in the title announces.

These sonnets illustrate the connection between Catholic meditation and poetic conception, but Alabaster's first sonnet sequence, *The Portrait of Christ's Death*, is even more instructive: it issues a direct challenge to the recent repudiation, the "new-found balk" of Christ's Passion by European Protestants. Repeatedly bemoaning their devotional failures ("Though all forsake thee, lord, yet cannot I"). Alabaster urges his Protestant contemporaries to return to the traditional meditation on Christ's suffering, to "show what he did bear, what thou hast fled." This sequence is Alabaster's personal counterreformation; its climactic ninth sonnet openly damns Luther for "hellish pride," for a dangerous indifference to Christ's torment.

From Alabaster's urgent, polemical voice, we can see that the comfortable symbiosis of Catholic poetry and meditation was threatened by the Reformation. In fact, Alabaster felt so torn, as he explains in his autobiography, that he renounced his Puritan upbringing, deserted his Protestant homeland, and converted to Catholicism: he was determined to preserve his own "greater tendernes of harte towardes Christes Crosse and Passion than . . . the protestantes weare wont to feele" (*Sonnets*, p. xii).

With this model of Catholic meditative poetry and Protestant resistance in mind, we should now be able to recognize the loyalties and developments of Herbert's poetry. His *Passio Discerpta* has notable similarities with Alabaster's devotional sonnets. For example, "Christus in cruce," like Alabaster's "Upon the Crucifix (2)," presents the speaker drinking blood as it drips from the Cross; and "In Clauos," like "Upon the Crucifix (3)," embraces Christ as he is nailed to the Cross. Like Catholic meditations and Alabaster's sonnets on the Passion, Herbert's Latin poems seek communion with Christ through Christ's pain. For example, in the fourth poem, "In latus perfossum," Christ's rod is a pathway which marks out the speaker's relationship with Christ. And in the central poem, "Christus in cruce," Herbert imagines himself joyfully drinking his own salvation as it drips in blood from the Cross. The poem envisions a continuous fountain of blood which flows directly from Christ's wounds to the speaker's open mouth. Although the speaker never quite feels Christ's bodily pain, he experiences salvation by his imaginative "presence" at the Crucifixion, by making an application of the senses and a "composition of place," as advised by the *Spiritual Exercises.*

Like Alabaster, Herbert blends time past with time present in order to imagine his real presence at the Passion. As Tuve observed of "The Sacrifice" and its medieval sources, *Passio Discerpta* is "abstracted from the world of historical events; it does not take place in a particular space or time; . . . parts of it are delivered as from the Cross . . . tenses vary, and there is no sense of a narrative being actually told" (p. 35). These poems dramatize the belief that Christ's sacrifice is an ongoing event, and the speaker prays for it to remain so: "Christe, fluas semper." His imagined presence at the Passion brings a feeling of direct, physical communion with Christ, enabling him to understand and trust in the present benefits of Christ's sacrifice.

Like Alabaster's sonnets, these poems enact a conventional meditation on the Passion; however, they betray none of Alabaster's polemical goals or theological anxiety. At this point, Herbert's attraction is clearly more aesthetic and less partisan than Alabaster's. Still, there are similar meditations on Christ's Passion in *Lucus,* which also contains poems courting Pope Urban VIII, so we know that Herbert associated this kind of devotional poetry with Roman Catholicism. Manuscript evidence has led F. E. Hutchinson to conclude that both *Lucus* and *Passio Discerpta* were written in 1623, the year Urban became Pope (pp. 590-91). The suggestion is plausible: Herbert's official activities as Public Orator were then at their peak, and King James was openly reaching out to Catholicism, proposing the much-discussed marriage between Prince Charles and the Spanish Infanta.

When Herbert resigned as Public Orator in 1627, his life was disrupted; his mother had died, and he himself faced several years of sickness, unemployment, and retirement. During this time, Herbert almost certainly began to write his English poems, which speak with a new intensity, with a new consciousness of strain, uncertainty, and loss. At first, the drama appears to be personal rather than doctrinal. But if we follow its story carefully, we will discover a definite theological plot and precise formal goals which confirm the generally accepted dates for the Latin poems and *The Temple*. Prompted by the fundamental doctrines of the English Reformation (and not the "curious questions and divisions" scorned by "Divinitie"), "The Church" rejects the Catholic traditions of *Passio Discerpta* and begins to search for a poetry of personal experience suited to Herbert's maturing Protestant faith.

Since "The Church" begins so noticeably with "The Sacrifice," a traditional imitation of Christ's Passion, most critics have assumed that Herbert was devoted to the methods of Catholic and medieval meditation; Martz, for example, believes that "Herbert's *Temple* displays a structure built upon the art of mental communion, and so designed, beyond any doubt, by George Herbert himself" (p. 288). Nevertheless, since "The Sacrifice" is spoken entirely by a persona, Christ, it could easily be "written in the language of, or using the 'norms' of, a genre in a formal refutation of the genre," as Frank Kermode says in another context.[11] In fact, once we begin to examine Herbert's own attitude, even the most conventional elements become problematic. The refrain, to take the most prominent example, is completely conventional: the question "Was ever grief like mine?" was frequently attributed to Christ in medieval poetry (Tuve, p. 24 *et passim*). Nevertheless, Herbert's unusual, drilling repetition calls attention to Christ's unusual grief and causes us to wonder whether Herbert intended to question the traditional participation in Christ's grief taught by Catholic meditation. Each time the refrain is repeated, this implicit reservation gathers strength until Herbert suddenly introduces an overt prohibition:

> Weep not, deare friends, since I for both have wept
> When all my tears were bloud, the while you slept:
> Your tears for your own fortunes should be kept:
> Was ever grief like mine? (149-52)

With all the bitter ironies behind this gentle advice, Herbert separates "my tears" from "Your tears," insisting that we should not attempt to share Christ's pain, even through a traditional meditation on the Passion. Still, the brief warning of this stanza and the guarded suggestion of the refrain may seem to be contravened by "The Sacrifice" itself, which does reenact Christ's Passion — although only in Christ's voice. Even as we read "The Sacrifice," these conflicting suggestions force us to ask what role this traditional, Catholic reenactment of Christ's suffering is meant to play in "The Church" as Herbert envisioned it. What is the reason for the commanding position of "The Sacrifice"? Why does Herbert choose to write exclusively in Christ's human voice here and never again? Does this make "The Sacrifice" atypical, stylistically and devotionally?

At the end of the poem many of these questions are answered when Herbert transforms Christ's traditional question into a command: "Onely let others say, when I am dead,/Never was grief like mine" (251-52). This resolution compels us to reconsider the traditional imitation of Christ's Passion, for Christ orders us to reiterate our decisive separation from his suffering, to "say" that his grief is inimitable.

To proponents of Herbert's conventional intentions, Christ's command has seemed like an endorsement of meditations on the Passion. Indeed, the text seems to support this interpretation. Since Christ's imperative to "others" is ambiguous, we can easily read the last line as if it were set off by quotation marks, as if each of us were being asked to suffer and to say that *my* grief is unprecedented. The phrasing encourages us to read the conclusion twice, and our second reading echoes and imitates Christ's pain, just as Catholic meditation says we should.[12] This reading creates problems, however, since the imitation depends upon allowing Christ to say the words first, and his words preclude any imitation. Such contrariety does not produce an illuminating Christian paradox, as the conclusions of Donne's Holy Sonnets so often do; but there is a simple solution: even as we say, "Never was grief like mine," we are insisting upon the uniqueness of our own experience and confirming our separation from Christ's Passion. Thus if we try to read "The Sacrifice" as a model of mental communion, and if we truly understand the meaning of Christ's command, we will be forced to undergo a complicated process of reassessment: ultimately "The Sacrifice" undermines the traditional meditative goal of communal suffering.

The conclusion of "The Sacrifice" requires us to perform a ritual. As Tuve has suggested, Herbert learned from his medieval sources that "poetry has quite as much kinship with ritual as with drama" (p. 36). Nevertheless, Herbert's ritual urges us to think about and separate Christ's grief from our own, past from present, history from commemoration. This distinction challenges the devotional "presence" which pervades medieval poetry, Catholic meditation, and even Herbert's

Passio Discerpta; and, as we shall soon see, it is precisely what Herbert learned from the Reformation.

In the following poems the speaker confronts the problems raised by "The Sacrifice": he asks, "Shall I weep bloud?" ("The Thanksgiving," 5): he tries to "say" Christ's refrain in various ways; and he assesses each subsequent attempt at "dealing with thy mighty passion" ("The Reprisall," 2). Martz assumes that this insistent concern with the Passion proves Herbert's commitment to Catholic meditation and the liturgy: "Most important of all, this practice of mental communion will help explain the significance of the four opening poems in Herbert's 'Church': 'The Altar,' 'The Sacrifice,' 'The Thanksgiving,' and 'The Reprisall,' which re-enact, through meditation, the eucharistic service ..." (p. 91). But a closer look at these poems shows that the juxtaposition of meditation and the eucharistic service only confirms and explains the difficulties raised by "The Sacrifice."

At the beginning of "The Thanksgiving" the speaker attempts to reenact the Passion through meditation; however, his questions are attenuated by theological uncertainty and self-questioning wit:

> Oh King of grief! (a title strange, yet true,
> To thee of all kings onely due)
> Oh King of wounds! how shall I grieve for thee,
> Who in all grief preventest me?   (1-4)

As the speaker evokes the details of Christ's suffering, he considers an Ignatian application of the senses to "beg for sorrow, tears, and fellowship with Christ in His sufferings." His initial exclamation seems to express conventional admiration and wonder at Christ's extraordinary grief. But under this naïve wonder is a searching attempt to define the exact nature of Christ's grief, and the extended definition immediately raises complications: the "title strange, yet true, / To thee of all kings onely due" recalls Christ's command in "The Sacrifice" and suggests that his grief may be inimitable. Moreover, this wondrous title disguises an even more knowing and critical wit, for in the seventeenth century *strange* meant not only "unfamiliar" and "singular," but also "surprising" and "queer."[13] This second meaning is stressed later in "The Crosse," when the speaker asks in horrified amazement, "What is this strange and uncouth thing?" (1); here it quietly hints that the conventional description of Christ's grief is not only truly unique but also truly unaccountable and troubling.

Thus the choice of ironic, paradoxical language creates a strange but true picture of Christ which immediately casts doubt upon the speaker's professed desire to imitate Christ's Passion. These double meanings may seem to resemble the paradoxical irony detected in "The Sacrifice" by both Tuve (pp. 19-99) and William Empson;[14] actually this ingenuous, cheerful, underlying wit reveals the speaker's growing distance from Christ's lordly, bitter, heavy irony. The speaker repeatedly considers a traditional participation in Christ's grief, but he counterpoints each advance with memories of Christ's sacrifice which question his own questions. For example, doubts about Catholic meditation hide cleverly but clearly within the second description of Christ in line 4, "Who in all grief preventest me." The speaker's ingenuous desire to imitate Christ is sustained by various seventeenth-century meanings of *prevent*: "to act before, in anticipation of, or in preparation for; to hasten, bring about." In this sense the speaker envisions Christ as a model who acts before him and prepares him to "grieve for thee." However, the rhetorical thrust of the sentence raises questions about man's capacity to share Christ's grief, and these questions are reinforced by a contrasting meaning of *prevent* — "to cut off beforehand, debar, preclude" — which suggests that Christ has cut man off beforehand in experiencing grief "for thee." The first meaning of *prevent* still supports a Catholic devotional participation in Christ's grief; however, the second focuses attention upon the difference between what Christ does for us and what we do for him which, like the focus on "mine" at the end of "The Sacrifice," ultimately distinguishes our grief from Christ's. The reformers claimed that the ancient concept of prevenient grace — a free gift of grace which precedes human action or need and predisposes man to repentance, faith, and good works — had been obscured by the increasing emphasis on elaborate ceremonies, sacraments, and human efforts. Therefore, Herbert's underlying question about what Christ "preventest," about what Christ precluded or brought about, begins to raise questions about the speaker's entire initiative.

After these portentous ambiguities, it is not surprising that the speaker stumbles upon even clearer preventions as he escalates the conventional imitation of Christ's grief. Although meditations on the Passion traditionally included mortification of the flesh — "to cause it sensible pain by means of wearing haircloth, cords, or chains of iron upon the body, by scourging or wounding oneself, or by other kinds of austerities" (*Spiritual Exercises*, p. 59) — the speaker's proposed actions have been regularly punctuated by reservations; and when the pains actually begin to spill out unabated, "Shall I be scourged, flouted, boxed, sold?" (7), they reach an abrupt and simple end: "'Tis but to tell the tale is told" (8). The perplexing power of this line arises from Anglican communion reforms which redefined the relation between history and ritual, between Christ's past sacrifice and the sacramental commemoration of it. The Anglicans insisted that "the tale is told," that Christ "made there (by his one oblation of himselfe once offered) a full, perfect, and sufficient sacrifice, oblation, and satisfaction for the sinnes of the whole world, and did institute, and in his holy Gospel command us to continue a perpetual memory of that his precious death, untill his comming againe." The Anglican liturgy celebrates the Lord's Supper in "perpetual memory" and not in perpetual repetition of Christ's sacrifice; the service is performed "in remembrance of his death and passion."[15] As the official explanation in the homilies warns, "We must then take heed, lest of the memory, it be made a sacrifice...."[16] Thus when "The Thanksgiving" calls attention to and insists upon the sacrifice as a "tale ... told" about a past event, it is imitating the Anglican reforms and rejecting the Catholic Mass and Catholic meditations like *Passio Discerpta* which assume that Christ's sacrifice is an ongoing event, reenacted by man's ritual celebration.

The Mass had always expressed thanksgiving, but the Church of England, like other Protestant churches, insisted that the Lord's Supper offered *only* a "sacrifice of praise and thanksgiving." Moreover, to protect against ritual reenactment of the Passion, the Anglican church banished the traditional Good Friday Reproaches. Consequently, any seventeenth-century Anglican would have found the poetic and liturgical tradition of Christ's complaint from the Cross less requisite and less holy than Tuve assumes. In "The Thanksgiving" the physicality and pain of Catholic meditation are finally rejected when the speaker recalls Christ's biblical complaint and Christ's parting words in "The Sacrifice": "*My God, my God, why dost thou part from me?*/ Was such a grief as cannot be (9-10). Together they teach the singular, past nature of Christ's sacrifice and preclude the traditional intermingling of past and present which Herbert found in Catholic meditations on Christ's life and practiced in *Passio Discerpta*.

In "The Thanksgiving" the regular counterpoint of naïve questions and detailed, troublesome recollections prepares us from the start for this separation of Christ's past grief and our present commemoration of it. Once the speaker finds an answer to his initial questions in the Anglican Lord's Supper, he begins to phrase his subsequent questions so that each conventional image of suffering is immediately transformed into his own artful and witty victory:

> Shall thy strokes be my stroking? thorns, my flower?
> Thy rod, my posie? crosse, my bower?
> But how then shall I imitate thee, and
> Copie thy fair, though bloudie hand? (13-16)

In these lines "The Thanksgiving" turns from thy "crosse" to "my bower," from the speaker's meditative presence at Christ's sacrifice to Christ's comforting presence in the speaker's life. Through wit he converts Christ's suffering into his own rhetorical success: he makes the "strokes" Christ received a cure (a common use of *stroking* in the seventeenth century) for his doubts. He even turns the thorns and rod which wounded Christ into a pleasantly prodding muse; now Christ's wounds flower into the speaker's "posie," his poesy on poetic offering, rather than his sympathetic blood and tears. Herbert subverts the poetic mode of "The Sacrifice" even further by his choice of verbs: "imitate" and "Copie" were technical terms for the writing of poetry as well as devotional terms for the imitation of Christ. The speaker will "Copie" Christ's "fair, though bloudie hand" in his handwriting and his poetry, but not in his suffering flesh or his weeping eyes. And transposed, his words even suggest the preparation of fair copy — a pure, new manuscript from which the speaker can copy a "fair," new imitation of Christ. The speaker has clearly transformed and subverted the Catholic meditation on the Passion. As an Anglican, he has discovered that grieving and weeping blood are not necessary to please God, to "write fine and wittie" ("The Forerunners," 12).

The speaker further undermines the premises of Catholic meditation when he asks, "Shall I then sing, skipping thy dolefull storie,/And side with thy triumphant glorie?" (11-12). Ignatius calls for a meditation on Christ's victory during the last week of meditation, but he rigorously excludes rejoicing from the week's meditation on the Passion, warning the retreatant "not to admit joyful thoughts, even though good and holy, as for instance of the Resurrection and of Heaven; but rather to excite myself to sorrow, suffering, and a broken heart, calling frequently to mind the toils, weariness, and sorrows of Christ our Lord" (p. 103). Thus the speaker's application of the senses fails completely when he blends the mortification and discipline of meditating on the Passion with the spontaneous song and free-flowing, "skipping" thoughts of Christ's triumphant joy. For the speaker, the sacrifice has become a strange story of the past rather than a real reenactment in the present; therefore, he can decide to skip the painful details of Christ's human suffering, skimming through those verses, until he comes to the victorious Christ who, in the words of the Lord's Supper, "sittest at the right hand of God the Father."[17] In so doing, the speaker again reveals his sympathy with the Reformation, for the Protestants, and especially Calvin, insisted upon Christ's past sacrifice in order to protect his present mediation in heaven. Citing the Epistle to the Hebrews 10:12 — "But this man after he

had offered a sacrifice for sin for ever, sat down on the right side of God"
— the reformers claimed that both the Catholic reenactment of the
sacrifice in the Mass and the physical presence of Christ in the Eucharist
violated the teachings of Scripture and undermined the heavenly state of
Christ. Therefore, when Herbert's speaker asks whether he shall "side
with thy triumphant glorie," he is considering the "side" of the reformers
and foreshadowing his final commitment to Christ as redeemer and
mediator, to "my deare Saviour Victorie" (48).

Having decided to "imitate" Christ in a new way, the speaker now
challenges the "victorious" Christ to a contest: "Surely I will revenge me
on thy love,/ And trie who shall victorious prove" (17-18). The speaker
is "surely" joking: the very idea of challenging Christ is unchristian since
ultimate victory is possible only through Christ's intercession. Although
the speaker will soon regret his heretical boldness in "The Reprisall," the
lighthearted challenge is necessary for the moment because it enables
him to consider yet another goal of Ignatian meditation: the election of
the second week, which teaches the penitent to redirect his life, his
marriage, honor, and riches, solely for the sake of God. As we might
expect by now, these next devotional efforts at "amending and reforming each his own life and state" (*Spiritual Exercises*, pp. 89-97) also
collapse into comic, self-defeating behavior. The speaker exaggerates
his "election," turning his promises into dramatic posturing. He even
offers to stage his own violent mini-sacrifice: "My bosome friend, if he
blaspheme thy Name,/ I will tear thence his love and fame" (25-26). He
is unusually impatient, broaching alternatives speedily and making
commitments that continually go awry:

> For thy predestination I'le contrive,
>   That three yeares hence, if I survive,
> I'le build a spittle, or mend common wayes,
>   But mend mine own without delayes.
> (31-34)

The speaker is so caught up in this "victorious" imitation of Christ that
he claims the divine capacity to mend his own ways: he even appro-
priates the most frightening sign of God's power, predestination. As he
"contrives" a three-year plan of good works and otherworldliness, he
proudly (and heretically) places all his trust in his own decisions and his
own works.

Thus "The Thanksgiving" compresses the entire spectrum of Ignatian
meditation. In the process the speaker loses interest in his original desire
to reenact Christ's Passion: "As for thy passion — But of that anon,/

When with the other I have done" (29-30). His efforts undermine the *Spiritual Exercises* and comically expose the failure of all his attempts to hasten salvation through his own exertions.

Finally, however, the speaker's earlier Protestant thoughts of a "tale" and a "dolefull storie" lead him to imagine a perfect union with God:

> My musick shall finde thee, and ev'ry string
>   Shall have his attribute to sing:
> That all together may accord in thee.
>   And prove one God, one harmonie.
> If thou shalt give me wit, it shall appeare,
>   If thou hast giv'n it me, 'tis here.
> Nay, I will reade thy book, and never move
>   Till I have found therein thy love,
> Thy art of love, which I'le turn back on thee:
>   O my deare Saviour, Victorie!   (39-48)

The speaker's visionary union with God through Christ and the Holy Scripture ends his hurried search for acceptable ways to "imitate" Christ. His voice gains prophetic confidence and self-irony, shedding its comic confusion and extravagant self-reliance. Thus the speaker's playful, excessive contrivances with predestination and his own regeneration finally prove the necessity of God's gifts: as all the Protestant reformers insisted, God must give man the power to do good works, to utter fine words, and to attain salvation. Justification is by faith alone. In his only extant theological commentary, the *Briefe Notes relating to the dubious and offensive places in the following Considerations*, Herbert confirms his commitment to this Protestant precept: let "a man presume not to merit, that is, to oblige God, or justify himselfe before God, by any acts or exercises of Religion" (p. 312).

After discovering his own helplessness, the speaker finally imagines himself victorious by following the chosen path of the Reformation, the retreat to the Bible in search of a personal way to Christ and, through Christ, to God. In his mature religious prose Herbert repeatedly explains the sustaining and comforting powers of the Bible, the voice of God's Holy Spirit. *The Country Parson* (which was clearly written after he was well established at Bemerton and thus in the last two or three years of his life) insists that "the chief and top of his knowledge consists in the book of books, the storehouse and magazene of life and comfort, the holy Scriptures. There he sucks, and lives" (p. 228). And in the *Briefe Notes*, written just five months before he died, Herbert repeatedly complains that Valdesso "slights the Scripture too much" (p. 306). Even more to the point, in Consideration 32 Herbert confronts Valdesso's comparison of Scripture to pictures of Christ crucified:

> "The unlearned man, that hath the spirit, serveth himselfe of *Images* as of an Alphabet of Christian Pietie; forasmuch as hee so much serves himselfe of the *Picture* of Christ Crucified, as much as serves to imprint in his mind that which Christ suffered.... In like manner a learned man, that hath the spirit, serveth himselfe of *holy Scriptures*, as of an Alphabet of Christian pietie...." (p. 309)

Valdesso's solicitude for the "unlearned man" explains the traditional justification for simple meditative procedures: visual images of Christ crucified enable even the illiterate to attain a sympathetic, imaginative understanding of Christ's sacrifice. Patrick Grant cites this passage among others to prove that Valdesso was the model for Herbert's own "remarkable emphasis on the passion of Christ" (p. 96), but Grant fails to notice that Herbert's note criticizes Valdesso:

> I much mislike the Comparison of Images, and H. Scripture, as if they were both but Alphabets and after a time to be left. The H. Scriptures (as I wrote before) have not only an Elementary use, but a use of perfection, neither can they ever be exhausted, (as Pictures may be by a plenarie circumspection) but still even to the most learned and perfect in them, there is somewhat to be learned more.... (p. 309)

Herbert emphasizes the Bible, not the picture of Christ crucified, either in church or in private meditation.

Again, Herbert's objections have a theological inspiration, for the Anglican reformers announced that pictures of Christ in the church were idolatrous, deceptive, and forbidden:

> ... no true image of God, our Sauiour Christ, or his Saints can be made: wherewithall is also confuted that their allegation, that Images be the Lay mens bookes. For it is euident ... that they teach no things of God, of our Sauiour Christ, and of his Saints, but lies and errours. (*Certaine Sermons*, II, 42)

In place of these comforting visible images, the Church offered the people an "Alphabet" of "perfection": the English liturgy. English paraphrases, and the homilies.[18] Thus when the speaker of "The Thanksgiving" finally turns away from the picture of Christ crucified toward "thy book," "Thy art of love," like Herbert he consciously places his trust in the Holy Scriptures, the way of the Reformation.

Feeling witty, exultant, and on the verge of union with God, the speaker makes one last attempt to consider the Passion: "Then for thy passion — I will do for that — / Alas, my God, I know not what" (49-50). But he fails again, and the final line trails off, melodramatically bemoaning a defeat which Herbert carefully arranged. In "The Thanksgiving" the speaker imagines a harmonic, painless resolution to his initial questions and doubts when he submits to God's "art of love," as set forth in the Bible, rather than his thorns and rod, as advised by Catholic meditation.

Once we understand the strictures of Ignatian meditation and of the reformed Lord's Supper, "The Thanksgiving" becomes a dramatic, witty poem of Protestant experience rather than a conventional meditation on Christ's Passion. Arnold Stein has revealed some of this "chatty glibness,"[19] while Vendler has noted the speaker's concern with personal experience (p. 232). But they have not explained the speaker's major discovery — that he must build *The Temple*, his personal life in the church and in God, on the Reformation and the solid, unadorned foundation of the Bible, not on the limited picture of Christ crucified and Catholic meditation. In this case, we can fully understand the purpose and order of what Herbert is trying to say only when we combine historical and theological knowledge with a careful study of poetic tone and structure.

Like Alabaster's first sonnet sequence, *The Temple* dramatizes a new consciousness that Catholic meditation and poetry conflict with the Reformation, but unlike the sonnets it assumes that Protestant doctrine is decisive. Since Herbert's mature religious prose confirms his Protestantism, *Passio Discerpta* and *Lucas* could not express a later attraction to Catholic meditation and Rome. Instead, the existence of these Latin poems (carefully preserved by Herbert in the Williams MS.) explains why he arranged "The Church" (and the Williams MS.) to dramatize immediately both the enticements and preclusions of reenacting the Passion: he knew from his own experience how distracting Christ's human suffering could be.[20] His dual purpose makes "The Thanksgiving" a complicated, elusive poem; its implicit debate has confused Martz and many subsequent critics. But Herbert recognized and guarded against these interpretive dangers, for the next poem, "The Reprisall" (called "The Second Thanks-giving" in the Williams MS. — which made the connection even more explicit), openly rejects the attempt to reenact Christ's suffering: "I have consider'd it, and finde / There is no dealing with thy mighty passion" (1-2). Since a primary meaning of *deal* in this period is "to take part in," the speaker here announces unequivocally that he cannot participate in Christ's Passion.

In "Good Friday" the speaker again evokes Christ's suffering, but he
has learned to avoid the dangers of reenacting the Passion:

> That when sinne spies so many foes,
> Thy whips, thy nails, thy wounds, thy woes.
> All come to lodge there, sinne may say,
> *No room for me*, and flie away.   (25-28).

Details like "Thy whips, thy nails" certainly have roots in the sensory
identification with Christ's suffering described by Martz and practiced
by Herbert in *Passio Discerpta*, but here they are disembodied,
fragmented, separated from any vivid re-creation of Christ's pain. The
Passion has been completely internalized, and the details of Christ's
pain have been lifted from their dramatic context to serve as indicators
of Christ's eternal activity on behalf of man.

Only in "Redemption" does the speaker successfully imagine himself
present at Christ's sacrifice, and the sense of "presence" is immediately
qualified by the point of view and the past tense. The speaker describes a
recent experience which reads like a simple narrative, but as he proceeds
he offers a confusing account which depicts a Protestant vision of
Christian history. Seeking his Lord "In heaven at his manour" (5), the
speaker learns that Christ has recently ("lately") left to take possession
of some land on earth which "he had dearly bought / Long since" (6-8).
Since this last description is the poem's only acknowledgment that
Christ has paid a costly sacrifice, and since Christ has been at home in
heaven since then, Herbert initially identifies Christ's suffering as an
event of the past. The narrative complications ensue when the speaker
returns to earth and finally arrives at the Crucifixion, because he then
sees Christ being sacrificed:

> At length I heard a ragged noise and mirth
> Of theeves and murderers: there I him espied,
> Who straight, *Yours suit is granted*, said, & died.
> (12-14)

Although the speaker is certainly present at the sacrifice, his experience
does not feel at all like a traditional meditational "presence." The scene
is characterized only from a distance. Wandering in at the last minute,
the speaker records absolutely no sensory details; and before he can even
make a petition, much less an "application of the senses," he receives
grace, prevenient grace. Although "Redemption" dramatizes the
natural desire for an imaginative presence at the Passion, the narrative
also shows us that the speaker has come too late to participate in the

sacrifice. The careful attention to details of time — "long," "new," "the old," "lately," "Long since," "straight," "At length," "straight" — clearly places the speaker in a Protestant world of history and sequence rather than a medieval or Catholic world of ritual reenactment and timelessness.

Herbert originally entitled this poem "The Passion," perhaps to show us that the speaker's presence at the sacrifice entails hardly any passion — the painful details of Christ's human suffering are expunged by the quickness and ease of the last line. Now Christ offers salvation without the bitter, ironic complaint of *Passio Discerpta* or "The Sacrifice," and the speaker receives redemption without even noticing Christ's grief. In fact, the whole story avoids the traditional language of blood and wounds. In "Redemption" Christ's Passion is not visualized; and he is seen not as a suffering man but as a gracious redeemer.

Since none of these poems was published during Herbert's lifetime, it is impossible to prove when they were written, but we can make some plausible speculations based upon the Williams MS. The poems about the sacrifice appear as a group at the beginning of that manuscript, and they are the only substantial group of poems which remain together — though retitled, revised, and reorganized — in the first edition; therefore, we can conclude that the problem of meditating on Christ's sacrifice was one of Herbert's earliest sustained concerns. And since "The Sacrifice" has such clear affinities in method and origin with *Passio Discerpta*, it seems logical that Herbert would have written it and dealt with it when his original attraction to Christ's sacrifice was recent enough to trouble him.

Herbert does return to comforting visual images of Christ's sacrifice later in *The Temple*, but he never departs from the strictures against Catholic meditation which the speaker discovers in "The Thanksgiving" and reconsiders in the following poems. He never again depicts a meditative "presence" at the Passion, and he never blurs the distinction between historical events and the ritual commemoration of them. The speaker remembers Christ's suffering, but he always yearns for Christ's spiritual presence in his life rather than his devotional presence in Christ's life. In "Home," for example, the speaker marvels that Christ, who once experienced such extreme suffering himself, can now fail to appear in sympathy:

> How canst thou stay, considering the pace
>   The bloud did make, which thou didst waste?
> When I behold it trickling down thy face,
>   I never saw thing make such haste. (7-10)

The speaker immediately acknowledges that the sacrifice is a past event; but then, for a moment, he attempts to find solace by imagining himself present at Christ's Passion, by seeing the blood "trickling down thy face." Yet the meditation is a failure — the speaker does not feel Christ's presence — and he is forced to consider how long ago the sacrifice took place: "He did, he came: O my Redeemer deare, / After all this canst thou be strange?" (25-26). Echoing "Oh King of grief! (a title strange, yet true)" from "The Thanksgiving," the speaker continues to plead for love, for the benefits of the sacrifice; but now Christ seems sadly unfamiliar and distant. The sacrifice has ended, and Christ has ascended to heaven.

In "Longing" the speaker also pleads for Christ's presence in the name of Christ's grief:

> Lord Jesu, thou didst bow
> Thy dying head upon the tree:
> O be not now
> More dead to me!
> (31-34)

Nevertheless, the speaker is clearly separated from Christ's redemptive suffering by time and place, and there is no comfort in view. When he finds relief in the following poem, "The Bag," he imagines Christ speaking to man from the Cross:

> If ye have any thing to send or write,
> I have no bag, but here is room:
> Unto my Fathers hands and sight,
> Beleeve me, it shall safely come.
> (31-34)

But as in "Redemption" Christ speaks as the mediator, not as the suffering man, and his address is carefully introduced as part of an old, strange story: "Hast thou not heard, that my Lord JESUS di'd? / Then let me tell thee a strange storie" (7-8).

Having learned in "The Thanksgiving" to ask, "Shall I then sing, skipping thy dolefull storie, / And side with thy triumphant glorie?" (11-12), the speaker continues to turn from Christ the suffering man to Christ the Saviour. In "The Dawning," for example, he openly chastises his "sad heart" (9) for dwelling on Christ's death:

> Thy Saviour comes, and with him mirth:
> Awake, awake;
> And with a thankfull heart his comforts take.

> But thou dost still lament, and pine, and crie;
> And feel his death, but not his victorie.
>   (4-8)

Thus *The Temple* does not, as Tuve and Martz have argued reenact Christ's Crucifixion according to medieval and Catholic devotional and poetic traditions. Instead, Herbert pauses to consider the proper way to commemorate the sacrifice in the Lord's Supper and in his poetry. Discovering an unbridgeable gap between his present suffering and Christ's past Passion, he turns away from the conventional complaint of "The Sacrifice" toward the story of Christ the redeemer and mediator, whose comforting words hover amidst the theological turmoil of the Reformation to mark out the way to God.

Although we cannot determine precisely when these more Protestant poems were written, they seem to assume and build upon the discoveries made at the beginning of *The Temple* (and the Williams MS.), because they no longer pause to explain why the speaker's participation in Christ's suffering fails. And it is interesting that none of these poems appears in the Williams MS., which suggests, although it does not prove, that they were written after Herbert had confronted and dramatized his doubts about Catholic meditation. We need not insist upon this order of composition, however; Herbert clearly arranged the poems of *The Temple* to teach us that Christ has been transformed from the ironic, suffering man of "The Sacrifice" to the gracious, heavenly redeemer of "Love (III)":

> Truth Lord, but I have marr'd them: let my shame
>   Go where it doth deserve.
> And know you not, sayes Love, who bore the blame?
>   My deare, then I will serve.
> You must sit down, sayes Love, and taste my meat:
>   So I did sit and eat.   (13-18)

At the end of *The Temple* the speaker clearly learns that Christ's past suffering was necessary to make this loving welcome possible, but he need not make his eyes weep tears and blood because Christ "bore the blame."

Alabaster converted to Catholicism out of intense sympathy with Christ's suffering, but Herbert moved closer to Christ the redeemer and mediator as he matured. *The Temple* frequently reconsiders "The Sacrifice" and the meditative practices which inspired it; but whenever the speaker seeks union with God by his own imaginative presence at Christ's Passion, he is stymied and frustrated. "The Sacrifice" is an important poem because it is questioning and transitional, not because it is conventional and typical; its frame, the beginning of "The Church," dramatizes the theological and poetic limitations of reenacting the Passion, not the traditional, medieval sympathies Tuve sees, nor the traditional, Catholic devotions Martz sees. After Herbert wrote *Passio Discerpta* and *Lucus*, his immediate sensual vision of the Passion dissolved in his former tears, reemerging as a "strange" and "dolefull storie."

Herbert's goal, like that of all Christians, is union with God ("That all together may accord in thee"). Prevented from reenacting the Passion, Herbert finds himself compelled, as did the men who envisioned the original Anglican Reformation, to seek an alternate way to Christ and through Christ to God. Many of the plans tested in "The Thanksgiving" and "The Reprisall" are immediately dropped, and the following poems encounter more questions, decisions, hesitations, and false starts. But Herbert was writing and revising *The Temple* until he died, and it repeatedly confirms the Protestant sympathies expressed in "The Thanksgiving." With God's help, Herbert soon learns to make his voice, with its flickering, variegated reflections of Scripture, a pathway for the saving light of the Anglican Reformation, "a window, through thy grace" ("The Windows," 5), which cannot "ever be exhausted, (as Pictures may be by a plenarie circumspection)."

II. RHETORIC, STYLE, FORM

HERBERT'S FORM

Joseph H. Summers

There is a certain irony in the fact that the most formal of seventeenth-century Anglican poems have been so much enjoyed by the anti-formalists in religion and art. The appeal of George Herbert's poetry to the opponents of ritual was a justifying triumph for Herbert's conception of form: in poetry as well as religion Herbert tried to work out a middle way between "slovenliness" and "superstition." It was by means of form that the material could be used in the service of the spiritual, that the senses could be properly employed for the glorification of God.

The problem of the relationship between objects of the senses and Christian worship had been introduced with the beginning of the ritual in the ancient church. In the England of Herbert's day there was a large and varied heritage of theory and practice.[1] For the extreme Puritan, the ritual and "adornments" in the church were only vestiges of Popish idolatry. They were considered sensuous barriers (similar to the priest's office) between the naked individual soul and God: the serious business of salvation left no room for them. It was presumptuous for sinful man to attempt to honor God through the creation of formal beauty within God's house. The proper method of honoring God, the essence of worship, was to confess one's unworthiness, to pray for forgiveness and God's grace, and to preach the gospel. Christian poetry had its practitioners and its appreciative audience outside the services, and certainly most Puritan preachers believed that the arts of logic and rhetoric (so long as they were not separated) were useful handmaidens for the instruction and moving of their audiences. But the idea that ritual or "ornaments" within the church could either aid the individual worshipper or honor God was alien to the largest segment of Puritan

Reprinted from *PMLA*, 66 (1951), 1055-72, by permission of the author and the Modern Language Association of America. This essay was later included in *George Herbert: His Religion and Art* (Cambridge, Mass.: Harvard University Press; London: Chatto & Windus, 1954), pp. 73-94.

thought. The light of the Spirit should reach the individual directly, like sunlight through pure glass; it should not be contaminated by "externals," as sunlight was colored by the pictured windows of the Papists.

Certain Catholics embraced an opposite attitude which might seem equally "enthusiastic" to one of Hooker's tradition. St. Ignatius Loyola had stated that "every meditation or contemplation about a bodily thing or a person, as for example, about Christ, demands the formation of a bodily place in vision,"[2] and his widely practiced "application of the senses" was influential in increasing exactly those sensuous details of Catholic worship to which the Protestants objected. The rich liturgy, rather than obscuring the way to God, came to provide the chief light. The Protestants insisted that the Catholics' engrossment in the sensuous details of worship was divorced from reason, from an understanding of the symbolism: it was idolatry.

Many members of the Church of England tried to find a way between the extremes. George Herbert took a firm and consistent position. As a believer in the Covenant of Grace, he could never allow the ritual to become a substitute for incorporeal experience. Yet Herbert also believed that the individual should not present himself, publicly at least, in disorder before God. God should be worshipped in "the beauty of holiness," and he had shown in the "two Books of His Revelation" that the arrangement of "objects of the senses" (whether things or words) into a pattern symbolic of divine order was the method of worship which pleased Him. It was also one of the most persuasive means by which men could be led to worship.

The ordering process was important in itself, and the Christian could create "significant form" in the church even where traditionally none had been intended. Izaak Walton tells that in Herbert's reconstruction of the church at Leighton Bromswold, "by his order, the Reading Pew, and Pulpit, were a little distant from each other, and both of an equal height; for he would often say, 'They should neither have a precedency or priority of the other: but that *Prayer* and *Preaching* being equally useful, might agree like Brethren, and have an equal honour and estimation'."[3] Reason and taste substantiated formal construction at every step. Nicholas Ferrar agreed with Herbert about the proper design for a church, and Herbert undoubtedly agreed with Ferrar's opinion of extemporaneous prayers: "*As for extempory prayers, he used to say, there needed little other confutation of them, than to take them in short-hand, & shew them sometime after to those very men, that had been so audacious to vent them. Ask, saith he, their own judgements of them (for I think they will hardly know them again), & see if they do not blame them.*"[4]

The use of reason as confutation of the extemporaneous implied that the ritual itself must be rational. The individual who participated in the services must understand the significance of each detail. According to Walton, Herbert's sermons at Bemerton were often devoted to a meticulous explanation of Anglican formal practice. The individual should understand the rational "fitness" of every phrase of the service, and he should apply that understanding to his own life. He should even know why particular passages of Scripture were read on particular days. He must understand the "reasons" for all the Holy Days and the symbolic significance of every physical movement of the priest and the congregation.

Walton described the times when Herbert was "too zealous": "And to this I must add, That if he were at any time too zealous in his Sermons, it was in reproving the indecencies of the peoples behaviour, in the time of Divine Service; and of those Ministers that hudled up the Church-prayers, without a visible reverence and affection; namely, *such as seem'd to say the Lords prayer, or a Collect in a Breath*; but for himself, his custom was, to stop betwixt every Collect, and give the people time to consider what they had pray'd, and to force their desires affectionately to God, before he engag'd them into new Petitions."[5] In the years at Bemerton Herbert appropriately reserved his outbursts of "passion and choler" for those who obscured the meaning of form. Such men offended both God and God's little ones. For the ritual could become a means of Grace. If every aspect of it was understood, it could teach the way of salvation and the beautiful pattern of God's creation. Proper worship resulted in an ethical and spiritual ordering of the worshipper's life. That was the ultimate method of honoring God.

Herbert's ideas were by no means original: it is difficult to ascribe to any one man — or civilization — the origins of the analogical habit of mind and the belief that order, measure, proportion, and harmony are both divine and beautiful. He could have found most of the concepts in St. Augustine, the only early Church father whose works he mentioned in his will. Karel Svoboda has insisted that Augustine's "aesthetic system" is the "most complete" that antiquity has handed down to us: it is "the crowning synthesis of the ancient aesthetic."[6] But the most important factor for the Christians who followed was that Augustine's "synthesis" was built around the central conception of the Christian God. Rightly understood, both ethics and aesthetics were only reflections (and not necessarily differing reflections) of the divine, creating Beauty:

What innumerable toys, made by divers arts and manufactures in our apparel, shoes, utensils and all sort of works, in pictures also in divers images, and these far exceeding all necessary and moderate use and all pious meaning, have men added to tempt their own eyes withal; outwardly following what themselves make, inwardly forsaking Him by whom themselves were made, and destroying that which themselves have been made! But I, my God and my Glory, do hence also sing a hymn to Thee, and do consecrate praise to Him who consecrateth me, because beautiful patterns which through men's souls are conveyed into their cunning hands, come from that Beauty, which is above our souls, which my soul day and night sigheth after.[7]

The ideas of God as the Great Artificer and as Absolute Beauty were theological conceptions with inevitable aesthetic corollaries, and the work of art could be valued exactly because it reflected the divine pattern. The ethical life was beautiful, and an unethical life or poem by definition represented that lack of order called "ugly" or "evil" — not a positive quality, but an absence of the good and the beautiful. In so far as an object lacked those qualities or had them imperfectly, it lacked existence; for everything which truly existed, in the sense that it fulfilled its proper nature, was good.[8] Any object or fact could therefore become a first term for almost any number of "true" metaphorical comparisons, since every "existing" thing derived from and reflected the divine creation. Long before Donne's playful poem, Augustine contemplated the flea seriously as an "aesthetic object."

There was, of course, an ambiguity in Augustine's thought (as in that of the Greeks before him and the Christians after) concerning both the value and the role of beautiful objects of the senses. They could be mortally dangerous. In the same paragraph of *The Confessions* in which he had stated the divine origin of those "beautiful patterns which through men's souls are conveyed into their cunning hands," Augustine had added, "And I, though I speak and see this, entangle my steps with these outward beauties; but Thou pluckest me out, O Lord, Thou pluckest me out; *because Thy loving-kindness is before my eyes.* For I am taken miserably, and Thou pluckest me out mercifully; sometimes not perceiving it, when I had but lightly lighted upon them; otherwhiles with pain, because I had stuck fast in them." Man fulfilled his proper nature only through the glorification of God. The fact that material objects of beauty had such power to intoxicate the senses could lead even a man who recognized the divine pattern in them to feel the danger of a sensuous engrossment without meaning and without God. It could also lead him to attempt to suppress sensuous response. A number of men in seventeenth-century England were not convinced, as Augustine was, that it was an error "to wish the whole melody of sweet music which is used to David's Psalter, banished from my ears, and the Church's too";[9] and there were Puritans who took more seriously than Robert Burton the attitude implied by his formulation, "And what is poetry itself, but, as Austin holds, the wine of error administered by drunken teachers?"[10] God was a spirit even though the Son had been incarnate, and one tradition of Christianity indicated that the mature soul anticipated the joys of heaven by rising above response to the matter of earth.

The more common emphasis, echoed throughout the seventeenth century, was that God's creation was second only to His Word as a source of truth and enlightenment. The danger that the individual might be blind to the truth of the created world, that he might "rest in Nature, not the God of Nature,"[11] was real, but it could be met. God had provided "repining restlessnesse" for the man who did not find Him:

> Not that he may not here
>   Taste of the cheer,
> But as birds drink, and straight lift up their head,
>   So he must sip and think
>   Of better drink
> He may attain to, after he is dead.
> ("Mans medley," *Works*, p. 131)

God could, moreover, grant the grace for man to perceive the essential relationships:

> Indeed mans whole estate
> Amounts (and richly) to serve thee:
> He did not heav'n and earth create,
> Yet studies them, not him by whom they be.
>
> Teach me thy love to know;
> That this new light, which now I see,
> May both the work and workman show:
> Then by a sunne-beam I will climbe to thee.
> ("Mattens," *Works*, p. 63)

One of poetry's greatest potential values was that God could employ it as a means through which man might perceive those relationships.

If poetry was an imitation of God's creation and possessed the divine power of moving the affections, the use of it for secular ends might come near to blasphemy. Although many Christians enjoyed secular or pagan poetry in a moral manner, there was little doubt that poetry with a Christian subject could be infinitely more pleasant and profitable. Not many men of the seventeenth century were buffeted black and blue by angels of God for their too great love of some profane writer as was St. Jerome, but a precisian or a parson with a vivid sense of his Christian calling might either abandon the arts of rhetoric and poetry entirely or consecrate their practice to the service of God.

To learn how poetry could be consecrated, Herbert had neither to engage in historical research nor to follow painfully those medieval writings which were read in his day. The religion, the poetry, and "the arts" of his own day were filled with manifestations of the hieroglyphic view of the universe and of experience, a view which could be basic to the practice of the Christian poet and which contained within itself a formal principle. More important for Herbert than the general notion of the microcosm-macrocosm or even the continual example of the ritual was the Bible.

The ancient four-fold interpretation of the Scriptures, which had inspired so much of medieval allegory and symbolism and had served Dante well, was attacked during the seventeenth century as a barrier to the clear perception of those "few things needful" to salvation and Christian charity. After all, some schoolmen had acknowledged seven and eight meanings, and such ingenuity obscured the simple "real" meaning of God's Word. But the older habit of mind was too deeply ingrained to be easily erased. As hermeneutics became a weapon in ecclesiastical controversies, the men who attacked the earlier "superstitious" interpretations sometimes derived the most metaphorical truths from their "plain" reading of the Bible. Such an outcome was almost inevitable, for the Bible was filled with metaphors and parables and types, and it declared the cosmological significance of almost everything from the heavens to the ant. In "Discipline" Herbert echoed the Protestant insistence that the Bible contained all knowledge and was a complete guide for every action in man's life:

> Not a word or look
> I affect to own,
>   But by book,
> And thy book alone.   (*Works*, p. 178)

The devout Christian attempted to "apply" almost every passage in the Old and New Testaments to his own moral and spiritual condition:

> Oh that I knew how all thy lights combine,
>   And the configurations of their glorie!

Seeing not onely how each verse doth shine,
But all the constellations of the storie.
This verse marks that, and both do make a motion
   Unto a third, that ten leaves off doth lie:
Then as dispersed herbs do watch a potion,
These three make up some Christians destinie:
Such are thy secrets, which my life makes good,
   And comments on thee: for in ev'ry thing
   Thy words do finde me out, & parallels bring,
And in another make me understood.
Starres are poore books, & oftentimes do misse:
This book of starres lights to eternall blisse.
       ("The H. Scriptures [II]," *Works*, p. 58)

Such an attitude made inevitable a symbolic exegesis of the text. The pattern for exegesis could be found in the Gospels, the Epistles of Paul, and the book of Hebrews, where it was shown how persons and events in the Old Testament had divinely prefigured the life of Christ and Christian doctrine and practice. There are references to almost every one of the specifically biblical types in Herbert's poetry. But once the method had been shown, neither the early Fathers nor the men of the seventeenth century were satisfied with the few types mentioned in the New Testament. Many discoveries of types were individual and eccentric; but there was general agreement, for example, that the twelve tribes of Israel had mystically prophesied the twelve Disciples, that Aaron's chief importance lay not in his historical role but in his embodiment of the type of God's priest, that the bride of The Song of Solomon was a type of the Church, the Bride of Christ. It is important to realize that the types were considered purposeful anticipations by God of the future unfolding of His Will, not merely imaginative analogies drawn by the reader:

For as the Jews of old by Gods command
   Travell'd, and saw no town;
So now each Christian hath his journeys spann'd:
   Their storie pennes and sets us down.
   A single deed is small renown.
Gods works are wide, and let in future times;
His ancient justice overflows our crimes.
      ("The Bunch of Grapes," *Works*, p. 128)

The idea of the types could be extended to profane literature and could partially sanctify it. The structure of the universe and the nature of

God's plan were so evident that even pagans had occasionally understood, however gropingly, many religious truths. Sure of the truth (like
the Freudians of a later day), the Christian readers welcomed the
perceptions of it which they found in classic mythology. Just as Paul had
been able to tell the Athenians the identity of their Unknown God, so
any educated reader could join Giles Fletcher in telling them the true
identity of Orpheus or Zeus or Hercules:

> Who doth not see drown'd in Deucalions name,
> (When earth his men, and sea had lost his shore)
> Old Noah; and in Nisus Lock, the fame
> Of Sampson yet alive; and long before
> In Phaethons, mine owne fall I deplore:
> But he that conquer'd hell, to fetch againe
> His virgin widowe, by a serpent slaine,
> Another Orpheus was then dreaming poets feigne.
>   ("Christ's Triumph over Death," st. 7)

The general assumption that "sensible images" "shadowed" intellectual or divine conceptions, in the present as well as in the past, made
for extraordinary formal parallels between religious and secular
"images," between, for example, the sacraments and the emblem books.
Richard Hooker noted "that many times there are three things said to
make up the substance of a sacrament, namely, the grace which is
thereby offered, the element which shadoweth or signifieth grace, and
the word which expresseth what is done by the element,"[12] and
Rosemary Freeman has recently defined the tripartite formal structure
of the emblem.[13] As a good Anglican of his time Herbert believed that
"The H. Communion" and "H. Baptisme" were the only two sacraments
which Christ had ordained for his Church; but that ordination had put
the stamp of divine approval on that hieroglyphic practice which the
Egyptians were believed to have known and taught to the Greeks, a
practice which the emblem books, those best-sellers of their day,
typified. Although most men of the seventeenth century would have
been shocked by the comparison, the Protestants at least considered
both the picture of the emblem and the element of the sacrament "visible
signs and symbols of internal and invisible things." The elements or
signs of the sacrament of communion were the bread and wine; the sign
of the emblem was a literal picture, a representation of some symbolic
figure or situation which could not be understood without the "word"
and the explanation. The "word" of consecration of the communion
service "which expresseth what is done by the element" was paralleled by

the "mot" of the emblem, which summarized the bit of moral wisdom which the emblem was to inculcate. That wisdom as it acted on the reader, like the actual grace of the sacrament, had no precise material counterpart. But the emblem's poem, which explained the exact relationship between the motto and the picture and rationally applied the moral to daily life, paralleled the sermon of explanation which usually preceded the celebration of the communion. The emblem book in England, like the Protestant theory of the two sacraments, insisted that the symbol be rationally explained and "applied."

The insistence on the interrelations of spiritual reality, the symbol, the word, and the explanation was not confined to the sacraments and the emblem books. The painters, the musicians, and the poets expressed those relationships, sometimes lightly and sometimes seriously, even when by modern canons those expressions seemed to involve violations of the rules of their crafts. Each developed varieties of what may be called hieroglyphic form. We should beware of interpreting their imitations according to modern standards. The composer no more attempted to convey the exact "curve of the feeling" of God's "exalting the humble and meek," the experience of falling, or the voice crying out of the deep,[14] than the poet tried to "recreate the experience" of "Trinitie Sunday," "Easter-wings," or "The Altar." Various artists and artisans did believe that symbolic representations which involved more than one sense in apprehension increased the pleasure and therefore the effectiveness of their works. That pleasure derived less from a delight in man's artfulness than from a recognition of the hieroglyphic nature of the universe.

Herbert had taken seriously the Lawyer's summary of the Law and the Prophets: "Thou shalt loue the Lord thy God with all thy heart, and with all thy soule, and with all thy strength, and with all thy minde, and thy neighbour as thy selfe" (Luke x.27). His conclusion he phrased in the terms of St. Paul: "Let all things be done decently, and in order," and "Let all things be done unto edifying" (I Cor.xiv.40, 26). In *A Priest to the Temple* that formulation applied specifically to the services of the church of England. The ritual of the Book of Common Prayer was to be followed because it provided a decent, orderly, and edifying form of worship which reflected that ordered beauty of the universe to which the individual strove to conform. In daily life the same criteria applied. The command of love to God and one's neighbor meant that each action must be decent, orderly, and edifying as well as charitable. It was impossible to distinguish the aims of specific actions for all was done to the glory of God: the aid both spiritual and physical of one's neighbor was also an act of worship of the productive life; and any individual act of public or private worship, once communicated, could become an act of edification to one's neighbor. The ultimate method of reflecting God's glory was the creation of a work of decency and order, a work of beauty, whether a church, an ordered poem, or an ordered life. This was not confined to the artist, but was the privilege and duty of every Christian. To do all actions "as for thee" was "The Elixir" "That turneth all to gold."[15]

Herbert intended the poems in *The Temple* as expressions of his love for God as well as his neighbor. In Herbert's characteristic imagery, they are both "fruits and flowers" of the Christian life, "wreaths" of worship for God's altar and the harvest of "fruits" of edification for others. As acts of worship they were to symbolize in their elaborate forms the beauty of the divine creation. As acts of edification they were to communicate to others the rational fitness of the symbolic forms, and to inflame them with the desire to follow the "beauty of holiness." The poems thus fulfilled for their readers the traditional classical aims, pleasure and profit. For nothing could be more pleasant than to contemplate the order of God's providence in the universe, the church, or the personal life; and nothing could be more profitable, since such contemplation should increase the reader's faith and cause him to order his own life after the divine pattern.

Any attempt therefore to find either in individual poems or in the sequence of the poems a direct revelation of autobiography will fail, for the primary purpose of the poems was not what we understand by self-expression. There is, of course, no question of sincerity. The poems are a "picture" of meticulously observed spiritual experience. But the self to Herbert was not the valuable thing which it became to a later age, and he desired that his poems should be burned if Ferrar did not think they could "turn to the advantage of any dejected poor Soul."[16] "Personality" and personal experiences were of interest to the poet exactly in so far as they could be profitably used in the objective creations which were his poems. In his "Dedication" to *The Temple* Herbert made a sharp distinction between his poems and himself, which still warns the reader:

> Lord, my first fruits present themselves to thee;
> Yet not mine neither: for from thee they came,
> And must return. Accept of them and me,
> And make us strive, who shall sing best thy name.
> Turn their eyes hither, who shall make a gain:
> Theirs, who shall hurt themselves or me, refrain.

For the conception which gives significance to the individual poems and to the organization of *The Temple*, a passage from one of Lancelot Andrewes' sermons is more revealing than most of the misty bits of Herbert's biography:

> So come we to have two sorts of Temples; Temples of flesh and bone, as well as Temples of lime and stone. For if our bodies be termed houses, because our souls, tenant-wise, abide and dwell in them; if because our souls dwell they be houses, if God do so they be temples: why not? why not? ... But then they be so specially, when actually we employ them in the service of God. For being in His Temple, and there serving Him, then if ever they be *Templa in Templo,* 'living Temples in a Temple without life.' A body then may be a Temple, even this of ours.
>
> And if ours, these of ours I say, in which the Spirit of God dwelleth only by some gift or grace, with how much better right, better infinitely. His body, Christ's, in Whom the whole Godhead in all the fulness of it, dwelt corporally![17]

We do not need to assume that Herbert knew this particular passage, for the conception of the Temple was present everywhere in Christian thought. But the passage gives to the modern reader the key to the meaning of Herbert's title. For the temple as a building was an hieroglyph for the body, particularly the human body in the service of God and the divine body of Christ. By implication of its constructive elements, "flesh and bone" and "lime and stone," the temple could become a symbol for all the types of order in the universe, both God's and man's. It is that symbol which pervades Herbert's volume.

Herbert's inclusion of many poems which refer to actual ceremonies or physical details of the English Church has led even so perceptive a critic as Helen C. White, who recognized the ambiguity of the title, to conclude that Herbert abandoned his initial plan for the organization of his poems.[18] No one would suggest that Herbert conceived of an abstract plan for something resembling "The Christian Year." Yet the order of the poems in the Williams MS. and the careful rearrangement of them in the Bodleian MS. and the 1633 edition indicate that Herbert did arrange the poems in what was to him a significant order which had little to do with biographical revelation.[19] If we conceive of *The Temple* as the symbolic record, written by a poet, of a "typical" Christian life within the Church, most of Miss White's perplexities concerning the meaning of the order of the poems disappear. "H. Baptisme," for example,[20] is a natural meditation after "Easter" and "Easter-wings" for the Protestant who remembers the symbolism of the death, burial, and Resurrection; and "Nature" and "Sinne" almost inevitably follow with the reminder that baptism does not free man from his sinful nature. "Affliction (I)" is more personal than most of Herbert's poems, but it also naturally follows "Sinne." "Repentance," "Faith," "Prayer," and "The H. Communion" are the means by which the Christian triumphs over affliction, and they are followed by the general rejoicing of "Antiphon (I)" and the more specific expressions of "Love (I)" and "(II)." The two poems called "The Temper" are prayers that God will not "rack me ... to such a vast extent," following the exaltation of "Love," and indicating the inevitable emptiness after the moment of illumination. "Jordan (I)" is Herbert's personal declaration of intent in writing his poems; the poem relates directly to the prayer of "Love (II)," and its general significance is partially indicated by "Employment (I)," which immediately follows. The Christian unsure of his calling turns to "The H. Scriptures," is moved by the account of the descent of the Holy Spirit on "Whitsunday," and prays that similar "Grace" may "Drop from above." Not all the sequences are so easily followed, but the central plan is clear. Long before Andrewes, Paul had indicated in 1 Corinthians vi.19-20 that "temple" had one primary meaning for the Christian. The Church of England, its doctrines, its services, and even the physical construction of its churches furnished spiritual sustenance for that "temple not made with hands," and it was filled with hieroglyphs of man's spiritual state. But it was the life of man within that Church which formed the principle of organization for Herbert's volume.

However symmetrical the ideal state of the Christian at any one moment, the pilgrimage of the Christian in time was not a broad and straight highway from the vales of sin to the Heavenly City. The very fluctuations between sorrow and joy, doubt and assurance, which caused George Herbert Palmer to believe that the arrangement of the poems was meaningless, seemed to the earlier readers of *The Temple* one of the most valuable evidences of Herbert's psychological realism. They saw in them the pattern of the Christian's life under the Covenant of Grace. Most of the men of the seventeenth century did not believe that sorrow was totally banished or that man achieved continuous beatitude on this earth. God had constantly to "create":

> Lord, mend or rather make us: one creation
>   Will not suffice our turn:
> Except thou make us dayly, we shall spurn
>   Our own salvation. ("Giddinesse," *Works*, p. 127)

Through Herbert's pictures of violently alternating spiritual change, however, they could perceive a deepening understanding of the "giddie" state of man. It is significant that all of Herbert's "Afflictions" (there are five poems so entitled,[21] although only the first is generally known today) occur within the early part of "The Church," the central body of lyrics within *The Temple*. Those "Afflictions" represent a developing spiritual maturity in the attitudes which they express. In the larger half of "The Church" the experience earlier described as "Affliction" is comprehended under new modes: as the "Dulnesse," "Complaining," "Longing," "The Search" or "Grief" of the individual; or as "Discipline," "The Pulley," "The Cross," part of "Josephs coat," the "Bitter-sweet" of the Christian life:

> Ah my deare angrie Lord,
> Since thou dost love, yet strike;
> Cast down, yet help afford;
> Sure I will do the like.
>
> I will complain, yet praise;
> I will bewail, approve:
> And all my sowre-sweet dayes
> I will lament, and love.

It was, perhaps, a perception of the pattern of *The Temple* which led T. S. Eliot to remark that Herbert's poetry "is definitely an *oeuvre* to be studied entire."[22]

The form of Herbert's volume is often the key to the understanding of individual poems. "Love (III)," one of Herbert's best known poems in the anthologies, has been generally interpreted as picturing the soul's welcome to the Communion or to salvation on earth:

> Love bade me welcome: yet my soul drew back,
>   Guiltie of dust and sinne.
> But quick-ey'd Love, observing me grow slack
>   From my first entrance in,
> Drew nearer to me, sweetly questioning,
>   If I lack'd any thing.
>
> A guest, I answer'd, worthy to be here:
>   Love said, You shall be he.
> I the unkinde, ungratefull? Ah my deare,

> I cannot look on thee.
> Love took my hand, and smiling did reply,
> Who made the eyes but I?
>
> Truth Lord, but I have marr'd them: let my shame
> Go where it doth deserve.
> And know you not, sayes Love, who bore the blame?
> My deare, then I will serve.
> You must sit down, sayes Love, and taste my meat:
> So I did sit and eat.

As the poem is in the Williams MS. it is probably "early," but both there and in the 1633 edition it is the last lyric within "The Church" and it follows "Death," "Dooms-day," "Judgement," and "Heaven." George Ryley, who had read *The Temple* in the early eighteenth century as the typical record of the Christian life, recognized that "the matter of it is equally applicable to the entertainment we meet with in Divine ordinances"; but because of the position of the poem in *The Temple* he believed, correctly I think, that it was intended as a description of the soul's reception into heaven: "A Christian's coming to Heaven is the effect of Divine Love. Therefore, after a contemplation on the state, it's proper to ruminate a little upon that which enstates us there."[23] The banquet at which Love serves personally is not that of the earthly Church, but that final "communion" mentioned in Luke xii.37, of which the present Communion is but an anticipation: "Blessed are those seruants, whom the Lord when he commeth, shall find watching: Verily, I say vnto you, That he shall girde himselfe, and make them to sit downe to meate, and will come foorth and serue them."

Within most of the individual poems the emphasis is on construction rather than pilgrimage. Herbert's imagery characteristically concerns the creator and the architect rather than the "nests" and "tears" of Crashaw, the "light" of Vaughan, or Donne's imagery of death. God is specifically the "*Architect*" in "The Church-floore,"[24] and He is almost everywhere the builder or the artist or the musician. One of the most convincing arguments against despair derives from the nature of God as artist: "As Creatures, he must needs love them; for no perfect Artist ever yet hated his owne worke."[25] Herbert rings all the traditional changes on "stone" as the chief architectural element, under its various guises as the heart of man, the tomb of Christ, the law of Moses, "the stone that the builders rejected." The hardness of the stone was generally recognized; it was the employment of that hardness in the construction of a true temple which appealed to Herbert's imagination.[26]

In "The World," "Love's" work is to build a "stately house."
"Fortune" attempts to disguise the house's structure; "Pleasure" ornaments it with "*Balcones, Terraces,* / Till she had weakned all by
alteration"; "Sinne" "The inward walls and sommers cleft and tore"; and
"Sinne" and "Death" combined "raze the building to the very floore";

> But *Love* and *Grace* took *Glorie* by the hand,
> And built a braver Palace then before.(*Works,* p. 84)

In "Vanitie (I)" the activities of the "fleet Astronomer," the "nimble
Diver," and the "subtil Chymick," divorced from the search for God, are
the search for death; life is found in the discovery of God, and creation is
its mark (*Works,* p. 85). In "Deniall" separation from God is compared
with the "breaking" of a bow, of music, of a blossom, of the heart — and
of rhyme and stanzaic structure (ibid., pp. 79-80).

There was for Herbert no one architectural pattern; there were almost
as many patterns as there were experiences. But Herbert could not
conceive of such a thing as a formless poem. "The Collar," one of his
most popular poems today, makes an immediate appeal to many readers
with its expression of revolt and with what appears to be its daring use of
"free verse." But the poem is not written in "vers libres"; it is one of
Herbert's most deliberate ventures in "hieroglyphic form." The object of
imitation is the disordered life of self-will which rebels against the will of
God and therefore lacks the order and harmony of art as well as of the
religious life: a strict "imitation" would be no form at all — and no poem
at all. Herbert has given a formalized picture of chaos.

> I struck the board, and cry'd, No more.
> I will abroad.
> What? shall I ever sigh and pine?
> My lines and life are free; free as the rode,
> Loose as the winde, as large as store.
> Shall I be still in suit?
> Have I no harvest but a thorn
> To let me bloud, and not restore
> What I have lost with cordiall fruit?
> Sure there was wine
> Before my sighs did drie it: there was corn
> Before my tears did drown it.
> Is the yeare onely lost to me?
> Have I no bayes to crown it?
> No flowers, no garlands gay? all blasted?

All wasted?
Not so, my heart: but there is fruit,
And thou hast hands.
Recover all thy sigh-blown age
On double pleasures: leave thy cold dispute
Of what is fit, and not. Forsake thy cage,
Thy rope of sands,
Which pettie thoughts have made, and made to thee
Good cable, to enforce and draw,
And be thy law,
While thou didst wink and wouldst not see.
Away; take heed:
I will abroad.
Call in thy deaths head there: tie up thy fears.
He that forbears
To suit and serve his need,
Deserves his load.
But as I rav'd and grew more fierce and wilde
At every word,
Me thought I heard one calling, *Child!*
And I reply'd, *My Lord.*

For readers accustomed to a different tradition in poetry, the picture of chaos may not at first be apparent. Except for some permissible extravagance of emotion and certain ideas which prove fallacious from the point of view of Christian doctrine, there is in the thought no obvious indication of the failure of rational control. The poem is clearly divided into four sections of argument: the original complaint of the heart, the answering assurance of the will that there is "fruit" if the heart would seek it, the repeated complaint and statement of purpose by the heart, and the final resolution. The heart originally rebels because of lack of "fruit," and, as Helen White has noted,[27] after the early "flowers" and "garlands" the imagery becomes more vulgar as the emotion becomes "more fierce and wilde." But the meaning of Herbert's poem, his evaluation of that revolt and its resolution, is clearly imaged in the elaborate anarchy of the patterns of measure and rhyme. The poem contains all the elements of order in violent disorder. No line is unrhymed (a few rhymes occur as often as four times) and each line contains two, three, four, or five poetic feet. (Herbert counted syllables. All the lines have four, six, eight, or ten syllables except lines 12 and 14, with their conventional feminine rhymes, and lines 15 and 16, with their daring but still "permissible" combination of short feet and feminine rhymes.) Although readers accustomed to Renaissance poetry might feel uncomfortable with the disorder of the first thirty-two lines, they could hardly divine the stanzaic norm which is the measure for that disorder until it is established, simultaneously with the submission of the rebel, in the final quatrain: $10^a 4^b 8^a 6^b$. That pattern of line lengths and rhyme does not occur until the final four lines; before those lines the elements of the pattern are arranged so as to form almost the mathematical ultimate in lack of periodicity. If we consider that the first thirty-two lines represent eight quatrains, we discover six different patterns of rhyme (the only repeated one is the unformed $a\ b\ c\ d$) and seven patterns of line lengths. "The Collar" is a narrative in the past tense. The message for the present concerns the necessity of order.

The Temple is almost a casebook of examples showing how "Order" gives "all things their set forms and houres."[28] It reflects Herbert's belief that form was that principle by which the spiritual created existence out of chaos, and Herbert assumed that that process could be rationally apprehended. Since the principle was divine and therefore universal, the understanding of the formal organization of any one object or state or action gave a clue to the understanding of the rest. The poet's duty was to perceive and to communicate God's form. In the process he would construct out of the chaos of experience and the mass of language another object which would reflect his discovery: literary form as we understand it was but a reflection of that form which was everywhere present, although often hidden to eyes that could not "see." It, too, in its material embodiment appealed to man's senses and moved his affections. The rational contemplation of it should lead to an understanding of its symbolic significance.

Such an undeviating effort to answer the question, "how are all things neat?"[29] ran the risk of over-neatness. For a person who did not scrutinize the heart, who attempted to formulate the answers before he had experienced them, such an external conception of the function of the priest and the poet would leave the craftsman and the logician admirably free, but it might also lead to triviality and inhumanity. That Herbert was deflected so rarely from the genuine was the result not only of his integrity as man and as artist, but also of the nature and depth of his experienced suffering. Suffering, both spiritual and physical, was the continuous challenge to the meaning of Herbert's existence and his art. Herbert believed that the Christian's life should be ordered in accordance with the will of God. As Austin Warren has remarked, the "marks" of that order were joy and "fruit" and peace.[30] When these were absent, a searching of the self and a passionate attempt at resolution were necessities. To Herbert it was not enough to present "honestly" the ugliness and the disorder either in the worship of God or in poetry. That desperate sorrow which seemed meaningless and for which no resolution could be conceived could serve neither for worship nor for edification. But poetry was not therefore to be left to the secular "lover's lute."[31] Suffering for which some resolution or evaluation could be envisaged was the subject of the most moving poetry. While Herbert had experienced the joy and peace of resolution, he had also experienced its momentariness. He knew that the Christian's and the poet's forms were only approximations within time which had constantly to be renewed. The composition of the poems, imitative as they were of that ordering which he had experienced and which he hoped to experience again, was the act of the craftsman who shapes the imperfect materials of his own suffering as well as joy into a pattern symbolic of the divine order.

GEORGE HERBERT'S RHETORICAL WORLD

Richard E. Hughes

"Rhetoric" is now one of the most used and abused words in the vocabulary of criticism. It can be taken to mean a commitment to persuasive intention in writing; it may refer to a specialized technique in writing; it may even (although this variant is quite antique) be used as a pejorative, implying woodenness and lack of conviction. In all three versions there lurks a suspicion that to be "rhetorical" is to be vaguely opposed to "creative," and that the writer who belongs in a tradition of rhetoric is academic, technique-ridden and unoriginal. The point of this essay is to argue that a commitment to rhetoric, instead of limiting a writer to a learned facility, actually involves him in a complex frame of reference; that rhetoric, properly defined, might better be called a *weltanschauung* than a *discipline*; and that to view rhetoric in this light is a considerable help in understanding and appreciating much of the poetry of George Herbert. The first emphasis in the essay will be generic and theoretical (necessarily), and then specific and analytic in its application to Herbert's poetry.

The first element in a genuinely rhetorical frame of reference is a belief in probability: a conviction that all non-factual apprehensions are not to be dismissed as merely opinionative or non-verifiable, but may occupy a sphere all their own. This sphere we call probability, and this acceptance of a middle ground between fact and opinion is the keystone of Aristotelian rhetoric (see *Rhetoric*, 1355^a). The willingness to admit probability to a scientifically or syllogistically indemonstrable proposition is the major distinction between Aristotelian rhetoric and (a) a rhetoric which ignores the doctrine of probabilities and sees all statement as either fact or opinion, like the sophistic rhetoric of Gorgias; and (b) a rhetoric which blurs the distinction between fact and probability,

Reprinted from *Criticism*, 3 (1961), 86-94, by permission of the author and Wayne State University Press.

and so eventually disposes of probability, such as the rhetoric of Agricola or Ramus. The Aristotelian-rhetorical frame of reference gives to abstractions, intuitions, and emotions the status of probable, even though they have no extension, no substance, no data to be empirically tested and passed as "fact."

The second element in this frame of reference is the belief that isolated phenomena, experiences and perceptions find their real value when they can be absorbed into or subordinated to the abstract realm of probability. An atomistic approach to experience, the consideration of any one experience as having an essential value or meaning, is overborne by the greater value such an experience assumes when it is so abstracted and subordinated. Consequently, it is not the rhetor-poet's function to give a dramatic account of a single experience; rather, he must abstract from the experience and locate for his abstraction a place in the whole company of probabilities.

It is for the purpose of implementing this subordination, abstraction and location that the *trope* exists. The ordinary distinction is between *trope* as a logical figure involving a displacement or transfer of meaning (irony, metaphor, metalepsis) and *figure* as a decorative device involving word schemes (anaphora, brachylogia, polysyndeton). But trope is far more than an arbitrary choice of oratorical device; for it is through trope that any single experience or sensation is established in a field larger than itself. Consequently, we must distinguish between two kinds of trope: the paradoxical and the signal. Each may be used to subordinate a single idea to a large abstraction, even though each operates quite differently.

The paradoxical trope establishes a real equality between the *definiendum* and the *definiens*, between the experience to be defined and the defining comparison. Understood thus, in metaphor the literal and the applied meaning co-exist; in irony the combative points of view co-exist; in oxymoron the contraries co-exist. This admission of co-existent planes of meaning, which we term paradox, assumes at least a bi-dimensional view of reality; things exist, not on one level, but on several.

The signal trope, on the other hand, does not aim at establishing a real equality between *definiendum* and *definiens*: the defining term does not co-exist with the term to be defined, but simply points to it. The signal trope is an indicator, merely a participant in what is being defined.

There is far more than a verbal difference between these two kinds of trope. "She has a garden in her face" and "My Love is like a red, red rose" cannot be identified as paradoxial and signal trope, respectively, simply because Campion dispenses with the simile form of the copula. Each of these lines presents the *definiendum* (the mistress, the love) not as identical to the *definiens* (the garden, the rose) but as being partially understandable in terms of the definer. The existence or non-existence of a *like* is no test of the difference between paradox and signal; the total world-view of a writer must be understood before we can determine which trope he is using — for the difference is not verbal but depends on whether he sees reality on several planes or on one plane. Both kinds of trope are most pertinent to the probability aspect of rhetoric, for the paradoxical shows individual experience to exist concurrently with abstraction or transcendence, while the signal subordinates individual experience to abstraction.

This is precisely the way in which Herbert's poetry is rhetorical. Rhetoric is not simply technique, not simply discipline, but is rather a way of looking at experience and ideas. A single probability dominates all, and the the tropes of rhetoric, both paradoxical and signal, are used as demonstrators of that probability. The dominant mode of this demonstration is, for Herbert, allegory: for allegory subordinates the specious world of appearances to the real world of abstractions, while at the same time admitting single details which may assert their single, unabstracted identity. Allegory can be made to function as both paradox and as signal, and this George Herbert does.

The single probability at the heart of all Herbert's poetry is, of course, the communion between the human spirit and its creator. This intuition, so graphically presented in Izaac Walton's life of Herbert, came to be the focus of all the poetry (even as Herbert promised in his first poems, "My God, where is that ancient heat toward Thee" and "Sure, Lord, there is enough in Thee"). His conversion was not like Donne's or Newman's, rationally acquired; like Paul, on the road to Damascus, Herbert was emotionally and instinctually converted. All the themes of Herbert's poetry (redemption, salvation, communion, conversion) are shoots from the main stem of this probability. The avowed intention of his poetry (as Walton quoted him) was to insist on this probability; and if he could not *prove* that probability, as a logician might, he could *demonstrate* it, as a rhetorician would: through trope, which presented both the attributes of and the uniqueness of God.

In those poems (and they make up, by far, the majority) in which Herbert demonstrates major attributes of God, the trope is signal. Not only is it *not* the experience of the speaker in the poetry which is important, but the historicity or the individuality of the event described is also unimportant. Human narrator and divine subject are both absorbed into an abstract framework, so that the material of the poem becomes a signal trope, a pointer to a transcendent probability. Thus, we observe that a poem like "The Collar," for all of its discordant technique signifying the soul's painful rejection and re-discovery of God, is yet an imaginative re-occurrence, not an account of a present involvement in any torment. "The Quip," with its refrain of temptations met and overcome, likewise adopts a past, abstract and impersonal point of view. The meaning of such a point of view is that the experience which took place outside the limits of the poem has already been resolved, and has consequently been subordinated to the dominant probability. The use of a certain time scheme as a symbol of subordination is one indication of Herbert's use of signal: along with this we must class other examples of abstraction which negate unique details in favor of a transcendent idea — the allegorical *débat* (as in "Humilitie"), the allegorical inference ("Vertue," "Life"), and certainly one of the most notable examples of trope as signal, the poem "Prayer," in which nothing is predicated of the details, the absence of any copula effectively transforming each detail into a pointer:

> Prayer, the Churche's banquet, Angel's age,
>   God's breath in man returning to his birth,
> The soul in paraphrase, heart in pilgrimage,
>   The Christian plummet sounding heav'n and earth;
>
> Engine against th' Almightie, sinner's towre,
>   Reversèd thunder, Christ-side-piercing spear,
> The six-daies-world transposing in an houre,
>   A kinde of tune which all things heare and fear;
>
> Softnesse, and peace, and joy, and love, and blisse,
>   Exalted manna, gladnesse of the best,
> Heaven in ordinarie, man well drest,
>   The milkie way, the bird of Paradise,
>
> Church-bels beyond the stars heard, the soul's bloud,
> The land of spices, something understood.[1]

The predication is absent from the poem, as it is absent from the temporal world: predication, meaning, is supplied by reference outside the poem, outside the temporal. The matter of "Prayer" is incomplete; the entire poem is a signal trope, pointing beyond itself to the area of final predication.

The same effect of diverting attention away from the immediate and the temporal to something transcendent and immutable is achieved still differently in a poem like "The Agonie." In these verses the physical agony of the crucifixion is not the focus of the poem. Instead, those details have their preface in a stanza which establishes an abstract problem:

> Philosophers have measur'd mountains,
> Fathom'd the depths of seas, of states, and kings;
> Walk'd with a staffe to heav'n, and tracèd fountains;
>   But there are two vast, spacious things,
> The which to measure it doth more behove:
> Yet few there are that sound them, — Sinne and Love.
>
>   (p. 33)

This deduction, this inference, this abstraction, now is supplied with examples; so that the details which follow are made to be demonstrators of the inference rather than details *sui generis*. Furthermore, both subsequent stanzas conclude with an additional abstraction, so that all details are subordinated to a prior and a posterior abstract idea:

> Who would know Sinne, let him repair
> Unto Mount Olivet; there shall he see
> A Man so wrung with pains, that all His hair,
>   His skinne, His garments bloudie be.
> Sinne is that presse and vice, which forceth pain
> To hunt his cruell food through ev'ry vein.
>
>   Who knows not Love, let him assay
> And taste that juice which, on the crosse, a pike
> Did set abroach; then let him say
>   If ever he did taste the like.
> Love is that liquor sweet and most divine,
> Which my God feels as bloud, but I as wine.   (p. 33)

The transformation of the physical act of suffering, first to the general theme of Pain and Sin and then to the liturgical symbol of the sacramental wine, moves the historical and the unique event far into the background and emphasizes the one spiritual reality.

Thus far, we have seen examples only of the signal trope in Herbert's poetry, as embodiments of the concept of a single reality. There are several examples of Herbert's awareness of a dual reality, of the single, unique, historical co-existing with the abstract eternal — the unique not absorbed into or subordinated to the abstract, but existing along with it. The rhetorical instrument which conveys this concept is, of course, the paradoxical trope. Such a trope is evident in several poems whose theme is the search of the soul for its God. In the process of the search, the point of view is abstractive and the tropes are signal; but at the conclusion of the search, the point of view is dual and the tropes are paradoxical. At the moment of discovery, the religious experience involves the double vision of two realities (one historical and unique, the other transcendental).

"Redemption" is perhaps the clearest instance of this ambivalence:

> Having been tenant long to a rich Lord,
>   Not thriving, I resolvèd to be bold,
> And make a suit unto Him, to afford
>   A new small-rented lease, and cancell th' old.
>
> In heaven at His manour I Him sought:
>   They told me there, that He was lately gone
> About some land, which he had deerly bought
>   Long since on Earth, to take possession.
>
> I straight return'd, and knowing His great birth,
>   Sought Him accordingly in great resorts —
> In cities, theatres, gardens, parks, and courts:
> At length I heard a raggèd noise and mirth
>
> Of theeves and murderers; there I him espied,
> Who straight, 'Your suit is granted,' said, and died.
>   (p. 35)

The first quatrain of this sonnet is a variation on the theme of "The Collar": the chafing of the soul under the covenant with God. Herbert's use of antonomasia, the epithet of landlord to signify Christ, effectively directs our attention not to the historical figure but to one of his attributes. The second and third quatrains extend this abstraction into allegory, with its characteristic disregard of temporality and definite space, signifying the eternal and ubiquitous. But in the final line of the third quatrain and in the couplet, even while the antonomasia is lightly continued (the landlord's grant to the freeholder), the historic accidents of the crucifixion are asserted, even though they are not likely extensions of the landlord figure (the ragged noise, the position with the thieves, the death). The process of deducing meaning from the crucifixion which takes place in the greater part of the poem is replaced by an insistence on the single act itself. Individuation, which is the identifying mark of dual outlook, becomes a factor in the poem. The landlord figure is clearly a signal trope; but the details of the death scene operate in an entirely different sphere. They focus attention on themselves, insist on their identity, and introduce a second reality: the physical reality of the crucifixion, which resists being submerged. To state it in previous terminology: the thing to be defined (Christ and the relationship between Christ and the human spirit) completely absorbs the definer *landlord*; whereas the details of the death do not function as definer only, but as a separate entity.

The poems "Christmas" and "Easter," which, considering their similar structure, ought to be compared, follow the same pattern of the search through allegory and abstraction for the single present act. Thus, in the sonnet-prologue of "Christmas," the Everyman-I rides through the allegorical no-where and no-time:

> All after pleasures as I rid one day,
> My horse and I, both tir'd, bodie and minde,
> With full crie of affections, quite astray,
> I took up in the next inne I could finde.

The closing quatrains and the couplet perform a metalepsis, transferring the idea of the inn from the haven of the traveller to the inn at Bethlehem to the inn of the human soul which ought to receive Christ:

> There when I came, whom found I but my deare,
> My dearest Lord, expecting till the grief
> Of pleasures brought me to Him, readie there
> To be all passengers' most sweet relief.
>
> O Thou, Whose glorious yet contracted light,
> Wrapt in Night's mantle, stole into a manger,
> Since my dark soul and brutish, is Thy right,
> To man, of all beasts, be not Thou a stranger:
>
> Furnish and deck my soul, that Thou mayst have
> A better lodging than a rack or grave.   (p. 72)

All this is the characteristic abstracting process, wherein the detail is dominated by the idea which it partially defines; and the historical scene of the nativity is displaced by the inference to be made from that scene. However, the poem does not end here. The sonnet is prologue only, and the rest of the poem is a hymn to the infant, sung in companionship with the shepherds. The scene at Bethlehem, which the prologue had metamorphosed into a signal trope, is allowed to stand forth, not as sign at all, but an event as real in its own terms as was the abstraction. "The shepherds sing; and shall I silent be": and even the time scheme has been altered, from past recollection to present observation. What had been simply definer or pointer has now been allowed its literal significance.

"Easter" also involves an allegorical prologue to the historical resurrection; and, as in "Christmas," this prologue converts the event into a signal. The song which follows the sonnet, however, reconverts the day of resurrection back into its original self, the single day to be celebrated rather than the implications of the resurrection on that day.

As a final indication of Herbert's method of first relegating a specific and literal detail to a signal trope, and then reversing the process and allowing literal significance to overcome signal, we may notice "The Pilgrimage." Once again, the single transcendent reality is first presented, all temporalities having been interpreted as an indicator of that reality: but at the end the dual reality of both transcendent and literal are allowed to come through. The poem begins with the allegorical traveller, seeking his resting place. Past the "gloomy cave of Desperation," "the rock of Pride," "Phansie's medow," "the wilde of Passion,"

> At length I got unto the gladsome hill,
>   Where lay my hope,
> Where lay my heart; and climbing still,
>   When I had gain'd the brow and top,
> A lake of brackish waters on the ground
>   Was all I found.

This moment of the Dark Night of the Soul is momentary:

> With that abash'd and struck with many a sting
>   Of swarming fears,
> I fell and cry'd, 'Alas, my King,
>   Can both the way and end be tears?'
> Yet taking heart I rose, and then perceiv'd
>   I was deceived,
>
> My hill was further; so I flung away,
>   Yet heard a crie,
> Just as I went, 'None goes that way
>   And lives.' 'If that be all,' said I,
> 'After so foul a journey death is fair,
>   And but a chair.'   (p. 128)

Until the second voice is heard, the hill of Calvary is a trope, a sign of the abstract hill of completion and the end of the journey. But the *none* which is voiced involves both the literal Christ on the ascent to crucifixion *and* the journey of the soul to an acceptance of that Death. The totality of *none* introduces the central paradox of the poem: Christ had to go that way to his death; through his death came redemption and life; the human spirit, if it goes the way of Christ, accepts death, which is Life. The sacrificial act was physical and real ("None goes that way and lives"), and at the same time metaphysical and abstract (the basic model for the text, "Except a corn of wheat fall into the ground and die, it abideth alone; but if it die, it bringeth forth much fruit," John, xii. 24). The death was real, final and concrete, and simultaneously implicative, abstract and apocalyptic.

This rhetorical world-view of Herbert's, with its complete acceptance of the probability of an eternal truth, certainly does not produce a wooden or unoriginal art. The transformation of temporal events or details into paradox, the presentation of single and dual concepts or details into signal tropes, the retransformation of those same events and reality — this is a fullness achieved not in spite of but because of the poet's acceptance of rhetoric.

THE PROVINCE OF ALLEGORY IN GEORGE HERBERT'S VERSE

Robert L. Montgomery, Jr.

THE RECENT ATTENTION given Herbert's symbolism has for the most part tended to explore its background in intellectual and religious tradition or to dwell on it as a form of hieroglyphic method.[1] The first approach, so well epitomized by the work of Rosemund Tuve, has been widely accepted in its fundamental assertion that Herbert consciously drew on long-standing and widespread religious analogies. The second approach, necesarily dependent upon the first and upon the demonstration of Herbert's relations to the emblem tradition, has been somewhat less successful in giving a full account of his figurative methods. Louis Martz and Joseph H. Summers have offered the best bases for further discussion — thanks to Mr. Martz, Herbert's meditative structures are very clear indeed, and thanks to Mr. Summers, the variety of his technique receives its due attention[2] — but a great deal remains to be done in the critical appraisal of the poet's symbolism.

That Herbert's symbols are, at bottom, analogies is hardly surprising: he shares with most writers of the age a fondness for similitudes, for precise and extensive correspondences. And in many of his poems he seems especially concerned with spelling out the analogy beyond the limits of necessity or of poetic propriety. But Herbert is more subtle than he appears, and it is doubtful that his symbolic method can be reduced to the translating and explaining of images. The context of the symbol within the poem is, I think, a better place to begin and a better place to make distinctions.

Broadly speaking, Herbert uses two kinds of context, the meditative and the allegorical, and it is the latter with which I am most concerned. Yet the meditative is the more frequent and, for purposes of the

From *TSLL*, 1 (1960), 457-72, Copyright © 1960 by the University of Texas Press. Reprinted by permission of the author and The University of Texas Press.

thoughtful religious lyric, the more normal. It develops the symbolic image directly out of the mind of the speaker in the poem, and the lyric center of the poem is the presence of a mind in the act of speaking and thinking. The substance of speech and thought may be symbolic, or more properly, may contain symbols. One way of developing such a context is to show the mind playing with hieroglyphs, as in "The Altar":

> A broken ALTAR, Lord, thy servant reares,
> Made of a heart, and cemented with teares:
> Whose parts are as thy hand did frame;
> No workman's tool hath touched the same.[3]

Herbert's precise and detailed emblem-making, his concern for the sharpest and most rigorous analogies spelled out with some fullness, are nowhere better demonstrated than here. Reduced to its essentials, the analogy seems little more than a static correspondence: altar equals heart. But Herbert develops the equation in terms of action (how the altar-heart is built) and of condition (it is imperfect). Even so, the discourse is essentially definitive and expository, moving toward the application of analogical truth and the prayer at the end of the poem.

"Sunday" is a more complicated example of this method, and it provides the first clear distinction between meditative and allegorical procedure. The title is first of all an event, an occasion and focus for meditation. But Sunday is also personified, and it has been the habit in some quarters to associate allegory and personification intimately, perhaps too intimately.[4] Yet, even though Sunday is addressed as a living entity by the speaker, that is not our clue to the symbolic method of the poem. In the first stanza, after addressing Sunday, he proceeds to define it:

> O Day most calm, most bright,
> The fruit of this, the next worlds bud,
> Th' indorsement of supreme delight,
> Writ by a friend, and with his bloud;
> The couch of time; cares balm and bay:
> The week were dark, but for thy light:
> Thy torch doth show the way.

In the second stanza the definition is shifted from a series of attributes to a fleshing-out of the analogy implicit in the original act of personifying Sunday. This and the following stanza are more consistent examples of the rhetorical figure *allegoria*, but the figure still does not control the poem.[5]

For in the fourth stanza Herbert shifts back to straight hieroglyphic definition: "Sundaies the pillars are." In other words, the *allegoria* of the first three stanzas is simply one of several modes of definitive correspondence, one of several rhetorical contexts in which to develop symbols. As a whole, "Sunday" gives the appearance of being loosely jointed, its discourse moving restlessly from one method to another as if the speaker were searching with difficulty for the proper definitive mode. There is a kind of associative order in the images — light in the first stanza, moving to "other dayes" in the second, which, with the third, concentrates on images of bodily gesture and effort, and so on — but there is nothing like the consistent rigor and logic between images drawn from the same general context that we find in "The Altar." And on the level of discourse Herbert again changes pace in the fourth stanza, abandoning personification entirely for an architectural similitude.

Thus, the symbolic procedure is shifting and accretive: Herbert deepens and extends his reading of Sunday as a symbol by adding definition to definition, attribute to attribute, and by keeping his meditative structure flexible and loose, at least in appearance. Only in the final stanza does he return to the original personification. Such a variety of figurative procedures has its purpose, or at least its effect. The first three stanzas, largely dominated by *allegoria*, are relatively emotive — celebratory and hortatory — although stanzas 1 and 2 are also definitive. The fifth through the eighth stanzas are not without emotion (Sunday is exploited as the day of the Resurrection and is therefore an occasion for joy), but Herbert has moved into largely general statement where feeling is an undertone. Only when he returns to the personal and openly emotive does he revive the allegorical mode.

This is not to suggest that we can always equate *allegoria* with heightened personal expression, although the coincidence of the two is frequent in the lyrics. What is more important is to see the meditative and allegorical procedures as distinct, and "Sunday" is a lyric where the meditative is in control and contains the other. Moreover, something besides personification distinguishes Herbert's use of *allegoria*. The second stanza will illustrate:

> The other dayes and thou
> Make up one man; whose face thou art,
> Knocking at heaven with thy brow:
> The worky-daies are the back part;
> The burden of the week lies there,

> Making the whole to stoup and bow,
> Till thy release appeare.

Herbert, illogically and deliberately, has reversed the process of personification, or, to put it another way, he has made one personification part
of another. Sunday is first a living entity in its own right, and then,
together with the other days, a corporate human figure. This is a rather
precarious method, but it allows the poet to set his animated occasion in
motion in such a way that he can distinguish the special role of Sunday
and effect a contrast between laborious suffering and release. The
implications here are fairly rich, and they are indebted to something
besides the complex analogical groundwork of the figure. The notion
that the seven days of the week can be represented as a man with Sunday
as the face and the others as the back works only if action is at least
implied. Here Herbert does not go much beyond implication; he does
not develop a story or fable but merely hints at one.

Nevertheless, it is the presence of action, even in embryo, that
validates the symbolism in this stanza and gives it a living suggestiveness, and it is action or fable by which Herbert's fully fashioned
allegorical poems may be distinguished. Most critics, past and present,
who have dealt with allegory have stressed its character as extended
metaphor, an analogy in which only one of the terms is explicit and
which is carried beyond the reach of a single word.[6] This emphasis is
most apparent in the brief discussions of allegory in Renaissance
rhetorics; Harington is one of the few to give full attention to the matter
of the fable.[7] It is entirely possible, as one modern critic says,[8] that
narrative is simply one of the means by which allegory can be developed,
but apart from examples of the figure in limited rhetorical use, it is
rather difficult to find a complete literary allegory without a fictional
structure.

There are a number of lyrics in *The Church*, about a fifth of the total,
where analogy, and therefore symbol, are developed out of a fictional
context.[9] If we can say that such a development controls an entire poem
and can describe the way in which it exercises control, we shall come
close to isolating a distinct lyrical method, and one, by the way, that few
poets before Herbert used to any significant extent.

To return for a moment to analogy, it presupposes some form and
degree of likeness between two distinct things, and its common strategy
is to place them side by side. But explicit juxtaposition and comparison
are not essential. One element may be represented fully, the other
inferred with more or less clarity. Herbert is capable of many degrees of

explicitness and inference. Moreover, we must decide, when confronted
by an image potentially capable of being exploited analogically, when it
has symbolic meaning and when it does not. For example, we might ask
whether Spenser's St. George is not simply St. George, a figure in a
quasi-historical romance, except that Spenser tells us outright that he
represents holiness. The poet's statement of intention is, of course, the
most comfortable way of establishing the allegorical character of a work
of art. But Herbert, although the discourse of his lyrics frequently
translates the images and specifies at least part of their symbolic
meaning, never openly admits that any given poem is an allegory. For
some poems the question is banal: no one would dispute the allegorical
character of "Humilitie," a dream-vision and beast-fable in familiar
Medieval fashion. And even if we were not accustomed to this type of
symbolic story, a literal reading would make little sense of it. Again, the
brief poem "Hope" demands that we find meanings for its images — the
watch, the anchor, the optick, the green eares, the ring — if we are to
make anything at all of it. Both "Humilitie" and "Hope" contain
obvious personifications, and these in combination with the fact that the
images must be read symbolically assure us of the allegorical structure of
the poems.

These reflections are simple and commonplace, and a number of
Herbert's lyrics yield to the allegorical label with no trouble at all. But
the issue of allegory as a definite symbolic method in the lyric becomes
complicated in "Love-Joy," a poem whose structure is fictional and
whose images are openly deciphered:

> As on a window late I cast mine eye,
> I saw a vine drop grapes with *J* and *C*
> Anneal'd on every bunch. One standing by
> Ask'd what it meant. I, who am never loth
> To spend my judgement, said, It seem'd to me
> To be the bodie and the letters both
> Of *Joy* and *Charitie*. Sir, you have not miss'd,
> The man reply'd; It figures *JESUS CHRIST*.

"Love-Joy" is clearly built upon a brief, compressed narrative moving
toward the double translation of the grapes and the initials. In fact their
reading is part of the action of the poem, and as Miss Tuve reminds us, a
whole complex of symbolic association lives in them.[10] But what of the
narrative itself? Although the focus of the verse is on the images, the
action casually reveals something of the character of the narrator: "I,
who am never loth / To spend my judgement, said." Moreover, the order
of the two interpretations gently contradicts his judgment and suggests

its incompleteness: he has failed to give the images their full significance. The poem thus becomes a presentation of and commentary upon the imperfection of one man's understanding of Christian truth, and a more general application is not difficult. But while this much is fairly obvious, I would add that the presence of such a structure for the explicitly symbolic images removes the discourse from the level of meditation to the level of drama, and because the strictly dramatic portion of the poem reveals something that the translation of the images and the typological tradition to which Miss Tuve refers us do not, we have a kind of lyric basically different from "The Altar" or "Sunday."

On the other hand, the implication toward which I have been moving, that thematically significant fable makes "Love-Joy" an allegory, is debatable. Obviously, non-allergorical fiction is capable of yielding meanings, and fairly explicit ones at that. Unlike the exegetical commentators of the high Middle Ages, we need not read every "history" both literally and figuratively, even though with Herbert the temptation is strong. "Love-Joy" may simply be interpreted as a fiction exemplifying a corner of human nature and framing symbols by which that exemplification is given a specific doctrinal focus. In other terms, the incidents in the fable need not be construed analogically as standing for something other than themselves. A typical event is not necessarily a symbolic one.

Nevertheless, the fable is the core of Herbert's allegorical method, and it is more than simply the means of extending analogies. "The Bunch of Grapes," another piece for which Miss Tuve has provided the explicit symbolic references,[11] has a fictional structure framing the symbols, and yet that fiction would be absurd if we took it literally. "The Bunch of Grapes" has a somewhat misleading beginning: "Joy, I did lock thee up" suggests that the fable might be an interchange between the speaker and the personification. But Herbert scarcely exploits this structure at all. Instead, the heart of the fable is the narration of what has happened to the speaker's emotions, largely in terms of the journey of the Children of Israel toward the Promised Land. But the personification does serve to warn us that the action of the poem is internal, that the fable is significant of what has happened within the mind and soul of the speaker.

Otherwise, Joy as a personification is largely conventional fantasy or conceit and plays no active, dramatic part in the fable. The allegory is largely concerned with narrating the speaker's past attempts to capture the fruits of religious devotion ("I did towards Canaan draw"), the lesson he learns from his initial disappointment ("A single deed is small renown"), his petulant begging for the blessings of piety as well as its sufferings ("Let me take up their joy, as sorrow"), and his final realization that he already has his reward ("Ev'n God himself being pressed for my sake"). This is the basic symbolic movement of the verse, and it is important to note that symbolism and fable combine. There is a dimension, allegorically reached, beyond the specific meanings of the separate typological images, the Exodus, the sojourn in the desert, the cluster of grrapes, and the sacrifice of Christ on the cross. The historical and chronological order of these images becomes an inclusive symbol for the progress of the speaker's internal meditation. The typological journey stands for the speaker's emotional and devotional career. One stanza will illustrate:

> For as the Jews of old by Gods command
> Travell'd, and saw no town;
> So now each Christian hath his journeys spann'd:
> Their storie pennes and sets us down.
> A single deed is small renown.
> Gods works are wide, and let in future times;
> His ancient justice overflows our crimes.

The application of the events of Exodus to the life of Christians (and more immediately of the speaker) is warranted by typological convention, and the fusion of the Old and New Testaments suggests both the difference between them occasioned by the sacrifice of Christ and the range to which the speaker's own experience may be extended. The order of the images, in this stanza and the others, defines the quality of the poet's quest for joy, and the traditional and deliberate confusion of the two Testaments generates his turning from a simple notion of reward for righteousness to the more difficult concept of Christian duty. Structurally, however, the fable of "The Bunch of Grapes" is uncertain. In the first stanza it carries the burden of discourse:

> I did towards Canaan draw; but now I am
> Brought back to the Red Sea, the sea of shame.

But the second stanza, quoted above, moves toward the rhetoric of meditation. The speaker's allegorical quest for joy still surrounds the poem, but it fails to exert full power within it.

Allegory as fiction contains an element of the improbable: in "The Bunch of Grapes" the speaker locks up joy and draws toward Canaan. Here allegory is conceit, but Herbert mutes the sense of fantasy in the poem by his persistent application of the symbols to his own, or the speaker's, case. On the other hand, "Hope" baldly displays its strangeness, the literal impossibility of its action:

> I gave to Hope a watch of mine: but he
>   An anchor gave to me.
> Then an old prayer-book I did present:
>   And he an optick sent.
> With that I gave a viall ful lot tears:
>   But he a few green eares.
> Ah Loyterer! I'le no more, no more I'le bring:
>   I did expect a ring.

The extreme compression here, the unexplained symbols, throw first emphasis upon the fiction, the action linking the symbols together. And the strength of the impression of oddity derived from the fiction finds its cause in the lack of explanations. We must seek them for ourselves (though perhaps a seventeenth-century reader, accustomed to the figure of Hope with an anchor in emblem books, could respond more quickly whan we), but the speaker acts as though they were obvious.[12] In broad terms we can read "Hope" as symbolic of a movement from confidence to chagrin, the loss of assurance in the achievement of perfection, of moral completeness, or even of union with God in this life. The fable and its separate images are interdependent: the acts of giving and receiving share symbolic status with the gifts and presents. We cannot avoid the symbolic nature of the poem because in fictional and human terms these acts are fantastic.

There are, then, three criteria for distinguishing Herbert's allegorical lyrics: a fable (or fictional structure) in control of the poem, the symbolic character of the fable, and fantasy or conceit. Generally, the appearance of fantasy is our clue to the symbolic nature of the fable. But allegory is never thoroughly absorbed by fantasy, or it ceases to be allegory; that is, it ceases to open a way to plausible interpretation of the fable. Moreover, fantasy and our sense of its working presence in the lyric are subject to degrees of variation. According to human convention some things seem more improbable than others, and the poet, as we have seen Herbert do in "The Bunch of Grapes," may rob fantasy of its impact by explicit interpretation, just as science fiction or the ghost story may be tamed by rational explanation. The particular blend of the fantastic and the plausible may be modified from poem to poem. Those we have considered so far exploit fantasy only to point up the symbolic character of what goes on. At the same time, they put no great stress on images or circumstances of familiarity. (I except, of course, "Love-Joy," which is not fantastic at all.)

"Love Unknown" introduces us to a group of poems where the
tension between the two elements is sharper and stronger, where the
mixture of the odd and the familiar seems to influence the reading of the
allegories more precisely and more subtly. Coleridge was provoked by
"Love Unknown" to admire its simplicity of language and deplore its
ingenuity of symbol and structure, but he failed to notice the insepara-
bility of the two and its significance.[13] The opening of the poem is
simple, plaintive, and casual:

> Deare Friend sit down, the tale is long and sad:
> And in my faintings I presume your love
> Will more complie then help.

Herbert's method emerges through the tale. The occasion of the poem is
a conversation between two friends, and the story is contained within
the framework of this circumstance. Herbert uses a situation that is
plausible, deliberately unremarkable, even somewhat commonplace,
and there are no personifications to injure the initial homeliness of tone
and circumstance.

Within the limits of dramatic colloquy, Herbert fashions a second
structure, a narrative of the speaker's experience, his "long and sad" tale:

> A Lord I had
> And have, of whom some grounds, which may improve,
> I hold for two lives, and both lives in me.
> To him I brought a dish of fruit one day,
> And in the middle plac'd my heart.

This action appears nearly as plausible as the opening lines until we
reach the last phrase, which suddenly lifts the poem well beyond the
limits of the credible or natural. The remainder of the paragraph
describes the painful cleansing of the speaker's heart, and his friend
suggests a reason: *"Your heart was foul, I fear."* The symbolic character
of the verse is at this point unmistakable.

Plainly enough, such a shift from the familiar to the fantastic, from
outward to inward event, is useful to announce the poet's allegorical
intention, but there is further point to the special means Herbert has
chosen to alter the nature of the discourse. Coleridge's charge of obscure
ingenuity and Rosemary Freeman's notion that "Love Unknown" is an
experimental exercise and therefore lacking in emotional power both
miss the point.[14] What happens to the speaker's heart first of all shocks
the reader into attention. A servant seizes the heart and throws it into a
font where it is washed in a stream of blood: in other words, it is
rebaptized by the sacrifice of Christ. The fruit, which the servant

ignores, may be taken as the speaker's good deeds offered to the Lord, and here the dramatic framework of the other images becomes crucial. More than the traditional meanings of the images is at work; in addition, the larger relationship between good deeds and the condition of the human soul is relevant, and the suddenness of Herbert's shift seems calculated to point this up. As in "The Bunch of Grapes" the sequence of the imagery is important, and the dramatic exposition of that sequence is essential to tie the sensations of the speaker to a general truth to be found in the Eucharistic symbols and their associations.

This much is clear if we notice that the surprise and shock are the speaker's as well as the reader's. The special tone of the drama and narrative are at the heart of Herbert's allegorical scheme, for the allegory is designed to reveal more than doctrine. As in so many of his lyrics, what the speaker learns and how he learns it are at the bottom of his presentation of Christian truth. In "Love Unknown" the protagonist tells his friend that he has passed through three stages of learning and suffering: purification, affliction, and quickening of the heart. The narrative of these events symbolizes a traditional pattern of Christian regeneration,[15] and surrounding this narrative are the friend's comments at each stage of the process and his final interpretative summary:

> *Truly, Friend,*
> *For ought I heare, your Master shows to you*
> *More favour then you wot of. Mark the end.*
> *The Font did onely, what was old renew:*
> *The Caldron suppled, what was grown too hard:*
> *The Thorns did quicken, what was grown too dull:*
> *All did but strive to mend, what you had marr'd.*
> *Wherefore bee cheer'd, and praise him to the full*
> *Each day, each houre, each moment of the week,*
> *Who fain would have you new, tender, quick.*

With this explanation and admonition the usefulness of the double fictional structure comes clear. The protagonist has failed to appreciate what has happened to him. After the bed of thorns he admits his imperfection, his "dullness," but makes excuses for himself by misinterpreting Christ's sacrifice:

> But all my scores were by another paid,
> Who took the debt upon him.

The speaker's avoidance of responsibility provokes the further lesson supplied by his friend, and to preserve the dramatic as well as the allegorical integrity of the piece the colloquy and final lesson are just as necessary as the narrative of the speaker's trials, for the friend appears to symbolize the speaking of Christ in the human heart.[16]

In her remarks on "The Bunch of Grapes" Miss Tuve calls attention to the symbolic traditions behind the imagery, and appears to think that the immediate dramatic or emotional elements in the poem are almost unnecessary. The latter she calls "the mere conveyance of a particular individual's emotion at a given time, that thin subject with which modern readers have come to be content."[17] But the particular experiences in "The Bunch of Grapes" and especially in "Love Unknown," with all the particular tonal and emotional qualities they generate, are inseparable from the traditional figures. Each makes the other valid, for while the Eucharistic associations of the separate images in "Love Unknown" magnify the effective range of the particular experience of the speaker, the dramatic and narrative frames allow Herbert to do more than generalize. At each stage of his suffering the speaker is bewildered and chagrined; at each stage what happens to him shatters his expectations. He must be taught and that teaching has no poetic validity apart from his very human impulses, which are significantly different as they appear in sequence. Moreover, the lesson delivered by the friend must be explicit, not for the sake of the reader but for the protagonist, whose reactions to his trials have been insufficient and need bolstering. Finally, the lesson rounds off the poem by neatly contradicting the speaker's early remark, "I presume your love/Will more complie than help."

This reading of the fictional structure of "Love Unknown" need not deny the validity of Miss Tuve's insistence that traditional images with conventional meanings be recognized. It simply means that such readings by themselves do not make the poem and do not yield a total understanding of it, any more than the fiction by itself is the only avenue to travel. And in others of Herbert's allegories he is even more committed to the total nuances of the speaking voice, even more concerned to give the foreground of the poem to the immediacy of individual experience. "Love Unknown" balances its Eucharistic images and dramatic or narrative immediacy about equally. Both action and meaning share the center of the poem, and as the sad tale moves forward, the oddity of the events and images seems to intensify. Elsewhere Herbert employs a different balance and a different strategy. "The Collar" still groups and orders a fair amount of imagery which is clearly symbolic, especially in the middle lines where the speaker's rebelliousness and frustration reach their highest pitch. But it is worth noting that the issue of obedience is resolved dramatically:

> Me thoughts I heard one calling, Child!
> And I reply'd, My Lord.

The final poem in *The Church,* "Love" (III), very nearly dispenses with typological imagery altogether, and places most of its weight on the narrative of a dramatic event:

> Love bade me welcome: yet my soul drew back
>   Guiltie of dust and sinne.
> But quick-ey'd Love, observing me grow slack
>   From my first entrance in,
> Drew nearer to me, sweetly questioning,
>   If I lack'd any thing.
>
> A guest, I answer'd, worthy to be here:
>   Love said, You shall be he.
> I the unkinde, ungratefull? Ah my deare,
>   I cannot look on thee.
> Love took my hand, and smiling did reply,
>   Who made the eyes but I?
>
> Truth Lord, but I have marr'd them: let my shame
>   Go where it doth deserve.
> And know you not, sayes Love, who bore the blame?
>   My deare, then I will serve.
> You must sit down, sayes Love, and taste my meat:
>   So I did sit and eat.

As much as any lyric of Herbert's this depends upon what is conveyed by the voices and the allusive imagery is correspondingly subdued.[18]

Herbert's method is to work a series of contrasts through the narrative and colloquy: Love's welcome is poised directly against the speaker's hesitation; Love's choice of the speaker's soul against his self-confessed ingratitude; Love's reminder of the divine creative power following the soul's inability to face her; Love's allusion to the Sacrifice, followed by the soul's offer to serve at table (here the contrast is modified, but the accord between the two actors is not yet reached); Love's insistence that the soul be a guest and its final acceptance. The entire force of the poem moves through these developed and resolved oppositions, and it is assisted by the tonal nuances of such phrases as "sweetly questioning," "Ah my deare" (which gives way in the final stanza to "Truth Lord" and then returns to "My deare"), the manner of the active gestures made by love and the speaker, and the patient tone of Love's questions. As a result, dramatically prompted tone seems to displace allusion in suggesting the proper approach of the soul to the ultimate gift of grace and the quality of its bestowal. A further indication that the weight of the allegory is borne by dramatic and narrative immediacy is the absence of any striking fantasy: only the personification "Love" (which is most thoroughly humanized) and the phrase "Who made the eyes but I?" stand out in this respect, and the personification is sufficient to indicate the symbolic character of the fable.

At the same time, the dramatic movement organizes the allusive imagery. The offer of welcome comes first and is, by inference, unsolicited. The speaker is immediately sensitive of his guilt and unworthiness, his mortality. This motif is pursued through general reference to his individual sins, until he is reminded that God is his creator. When he then answers that he had "marr'd" this creation, Love reminds him of the Sacrifice. This in turn provokes the speaker's grateful humility, which Love refuses, thus magnifying the importance of grace. The sequence, as well as its components, has broad reference to Christian doctrine, putting grace in a penitential context and interpreting it as a reflection of divine power and especially love. (It seems important that the speaker's altered form of address, "Truth Lord," directly follows Love's question, "Who made the eyes but I?") In other words the structure of "Love" (III) is shaped by a pattern at once expository and dramatic, argumentative and active, specifically personal in its tone and psychology and broadly traditional in fixing the manner and meaning of the love that welcomes the soul into heaven. Herbert has moved as far as he ever does from the hieroglyphic or meditative framing of symbols, and yet in using the devices of dramatic and vocal immediacy he preserves his usual symbolic clarity and precision. Once again the blend of the fantastic and familiar (the probable as well as the informal) is a strong clue to his purpose and a measure of his ability to tailor his allegorical method to the particular task at hand.

William York Tindall points up an important consideration if we are to accept allegory as an independent mode of symbolism of more than rhetorical significance. Noting the difference between the "Romantic" concepts of the symbol as a meaningful object for which it is dangerous and even wrong to substitute exact meanings (the vitality, suggestiveness, and emotional resonance of the symbol are thereby violated) and the Medieval and Renaissance preference for more or less explicit analogical construction, Mr. Tindall thinks that even the signlike images of these periods are never fully grasped in rational interpretation.[19] I am inclined to agree. In the rhetoric of the Renaissance all figurative language is an embellishment or decoration, an instrument of heightened color or vividness, but never abolutely necessary to meaning. But before we accept such a view and conclude that Herbert's allegorical method is simply another means of pleasing, we must remember that Sidney (though he may at times think in terms of embellishment) recognizes the necessity of the poetic fiction and considers it superior to fact and philosophy.[20] Elsewhere he derides allegory's "curious frame,"[21] but allegory as Herbert uses it is not inconsistent with the Sidneian doctrine of the fiction as the best imitative, and instructive, method. According to this view, poetry tells the truth as no other verbal context can, and when we arrive at the point of seeing the poetic fiction as itself analogical and symbolic, as yielding a high degree of meaningful formulation and yet retaining its vital integrity, we must conclude that Herbert as an allegorist has used the method for more than delight or ingenuity.

At the same time, his allegory (although I have kept it distinct from the meditative form) is at bottom a form of systematic discourse in which the fictional order conceals the meditative underpinnings. And, as we have noted, Herbert points to his meanings with varying degrees of openness; yet he always holds something in reserve. The curious thing about a poem like "Love Unknown," concrete and explicit in translating its symbolic images, is the fact that its fable, by embodying a human event, dramatically and narratively, is not lost in the process of translation. The source of the vitality of the poem is here: the fable makes the symbols it orders and contains poetically valid, just as in a different fashion Herbert's patently meditative lyrics justify their symbols by giving them order.

Finally, allegory as a kind of larger symbol and vital form is, in Herbert's hands, his most versatile poetic tool. The poems that have attracted the greatest concentration of modern critical attention are, with a few exceptions, allegories: "The Collar," "The Pulley," "Love" (III), "Affliction" (I), and "The Flower," to name the most prominent. "The Sacrifice," the nature of whose structure is fictional, but not allegorical, at least demonstrates Herbert's nearly constant gravitation toward the vocally dramatic or narrative form, and like the allegories, it embodies the peculiar tension between the dramatic and expository Herbert achieved. "Love" (III), for example, cannot but interest us tonally, emotionally, dramatically, even as we search for the doctrine behind it. "The Collar," with its free metric structure and strong colloquial power, is nevertheless continually mediating between vitality of its fable and the sharp lesson of doctrine to which it points. Herbert's allegorical method again and again seems to achieve this delicate balance between the levels and purposes of discourse, and it is in his manipulation of what the Middle Ages called the literal level, the fiction as symbol, that balance is sustained.

SACRED "PARODY" OF LOVE POETRY, AND HERBERT

Rosemond Tuve

Some conceptions held by Herbert and his predecessors of the relations between sacred and profane love poetry are the matter at issue in this essay — yet it is particularly directed to the attention of two kinds of special students not likely to be especially interested in that issue. I wish it might be read by those who know unpublished Renaissance music, and those who work with semantics and early dictionaries in various European languages. It is written with the hope that some one else may run across an unfound musical setting, and that some one else may adduce earlier uses of a puzzling word. Its main concern, however, is to present certain materials and ideas of rather broader interest to students of Renaissance poetry.

Herbert gave the title 'A Parodie' to a poem addressed to God, beginning:

> Souls joy, when thou art gone,
>   And I alone,
>   Which cannot be,
> Because thou dost abide with me,
>   And I depend on thee;
>
> Yet when thou dost suppresse
>   The cheerfulnesse
>   Of thy abode,
> And in my powers not stirre abroad,
>   But leave me to my load:
>
>   O what a damp and shade
>   Doth me invade! . . .

He has imitated a secular lyric addressed by one lover to another and early attributed to Donne,[1] as recent editors of both poets have observed. Another attribution, to William, third earl of Pembroke, is

Reprinted from *SRen*, 8 (1961), 249-90, by permission of the author's executor, Mr. Richard L. Tuve, and the publisher. This essay was reprinted in *Essays by Rosemond Tuve*, ed. Thomas P. Roche, Jr. (Princeton: Princeton University Press, 1970), pp. 207-51.

that preferred by Grierson, and I shall call the original piece 'Pembroke's poem' to save awkward reiteration.[2] It begins:

> Soules joy, now I am gone,
> And you alone,
> (Which cannot be,
> Since I must leave my selfe with thee,
> And carry thee with me)
> Yet when unto our eyes
> Absence denyes
> Each others sight,
> And makes to us a constant night,
> When others change to light;
> O *give no way to griefe,*
> *But let beliefe* . . .

But Herbert's title will not bear the meaning which the word *parody* has in seventeenth-century dictionaries of the learned or vernacular tongues, nor does it square with Latin or Greek or English or French usage of the word in literary contexts. These, like our own use of the word, stress the element of mockery, burlesque, or at the least some sidelong denigrating comment on the original author's sense; something on the order of Ben Jonson's 'a *Parodie!* a *parodie!* ... to make it absurder then it was' (*Every Man in his Humour*, V.v.26), or on the order of N. Pasquier's 'parodier, parodiant' in a violently polemical letter answering a detractor of his father's who had written scurrilously, and scoffing at that user of these words. For an actual dictionary definition, the early English-only dictionaries do not provide us with evidence (see below note 9). The earliest citation in von Wartburg's *Wörterbuch*[3] of the French substantive, 1614, confirms the meaning of 'travestissement burlesque', and when we consult, *faute de mieux*, the later seventeenth-century French dictionaries — Furetière, Richelet — we find the same elements of 'raillerie' or burlesquing of 'ouvrages serieux'.[4]

Its derivation in modern tongues from Greek παρωδια, probably by way of Latin *parodia*, is agreed upon in the historical dictionaries. The word in classical Greek apparently kept to the kind of connotations just given (see Liddell and Scott); and in sum the *Oxford Classical Diction[ary's* articles on *Parody: Greek* and: *Latin* seem to cover the matter: exaggeration and incongruity (often through the use of high language for trivial things) are essential elements, and examples show that what we might call a 'take-off' is the root idea, whereas exaggeration to bring out 'salient features of an individual's style ... was seldom attempted by the Greeks'; while in Latin usage we find both pastiche ('caricature of manner without adhering to the original words') and parody proper, in which 'distortion' of an original with but few verbal changes provides a new sense 'often incongruous with the form'.

Not any of these descriptions accurately describe the relation Herbert's poem bears to its original, though he has declared the relation to be that of 'A Parodie'. Obviously he is not mocking Lord Pembroke's poem in any usual way, nor caricaturing its manner, nor distorting or exaggerating its sense, with a view to the humor or irony of an incongruity we are expected to notice either in his original or in his imitation. To explain the anomaly of the title, Herbert's editor Hutchinson offers Dryden's definition of parody in the 'Discourse concerning ... Satire' in the *Juvenal* (1693). This is repeated by L. L. Martz, when in an extended treatment of 'Herbert's art of sacred parody' he adds that the poet's title is an illustration of 'this neutral usage' as defined in Dryden.[5] But quite aside from the two-thirds-of-a-century gap in time, an examination of Dryden's context shows that if Herbert were neutral after Dryden's fashion, his so-called neutrality would be what Dryden finds in 'songs, which are turned into burlesque, and the serious words of the author perverted into a ridiculous meaning'. Herbert scarcely intended such an effect when he so turned Pembroke's phrases that they decorously suit an address to God, and Dryden's other example of Ausonius' joke on the modest Virgil is quite as malapropos. For Dryden's definition and usage are neither one neutral; he is discussing the satyric *silli*, 'full of parodies', of scoffing and petulancy and invective. And Herbert is not doing any of the things Dryden describes.[6]

So far as I can discover, in seventeenth-century literary usage, if an imitation of a poem was 'parody', it was not neutral. The vital point here is whether or not we can take Herbert's title as proof that he has intended a series of sidewise derogatory comments on the ideas and theme of Pembroke's poem. The answer is of some moment, in our whole understanding of Herbert's attitude toward sacred and profane love. Neither do I know (some one else may) *examples* of such subtly covert literary parodying, that is, of imitations neither burlesque nor yet truly innocent, which would furnish evidence of a *practice* — however silent the dictionaries are — that could be responsible for Herbert's title. There are examples in plenty of something close to this: for there is another reason than raillery, or mockery of a style, for writing sacred imitations of secular poems — substitution. Both scholars I have mentioned claim it as part of Herbert's intention. Shoals of poems were written in Europe with this intent, before and just after Herbert. Was he in truth following in the path of 'Southwell's campaign to convert the poetry of profane love into poetry of divine love"? (Martz, p. 184). If so, Herbert's use of the word *parody* is no more innocent than would be the case if his poem exhibited the constant mocking parallelism of travesty or burlesque; no attitude toward another man's work is much less neutral than an intention to displace it entirely.

An interest in this displacement of the profane by the sacred has been widely accepted in modern times as a prime motivation for much of Herbert's writing of religious poems, and few are the treatments of him which do not mention the tensions which thence accrue, especially if the poet is thought to be not quite ready, himself, to make the substitution of one love for another. It is not impossible that this is a peculiarly subtle form of the fallacy of attributing a certain character to poems in order that they should suit with an intention which we would fine psychologically interesting in their author. Their purport and bent is deduced from an assumed intention, whereas criticism properly uses the latter rather as a hint to try out hypotheses about meanings. We can never know the answers to such questions with certainty, but we can look for evidence. If we look first at the poem in hand, we find that the seemingly tendentious title stands almost alone as proof. (The text of both poems is given at page 279.)

Herbert seems to drop anything we could call a paralleling of ideas concerning profane and divine love after the first stanza or so. Lord Pembroke's poem is a forthright secular love lyric concerning the powerlessness of absence over true love. But Herbert's is not even 'a sacred love poem' except in so far as any poem about man's relation to God is a poem about love. There is no indication that he disbelieves what Pembroke says about absence being for mutually true human lovers a wound only sense-deep (whether we read Pembroke as serious or as over-easy); nor is there any comparison between Pembroke's human lovers and God who is by definition always spiritually present (a foolish comparison). He neither says nor implies anything about the validity of Pembroke's different kind of claim; it is simply clear that this statement about absence and mutual human love was a point of departure for his thoughts about the damps and cold which invade him when God's light seems to be eclipsed. He leaves quite behind him the ideas about love, over against which modern interpreters say he intended to set a sacred parody on a parallel theme, to consider instead the treachery with which his sinful lying mind denies the constant abiding presence of God. Editors of course have perceived his departure from his model, but nevertheless both Grierson (II, 267) and Hutchinson (like Martz later) attribute to Herbert the 'aim' or 'intention' of turning the muse 'from profane love verses to sacred purposes', meanwhile commenting that the parody does not extend beyond the opening lines.

This, however, is untrue. There is a parallelism between the two poems extending throughout their length, but it is not conceptual, and I think had little to do — in origin or intention or effect — with 'turning' another poet's sense and thus obliquely commenting thereon, or with the intention of substituting good loves for bad by displacing naughty verses.

One kind of *parody* really did include a neutral relation of imitation to original. The first meaning in Hatzfeld-Darmsteter is: 'couplets composés sur un air connu'; recurring in the eighteenth-century Academy dictionaries, and familiar from Littré, this common musicological term, in several European languages, for an ancient practice is hard to date precisely. In Apel's article in the *Harvard Dictionary of Music* the term's use, earlier, to denote simply 'replacement of text for a known tune' is explicitly distinguished from later musical usage with a necessary connotation of caricature. Herbert may have confused the early practice (*contrafactum*) with parody, as others did; moreover we must remember that the seventeenth century used many musical terms with more flexibility than do modern scholars. The really often-met early musical use is the related one in *missa 'parodia'*; the great number of parody masses, and their great beauty, may quite possibly have been known to Herbert. He was a musician of such competence as to elicit contemporary remark even in days when such abilities and tastes were common, certainly among men of his kind of family,[7] education, and pursuits, and his special zeal for ecclesiastical music is common knowledge, as are Walton's references to his composing and his bi-weekly rides into Salisbury to sing after services in a private 'Musick-meeting'. That cathedral's music and roster of singing-men had its ups and downs, but its not undistinguished annals show us during Herbert's time names like Thomas Lawes, the father of the two brother composers, Francis Sambrooke, and Giles Tomkins of the Cambridge and west-country musical family; and Herbert knew the music both of Cambridge and the court. The longish development of parody masses came to its peak just before Herbert's lifetime; his liturgical sympathies make it the less likely that he was ignorant of them, and their very names, unmistakably references to secular originals, advertise their character; moreover other works show that England did know the parody technique. The older and simpler phenomenon of musical parody mentioned first in this paragraph, was yet more everyday, whatever a gentleman musician of the 1620s called it.

It is properest to think first about this simpler musical kind of parody (whatever the term), the supplanting of a text set to music by fitting the melody to new words. In the edition of Pembroke's and Ruddier's poems wherein the original 'Soules joy' is printed, headed '*Song. P.*' (i.e. by the Earl of Pembroke), the younger Donne's prefatory remarks 'To the Reader' run thus:

> In the collecting of these poemes (which were chiefly preserved by the greatest Masters of Musick, all the Sonnets being set by them) I was fain to send to Mr Henry Laws, who furnishing me with some, directed me for the rest, to send into Germany to Mr Laneere, who by his great skill gave a life and harmony to all that he set.

Surely it seems very likely that there existed a musical setting for William Herbert's 'Soules joy, now I am gone', to which music George Herbert his cousin, who knew him and frequented his household, composed the new set of religious words in 'Souls joy, when thou art gone' — in strict accordance with the musical usage noted above for 'a parodie'.

I cannot find out exactly when this term came to be applied to this habit. The inclusion of special uses is not to be counted on in early dictionaries, and the absence from them of this sole use showing the 'neutrality' which would best explain Herbert's own use does not mean much more than the absence of the word itself from so many of them. As I have pointed out, known occurrences (as in Jonson), literary practice, and gradual dictionary appearance with the 'burlesque' meaning show this to have been its *literary* connotation. The commonly known musical treatises in English[8] do not treat the term or the habit, and roughly contemporary English dictionaries (Cooper, Bullokar, Blount, Phillips) are of small use on the whole matter.[9]

If it is hard to run down the earliest date for use of the *term* 'parody', for new words framed to a melody, it is certainly not hard to find hosts of examples. One important point is that as soon as the element of music is involved in the imitation the pleasure becomes far less dependent upon mockery or 'showing up'. Strictly formal imitation pleases. Common sense observes also that sung 'parodies' are less likely to show ironic, refined, or thoughtful oblique commentary on the ideas in an original text than those written to be read. Quite aside from the added formal hurdles to be cleared by an imitator, there is not time for either a singer or his auditors to catch esoteric relationships between two *texts*, only one of which can be present to the ear. The main source of the pleasure and interest lies elsewhere. Indeed one has only to sing successively Marlowe's, Ralegh's, and Donne's words to the tune for 'Come live with me and be my love' which Chappell gives,[10] and many of the fastidious comparisons between those much-discussed poems will explode and disappear. The Elizabethan and Jacobean habit of writing vastly different lyrics to be sung to the one air should temper some of our too-meticulous claims about the intended strategies touching the 'tone' of this or that poem — unless music has naught to do with mood. And if any persons at Wilton, or a mile and a half away at Bemerton, heard both poems beginning 'Souls joy' sung to one setting, it is difficult to believe that their reactions would indeed have had the character of serious responses to a serious attempt to supplant profane loves with divine and turn the devices of secular art to better because more pious uses.[11]

That there were such serious attempts is of course questionless. There is a truly huge corpus of 'parodies' in the sense we are examining which are not 'neutral' imitations of their originals in the way I think Herbert's was of his. There was indeed a time when men systematically transposed great numbers of secular songs into spiritual ones as a deliberate move in a campaign of substitution — but the great flowering time for this phenomenon ws the time of Luther and of Marot and of Bourgeois. It may quite well be that with Southwell's 'Epistle Dedicatorie' 'the aesthetic of the Counter Reformation establishes itself on English soil'.[12] But as far as this special element — the diverting of men's minds from profane to sacred poetry by using the former's arts — is concerned, the aesthetic was shared by individuals of a considerably different color of thought, and if such a zeal is to distinguish for us a tradition running from Southwell through Herbert to Vaughan, we shall have to bear with the awkward results of the fact that the tradition and the aesthetic are attached at the farther end to (for example) Coverdale or *The Gude and Godlie Ballatis* and the immediate circles of both Calvin and Luther. An aesthetic which is uncompromisingly 'Reformation' before it is 'Counter Reformation' is likely to be imputed to Herbert with considerably less ardor. These ideas and the practice of 'sacred parody' with substitution as an aim[13] can have been no news to the England of the 1590s, though the ferment and excitement of concerted efforts in this direction had been continental.

It is well known that Luther and his immediate followers took the music for their hymns from wherever they could lay hand upon songs known to the people; since the fairly restricted number of thoroughly familiar melodies for Latin hymns, adaptable for congregational singing, could not take care of the tremendous output of vernacular compositions, they used secular tunes, popular melodies, as well as the modified liturgical chants and extant hymns Latin and German. In countries where Puritanism was to be strong, and in the history of the

Huguenot psalter and its descendants and translations, we encounter as a declared purpose in prefaces the intention of substituting sacred songs for ribald or frivolous ones,[14] stated in terms often resembling Southwell's. Singing was as well recognized a means of spreading the ideas and the renewed devotional fervor of the reformers as was preaching; the virtue of the borrowed secular melodies was that they were well known and singable, and new words framed to them sprang up in a huge and fertile crop. The far from neutral intention — substitution of sacred lyrics for secular — of *such* 'parodies' is directly attached to the governing purpose of the men who wrote them: the reforming of a faith. A similar intention has much to do with the later efflorescence of a similar practice among authors of the Counter Reformation. This is shared by a Southwell, but only very little if at all by a Herbert. In case we are determined to find such substitution so important to his poetry, I suppose that we might conceivably attribute to him a general aim touching the improvement of men's moral sensibilities, but Herbert was not concerned to remake the faith of Anglicans. His own attachment to that communion was serene. Convinced 'sacred parodists' anxious about the substitution of the sacred, to the best of my knowledge, have either such reformers' aims or else the narrowly moral fervor of puritanical piety, Catholic or Protestant. Herbert's religious verse smacks of neither.

It is not that the reformers had gone about to do any new thing; musically, the procedure had been common practice for some centuries. What they did was to use a musical practice to fulfill intentions they had as religious leaders; the intention does not inhere in the practice and we cannot use the latter to support guesses about Herbert's intentions. The writers of medieval *contrafacta* and the numerous composers who had built sacred motets for liturgical use on secular *chanson* themes did not intend either to kill the *chansons* or wake the people to a 'Reformation'. It seems to me just as difficult to believe that Herbert wished oblivion to overtake Lord Pembroke's innocent small song, and although to be sure he grieved over the way men wilfully allow their worldly loves to usurp all place in hearts that should turn even through those to the source of all love, it is a grief he shares with all serious Christian thinkers. This is not to be cured by a substitution; the Country Parson would perhaps have spoken rather of putting on Christ. It is a different thing from cutting out secular songs, or human love. Those who are ready to whip human love out of the heart are commonly very sensitive to the idea of an ineradicable incongruity between earthly and heavenly loves. We must ask for a considerable body of evidence before we attribute this, either, to Herbert.

When it comes to the presence or absence of self-consciousness or tension concerning the use of secular models, the 'spiritualizing' of secular songs during the mid- and later 1500s shows an especial likeness to the medieval practice of *contrafactum* which preceded it; the likeness is shared by the already prominent somewhat different technique of the *missa parodia*. For in them all it is apparent that the *musical* part of the imitation was truly felt as neutral. The term *contrafactum* refers to a vocal composition framed to a new text which is substituted for the old one, and although the setting of a new sacred text to existing secular melodies is common, the replacement can go either way, trouvère *chansons* being fashioned for example upon liturgical plainsong melodies.[15] Neither in this medieval conversion of secular music to religious use, nor in the closely similar widespread sixteenth-century practice which provided the large literature of Protestant hymns and influenced the psalmody of Huguenot countries and others, nor in the *cantus firmus* mass which resembles *contrafactum* (in that a monodic borrowing, often from a secular *chanson*, provides the tenor) do we find any nervous indication that incongruousness was felt between *the known* secular provenance and the new religious use. The singers knew both uses, and listeners are very generally expected to recognize the secular originals; their attached names usually serve as identifying titles, or as indications of what tune to sing to, where songs are printed without music. And in *cantus firmus* masses and motets portions of older secular text show how the musical structure was contrived and were evidently sung by some of the voices. Like florid descant, this confusion of texts (*of two sacred texts as well*) was felt to be an evil, and both were censured at various times during the fourteenth and fifteenth centuries; Pope John's famous bull is primarily concerned with purely musical decorum, but confusion of texts was prohibited at the Council of Trent, in 1562.[16]

Sir Richard Terry's claim that 'in the sixteenth century the sharp line of demarcation between "sacred" and "secular" music did not exist'[17] could well be pondered when we consider the interchanges and borrowings of other similar 'arts' and 'devices' and techniques — those rhetorical arts which govern the musical management of verse whether it is secular or religious. The sense of sharp demarcation may belong more, as it does in the musical historians, to the nineteenth century than it does to the sixteenth and seventeenth.[18] Clearly we cannot apply our common notions about felt incongruities between profane and religious 'worlds' to times when even a Beza himself expected men to sing his translation of the canticle 'Voici que dit David' to an air he chose and set, 'De retourner mon ami je te prie'; when the 1540 Flemish psalter directed men to sing Psalm xxvi to the tune of 'Ick weet een vrouken amoreus', or the Antwerp psalter of 1541 set Psalm cviii to 'Faulte d'argent c'est douleur non pareille'; when it was entirely in line with long-followed practice to fit a 'Kyrie eleison' to the initial portion of the madrigal 'Reviens vers moi', or to sing Luther's 'Nun freut euch lieben Christen g'mein' to the secular tune he chose for it.[19] Nor should we attribute to insensitivity such absence of strain, touching the medieval religious use of formal arts or elements familiar in secular contexts, or touching the Protestant reformers' use of familiar music without hesitating at connotations either worldly or popish. A likelier explanation would be the sensible assumption by most of these men that formal elements in an art do not have a Protestant or a Catholic soul, a profane or a sacred 'nature' except as their *formal* character provides tangible distinctions; and one would incline to the judgment that Herbert's or other poets' uses of rhythms, devices, and rhyme-groups with a largely secular history show a similar understanding of decorum. One halts before a godly stanza-pattern, or an unchaste feminine rhyme, as before a Christian vowel-quantity, or a Mahometan alliteration. As well say — as some one did — all that pale mauve is un-American.

Certainly the English and Scottish 'parodies' of the sixteenth century show very little sense that formal borrowings would bring their secular flavor with them, to provide a secret ambiguity in men's responses. To our unaccustomed minds the 'incongruities' arising from such imitation do often seem more like camels than gnats; yet, had they been strained at, the whole purpose of the reforming 'sacred parodists' would have been set at nought. It is not possible to call in question the single-mindedness with which men were able to accept the spiritual songs in, for example, the *Gude and Godlie Ballatis*. This much reprinted book, though it contains translations of psalms and canticles, is not a collection of hymns used in services, rather of sung religious lyrics. Yet the historian of the Scottish psalter calls it 'a book which, next to the Bible itself, did more than any other to further in Scotland the Reformation cause'.[20] These are sung, not read, lyrics, though no music is printed, the secular tune being simply cited. Hence, a singer who knew what tune to use for the spiritual song I quote below did know the secular song at the left. Thence, for example, it was present to the mind (if not at the instant of singing) that the melodic phrase for I-the-pined-lover-of-my-lady now fits itself to Christ-the-pined-lover-of-mankind, and evidently this fact did not carry with it the sense that earthly and heavenly lover could both be suggested, with the disturbances of tone and temper that would result.

Into a mirthfull May morning   In till ane myrthfull Maij morning,

As Phebus up did spring	Quhen Phebus did vp spring:
I saw a May both fair and gay,	Walkand* I lay, in ane garding gay,
Most goodly for to see!	Thinkand on Christ sa fre:
I said to her be kind	Quhilk meiklie for mankynde,
To me that was so pyn'd	Tholit to be pynde,
For your love truly.	On Croce Cruellie, La. La.
(*GGB*, p. 270)	(*GGB*, p. 137; *variant 'Waking')

Without the least attempt at disguise of provenance, men were expected to (and hundreds did) sing 'Grievous is my sorrow', a long lyric of the kind called Christ's Complaint to Man, to the music of a song which Ritson reprints as 'The Dying Maiden's Complaint'. Hers too begins

> Grevus ys my sorowe,
> Both evyne and moro,
> Unto myselffe alone,
> *Thus do I make my mowne*, ...

— but with the last clause we change to 'Thus *Christ* makis ...'.

... Thus Christ makis his mone,	... Thus do I make my mowne,
Saying, Vnkyndnes hes killit me,	That unkyndnes haith kyllyd me,
And put me to this paine:	And putt me to this peyne,
Allace! quhat remedie,	Alas! what remedy
For I wald nocht refraine.	That I cannot refreyne!
(*GGB*, p. 151)	(Ritson, *Ancient Songs & Ballads*,
	ed. Hazlitt, p. 171)

The secular song as an ultimate source for the theme and characteristic structure of such a religious poem is out of the question; this is not strictly a *popule meus* poem, but the details of the 'unkyndnesse' suffered during Christ's life and Passion contrasted with the 'Kyndnesse' of the Atonement, are usual in this small poetic kind.[21] Nevertheless, to those who knew both well enough to sing both, the identity of commencement, refrain, and melody could conceivably be constant reminders that the author seemed, at least, to be simply translating a profane into a heavenly love; moreover, images using the same terms occupy the same musical place (the heart, the tomb, the bequeathing) and frequently show an identical series of rhymes. The types of rhetorical formal relation are very like those which attach Herbert's poem to Pembroke's, though closer and more frequent. But nothing in Herbert's imitation shows the interesting effect below:

(the maiden's complaint)	(Christ speaks)
O harte I the bequyeth	Go, hart, I the bequyeth
To hyme that is my deth,	To hir that was my deith,

Yff that no harte haith he	Mannis Saule is scho [she] trewlie,
My harte his schal be;	My hart hir hart sall be,
Thought unkyndnes haith kylled me,	Thocht scho maist unkyndlie slew me,
And putt me to this payne,	And put me to greit paine:
Yett, yf my body dye,	ʒit thair is na remedie,
My hertt cannott refrayne.	My hart will nocht refraine.

Despite precise verbal imitation, these are not the same image at all. The prior existence of the traditional spouse image allowed the adaptation, but the sense in which Christ's bequeathed heart '*hir* hart sall be' quite alters the function and nature of the figure, and the same thing happens because of the special theological meanings of 'unkindness' (in a special way un-natural and in-grate), as the changes are rung on this in the fifth line of each stanza. The same real transformation, not imitation, of *meaning* occurs in the changing relevance of the refrain — both melody and words meanwhile providing a strict formal identity. This phenomenon furnishes us with the reason why 'incongruities' were not felt as such, for they are apparent, not real. The question of congruity does not arise where subjects are not parallel but, simply, different.

This is also the reason why it is superficial to speak as if parodic imitation in which the secular is converted to the sacred *of itself* brings in a baroque tension or ironic dissonance between two 'worlds'. Form can straddle two worlds without tension; it is conceptual identifications (within images, for example) which bring in the likelihood of ambiguous doubleness, and our tools for detecting such identifications in users' minds (let alone readers' minds) are very blunt. If we met, in a poet whose date led us to expect such complications, the use of an *aubade*, tune and all, for a religious 'parody', voices would not be wanting to call attention to the witty doublenesses surely intended by one who would use the situation enclosed in that particular small form for a sacred lyric.

> The thissel-cok cryis
> On louers vha lyis,
> Nou skaillis the skyis:
> The nicht is neir gone.

As the parody below advances beyond the initial identical lines, we see that when in it Christ has become the cock announcing 'dawn', then the dawn takes on a meaning which totally ousts the usual *aubade* situation. The warning voice of a cock in an *aubade* awakens lovers so that the idyl need not come to a violent end but may continue when jealous day in its turn is near gone. But Christ has not become *that* cock, and *night* has turned into a *figure*, making an 'identical' line an utterly dissimilar line:

Hay! nou the day dauis;	Hay now the day dallis,
The jolie Cok crauis;	Now Christ on vs callis,

Nou shroudis the shauis,	Now welth on our wallis
Throu Natur anone.	Apperis anone:
The thissel-cok cryis ...	Now the Word of God Regnes: ...
The nicht is neir gone.	The nycht is neir gone.
(*GGB*, p. 289)[22]	(*GGB*, p. 192)

This parody could, but does not, pull over some of the original point of
the warning voice which wakens lovers in the *aubade*; it could, but does
not, thereby introduce baroque dubieties, as though the author were
implying some sorriness that the 'night' (here, of ignorance, often of
sensual love) was brought to a conclusion by Christ's 'reign'. I am not
sure how a later religious poet with a different type of sensibility would
manage to convey the notion that he was not quite ready to be so
delighted that his night of natural sensuality was brought to an end by
Christ's wakening cry. But I am sure that such ambiguities, in baroque
poets either, should not be claimed on verbal identity alone, but depend
on their retaining, provably, some of the original's *reason for using* the
images of cock and night. In our instance, those images have been
displaced; the new cock, and the night whose going is unequivocally
welcomed (as 'Christis flock singis' what they are taught by the 'Word' of
God who is 'King of all Kingis') are new images.[23]

They happen also, of course, to be very old ones. The ancient
Christian symbolism of Christ as cock, thence priest or preacher as cock,
perhaps started this poem (it is a criticism of clerics) on its way; but it is
not very important to it. Only so much of a symbol is 'in' a poem, even a
poor one, as can be seen to serve some end there. A different situation
appears in another song related to the *aubade* form, one of the
'spiritualizations' written to the prodigiously popular sixteenth-century
tune of 'The hunt is up'. The symbolic figure of Christ the king-
huntsman, and the resulting figures playing on *his deer — his dear*, are
sustained through eighteen stanzas. They tell of God's creation and
enclosure of his grounds, of how the deceiver caused God's chosen Dear
to leap the pale, how He

>   ... sent his owne soone,
>   Who strongly begoon
>   To hunt both hill and playne;
>   No one kynd of payne
>   But he dyd systayne,
>   To wyn his deare agayn.

And of how He then enclosed a 'park', and taught twelve 'To blow so just
a note' as brings all deer within it; and the poem ends with injunctions to

keepers, and promises to those who will 'be his deere for ever'. There were many sets of secular words, so familiar that I quote none, and similarly this is only one of the 'moralizations' written to the tune.[24] Indeed, 'a hunt's-up' became a substantive, and what witty ambiguities might we not introduce into the godly parody when we learn from Cotgrave's Renaissance dictionary that the synonym for French *resveil*, a morning song *for a new-married wife*, is 'a hunt's-up'? But for the fact that there is no evidence that it was intended, this connotation could provide an interesting shock in the final use of that anima-spouse image which of course is present throughout:[25]

> The hunt is up,
> The hunt is up,
>   Loe! it is allmost daye.
> For Chryst our kyng
> Is cum a huntyng,
>   And browght his deare to staye.

It seems worth while to remind ourselves frequently that 'music is at the bottom of it', in this establishment of a widespread habit of 'sacred parody' — widespread long before we can expect, or find, anything at all close to a baroque sensibility demonstrated in the parodic relation between secular and sacred texts. To be sure, plenty of music of this same period has the habit of pointing secretly at some hidden doubleness of meaning,[26] but its characteristics are not shared either by that which arose from the quite usual medieval practice of *contrafactum* or that which we trace during the sixteenth-century wave of borrowing tunes for sacred songs. But for the still-maintained ancient tie between lyric poem and music, we might have had very little of the phenomenon of parody, so far as the English poetic scene exhibits it; its far greater seventeenth-century strength in some other countries may support very different conclusions from those I have stressed.

One point should be recalled: that early 'popular music' had a character so different from that of popular music as we have been accustomed to it since the eighteenth century, and was formally so much more truly suitable to sacred themes and moods, that nothing but singing two texts to a melody shows how natural the interchange was. Luther's 'Num freut euch', like other chorales less universally recognized as popular tunes, takes and has kept its place in the most dignified of all hymnologies with no sense of alienness; it was one of those Coverdale reproduced with the music, and translated, in his attempt to introduce into England words and music from the Wittenberg and other chorale books from 1524 onward.[27] England shared least in this enrichment of ecclesiastical music through deliberate borrowing; even Protestant France, though less eminent and less alive musically, benefitted more, through the Huguenot psalter of 1562 and its predecessors for which Bourgeois found and arranged so many magnificent settings for Marot's vernacular metrical psalms. One may sing through the whole without noting flaws in decorum attributable to provenance, and usually only the asterisk affixed by an editor would apprise one of secular origin. Wynkyn de Worde printed in 1530 this sacred song with its music:

> And I mankynd haue not in mynd
> My loue that mornyth for me for me.
> Who is my loue but god aboue
> That born was of Mary . . .
> That king of blys my loue he ys
> That mornth so sor for me.

The melody is almost certainly from a secular song of which these words are a parody, but it is entirely suitable to its present text.

Only occasionally can one pass off the practice as a revivalist device — suitable to naive singers, musical stuff for Flemish weavers. This does seem to me to fit the remaking of the famous song 'Who is at my window, Who? Who?'. The tune had an interesting history of instrumental settings. Chappell's text of the sung tune is rather a jingle, *formally* suitable instead to its original secular words, and we need not ask ourselves seriously why those who enjoyed singing such a parody felt no formal incongruity as they went through the long dialogue-song. 'Ane wratcheit mortall' sings verses which end 'Se Quho is at thy windo, quho', and his 'Lord Celestiall' sings those which end 'Go from my windo, go' (the refrain later shifts to a series of changes rung on 'In at Thy door let me go' ('. . . at My door thou shalt go')). The conception of the deity's nature is as relaxed as the tune, but apparently nothing very early remains[28] to give us an actual secular text for comparison save other 'real' parodies (take-offs) in various snatches in plays. In the main however, there is singularly little in this whole sixteenth-century exchanging of melodies that encourages us to check up the entire affair to the same account as '*OH* come, *to* the church in the wildwood | *THE* lit-tle brown church in the vale'. Even for 'Who is at thy window', as also for the pious text to the tune of 'John come kiss me now' (*GGB*, p. 158, and Chappell I, 147), we should doubtless remind ourselves that this Scottish collection was a book of songs for household hearths and for jogging about, not for church and service.

For many sacred parodies we have only the names of original secular texts which served to identify the tunes — evidence of the practice but of no use for judging of relations. Or we have the numerous references to 'a moralization of' this or that, entered in the Stationers' register, references such as are scattered through the pages of Chappell and which attest to the habit of 'spiritualizing' secular songs whose texts we possess, but which can tell us nothing of the nature of the imitations. On the other hand, the long text of the extremely well-known 'Nut Brown Maid' can be compared stanza after stanza with the parody in which it becomes a dialogue between Mary and Christ the 'banished man' (c. 1520: printed by E. F. Rimbault, *Ancient Poetical Tracts*, 1842, Percy Soc. VI, pp. 33 ff.; chiefly alike in rhyme-words preserved).

In stressing religious-from-secular borrowings only, for their obvious pertinence to our special questions, I have introduced a division into categories which does not stand out so sharply during the periods concerned. It is also pertinent to recall the large amount of parody in which a secular text replaced another secular text, since we are interested in gauging the extent to which melodies were felt to be a divisible formal element, not inescapably tied to one kind of meaning or another. This should shed light on the extent to which certain other formal devices were similarly regarded. Recalling that parody involves deliberate modeling (though of course singers as well as authors can be parodists), one still has only to leaf through the row of Elizabethan miscellanies for examples; in *A Gorgeous Gallery* (1578): 'The Lover wounded with his Ladies beauty craveth mercy. To the Tune of where is the life that late I led', i.e. 'If pitty once may mooue thy hart' (p. 39);[29] or 'Not light of loue lady' (p. 38), 'To the Tune of Attend thee go play thee'; or 'Passe forth in doulfull dumpes my verse' (p. 31), 'To the tune, when Cupid scaled first the Fort'; or 'The glyttering showes of *Floras* dames' (p. 26), to the famous tune of 'lusty Gallant'. Singing it to that tune (in Ward, pp. 176, 170), one may enjoy the exercise of seeking any comparable element which made the tune seem suitable also to 'Fain would I have a pretie thing, to giue vnto my Ladie', in *A Handful of Pleasant Delights* (1584), p. 57. One may also try to imagine how a 'moralization' can possibly have gone onward following the first line we have from its 1566/1567 entering, 'Fayne wolde I have a *godly* thynge to shewe unto my ladye', and how it can have used the engaging part of the tune that goes with this part of the song in the *Handful*:

> I name no thing, nor I meane no thing,
> But as pretie a thing as may bee.

But these citations could go on for pages, showing us how usual a thing was 'parody' (whether called by that term or not) in the first and simpler musical sense which we set out to examine.

Much more could be presented. My object has been simply to indicate the existence and extent of a practice which descended to seventeenth-century 'parodists' without break, a long history of formal imitation and exchange, unself-conscious and ordinary, provocative neither of ambiguities nor ironies. This long development has to be taken into consideration when we wish to determine *what* precisely allows us to think of seventeenth-century religious uses of secular formal elements as something characteristically baroque, something related to the marriage of two incompatible worlds, with all the unresolved tensions, the ambiguities and oblique double intentions which thence accrue. If it be the presence of ironic dissonances that allows this categorizing, our readiness to find these must depend on something other than the mere practice of 'spiritual parody' itself, for scores of examples of the spiritualizing of secular poetry are not baroque at all in this respect or others. The practice alone of 'spiritual parody' is fairly generally accepted as a criterion for such categorizing, but the category itself breaks down if we include what the criterion would admit.

Touching Herbert in particular, these details of literary history are evidence for the fact that even if numerous forms of converting the secular were more important in his poetry than they are, this would not declare to us the nature of his motives or the kind of attitude he took toward secular arts and profane love. It would be no more legitimate, and no service to him, to substitute — for an alignment with a Counter Reformation Southwell on grounds of shared aesthetic — an alignment with the Coverdales and Wedderburns and Sternholds whose motives were more typically puritan. We must look elsewhere than to his 'sacred' use of the formal arts and devices of profane love poems for evidence that he condemned their subject. He had many predecessors in the practice who also shared these reformers' habit of borrowing without sharing their puritan or pietistic reasons for doing it. Surely it somehow lessens Herbert as a poet to conceive of him as nervously and tensely anxious to convert whatever hinted at the power and interest of love between human beings to pious uses. If this be true, it has very real connections with his theology, particularly with his conception of the definition of the love of God, the center of a Christian life as of a Christian theology. Such interpretations do not seem to me to square with the rest of his poetry, nor with his notably sane and balanced understanding of the close relation between heavenly love and all the many kinds of human love which he dealt with, knew, and apparently wove into a life distinguished for its practice of loving-kindness.[30]

Yet once at least he indubitably did remake an extant secular poem into a sacred one, and his title 'A Parodie' constitutes *his* definition of what he has done. But instead of assuming, from his act, a campaigner's intention, should we not rather follow his title's suggestion and relate the poem to the history, including the musical history, of such remakings? They were *formal* imitations; they were not ways of declaring a position through oblique commentary upon another text whose different *concepts* were thus derogated, or whose concepts were the source of hidden ambiguities because these were felt to be still present in the borrowed *form*. Where reformers used parody for their special intentions, it is abundantly clear that the formal elements borrowed are not the carrier for these. However, though one may be convinced that Lord Pembroke's *Song* was sung, and that Herbert followed a musical convention of some centuries' standing in writing a 'parody' of it, the only way to make sure that that conviction stands upon a fact would be to find the piece of music. This I have not succeeded in; and because I hope some one else will, I shall set down with some exactness just how and where I have looked for it.

Because of the younger Donne's reference to Lawes and Laniere (thought to be Nicholas, 1588-1666), in the 1660 edition of Pembroke and Ruddier containing 'Soules joy', one would seek first in them. One would expect a later public appearance of such an air, not one contemporary with Pembroke and Herbert — always provided it were thought to be worth publication. The printed collections were examined, beginning with those mentioned in Grove's *Dictionary* as important for Lawes; this is made easier by the fact that the several collections printed for Playford[31] are indexed in Day and Murrie's first-line index of *English Song-Books 1651-1702* (1940), with a check made possible by the more recent *Music at the Huntington Library* by E. Backus (1949).[32] The knotty problem of music still in manuscript is not taken care of by the first-line indices which fortunately exist (for the British Museum, for manuscripts at Christ Church, Oxford and at the Music School, supplemented for Oxford by the first-line card-index of manuscript poems in the Bodleian, in process[33]); there is still the matter of manuscripts acquired since those listings. This is easier to handle for Lawes, and in particular the important privately-owned 'Lawes Autograph MS,' often mentioned in connection with work on the *Comus* music is now at the British Museum (B.M. Loan 35) and was examined. But despite the helps like the British Museum class catalogues and Bodley's slip-catalogues, my checking of Laniere seems uncomfortably inadequate.[34] At this point, however, one may recall that all we know from Donne's preface is that Lawes and Laniere are good risks — the song may be any one's. To meet such a problem, we have only things like

Fellowes' numerous publications, such collection listings as go by first line rather than composer, and the possibility of covering through reading-room handlists such recent acquisitions as the extraordinary huge two-volume MS. Egerton 3665. There is still, so to speak, a hole between Fellowes and Playford[35] — and I hope Lord Pembroke's song is in it.

The musical literature, and particularly the manuscripts, which contain much that can never be got into print completely (like the format of lyrics), can illuminate many of the questions and possibilities which make difficulties for the critic of lyrical writing. This is especially true for poems written for extant music (as compared with those merely set by a later composer). One learns much about such matters as relations that cross language barriers, including the importation of lyric patterns (many manuscripts are half Italian, or sprinkled with French texts; a song of course is borrowable from any model). Or about special 'kinds' like the dialogues, secular and 'spiritual'; about conventional metaphors given more durability by the popularity of kinds of settings (for example the lady as besieged fortress, set from the fourteenth century to the seventeenth in the style of battle pieces; see Reese, *Renaissance*, pp. 12, 56). Or about the particular type of parodic composition paired with its original as an 'answer'; about the popularity of pieces, often to be attributed to a musical setting, and the changes in them to suit later tastes and later musical styles; about the repetition of portions as 'refrains', and other subtler ways in which the contour of poems affects our judgments of their structure; and about conceptions of formal fitness, especially of what formal elements are assumed to be largely indifferent to mood or conceptual content, hence to be changed or exchanged at will.[36]

It is no easier for a student of music to recognize the possible solution of literary cruxes, unless he knows the lyrical works of several decades almost by heart, than it is for a literary student to perceive — as he reads some setting — that a contemporary musician is overturning some of our most orthodox assumptions about literary decorum, touching tone perhaps, or tempo, or the contribution of rhetorical devices (repetition, inner rhyme, assonance). I allow space to the perhaps overprecise bibliographical materials above partly to emphasize the difficulties and pitfalls which come in the way when literary or musical students need to ask, of the others' expert knowledges, answers to their own respective kinds of questions. And partly to suggest how much remains to be done before we shall have a true sense of what the living reality was that corresponds to the literary phenomenon we refer to as the development of the seventeenth-century lyric.[37]

One aspect of this is small but it is unlikely to receive comment in any other connection: the extent to which the numerous minute facts brought to light in these slow and desultory ways affect our notions of the groupings and exchanged influences between authors. The web of interrelations between writers, and between works, which the living men experienced, would not look at all like our set of logical and schematized critical divisions. The musical popularizing and transmission of texts provided a different kind of viability, and influences unlike those of printed whole editions; the single poem, and not always the most characteristic or 'best' poem, is more important, and moreover what men learn from others' poems depends on what form they meet them in. (This holds for literary critics as well.) A network of ties we are largely unaware of made poets answer each other's poems, try out each other's new modes, proclaim improbable admirations and dislikes, pay the compliment of imitation to attractions we do not see, produce a sudden spate of 'blackamoor' poems or pastoral invitations, pursue some motif to an early, final, and absurd death. Of this network we once had only fairly gross notions — on the order of 'Herrick, son of Ben', 'young Herbert and young King, inside the dean's circle', 'Browne, Spenser, Daniel: another world'. Biographical research has confused our once neat critical alignments, and particularly some of the old assumed antipathies have had to go; the allowed patterns would be further shaken by a detailed history of musical settings.

Odd single relationships can sometimes afford a safer glimpse into special 'influences' and the judgments men made of each other than our ideas of what would be plausible. Who could easily say why, of all the poems Herbert might have imitated, he chose to leave us this one close echo? Not that we lack evidence of connections between the two cousins. We have fairly continuous evidence of the friendly relations between the several Herbert brothers, including Edward and Henry also, and their fourth cousin William Lord Pembroke, and of his favors to George. Pembroke's close friend Ruddier (commonly paired with him touching authorship of poems long before the joint editing of the two in 1660) is the Sir Benjamin Ruddyard to whom Herbert says he is writing for support of his candidacy for the oratorship, as well as to 'my Lord' (pretty certainly Pembroke; letter VIII in Hutchinson, p. 370). Ruddyard was returned for the borough of Wilton, 'again', in June 1625. Herbert evidently owed his own seat as M.P. for Montgomery to Lord Pembroke and his brother Philip (1624; Herbert's term overlapped that of his important earlier patron, for he was not succeeded in the seat by his brother Henry until 1626).

It is a little difficult to disentangle actions in his behalf by the two Lords Pembroke, especially in the matter of the Bemerton living, the deed of presentation of which (16 April 1630) is dated six days after William's sudden death made Philip fourth earl. The story in Walton of King Charles, the Earl of Pembroke, and Laud, at Wilton or Salisbury, together persuading Herbert to acceptance, is properly called in question, but Hutchinson accepts the statement that Pembroke 'requested the King to bestow it upon his Kinsman *George Herbert*' (it was a living in the earl's gift, but fell to the crown this time through promotion of the incumbent). All Herbert's movements center in Wiltshire for several months around these dates. We may not fix a precise date for the late poem 'A Parodie'; but close connections with Wilton, with the Herberts who came and went there, and with the interests of that third earl who was so well known a patron of poetry and music, do not have to wait for residence at Bemerton. Nor need they depend on whether Herbert was chaplain at Wilton House (as Aubrey says), or on his good friendship with its famous later mistress, Philip's wife Anne, countess of Cumberland.[38]

Lord Pembroke's interest in music is a little less well known than his patronage of poets.[39] Lawes and Laniere most likely did their settings of numerous pieces by him and his friend Ruddier during a connection of long standing — a kind of patronage-partnership which is not unusual, and all the more natural given Lawes' Salisbury boyhood and continued connections there through his father Thomas, vicar choral.[40] The incomparable Dowland set a song of Pembroke's. Tobias Hume, that strange and finally piteous character, would no doubt have liked to have set one too; his dedication of his *Musicall Humours*, 1605, sounds too formal for the friendship we sense in the Lawes connection, and by 1642 he is thanking a later Lord Pembroke for 'a meal's meat' now and then.[41] Other musicians testify to Lord Pembroke's interest in music of other kinds than songs of profane love; Thomas Tomkins' dedication to the earl of his *Songs*, 1622, after alleging ties with him as another west-country man, speaks of his 'often frequenting and favorable attention to the Musicke in the Chappell', music which raises the soul above the body (this would be in the court's Chapel Royal). *The Just Mans Memoriall* is a printed sermon preached by 'T.C.' (his London chaplain?) 'before the interment of the Body' at Baynard's Castle, the earl's London house where he died suddenly 10 April 1630; its description of 'my dead Master', including his daily attendance at prayers, suits ill with the bad reputation Pembroke has had, falsely it now seems, in some modern comment.[42] It takes no flight of the imagination to think that the alleged author of the first 'Soules joy' was a congenial friend as well as helpful kinsman of the author of the second, and that both amateurs of music and of poetry did not live in the same county so many months of several different years connected only by letters and the memory of past obligations. A poem with or without music, in manuscript at Wilton when Herbert came at the earl's persuasion to live so near by,[43] is enough to explain why a good musician should write 'A Parodie'. It is a disappointingly common sense explanation compared with the picture of a Herbert torn by anxieties and determined to turn all secular love into sacred channels, but it suits the man better.

Much of this information, like so much information, simply changes our expectations a little. For the chief support for understanding the poem in the matter-of-fact way I have suggested lies in the nature of the relation between it and its model. It is a formal imitation.

I reproduce the two poems in a format which allows easier comparison.

Song	*A Parodie*
Soules joy, now I am gone,	Souls joy, when thou art gone,
And you alone,	And I alone,
(Which cannot be,	Which cannot be,
Since I must leave my selfe with thee,	Because thou dost abide with me,
And carry thee with me)	And I depend on thee;
Yet when unto our eyes	Yet when thou dost suppresse
Absence denyes	The cheerfulnesse
Each others sight,	of thy abode,
And makes to us a constant night,	And in my powers not stirre abroad,
When others change to light;	But leave me to my load: 10
O give no way to griefe,	O what a damp and shade
But let beliefe	Doth me invade!
Of mutuall love,	No stormie night
This wonder to the vulgar prove	Can so afflict or so affright,
Our Bodyes, not wee move.	As thy eclipsed light. 15
Let not thy wit beweepe	Ah Lord, do not withdraw,
Wounds but sense-deepe,	Lest want of aw
For when we misse	Make sinne appeare; [cleare,
By distance our lipp-joying blisse,	And when thou dost but shine lesse
Even then our soules shall kisse,	Say, that thou art not here. 20
Fooles have no meanes to meet,	And then what life I have,
But by their feet.	While sinne doth rave,
Why should our clay,	And falsly boast,
Over our spirits so much sway,	That I may seek, but thou art lost;
To tie us to that way?	Thou and alone thou knowst. 25

O give no way to griefe,
   But let beliefe
   Of mutuall love,
This wonder to the vulgar prove
Our Bodyes, not wee move.

O what a deadly cold
   Doth me infold!
   I half beleeve,   [grieve,
That Sinne sayes true: but while I
Thou com'st and dost relieve.

The usually careful and meaningful format in Herbert is not disturbed, except to point up by deeper indentation how the parallel third and sixth stanzas would have been sung to what was probably set as a refrain in Pembroke's, twice following upon ten lines (two identically patterned fives). We do not know the format of Pembroke's *Song*. Grierson evidently takes the format, in two ten-line stanzas with an italicized refrain separating these and recurring at the end, from the 1635 Donne (and parallel later editions). In neither of the two manuscript copies (Lansdowne 777, Stowe 962) nor in the 1660 edition of Pembroke is there any indication that the five lines 'O give no way . . .' are a refrain;[44] but if the edition (a bad text) is a careless copy from a music manuscript, this 'refrain', if it is one, might have been sung after each five, not each ten, for the lines appear as the second five.[45] But there is no trusting this editor. The 1635 Donne probably got this poem, as it got other additions to 1633, from the O'Flaherty MS. (now at Harvard), for that carefully arranged text gives us a two-stanza song, each of ten lines, with refrain (to repeat at end) as in Grierson, with the additional care, as in Herbert, of showing by lesser indentation that the fourth line, in each stanza and in the refrain, is a longer one. But its verbal blunders are only a little less absurd than those of 1660, and Grierson had to correct them from the Lansdowne MS. (see Grierson, II, xcviii). Syllabically, each stanza (or half-stanza) is 6-4-4-8-6, and the same music will suit the same completed song, whether in six separate fives as in Herbert or two tens with inserted and final refrain as in Pembroke. This explanation was necessary in order to see that Herbert suits a text to a pattern, not a text to a text.

The conceptual structure of the *Song*, quite different from Herbert's, allows the parallel ideas about absence in stanzas one and two to be laid at rest each time by the asseveration repeated in the identical 'refrain', truly one in this respect at least. The thought of 'A Parodie' is not built like this; it proceeds in one line from the impossibility of God's absence, to His seeming absence, to 'O what a damp and shade' that induces, to a plea not to seem absent, to the dangers that involves, to a climactic final five lines that begin *formally* (and with great propriety musically) 'O what a deadly cold . . .', as before, but end '*Thou com'st* and dost relieve'. Conceptually there is and can be nothing in Pembroke's poem for this thought-structure to be a 'parody' of, neutral or otherwise. It is not a parody of ideas or style; it is the use of a strictly formal pattern to write one's own poem to. Whether there was music or not, or whether both poems were sung to some music for a third which we therefore do not find in our searches, Herbert's poem is set 'to' the form, in the way words are set 'to' music. Herbert does not 'leave' Pembroke's subject; he has never picked it up. His poem is on a different subject, which is not the nature of love.

This statement may sound foolhardy in the light of five lines of near verbal identity between the two poems. But concepts do not build up with words as with bricks, and even closer verbal identity would not make the same idea out of 'my self left with thee' said of a relation to another human being, and 'thou abiding with me' said of God's relation to the soul. Change of referents changes the meaning even of identical words, and this interesting aspect of the relations which obtain between form and meaning provides part of the pleasure in all types of parody. But instead of watching how Herbert talks about seeming absence without talking about Pembroke's subject of seeming absence, we may more profitably follow with some care the formal echoings which relate the two poems well beyond the point where verbal parallels cease.

In doing this I shall make several references to the technique of the *missa parodia*. This is illegitimate in that music alone can show the technique. For any poem is, like a song, monodic, whereas the whole burden of a good deal of fairly recent work on the parody mass is to show its difference from its ancestors, the practice of *contrafactum* (also monodic) and the *cantus firmus* mass, and the difference lies in the fact that a parody mass is based on a polyphonic model and uses its borrowings polyphonically. The *missa parodia* borrows not just a line of melody, augmenting and inverting it and treating it contrapuntally, but borrows consonances, hormonic phrases and entries, polyphonic inter-weaving of melodic elements. Obviously this can have no precise literary analogue. Yet the effects thus gained, and their obscured but present relations to their model, are more useful to bear in mind than straightforward monodic imitations when one looks at the way com-bined literary elements of vowel and consonant quality, accent, rhythm, and echo produce a texture related to an imitated texture. In addition, because we need not doubt that Herbert had an ear made alert to this contemporary technique through singing and listening, and because even if he did not know such masses the parody technique was otherwise known in England (see e.g. some of Morley's madrigals and canzonets),[46] and because *missa parodia* may be the term which gave earliest currency to the *term* used in his title, it is proper to make some references thereto. It remains true that his probable confusion of *contrafactum* and *parody* may account for his name, thus harking back to a yet more common technique.

The definite and recognizable use of the original for the opening is universally characteristic. As in 'Souls joy', this is an imitation, often very close, of a largish formal portion, a near-quotation. Every Kyrie in a mass showing either the earlier or the later kind of imitation 'states', as does Herbert's beginning its parodic character, but it is just as much a Kyrie for all that, and no notion can really enter of a reference to the *ideas* the composer had to hand in his secular musical models, in 'L'homme arme', 'Fortuna desperata', 'Malheur me bat', 'Douce memoire', 'Ite rime dolenti', 'Ultimi miei sospiri', 'Cara la vita mia', 'Puisque j'ai perdu', or whatever else. I simply take names of extant masses by the best-known composers of sacred music;[47] these do not differ in their 'spirituality' from other masses by the same writers based instead on sacred motets[48] — and the same is true if one compares Herbert's 'Souls joy' with his independent or liturgically based sacred poems. Where masses seem 'secularized', as is sometimes said of di Lasso or Victoria, there are formal reasons for it — declamation, 'skipping rhythms', and so on — not this practice of parody which they share with Josquin, Clemens non Papa, Philippe de Monte, Gallus (Handl), Palestrina, and others renowned for their deeply religious quality. Several of these were notably devout men, and if they thought possible the intrusion of secular connotations through formal likenesses, they did ill in usually choosing secular models made famous by recent or noted settings. Taverner's mass founded on and called after 'The Western Wynde' uses *cantus firmus* rather than parody technique, the reworking thus being all the more eminent, but it would be equally idle to suppose that he either feared or desired any tensions set up in his auditory by the fact that in his Benedictus the trebles sing 'qui venit in nomine Domini', in the Gloria the tenors sing 'peccata mundi', in the Credo 'Patrem omnipotentem' — to that part of the melody every one knew was occupied by 'Christ, that my love were in my arms | And I in my bed again'.

The formal parallelism between Pembroke's *Song* and the 'Parodie' is again peculiarly marked where 'O give no way to griefe, | But let beliefe | Of mutuall love ...' is echoed by Herbert's 'O what a damp and shade | Doth me invade!' and 'O what a deadly cold | Doth me infold!' This would be a natural way to make the most of a musical phrase, in case Herbert wrote to a setting composed for a text whose 'refrain' had this accentual pattern (therefore occurring twice). The textural likenesses (they are in contrast to his own other fives) are apparent in tempo, shifted accents, falling cadence after the first 'O', long and heavy words, with long vowels in rhyming positions — though the feeling and meaning of the two five-line units are simply not related, not even opposed.

In musical parody, the fact that one formal structure is being used to bring another one into being results in the appearance of a great many small semi-quotations of partially parallel motifs — ranging from harmonic coloring to *Nebentheme*, sometimes a figure quoted with a slight but transforming change in rhythm or in the time, a lengthened or contracted near-repetition. These are not true analogues to what we find in Herbert's or any literary imitation except that a similar effect of a likeness that is not quite a likeness results from the numerous all-but-parallel rhetorical effects: the same poised hesitation before a cadence in several lines, near-assonance and parallel endings in each 14th line ('this *wonder* to the *vulgar* prove'; cf. Herbert's alliteration and final consonance in slightly altered accent-positions in 'Can so afflict or so affright'; similarly both 21st lines: '*meanes* to *meet*'; '*life* I *have*'); the same high slow emphasis ('Even then ...', 'Say, that ...', both lines 20), continuing into a row of fastidiously separated syllables. These relations, like the subtly similar winding of the run-ons, are quite different in effect from outright repetitions like 'Yet when ...' (6), or the mere clang of rhyme-words in the memory which is most likely responsible for the last stanzas' 'griefe ... beliefe': 'beleeve ... greeve'. The contour of 'Let not thy wit beweepe' (16) is reflected, though with a pebble just moving the image in the pool, in 'Ah Lord! do not withdraw' (16), but they share nothing conceptually except a wordless sense of the mental posture of pleading. One does not think these planned tricks, but the result of a sensitive ear accustomed to notice and take pleasure in artistic imitation, accompanied by a disposition to regard formal imitating as a thing quite separable from following the line of another man's thought.

Perhaps it is necessary to remark in concluding this comparison that its relevance does not depend on our envisaging England as full of men singing foreign polyphonic masses. To be sure musicians — going either way — did not stop at the channel, nor the tastes of cultivated men pull up short before popish music like pledge-signers, and musical Englishmen were not at this epoch writing or listening to native wood-notes wild; also, in a time of such unusual mobility among performers and composers no great household or cathedral town (or even Cambridge) can be safely placed in the category 'just out in the provinces'. But this is not the essential element in my reason for noting these comparisons. They demonstrate usefully the nature of a parodic relation which imitates *form*, and is unarguably divorced from the interest in evoking conceptual ambiguities which we attribute to practically all literary interactions of the sacred and the profane, especially in the seventeenth century.

That Herbert is one for whom the musical comparisons are particularly apt because of his special interests and competences is so much extra good fortune. It should not need to be said (but experience shows that it does) that the idea of Herbert setting himself to compose 'Souls joy' as if he were writing a parody mass or a parody of a polyphonic canzonet would be a laughable one. Rather we realize that he was used to what it meant to 'parody' formally, and that he had an exquisitely sensitive ear, with complete integrity as far as keeping his eye on his own subject was concerned.

I would suggest that this was his attitude also with respect to the more inclusive matter of his use of arts learned from secular poetry, and that his poems support it. This is not to deny that tensions and wry ironies accompany men's attempts to relate or combine what is sacred to them and what is not, and that these are sometimes expressed in ambiguous juxtapositions or a bizarre relation between form and *raison d'être* of a work of art. That such tensions were peculiarly acute in the early seventeenth century is true, and there is no doubt some virtue in taking over the art historian's terms to call such expressions baroque.[49] Such analogous terms have come to limit overmuch our ideas of what authors can be like, nailing them down often to the insights of their lesser contemporaries. Obviously if a particular practice or a way of using secular arts in sacred art works has had a long history, being used by men who subscribed to a variety of aesthetic positions, its mere presence in an author can tell us little about his particular aesthetic. To ignore this is simply to assume intentions for an author and proceed as if he had declared them. It is necessary to find the declaration of them in the nature of his peculiar expression, and it is hard to find poems by Herbert wherein his uses of arts learned from secular poetry operate as a cause to produce a baroque tension born of straddling two worlds and giving up neither. Or giving up either.

That other men of his date so wrote and had such intentions is only to the purpose in that it warns us to scrutinize his carefully. An author's date can never declare what he meant. Any good writer (and to some extent any writer, and any man) has the freedom of all the history he knows. The history of how other men of other dates used practices he uses is again only to the purpose in that it moves us to careful scrutiny. We have seen that Herbert in turning secular arts to sacred purposes and specifically in writing 'parody' is doing something many generations of men had done before him, and yet that this is not evidence for thinking either that he must share the intentions of the puritan reformers or must resemble in style the pious parodists.

One does not use history to discover uniformities, but possibilities. It is dangerous nowadays to call attention to likenesses between artistic events or habits in different historical eras, since some one always arises to declare that the events are not identical. One thinks of this as a point of departure so accepted that intelligent men do not remark upon it to each other. Artistic expressions are incurably single. It yet remains necessary to demand that writers' differences should be found in that wherein they differ, not in that which they share. Herbert's great differences in style and feeling from his predecessors should not throw dust in our eyes concerning his differences in some elusive but basic ways from his contemporaries. A poet shares much with these, like all men, perhaps more deeply and more variously than most. If he is a good poet he is different from any one — and also if he is a good poet an enjoyment of his uniqueness is inseparable from the sense of his transcendence of it.

This transcendence of their uniqueness and their unique historical moment is not peculiar to poets but to men. It is not the historian among critics who is likeliest to put an author into the strait jacket of a 'time' or a 'milieu' or a 'tradition', but the critic or reader who by reason of a false sociology does not see writers as men who make choices.[50] Their freedom from time in this respect they communicate directly to us who share it. This does not mean that we need retreat to the obscurantist and at bottom sentimental position that merely by being men — and a poet one who is 'a man speaking to men' — we shall straightway understand all. It is rather when we know enough history not to impose ephemeral distortions (its creator was able to elude them) that a poem reveals to us both its historical uniqueness and its non-historical permanence, and this caveat applies generally to Herbert's and many others' close relation to several kinds of earlier traditions; we hear in Herbert's poems the arts he learned from others, even the words he copied from others, but as it was not these — his history — which finally determined what he made, so also it is not his own historical uniqueness (a true and valuable thing) which alone makes him valuable to us in ours. These very borrowed things themselves in any art speak with a voice that was unique and yet is not silenceable in the way everything unique is silenced.

In parody, an extreme and deliberate form of imitation, this can be all the more apparent. I shall now append a parody of my own. It is a tour de force, and not satisfactory, but it will show that borrowings do not account for the things they help to make, that the long history behind a relation between two poems helps us to see what it is and the limits of it, and that the ways in which parodic relations are interesting and pleasurable are too varied to be assigned to any single simple intention in a poet. Lacking a setting for 'Soules joy', I have appropriated and adapted an originally secular composition remade to a sacred use, before 1561, by 'the continuator of Bourgeois', who completed the latter's work on the settings of the Huguenot psalter.[51] The reader is asked to perform this with all the secularity of which he is capable, singing Lord Pembroke's words. And then to see whether, as he sings Herbert's words to the same music, he does not find that a formal imitation is the sole relation between the secular work of art he first produces and his own production of a sacred Parodie.

Texts: 'Song', probably by the Earl of Pembroke. 'A Parodie' by George Herbert

Hypothetical setting with music adapted from Goudimel's treatment of Psalm 96 in *Les Pseaumes ... mis en musique a quatre parties*, 1565. The Genevan melody is in the tenor.

But let be-lief Of mu-tual love, —— This won-der to the
Doth me in-vade! No storm-y night —— Can so af-flict or
Doth me in-fold! I half be-lieve, —— That sin says true: but

vul-gar prove, Our bod-ies, not__ we__ move.__
so af-fright, As thy e-clip - - sed light.__
while I grieve, Thou com'st and dost__ re-lieve.__

GEORGE HERBERT: THE ART OF PLAINNESS

Arnold Stein

As a religious poet Herbert addresses God directly or writes with the intention of being overheard by Him. For traditional and for contemporary reasons, both religious and secular in origin, he aspires to an art of plainness that can achieve absolute sincerity. He is impatient with art but must practice patience. He distrusts rhetoric — as who does not? — but in order to speak sincerely he must master the rhetoric of sincerity.

Some of his more severe claims, assertions, and rejections lend themselves, a little too easily, to the purposes of critical definition. But we do not need to take him at his word in poems like the two sonnets which, according to Walton, were addressed to his mother, or in the pair of sonnets entitled "Love" (I and II). In these poems the contest between human and divine love is presented as if it were a moral scandal, to be treated only in terms of extreme contrasts and a single range of emotion. Everything is externalized, as if a safe imaginative distance were the only proper course. If plainness has anything to do with forthrightness and with the manner attributed to plain dealers, then we must acknowledge a kind of plainness in these poems, though they lack something in art. The case against their sincerity would have to point out that the attitude assumed by the author, and eloquently expressed, does not cost him very much. The desire to believe lends energy, vividness, sharpness, but not precision, depth, or fineness to the expression. When we speak of the rhetoric of sincerity, it is not with such poems in mind.

Let us turn to a poem which does not offer a stiff rejection but raises questions, and in a very mild and casual manner seems to present a

From *The Poetic Tradition: Essays on Greek, Latin, and English Poetry*, edited by Don Cameron Allen and Henry T. Rowell (Baltimore: The Johns Hopkins University Press, 1968), pp. 99-122, © Copyright 1968 by The Johns Hopkins University Press. Reprinted by permission of the author and The Johns Hopkins University Press. This essay appears in an expanded form in *George Herbert's Lyrics* (Baltimore: The Johns Hopkins University Press, 1968), pp. 1-44.

radical solution. The poem is "A true Hymne," which begins:

> My joy, my life, my crown!
> My heart was meaning all the day,
> Somewhat it fain would say:
> And still it runneth mutt'ring up and down
> With onely this, *My joy, my life, my crown.*

Herbert then goes on to defend these words, which "may take part/ Among the best in art" if they are "truly said." We may suspect that the naïvety is in part cultivated; it is plainly meant, however, and comes from a refinement of knowledge rather than a lack of knowledge. These words are symbols; they represent precious wisdom, the soul of living truth which the speaker may pronounce without possessing. It is hard to say them "truly"; the heart was "meaning" them all the day, but even the heart is uncertain — "Somewhat it fain would say," and it runs "mutt'ring up and down." The value of these words, whether in private thought or in art, depends on understanding what they mean and saying them truly.

Herbert ends the second stanza with a firm declaration:

> The finesse which a hymne or psalme affords,
> Is, when the soul unto the lines accords.

This, though it has an admirable ring and expresses one clear concept of poetic sincerity, does not quite face the problems that have been raised. The accordance of the soul may assume that the heart has understood and that the words have been "truly said," but we are not told how these vital steps are taken, or even that they have been taken. Instead, we have been given a partial definition, which is then extended by a charming example of negative illustration — a whole stanza that shows how not to do it:

> He who craves all the minde,
> And all the soul, and strength, and time,
> If the words onely ryme,
> Justly complains, that somewhat is behinde
> To make his verse, or write a hymne in kinde.

The amused incoherence of the stanza parodies the ambitious poet who starts with high resolution and finds himself hung up, forcing rhyme, splicing syntax, and barely staggering through. After the brave opening, the only words that ring true are "Justly complains." Furthermore, the grounds have been shifted, and we have not followed up the problem of how the words are to be "truly said" or how that accordance of the soul is to be achieved.

The last stanza presents a solution that is indirectly relevant to the problems of literary expression but directly relevant to the heart seeking to address God:

> Whereas if th' heart be moved,
> Although the verse be somewhat scant,
> God doth supplie the want.
> As when th' heart sayes (sighing to be approved)
> *O, could I love!* and stops: God writeth, *Loved.*

We come to see that the writing of poetry has not been at the center of the poem after all. Instead, Herbert has used art as a metaphor to express an experience of religious life. In life, if not in art, the "somewhat scant" expression of the sincere heart may be amended and completed by God. When God writes "Loved," the desire to articulate and the desire to love are at once fulfilled. Their ends are achieved without the ordinary steps of a humanly conducted process. By authoritative acknowledgment virtual expression becomes actual.

If we look at the poem from one point of view, a miracle has taken place: but from another point of view we need recognize only an inspired compression — always possible in dialogue if the correspondent understands the intention, approves it, and fully reciprocates. We may observe, therefore, that Herbert is not simply invoking a miracle, for the ends of expression may often be realized without the full use of normal means. What we cannot do, however, is take the metaphorical analogy of writing poetry as if it were literal. Sincere feelings do not of themselves produce good poems. Herbert surely knew this as well as we do. But he must also have believed that whenever he felt a poem of his to be successful, God's hand had guided his in the composition; and if he felt a poem to be successful that feeling was the sure sense that the expression had realized its end, that God had blessed the end and given him the feeling by reflection. The humility of the man of God and the humility of the artist might both acknowledge that a fumbling, "muttering" intention had by some unexpected swiftness been clarified, and that the awkward wrongness of initial and intermediate stages had somehow been transformed into the triumphantly graceful and right. In retrospect, even the labor of composition — like some fictional by-product of the creative process — might seem to be compressed into a decisive instant of time. (Poets are notoriously inaccurate in reporting on these matters and prefer to believe that their perfect poems were "dictated":

which is what we prefer to believe when the evidence to the contrary does not interfere.)

There are at least two ways, then, of looking at the issues raised by this poem. I have been emphasizing the "normal" conditions of the creative process because I am primarily interested in the poet Herbert; and because I am convinced that the religious lyric, though it must fulfill special conditions, must also, and does, answer all the questions we ask of other lyrics. From a literary standpoint the central metaphor of the poem can be interpreted as analogous to the ways in which inspiration figures in the writing of poems. Inspiration is of course the kind of concept that easily crosses a line between the secular and the sacred, and for Herbert so too does the act, or the metaphor, of writing poems. In this poem we are free to interpret the analogy, so long as we recognize that it is a metaphor and is not to be taken literally. But we must also recognize that, for Herbert, though the metaphor may apply to the writing of poetry it has been superseded, as it were, by the higher form of expression to which it refers. The wisdom descending from God crowns, not with understanding but with love, an apparently clumsy human effort to understand and express. We do not expect Herbert to be dissatisfied with the attainment of such an end simply because the means do not seem to justify it. But we do not therefore think Herbert believed that this was the way to write poems, and that the individual details of thought and expression might safely be ignored because they would leap intervening stages if only "th' heart be moved." Herbert knew better, both as poet and as man of God. That he hoped, humbly, for the easier path of inspiration — one does not need to be either poetic or religious to feel the attraction of that course.

But Herbert's metaphors are capable of moving in more than two directions. The central fiction of writing poetry, which may refer to the real writing of poetry and to something real in the experience of religious life, may have still a third reference. In presenting the fictional account Herbert is at the same time confessing his own unworthiness, his own desire, and intimating the authentic joy which he would feel if what he is describing should happen to him. In other words, the narrative is also a concealed prayer, composed by one of the modern masters of that difficult decorum and rhetoric by means of which one may properly address God and suggest to Him certain courses for human affairs.

And so the cultivated clumsiness of the poem, the shifting of grounds, the apparent naïvety, and what may have seemed to be a radical solution to the problems of writing poetry, when taken together are something else, or several things else. But if we are at all right about the poem it cannot be taken as a simple assertion about poetry; what seems to be assertion is ultimately part of a complex and tactful statement. Yet we cannot stop here, at the satisfying literary position. We must remember that, for Herbert, the metaphor of writing is in the poem superseded by the fulfillment of the end of expression — here a confirming act which writes and rhymes as poetry but means as metaphor. If he himself believes in the fiction of his poem, then he will find its conclusion a happier one than most of his poems provide, and toward the slower, labored uncertainties of most composition he will feel some understandable impatience.

At this point, if there were time, I should want to comment on the kind of plain style we find in "The Church-Porch," and to look at some poems in which Herbert accepts, or even flaunts, a division between truth and beauty. But these poems do not finally say anything distinctive or resonant. The gestures of sincerity by which art is used to expose art can at best make but limited points. A better and more characteristic performance is "The Forerunners." Whatever else he is saying in the poem, Herbert is also bidding a fictional farewell to poetry, to the "sweet phrases, lovely metaphors," which he has rescued from the poetic "brothels" in order to bring into the church, repentant and renewed: "My God must have my best, ev'n all I had." The excitement and affection of his address could serve as well for arrival as for departure: "Lovely enchanting language, sugar-cane,/Honey of roses," he exclaims, as preface to imagining the unfortunate relapse of poetry returns to its old ways. He argues against what he knows will happen, and in doing so marks both a separateness of truth and beauty and the bridge of normal relations that leads to their unity:

Let follie speak in her own native tongue.
True beautie dwells on high: ours is a flame
    But borrow'd thence to light us thither.
Beautie and beauteous words should go together.

Here Platonic solution is emphasized, rather than Platonic division. The statement is handsome and, as well as we can judge from the context and from other poems, heartfelt — a major poetic belief, but not therefore the guiding inspiration of every lyrical utterance.

"Yet if you go," he adds, meaning, when you go, as the poet prepares to settle down for a final accounting:

Yet if you go, I passe not; take your way:
For, *Thou art still my God*, is all that ye
Perhaps with more embellishment can say.

And so a significant division appears, if not between truth and beauty, at least between "true beauty" and what can be said in words. That words are treated as no more than a conventionally detachable garment of style may seem a little disappointing, but Herbert does at least say "perhaps." Besides, in the context of the poem "Thou art still my God" *is* an ultimate expression, one that can be and is developed in other poems but cannot be here. Its meaning cannot be improved upon, and the man preparing to give up everything will not need anything else. The expression is complete, syntactically and otherwise, as the plain saying of "My God, my King" and "My joy, my life, my crown" are not. Nor does the poet's own attitude toward poetic language remotely resemble the stiff certitude with which he elsewhere rejects the misguided efforts of misguided poets. He is not rejecting here but parting, and with fine reluctance and such sweet sorrow.

In "The Forerunners" the act of writing poetry stands for the means, made visible and audible, of communing with God; it is a human invention motivated by a borrowed flame "to light us thither," a means of returning to the source of beauty. The house of the church, the house of poetry, and the house of life, the "best room" of which is the heart, are in the poem all reduced to an essential state. As the visible church stands truly, beautifully, but imperfectly for the invisible church, so do the "sweet phrases, lovely metaphors" express imperfectly the "True beautie" on high. In its plainness the essential expression, "Thou art still my God," will fulfill the end of expression, "And if I please him, I write fine and wittie." The essentiality of the expression, when one contemplates its meaning, by itself and in the context of the poem, would seem to be better established than the poet's assurance of writing "fine and wittie." That claim one may perhaps regard as a little assertive, markedly different from the persuasive tact with which art demonstrates the limitations of art in the argument of the poem.

The distinction is a fine one but it needs to be made. I mentioned earlier that if Herbert felt a poem to be successful he would need to believe that the expression had realized its end of pleasing God, and that God had given him his feeling by reflection. But he does not practice the art of silence or the art of discovering only the essential expression, which he can then merely "mutter." He writes poems, even when their aim is to express, or transcend, the inadequacy of poetic expression. We may perhaps regard "Thou art still my God" as a symbolic plainness, an ideal to which his poetic art of plainness may aspire, but it is not itself an expression of that art.

I think we can put matters in the right perspective by drawing a distinction between the symbolic plainness of an ultimate expression and the plainness of a complete poetic action. The latter may (and in Herbert often does) move toward a clarification that resembles the symbolic plainness. But if the poetic action is complete its conclusion will be the result of a process of expression. Though the "true beauty" of "Thou art still my God" may be traced to the compressed inner meaning the expression holds for Herbert, nevertheless that statement does appear three times in the poem, and it works both with and against other statements. In "The Flower" Herbert makes another absolute statement: "Thy word is all, if we could spell." Some of his poems are advanced spelling lessons. If "The Forerunners" were, say, a poem like "Aaron," its process might have included some parsing of the implicit relations between "thou" and "my," or between "art" and "still."

Herbert is acutely aware, as poet and as Christian, of deception, evasiveness, and inadequacy within himself — and, for these, traditional attitudes toward language and art provide useful and established symbols. Besides, many of his more assertive poems take up positions that he does not intend to carry through uncritically. A paradox that furnishes much of his poetic material may help explain why the single attitude is often countered within its own poem and opposed by other poems. The "grosser world," toward the beauty and importance of which the poet feels conflicting emotions, is, in spite of his feelings, a fixed and orderly world regulated by the "word and art" of God. It is the "diviner world of grace" which suddenly alters, and of which God is every day "a new Creatour."[1]

What Herbert writes in "Superliminare" may be applied to all instances when he engages himself to "Copie out onely" this or that. He will admit

> Nothing but holy, pure, and cleare,
> Or that which groneth to be so.

That is a program which leaves room for and grants validity to the hopes of individual effort, without regard to cost and efficiency. Herbert's most important subject is the mystery of God's art with man, a subject he confronts with patience and imagination, both passionately involved and scrupulously detached. That God's art with man reveals God's nature he takes for granted, and he assumes that the mysteries which God has concealed in man encourage the study of things human as an authorized reflection of things divine.

We may put these observations together by saying that Herbert does not give us a single, consistent attitude toward expression, that his art of plainness does not bear a single stamp, and that his arguments with God are conducted with great freedom and inventiveness. Whenever as critics we take a single example as our model to copy, we become aware of statements on the other side and of stylistic demonstrations that force us to widen our definitions. From one point of view we may be satisfied to locate the essential Herbert in the ringing declarations of "H. Baptisme" (II): "Let me be soft and supple to thy will.... My soul bid nothing.... Childhood is health." But softness must be "tempered" and suppleness must exert itself in order to be what it is. We do not know enough when we know that the goal expressed so simply is a difficult one to achieve, and that the verbal summation stands for detailed, strenuous efforts by an individual conscious that millions of human beings have in effect said the same thing and have both failed and succeeded. Our general knowledge must also "descend to particulars," for exactness lies not in any general statement but in the clarified order which poetry may achieve when particular expressions work with and against each other. In Herbert's poetry the soul has other lessons to learn, not all of them compatible with what is here presented as the sum of wisdom. For the soul that bids nothing may hear nothing; nor is that spiritual state exempt from posing and artful presumption. Childhood is not health at all in "Mortification," but is only one of several stages in the art of dying. That art would seem to be more valuable than spiritual health itself; for the art of knowing possesses more fully whatever it desires and gains, and Herbert never deviates long from this old principle, which represents the uneasy, but enduring and fruitful, marriage of Athens and Jerusalem. Childhood generally symbolizes the will in his poems, but the education of the will is the patient task of intelligence, and Herbert, to his honor, seldom trusts for long any of the attractive substitutes for intelligence. Even that most famous conversion of "The Collar" — "Me thoughts I heard one calling, *Child!*/And I reply'd *My Lord*" — rests on the demonstration of an argument that has ruined itself.

As for his plainness, which is not all of one kind, it is above all a rhetoric of sincerity, an art by which he may tell the truth to himself and God. The major devices are not traditional figures but psychological gestures and movements. The excesses of cheerful confidence and the defections of faith decked out as humility are given their full human voice, not as exotic monsters of thought and feeling, but as common faults "whose natures are most stealing, and beginnings uncertain," faults which are most tenacious when they are not allowed to expose themselves by speaking in their "own native tongue." Belief in the divine desire for human desire grants the human feelings an essential dignity, even in error, and encourages a vigorous freedom of expression. That freedom comes under the general laws of art, and is enlarged, not restricted, by the necessities of religious tact and discipline — as it is enlarged by realizing the complex demands of poetic form.

I propose now to offer more than a token and less than a complete demonstration of his art of plainness by drawing upon three poems: "The Temper" (I), "The Pearl," and "Death."

"The Temper" (I) begins with a declaration:

> How should I praise thee, Lord! how should my rymes
> Gladly engrave thy love in steel,
> If what my soul doth feel sometimes,
> My soul might ever feel!

And ends with a declaration:

> Whether I flie with angels, fall with dust,
> Thy hands made both, and I am there:
> Thy power and love, my love and trust
> Make one place ev'ry where.

The "plain intention" of the poem is to transform its initial attitude into its concluding one. Our best approach, I think, is from the lines in "Love" (II) where God is asked:

> And kindle in our hearts such true desires,
> As may consume our lusts, and make thee way.

Most of "The Temper" is devoted to the consuming of false love, but the kindling of true desire coincides with the opening lines of the poem, which speak in the high hortatory voice of love convinced that it is sincere and deserves to have its way. The "how should" and the "if" mark the fiction that represents real desire and invokes the conventions of literary and religious praise. Although the power and sweep of the language obscure the personal motive, which is not in the conventions of praise an illegitimate one, Herbert's characteristic exercise of religious propriety never allows personal desire to speak for the whole man without some discriminating process of clarification. "Gladly engrave thy love in steel" rings beautifully, but pretends to forget that the only standard is God's approval of the offering. The poet's desire is not absurd, but he knows that its expression is, and he compensates in the second stanza by acting out his pretentiousness. If there are forty heavens, or more, when things are right with him he can "peere" over them all. At other times "I hardly reach a score." And sometimes there is a general minus, without arithmetic: "to hell I fall." The kindling and consuming are most intense in the next three stanzas, which clarify the issues and stand apart from the first and last two stanzas. In these middle

three stanzas the excesses of pride and humility strive against each other
in images of expansion and contraction, and in the movements up and
down of actual and psychological space:

> O rack me not to such a vast extent;
>   Those distances belong to thee:
> The world's too little for thy tent,
>   A grave too big for me.

> Wilt thou meet arms with man, that thou dost stretch
>   A crumme of dust from heav'n to hell?
> Will great God measure with a wretch?
>   Shall he thy stature spell?

> O let me, when thy roof my soul hath hid,
>   O let me roost and nestle there:
> Then of a sinner thou art rid,
>   And I of hope and fear.

This last stanza (the fifth) is like the first in advancing personal desire
while paying tribute to God. We may note that the eloquence of humility
is no less moving, no less an expression of real desire, and no less wrong,
than the eloquence of pride. By now the two extremes have exhausted
each other, and some *tertium quid* must be called on to make peace. The
sixth stanza explains the emblematic title, declares acceptance of the
divine will, and advances the metaphor of music as a solution to the
problem of praise:

> Yet take thy way; for sure thy way is best:
>   Stretch or contract me, thy poore debter:
> This is but tuning of my breast,
>   To make the musick better.

And so the stanza completes the action of consuming false love by
translating the experiences of the poem into terms of acceptance which
draw a moral. The metaphor of music discovers a retroactive purpose in
the contradictions, a purpose which may also govern present and future
action. But Herbert does not stop here, for the kindling and consuming
have served "to make thee way," and the seventh stanza is the
demonstration of what can happen when way has been made for God:

> Whether I flie with angels, fall with dust,
>   Thy hands made both, and I am there:
> Thy power and love, my love and trust
>   Make one place ev'ry where.

One may perhaps describe the metaphor of music as a rational discovery which orders in a quiet, reasonable way the passionate contradictions which have been expressed. But the final stanza establishes, without reference to music, a concord that is more comprehensive. In the language of religion the difference resembles that between intellectual acceptance and entire resignation. Herbert himself might well have thought that the old, restrictive terms were consumed in order to make way for the new, and that he was himself, in a minor, personal way, copying the process by which truth had once come to light — in Augustine's summary statement: "the New Testament reveals what was concealed in the Old."[2] In "The Quip" Herbert refuses the arguments of his opponents for he has a single answer ready penned; here the arguments come from his own soul and he must work through them to reach his answer. The simple perfection of that answer cannot be anticipated but comes suddenly, and after a slight pause.

Although the final stanza may be said to express and to demonstrate religious resignation, we may approach it from the traditions of rhetoric. First, we may draw on Aristotle's point that of the three "modes of persuasion furnished by the spoken word" the most important, by and large, is "the personal goodness revealed by the speaker"; in fact, "his character may almost be called the most effective means of persuasion he possesses."[3] Christian rhetoric accepts the point and advances it; where the unity of eloquence and wisdom occurs we may assume the effective presence of inspiration as a proof of character. The chief goal of eloquence is to move, and Christian high style could be thought of as assimilating all the characteristics of the plain style, deriving its elevation primarily from the personal fervor with which the saving truth was expressed.

The last stanza will not fit into a rhetorical category of style. It is adorned and elevated, but the dominant effect is that of plainness and simplicity. The graces of art are subtle though not inscrutable; and we could point to devices not in the handbooks of rhetoric (as Augustine is pleased to note of a passage from the Book of Amos),[4] and perhaps not even in the annals of microlinguistics. But we may spare that demonstration for now. The issues of the poem are resolved in a final expression that unites beauty and truth, eloquence and wisdom. There is no point of leverage for distinguishing between what is said and the authoritative gift of being able to say it: inspiration is the proof of character. An expression as complete and as final in its way as "Thou art still my God" has emerged from a developing pattern of conflict; and although that expression can stand alone, it was created in the act of completing the poem, and it answers all the immediacies of conflict and form. It can stand alone but does not insist on its privilege, as a few ready-penned expressions make some show of doing. We may perhaps apply Herbert's metaphor of wisdom descending from above, the silk twist let down; though in "The Pearl" inspiration must precede and direct the poem in order to be present for the final confirmation. Or we may say that in "The Temper" when the poet stopped God wrote "loved" and spelled it out in a whole stanza.

Our next example is "The Pearl," a poem with a simpler argument and a basic plot — that of rejecting the ways of the world, the flesh, and the devil, each in a stanza. A final stanza explains why, clarifies the issues, confirms the character of the speaker, and in a simple statement organizes the procedures of the poem into their completed form. We find no acting out of inspiration at the end, but instead a quietly effective definition of the ways of love and understanding. In the penultimate stanza, for the sake of an ultimate plainness the poet unexpectedly elevates the plain style that has been serving him with perfect ease and variety.

The plot is basic and the formula for human temptation is the standard one, but Herbert's conception and performance are markedly fresh and individual. The temptation of the devil, as intellectual pride, he puts first. It is not a temptation at all but little more than an inventory, and not even an explicit rejection. By putting intellectual pride first but not treating it as pride, and by his casual manner and racy diction, he exhibits a surprising and witty indifference to the traditional power of that temptation. Indeed, if we do not recognize the historical issue, the first appearance of the refrain, "Yet I love thee," may seem a little forced and overemphatic. As the poem develops, and as we collect our bearings in motion, we are supposed to recognize that pride is not being located in the intellect alone but is distributed throughout all decisions involving a choice between the love of self and the love of God. In the second stanza the temptations of the world are rejected, without the dignity of a formal recognition but in the course of drawing up an inventory of the ways of honor. The casual raciness becomes intensified, and the tone advances to open mockery:

> I know the wayes of Honour, what maintains
> The quick returns of courtesie and wit:
> In vies of favours whether partie gains,
> When glorie swells the heart, and moldeth it
> To all expressions both of hand and eye,
> Which on the world a true-love-knot may tie,
> And bear the bundle, wheresoe're it goes:

> How many drammes of spirit there must be
> To sell my life unto my friends or foes:
>   Yet I love thee.

Then the third and climactic stanza presents the temptation of the flesh, the ways of pleasure. One does not expect to meet sensitively intelligent Christians who are confident that they are untempted by intellectual pride and the subtle allurements of the world; one expects even less to learn that so rare a person is frankly responsive to the appeals of pleasure:

> I know the wayes of Pleasure, the sweet strains,
> The lullings and the relishes of it;
> The propositions of hot bloud and brains;
> What mirth and musick mean; what love and wit
> Have done these twentie hundred yeares, and more:
> I know the projects of unbridled store:
> My stuffe is flesh, not brasse; my senses live,
> And grumble oft, that they have more in me
> Then he that curbs them, being but one to five:
>   Yet I love thee

These are not, to be sure, the common temptations of the flesh but reflect a refined, more philosophical, concept of pleasure — as if Herbert were revising Socrates' fable in the *Phaedrus* and attributing rebelliousness to the spirited horse of the psychic team. A twentieth-century reader might resent the antique novelty of assigning the products of culture to the ways of pleasure, but he might find some compensation in the formal emphasis on knowledge that echoes through the stanza: "mirth and musick *mean*," and the introductory expression, "I know," is used a second time only in this stanza. What is most distinctive, however, is the passionate immediacy, the full identification of the poet with the feelings expressed. The nonchalance of witty indifference abruptly disappears; and the stanza excludes, for the moment, those quantitative images of profit and loss which partly reflect the amused detachment and superiority of the speaker — the "stock and surplus," "quick returns," "gains," and "drammes of spirit." The controls of knowledge and love are not broken down, but they remain external and neither repress the feelings nor enter into their expression. As for the temptation itself, it is not considered in a formal way, but its presence and force are amply represented by the language of the speaker.

As a measure of Herbert's boldness and candor it is useful to quote an authoritative diagnosis of the symptoms and etiology of imaginative self-temptation. When, according to Augustine, the soul slackens in its powers of determination, the body will try to advance its own interests. Delighted by "corporeal forms and movements," the soul then "becomes entangled with their images which it has fixed in its memory, and is foully defiled by the fornications of the phantasy." When the soul places the end of its own good in the sensuous, it "snatches the deceptive images of corporeal things from within and combines them together by empty thought, so that nothing seems to it to be divine unless it be of such a kind as this."[5] Augustine's diagnosis, with its adaptation of Platonic and Stoic features, may describe the rebellious imagination as we see it, for instance, in "The Collar," and it may help identify an occasional lapse in Herbert's spiritual nerve, but it is remarkably irrelevant to the "corporeal forms and movements" of his third stanza. The feelings expressed there have dignity; they are immediate and real, without defilement and resulting self-hatred, and without confusions of the divine. In fact, only the ways of honor come directly under Augustine's analysis, for they are the artificial products of illusive symbolizing, the "deceptive images" patched together with "empty thought."

The first and second stanzas, we noted, resemble each other in their amused detachment. Their plain style is that of argument, which demonstrates indirectly, by witty analysis, that the major temptations do not tempt at all. The greater intensity of the second stanza by moving toward mockery increases the imaginative distance between the objects discussed and the speaker. The plain style of the last stanza will reverse that direction. It is argument, and intellectual, but not detached. Everything is drawn together, and toward the poet at the center of his experience. But the decisive change is initiated by the third stanza with its personal fervor and elevated style.

Let us compare in their relations these last two stanzas and the last two stanzas of "The Temper" (I). In that poem the penultimate stanza ("Yet take thy way; for sure thy way is best") presents an intellectual acceptance which is rather dry and detached but provides the necessary bridge to the comprehensive solution of the last stanza, which is highly charged with feeling but registers as an inspired clarification. In "The Pearl" the general procedure is the same but the parts are reversed. The conflict does not take shape until the penultimate stanza, where the climax also occurs; that stanza brings about the shift in direction from analytical distance to synthetic immediacy, as the necessary bridge to the comprehensive solution of the last stanza. In "The Pearl" it is the penultimate stanza which is elevated in style and charged with feeling. But its expression is, though intense and candid, consciously limited by the external controls of the context; it cannot speak for the whole man in the poem. Though eloquent and moving, the voice of the stanza cannot possibly bring eloquence and wisdom into the unison of a single speech. The last stanza names inspired wisdom as a presence which has governed the whole action of the poem, but which does not, as in "The Temper" (I), make a personal appearance. The clarification of love and understanding is quietly intellectual, not passionate, and includes the humble disclaimer that whatever has been accomplished by the poem was merely by following instructions:

> Yet through these labyrinths, not my groveling wit,
> But thy silk twist let down from heav'n to me,
> Did both conduct and teach me, how by it
> To climbe to thee.

In this poem there is no pause inviting God to write the last stanza; an affirming act of the intellect builds on a moment of passion, rather than the reverse. But the proof of character lies in the integration and in the poet's being at one with what he says. There has been no spectacular inspiration, but everything has been drawn together, and the silk twist which has led him through the labyrinths has brought him to the expressive center of what he concludes.

Our final example is the poem "Death," which acknowledges no conflict. The fictional pretext is a slight and transparent one: the difference between the way we used to look at death and the way we look at it now. The plot is not likely to surprise, and since there is no formal conflict the poet's own feelings do not directly participate in the action. Coming to the poem after "The Temper" (I) and "The Pearl," one is at first perhaps more conscious of the differences, but the similarities are more significant.

As in many poems that are relatively straightforward and simple in statement, Herbert invents fine devices on which the materials turn, move, and develop — as if they were proceeding by means of the more visible structures of argument, dramatic conflict, or narrative plot. Each stanza of "Death" is a kind of self-contained scene, into which the last line brings an unexpected effect. The reader is not likely to be aware that an argument is also being produced, until he encounters the open "Therefore" at the beginning of the sixth and last stanza. There are three parts of the argument, arranged in a formal diminution of 3:2:1. The first three stanzas give us the old wrong views of death, the next two corrected present views, and the conclusion is drawn in a single stanza. Let us begin with the first three:

> Death, thou wast once an uncouth hideous thing,
>   Nothing but bones,
>   The sad effect of sadder grones:
> Thy mouth was open, but thou couldst not sing.
>
> For we consider'd thee as at some six
>   Or ten yeares hence,
>   After the losse of life and sense,
> Flesh being turn'd to dust, and bones to sticks.
>
> We lookt on this side of thee, shooting short;
>   Where we did finde
>   The shells of fledge souls left behinde,
> Dry dust, which sheds no tears, but may extort.

The mementos of death are handled with remarkable verve and gaiety. Of "The Temper" (I) we could say that the intention of the poem was to transform its initial declaration into its concluding one. Here we have attitudes rather than declarations; and that strange, bluff greeting to death, though startling, original, and arbitrary, does not register at once as a "wrong" attitude asking for correction. Nevertheless, the tone is the exaggerated one of an extreme which the development of the poem will transform. If we borrow an observation from our study of "The Pearl," we may describe the speaker's opening attitude as detached and superior, as if enjoying his analytical distance from the object of his attention. In the fifth stanza the tone will be countered by an opposite extreme of immediacy and identification. Then the argument, expression, and tone of the last stanza will transform the extremes of psychic distance and immediacy into a final attitude.

The second and third stanzas drop the concentrated focus on skull, bones, and grinning jaws, and drop the harsh, summary definition of life as a music of groans, and death as the arrested image of that music. The reason now given for that hideousness is not concentrated and shocking but leisurely and general, as befits an intellectual speculation prefaced by "For we consider'd." The error in human understanding is caused by our faulty sense of time. We think in spans of six or ten years from now and judge death by its appearances then. The detachment is quietly intellectual but does not therefore eliminate some tension of divided attitude. The reader will not find that the studied casualness of rhythm, tone, and detail prevents him from considering any thought of his own

death, "some six / Or ten years hence." Furthermore, the ironic turn in
the last line of each stanza reintroduces the opportunity for personal
concern and relation: "Flesh being turn'd to dust, and bones to sticks. . . .
Dry dust, which sheds no tears, but may extort." And that beautiful
euphemism for skeletal remains, "The shells of fledge souls left behind,"
is a little too successful; we admire the imaginative act and in so doing
are reminded of the natural state of the material thus translated.

In addition to these psychological movements which endue a sense of
developing conflict, we may note the presence of significant attitudes
toward time. The first stanza greets death as it was, not once upon a time
but "once," as it was in time past. But the imaginative time of that stanza
is the feeling-present, which the shock of the image produces, in spite of
the summary intellectualizing of the cause in the immediate past and the
assertion that all of this visible effect is not what it seems to be but is
what it was "once." The assertion is left dangling as a challenge that is to
be made good, but not in the formal time of the second and third
stanzas, which does not go all the way back to the "once." The feeling-
present returns, though less emphatically, in the suggestions of personal
death and in the reference to the dust "which sheds no tears, but may
extort." Still more elusively, the sense of future time enters these stanzas.
There is an ambiguity in the "six / Or ten years hence" — depending on
whether we were considering the case of stanza one, or were considering
some case, perhaps our own, from a point in the past identical with our
consideration and extending six to ten years into the future. But since
the point in the past is not located firmly, the sense of future time is at
best weak. Similarly, the flesh and bones "being turn'd" to dust and
sticks presents us with a free composition of past, present, and future;
any single dimension of time can dominate in that formula, depending
on the formal perspective. Finally, the "fledge souls" do evoke the future
in a definite but small way; the transaction itself points ahead, and the
habits of metaphorical thought on this familiar subject move naturally
from the place "left behind" to the far future.

Everything we have considered thus far will reappear, with changes,
in the next step of the argument, which begins in the fourth stanza:

> But since our Saviours death did put some bloud
> Into thy face;
> Thou art grown fair and full of grace,
> Much in request, much sought for as a good.

The verve and gaiety continue, but now the mementos of death are
looked at from the perspective of life after death. Out of the conventions

of that perspective Herbert draws details that emphasize the imaginative nature of his presentation. The hideousness of the skull in the first stanza was the product of its appearance, our perspective, and the grotesque associations brought to bear. In the fourth stanza the perspective and associations are changed; a show of appearance is made, but the literal, physical terms are dominated by their symbolic and metaphorical meanings. The language is matter-of-fact. "But since our Saviours death did put some bloud / Into thy face," and more comforting than "Thy mouth was open, but thou couldst not sing"; but both statements are self-consciously imaginative, two opposing ways of looking at death, each an exaggeration based upon a different view of the truth. The stanza continues to emphasize its imaginative play as it moves further from the possibility of literal presentation. Both the face which is now "fair and full of grace" and the beholder's eye are altered, and the newness of the relationship is underlined by the pleasantry of "grace." The last line of the stanza draws back a little, with a kind of wry humor far gentler than the irony in each of the preceding last lines. Death is "Much in request" — as if by a change in fashion. That death is "much sought for as a good" moves the significance further from its physical base and advances the dignity of its attractiveness by the deliberate introduction language that has philosophical associations.

The "But since" which opens the fourth stanza is the sign both of argument and of time. Though the dominant time-sense is present it is derived from the Savior's act in the past and lightly suggests the future in "sought for as a good." The sense of the present, however, is not *felt* as in the first stanza but serves mostly as a kind of intellectual transition to the strong present of the fifth stanza. Finally, to touch again on the point of imaginative distance: the fourth stanza maintains a distinctive kind of detachment, because of its intellectualized emphasis on the metaphorical and the witty.

The fifth stanza completes the corrected view of death, bringing the poem to a sudden climax:

> For we do now behold thee gay and glad,
>   As at dooms-day;
>   When souls shall wear their new aray,
> And all thy bones with beautie shall be clad.

Each of the first three stanzas presents a thesis abruptly at the beginning and then makes additional points to tighten and complicate the scene. In the fourth and fifth stanzas the thought requires the whole four lines for its development, and in the fifth stanza rises to a declarative climax in the last line, reversing the established ironic twist of the first three stanzas and the mildly humorous withdrawal of the fourth. More important, all of the motions of detachment, all of the varieties of analytical distance in the poem are reversed in the sudden rush of imaginative immediacy.

The developing attitudes toward time are also brought to a climax, but the details are more involved and cannot be seen without analysis. Let me summarize briefly. In the first three stanzas the formal time was past, the finished past of "once" in the first stanza and a less definite, recent past in the second and third stanzas. But in the first a sense of the feeling-present dominates; in the second and third present and future both enter, but elusively. In the fourth stanza a similar blend occurs, though the formal time is present. But when we come to the fifth stanza, suddenly there is no sense of the past. The present dominates but draws its intensity from a prophetic vision of the future. That future comes into the poem strongly and positively at this one point, and fully answers the finished past of stanza one. Since that future is imagined as intensely present, the effect is a formal reply to the feeling-present of stanza one.

These answers composed of the oppositions of time and the opposi- tions of psychic direction are not conclusive. A quiet "Therefore" converts their striking emphasis into mere transition, as if the real answer has been waiting for the commotion to subside:

> Therefore we can go die as sleep, and trust
> Half that we have
> Unto an honest faithfull grave;
> Making our pillows either down, or dust.

Now the time is wholly present: it is the unique product of imagined past and future, but emerging also from the varying stresses on the present which have been drawn like a thread through the labyrinth to this open place. As for either analytical detachment from death or imaginative identification — the final attitude rejects the terms of the contradiction, but draws an essential indifference from detachment and an essential acceptance from identification. The human present of the last stanza copies the calm of eternity, into which no agitations of past or future intrude. Death is not an alien object exciting mixed emotions, nor a lover to be sought and embraced. The imagination of the poem has made death familiar and neutral; it can have no place even in dreams when it has been made subject to a common, everyday idiom which says, "we can go die."

The activity of the mind is less prominent than in the conclusion of

"The Pearl," but as in that poem an affirming act of the intellect quietly builds on a moment of passion, and the mind that dismisses itself has demonstrated the power and clarity of its self-possession. There is no pause, as in "The Temper" (I), inviting God to write the last stanza. The spectacular inspiration comes in the prophetic vision of doomsday, which is followed by the rarest kind of personal clarity, casual and laconic, as if inspiration were part of the everyday order and could be taken for granted. The final state of simplicity is not one of reduced but of alert, refined consciousness. One sign is the attitude toward the body, which is no less than "Half that we have." And even more remarkable than calling the grave "honest" and "faithfull" is doing so with the air of not saying anything unusual. As in "The Pearl," the excited elevation of style in the penultimate stanza is followed by an authoritative descent to the plain style. In "Death" it is an assimilative plain style, confidently challenging comparison with the height of the preceding stanza. The power of that plain style lies in the passion excluded, in the resistance mastered, and in the deliberate grace of saying difficult things with ease. The grandeur and force of the high style are achieved while talking in an off-hand, humble manner in the common imagery of going to bed. An enlightened rhetorician would observe that this plain style does not austerely reject ornament, which may persuade but must first provide esthetic pleasure. He would add, I am sure, that these graces of style are so natural and fine as to seem in the very grain. The last line, "Making our pillows either down, or dust," awakens a delicate echo of the earlier ironies, as a farewell touch of recognition. And the order of "die as sleep" is beautifully reversed and balanced by "down, or dust."

I shall end by introducing another viewpoint for a moment. In reading Donne Coleridge described the delight of "tracing the leading thought thro'out the whole," by means of which "you merge yourself in the author, you *become He*."[6] Herbert he declares to be "a true poet, but a poet *sui generis*, the merits of whose poems will never be felt without a sympathy with the mind and character of the man." A true poet who requires a conscious act of sympathy would seem to have a different and lesser merit than the poet who compels you to *"become He."* Coleridge justly admires Herbert's diction, "than which nothing can be more pure, manly, and unaffected." But some of the thoughts are "quaint," and he does not try to follow a leading thought throughout. Identifying oneself with the author would seem to be a modern extension of the most important mode of rhetorical persuasion, "the personal goodness revealed by the speaker" in ancient rhetoric, or the inspired unity of wisdom and eloquence in Christian rhetoric. The merits of identifying oneself with the poet are debatable. But we can draw two firm points from Coleridge's remarks. First, it is clear that Herbert is a master who draws a leading thought through authentic obstacles which both test and refine the ultimate expression of that thought. Secondly, the rhetorical proof of character lies in the poet's convincing demonstrations that *he* becomes what he says, that the flow and shape of his words lead to a unity of eloquence and wisdom, and that he is at the expressive center of what he concludes.

It is tempting to end here, adding only that there are many true poets but few masters of this art of plainness. But it may be well to back up and remember that Herbert's art of plainness is an art and not a summary feature. If we have touched on the essential quality, good; but we can no more do without a full apparatus for understanding his art than he could write poems by plainly saying "Thou art still my God."

THE RE-INVENTED POEM:
GEORGE HERBERT'S ALTERNATIVES

Helen Vendler

One of the particular virtues of Herbert's poetry is its extremely provisional quality. His poems are ready at any moment to change direction or to modify attitudes. Even between the title and the first line, Herbert may rethink his position. There are lines in which the nominal experiences or subjects have suffered a sea-change, so that the poem we think we are reading turns into something quite other. The more extreme cases occur, of course, in Herbert's "surprise endings," what Valentina Poggi calls his "final twist,"[1] where, as Arnold Stein says, Herbert "dismisses the structure, issues, and method" of the entire poem, "rejecting the established terms" on which the poem has been constructed, as he does in "Clasping of Hands," which ends, after playing for nineteen lines on the notions of "thine" and "mine," with the exclamation, "Or rather make no Thine and Mine!"[2] In cases less abrupt, Herbert's fluid music lulls our questions: we scarcely see his oddities, or if we see them, they cease to seem odd, robed as they are in the seamless garment of his cadence. When in "Vertue," he breathes, "Sweet rose," we echo, "sweet rose," and never stop to think that nothing in the description he gives us of the rose — that it is angry in hue, that it pricks the eye of the rash beholder, that its root is ever in the grave — bears out the epithet "sweet." Is the stanza about a sweet rose, as the epithet would have us believe, or about a bitter rose? This is a minor example of Herbert's immediate critique of his own clichés ("The Collar" may serve us as a major example) and poses, in little, the problem of this essay: how can we give an accurate description of

Reprinted from *Forms of Lyric: Selected Papers from the English Institute*, ed. Reuben Brower (New York: Columbia University Press, 1970), pp. 19-45, by permission of the author and the publisher. This essay appears in a revised form in *The Poetry of George Herbert* (Cambridge, Mass.: Harvard University Press, 1975), pp. 25-56.

Herbert's constantly self-critical poems, which so often reject premises
as soon as they are established?

Herbert's willingness to abolish his primary terms of reference or his
primary emotion at the last possible moment speaks for his continually
provisional conduct of the poem. After begging, for twenty lines, for
God's grace to drop from above, Herbert suddenly reflects that there is,
after all, another solution, equally good: if God will not descend to him,
he may be brought to ascend to God:

> O come! for thou dost know the way:
> Or if to me thou wilt not move,
> Remove me, where I need not say,
> *Drop from above.*   ("Grace")

In part, this is simply the cleverness of finding a way out of a dilemma;
but more truly, in Herbert's case, the ever-present alternative springs
from his conviction that God's ways are not his ways — "I cannot skill of
these thy wayes." If man insists on one way — that his God, for instance,
drop grace on him — it is almost self-evident that God may have a
different way in store to grant the request, and Herbert bends his mind
to imagining what it might be — in this case, that God, instead of
moving himself, should *re*move Herbert. The pun in the "solution"
shows verbally the pairing of alternatives to accomplish the same object.
Precision is all, and when Herbert catches himself in careless speech, he
turns on himself with a vengeance. In "Giddinesse," human beings are
reproved for fickleness, and God is asked, first, to "mend" us; but no, we
are beyond mending, and so Herbert must ask God to "make" us anew;
but no, one creation will not suffice — God will have to "re-make" us
daily, since we sin daily:

> Lord, *mend*
> or rather *make* us; one creation/Will not suffice our turn;
> Except thou *make us dayly*, we shall spurn
> Our own salvation.

Equally, when Herbert finds himself lapsing into frigid pulpit oratory,
he pulls himself up sharply from his clichés about "Man" and in the last
breath turns inward, "My God, I mean myself." These second thoughts
are everywhere in Herbert. The wanton lover, he says, can expend
himself ceaselessly in praising his beloved; why does not the poet do the
same for God? "Lord, cleare thy gift," he asks in "Dulnesse," "that with a
constant wit/ I may —" May what? we ask, and if we continue the
analogy we would say, "That I may love and praise thee as lovers their

mistresses." Something like this must have passed through Herbert's mind, and have been rejected as overweening, so that instead he writes:

> Lord, cleare thy gift, that with a constant wit
> I may but look towards thee:
> *Look* only; for to *love* thee, who can be,
> What angel fit?

The italics on "look" and "love" show Herbert, as it were, doing the revision of his poem in public, substituting the tentative alternative for the complacent one. He takes into account our expectation, prompted by his analogy with lovers, of the word "love," and rebukes himself and us for daring to ask such a divine gift. The proper reading of the poem must realize both the silent expectation and the rebuke, as Herbert changes his mind at the last moment.

Some of Herbert's most marked and beautiful effects come from this constant re-invention of his way. One of the most spectacular of these occurs in "A True Hymne": Herbert has been praising the faithful heart over the instructed wit, and says:

> The fineness which a hymne or psalme affords,
> Is, when the soul unto the lines accords.
>
> ... If th'heart be moved,
> Although the verse be somewhat scant,
> God doth supply the want.

He then gives us an example of God's supplying the want:

> As, when th'heart sayes (sighing to be approved)
> *O, could I love!* and stops: God writeth —

Logically, what God should write to reassure the soul, is *Thou dost love*. To wish to love is to love; but to love God, Herbert bethinks himself, is first to have been loved by God, (as he tells us in the first "Affliction") and so God, instead of ratifying the soul's wish, *O could I love!* by changing it from the optative to the declarative, changes instead the soul from subject to object, and writes *Loved*. If we do not intuit, as in "Dulnesse," the "logical" ending *Thou dost love*, we cannot see how Herbert has refused a banal logic in favor of a truer metaphysical illogic, conceived of at the last possible utterance of the poem. He stops in his course, veers round, writes *Loved*, and ends the poem in what is at once a better pride and a better humility.

What does this mean about Herbert's mind, this rethinking of the poem at every moment? It means that he allows his moods free play and knows that logic is fallible: one may want one thing today and quite another on the Last Day, for instance. When Herbert is tormented in turn by the jeering of worldly Beauty, Money, Glory, and Wit, he remains silent, but says in his heart that on the Last Day he will be revenged, when his God will answer his tormentors for him: "But thou shalt answer, Lord, for me." And yet, as soon as he truly thinks of that scene on the Last Day, he re-invents it: the last stanza of "The Quip" shows Herbert's God, not vindicating at large the now-triumphant soul, not administering an anathema to the defeated worldly glories, but engaging in an almost silent colloquy alone with the faithful soul:

> Yet when the houre of thy designe
> To answer these fine things shall come;
> Speak not at large; say, I am thine:
> And then they have their answer home.

When we hear, in "Love Unknown," of God's wishes for Herbert (which of course amount to Herbert's best wishes for himself) we learn that "Each day, each houre, each moment of the week,/ [He] fain would have [him] be new, tender, quick." Nothing is to be taken for granted, nothing should be habitual, nothing should be predictable: every day, every hour, every moment things have to be thought through again, and the surface of the heart must be renewed, quickened, mended, suppled.

An accurate description of Herbert's work implies a recognition of where his true originality lies. A few years ago this was the subject of some debate between William Empson and Rosemond Tuve, when Empson claimed as "original" images which Miss Tuve proved traditional in iconographic usage. Empson retorted that traditional images could nevertheless bear a significant unconscious meaning, and that choice of image in itself was indicative, a statement which deserves more attention. The attic of "tradition" is plundered differently by differnt poets, and each poet decides what décor he will choose from the Christian storehouse in order to deck his stanzas. Though every single image in a poem may be "traditional," the choice of emphasis and exclusion is individual and revealing. Herbert, of course, often begins poems with, or bases poems upon, a traditional image or scene or prayer or liturgical act or biblical quotation; and our knowledge of these bases has been deepened by Miss Tuve's book. But a question crying out to be answered is what he makes of the traditional base. A similar question would ask what he does with the experiential *donnée*, personal rather than "traditional," of an autobiographical poem. In short, what are some of Herbert's characteristic ways of "conducting" a poem? My answer, in general, appears in my title, and in the examples I have so far offered: Herbert "re-invents" the poem afresh as he goes along; he is constantly criticizing what he has already written down, and finding the original conception inadequate, whether the original conception be the Church's, the Bible's, or his own. Nothing is exempt from his critical eye, when he is at his best, and there is almost no cliché of religious expression or personal experience that he does not reject after being tempted into expressing it. A poem by Herbert is often "written" three times over, with several different, successive, and self-contradictory versions co-existing. A different sort of poet would have written one version, have felt dissatisfied with the truth or accuracy of the account, would then have written a second, more satisfactory version, have rethought that stage, and have produced at last a "truthful" poem. Herbert prefers to let his successive "re-thinkings" and re-inventions follow one another, but without warning us of the discrepancies among his several accounts, just as he followed his original qualification of the rose as sweet with a long description of the rose as bitter, without any of the usual "buts" or "yets" of semantic contradiction. (I should add that the evidence we have in the Williams manuscript, which gives Herbert's revisions of some poems, supports these conjectures on Herbert's rethinking of his lines, but what I wish to emphasize is not his revisions before he reached a final version but rather the re-invention of the poem as it unfolds itself.)

The rest of this essay will be concerned with larger examples of Herbert's re-inventing of different sorts; and I begin with a combination of the liturgical, the ethical, and the biblical, in the poem called "The Invitation." In this poem, Herbert the priest is inviting sinners to the sacraments. He is probably remembering, in the beginning, St. Paul's statement (in Romans 14:21) that it is good neither to eat flesh nor to drink wine, and he begins his invitation with the Pauline view of sinners as prodigal gluttons and winebibbers, whose taste is their waste, and who are defined by wine:

> Come ye hither All, whose taste
>   Is your waste;
> Save your cost, and mend your fare.
>   . . .
> Come ye hither All, whom wine
>   Doth define,
> Naming you not to your good.

For Herbert, though, St. Paul's revulsion is not congenial; Herbert, who "knows the ways of pleasure" and knows as well the pains of remorse, begins to alter his portrait of swinish and sensual sinners in a remarkable

way. In the third stanza, the sinners become "All, whom pain/ Doth
arraigne"; in the fourth stanza they are people who are misled by their
delight to graze outside their bounds; and by the astonishing fifth stanza
the sinners are positively seraphic:

> Come ye hither All, whose love
>   Is your dove,
> And exalts you to the skie:
> Here is love, which having breath
>   Ev'n in death,
> After death can never die.

Sinners, in fact, are finally seen in the poem as people with all the right
instincts — they want joy, delight, exaltation, and love; and that,
Herbert implies, is what the redeemed want too. The sinners, misled in
their desires, seek the carnal and the temporary, Venus' doves instead of
the Holy Spirit, sky instead of heaven. The equation of wants in saints
and sinners permits Herbert's final startling stanza:

> Lord, I have invited all ...
> For it seems but just and right
>   In my sight,
> Where is All, there All should be.

The liturgical "dignum et justum est" and the verbally indistinguishable
"All's" (both capitalized) give the sinners a final redeemed and almost
divine place at the banquet. The poem amounts, though implicitly, to a
total critique of the usual scorn toward sinners, a scorn which Herbert
himself began with, but which in the course of the poem he silently
rejects. He makes no announcement of his rejection as he changes his
view, and therefore we are likely to miss it, as we miss other changes of
mind in his poems. Nevertheless, over and over, Herbert re-invents what
he has received and embraced, correcting it to suit his own corrected
notions of reality.[3]

Our received notion of Doomsday, for instance, is a severe one, the
Dies Irae when the whole world, as Herbert says elsewhere, will turn to
coal. That day is sometimes thought of from God's point of view, as
when we say, "He shall come to judge the living and the dead," or from
the human point of view (as when St. Paul says, "We shall be changed,
be raised incorruptible"), but Herbert chooses to think of it via the
fanciful construct of the emotions felt by the bodies already-dead-but-
not-yet-raised, unhappy in their posthumous insensibility, imprison-
ment, noisomeness, fragmentation, and decay. The "fancy" behind the
poem is that it is not so much God who awaits the Last Day, nor is it

those on earth who wish to put on immortality, nor is it the disembodied souls in heaven, but rather it is those poor soulless corrupting bodies confined in their graves. It is they who really yearn after a lively and sociable Judgment Day, when they can each "jog the other, each one whispring, *Live you, brother?*" A poem like this begins with a poet thinking not "What are the traditions about Doomsday?" but rather, "I know what is usually said about Doomsday, but what would it really be like, and who really longs for it?" Herbert's poem is very different from Donne's more conventional "At the round earth's imagined corners, blow/ Your trumpets, Angels, and arise, arise/ From death, you numberless infinities/ Of souls," a poem in which we at once recognize the Doomsday conventions at work.

Herbert's corrections extend, of course, to himself as well as to his liturgical or biblical sources, and these self-corrections are his most interesting re-inventions. Some of them do not at first sight seem personal, and since these are rather deceptive, I should like to begin with one of them — his self-correction in the sonnet "Prayer." This famous poem is impersonally phrased, and is, as everyone knows, a definition poem consisting of a chain of metaphors describing prayer. "Rethinking" is in fact most likely to occur in ordinary life in just this sort of definition-attempt, but whereas in life this rethinking and refining is generally an exercise in intellectual precision, in Herbert it is an exercise in the affections. Herbert's images cannot be said to be ambiguous; they are, though sometimes recondite, in general perfectly clear. It is the whole which is complex, a something (prayer, in this instance) which can be any number of things, not only at different times, but even at once. This tolerance of several notions at once appeals to us in Herbert nowadays, just as his profusion of images appeals. As Rosemond Tuve pointed out in *Elizabethan and Metaphysical Imagery*, an attempt to make clear the logical actions or passions of a subject will all by itself engender images, as it does in "Prayer." These twenty-six or so images of prayer tell us several things. To begin with the easiest, we know the sort of prayer which is an engine against the Almighty, which reverses the Jovian thunderbolt and hurls it back at its source. It is not too much to call this the prayer of resentment uttered by the wounded soul; it is the sinner's tower (with overtones of Babel) raised against a seemingly unjust God. We have any number of these "rebellious" prayers in the Herbert canon. To pray in this indignant warlike way is scarcely a sign of perfection; it is an emanation of the lowest possible state above the outright rebellion of sin. The next easiest group of images in the poem, by all odds, is the group toward the end — the Milkie Way, the Bird of Paradise, the Land of Spices. When prayer seems like this to the soul,

the soul is clearly experiencing an unearthly level of feeling quite
without aggressive elements. The poem, then, arrives at this state of joy
from an earlier state of anger and rebellion; so much is clear as soon as
we assume a single consciousness behind the metaphors of the poem.
But what, then, are we to make of the beginning of the poem, which
seems neither aggressive nor exalted?

> Prayer, the Churches banquet, Angels age,
>   God's breath in man returning to his birth,
>   The soul in paraphrase, heart in pilgrimage,
> The Christian plummet sounding heav'n and earth.

In what state is the soul when it speaks these lines? It must be a state
which precedes the sudden rise of injured "virtue" in the use of engines
and thunderbolts and spears against God; it is certainly not the heavenly
state of the sestet. These lines which begin the sonnet are, in fact, without
affect; they are the lines of the man who sets himself to pray frigidly, out
of duty, drawing his metaphors not from feeling but from doctrine.
What has he been taught, theologically, in dogma, about prayer? That it
is the banquet of the church, that angels determine their age by how long
they have been praying, that it engages both the heart and the soul, that
it is "the Christian plummet" connecting the church militant to the
church triumphant. When, from these artificialities, the speaker turns to
his own feelings and takes stock of his own state and lapses into his own
resentment, the poem takes on human reality: what, thinks Herbert,
aside from these stock phrases, is prayer really? to me? now? A weapon,
a spear, against the God who cripples my projects and cross-biasses me;
and the aggressive images multiply. But that weapon (in the traditional
image on which the entire poem hinges), by piercing Christ's side,
initiates a countermovement, not of Jovian thunder this time but of
grace, an infusion transforming the workaday world into the Sabbath
(or rather, a transposing not a transforming, says Herbert with his usual
precision; we are not changed but glorified). Whereas earlier the man
praying had been active, launching engines, building towers, piercing
with spears, he now relaxes in an ecstasy of passivity; prayer becomes a
constellation of experienced essences, "softness and peace and joy and
love and bliss." But Herbert cannot rest in that passivity of sensation;
with a remarkable energy he introduces, again just as the poem is about
to end in its celestial geography, the hitherto neglected intellect. Prayer,
he says, correcting his delighted repose, is in the last analysis not simply
a *datum*, something given, but a *comprehensum*, something understood. This phrase is at once the least and the most explicit in the poem.
Finally the poet understands, and is no longer the frigid reciter of

theological clichés, the resentful beggar, the aggressive hurler of thunderbolts, the grateful receiver of Manna, nor the seeker of a Land of Spices. As a final definition, "something understood" abolishes or expunges the need for explanatory metaphors. Metaphor, Herbert seems to say, is after all only an approximation; once something is understood, we can fall silent; once the successive rethinkings of the definition have been made, and the truth has been arrived at, the poem is over.

To arrive at that truth, to be able to end the poem, is often difficult. "The Temper" (I) has to try three different endings before it succeeds in ending itself satisfactorily, or at least to Herbert's satisfaction. He has complained that God is stretching him too hard, subjecting him to exaltations succeeded by depressions:

> O rack me not to such a vast extent!
> Those distances belong to thee.

God's stretching and then contracting him suggests to Herbert another image, not this time the rack but another image of equal tension, introduced with a characteristic concessive "yet" —

> Yet take thy way; for sure thy way is best:
> Stretch or contract me, thy poore debter:
> This is but tuning of my breast,
> To make the musick better.

If Herbert had been content (as he sometimes could be) with resolution on an easy level, there it was. Herbert's pain does not diminish, but he has found a new vision of God to explain it by: God is no longer the inquisitor torturing his victim on the rack; he is rather the temperer, the tuner of Herbert's heartstrings. The ending is adequate enough, and in fact Herbert's unknown adapter of 1697 stopped here, deleting Herbert's final stanza: to him the poem was finished, since Herbert had rediscovered the true "corrective" meaning of suffering.[4] But for Herbert the poem was not finished. The image of tuning still adhered to the poem's original primitive and anthropocentric notion of being stretched, of being first lifted by God to heaven and then dashed to earth. From a more celestial point of view, of course, heaven and earth are equally in God's presence and of his making, so Herbert repents of his shortsightedness, and invents a brilliant coda to his poem, expunging all its former terms of spatial reference:

> Whether I flie with angels, fall with dust,
> Thy hands made both, and I am there.

The compact use of the one adverb — "there" — to stand for two places, heaven and earth, because both were made by God's hands, seems yet another final resolution of the distances in the poem. Still, Herbert is not satisfied. He continues with what seems at first to be a reiteration; we expect him to say that God's power makes everywhere, heaven and earth alike, one place. Instead, he says the reverse:

> Thy power and love, my love and trust,
> Make one place everywhere.

In short, Herbert first rewrote racking as tuning, then he rewrote distance as unity ("there"), and then he rewrote unity ("one place") as immensity ("everywhere"). We should not forget that he was rewriting at the same time the cause of this transformation: at first everything was his God's doing, but at the penultimate line the change becomes a cooperative act in which two loves intersect, and God's power is conjoined with man's trust.

In addition to correcting himself, whether in the impersonal terms of "Prayer" or in the terms of repeated experience in "The Temper," Herbert corrects his autobiography, as usual not flaunting his re-inventions. They are for us usually the discoveries of a second reading, since at first we take them wholly for granted. The blandness of most critical paraphrase of Herbert indicates that readers have been misled by the perfect grace of the finished poem, and have concluded that an uninterrupted cadence means an uninterrupted ripple of thought. Herbert knew better: he said his thoughts were all a case of knives. The wounds of those knives are clearest in the autobiographical poems, those three great statements — "Affliction" (I), "The Flower," and "The Forerunners." In "The Forerunners," the simplest of the three, Herbert complains that in age he is losing his poetic powers, and he offers several alternative explanations of the loss, which a more anxious poet would be at pains to reconcile with each other. Herbert simply lets them stand; truth, not coherence, is his object. First, the harbingers of age come and evict his "sparkling notions," who are of course guiltless since they are forcibly "disparked." They and Herbert suffer together. Next it seems as though the "sweet phrases, lovely metaphors," are not being evicted but are leaving of their own free will; echoing Wyatt, Herbert asks reproachfully, "But will ye leave me thus:" accusing them of ingratitude after all his care of them. Next, they are no longer ungrateful children leaving home but rather fully of age, seduced virgins: "Has some fond lover tic'd thee to thy bane?" Finally, they are debased, willingly prostituting themselves in the service of the lover who loves dung, and, in Herbert's last bitterness, even their essence and power are denied them. They are no longer creative "enchanting" forces but only "embellishments" of meaning. There is no resolution to these successive metaphors of loss — no comprehensive view is taken at the end, and we suffer with Herbert the final pretended repudiation of those servants who have in fact deserted him. His powerful love of his "beauteous words" has its own independent force within the poem, but so does his gloomy denial of value to those words at the end. The only true critical description of poems such as this must be a successive one; a global description is bound to be misleading.

"Affliction" (I) is too long a poem to be taken up in detail here, but it, like "The Forerunners," depends on a series of inconsistent metaphors for a single phenomenon, God's treatment of his creature. Herbert's ingenuity is matched only by his frankness. His God is at first a seducer, "enticing" Herbert's heart; next he is a sovereign distributing "gracious benefits," then an enchanter "bewitching" Herbert into his family; he is an honest wage-paying master; he is a king dispensing hope of high pleasure; he is a mother, indulgent:

> At first thou gav'st me milk and sweetnesses;
> I had my wish and way.

But then God becomes one who inflicts sickness, and the poet groans with the psalmist, "Sicknesses cleave my bones." Worse, God becomes a murderer — "Thou took'st away my life" — and an unfair murderer at that, leaving his creature with no means of suitably vengeful retaliation — "A blunted knife/ Was of more use than I." God sends famine, and Herbert becomes one of Pharaoh's lean kine: "Thus thinne and lean without a fence or friend,/ I was blown through with ev'ry storm and winde." In two lines of sinister genius, God is said to "betray" Herbert to paralysis (a "lingring" book) and death (he "wraps" Herbert in an unmistakably shroudlike gown). Next, God becomes a physician, deluding Herbert with his "sweetned pill," but then cruelly undoing his own healing, he "throws" Herbert into more sicknesses. God's last action seems his wickedest, surpassing all his previous enticements and tortures; he "clean forgets" his poet, and the abandonment is worse than the attention. These indictments of God are only one strain in this complaint, with its personal hesitations, accusations, self-justifications, and remorse, but they show Herbert's care and accuracy in describing his own notions of God as they changed from episode to episode. There is a remarkable lack of censorship; even with the Psalms as precedent, Herbert shows his absolute willingness to say how things were, to choose the accurate verb, to follow the truth of feeling. We can only guess at Herbert's inconsistencies of self-esteem which underlie the inconsistencies in this portrait of God. This God, changeable as the skies, first lightning then love and then lightning again, is reflected from a self first proud then craven and then proud again, a self which does not know whether it is a child or a victim or a dupe, a self for whom all self-assertion provoked a backwash of guilt.

With that guilt came a sense of God's absence, and that experience, habitual with Herbert, is the central topic of the third of these autobiographical poems, "The Flower." Just as the sonnet "Prayer" had redefined, over and over, with increasing approximation to the truth, what prayer is, so "The Flower" redefines, over and over, with increasing approximation to the truth, what has in fact been happening to Herbert. We are told that he has suffered a period of God's disfavor, during which he drooped, but that God has now returned to him and so he flourishes once again. This simple two-stage event could have been told, presumably, in a simple chronological account; but no, we are given several versions of the experience undergone. It is this repetitiveness, incidentally, here and elsewhere in Herbert, which caused George Herbert Palmer to class this poem together with others as redundant, lacking that fineness of structure he saw in Herbert's simpler two-part and three-part poems.[5] The redundancy is apparent, but not real; each time the experience is redescribed, it is altered, and each retelling is a critique of the one before.

The first version of Herbert's experience is a syntactically impersonal one, told without the "I": Herbert could be meditating on some universally known phenomenon:

> How fresh, O Lord, how sweet and clean
> Are thy returns! ev'n as the flowers in spring;
> To which, besides their own demean,
> The late-past frosts tributes of pleasure bring.
> Grief melts away
> Like snow in May
> As if there were no such cold thing.

Now these last three lines say something not strictly true. We do keep a memory of grief. But in the first flush of reconciliation, Herbert generously says that God has obliterated all past grief in the soul. This version of the incident also says that God has been absent and has now returned, just as spring absents itself and then returns, in a natural cyclical process. We, and Herbert, shall discover in the course of the poem how untrue these statements, about the cyclical absence of God and the obliteration of grief, are.

The second stanza gives us yet another, and almost equally rosy, view of Herbert's experience, this time in the first person:

> Who would have thought my shrivel'd heart
> Could have recover'd greennesse? It was gone
> Quite under ground; as flowers depart
> To see their mother-root, when they have blown;
> Where they together,
> All the hard weather
> Dead to the world, keep house unknown.

Here the period of grief is represented as, after all, not so difficult; it was not God who went away, really, but rather Herbert; and his absence was on the whole cosy, like the winter hibernation of bulbs, where the flowers, in comfortable company, visiting their mother the root, keep house together with her, while the weather is harsh aboveground. This certainly does not sound like a description of grief, but like a situation of sociable comfort; the only ominous word here, keeping us in touch with the truth, is "shrivel'd," which sorts very ill with the familial underground housekeeping.

So far, a cloak of palliation lies over the truth. But when Herbert has to summarize what this experience of grief followed by joy has taught him, he admits that he finds the God who lies behind such alternations of emotion an arbitrary and incomprehensible one, who one day kills (a far cry from absenting himself) and another day quickens, all by a word, an absolute fiat. We are helpless to predict God's actions or to describe his intent; we await, defenseless, his unintelligible decisions, his arbitrary power:

> These are thy wonders, Lord of power,
> Killing and quickning, bringing down to hell
> And up to heaven in an houre;
> Making a chiming of a passing-bell.
> We say amisse,
> This or that is:
> Thy word is all, if we could spell.

An early anthologist of Herbert cut off the poem here,[6] for him, and we may suspect for George Herbert Palmer, too, the poem might just as well have ended with this summarizing stanza. For Herbert, it could not; he has presented us with too many contradictions. Does God absent himself cyclically, like the spring, or arbitrarily and unpredictably? Is God only benevolent, or in fact a malevolent killer as well? Was it he that was absent, or Herbert? Was the period of absence one of hellish grief or one of sociable retirement? The poem had begun in earthly joy, but now, with the admission that we cannot spell and that God's word is arbitrary and incomprehensible, Herbert's resentment of his earthly condition has gained the ascendancy, and he repudiates wholly the endless emotional cycles of mortal life:

> O that I once past changing were,
> Fast in thy Paradise, where no flower can wither!

Not God's changeableness, but his own, is now the issue; the "withering" and "shriveling" are now uppermost in his mind, as his past grief, tenacious in memory and not at all melted away, comes once again to his mind.

Yet once more, for the fourth time, he recapitulates his experience. This time he does it in the habitual mode, the present tense of habit, emphasizing its deadly repetitiveness:

> Many a spring I shoot up fair,
> Offring at heav'n, growing and groning thither....

> But while I grow in a straight line,
> Still upwards bent, as if heav'n were mine own,
> Thy anger comes, and I decline.

This habitual recapitulation leads Herbert to realize that his God's actions are in fact not arbitrary, as he had earlier proposed, but that his punishments come for a reason: Herbert has been presumptuous in growing upwards as if Heaven were his own, and therefore he has drawn God's terrible cold wrath upon him. We must stop to ask whether this confession of guilt on Herbert's part is in fact a realization or an invention. The intolerable notion of an arbitrary and occasionally malevolent God almost necessitates the invention of a human fault to explain these punishments. That is Herbert's dilemma; either he is guilty, and therefore deservedly punished, or he is innocent, and God is arbitrary. Faced with such a choice, he decides for his own guilt. We cannot miss the tentative sexuality of his "budding" and "shooting up" and later "swelling" — one question the poem puts is whether such self-assertion can ever be guiltless, or whether every swelling is followed by a punishing shriveling. The answer of the poem is equivocal; his present "budding" seems innocent enough, but the inevitable alternation of spring and winter in the poem, of spring showers and icy frowns, tells us that we may always expect God's wrath. When that wrath directs itself upon the sinner,

> What frost to that? What pole is not the zone
>   Where all things burn,
>   When thou dost turn,
> And the least frown of thine is shown?

There is no more talk about keeping house snugly underground through all the hard weather. Herbert, on the contrary, has been nakedly exposed to the hard weather, has felt the freezing cold, has felt the tempests of God. The truth is out; he *has* suffered, and he still remembers his grief. Oddly, once the truth is out, Herbert has no more wish to reproach his God; he feels happier considering himself as guilty than indicting God. It is not God, he says, who is arbitrary and capricious, but we; his actions only follow ours; he is changeless, and we are the changeable ones. Herbert, having put off the old man, scarcely recognizes himself in the new man he has become:

> And now in age I bud again;
> After so many deaths I live and write;
> I once more smell the dew and rain,
> And relish versing: O my only light,
>   It cannot be
>   That I am he
> On whom thy tempests fell all night.

In the unearthly relief of this stanza, Herbert returns to the human norm. His two constant temptations are to be an angel or a plant, but the second half of "The Flower," like the second half of "Prayer," is the discovery of human truth after the self-deceptive first half. With the unforced expression of relief, Herbert can acknowledge that in truth he was not comfortably visiting underground, but was in fact being beaten by tempests. The paradisal experience of "budding again," like any paradisal experience in life, is in fact forfeit if the reality of past grief is denied: the sharpened senses that once more smell the dew and rain are those of a Lazarus newly emerged from the sepulchre; to deny the cerements is to deny the resurrection. At this point, Herbert can engage in genuine "wonder." The previous "These are thy wonders, Lord of power," may be translated "These are thy tyrannies," but now that Herbert has assuaged his anxiety by deciding that power is not arbitrary and perverse but rather solicitous and redemptive, he can say, "These are thy wonders, Lord of love." The poem is one of perfect symmetry, marked by the two poles of "wonder"; it is redundant, if one wishes to call it that, in circling back again and again to the same experience, but each time it puts that experience differently.

The end of the poem embodies yet another self-reproof on Herbert's part, put this time as a warning to all who, like himself, may have been presumptuous in thinking heaven their own:

> These are thy wonders, Lord of love,
>   To make us see we are but flowers that glide:
>   Which, when we once can finde and prove,
>   Thou hast a garden for us, where to bide.
>   Who would be more,
>   Swelling through store,
>   Forfeit their Paradise by their pride.

This homiletic neatness is probably a flaw in the poem, and the very harsh judgment which Herbert passes, in this impersonal and universal way, on his earlier presumption makes this one of the comparatively rare Herbert poems with an "unhappy" ending. Since the fundamental experience of the poem is one of resurrection, and since the best lines of the poem express that sense of renewal, we may reasonably ask why these last lines are so grim. They are so, I think, because of the two truths of experience at war in the poem. One is the immediate truth of renewal and rebirth; the other is the remoter, but larger, truth of repeated self-assertion, repeated guilt, repeated punishment. Until we are "fast in Paradise," the poem tells us, we are caught in the variability of mortal life, in which, however intense renewal may be when it comes, it comes uncertainly and not for long. Intellectually, the prospect is depressing, with innocence and relish spoiled by guilt and punishment. The hell of life may continue into a hell after life. But this, since it is an intellectual conclusion, cannot fundamentally damage the wonderful sense of restored life which has made this poem famous. It speaks, however, for Herbert's grim fidelity to fact that he will not submerge the gloomy truth in the springlike experience.

The inveterate human tendency to misrepresent what has happened is nowhere more strongly criticized than in Herbert. Under his repetitive and unsparing review, all the truths finally become clear. Herbert knows that to appear pious is not to be pious; to pay formal tribute is not to love; to servilely acknowledge power is not to wonder; to utter grievances is not to pray. His readers, often mistaking the language of piety for the thing itself, are hampered by dealing with an unfamiliar discourse. We have a very rich sense of social deception in human society and can detect a note of social falseness in a novel almost before it appears; but it sometimes does not occur to us that the same equivocations, falsenesses, self-justifications, evasions, skirtings, and defensive reactions can occur in a poet's colloquies with his God. We recognize defiance when it is overt, as in "The Collar" or the first "Affliction," but other poems where the presentation is more subtle elicit bland readings and token nods to Herbert's sweetness or humility. Herbert spoke of himself as "a wonder tortur'd" and his own estimate of himself can be a guide in reading his poems.

Even in that last and most quietly worded poem, "Love," which is spoken in retrospect by the regenerate soul from the vantage point of the something understood, the old false modesty lingers. There is, as Herbert says elsewhere, no articling with God, but in this poem the soul is still refusing, in William James's words, to give up the assertion of the "little private convulsive self."[7] When Herbert catches glimpses of God's order, which we may if we wish call the best order he can imagine for himself, he finds it almost unnatural, odd — even comic. His impulse is to deny that he has any connection with such a disturbing reordering of the universe, to feel a sense of strain in attempting to accommodate himself to it, and at best, he prays that his God will remake him to fit in with that scheme, if he please: "Lord, mend or rather make us." But sometimes Herbert rejects this claim on God's indulgence. At his best, and at our best, says Herbert, God refuses to indulge the view we like to take of ourselves as hopelessly and irremediably marred and ignorant creatures. Herbert's protests that he is not capable of glory are not catered to; instead of a gentle solicitude by God, he is confronted by an equally gentle but irreducible immobility. Each of his claims to imperfection is firmly, lovingly, and even wittily put aside, and he is forced to accept God's image of him as a guest worthy of his table. What Herbert wants is to linger in the antechambers, to serve, to adopt any guise except the demanding glory of the wedding garment, but Love is inflexible, and the initial "humility" of the Guest is revealed as a delusive fond clinging to his mortal dust and sin. Herbert's God asks that he be more than what he conceives himself to be. Herbert invented this sort of God, we may say, to embody the demands that his own conscience put upon him, a conscience formed by that "severa parens" his mother. But even in such a brief poem as "Love," Herbert's originality in transforming his sources, in re-inventing his topic, strikes us forcibly. We know that the poem depends on St. Luke's description of Jesus' making his disciples sit while he served them, and on the words of the centurion transferred to the Anglican communion service, "Lord, I am not worthy that thou shouldst enter under my roof," and on Southwell's "S. Peter's

Complaint" (cxviii), in which St. Peter knocks on sorrow's door and announces himself as "one, unworthy to be knowne." We also know, from Joseph Summers, that Herbert's actual topic is the entrance of the redeemed soul into Paradise. Now, so far as I know, this entrance has been thought of as an unhesitating and joyful passage, from "Come, ye blessed of my father," to "The Saints go marching in." The link between St. Peter knocking at a door and a soul knocking at St. Peter's door is clear, but it is Herbert's brilliance to have the soul give St. Peter's abject response, and stand hesitant and guilty on the threshold, just as it is a mark of his genius to have the soul, instead of being the unworthy host at communion, be the unworthy guest in heaven. When we first read "Love," it strikes us as exquisitely natural and humanly plausible; it is only later that the originality of conception takes us aback. As in "Doomsday," Herbert looks at the event as it *really* would be, not as tradition has always told us it would be. If the redeemed soul could speak posthumously to us and tell us what its entrance into heaven was really like, what would it say? and so the process of re-invention begins.

Herbert's restless criticizing tendency coexists with an extreme readiness to begin with the cliché — roses are sweet, redeemed souls flock willingly to a heavenly banquet, sinners are swinish, Doomsday is awesome, past grief was really not too painful. On the cliché is appliquéd the critique — roses are bitter and smarting, the soul would in reality draw back from Love's table, sinners are, in desire, indistinguishable from saints, Doomsday would in fact be agreeably social, past grief was, if truth be told, intolerable. It makes very little difference to Herbert where he finds his *donnée* — in the clichés of courtly poetry, in the Bible, in his personal experience. The artless borrowed beginning becomes very soon the scrutinized personal statement. The anxiety which must have made Herbert want to begin with the safe, the bland, the familiar, and the taken-for-granted coexists permanently with the aggression which impels him almost immediately to criticize the received idea. He seems to have existed in a permanent reversible equilibrium between the two extremes of tradition and originality, diffidence and protest, the filial and the egotistic. His poems do not "resolve" these extremes into one attitude; rather they permit successive, and often mutually contradictory, expressions of the self as it explores the truth of feeling. At any moment, a poem by Herbert can repudiate itself, correct itself, rephrase itself, rethink its experience, re-invent its topic, and it is in this free play of ideas that at least part of Herbert's true originality lies.

CATECHIZING THE READER:
HERBERT'S SOCRATEAN RHETORIC

Stanley E. Fish

1

The distance travelled by Herbert criticism in the past thirty-five years can be measured if we juxtapose two statements by Helen White and Helen Vendler. In 1936, Professor White wrote that "there is less of surprise in [Herbert] than in most of the metaphysicals, more of inevitability."[1] In 1970, Mrs. Vendler opened her essay "The Re-invented Poem" by declaring flatly that "one of the particular virtues of Herbert's poetry is its extremely provisional quality; his poems are ready at any moment to change direction or to modify attitudes."[2] A survey of the current scene suggests that Mrs. Vendler's view now prevails and that the older view of a calm and resolute Herbert (attached, more often than not, to an over-drawn contrast between Herbert and Donne) is no longer in fashion. Even Rosemond Tuve, who emphasizes what is traditional and familiar in Herbert's art, remarks that "his Jordans never stayed crossed."[3] Writing partly in response to Tuve, Robert Montgomery focuses on the establishing, in many of the poems, of a "fictional context," the effect of which is to "remove the discourse from the level of meditation to the level of drama."[4] The "symbolic images" documented and explicated by Tuve function in the action of a "fable," and what is significant is what happens "within the mind and soul of the speaker" (463). What happens, according to Valerie Carnes, is a succession of "vacillations" and "alternations," "psychological shiftings" which reflect the "'double motion' of the soul that yearns simultaneously for heaven and earth."[5] The result is a poetry in which understandings

From *The Rhetoric of Renaissance Poetry*, ed. Thomas O. Sloan and Raymond B. Waddington (Berkeley, Los Angeles, London: University of California Press, 1974), pp. 174-88; Copyright 1974 by The Regents of the University of California, reprinted by permission of the University of California Press and of the author.

are continually being revised as "the poet's symbolic consciousness is . . . turned back upon itself with highly ironic effect" (519). This is precisely what Mrs. Vendler intends by her phrase the "re-invented poem." Herbert "is constantly criticizing what he has already written down, and finding the original conception inadequate" (204); "at any moment, a poem by Herbert can repudiate itself, correct itself, rephrase itself, rethink its experience, re-invent its topic" (45), as the poet, in effect, does his revising "in public" (22). For Coburn Freer, this re-thinking or correcting is one manifestation of what he calls "tentative form," the result of a "discrepancy between the way a Herbert poem behaves and the way it says it behaves."[6] The form of a poem, Freer asserts, often argues with its "literal meaning" and the argument is reflected in an alternation between confident assertion and "bathetic falterings" (213), between "grace and fumbling" (214).

All of these critics, then, make essentially the same point, but even as it is made, they gesture (sometimes nervously) in the direction of the other Herbert, the Herbert of a mature and unshakeable faith, who writes always from a center of certainty. The usual strategy is to place this Herbert in a separate category — "orchestral form" as opposed to "tentative form," the "meditative" as opposed to the "dramatic" mode — but these artificial divisions only displace the central question that confronts the critic, a question that is precisely (if indirectly) posed by Freer when he speaks of that "uniquely Herbertian quality of order and surprise" (218). How is it that a Herbert poem can contain and communicate both? This question, when it is asked, is usually answered by suggesting that the surprise is staged; either it is a fiction designed to illustrate dramatically a truth known to the poet from the beginning, or it is a recreation, in verse, of a spiritual crisis he has successfully weathered.[7] Explanations like these, however, solve one problem by creating another; for while they exalt Herbert the craftsman, they raise questions about Herbert the man, who is either completely separated from his speakers or made to stand in relation to them as a player of roles, a posturer. In either case he is distanced from their concerns, becoming that much less of a Christian as he is acknowledged to be that much more of a poet. We seem, then, to be at an impasse: on the one hand the order in Herbert's poetry is denied; on the other it is acknowledged, but at the price both of his sincerity and of his wish to make his art self-consuming.[8]

The problem then is to find a way of talking that neither excludes Herbert from his poems (by emphasizing their order), nor makes them crudely autobiographical (by making them all surprise). That way is provided, I believe, by Herbert himself in Chapter XXI of *A Priest To*

The Temple. The title of the chapter is "The Parson Catechizing," but it is largely a praise of "the singular dexterity of Socrates," who held "that the seeds of all truth lay in everybody, and accordingly by questions well ordered he found Philosophy in silly Trades-men."[9] That position, Herbert admits, "will not hold in Christianity, because it contains things above nature," but the general method or "skill" can be adapted and imitated, for it consists "but in these three points":

> First, an aim and mark of the whole discourse, whither to drive the Answerer, which the Questionist must have in his mind before any question be propounded, upon which and to which the questions are to be chained. Secondly, a most plain and easie framing the question, even containing in vertue the answer also, especially to the more ignorant. Thirdly, when the answer sticks, an illustrating the thing by something else, which he knows, making what hee knows to serve him in that which he knows not.
>
> (256-257)

Here, I think, is a perfect formula for the order and surprise of Herbert's poetry. The order belongs to the Questionist-poet who knows from the beginning where he is going. The surprise belongs to the reader who is "driven" by "questions well ordered" to discover for himself "that which he knows not."[10] Herbert's questions are not always posed directly, in the conventional grammatical form, any more than are the questions of Socrates. Like the philosopher he strikes deliberately naive poses that are calculated to draw a critical or corrective response from an interlocutor; that is, he makes assertions which *function* as questions because they invite the reader to supply either what is missing or what is deficient. Consider, for example, the poem "Love-Joy":

> As on a window late I cast mine eye,
> I saw a vine drop grapes with J and C
> Anneal'd on every bunch. One standing by
> Ask'd what it meant. I, who am never loth
> To spend my judgement, said, It seem'd to me
> To be the bodie and the letters both
> of *Joy* and *Charitie*. Sir, you have not miss'd,
> The man reply'd; it figures *JESUS CHRIST*.

For Montgomery, "Love-Joy" is "a brief compressed narrative," "a presentation of and commentary upon the imperfection of one man's understanding of Christian truth." The imperfection is the narrator's and it is revealed by "the order of the two interpretations" which "gently contradicts his judgment" (462). But if any judgment is contradicted in this poem, it is the reader's, even though the second interpretation is the one he has all the while been ready to deliver. Even before the poem's official questioner ("One standing by") appears, a question is being asked by the hieroglyphic riddle of lines 1 and 2: what do J and C annealed on a bunch of grapes mean? The obvious answer is "Jesus Christ," and it is the answer the reader expects to hear, especially since the word "bodie" would seem to allude directly to the typological identification of the bunch of grapes in Numbers with the wine press of the Passion.[11] Thus for fully seven-eighths of the poem it is the reader who is spending his judgment, and it is with some surprise that he hears the narrator in line 7 give what is apparently the wrong answer. This, however, is only the first of three surprises. The second occurs when the Questionist appears to approve the narrator's answer, for then it seems that the reader has spent his judgment unwisely; but when the answer is expanded and completed (this is the third surprise) it turns out to be exactly what the reader has been expecting: "It figures *JESUS CHRIST.*" The point is not, as Montgomery suggests, that one interpretation is superior to the other, but that properly understood they imply each other. It is a point the reader is left to make for himself, and he *will* make it, if only because the method of "questions well ordered" has given him a stake in the solving of the riddle, both the riddle as initially posed, and the interpretative riddle of the final two lines. In short, the reader is brought by means of "what hee knows," by "a most plain and easie framing the question," to "that which he knows not" (or at least doesn't know consciously), not merely what J and C stand for, but what JESUS CHRIST stands for, *Joy* and *Charitie.*

2

"Love-joy," then, is not "a brief compressed narrative"; rather it is a dialogue, with the poet (in two roles) as Questionist and the reader as (silent) respondent. Montgomery contrives to turn Herbert into a seventeenth-century Browning, a dramatic monologist who does not necessarily hold the opinions expressed by his first-person speakers; but the distinction between poet and persona need not be made if Herbert is understood to be speaking in his own *pedagogical* voice; for then it is not a question of recollecting in tranquility a previous experience, or of fictionalizing an experience he has never had, but of sincere role-playing, that is, of straightforwardly adapting the rhetorical strategy described in *A Priest To The Temple.*

That strategy, as Herbert elaborates it, is characterized by its flexibility. The country parson does not employ set forms, for these create a situation in which the catechized deliver answers by rote and perform "as parrats" (256). The better practice is one in which the order and the method of questioning are "varyed," as the catechizer responds to particular circumstances and to the differing capacities of his pupils. (Here Herbert would seem to be following the counsel of Augustine in *De catechizandis rudibus*.) In this way the Answerer is brought not only to a knowledge of the "dark and deep points of Religion," but to a knowledge of himself; he is led, as Herbert puts it, to "discover what he is" (257).

In *The Temple*, this flexibility of method is reflected in the varying relationships into which readers and speakers enter. In "The Holdfast" reader and speaker are catechized together by a third person, and their responses, as I have argued elsewhere,[12] trace out parallel careers. Both are "driven" to the realization that Christ is and does all things when an unidentified voice refuses to allow them the things and actions (including the action of interpreting) they would reserve to themselves. As the poem ends, they have fallen silent, and that voice is summarizing the lesson that has been "the mark of the whole discourse." In "Love-Unknown" the same three-cornered situation results in a different set of relationships. Here the reader is not allied with the speaker, but runs ahead of him, answering the questions raised by his tale, supplying the typological significances to which he seems blind, solving the puzzle of the title, anticipating the responses of the "Deare Friend" before they are offered. The context is still catechistical, but it is one stage removed, a *re*learning of a lesson by watching and reacting to the instruction of another.[13] (Writers of catechisms regularly urge the benefits of attendance at public catechizings.) In "Love-joy" the relationship between speaker and reader is continually changing. At one point , the reader is encouraged to think himself superior, because it appears that the speaker has given the wrong answer; but then the positions are reversed when that answer is approved by the catechizer. In a final reversal, the reader learns that he was correct after all, but his understanding of his own response is now deeper because of the sequence he has negotiated.

In each of these three poems, the shape of the catechistical experience is different, but the basic pattern remains the same: the reader, in the company of a fellow pupil, is driven by the singular dexterity of a Questionist to one of the deep and dark points of religion. In another group of poems, the same pattern unfolds in the absence of a fellow pupil; the confrontation between catechized and catechizer is unmeditated and direct. The mode of catechizing, however, is *in*direct, since the dialogue is not built into the form, but is initiated when the reader is moved to correct or complete the speaker's statements in the light of that "which he knows."

What he knows as he begins "The Bunch of Grapes" has been nicely summarized by Joseph Summers:

> That "branch with one cluster of grapes," which was so large that "they bore it betweene two upon a staffe," had represented a joy which the Israelites refused. To them the bunch of grapes substantiated the report that it was "a land that eateth up the inhabitants thereof, and all the people that we saw in it, are men of a great stature. And there we saw the giants, the sonnes of Anak, which come of the giants: and we were in our own sight as grashoppers, and so wee were in their sight" (Num. xiii.32-33). From fear they turned to the rebellion which caused God to decree the wandering of forty years. Of all the adults who saw the grapes, only Caleb and Joshua entered the Promised Land. The image of the bunch of grapes suggests, then, not only the foretastes of Canaan and heaven, but also the immeasurable difference between those foretastes under the Covenant of Works and the Covenant of Grace.... The bunch of grapes is a type of Christ and of the Christian's communion. "I have their fruit and more," for the grapes, of which the promise was conditional upon works, have been transformed into the wine of the New Covenant: "I" have both the foretaste and the assurance of its fulfilment.[14]

All of this is potentially contained in the title of the poem, but, paradoxically, it is brought out only because it is suppressed. As in "Love-joy" Herbert works *against* the expectations of his reader so that in the end they may be more meaningfully confirmed. He begins with a complaint: "Joy, I did lock thee up: but some bad man / Hath let thee out again." On the surface, this is simply a testimony to the unevenness of the Christian's spiritual life, but to the reader who, like Miss Tuve, has seen one of the many "vivid representations of Christ pressed in the winepress of the Passion" (116), the note sounded here will not ring true. The language is the language of enclosures and confinements ("lock up," "let out"), but the joy of Christ's inheritance is boundless and free. It is not possessed, but possesses. We do not have it, we share in it and live in it; it contains us rather than the reverse. Of course the statements I have been making in the previous sentences are more precise than anything the reader is thinking at this point. His misgivings are more inchoate, a slight and largely undefined uneasiness that springs from his unawareness of the contexts invaded by the title. In the course of the poem, that uneasiness acquires form and substance, as the poet's assertions continue to invite a critical and corrective response. The invitation is sharpened as this first stanza proceeds:

> And now, me thinks, I am where I began
> Sev'n yeares ago: one vogue and vein,
> One aire of thoughts usurps my brain.
> I did towards Canaan draw; but now I am
> Brought back to the Red sea, the sea of shame.

(lines 3-7)

Again the lines assert one thing, but the reader extrapolates something else. The poet's complaint is carried by two spatial images, one linear ("I did toward Canaan draw"), the other cyclical ("I am where I began"), the first figuring forth the direction of his hopes, the second emblematic of their frustration. Yet even as this plain sense registers, it is undermined by the typological associations of its components. Canaan, of course, is a figure of salvation, while the passage way to Canaan, the river Jordan, is a type of baptism, and this is perfectly consistent with the statement Herbert is making. The Red Sea, however, is also a type, a type of the crucifixion and more specifically of the blood that flowed from Christ's side:

> For the watyr yn the fonte [Red Sea] betokeynth the red blod and watyr that ran down of the wondys of Cristis syde in the wheche the power of Pharo, that is, the veray fend, ys drowned, and all hys myght lorne, and all cristen pepull sauet.[15]

> All our waters shall run into Jordan, and thy servants passed Jordan dry foot; they shall run into the red sea (the sea of thy Son's blood), and the red sea, that red sea, drowns none of thine.[16]

The Red Sea, then, is "the sea of shame" only under the Law when it is the passageway to forty years of wandering; but typically understood, under the New Dispensation of the Spirit, this same "font" signifies a *release* from shame, a release that has been effected by Christ's blood, simultaneously the passageway and the vehicle of passage. In the light of these significances, the poet's complaint denies itself in the uttering — I did towards Canaan draw but now I am brought back toward Canaan — and the spatial metaphor which has been carrying his argument is discredited. The inadequacy of that metaphor inheres in its rigidity, its inability to accommodate a God who is everywhere and from whom one can not move away, and that limitation is in turn a reflection of the limitation of the Law (an inflexible system of rewards and punishments) and of the minds in bondage to it.

None of this is in the poem; it is supplied by the reader who is responding to the question the stanza indirectly poses: what is wrong with these statements? What is wrong, of course, is that they betray a misreading on the speaker's part of typological significances, a misreading that becomes even more obvious when typology itself becomes the poem's explicit subject:

> For as the Jews of old by Gods command
> Travell'd, and saw no town;
> So now each Christian hath his journeys spann'd:
> Their storie pennes and sets us down.
> A single deed is small renown.
> Gods works are wide, and let in future times;
> His ancient justice overflows our crimes.
>
> (lines 8-18)

The basis for these lines is I Corinthians 10; but while the doctrine proclaimed in that espistle is liberating — release from the letter of the law — it is here confining and legalistic, confining even in its language — "spann'd," "pennes," "set ... down" and legalistic in its assumption of a one-to-one correspondence between the careers of the Old Testament wanderers and the lives of modern Christians. In this formulation, typology becomes a veritable prison within which we are condemned to repeat the errors and idolatries of the Israelites, and the "wideness" of God's works only serves to prevent us from escaping his "ancient justice."

Such a view of the matter, however, ignores, and by ignoring calls attention to, the distinction central to this way of reading history, the distinction between the type and the antitype, the shadow and the substance, the promise and fulfillment. The very point of bringing together the events of the Old Testament and the New is to assert the superiority of the dispensation under which the latter occur. (Noah's ark, for example, is a type of baptism, but its antitype is better because by it more are saved.[17]) Rather than penning us down, the stories of the Israelites provide a counterpoint to our happier situation.

It is this gracious difference that is denied by Herbert's determined literalism, but it is that same literalism which pressures the reader-Answerer to recall it; and the pressure becomes irresistible in the final two lines of the stanza: "Gods works are wide and let in future times; / His ancient justice overflows our crimes." The plain sense of this couplet is negative and constricting, but its experience is liberating. In place of "lock," "pennes," and "set down," the vocabulary of confinement, we are now given "wide," "let in," and "overflows," the vocabulary of release. The language is pointing us away from what it literally asserts and toward a recognition of the freedom we now enjoy as a result of the greatest of God's works, the work of self-sacrifice. (This "linguistic release" is an analogue, in the reading experience, of the release from the Law effected for us by the New Covenant of the Spirit.) This is particularly true of the word "overflows" which reaches back to the water imagery of the first stanza, and, more impor:antly, to the typological significance of the Red Sea, "the red blod and watyr that ran down of the wondys of Cristis syde in the wheche ... all cristen pepull [are] sauet." It is this that overflows all our crimes, inundating and submerging them in endless waters of forgiveness and redemption, and this interpretation of the word is made inescapable by what is so obviously *missing* from the line: "His ancient justice overflows our crimes." In any seventeenth-century discussion of the attributes of God, when "justice" is mentioned, "mercy" cannot be far behind. They are, as Milton declares, "colleague," and by citing the one, Herbert invites us to supply the other, and to attach it to the image which, even though it is absent, is slowly taking possession of the poem, the image of the bleeding (mercy-showering) Christ. In other words, we are provoked to remember mercy because Herbert so ostentatiously forgets it, and, as the poem continues, every detail points unmistakably in the direction he refuses (overtly) to take:

> Then have we too our guardian fire and clouds;
> Our Scripture-dew drops fast:
> We have our sands and serpents, tents and shrowds;
> Alas! our murmurings come not last.
> But where's the cluster? where's the taste
> Of mine inheritance? Lord, if I must borrow,
> Let me as well take up their joy, as sorrow.

> (lines 15-21)

The "guardian clouds and fire" are evidences of God's providence; they hover over the Tabernacle (Numbers 9:15-23), which is a type both of the church and of the believer as a temple of the living God. The "brazen serpent" and manna ("Our Scripture-dew drops") are alike types of eternal life that is the reward (the "fruit") of those who believe in Christ.[18] The questions — "But where's the cluster? where's the taste / Of mine inheritance" — carry an implied accusation — it isn't fair — but the answers they draw from us deny the accusation by validating it. It *isn't* fair, but the disproportion is all in our favour: God does not treat us exactly as he did the "Jewes of old," he treats us better; we do not receive their portion of joy; we receive more, and receive it not as a reward nor upon conditions (as they did), but as a gift, freely given at great cost to him and in gracious (merciful) *dis*regard of our deserts; we do not borrow *their* inheritance, *their* cluster, we share in our own, in the fruit of the "true vine" planted and nourished by God (John 15.1). This, then, is the "immeasurable difference" between the two foretastes, one under the Covenant of Works, the other under the Covenant of Grace, but it is a difference that is realized not in the poem (where it is resolutely ignored), but in the response of the reader to the poet's deliberately narrow assertions.

If we turn once again to the account in *A Priest To The Temple* of the parson catechizing, we can see how closely it corresponds to the experience of this poem. By means of a progressively "plain and easie framing" of the question ("what is missing here?") the reader has been "driven" to discover for himself the "aim and mark of the whole discourse," that is, the full significance of the bunch of grapes. The function of catechizing is, in Herbert's words, "to infuse a competent knowledge of salvation in every one of [the parson's] flock" (255). In this case, we are his flock, made competent in exactly that knowledge by a poetic variation of "the singular dexterity of *Socrates*"; and like Socrates, Herbert abandons his deliberately naive pose when it has done its work:

> But can he want the grape, who hath the wine?
> I have their fruit and more.
> Blessed be God, who prosper'd *Noahs* vine,
> And made it bring forth grapes good store.
> But much more him I must adore,
> Who of the Laws sowre juice sweet wine did make,
> Ev'n God himself being pressed for my sake.
>
> (lines 22-28)

At this point Mrs. Vendler might say that the poem is re-invented, while Montgomery is forced to conclude that "structurally ... the fable of 'The Bunch of Grapes' is uncertain" (464) since it equivocates between the fictional and meditative modes. But there is no equivocation or re-inventing if the mode of the poem is acknowledged to be rhetorical; for then the change in tone and direction one feels here marks the moment when the catechism has ended and Questionist and Answerer share a level of understanding, an understanding one has earned and the other has laboured to give. Indeed, line 22 functions here much as "Sir, you have not missed" functions in "Love-joy"; for by voicing precisely the counterarguments that he has drawn from the reader, the poet implicitly approves them, and from this point on the participants in the poem's dialogue proceed in unanimity, openly proclaiming the truth they now share. The vocabulary which was the vehicle of their temporary divergence remains, but it is transformed by the single perspective that now rules the poem and its experience. For a moment, the first half of line 23 — "I have their fruit" — suggests the narrow literalism of the opening lines, but the phrase "and more" is liberating for it literally overflows the spatial boundaries suggested by the verb of possession. This "having" is finally very different from the "locking up" of line 1; it is the result of realizing that such a locking up is at once impossible and unnecessary. The sense of liberation is also communicated by the rhythms of the verse. The questions and exclamations of the previous stanzas had resulted in a choppy reading experience with mandatory breaks and pauses (pauses which were to be filled by the answers of the reader); here we move smoothly and without interruption through what is essentially one long flowing sentence. The climax of that sentence and indeed of the entire poem is the verb "pressed" which, while nominally of the same class as "lock" and "pennes" and "set down," is not constricting at all; for in this context, the action of pressing is equivalent to an *out*pouring, an outpouring of red wine, red sea, red blood, mercy, love; and it is this that the poet and reader see, feel, taste, as all the significances which have been accruing to the title emblem, in the tradition and in the poem, are compressed into this sublimated image of the crucifixion.

3

It might seem that all I have done in this essay is substitute one set of terms for another, Questionist for persona, Answerer for reader, and dialogue for narrative. The new terms, however, are I think qualitatively superior to the old, not only because they are Herbert's but because by bringing the reader into the center of the poem's action, they make it possible to account for the "Herbertian quality of order and surprise." If the reader is not considered a party to the transaction, the critic, as we saw, has only one of two choices: if he wishes to keep Herbert the man at the center of his poetry, he must deemphasize order and design; and if he accommodates order and design by positing a succession of personae, he removes Herbert the man from the center of his poetry. Acknowledging the role of the reader cuts across these choices and dissolves the dilemma. The poet is granted "the singular dexterity" and skill of a Christian pedagogic design, and that design is realized in the series of surprises experienced by the reader. This solution also has the advantage of being true to Herbert's own hopes for his verse, hopes that are, in the

best sense of the word, rhetorical. Even if Walton is writing hagiography,
his report of Herbert's direction to Ferrar at the very least reflects an
accepted view of the poet's intention: "desire him [Ferrar] to read it, and
then if he can think it may turn to the advantage of any dejected poor
Soul, let it be made publick; if not, let him burn it."[19] This concern for
the soul of the reader is voiced in the poems themselves. In "The
Dedication" God is petitioned to "Turn their eyes hither, who shall
make a gain"; in "Praise III" the poet cries "Oh that I might some other
hearts convert" (39); and in "Obedience" this wish is given its strongest
expression:

> How happie were my part,
> If some kinde man would thrust his heart
> Into these lines; till in Heav'ns Court of Roll
> They were by winged souls
> Entred for both, farre above their desert.

(lines 41-45)

In Herbert's own century, this invitation was accepted by "many
pious converts" (the phrase is Vaughan's).[20] Crashaw not only thrusts
his own heart in, but would extend the benefits by sending "Mr.
Herbert's book" to another; she, in turn, is warned that the reading of
these poems is no passive experience: "Know you faire, on what you
looke; / Divinest love lyes in this booke: / Expecting fire from your eyes,
/ To kindle this his sacrifice."[21] Christopher Harvey is moved to build a
synagogue in imitation of The Temple and is rewarded when Walton
groups him with Herbert: "These holy hymns had an ethereal birth; /
For they can raise sad souls above the earth, / And fix them there, / Free
from the world's anxieties and fear. / Herbert and you have pow'r / To
do this; ev'ry hour / I read you, kills a sin / Or lets a virtue in."[22] The
most eloquent testimony comes from Henry Vaughan who speaks for
others as well as himself when he bears witness to the effect of Herbert's
"holy, ever-living lines":

> Dear friend! whose holy, ever-living lines
> Have done much good
> To many, and have chect my blood,
> My fierce, wild blood that still heaves, and inclines,
> But is still tam'd
> By those bright fires which thee inflam'd;
> Here I joyn hands, and thrust my stubborn heart
> Into thy Deed.

("The Match," lines 1-8)

It is more than likely that Vaughan alludes here not only to "Obedience" but to the opening stanza of "The Church-Porch" where the reader is promised verses that will rhyme him to good:

> Thou whose sweet youth and early hopes inhance
> Thy rate and price, and mark thee for a treasure;
> Hearken unto a Verser, who may chance
> Ryme thee to good, and make a bait of pleasure.
> A verse may finde him, who a sermon flies,
> And turn delight into a sacrifice.

Surely it is no accident that the terms in which poetry is praised here are the terms in which catechizing is praised in *A Priest To The Temple*: "at sermons . . . men may sleep or wander; but when one is asked a question, he must discover that he is" (257). It is not simply that in both texts a comparison is made at the expense of sermons, but that the virtues of poetry and catechizing are the same: they do not allow the reader-auditor to escape; he is found, he is discovered, he is drawn in, and once in he is remade into the "spirituall Temple" which both catechism and poems "build up" (255).

I am not arguing, as others have,[23] that Herbert's remarks on catechizing provide an interesting analogue to his poetical practice. I believe that the connection is much firmer, and that Herbert consciously composed *The Temple* on a catechistical model. That however will be the argument of a longer work[24] and within the limits of the present essay it is enough to point out that the experience of the poetry is in every way answerable to the description of catechizing: its questions are "chained" so that they lead inexorably to the "aim and mark of the whole discourse"; the leading — the order — is the poet-Questionist's, while the discovery — the surprise — belongs to the reader-Answerer; and the whole is "an admirable way of teaching, wherein the Catechized will at length finde delight, and by which the Catechizer, if he once get the skill of it, will draw out of ignorant and silly souls, even the dark and deep points of Religion" (256). Herbert has got the skill of it.

III. IMAGES AND ALLUSIONS

GEORGE HERBERT AND THE EMBLEM BOOKS

Rosemary Freeman

The Emblem Book was a literary form which had much vitality in the sixteenth and seventeenth centuries. Although little is heard of it now, it was serious enough then to attract men of some minor ability, and people like Henry Peacham, George Wither, and Francis Quarles added books of emblems to their many other publications. The nature of the convention was, however, such as to make it more valuable as a means to an end than as an end in itself, and consequently its greatest success lay in its applications and transformations in other poetry and not in its use in the Emblem Books proper. It had considerable influence on the poets of the period: Donne, Crashaw, and Vaughan — to name only the outstanding figures — all owed something to the Emblem Book, and among the lesser writers there are many traces of a similar interest. An extreme example is Mildmay Fane, Earl of Westmorland, whose *Otia Sacra* (1648) is a collection of poems consciously, and often indeed fantasticaly, emblematic. But the poet whose work comes nearest to that of the emblem writers, while at the same time being infinitely more distinguished, is George Herbert; and I wish here to show how a convention which in itself produced only mediocre writing was modified to suit the purposes of a great poet.

I

Of the history of the emblem convention not much need be said. In 1531 an Italian lawyer, Andrea Alciati, published an *Emblematum Liber*, a small volume containing ninety-eight woodcuts, with mottoes and short poems attached to each. This formed the model upon which innumer-

Reprinted from *RES*, 17 (1941), 150-65, by permission of Oxford University Press. A revised and expanded version of this essay appeared in *English Emblem Books* (London: Chatto and Windus, 1948), pp. 148-72.

able other books of emblems were constructed. The *Emblematum Liber* itself was enlarged and reprinted again and again; it went into ninety editions in the sixteenth century alone; it was wedged between solemn and cumbrous annotations, translated into French, Italian, English, and Spanish, and modified and imitated everywhere. Independent French Emblem Books were written soon after the first publication of Alciati: de la Perrière's *Théâtre des Bons Engins* was published in 1539, Corrozet's *Hecatongraphie* in 1540, and Paradin's *Devises Héroiques* in 1557. English reaction was slower; partly because of the backward state of engraving in this country and partly because Latin and French presented no barriers to the class of readers for whom the books were written, Emblem Books did not appear in the vernacular until 1586, when Plantin published Geoffrey Whitney's *A Choice of Emblems and Other Devises*. This was in the main an anthology of foreign emblems, the pictures being provided from Plantin's large stock of plates. It was, however, quickly followed by attempts at original work, and besides translations of Paradin and de la Perrière,[1] there were several Emblem Books in English which had no immediate foreign source; the *Sacrorum Emblematum Centuria Una* of Andrew Willet, a prodigy of learning and industry who poured out books in such profusion that an astonished contemporary was provoked to remark that he 'must write as he sleeps, it being impossible he should do so much waking!' is one of these, and another is Henry Peacham's *Minerva Britanna*, published in 1612. Peacham had the greatest enthusiasm for emblems, and he also made three manuscript collections, one of which was coloured for presentation to Prince Henry.

These Emblem Books all have the same characteristics. Each emblem was made up of a symbolical picture, a brief motto or *sententia*, and an explanatory poem. The purpose of the motto was to complete and interpret the picture, while the picture gave meaning to the motto: neither could stand without the other. The purpose of the poem, the third essential feature, was to explain the whole and to point the moral. The three parts were called by the emblem writers and their critics the 'picture', the 'word', and the 'explanation' or 'mind' of the emblem, respectively. For example, the first emblem in Whitney's *Choice* was taken from Paradin's plate of the device of the Cardinal of Lorraine. The picture represents a pillar round which is twined a stem of ivy; the motto or word is TE STANTE VIREBO. The poem interprets the symbolism and at the same time pays a graceful compliment to Queen Elizabeth:

> A mightie Spyre, whose toppe doth pierce the skie,
> An iuie greene imbraceth rounde about,

> And while it standes, the same doth bloome on highe,
> But when it shrinkes, the iuie standes in dowt:
>> The Piller great, our gratious Princes is:
>> The braunche, the Churche: whoe speakes unto hir this;
>
> I, that of late with stormes was almoste spent,
> And brused sore with Tirants bluddie bloes,
> Whome fire, and sworde, with persecution rent,
> Am nowe sett free, and ouerlooke my foes,
>> And whiles thow raignst, oh most renowmed Queene
>> By thie supporte my blossome shall bee greene.

The subjects treated by the emblem writers were drawn from all sources. Whitney divides his into three groups, natural, historical, and moral, natural being the wonders of nature, usually the wonders of Pliny and Æsop; historical, tales from classical history and myth; and moral, anything that will not fit into the other categories. In the work of Peacham, and to a lesser degree in Whitney, a number of personifications were also used, the motto then being replaced by the name of the figure personified. Such figures were always easily recognizable by external marks: Whitney's *Invidia* has a forked tongue, *Occasion* a long forelock, *Temperance* a bit and bridle. These personifications form one of the links between the Emblem Books and other literature; Peacham, for instance, drew some from Spenser, and others from the *Iconologia* of Cesar Ripa, which was used by Ben Jonson and Inigo Jones as a source-book for figures for masques.

A later development of the emblem convention, which must be mentioned for its relevance to the work of Herbert, is seen in the Emblems of Love, love profane and love divine. These emblems flourished particularly in Holland, and were used by the Jesuits as a means of teaching ethical and religious doctrine.[2] It is to this branch of the convention that the work of Quarles belongs. The technique remained substantially the same as in the earlier type of Emblem Book, but the material was new. In Quarles's *Emblemes* (1635) two figures, Amor, representing divine love, and Anima, the human soul, walk the world together. Anima falls into the snares of the devil and is restored by Amor, and reunited to him; she is shipwrecked and moves through the waters towards his outstretched hand; or she is brought to judgment before him by Justice. Another type of Jesuit Emblem work is exemplified in Christopher Harvey's *Schola Cordis* (1647), which was adapted from B. van Haeften's book of the same name. In this the human heart becomes the centre of interest. The emblems depict the fall of man in Eden, and the ensuing darkness, vanity, covetousness, hardness, and insatiability of his heart, which is, however, persuaded to return to Christ; and in the series of emblems which follow it is purified and prepared for heaven. The plates show the actual processes of redemption. The heart is burnt on a sacrificial altar, washed in a fountain of blood, ploughed and sown with good seed; it is portrayed as infested with serpents, crushed flat beneath a press, hung round with symbols of this world's vanity, or given an ever-open eye in accordance with the text *I sleep but mine heart waketh*. This curious symbolism was more successful than might at first be expected in a Protestant country, and Harvey's book was reprinted twice in the seventeenth century and later attributed to Quarles, with whose *Emblemes* it was afterwards bound up. Another English Emblem Book which belongs to the same category as these is Edmund Arwaker's version of one of Quarles's sources, Herman Hugo's *Pia Desideria*,[3] which was made because the translator considered that 'Mr. Quarles only borrowed his emblems to prefix them to a much inferior sense'.

There were probably a number of different reasons for the popularity of the Emblem Book in general and of Quarles in particular. Walpole, indeed, remarked that even Milton had had to wait until the world had done admiring Quarles; but then Quarles had an unusual gift for popularity. The Emblem Books did, however, make an appeal as a literary form, quite apart from the individual merits of Quarles's work. They had the attraction of pictures, and those sometimes of a high standard — Wither's Emblem Book, for instance, is illustrated with engravings by Crispin der Pass; they taught a moral lesson; and, finally, their symbolism was just difficult enough to make the discovery of its meaning an intellectual adventure of a not too strenuous kind. (It was considered a fault to make an emblem too obscure; Shakespeare's only recorded experiment in the field failed because nobody understood it.[4]) Their charms were, in fact, various, and there is no doubt that, for one reason or another, many seventeenth-century readers were familiar with the convention in its different forms.

A convention so popular was ready to hand for any poet to use. The material — the classical myth and legend, fables, natural history, heraldry, in the earlier type, and the regeneration of the human heart or the adventures of Amor and Anima in the later — was easily accessible. The technique was simple and required no great imaginative powers. There was never any necessary essential likeness between the picture and its meaning. Quarles delighted in choosing some entirely arbitrary symbol, and then piling up likenesses which must depend for their validity upon the acceptance of the original comparison; once it is granted that man's soul is an organ, or our life the image of a winter's day, detail upon detail may be added and the original point of resemblance indefinitely expanded. The details, however, never illuminate the image: they merely extend it. The more curious and unusual the comparison the better the 'wit'. Thus Bunyan, in his Emblem Book, *A Book for Boys and Girls* (1686), chooses an egg and finds no less than fourteen points of resemblance between the state of man and that unpromising symbol.

The literature of the first half of the seventeenth century shows how often and how variously the convention was adapted to the purposes of poetry. Crashaw's bleeding and flaming hearts recall one of its main themes, and there is much, too, in the work of Vaughan that can be related to the genre. In his love poems he introduces what are unmistakable emblems:

> And on each leafe by Heavens command,
> These Emblemes to the life shall stand:
>   Two Hearts, the first a shaft withstood;
> The second, shot, and washt in bloud;
> And on this heart a dew shall stay,
> Which no heate can court away;
> But fixt for ever witnesse beares,
> That hearty sorrow feeds on teares.
>   Thus Heaven can make it knowne, and true,
>   That you kill'd me, 'cause I lov'd you.[5]

Like other poets he is more successful, however, when he does not keep strictly to the rules of the convention he is using. In the *Palm-Tree*, for instance, the favourite emblematic image of the palm which will still flourish under a heavy weight is used to signify those who aspire towards heaven though bowed down by the heavy weight of this world's sin. The image is treated emblematically in that it is first presented and then interpreted, but Vaughan gives it a much fuller and richer meaning by working out the other associations of the palm, its connection with victory and its connection, as a tree, with the Tree of Life, and consequently builds up a complex poem upon the original simple basis. Other parts of *Silex Scintillans* bear in a more general way upon the convention. Vaughan's method is to handle abstract ideas as if they were tangible and visible objects. In *The World*, for instance, the lover is surrounded by

> His Lute, his fancy, and his flights,
>   Wits sour delights.

These are set out pictorially as emblems of his folly, though it is only the first that can be visualized. It is this kind of presentation that gives Vaughan's poetry its mixture of vagueness and precision; and it depends in part on the technique developed in the Emblem Books where the abstract lent itself so readily to formulation in visual terms.

The real triumph of the convention was, however, achieved for it by George Herbert. For the emblem method did not on the whole encourage good work; the pictures freed the poet from the obligation of making his poem stand up by itself, and required so simple an equation between the image and its significance that neither subtlety of tone nor richness of meaning was possible. Good poets, therefore, generally used the emblem as one device among many, and their poems are most successful when they do not cling too closely to the principles of the convention. Herbert, however, accepting the technique in its entirety, was able to turn to advantage both its pictorial quality and its simplicity; and in his work it migrates from what was merely on the level of verse and becomes poetry.

II

The Temple, which was published in 1633, comes very close to that mode which Quarles and his followers were to develop in England a few years later. A poem such as *The Churche Floore* is emblematic, although it has no direct dependence on the Emblem Books for its content:

> Mark you the floore? that square and speckled stone,
>   Which looks so firm and strong,
>   Is PATIENCE:
>
> And th'other black and grave, wherewith each one
>   Is checker'd all along,
>   HUMILITIE:
>
> The gentle rising, which on either hand
>   Leads to the quire above,
>   Is CONFIDENCE:
>
> But the sweet cement, which in one sure band
>   Ties the whole frame, is LOVE
>   And CHARITIE.

> Hither sometimes Sinne steals, and stains
> The marble's neat and curious veins;
> But all is cleansed when the marble weeps.

Sometimes Death, puffing at the doore,
Blows all the dust about the floore;
But while he thinks to spoil the room, he sweeps.

Blest be the Architect Whose art
Could build so strong in a weak heart![6]

In some seventeenth century editions[7] of *The Temple* two engravings were included, one as a setting for *The Altar* and the other for *Superliminarie*, but the method of this poem makes it clear that pictures could not offer any fundamental contribution to the book. They might serve as marginal notes indicating the nature of the poems they illustrate, but they could never become an element in their structure. The visual image is certainly present: it is , in fact, the basis of the poem: but it is present only in complete fusion with its meaning. There can be no elementary separation into 'picture' and 'word' where the floore 'so firm and strong', the 'gentle rising' of the chancel, and the dust of death are involved; they must be understood, to take a phrase from Vaughan, as 'bodied ideas'. Quarles's poetry simply deduces ideas from a given image; and it therefore demands the presence before the eye of an actual picture which can be explored in detail in the verse. Herbert sets out a picture which has already been explored in the mind and which, accordingly, brings with it the knowledge of its own implications.

Herbert's poetry remains primarily visual, and visual in the special sense that has been defined as emblematic. Few of his poems could be labelled 'Emblems' because too much is generally involved in each to allow the unwinking concentration upon one image which characterizes such work. It is, indeed, usually the less successful poems, such as *Lovejoy*, which are closest to the stock pattern. But everywhere in the formulation of ideas, in lines like this:

Thy root is ever in its grave:[8]

in poems consciously patterned such as *Easter Wings* and *The Altar*, and in poems like *The Church Floore* which develop a series of images, a use of language asserts itself that can only be described as emblematic. It is a quality not limited to single lines and scattered phrases but is expressed in the structure of the poems, in the accumulation and inter-relation of their images. This use of language indicates a habitual cast of mind, and becomes central in the verse. To confine a connection of *The Temple* with the Emblem Books to the few poems which can be classified as emblems in strict definition would be not only to ignore much else that is the strength of Herbert's poetry, its range of tone, the complexity of its rhythms, its power of resolving the personal in the liturgical, but even to distort the perspective in which these few are to be seen. For Herbert's work as a whole constitutes the transformation of the methods of the emblematists into a form for poetry.

This poetry is characterized by a simplicity of image, an extreme unobtrusiveness, and a concentration of meaning in which the complexity becomes only gradually apparent. It has not, conspicuously, either the intensity of Donne or the shining brilliance of Vaughan; its strength lies rather in rhythm, in imagery that is essential but rarely rich in itself, in language whose austerity does not preclude abundance. This verse from *Peace*, for instance, is as powerful in its way as the more spectacular kinds of metaphysical poetry:

> Sweet Peace, where dost thou dwell? I humbly crave,
> Let me once know.
> I sought thee in a secret cave,
> And ask'd if Peace were there.
> A hollow winde did seem to answer, "No;
> Go seek elsewhere".

All the emptiness and privation of the life of solitude is conveyed in the last two lines, but they depend for their force on their context; taken in isolation they lose half their meaning. Writing of this kind can, however, easily be underestimated, and Herbert's poetry has sometimes been accused of the lack of any real power of thought or imagination. It is useful for this reason to set it beside the fourteenth-century religious lyric, which possesses both the simplicity and the intensely personal note which are usually considered to be Herbert's main virtues. A poem like this fulfils the claims often made for his verse:

> Louerd thu clepedest me
> an ich nagt ne ansuarede the
> Bute wordes scloe and sclepie:
> "thole yet! thole a litel!"
> Bute "yiet" and "yiet" was endelis,
> And "thole a litel" a long wey is.[9]

If we are to believe Herbert's critics, his work is not more complex than this. Clearly his simplicity is of a different order. In the first place it disguises a remarkable mastery of tone. So much is done dramatically and by implication:

> Then Money came, and chinking still,
> "What tune is this, poore man?" said he;
> "I heard in Musick you had skill".[10]

There is the shrug of the shoulder implied in:

> How canst Thou brook his foolishnesse?
> Why, he'l not lose a cup of drink for Thee:
> Bid him but temper his excesse,
> Not he: he knows where he can better be —
> As he will swear —
> Then to serve Thee in fear.[11]

Secondly, behind seeming simplicity and directness there is often great strength which has its roots in the liturgy. The poem *Peace*, for instance, is a brief allegory of human life. The economy with which the story is told is witness not to poverty of material but to a hand that knows its own resources. In the last verse, accordingly, the references to the Garden and to the bread of life are felt to suggest something more complicated and more universal than would be possible if its brevity were the measure of content:

> "Take of this grain, which in my garden grows,
> And grows for you;
> Make bread of it; and that repose
> And peace, which ev'rywhere
> With so much earnestnesse you do pursue,
> Is onely there."

This is all done so quietly and unemphatically that there is nothing in it that can be isolated. The complexity is evident only in the rhythm, and that is difficult to fasten on. But what establishes the point of the allegory more distinctly than the images alone can do is the cadence of the first two lines which so clearly echoes that of the words of administration in the Mass. Many of Herbert's poems are directly liturgical in this way. *Repentance*, for example, seems to have a general background of psalms and intercessions behind it, and lines like these —

> Yet still Thou goest on,
> And now with darknesse closest wearie eyes,
> Saying to man: "It doth suffice;
> Henceforth repose, your work is done."[12]

have a finality that suggests the Burial of the Dead, although the expressed intention is only to convey day and night. But the reference to the 'ebonie box' in the next line recalls the same undercurrent of ideas. Other poems have an acknowledged connection with the Prayer Book in that some part of the service is turned into verse; as in the paraphrase of

the 23rd Psalm in *The God of Love my Shepherd is*, and, most
remarkable of all, *The Sacrifice*, where Herbert achieves a personal and
moving effect within a framework that has all the abstractness of ritual.

III

These are some of the virtues of the poetry of *The Temple* and it is to
their attainment that the emblem method makes a contribution. For
Herbert's images remain emblems and nowhere encroach on the
province of symbol. There is no necessary likeness between the church
floor and the human heart, between stained glass windows and preachers,
or between two rare cabinets filled with treasure and the Trinity and the
Incarnation. His method is always to evolve meaning by creating
likenesses; the likenesses are rarely inherent or to be seen from the
outset. His writing, that is, is inductive not deductive. Each of the
epithets in *The Church Floore* adds simultaneously to the image and to
the generality behind it, creating the picture in the moral and the moral
in the picture, and at the same time maintaining the sharp outlines of
both. Out of these is built up the central parallel which is allegory made
explicit only in the last couplet:

> Blest be the Architect Whose art
> Could bulid so strong in a weak heart!

Herbert himself sums up his method in the poem called *The Rose*:

> But I will not much oppose
> Unto what you now advise;
> Only take this gentle Rose,
> And therein my answer lies.

It is chiefly in the principles underlying the work that Herbert's
affinities with the Emblem Books are most clearly to be seen, but there
are, here and there, references to familiar themes. In *The Church Porch*,
for example, one of Alciati's problems appears. It is that of the ass who,
seeing worshippers kneeling to the shrine of Isis on his back, thought
they were adoring him:

> The shrine is that which thou dost venerate,
> And not the beast that bears it on his back.

In *The Size* an emblem is used to clinch the argument of the poem:

> ....Call to minde thy dreame,
> An earthly globe,

> On whose meridian was engraven,
> "These seas are tears, and Heav'n the haven".

But apart from one noteworthy exception Herbert uses the actual material of the emblematists very little, and then not directly. Memories of Amor and Anima are perhaps behind the *Dialogue* and the better known 'Love bade me welcome but my soul drew back', and *Good Friday* may have been written with the imagery of the heart in mind:

> Since bloud is fittest, Lord, to write
> Thy sorrows in and bloudie fight,
> My heart hath store, write there, where in
> One box doth lie both ink and sinne:
>
> That when Sinne spies so many foes,
> Thy whips, Thy nails, Thy wounds, Thy woes,
> All come to lodge there, Sinne may say,
> "No room for me", and flie away.

But in all these the connection is only general. The one exception is *Love-Unknowne*. It was quoted by Coleridge in support of his contention that the characteristic fault of the earlier poets was to convey 'the most fantastic thoughts in the most correct and natural language' and, without its context in the tradition to which it belongs, it certainly reads obscurely, and presents, as Coleridge says 'an enigma to thought'.[13]

The pursuit of the unintelligible never was an interest of Herbert's, and there is no suggestion of it in the tone of the poem. He is merely attempting to do briefly what had already been done at greater length on the Continent and what was to find its way to England in Christopher Harvey's *The School of the Heart*. The poem is an allegory made up of three incidents:

> ... a Lord I had,
> And have, of Whom some grounds, which may improve,
> I hold for two lives, and both lives in me.
> To Him I brought a dish of fruit one day,
> And in the middle plac'd my heart....

The Lord, however, rejects the offering and summons instead a servant to wash and wring the heart in a font. Then,

> After my heart was well,
> And clean and fair, as I one even tide,
> I sigh to tell,
> Walkt by myself abroad, I saw a large

> And spacious fornace flaming, and thereon
> A boyling cauldron, round about whose verge
> Was in great letters set, "Affliction."

Again the heart is made subject to restoration and the poet hastens home:

> But when I thought to sleep out all these faults,
>   I sigh to speak
> I found that some had stuff'd the bed with thoughts,
> I would say thorns....

The previous references to *The School of the Heart* indicate the convention out of which the poem was built. There were already a number of publications of this kind available and Herbert may well have seen one. Before his decision to enter the Church he had studied French, Spanish, and Italian in the aspiration of following the example of his predecessor, Sir Francis Nethersole, and obtaining a secretaryship abroad. But another and more immediate background for the poem is to be found in the *Little Gidding Concordances*. In the Book of Revelation there are a number of plates taken from Emblem Books, many of which are in the manner of *The School of the Heart*. Among them is an engraving of a font full of Hearts into which the blood of Christ is streaming; another represents Christ with a lantern entering a Heart crowded with salamanders and other creeping creatures; in others he is enthroned in the Heart, or knocking at its door. All these indicate the kind of collection which Ferrar made when he was abroad and the type of illustration with which the concordance he presented to Herbert would have been decorated.[14] Certainly the structure of *Love Unknowne* suggests a series of three of this kind visible before the eye. Herbert draws upon the same tradition in the poem *Grace*:

> Sinne is still hammering my heart
> Unto a hardnesse void of love:
> Let suppling grace, to crosse his art,
>   Drop from above.

But *Love-Unknowne* is the only poem in which all the assumptions of that particular group of Emblem Books is made explicit. It is *The School of the Heart* in little. It has been suggested by Herbert's editor, Mr. G. H. Palmer, that the poem is largely autobiographical, the dish of fruit being an allusion to Herbert's poetry and scholarship at Cambridge, and the cauldron an echo of the state of mind out of which the five poems called *Affliction* were written. It seems injudicious, however, to attribute such interests to any of Herbert's poems; certainly in this the conventional elements outweigh the personal to the extent of suggesting an academic exercise.[15]

These connections with specific Emblem Books are only occasional, and while they do establish incontrovertibly Herbert's closeness to the form, scattered parallels are never a very fruitful method of comment. And the emblem mode has here a more universal application. What is displayed in every poem is the habitual formulation of ideas in images, each brief and completed yet fully investigated. Poems like *Prayer* which consist wholly in images are only specialized versions of a process that is active everywhere. In the last two stanzas of *Faith*, for example,

> That which before was darkned clean
> With bushie groves, pricking the looker's eie,
> Vanisht away when Faith did change the scene;
> And then appear'd a glorious skie.
> What though my bodie runne to dust?
> Faith cleaves unto it, counting ev'ry grain
> With an exact and most particular trust,
> Reserving all for flesh again.

the close particularization of the phrase 'pricking the looker's eye' and the last three lines show how fully the image has been explored. In the *Country Parson*[16] Herbert had advocated the 'diligent collation of Scripture with Scripture', and in the poem called *The Pearl*, the ways of Learning, of Honour, and of Pleasure are all present in the mind:

> I know all these, and have them in my hand:
> Therefore not seeled, but with open eyes
> I flie to Thee ...

It is on this habitual completeness of knowledge that the simplicity of Herbert's poetry is based. Speculation which has travelled far and felt intensely is contracted into a single image; and the poem offers a picture that is deceptively precise and clear-cut. In some poems the stanza form supplies in itself an unacknowledged central image. *Easter Wings* and *The Altar*, for instance, are written in those actual shapes; *Sunday* has stanzas of seven lines; and in *Sinnes Round* his 'offences course it in a ring', each verse beginning with the last line of the preceding one; in *A Wreath* the same method is repeated and Herbert achieves a remarkable *tour de force* in building up a poem of overlapping lines:

> A Wreathed garland of deserved praise,
> Of praise deserved, unto Thee I give,

> I give to Thee, Who knowest all my wayes,
> My crooked winding wayes, wherein I live.

In all these the title describes what has been done by the stanza form, demonstrates the picture which the actual set-out of the poem on the page would offer to the eye. In others the same method is used more subtly. In *The Pulley* the image of a pulley is nowhere present in the substance of the poem; yet the title makes its whole point:

> When God at first made man,
> Having a glass of blessings standing by,
> "Let us," said He, "poure on him all we can;
> Let the world's riches, which dispersed lie,
> Contract into a span".
>
> So strength first made a way;
> Then beautie flow'd, then wisdome, honour, pleasure;
> When almost all was out, God made a stay,
> Perceiving that, alone of all His treasure,
> Rest in the bottome lay.
>
> "For if I should," said He,
> "Bestow this jewell also on My creature,
> He would adore My gifts instead of Me,
> And rest in Nature, not the God of Nature:
> So both should losers be.
>
> Yet let him keep the rest,
> But keep them with repining restlessnesse;
> Let him be rich and wearie, that at least,
> If goodnesse lead him not, yet wearinesse
> May tosse him to My breast".

In the same way in *The Collar*, that one image informs the whole. All through the poem an active profession of violence and confusion is made, and yet, collarwise, it is controlled by a single line at the end:

> But as I rav'd and grew more fierce and wilde
> At every word,
> Methought I heard one calling, "Childe";
> And I reply'd, "My Lord".

The care with which Herbert named the poems is obvious from the poems themselves. In *The Temple* even the incomplete *The Size* has a title, and some had been re-named to make their meaning clearer. *Prayer* in the Williams Manuscript[17] becomes *Church Lock and Key*;

The Passion, Redemption; and *Invention, Jordan*. It seems that all the changes were towards the concrete; the original title for the poem which begins 'Teach me my God and King ...' was *Perfection the Elixir*, but in the final version the generalized idea has been dropped and only the second half of the title preserved.

The personifications in *The Temple* also reflect Herbert's modification of the ways of the emblematists. It was not a device that he used very often and his figures are entirely his own. They carry no bit, bridle, anchor or other recognizable paraphernalia, nor is any single one of them described directly. Any attributes they may have are shown by implication: Glorie comes

> puffing by
> In silks that whistled; who but he![18]

Religion and Sinne are contrasted:

> Religion, like a pilgrime, Westward bent,
> Knocking at all doores ever as She went.

and Sinne:

> travell'd Westward also: journeying on
> He chid the Church away where e're he came,
> Breaking her peace and tainting her good name.[19]

Yet figures like these are much more fully realized than those which are described at such length by the emblem writers. Their attributes are not hung upon them from outside like the clothes of a cardboard doll, but are intrinsic. They appear only briefly, but their function is always completed. In *The Quip* a series of figures is introduced, each of which has his characteristic speech and gesture:

> First Beautie crept into a rose,
> Which when I pluckt not, "Sir," said she,
> "Tell me, I pray, whose hands are those?"
> But Thou shalt answer, Lord, for me.

The poem describes a trial of faith. It is also a definition of faith. The strength of the resisting virtue is measured by the plausibility of the figures who confront it; and there emerges at the same time a clear conviction of the nature of that virtue. For each figure is the single embodiment of both tempter and temptation. Once again the image has been explored to its farthest limits.

The ability to express complex thoughts and sensations in poetry was typical of the metaphysical poets as a whole, but the precision and simplicity which Herbert achieved in his expression of them was perhaps attainable only when the emblem convention flourished. Certainly no other poet has been able to concentrate so rich a meaning within so simple a framework.

HERBERT'S SEQUENTIAL IMAGERY: "THE TEMPER"

Fredson Bowers

Two allied propositions may be advanced. First, the order of the poems in George Herbert's *Temple* is not random but is planned according to developing sequences that work out major themes. Second, within these sequential poems Herbert develops clusters of images that are appropriate not only for the poem in which they appear but also — in some sense — exist coincidentally with the individual poems and apply independently to the great central theme of the section and then of *The Temple*. I take it that Herbert, quite properly, intended any separate poem to be read as a sufficient unit; but, in addition, that he planned large sections of *The Temple* for a cumulative effect that could be gained only by reading a sequence in order and understanding its larger theme.

Evidence that the collection opens with an ordered sequence is abundant. The main section of *The Temple*, called by Herbert "The Church," begins with what is in effect a dedicatory poem, "The Altar," and this poem ends:

> O lett thy blessed sacrifice be mine,
> And sanctify this Altar to be thine.[1]

It is not, therefore, an accident that the next poem is "The Sacrifice" — that central fact in all Christianity. "The Thankes-giving" properly follows, for without Christ's sacrifice there could have been no salvation. Again, there is a link between the last line of the one poem and the first of the other. "The Sacrifice" ends with Christ's lament, "Never was greif like mine," to be followed by the first line of "The Thankes-giving," "Oh King of greif — a title strange, yet true." At the end of "The Thankes-giving," Herbert confesses defeat in his attempt to match Christ's love:

> Then for thy passion — I will do for that —
> Alas, my *God*, I know not what.

From *MP*, 59 (1962), 202-13, © 1962 by The University of Chicago, Reprinted by permission of the author and The University of Chicago, Press.

"The Reprisall" coming next (originally entitled "The Second Thanks-giving") carries on the argument, and though it begins in the mood of the close of the first "Thankes-giving" with

> I have considered it, and find,
> There is no dealing with thy mighty passion.

it ends with the triumphant conclusion,

> though I can doe nought
> Against thee, in thee I will overcome
> The Man, who once against thee fought.

This reference to the sinful antagonism of man to Christ, especially as found in its most terrible moment on the cross, circles us back once more to "The Sacrifice," in which it is the central theme; and it is clear that Herbert intends us to see this connection in his next poem, "The Agony." These verses attempt to measure Christ's love for man, which has been in discussion ever since "The Sacrifice"; and in "The Agony" we are again called on to contemplate the Crucifixion, ending in the final irony, the healing blood and water that gush from Christ's side following the last cruelty of the spear.

And so on — the connected ideas progress through "The Sinner" to "Good Friday," to "Redemption," and to the Easter subjects of "Sepulcher" and "Easter," and then we have the path which a Christian treads for his redemption: the sacrament of "Holy Baptisme," man's fall in "Nature," his "Sinne," followed necessarily by "Affliction," then "Repentance" and a rise to "Faith," his proper communication with God through "Prayer" and the second sacrament of "The Holy Communion," his rejoicing in "Antiphon" as the Easter promise is fulfilled, his double analysis of divine "Love" — especially in relation to the subject for poetry — and then follow the two "Temper" poems, with the first "Jordan," again concerned with poetry, succeeding them.[2]

The development of the subject in this series is quite clear, and the occasional linking of poems by reference in first lines to the last lines of the preceding poem is an obvious device to secure narrative continuity. However, much more continuity is discoverable in the poems of this sequence than is found merely in the progression of formal idea or in links at end and beginning. Very subtle, but important, is the development of certain strains of images that independently form a commentary on the announced theme for any poem. Moreover, these images are not mere echoes or formal links but instead a developing and dynamic force in their own right, so much so that occasionally their significance, or application, in a poem cannot be fully understood except by reference back to their sequential development. And, frequently, when seen and understood, these sequentially developed images add an ironic or subtly emotional deepening to what might otherwise seem to be a casual and colorless phrase. These images (we may hesitate to call them symbols) are often of the nature of emblems, for it is possible to maintain that Herbert consistently thought and wrote in an emblematic manner. Although some of these images may have profound typological values,[3] my concern is not with such matters but instead with Herbert's method of using this poetic device. Moreover, I am also concerned with illustrating the possible uses of following this Herbertian device, which we were surely intended to do, as a means of checking our inferences about the so-called total meaning of any poem and also as a means of securing precision in the explication of lines affected by these sequential images.

As illustration we may survey an example or two from "The Temper" (I) without attempting to examine the whole intricate fabric of this complex poem. Neglected, therefore, is the significance in this poem of writing or engraving; the use of meditation as a telescope; neglected is any consideration of Herbert's interesting use of container images, ranging from boxes of sweets to graves or even to God's tent, with the allied subject of God the architect. I neglect the bird images of roosting and nestling, and the commercial or bargain images present in the phrase "thy poore debter." Instead I shall try to give — even though only in skeleton form — some of the accumulated meanings of the title "The Temper" as they are worked out either in the poem itself or as ascertainably present from the evidence of the preceding sequential imagery. We are faced with layer after layer of puns in this title. But we do not need to rely on our ingenuity in seeing these puns or to avouch the hypothesis that they *may* exist as proof of their existence, in the manner of subjective criticism. If only saying makes a thing so, criticism becomes so facile as to be meaningless. Instead, we can in effect demonstrate what Herbert consciously intended by checking the various possibilities against his preceding (and sometimes his succeeding) imagery.

The primary, and certainly the most obvious, reference in the title "The Temper" is to the hardness and the elasticity imparted to steel by the tempering process of heating and then chilling. Herbert has given this hint in his use of "steel" in the second line. The heat is "divine love." In "The Sacrifice" Christ speaks:

> I answere nothing, but with patience prove
> If stony hearts will melt with gentle Love.

It is the love that Herbert addresses in "Love" (II):

> Immortal heat, o let thy greater flame
>   Attract the lesser to it: let those fires,
>   Which shall consume the world, first make it tame,
> And kindle in our hearts such true desires,
> As may consume our lusts, and make thee way.

In this instance the coldness that counters the melting power of the heat and combines with it to produce the temper of the metal is not the cold hardness of the stone (man's sinful heart) but instead the coldness of God in withdrawing this love, as in "The Temper" (II):

> It cannot be. Where is that mightie ioy,
>   Which iust now tooke up all my heart?

The coldness of the tempering process, however, extends beyond the mere absence of love and is equated with God's sending afflictions to man. These positive ills macerate his flesh:

> Thou didst so punish sinne,
>   That I became
>   Most thinne
>   ["Easter Wings"].

They are

> sorrow dogging sinne,
> Afflictions sorted, anguish of all sizes
>   ["Sinne" (I)].

We read in "Affliction" (I):

> My flesh began unto my soule in paine,
>   Sicknesses cleave my bones....
> Thus thinne and leane without a fence or freind,
>   I was blowne through with every storme and
>   wind.

In the heat of divine love, Herbert can peer above some forty heavens. When afflicted with divine cold, his insight fails and he suffers punishment for his sins. The title indicates that this alternating process is ultimately beneficent, and in fact at the end of the poem Herbert accepts its necessity.

However, there is more we can learn of Herbert's ideas about the tempering process as applied to metals. Not only is hardness imparted to steel; it is also given elasticity and resilience. In "Holy Baptisme" (II) Herbert had prayed, "Let mee be soft and supple to thy will"; and though here he was working with an image describing childhood, this pliancy and suppleness in bending to God's will is applied to metals or to the softening of the hard stone of the heart ("sinne turn'd flesh to stone": "The Holy Communion"). Sinful man is brittle: "He is a brittle crazy glasse" ("The Windowes"). Such brittleness characterizes the hardness of stone (sin), and of glass (man's flesh), not that of steel tempered by adversity. And so Herbert prays, "Give mee the plyant mind" ("Content"), and in a metal-forging image that is applicable to "The Temper":

> Sinne is still hammering my heart
> Unto a hardnes, void of love:
> Let supling grace to crosse his art
> Drop from above
> ["Grace"].

I take it that the images of stretching and contracting in "The Temper" are intended to represent the action of the metal in the tempering process expanding under heat, contracting under cold. Yet it is more than possible that Herbert is protesting not only the painfulness of this process but also the subsequent stresses and strains put on him when he is tempered and is pliant enough so as not to break under the strain as if he were brittle glass. The resiliency of tempered metal is surely typified in man, the great amphibian, who must be stretched between a world of grace and one of sin, the world of the spirit and that of the flesh.

At first Herbert protests that raising him by love and dropping him by punishment the distance from heaven to hell is to stretch a crumb of dust over the spaces of infinity that only a divine being can fill. The images here are interesting. The "distances that belong to thee" have been foreshadowed in "The Agony" in somewhat similar language:

> But there are two vast, spacious things,
> The which to measure it doth more behove.
> Yet few there are, that sound them, Sinne, and
> Love.

Later, the subject is to be elaborated. In "Affliction" (IV) Herbert is very precise in his description of a brittle man who has been broken by such stretching:

> Broken in peices, all asunder,
> Lord hunt mee not,

A thing forgott,
Once a poore creature, now a wonder,
A wonder tortur'd in the space
Betwixt this world and that of grace.

The heart of the comparison lies in the protest that a temper, or elasticity, proper only for divinity has been imposed on man. Herbert argues that, if man is capable of meeting God's demands in this respect, as a result of this agonizing tempering, God will be revealing more of His mystery than is proper. Two similar images occur: "Wilt thou meet armes with man" and "Will great *God* measure with a wretch?" Canon Hutchinson[4] suggests that in "meet armes" there is a pun on *mete*, or measure, and that the figure is drawn from fencing and the measurement of weapons to secure equal lengths. Just possibly some word play on *mete* is present, but the repetition of *measure* two lines below indicates that any such pun must be distinctly subsidiary to some other sense. It is true that "meet armes" seems to be Herbert's own idiom. To "meet with," as to "meet with man" is common for to fight a duel with, or to oppose in battle; and perhaps "meet armes with" could mean "to combat armed." I do not really think so, however. Hutchinson does not explain how measuring weapons can stretch a crumb of dust from heaven to hell; and it would be absurd to argue that the crumb is stretched in order to be able to hold a sword as long as that of the Lord of Hosts. The same objection holds to the armed-combat explication, especially since these terms for combat would be unique in Herbert's frequent use of the combat idea.[5]

The primary meaning is still to seek. Whatever it is, it should appear earlier in the sequence. In "Faith" we find:

If blisse had lien in art or strength,
None but the wise, or strong had gained it:
Where now by fayth all arms are of a length,
One size doth all conditions fitt.

Several references make it clear that "arms" here are not weapons but man's own arms. The next stanza continues, for instance,

A peasant may beleive as much
As a great cleark, and reach the highest stature.

With this we may profitably compare "The Temper": "meet armes with," "measure with a wretch," and "Shall be thy stature spell?" That all arms are of a length, made so by Faith, clearly means that no man because of natural or acquired endowments has a longer arm to reach up for grace (presumably with the upstretched arms of supplication) than another of equal faith. Length of arm is clearly signified here. Elsewhere, in "Praise," man's arm is described thus:

> His arme is short; yet with a sling
> He may doe more.[6]

On the other hand, in "Prayer" (II) we read, about God,

> Of what supreme almighty powre
> Is thy great arme, which spans the east and west,
> And tacks the centre to the sphere.

The general equation, then, is made between the length and strength of an arm. If God racks a crumb of dust from heaven to hell, he is meeting, or matching length of arms with man, and the measure is the span from east to west, from pole to pole, from heaven to hell, with One Who, in the words of "The Sacrifice," "grasps the earth and heaven with his fist." If there is a combat implied, as doubtless there is in one sense, it is not that of dueling or armed combat but instead that of wrestling. This interpretation is almost certain, even though no very specific reference for it may be found. When in Herbert man and God are in rivalry, or combat, the language is not that of formal warfare but of a trial in which God tempers his strength to just that necessary to overcome man. For example, in "Artillerie" such a combat takes the form of an archery match:

> Then wee are shooters both, and thou dost daine
> To enter combate with us, and contest
> With thine own clay.

In "The Reprisall" we have somewhat similar language:

> Ah was it not enough that thou
> By thy eternall glory didst outgoe mee?
> Couldst thou not greifs sad conquests mee allow,
> But in all victories overthrow mee?

I suggest, though there is no specific evidence for it, that Herbert had in mind in these friendly contests the type of Jacob wrestling with the angel. And the association of strength of arms with wrestling is clearly indicated in "A Dialogue Antheme" when Death speaks:

> Let loosers talk: yet thou shalt dy,
> These Armes shall crush thee.

Since "armes" are not weapons, it would seem that Herbert in "meet armes with" and "measure with a wretch" has partly in mind some such friendly match on God's part as a contest of strength, like wrestling.

The stretching of the crumb of dust so that his arms might be of a length with those of Christ, "which span the Poles, And tune all spheares at once" (the quotation is from Donne's "Good Friday, 1613") calls to mind in "Easter," Herbert's combination of the stretching of Christ on the cross with the tuning of the lute string, which stands for praise and prayer, and thus for religious poetry as well:

> The *Crosse* taught all wood to resound his Name,
>   who bore the same.
> His stretched *sinews* taught all strings, what key
> Is best to celebrate this most high Day.

Herbert also probably had in mind in the matching-of-arms images in "The Temper" the protest of mortal man at being stretched above his capacities so that his measurement of arms with those that span "the east and west" ("Prayer" [II]) is intended, as well, to refer to the impossibility of his enduring the agonies of Christ on the cross or by such agonies to achieve the salvation that only the death of divinity could bring. Herbert had earlier protested in another manner against the imposition of divine emotions on incapable and sinful man:

> Such sorrow, as if sinfull man could feele,
> Or feele his part, he would not cease to kneele,
> Till all were melted, though he were all steele
>   ["The Sacrifice"].

The interesting use of steel here as a sign of hardness instead of the usual stone indicates, to my mind, the impossibility even of tempered man feeling the depth of divine sorrow.[7] The stretching of Christ's sinews on the cross in Herbert's "Easter" compared to the stretching of lute strings being tuned to the proper key, or temper, to celebrate the Resurrection, spells out to us, in anticipation, the tacit use of the same image in "The Temper." The space images, therefore, that rack man to such a vast extent, that stretch a crumb of dust the distance between heaven and hell through the spaces of infinity suitable only for the reach of the divine Christ, these — through the tuned lute strings stretched to the temper or key of celebration (these in turn typified by the stretched nerves of Christ on the cross) — combine ultimately to suggest the vast distance actually encompassed by the outstretched arms of the crucified Christ, and the seemingly impossible demands made on man (who is not a God-Man) to stretch himself between the world of the spirit and the world of the flesh.[8]

The image of "the tuning of my brest / To make the musick better" is a very common one in Herbert. It has two main significances. First, in the tuning of the instrument the preparation for the music that is to follow is conceived as groans ("Affliction" [I]), which are the necessary pre-requisite for repentance.

> All *Solomons* sea of Brasse and world of stone
> Is not so deare to thee, as one good grone. ...
> ... grones are quick, and full of wings,
>   And all their motions upward bee;
> And ever as they mount like larks, they sing,
> The note is sad, yet musique for a *King*
>   ["Sion"].

As man is stretched by his afflictions to promote repentance, so a lute string is tuned to produce harmonious chords of praise and thankful-ness. This tuning of a musical instrument to adjust its pitch, and to bring its various strings into correct harmonic relationship, is known as *tempering*; and here it is obvious that we have one of the underlying puns on the title. Then when each string is properly tuned, or tempered,

> My Music shall find thee, and ev'ry string
>   Shall have his attribute to sing.
> That all together may accord in thee,
>   And prove one *God,* one Harmonie
>   ["The Thankes-giving"].

Moreover, the tempering, or harmony, of music is not confined only to man as the lute: in sign of reconciliation God Himself may make up the third voice of the polyphony:

> Consort both *Heart* and *Lute*, and twist a song
>   Pleasant and long:
> Or since all Musick is but three parts vyed
>   and multiplied
> O let thy *blessed Spirit* beare a part,
> And make up our defects with his sweet art
>   ["Easter"].

The universality of song is indicated in "Repentance," following on a medical description of the way in which a punished sinner wastes away,

> But thou wilt sinne and greif destroy,
> That so the broken bones may ioy,
> And tune together in a well sett song,
> Full of his praises,
> Who dead men raises:
> Fractures well cur'd make us more strong.

Besides the interest in these lines from the equation of repaired lute with broken bones of brittle humanity knit together, the association of a medical with a musical image is of particular significance. With the medical meaning we come to the first of the understood puns in the title that are only indirectly suggested in the text but which we can read into the poem with confidence on the basis of Herbert's use of similar images in the preceding sequence.

In medical terms the "temper" is the "temperament," which can be both mental and physical. When the four humours of the body are in equable relationship, a man is properly tempered. Thus "to temper" means to restore the proper temperament to, to bring into a good or desirable state of health; to cure, heal, or refresh. For the physical, the use of "temper" to refer to the correct proportioning of the four humours is associated with another meaning, in which one "tempers" by mixing ingredients together, or one with another, in proper proportions. And, since in mental states "temper" follows the physical, it comes to mean a mental balance or composure, a command over excessive emotions. Acceptance of God's will is thus a tempered state.

In this sequence in which "The Temper" occupies such an important place, Herbert has used a very common image cluster concerning God, or Christ, the physician. The note was first struck in "The Sacrifice":

> Now heale thy self, Physitian, now come downe.
> Alas, I did so, when I left my crowne,
> And fathers smile for you, to feele his frowne.
> Was ever greif like mine?
>
> In healing, not my self, there doth consist
> All that salvation, which ye now resist.
> Your safety in my sicknes doth subsist.
> Was ever greif like mine?

The chief medicine of Christ the physician is, of course, the blood and water that issued from his pierced side; and in "Holy Baptisme" (I) Herbert addresses this medicine:

> O blessed streames, either ye doe prevent

> And stop our sinnes from growing thick and wide,
> Or els give teares to drown them, as they grow.
>   In you Redemption measures all my time,
>   And spreeds the plaister equall to the crime.

Christ's blood, as transmitted in the Eucharist, is of course the great healer. In "The Holy Communion" Herbert remarks how "by way of nourishment and strength / Thou creep'st into my brest"; and, later, in "Conscience" he addresses Sin:

> If thou persistest, I will tell thee,
> That I have physick to expell thee.
>   And the receit shall bee
> My *Saviours* blood: ...
>   The bloody crosse of my deare *Lord*
>   Is both my physique and my sword.

Again, in "An Offering":

> There is a balsome, or indeed a blood,
> Dropping from heaven, which doth both clense
>   and close
> All sorts of wounds.

On the other hand, God has another medicine that Herbert dreads:

>   O doe not fill mee!
> With the turn'd viol of thy bitter wrath:
> For thou hast other vessels full of blood,
> A part whereof my *Saviour* emptied hath
> Even unto death: since he dy'd for my good,
>   O doe not kill mee.
>   But O repreive mee.
> For thou hast life and death at thy commande:
> Thou art both *Judge* and *Saviour, feast* and *rod,*
> *Cordial* and *Corrosive*: put not thy hand
> Into the bitter box, but O my *God,*
>   My *God,* releive mee.

Here in "Sighs and Grones" we have the clearest statement of God the physician, with his cordial box of Christ's blood, which stands for Love; and his corrosive box of Punishment for sin by purgation. In the light of this image we can see more clearly the meaning of the lines in "Repentance," a poem that comes shortly before "The Temper":

> Sweeten at length this better boule;
> Which thou hast pourd into my soule;

> Thy wormewood turne to health, ...
>   When thou for sinne rebukest man,
>   Forthwith he waxeth woe and wan.
> Bitternes fills our bowells: all our hearts
>   Pine and decay,
>   And drope away,
> And carry with them th'other parts.

In view of the common medical sense of "temper" and the various references in the preceding poems to the bitter medicine of affliction that purges man of sin and prepares him for the cordial box of Love, it is reasonable to equate with a medical pun in the title the presence and the withdrawal of God, the racking between exaltation and punishment, and *the final acceptance* by which Herbert arrives at a state of perfect *temper*, or balance, by the operation of these two medicines. The pun is nicely balanced between, on the one hand, the physical purgation and healing process and, on the other, the mental balance and composure resulting from the *temper* or middle course as in Hooker, quoted by the Oxford Dictionary: "A moderate, indifferent [i.e., balanced] temper betweene fulnesse of bread, and emptinesse." One may, again, bring forward the definition: to mix or blend ingredients with one another in proper proportion (here bitter and sweet), the result being another kind of *temper*: to manage in good measure, to regulate, govern, rule — what at the end Herbert does to his excessive passions of joy and fear.

We may revert now to the source of a deeper lying pun. Given the prevalence of Eucharistic imagery in Herbert, as in other religious poets of his time, it is no cause for surprise that there should be a pun on the way in which God tempers man by the operations of justice and mercy, and another on the way in which one tempers the other, as the New Law tempers the Old. And that the Eucharist is specifically associated with mercy, or love, is quite conventional and is emphasized in "The Sacrifice," as in "The Agony":

> Love is that liquor sweet and most divine,
> Which my *God* feels, as blood, but I, as wine.

The Eucharist itself may properly be called a tempered drink in the sense that two elements are mixed together in proper proportions: wine and water. Such tempering was ordered as early as the second century by Pope Alexander I to commemorate the blood and water that issued from Christ's pierced side. This mystical union of water and of wine became a symbol of Christ Himself. He was Man and God. He had two natures, the human and the divine, so closely joined like the water and the wine that nothing could divide them. The wine shows Christ's divine nature joined, or tempered, with His human nature (water). The tempering, however, is even further allegorized. According to Cyprian, just as the wine receives the water in itself, so has Christ taken to Himself us and our sins. Therefore the mixing of the water with the wine symbolizes the intimate union of the faithful with Him to whom they have bound themselves in faith; and this union is so firm that nothing can sever it, just as the water can no longer be separated from the wine.[9]

Herbert has no strongly developed image cluster that concerns the mixture of the human and divine in Christ typified by the addition of a little water to the Eucharist wine, nor does he usually typify the union of men with Christ in the Church as the water and wine, although this concept certainly appears in "The Sacrifice." Nevertheless, the water plays an important part in his thinking, and does in fact have a Eucharistic significance in the title "The Temper." For example, the difference between the Old and the New Law is epitomized in "The Sacrifice" as the difference between the non-saving gush of water that issued from the rock struck by Moses, a man, as compared with the saving blood from the side of the pierced divinity:

> He clave the stony rock, when they were dry.
> But surely not their hearts, as I well try.

In this sense, therefore, the wine of mercy-salvation tempers, or mollifies, the water of justice-punishment, the New tempers the Old Law; and it would seem that we are back at Herbert's rack operated by love and punishment.

But there is a more intimate and secret manner in which the water mixed with wine may be linked with tempering. For Herbert, tears are always associated with repentance; and it is by repentance that man puts himself in the proper frame of mind to receive grace and the sacrament. In "Holy Baptisme" (I) the water issuing from Christ's side seems to be associated with the baptismal sacrament, as the blood is with the sacrament of Communion. Both are spoken of as giving "teares to drown them [our sins], as they grow." It may be, though he never says so, that Herbert had in mind some such equation as the tears of repentance being changed into salvation as the water was changed to wine in Christ's miracle. Certainly his frequent association of tears with blood suggests that he at least had some notion that tears, imputed for deeds, brought down the miracle of cleansing grace.[10]

Two interesting passages occur in "The Sacrifice," both being concerned with another form of tears, the sweatlike blood from Christ in Gethsemane.[11] In the first, his disciples sleep, and he says,

> Therefore my soule melts, and my hearts deare treasure
> Drops blood (the onely beads) my words to measure.
> O let this cup passe, if it be thy pleasure.
>   Was ever greif, &c.
>
> These drops being temper'd with a sinners teares
> A Balsome are for both the Hemispheres;
> Curing all wounds, but mine; all but my feares.
>   Was ever greif, &c.

In the second, at His trial Christ addresses His weeping followers:

> Weep not, deare freinds, since I for both have wept
> When all my teares were blood, the while you slept:
> Your teares for your owne fortunes should be kept.
>   Was ever greif, &c.

There cannot be the slightest doubt that in the first of these quotations:

> These drops being temper'd with a sinners teares
> A Balsome are for both the Hemispheres;
> Curing all wounds, but mine; all but my feares

the sacramental blood of Christ is prefigured and the blood from His heart is as Eucharistic as the blood from His side. Only the communion wine miraculously turned to Christ's blood can be called a balsam (the medical term) or spoken of as curing all wounds as well as fears. It would seem, then, that Herbert allegorized here the water in the Eucharist, through its common meaning representing man, as the tears of repentance. This mixture, or temper, of human tears (repentance from sin) with Christ's blood (love and grace), as the ultimate expression of love is the deepest significance in the title "The Temper," a poem that following hard on "Holy Communion" and two poems on "Love," continues in the sequence the reconciliation of man and God. This reconciliation as an important element in "The Temper" (and one of the important senses in the title) is clear not only by reason of the theme of acceptance in the final stanza but by a significance that has been latent in the whole series of images about distance and is emphasized in the first line of the last stanza, "Whether I flye with Angels, fall with dust." In flying with angels man is exalted by love; in falling with dust, he is thrown down in punishment by the exercise of God's power. In "Providence" Herbert had said:

> Wee all aknowledge both thy powre and love
> To be exact, transcendent, and divine.

In "The Temper" it is the exercise of this power and love, the stretching and contracting, that seems so incomprehensible. Thus, it is no accident that, later, in "The Search" we have in some important lines the enormous universal spaces, a theme on which "The Temper" is built, typified as the distance between God's will and man's understanding of it:

> Thy will such a strange distance is,
> > As that to it
> East and West touch, the poles doe kisse,
> > And parallels meet.

"The Search" thereupon continues with what is a useful commentary on "The Temper": when God is withdrawn from man in the exercise of His will, man's grief is equal to the immense distance of the withdrawal. On the contrary, when God comes close to man in love, the two are united:

> For as thy absence doth excell
> > All distance knowne;
> So doth thy neerenes beare the bell,
> > Making two one.

The union is not alone that which man feels in the plenitude of God's love, but, more specifically, the tempered union of man within the Church in the body of Christ, the tempered mixture of mortal water and divine blood in the Eucharist cup, in which the water, as tears of repentance, or mortal love and sorrow for sin, is willingly lost and no longer is separate from the great will of divinity. The tempered Eucharist, therefore, as suggested by "The Sacrifice"

> These drops being temper'd with a sinners teares
> A Balsome are for both the Hemispheres;
> Curing all wounds

not only recognizes the essential that man must come to the Communion in a state of grace as represented by repentance but also typifies the great reconciliation of God with man as represented by man's complete acceptance of divine will.[12]

In *The Temple* the order of the poems following "Easter" is interesting, for it seems to epitomize the life of a Christian under the New Law brought in by the sacrifice celebrated at Easter. We have first "Holy Baptisme," then "Nature," then "Sinne," then "Affliction," followed by "Repentance," "Faith," "Prayer," "Holy Communion," "Antiphon," two poems on "Love," and then the two "Temper" poems, and "Jordan." We should notice that after the reconciliation following sin expressed in "Holy Communion" and its triumphant "Antiphon," the celebration of "Love" in both poems is concerned with the proper subject for love poetry, the decision being made in favor of that verse celebrating divine rather than earthly love. On the other side of the two "Temper" poems is "Jordan," also concerned with the pre-eminence of religious over secular poetry. Given this position, it would be odd if there were no literary references implied in "The Temper."

I suggest that at their most personal level the two "Temper" poems are also concerned with poetry, and that this concern involves a final — and private — reference in the title. We know that the opening lines of "The Temper" (I) link this poem with the preceding poem on "Love":

> How should I praise thee, *Lord?* how should my rimes
> Gladly ingrave thy love in steele,
> If what my soule doth feele sometimes,
> My soule might ever feele.

The poem then continues with what is, in effect, a complaint that the poet cannot write of love when he is stretched between the extremes of exaltation and of depression. He prays for the steady feeling of security but then decides that he must accept God's will and be heated and cooled, stretched and contracted, accordingly. The reconciliation is then complete when he sees that, in truth, the joy and the pain he feels in extremes are tempering him to write better poetry on his subject. The association of music with poetry in Herbert is fairly constant, especially if divine poetry be thought of in Herbertian terms as only another form of prayer. Then in the final stanza, we may take it, he attempts to reach another sense of "The Temper." We have had the metal-working images of heat and cold, expansion and contraction; the process of changing the brittleness of iron to the pliancy and strength of steel. In the tuning of the lute we have the harmonious temper of music applied to the production of divine poetry. And, finally, Herbert as man attempts to rise to the equable or medical sense of temper, the middle way achieved by acceptance and balance.

This progression is accomplished within the tacitly understood imagery of the tempering of wine and water, so that Herbert in writing of his divine poetry is not distinguishing the poet from the priest, both of whom make their offering. Here we must revert to the opening poem of the sequence, "The Altar," in which the natural altar untouched by tool, which marked the Promised Land, Herbert's heart, is cemented with tears and dedicated to God's praise. This praise is performed by his religious poetry, which, at the start of *The Temple*, hymns Christ's sacrifice in a series of Eucharistic poems before celebrating Herbert's progress from the secular to the religious life as paralleling the life and regeneration of a Christian from baptism to the exalation of love. In this sequence it would seem that "The Temper" holds a key place in the sequence of five poems which discuss the proper subjects for poetry. Only when the poet has been tempered by divine love and has passed, as in the two "Temper" poems, through the strengthening and suppling process can he come to "Jordan." And that "Jordan" in its title can have a reference also to the water that is blessed and mixed with wine in the Eucharist cup is not without significance. Finally, for the conjecture that Herbert in "The Temper" is associating his fitness as priest with his fitness as divine poet, his revolt at, and then his acceptance of, the distances in this poem is interestingly paralleled later in "The Preisthood," apparently written before he took holy orders, which begins:

> Blest Order, which in powre dost so excell,
> That with th'one hand thou liftest to the sky,
> And with the other throwest down to Hell
> In thy just censures.

The language here is too close to "The Temper" (I) to be accidental, and leads to the view that "The Temper" also discusses the responsibility of the priest, in the distance-space images, as against the simple roosting and nestling of the laity within the Church.

These responsibilities are mixed with Herbert's mental states reflecting the difficulty encountered when each priest is supposed to act out Christ's story in his own life and to match arms with the crucified Christ, those arms that extend from pole to pole, or heaven to hell. The purgation and healing that he performs as priest to his own flock he must first undergo himself, and come to an equable, tempered acceptance of God's will. His temper or balance must acquire the resilience of steel, the health of the purified soul, and the experience of the racking distances between God's will and man's understanding of it. Only when he can learn to comply with God's will can he, like David, celebrate his God in prayer — or in poem. For this is also the preparation necesary for the divine poet who, tempered by heat and cold, like steel, beyond the capacities of Venus' men, and tempered like the water of the communion cup by being mixed beyond the possibility of separation with the wine of Christ's Church, finally rears his altar of unhewn stone, rounding the sequence, this side of Jordan.

GEORGE HERBERT: PRIEST, POET, MUSICIAN

Amy M. Charles

The fellowship of music is always open to kindred spirits, and the boundaries of time and place form no barrier. Those whom love of music carries back to the seventeenth century inevitably learn of the musical interests of George Herbert (1593-1633), the rector of Bemerton, near Salisbury, in Wiltshire, England, and surely one of the most musical of English poets. Herbert played both the lute and the viol (both represented in Christopher Webb's modern memorial window in Salisbury Cathedral), and his love of music recurs throughout the poems in *The Temple*, published in the year of his death by his good friend Nicholas Ferrar.

To understand how thoroughly music pervades many of Herbert's poems requires some knowledge of seventeenth-century musical practice; and of course gambists are especially well prepared to interpret many of his musical allusions. But the player who comes to Herbert expecting to find poems that frequently employ musical terms may be disappointed at first, because Herbert's open use of musical language and imagery is less than would be expected, if one looks only for the terms in a musical glossary. Herbert's use of music is both more subtle and more pervasive.

Herbert names the viol only once — and then not in a poem at all, but in a prayer included in one of his prose works, *A Priest to the Temple:* "Blessed be the God of Heaven and Earth! who onely doth wondrous things. Awake therefore, my Lute, and my Viol! awake all my powers to glorifie thee!"[1] Lute and viol are juxtaposed also in a famous passage by Izaak Walton, Herbert's first biographer:

> His chiefest recreation was Musick, in which heavenly Art he was a
> most excellent Master, and did himself compose many *divine*
> *Hymns* and Anthems, which he set and sung to his *Lute* or *Viol*;
> and, though he was a lover of retiredness, yet his love to *Musick*

Reprinted from *Journal of the Viola da Gamba Society of America, 4 (1967), 27-36,* by *permission of the author and the publisher.*

was such, that he went usually twice every week on certain appointed days, to the *Cathedral Church* in *Salisbury*; and at his return would say, *That his time spent in Prayer, and Cathedral Musick, elevated his Soul, and was his Heaven upon Earth*: But before his return thence to Bemerton, he would usually sing and play his part, at an appointed private Musick-meeting; and, to justifie this practice, he would often say, *Religion does not banish mirth, but only moderates, and sets rules to it.*[2]

To Herbert, accustomed to the musical services at Westminster Abbey (as a schoolboy) and at Cambridge University (as an undergraduate and, later, as University Orator), the opportunity to hear cathedral music and to take part in the private musical gatherings that followed evidently was a necessary part of life; and on occasion his curate, Nathaniel Bostock, conducted the services at Bemerton so that Herbert would not have to forego his musical sustenance. One of the most delightful of Walton's anecdotes relates how Herbert's friends twitted him when he arrived at one of their sessions disheveled and soiled from helping a poor man and his horse. Herbert explained to them carefully "*That the thought of what he had done, would prove Musick to him at Midnight*," then turned rather briskly to the business at hand with "And now let's tune our instruments."[3]

Tuning, as a matter of fact, is as important in Herbert's poems as it is in playing any stringed instrument. Pegs are mentioned only once (in a line later rejected from "The Pearl"[4]), but strings and tuning provide the basis for some of Herbert's most effective musical figures. In "Deniall," when Herbert's prayers are unheard, his soul is "Untun'd, unstrung"; and he implores God: "O cheer and tune my heartlesse breast." Musical imagery ("sing," "strokes," "imitate," "harmonie") recurs in "The Thanksgiving," most memorably in

> My musick shall finde thee, and ev'ry string
> Shall have his attribute to sing ...

The reader is reminded of the physical origin of the strings in *"Grieve not the Holy Spirit"*:

> Oh take thy lute, and tune it to a strain,
> Which may with thee
> All day complain.
> There can no discord but in ceasing be.
> Marbles can weep; and surely strings
> More bowels have, then such hard things.

The physical aspect of Christ's suffering on the cross is emphasized in one of the most musical of Herbert's poems, "Easter." In the first part of this poem Herbert calls to his heart to rise as Christ has risen, calls for his lute to take its part in his celebration, and asks the Holy Spirit to bear the third part (a reflection of the Trinity in keeping with attitudes from medieval times) in his consort; then in the second he sets forth their song, a song at once heart-breaking in its simplicity and heart-raising in its triumph. In calling on his lute he reminds it that

> The crosse taught all wood to resound his name,
> Who bore the same.
> His stretched sinews taught all strings, what key
> Is best to celebrate this most high day.

Here the strings, likened to the sinews of Christ, are both taught and taut as the key is raised for the high holy day of the Christian year.[5]

The necessity of being well prepared, never far from Herbert's mind, is set forth in two favorite figures, being dressed and being tuned (occasionally used together). Sometimes, as in "Gratefulnesse," Herbert does the tuning. (Several times he tunes sighs into groans, as in "The Search," in effect creating a figure appropriate to both vocal and wind music.) More often, however, he is the instrument that is tuned, usually by Christ. Of the command or permission of the "most sacred Spirit," he acknowledges in "Providence,"

> Nothing escapes them both; all must appeare,
> And be dispos'd, and dress'd, and tun'd by thee,
> Who sweetly temper'st all. If we could heare
> Thy skill and art, what musick would it be!

In "Aaron," a poem noteworthy for its devices of sound, the third line of each stanza moves through various appeals to the ear ("Harmonious bells below," "A noise of passions ringing me for dead," "Another musick," "My onely musick") to culminate in "My doctrine tun'd by Christ." In a poem particularly rich in musical allusion, "The Temper," Herbert employs such verbs as "rack" and "stretch" before he makes the figure of tuning explicit:

> Yet take thy way; for sure thy way is best:
> Stretch or contract me, thy poore debter:
> This is but tuning of my breast,
> To make the musick better.

No string player need be reminded of the necessity for meticulous care in tuning; and Herbert's varied and frequent use of the figure of tuning shows how naturally he drew on the musical knowledge in writing his poems.

No other image is used so generally — but then, no idea is more important to Herbert than that of man's being well prepared to learn and to follow God's will. This attitude is made most explicit in the conclusion of "Deniall," a poem in which Herbert has intensified the sense of disorder and being out of harmony with God by ending each stanza with an unrhymed trochaic fifth line; then in the final stanza he brings the fifth line into harmony of pattern, as the mind and the spirit are brought into harmony with God. The fifth line, turned into the dominant iambic rhythm, is made to complete the rhyme scheme of ABABB:

> O cheer and tune my heartlesse breast,
> Deferre no time;
> That so thy favours granting my request,
> They and my minde may chime,
> And mend my ryme.

This subtle underlining of thought through form is only one means of enriching the verse, but one particularly apt for a poet of musical interests.

Herbert employs a variety of musical terms in his poems, sometimes in an unequivocally musical sense (as in the line in "Vertue," "My musick shows ye have your closes," or cadences), but often as the basis of the serious pun so widely used in the Renaissance (as in "Grace," for example, where he puns on "grasse" and the quality of grace, and may or may not use "grace" in a musical sense). Like other poets of his day, Herbert speaks often of his poetry in terms of "praise" or "sing", and he chooses terms that might apply to either verse or music. There is no question of the musical application of these lines in "Employment (I)":

> Lord place me in thy consort; give one strain
> To my poore reed.

The lute tuned to a strain in "*Grieve not the Holy Spirit*" and the "notes and strains" of "Dooms-day" unquestionably allude to musical strains; and the embellishments called relishes[6] assure us that Herbert intended a musical application of these lines in "The Pearl":

> I know the wayes of Pleasure, the sweet strains,
> The lullings and the relishes of it . . .

But it is less certain that he intended a musical interpretation of these lines in "Dulnesse":

> The wanton lover in a curious strain
> Can praise his fairest fair...

Later lines in this poem (especially "Where are my window-songs?") suggest that the lover's strain was at least words to be set to music; but this sort of allusion, particularly when vocal music may be involved, is less simple to label with certainty.

Even when a word that may be a musical allusion occurs in conjunction with other words that may be used in musical senses, we have no assurance that Herbert so intended it. The musical "fall" Orsino asks to have repeated in the opening speech of *Twelfth Night* is not likely to be the sense of the word Herbert uses in several poems: "And measure not their fall" ("Miserie"). "Sometimes I hardly reach a score, / Sometimes to hell I fall" ("The Temper (I)"). "Let th' upper springs into the low/ Descend and fall, and thou dost flow" ("The Size"), and "Or shall each leaf,/ Which falls in Autumne, score a grief?" ("Good Friday"). The presence in each of these passages of words that *might* be musical terms ("measure," "score," "springs" as word play on the ornament called a "springer," "grief" as a pun on the musical term "grave") should not mislead us into what was probably not intended as musical allusion.

Among the numerous other terms that may at one time have had a musical application but have now been dulled by frequent use we may include "accord" as in "accord in thee,/ And prove one God, one harmonie" ("The Thanksgiving"), "aire" in "one aire of thoughts usurps my brain" ("The Bunch of Grapes"), "bar" in "O take these barres, these lengths away;/ Turn, and restore me" ("The Search"), "bear" in "the heart/ Must bear the longest part" ("Antiphon (I)"), "diminishings" in "Yet must there such proportion be assign'd/ To these diminishings" ("The Church Militant"), "divisions" in "Could not that Wisdom ... Have ... jagg'd his seamless coat ... With curious questions and divisions?" ("Divinitie"), "flat delights" and "sowre displeasure" ("Vanitie (II)"), "fancy" in "'Tis a thin webbe, which poysonous fancies make" ("The Church-porch", in a stanza using also "toy," "compose," "shake," "plays," and "rest"), "measure" in "For mine [grief] excludes both measure, tune, and time" ("Griefe"), even "musick" in "Me thinks delight should have/ More skill in musick, and keep better time" ("The Glimpse"), "note" in "The note is sad, yet musick for a King" ("Sion"), "part" in "Sinne and Satan ... use much art/ To gain thy thirds and little

part" ("Decay"), "rest" in "Making my way thy rest, / And thy small
quantities my length" ("The H. Communion"), "set" in "a well-set song"
("Repentance") or "Thy passions have their set partitions" ("An Offering"), and "shake" in "endure a shake" ("The Church-porch"). Many
other examples might be adduced, but these are typical and demonstrate
the point that it is as important not to infer a non-existent musical
allusion as to recognize one that Herbert clearly intended.

Herbert's involvement in music extended beyond the use of active
figure and passing allusion, and a number of his poems are clearly
intended as songs. In three poems — "Easter", "Christmas," and "An
Offering" — one poetic form is used in the first section to introduce the
song (in a different poetic form) that makes up the second part. Poems
like "The Rose," some of them the sacred equivalents of the secular love
song, were unquestionably intended to be sung, probably to the
accompaniment of lute or viol, perhaps at one of the gatherings in
Salisbury. We may suppose that these music meetings were similar to
those Thomas Mace described in the 1670's as having taken place during
his "*Younger Time*":

> We had (beyond all *This*) a *Custom* at *Our Meetings*,
> that commonly, after such *Instrumental Musick* was
> over, we did *Conclude All*, with some *Vocal Musick*,
> (to the *Organ*, or (for want of *That*) to the Theorboe.[7]

The accompaniments for such songs may have been extempore, or, if
they were written out, they may have been destroyed, along with
Herbert's other papers, in the fire during the Civil War at Highnam,
where Jane Herbert lived after her second marriage, to Sir Robert
Cook.[8]

Herbert's poems have not lacked musical arrangements by other
musicians. The Tannenbaum bibliography[9] lists fifty-three arrangements of twenty-four different poems by Herbert. In our own time, the
most distinguished setting is that by Vaughan Williams in *Five Mystical
Songs* (1911): "Easter," "I Got Me Flowers" (the second part of
"Easter"), "Love Bade Me Welcome," "The Call," and "Antiphon." As
hymns, however, Herbert's poems have fared less well; only two of his
poems are in use in the current edition of the *Episcopal Hymnal*: "The
Elixir" ("Teach me, my God and King") and "Antiphon (I)" ("Let all the
world in every corner sing"). *Hymns Ancient and Modern*, used by the
Church of England, also includes two of Herbert's poems as hymns:
"Antiphon (I)" and "Praise (II)" ("King of Glorie, King of Peace").
Herbert's delight in developing a variety of stanzaic patterns is probably
the reason that his poems are more readily adaptable as anthems or for

solo voice but are more difficult to fit to the patterns of hymn tunes in common, long, or short meter.

A casual reader of Herbert's poems, remembering Walton's words about Herbert's hymns and anthems, may be surprised to find that so few of them are in general use as hymns today. Although the appearance of Herbert's verse on the page conveys a strong sense of form and order, closer examination of these forms reveals unexpected complexity in stanzas that, at first glance, may have looked simple. Matching line-length to thought is characteristic of Herbert, and (aside from the sonnets) the poems in which the line-length remains constant are far out-numbered by those in which he combines lines of two or even three different lengths, and in unusual patterns. "Longing," for example, has iambic lines of 342241, "Peace" of 524352, "The Bunch of Grapes" of 5354455, and "Frailtie" of 52524352.[10]

The complexity of Herbert's verses is not limited to their form. Although these poems at first convey the impression of utter simplicity in form, in diction, and in their avoidance of the sort of classical allusion that adorned the verse of many of Herbert's predecessors, their diction is richer in appeal to both eye and ear than that of many other poets writing in the English language: Rosemond Tuve has suggested a remarkable range of visual imagery in Herbert;[11] and the range of his aural devices is far more extensive than the musical language, allusions, and figures here mentioned. Herbert was far too subtle a poet and his musical knowledge far too deeply ingrained to be confined to such diction and imagery. John Hollander has aptly commented, "If we can believe Walton, Herbert's almost constant use of 'sing' and 'pray' represents a personal as well as a conventional figure: it is the actual image of the poet-divine playing and singing in secluded retirement that lurks behind so many of the musical conceits in his poetry."[12]

All poets are keenly aware of sound; in Herbert, music seems to have intensified this awareness to the point where the words of poem after poem sound in their own right, but (as we have already observed in "Aaron") sound also to the accompaniment of other aural appeals. The verbs "sing," "praise," "sound," "ring," and "hear" occur frequently; bells toll or chime; trembling shows "inward warblinge" ("A Paradox"); the soul "accords to the lines of hymns or psalms" ("A true Hymne"); the cries of the Church drown the sound of the trumpet ("The Jews"). Several titles suggest sound of one kind or another: "The Answer," "Antiphon," "The Call," "Complaining," "Deniall," "A Dialogue-Antheme," "Even-song," "A true Hymne," "The Invitation," "Mans medley," "A Parodie," "Praise," "The Reprisall," "Sighs and Grones," "Sinnes round," "The Storm," "The Knell." Even silence is related, in a paradox, to sound: "There can no discord but in ceasing be" ("*Grieve not the Holy Spirit*"); Herbert's devotions fail to pierce the "silent eares" of God ("Deniall"); and he asks in "The Familie" a question Henry Vaughan was to echo in "Admission" — "What is so shrill as silent tears?" Pleasures "gloze" falsely in "Dotage"; and in "The Quip," which opens to the sound of jeering, Herbert uses onomatopoeia with memorable effect in describing Money and Glorie:

> Then Money came, and chinking still,
> What tune is this, poore man? said he:
> I heard in Musick you had skill.
> *But thou shalt answer, Lord, for me.*
>
> Then came brave Glorie puffing by
> In silks that whistled, who but he?
> He scarce allow'd me half an eie.
> *But thou shalt answer, Lord, for me.*

These more general uses of sound are less readily marked than Herbert's musical allusions; but it is doubtful that he would have used them so widely had his sense of the sound of words not been developed and refined by his music.

Music and poetry continued to bring Herbert comfort almost to the end of his life. Walton tells how, on the last Sunday of his life, Herbert rose suddenly from his Bed or Couch, call'd for one of his instruments, took it into his hand, and said —

> *My God, My God,*
> *My Musick shall find thee,*
> *   And every string*
> *shall have his attribute to sing.*

And having tun'd it, he play'd thus and sung:

> *The Sundays of Mans life,*
> *Thredded together on times string,*
> *Make Bracelets, to adorn the Wife*
> *Of the eternal glorious King:*
> *On Sundays, Heavens dore stands ope;*
> *Blessings are plentiful and rife,*
> *   More plentiful than hope.*[13]

The cathedral music he loved formed a part of his funeral service the following Sunday, Quinquagesima, in the little church of Bemerton St. Andrew's: "He was buryed (according to his owne desire) with the singing service for the buriall of the dead, by the singing men of Sarum."[14]

Not even here, however, have we fully described the significance of music in George Herbert's life, nor could we ever do so even by examining every possible musical allusion in his writing. The influence of music pervaded Herbert's life to a rare degree. Having brought himself to set aside the ways of Learning, Honour, and Pleasure he had known in the world (as he tells us in "The Pearle") to live the simple life of a rector of a country parish, he set aside virtually all the accoutrements of that fine life: he said farewell to the pretentious and florid style of preaching; he settled into a simple community removed from university and court; he changed his clothing from court fashion to canonical garb. He continued the strict restraint of his poetic diction that marked the earlier poems in the Williams manuscript (probably written before he came to Bemerton). In only two points did he refrain from strait simplicity — and they were related points: the metrical skill in his poems and the continued participation in music as listener, composer, and performer. In both poetry and music he found the discipline, the form, and the sense of order that gave direction to his life, even as he found these qualities in his service to God through his vocation. His poetry and his music were no mere indulgence, however, no reluctance to forego his own pleasures. In a very real sense, music *was* Herbert's sustenance on earth and its upward movement his most treasured avenue to God:

Church-musick.

Sweetest of sweets, I thank you: when displeasure
    Did through my bodie wound my minde,
You took me thence, and in your house of pleasure
    A daintie lodging me assign'd.

Now I in you without a bodie move,
    Rising and falling with your wings:
We both together sweetly live and love,
    Yet say sometimes, *God help poore Kings*.

Comfort, I'le die; for if you poste from me,
    Sure I shall do so, and much more:
But if I travell in your companie,
    You know the way to heavens doore.

In the service of the Anglican Church and in *The Temple* George Herbert — priest, poet, and musician — found both the harmony and the sense of order he sought.

"SOLOMON VBIQUE REGNET": HERBERT'S USE OF THE IMAGES OF THE NEW COVENANT

Florence Sandler

When Herbert chose for his book of devotional poems the title of *The Temple*, his reference was in the first instance biblical. Mary Ellen Rickey has pointed out that in both text and arrangement of the poems Herbert has made substantial reference also to the classical *fanum*. Nevertheless, as one would expect in a volume of Christian poetry, the biblical reference predominates; as I hope to show, it is probably by the application of a biblical thesis that the pagan temple has any place there at all. But to say that the temple is biblical is not yet sufficiently precise: one must make a distinction between the significance of the temple in the Old Testament and the New. Rosemond Tuve and Joseph Summers have pointed out the importance for Herbert's poetry of the New Testament thesis that the temple which God had inhabited upon Mount Sion from the days of Solomon was intended to prefigure his new "temple," namely, the heart of man. As Herbert laments in "Sion,'" the new temple is hardly as glorious as the old; moreover, God's occupancy there is obstructed by Sin. Even so, the heart is the fit house of God, and the "grones" which come from its yearning and purification are God's proper music, like the psalms in the temple of old.[1]

The explicit statement in "Sion" of God's habitation of the human heart is supported in other poems, for example, "Man," "The World," "A Parodie," and "The Temper" (II). In this last poem it is clear from the allusion to the "chair of grace" (or "mercy seat," as it is called in the King James Old Testament) that Herbert has the Hebraic temple in mind. Elsewhere, he may call God's habitation not "temple" but "palace." It is doubtful that these two words are intended to represent alternatives: since God is King, his temple — upon Mount Sion or in the human heart — is also a palace wherein he maintains his court in majesty. Indeed, Herbert, like Peter Sterry, may have been aware that "the same word in Hebrew signifieth a Temple, and a Pallace."[2]

Reprinted from *PLL*, 8 (1972), 147-58, by permission of the author and the publisher.

Recognizing the Hebraic allusions in certain poems, some readers of Herbert have been disappointed to discover that in the volume as a whole such allusions are infrequent. J. D. Walker some time ago went so far as to insist upon a structural analogy between the architecture of Herbert's temple and Solomon's, thereby neglecting Herbert's specific designation of parts of his "Hebraic" temple as *Church* and *Church-porch*, and misreading the argument of "Sion."[3] In that poem Herbert is careful to distinguish between two temples, one "of old" and the other "now," the temple of the Old Covenant being significant not for its own sake but only insofar as it prefigures that of the New. For his allusion to God's "mercy seat" fixed in the heart, Herbert had New Testament precedent; other specifically Hebraic temple furnishings, for example, the menorah and oracle, receive no mention in Herbert's poetry simply because no significant use is made of them in the New Testament.

The concept of the New Covenant (or New Testament, since the words mean the same) explains not only Herbert's use of the temple but also his use of the related figures of the Law and the Sacrifice, for just as the Hebraic temple had been replaced under the New Covenant by the temple of the heart (or, in the collective aspect, by the temple of the Church, Christ's Body), so also the Law of the Decalogue had been replaced by the Law of Christ, and the sacrifice of animals under the Mosaic Law by the Sacrifice of Christ upon the Cross. In a sense, the type of the temple includes the other two, for Solomon's temple upon Mount Sion contained both the altar on which the Mosaic sacrifices were offered and the tablets of the Law which were stored in the ark in the Holy of Holies. Similarly, Christ's new temple, the Church, "contains" Christ's Law in her doctrine and his Sacrifice in her Eucharist; and the individual heart, insofar as it too becomes Christ's temple, must become also the repository of his Law and Sacrifice.

It would seem worthwhile briefly to reexamine the images of the New Covenant which Tuve and Summers have traced in Herbert's poetry in order to make a point not generally appreciated: that is, that these images, seen in the light of their scriptural derivation, fall regularly into the three categories of the Temple, the Law, and the Sacrifice. Nor are these categories arbitrary, for, as I shall show, they are to be correlated with the three traditional offices of Christ, as Prophet, Priest, and King.

The first group of images, that which concerns the heart of man as the proper house or temple of God, is associated in the biblical context with the doctrine of Creation. Thus, in the poem "Man," Herbert praises the Lord of Creation who, in giving man a special dignity and dominion on earth, has made of him "a stately habitation" and a "brave Palace." From the Book of Genesis it is clear that the purpose of the God who created all men is to be understood in the light of his specific dealings with the people of Israel, and the Book of Exodus, following Genesis, proclaims God's intention to dwell forever in the midst of his people. Though God sits enthroned in the heaven, he will also have his throne in Israel. Moses is therefore commanded to make on top of the ark of the Covenant and between the wings of the cherubim a mercy seat from which God shall reign (Exodus 25:17-22).

That God's habitation with Israel (first in the tent in the wilderness and later in the temple on Mount Sion) is a pattern for his dealings with all mankind is made explicit again by Deutero-Isaiah and later by Paul, the Apostle to the Gentiles. All men, Gentiles and Jews, may receive the Covenant in Christ and, being "fitly framed together," grow "unto an holy temple in the Lord: ... an habitation of God through the Spirit" (Ephesians 2:21-22).[4] Indeed, so Paul argues in his Letter to the Romans, the Gentiles have their own separate history of the experience of God which is now fulfilled in the New Covenant; the temple of the classical world may, as it were, take its place alongside the temple on Mount Sion as a type of the new temple of the Spirit.

From the history of the temple in Israel an analogy can be drawn with the present condition of the heart as God's dwelling. The temple had been built by Solomon, preserved through the siege of the Assyrian armies, razed by the Babylonians, and later rebuilt by Zerubbabel, only to be defiled by Antiochus Epiphanes, restored by Judas Maccabeus, and finally destroyed by the Romans. All these vicissitudes had been directed by God in the course of chastising and refining his people. So too, God raises, and as often razes, the heart where he now dwells, Herbert proclaims in "The Temper" (II).[5] It is a paradox that God must constantly destroy his habitation in order to save it (or, as the theme emerges in the Affliction series, that the Lord of life must kill every day in order to re-create). Whereas in "Man" the Order of Nature had been used to support the Order of the Spirit and of Grace, here Herbert draws a contrast: the miracle of Creation, required once and once only in "the grosser world" of nature, is required every day for the new Creation in "the diviner world of grace." But the creation of the new man — or the new heart — is posited upon the destruction of the "old man" of Sin. To reconsider the figure of the temple: just as God's habitation with Israel was affronted by idolatry and even the presence of idols within the temple itself, so now inside the heart there are "unruly powers" which would dispute God's occupation and sovereignty there. Like the psalmist, Herbert in this poem prays that God will indeed confound his enemies, discipline the insubordinate, and "keep a standing Majestie in me."

Not to recognize God's sovereignty and allow his habitation invites instead, as the prophets had proclaimed, his adverse judgment and wrath. The theme of the avenging God is rare in Herbert, but it occurs in "Decay." When he compares God's free and spacious movements across the land in the days of Moses and the patriarchs with his present confinement in "some one corner of a feeble heart" and finds that God's occupation of even this restricted territory is disputed, he can see no outcome short of the apocalypse: the heat of God's love will "still retreat, / Cold Sinne still forcing it, till it return, / And calling *Justice*, all things burn."[6]

One of Herbert's most explicit statements of the heart's holiness as the house of God under the new dispensation is to be found in the poem "*Velum scissum*" from *Passio Discerpta*.

> Frustra, Verpe, tumes, propola cultûs,
> Et Templi parasite; namque velum
> Diffissum reserat Deum latentem,
> Et pomoeria terminósque sanctos
> Non vrbem facit vnicam, sed Orbem.
> Et pro pectoribus recenset aras,
> Dum cor omne suum sibi requirat
> Structorem, & Solomon vbique regnet.
> Nunc Arcana patent, nec inuolutam
> Phylacteria complicant latrîam.
> Excessit tener Orbis ex Ephebis,
> Maturúsque suos coquens amores
> Praeflorat sibi nuptias futuras.
> Vbique est Deus, Agnus, Ara, Flamen.[7]

Herbert is meditating here upon the significance of the statement in the Gospels that, when Jesus yielded up the ghost, "the veil of the temple was rent in twain from the top to the bottom" (Mark 15:38; cf. Matthew 27:51). The meaning of the event, as it had been explained by the author of the Epistle to the Hebrews, is that God is no longer confined within the Holy of Holies behind the veil in the temple where he was accessible only to the high priest and then only on the Day of Atonement. With the rending of the veil, the Holy of Holies and the presence of God in Christ are extended everywhere. Christ, the new Solomon, has founded the new temple which is nothing less than the Church Universal ("Solomon vbique regnet"), and, since God is now to be worshipped not on Mount Sion nor on any other mountain but in spirit and in truth (for so Christ had declared in John 4), the altars of Christ's temple are the hearts of men ("pro pectoribus recenset aras"). Those members of the Old

Covenant whose special and exclusive mark is the circumcision (the "Verpe" of the poem) have not caught up with the reality of the New Covenant which extends over the world and which has as its mark the union here and now of God and man in the Spirit ("Praeflorat sibi nuptias futuras").

The last line of "*Velum Scissum*" is apparently unrelated to the lines that immediately precede it, for what has marriage to do with sacrifice? But in the format of the poem it can be seen that "Vbique est Deus, Agnus, Ara, Flamen" provides a parallel with the earlier phrase, "Solomon vbique regnet." Those two phrases indicate two major functions of the temple, that it is the palace of God the King and also the place where sacrifice is performed. A third function is to effect a union between man and God, and this function Herbert has accommodated in the intervening lines about the marriage. The poem thus provides comment on all the major functions of the temple and the manner in which they are extended and transformed upon the death of Christ and the inauguration of the New Covenant.

That "God is everywhere" would be a sufficient statement of the new reality. Herbert, however, does not stop there. "God," he says, "is everywhere the Lamb, the Altar, the Priest," and thereby he gives his characteristic perception of the presence of God as a *sacrificial* presence. But if God in Christ himself provides all the materials for the sacrifice (being the Offerer, the Offering, and the Place of Offering), there is still the scope — and indeed, the necessity — for man's participation. Specifically, though God himself is the Altar, he also looks for altars in men's hearts. Here is evident that aspect of Herbert's thought which is concerned with man's obligation to imitate God in love and sacrifice.

The second group of images of the New Covenant treats of the heart as the altar for Christ's Sacrifice. The idea occurs in the Epistle to the Hebrews where the author has in mind that the Old Covenant, according to the account in Exodus, chapter 24, was inaugurated with the offering of a sacrifice of oxen and the sprinkling of the blood upon the altar and the people. The New Covenant likewise is inaugurated with the Sacrifice of Christ upon the Cross and the sprinkling of Christ's blood upon the altar of the heart. We may therefore, says the author of the Epistle, come back into reconciliation with God in the New Covenant, "having our hearts sprinkled" by the blood of Jesus (Hebrews 10:22).[8]

Since the idea of the heart as altar concerns the foundation of the New Covenant and of the Church, it is appropriate that Herbert's most elaborate treatment of the idea is to be found in the poems at the beginning of the section called "The Church." It is not only the historical

Church to which Herbert alludes, but to the "Church" or house of God which a man himself may become through grace and devotion. Thus, in "Superliminare," which immediately precedes "The Church," Herbert delivers the injunction "Avoid, Profaneness" — that is, let what is fit to remain on the outside of the temple be dismissed — for "nothing but holy" belongs here. He proceeds then in "The Altar" to raise in the "Church" which is his own life of devotion a "broken ALTAR, . . . Made of a heart, and cemented with teares."

As Miss Tuve has pointed out, this altar made of stone which "no workmans tool hath touch'd" conforms to the instructions for a stone altar which God gives Moses in Exodus, chapter 20. (At the same point there are instructions concerning an altar of earth which may have provided Herbert with the inspiration for the poem Λογικὴ Θυσία "Reasonable [for "Logos-like"] Sacrifice" in *Lucus*, where man, the creature of earth, has become through Christ's covenant the living altar of God.)[9] Exodus does not, however, give the origin for the other parts of the description of Herbert's altar, that it is made of a stony heart, the stone having been "broken" and then "cemented with teares." The obdurate heart shattered by the touch of the divine love and power and healed by penitential tears is a common enough theme in Christian devotion and familiar in particular from the frontispiece of Vaughan's *Silex Scintillans*. For Herbert, the direction of the devotional life is summed up by the prayer with which the poem ends: "O let thy blessed SACRIFICE be mine, / And sanctifie this ALTAR to be thine." To the penitential and grateful contemplation of that blessed Sacrifice of Christ, the "readie Paschal Lambe," he proceeds in the next poem, "The Sacrifice," with the rich liturgical allusion which Miss Tuve has documented.[10]

It should be noted that the offering up of Christ's Sacrifice is central to the Eucharist which Herbert knew intimately throughout his life and which, as priest, he celebrated. Indeed, Herbert could hardly write upon the Sacrifice without having in mind the service which derives from that event. Picking up Martz's clue to the sacramental nature of the introduction to *The Temple*, one can see that "The Altar" and "The Sacrifice" are part of a sequence which suggests the Communion Service. They are preceded by "Superliminare" which, like the Exhortation and the Bidding, serves notice that all unworthy thoughts must be dismissed because the worshippers are here approaching "the churches mysticall repast." At the heart of the matter, "The Altar" and "The Sacrifice" may be compared with the Prayer of Consecration which represents Christ's "full, perfect, and sufficient sacrifice [and] oblation . . . for the sins of the whole world."[11] The sequence ends with "The

Thanksgiving" and "The Reprisall," two poems paralleling the post-Communion prayers which not only give thanks for the Sacrifice and the grace flowing from it but also ask that the partakers be enabled to imitate it (take their "reprisal," as it were) by making of themselves "a lively sacrifice" unto God (cf. Romans 12:1).

In "The Reprisall," the poet, who has first tried to "turn back" on God his "art of love," but cannot, reaches the conclusion that

> by confession will I come
> Into thy conquest; though I can do nought
> Against thee, in thee I will overcome
> The man, who once against thee fought.

When the Crucifixion is considered as a conquest, the response of the follower must be that he also will conquer in Christ's name his own worse self. But when the Crucifixion is considered under the aspect of sacrifice, then the response must be that, like Christ, one will make of oneself a sacrifice, or, by another turn of speech, one will make of one's heart the altar on which the Sacrifice of Christ may be offered. Thus, on the one hand, in "Since my sadnesse," Herbert offers to God "this poore oblation," his heart, and, on the other hand, in "The Altar," he rears an altar of his heart and prays that God himself will provide the Sacrifice to be offered upon it.

The heart of stone may be converted not only into an altar for sacrifice but, under the third category, into tablets on which the Law may be inscribed, the New Law being as integral a part of the New Covenant as is the New Sacrifice. After lamenting how little "holinesse" his heart contains in comparison with "quarries of pil'd vanities," Herbert ends his sonnet "The Sinner" with the plea: "though my hard heart scarce to thee can grone, / Remember that thou once didst write in stone." God had written on stone on that occasion when he inscribed the commandments for Moses upon the two stone tablets (Exodus 32 and 34, cf. Deuteronomy 4 and 10). The tablets were to be stored within the ark of the Covenant, and around the ark the sanctuary of the tabernacle was to be built. The later temple on Mount Sion also received its sanctity from the presence in the sanctuary of the ark of the Covenant with the inscribed tables, which David had had transported up to Jerusalem (2 Samuel 6; cf. Psalms 132).

But for the prophets and psalmists of Israel the sanctity of the temple and the services of worship there availed nothing, unless Israel were also prepared to serve God with her whole heart and make of herself a sanctuary to enshrine the Law. After the days of affliction which Jeremiah foretold for Israel, "saith the Lord, I will put my law in their inward parts and write it in their hearts; and will be their God, and they shall be my people" (Jeremiah 31:33). These are the words of the New Covenant which were later to be quoted by the author of Hebrews and by Paul in his Second Letter to the Corinthians as evidence that throughout the history of Israel God had been preparing the New Covenant in Christ. The same passage from Jeremiah is a source of reference for later Old Testament writers also, particularly Ezekiel and Zachariah. A passage from Ezekiel is worth quoting for the sake of the additional elements which, as I shall show, are incorporated into Herbert's poems. "A new heart also will I give you, and a new spirit will I put within you: and I will take away the stony heart out of your flesh, and I will give you an heart of flesh. And I will put my spirit within you, and cause you to walk in my statutes, and ye shall keep my judgments, and do them" (Ezekiel 36: 26-27). It can be seen that the lines from "The Sinner" rely on both these passages: the poet's heart is hard and stony (as in the Ezekiel passage), but if God will write the Law in his heart (in accordance with the other passage quoted from Jeremiah) then even he will become enrolled in the New Covenant inaugurated by Christ's Sacrifice on the Cross. Herbert takes up the idea again in "Nature," where the engraving of God's Covenant Law upon the heart, as in Jeremiah, is followed by the alternative given by Ezekiel, namely, that God will give a new heart that is fresh and responsive, not obdurate like the old. In fusing these elements, Herbert is no innovator; he is again following Paul where, in the Second Letter to the Corinthians, the Apostle refers to his community of converts as "the epistle of Christ ministered by us, written not with ink, but with the Spirit of the living God; not in tables of stone, but in fleshy tables of the heart" (3:3).

In "Since bloud is fittest," Herbert is inspired by his meditation upon the Blood of the New Testament (to use the phrase of the Gospels and the Communion Service) and upon God's promise that he will write his Law in men's hearts, to proffer his own heart's blood as the "ink" for the writing. Because God's writing in the heart is the same thing as the Spirit's dwelling there (because, that is, the image of the heart as the tablet of the Law has the same significance as that of the heart as temple), the poet's thoughts turn next to the sort of lodging he can offer his Lord. The heart had given nearly all of its accommodation to Sin and little to the Spirit, he had decided in "The Sinner." But if the Lord now comes to lodge there — and this is the Crucified Lord with his nails and wounds and woes — then Sin will flee and will not return as long as the Lord keeps possession.

Writing and lodging occur again in "Sepulchre," in which the stone which forms the sepulchre for Christ's body becomes assimilated to those other "stones" already mentioned: the heart of stone in Israel and the tables of stone on which the Law of the Old Covenant was inscribed. As the significance of the "stone" changes through the poem, so does the role of Christ. When, in the first stanza, the stone is the sepulchre, Christ is the One laid inside it; when in the last stanza the stone becomes the tablet, Christ supplies (or, rather, as the Logos-Christ of the Fourth Gospel, he *is*) the letter of the Law. The receiving of the Law by Israel at Sinai was paralleled — indeed, fulfilled — when flesh received the Word at the Incarantion. But the mystery of the Incarnation must still be reenacted in the heart of each man. Just as at the Incarnation, according to the Fourth Gospel, although the Word "came unto his own, ... his own received him not" (John 1:11), so now the poet can see "So many hearts on earth, and yet not one / Receive thee." Such a bitter realization belongs to that part of *The Temple* in which Herbert is engaged in what Professor Martz has called the "Body of Conflicts."[12] Later, in the poem "Jesu," the image of the heart as tablet will be used to express a calm assurance: "JESU is in my heart, his sacred name/Is deeply carved there."

From even a selective discussion of the way these images of the temple, the altar, and the tablets of the Law operate in Herbert's poetry, it is apparent that Herbert invokes the temple of Solomon not for its own sake but only insofar as that enables him to talk about the presence of Christ. From the scheme of the literal, historic temple, one could not explain why the poet gives such prominence to the altar and the tablets and neglects, for example, the menorah. In fact the peculiar significance of these three images (that is, the images of the altar, the tablets, and the temple itself) is to be explained by their correlation with the three traditional offices of Christ (the "three offices" of "The Church Militant").[13] Christ is Prophet, Priest, and King. As Prophet, he is the exponent, even the embodiment, of the Law. The heart therefore becomes the tablet on which the Law is written. As Priest, ("after the order of Melchisedec," according to the thesis in the Epistle to the Hebrews), Christ offers up the Sacrifice of himself as Victim. The heart then becomes the altar on which Christ is offered and at which he officiates. As King, Christ subdues his enemy and reigns from the throne situated in his palace. The heart then is seen as both the arena in which Christ defeats Sin, and also the palace or temple where he sits enthroned.

That Herbert uses New Testament, especially Pauline, typology with such consistency and precision is a point not generally appreciated in his poetry. The clarity and immediacy of his religious devotion are achieved not by the neglect of doctrine but by its thorough assimilation; the doctrine, moreover, shows the influence of the Reformation in its rigorously biblical character. Herbert's poetry attests his practice of the principle which he enunciated in his Notes on Valdesso: "The H. Scriptures ... have not only an Elementary use, but a use of perfection, neither can they ever be exhausted, ... but still even to the most learned and perfect in them, there is somewhat to be learned more."[14]

IMAGES OF ENCLOSURE IN GEORGE HERBERT'S *THE TEMPLE*

Robert Higbie

THE QUESTION OF HOW COMPLETELY AND SYSTEMAT-
ICALLY GEORGE Herbert organized *The Temple* as a whole has
frequently engaged the attention of critics.[1] One indication that the
poems which make up the work are linked together according to some
system is the recurrence of similar images. Among such groups of
images, one of the commonest is the imagery of enclosure. Throughout
The Temple Herbert refers to walls, locked doors, houses, or to smaller
but similar enclosures such as boxes and cabinets. By returning to this
idea of containment he is, I think, trying to induce us to make larger
connections than those we make within the individual poems and thus to
perceive an overall progression in which each poem is merely one step.

There are several reasons for choosing this particular image, and
Herbert seems to have chosen it consciously, to have been especially
attracted to the idea of enclosure and confinement. Accepting God's
control for him seems to have meant accepting some sort of containment, some boundaries within which God would protect him. Furthermore, a temple itself is a kind of enclosure, and Herbert seems to have
chosen the enclosure image for its relation to his concept of the temple,
which I think represents for him God's perfect enclosure, the ideal of
which all his earlier enclosure images are imperfect reflections.

The imagery of *The Temple*, then, seems to follow a progression from
the earthly, man-made enclosure, the house and the church, to the divine
enclosure of the temple, the perfection that the church tries to embody
on earth. This is not, however, an obvious, direct progression; on the
contrary, it moves through conflict, as the Christian himself must before
he can reach God: poems contradict each other, affirmation alternates
with despair. Nevertheless the work does move to a final sense of God's
grace, and the progression from earthly church to divine temple can be

From *TSLL*, 15 (1974), 627-38. Copyright © 1974 by The University of Texas Press.
Reprinted by permission of the author and The University of Texas Press.

taken as a representation of the movement from the old dispensation to the new, from punishment to redemption. Herbert accomplishes this movement by making us feel the inadequacy of the merely earthly. It is for this reason, I think, that he finds the enclosure image particularly appropriate. Man's state is described as an enclosed one because Herbert wants to make us aware of how limited it is; he wants to give us a sense of the straitness of our earthly dwelling-place, to make us feel imprisoned in it, and by doing so to make us want to transcend the earthly and seek the divine. The conflict and contradiction within the central part of *The Temple* thus serve the purpose of forcing us to look beyond the individual poems to something higher.

Finally, as I hope to show, this interpretation of the organization of *The Temple* tells us something about Herbert's concept of poetry and has certain implications for the interpretation of individual poems. There is a tendency in *The Temple* to emphasize the enclosed nature of the poems, their tight confinement within strict forms; Herbert seems at times to have tried to impose as much formal control on poems as possible. I think one reason he does this is to induce in us a degree of ironic detachment, a realization that mere man-made poetry, like other human structures, is inadequate to lead us to God. It is only when we are looking at the poems not as separate entities but as parts of *The Temple* as a whole that we are thus led to feel that Herbert is deliberately playing with the limitedness of poetic form to force us to look beyond the individual poems. Once we realize he is doing this, various contradictions within *The Temple* are explained, such as Herbert's desire for poetic simplicity (as expressed for example in "Jordan" I and II) in contrast with the actual complexity of many of his poems.

Herbert's progression begins with "The Church-Porch," in which he uses the image of an orderly enclosure to give us a definition of the Christian, a definition we can take with us into the more complex structure of *The Temple* and there modify as we move toward a fuller understanding of God. Man, he tells us here, should live by rule as "houses are built by rule" (l. 135).[2] Enclosure is thus associated with order; an enclosure is the physical embodiment of "rule." Like the enclosure, man's mind should be regulated; what is inside it should be kept in its proper place. For the enclosure is not empty; Herbert is aware of what it contains. He describes man as "a shop of rules, a well truss'd pack" (l. 141) of parcels, and tells him "stuffe thy minde with solid braverie" (l. 208). Like a shopkeeper, man should "husband" (l. 302) his "goods" (l. 283). But he should do this only in order to "Submit" (l. 284) them all to God; for it is God, not man, who makes this enclosure and provides it with contents. God, we are told later, is "the *Architect*, whose art / Could build so strong in a weak heart" ("The Church-floore," ll. 19-20), who not only creates man's enclosure but furnishes it with "glorious household-stuffe" ("Affliction" [I], l. 9). In other words, if man accepts the limits God sets him, the contents of his mind will have value, for the order imposed on them will make the mind devout, will enable it to use what is within to reach God.

There seems to be something childlike about this desire for self-enclosure, for a home, a space within which the poet can be protected by an all-providing Father. In fact Herbert often takes a child's role in his relationship with God (as at the end of "The Collar"), surrendering to God's control; and in several poems he speaks of the enclosure he desires as the sort of enclosure a parent provides for a child. In "The Temper" (I) he wants to "roost and nestle" under God's "roof" (ll. 17-18); in "Paradise" he wants to be safe within "the inclosure" of God's arm (l. 6); in "Content" he wants to "sweetly sleep," lying "warm" like a child in a "bed" (ll. 3 and 20); and in "Home" Heaven is a "nest" in which God's son "lay" (l. 19).

However, the enclosure image is not as simple and stable as it at first appears to be. This kind of a retreat into God's sanctuary is not as easy as it would be for a child, since the poet no longer has the child's purity. Already in "The Church Porch" there is the sense of a threat to man's enclosure, the sense that there is something outside it which is dangerous. Sin is described as "Blowing up houses" (l. 204), and man must therefore keep "guard upon himself," keep himself "under lock and key" (ll. 139 and 144). The man who does not hold himself in properly "breaks up house, turns out of doores his minde" (l. 150). There is a fear of what lies outside the enclosure here, a sense that it is in opposition to what is inside, is in opposition to order itself. It is this destructive outer force that makes Herbert feel the need for some enclosed sanctuary, a place within which man can keep his goods safe. The "doores" of the eyes should thus be "shut" (l. 418) so that the physical world cannot gain admittance into the soul and corrupt what is within it. Herbert hopes to use the enclosure as a place from which the physical and unclean can be excluded, so that if he stays within its walls and renounces all that is impure in himself God will condescend, as he says in "Man," to "dwell in" the enclosure God originally "built" (l. 50).

The sense of some danger outside betrays the fact that the ideal enclosure the poet desires has not yet been reached, that it is still precarious. In several later poems Herbert returns to this fear of what is outside. In "The Discharge" death "environs and surrounds" (l. 36); in "The Holy Communion" sin is pictured as trying to leap "the wall that parts/Our souls and fleshy hearts" (ll. 14-15); in "Assurance" we are warned not to "unlock the doore / To cold despairs and gnawing pensiveness" (ll. 15-16); and in "Content" — whose punning title itself equates containment with contentment — "mutt'ring thoughts" should "keep / Within the walls of your own breast" though called "abroad" by "passion" (ll. 1-2, 5-6). In each of these cases the enclosure is defined in terms of what opposes it, so that man is felt to be at the mercy of larger forces.

Although these images try to make the danger seem exterior to the mind, it is clear that what Herbert fears — sin, passion, thoughts, despairs — is actually within him; he is trying to defend one part of his mind against another part. These two parts are imaged in terms of economic forces in "The Church Porch," where "worldly thoughts" are described as "theeves" which threaten the "goods" contained within the "shop" of the mind (ll. 424, 283, 141). This awareness of the economic implications of his imagery is typical of Herbert, and suggests that one way we can see his religiousness is as a reaction against commercial acquisitiveness and competitivity. He values the shopkeeper and fears his opposite, the thief. The shopkeeper is good because he stays within the enclosure, or at least he ought to do so, submitting his goods to God's ownership, acting as God's "tenant" ("Redemption," l. 1) or "debter" ("The Starre," l. 7). The thief on the other hand does not submit to such control: he is what the shopkeeper would become if he did not stay within his enclosure. He embodies the assertion of the self, the desire not to give up property but to obtain it. In other words, there is one part of the mind that desires to accept a higher control and renounce selfishness, but there is another part that opposes all such restraint, that wants to break and enter, not to surrender but to seize. This is the "quick-piercing minde" Herbert describes in "Vanitie" (I) (l. 2), the mind that penetrates the walls that oppose it, passing "from doore to doore" (l. 3), unlocking them all. It is this side of the mind that Herbert seems to fear: the thief that can break down the enclosure and let in sin and death — acquisitive, unsubmissive Reason, the desire for the fruit of knowledge.

This is not to say that Herbert is hostile to the powers of reason. Rather he seems to feel the need to limit it, to create some sort of wall in his mind, to keep it under lock and key. He allows reason into the enclosing part of the mind, trying to control it and consecrate its energy to spiritual ends. We can see this in "The Pearl" where the treasure he seeks to obtain is contrasted with the false, merely earthly pearl of knowledge. Here again reason is pictured as penetrating walls: "All these stand open, or I have the keyes" (l. 9). But here reason is itself enclosed, kept within bounds by the ending of each stanza, which brings its action back to God. Reason is a "good huswife" (l. 4): it keeps within the house of Nature, enclosed within a larger framework. And it in turn is used here to enclose the activities of the mind by knowing them: "I know all these, and have them in my hand" (l. 31), containing them, measuring like a prudent shopkeeper "How many drammes" (l. 18) of things there are, "the stock and surplus" (l. 8). Thus reason has here been brought under control, enclosed, and therefore made unselfish.

There is, however, a danger in allowing this penetrating, potentially destructive force inside the mind's enclosure. Herbert usually pictures this force not as submissive but as opposing limitations, "unbridled" ("The Pearl," l. 26), "swelling through store" ("The Flower," l. 48). Swelling implies an effort to burst one's bounds, and both here and in "Jordan" (II), where "swell" is rhymed with "sell" (ll. 4 and 6), the word has an economic significance. It suggests someone who wants to get control of God's goods for himself and by doing so become like God, controlling his own soul and thus forfeiting his right to God's control. The danger in allowing reason into the enclosure of the mind, then, is that instead of its being the enclosure that controls reason, reason is likely to gain control itself and pervert the enclosure to its own purposes.

When this happens, the enclosure ceases to be a desirable one. The shopkeeper is transformed into a miser, using the enclosure he has taken over to hoard up goods for himself and to close God out. We can see this transformation in the enclosure imagery taking place in many of the poems in the central part of *The Temple*, poems concerned with the difficulty of attaining union with God. In "Confession" the enclosure is turned into a hiding-place like a miser's: "within my heart I made / Closets, and in them many a chest; / And, like a master in my trade, / In those chests, boxes; in each box a till" (ll. 2-6). Here reason, like the carpenter's art, is losing itself in the kind of "curling" complexity Herbert mistrusts in "Jordan" (II) (l. 5); it is becoming an end rather than a means, and thus erecting artificial walls that try to exclude God rather than include him. Again in "Good Friday" the heart is like a "box" containing a "store" of sin (ll. 23-24), and in "Dotage" man tries to possess "casks" of false pleasures (l. 1). The enclosure has lost its value here and become something narrow and constricting, something that belongs to man alone and is no longer given worth by God.

We can further see this change in value in the way the contents of the enclosure image have been transformed from "solid braverie" ("The Church Porch," l. 208) to a hoard of bitter, poisonous, or even excrementlike things. In "The Sinner," for example, the "quarries of pil'd vanities" that have been "treasur'd" turn out to be not "quintessence" but "dregs" (ll. 2, 5, and 9); in "Nature" the "strongholds" of men's hearts contain "venome" (1. 6); and in "Lent" the pursuit of "fulnesse" for its own sake causes one to be filled not with good things but with "sluttish fumes, / Sowre exhalations, and dishonest rheumes" (ll. 22-23). There is a sense here that without God's control things become merely physical, and physical to an exaggerated, intense degree so that they are even physically sickening. For if God is excluded from the mind, man becomes merely physical himself, body rather than soul — a danger that Herbert reacts to with revulsion.

If God is thus excluded from the mind's enclosure, it becomes not a "house" but a "dungeon" ("Grace," l. 6) or a "cage" ("The Collar," l. 21). Sin "locks" the ears against God ("Church-lock and key," l. 1), and man becomes "close, reserv'd" — "In his poore cabinet of bone / Sinnes have their box apart" ("Ungratefulnesse," ll. 25 and 28-29). Man's "house and home" become a "dumbe enclosure" ("Mortification," ll. 20 and 23), "A narrow cupboard for [his] griefs and doubts" ("Grief," l. 11).

When man's selfishness leads him thus to change his relationship with God and lock himself up, God in return takes on a new attitude toward man. God is now on the outside of the mind's enclosure and is thus opposed to its walls, since they have been turned against him. He is turned "out of doore" ("Sepulchre," l. 7). Therefore in trying to return to a union with God the poet must ask God to "captivate" the stronghold of the heart ("Nature," l. 5), to "take these barres . . . away" ("The Search," 1.49), for only God "hath the privie key, / Op'ning the souls most subtile rooms" ("The H. Communion," ll. 21-22). Similarly in "Love unknown" he says "I fled / Unto my house" (ll. 46-47), an enclosure to which God has the "key" (l. 55). And in "Confession" God has a "piercer," Grief, "too subtill for the subt'llest hearts" (ll. 7 and 11); God's afflictions always enter the mind's enclosure: "No smith can make such locks but they have keyes: / Closets are halls to them; and hearts, high-wayes" (ll. 17-18). The very narrowness and imperfection within which the mind is enclosed thus become a way toward God, since the more man tries to take over his enclosure and assert himself the more tightly he becomes encaged, the more his enclosure becomes a punishment instead of a protection, and thus the more he becomes aware of the need for a higher control than his own. It is only by becoming thus aware of how enclosed he is in his own limitations that he can discover how much he needs something beyond those boundaries, namely God.

The poet's next step then is to leave this cage behind, since it has ceased to fulfill the function for which it was originally constructed, and to replace it with a new, ideal enclosure. Since God's "Architecture meets with sinne" ("Sion," l. 11), it must be destroyed; the "little frame" of the heart is broken "all to pieces" by the affliction God sends, and the heart is in "parcels," desiring to return to the "whole" that is God ("Jesu," ll. 3-4, 7, and 10). Once this demolition work is done, God's house must be rebuilt "a braver Palace then before" ("The World," l. 20). Since the merely human enclosure is imperfect and falls into abuse, this "braver Palace" must be more than human — it must be not man's but God's.

This is the final metamorphosis the enclosure imagery undergoes as we move toward the poems of resolution at the end of "The Church." Now instead of asking God to let him out of his own imperfect enclosure, the poet is asking God to let him into God's perfect enclosure, into an ideal home in which he can attain a union with God. He does not give up the idea of enclosure, of an orderly, controlled space, even though he has found its earthly manifestations inadequate; rather he transfers the concept to the level of the ideal. Herbert seems to abhor a vacuum; in "Affliction" (IV) he says that to be caught in the open "Space" that lies "Betwixt this world and that of grace" is torture (ll. 5-6). He needs some kind of containment and if he cannot find it in this world" then he must turn to "that of grace."

Before he can be allowed into God's house he must not only give up his own walls but must humbly petition for admission. Several poems picture the poet outside God's house wanting to be let in. In "Whitsunday" he says that God used to "Keep open house" but now "Thou shutt'st the doore, and keep'st within; / Scarce a good joy creeps through the chink" (ll. 7 and 20-21). In "Holy Baptisme" (II) "A narrow way and little gate / Is all the passage" to God (ll. 2-3). In "Gratefulnesse" he talks about "Perpetuall knockings at thy doore, / Tears sullying thy transparent rooms" (ll. 13-14); in "The Storm" he "Dares to assault thee, and besiege thy doore" (l. 12); and in "Longing" he cries "is all lockt? hath a sinners plea / No key?" (ll. 47-48). God seems here to have shut his door in retaliation, to have walled himself up because man has done so, to force man to realize that to be allowed inside he must surrender his own selfish enclosure.

Once this surrender is complete we reach the final stage, the entrance into God's ideal enclosure. Here the enclosure imagery is transformed, and we are given the picture of an enclosure that paradoxically does not constrict but rather liberates man from the narrowness of his own enclosure. Furthermore, its contents are transformed from poisonous things to food and objects of wealth and beauty. The ideal enclosure is pictured as a cask of treasure, a box of sweets, a garden of flowers, or a palace in which a feast is laid out, many strands of imagery combining to produce an effect of final harmony and richness.

Early in *The Temple* this ideal is merely glimpsed, a memory of something the poet once had and lost, but as we reach the end it becomes more and more accessible. In "The Familie" the poet describes God's "house" as a place within which God's "controll" gives "all things" their "set forms" and makes all "neat" (ll. 5 and 8-11). When this control can be accepted, the enclosure becomes an "open house" in which God is pictured as "feasting all comers" ("Whitsunday," ll. 7-8). God's containment, then, unlike man's, is transformed into openness, and what it contains becomes a feast. This image of the feast seems to evoke for Herbert the feeling of joy that results from reconciling enclosure with openness. Again in "Ungratefulnesse" God has "rare cabinets full of treasure" which are "unlockt" and in one of which "all thy sweets are packt up" (ll. 7, 9, and 19). In "Home" Heaven is a "hive of sweetnesse" (l. 20), and in "Providence" God's "cupboard serves the world: the meat is set, / Where all may reach" (ll. 49-50). These images of God's house as a place where one can feast all seem to be leading toward the final poem of "The Church," "Love" (III), in which the ideal is no longer merely glimpsed but is at last brought within reach. Here God's banqueting hall not only stands open, but the speaker is actually brought inside and given food. This seems to be the climax toward which the imagery has been developing, the final attainment of the ideal, acceptance into God's enclosure.

This transformation of the hoard of bitter things into a feast seems to express the purification that takes place when man is purged of the self-assertive, acquisitive side of the mind that originally led to his affliction. As bitterness is associated with affliction, sweetness is associated with surrender, with "sweet sacrifice" ("The Sacrifice," l. 19). It is the mind's acquisitiveness that is being surrendered, the desire to know and control things for oneself. This surrender of reason's control becomes in the end an almost mystical surrender to the senses, to a purely sensory perception of God, as in "The Glance": "I felt a sugred strange delight, / Passing all cordialls made by any art, / Bedew, embalme, and overrunne my heart" (ll. 5-7). The speaker feels; what happens is in his heart not his mind, so that reason can only find it "strange," cannot comprehend it since it passes beyond "art." Reason must therefore surrender, must become passive, content to be "overrunne" by the sweetness the soul senses.

The surrender to sensory imagery and at least partial abdication of reason are probably what make Herbert seem childlike at times. The fondness for sweets is itself a childlike characteristic — in "Mortification" the "chest of sweets" is associated with "infants" (ll. 2-3), and the picture of "a masse / Of strange delights, where we may wish & take" in

"The Holy Scriptures" (I) sounds very like a child with candy. It is by becoming childlike in this way that man can be allowed back into God's enclosure: to reach God one must become "Small" as in "infancie" ("Holy Baptisme" [II], ll. 3 and 9).

The relationship between the sense of enclosure and that of sweetness is explored in several other poems. In "The Forerunners" sweet and "beauteous" things like "sugar-cane, / Hony of roses" must be "within" not outside "the doore" to have value (ll. 19-20, 30, 35-36), must be under God's control rather than part of the competitive, selfish world outside. The poet's "sweet phrases" must be purified by his suffering, must be submitted to God's control, which will enclose them properly, make them "well drest" rather than mere "embellishment" (ll. 13, 17, 33), mere surface without the inner sense of God to give them meaning, like the "sugred lyes" mentioned in "Dulnesse" (l. 21). In "Paradise," which describes another kind of enclosure full of sweet things, a garden, he again says that only if what is within is enclosed and controlled, pruned and pared, will it bear fruit (ll. 11-12). When this happens, the garden can become God's "Paradise" where men can "bide" like the flowers that "keep house unknown" ("The Flower," ll. 23, 46, and 14). In other words, by accepting God's enclosure one can enter into a "peaceable" state in which "things of ordinary use" are "washed, and cleansed, and serve for lights even of Heavenly Truths," and in which "the Angels minister to us their owne food, even joy, and peace."[3] The process of purification transforms everyday objects, like the ones Herbert so often uses for his imagery, into sweets, the "food" of joy.

It is toward the Eucharist that all this development has been leading, and the final climax in "Love" (III) when "I did sit and eat" (l. 18) is what gives meaning and direction to the long process of purification that has preceded it. It is for this final "entrance" (l. 4) into God's enclosure that the enclosure imagery has been constructed, and this ritual act representing union with God is what it was meant to enclose. It is not merely a physical but a spiritual enclosure, the place within which the union can be consummated. And this enclosure, I propose, is the temple to which Herbert's title refers — not an earthly temple, any more than the Eucharist taken inside it is earthly food, but rather an ideal, a temple raised in the heart: "Christ purg'd his temple; so must thou thy heart" ("The Church Porch," l. 423). This enclosure contains all the separate poems within it, giving them meaning by relating them all to the ideal toward which they all strive.

Herbert reaches this sense of an ideal enclosure by means of a progression through a series of less perfect ones that suggest the need for the ideal. This process does not take place only in his imagery; the poems themselves can be seen as enclosures, cleverly worked containers, boxes "where sweets compacted lie," and *The Temple* as a whole can be seen as the ideal enclosure they lead to. If we see the poet's surrender to God as a process of self-enclosure, we can say that his poems are a way of enclosing himself, of imposing strict control on his mind. We can see this in the tight, neat structure of the poems. He takes a delight in "configurations," in the way "dispersed" things "combine" ("The Holy Scriptures" [II], ll. 1-2 and 7), as all the images dispersed throughout *The Temple* finally combine at the end. Like music, his poetry creates a "house of pleasure" where he can take a "daintie lodging" ("Church-musick," ll. 3-4). He seeks an art like God's: "I adore / Thy curious art in marshalling thy goods" ("Providence," ll. 93-94), the poem itself marshalling a list of goods, carefully packing them within its enclosure, in the same neat way God can "the world's riches, which dispersed lie, / Contract into a span" ("The Pulley," ll. 4-5). Again, in *"Our Life is hid with Christ in God"* the meaning is "hid" and "compacted" in the poem as in a child's puzzle, everything tightly packed together, cleverly interlocking. He wants to "contract" all that has value, give it "measure" and a sense of "strict yet welcome size" ("The Rose," ll. 3-4), and by using poetic form in this way to bring about a similar kind of tight self-enclosure within himself. The control exercised over the poem is what gives its contents meaning by making them all part of a pattern, a configuration, that leads to God by showing the beauty of the order he imposes on the world. Similarly, the discipline the poet exercises over his mind is what keeps the rebelliousness some poems reveal under control: the rebelliousness is also part of a pattern that reveals God's plan, for it brings the affliction that humbles the poet so that he can accept God.

Although there are order and control exercised through the individual poems, the complete pattern combining all the dispersed parts of the poet's creation must be found in *The Temple* as a whole. The structures of individual poems, like the individual enclosure images, are merely attempts to approach an ideal structure; they are not themselves ideal. They are another kind of man-made enclosure, created by imperfect human reason, and are therefore limited in comparison with the perfect enclosure only God can create. The poem is something "small" and "poore"("Praise" [II], l. 25) compared with the vastness of what that poet wants fo express. To lead us beyond the individual poems to this ideal, Herbert exploits our sense of the poem as an enclosure, makes us aware that it is limited and thus forces us to look for something beyond it. His poetry often points to something outside itself, something too big for it to contain. For example, one poem often points to another by echoing imagery or wording. Again, poems are given titles like "Home," "The Collar," "The Pulley," and "Content" that lead away from the poem itself to ideas the poem only hints at.

Sometimes Herbert uses the poetic structure itself to express the contrast between God's power and art on the one hand and the imperfection of his own art on the other. In "The Collar" he desires to escape enclosure, to go "abroad" and become "free" and "Loose" (ll. 2, 4-5), but the very looseness of the poetic form in which he expresses this rebelliousness makes us feel the need for some control, so that it comes as a relief at the end when God abruptly pulls the speaker up short and brings him back within the enclosure of a regular rhyme-scheme. The ending of this poem may be considered unconvincing if it is taken by itself, but once we put it in the context of *The Temple* as a whole we can see that the way in which God suddenly enters at the end here, as in other poems, is not to provide a conclusive ending to the poem but rather to beckon to us to pass beyond the poem itself, to see the inadequacy of the mood the poem indulges and look upwards, ahead towards some more inclusive solution, one which will see this poem as part of the entire progression.

Again at the end of "Home" Herbert uses the poetic form to make us feel the existence of some force more powerful than the speaker's own imperfect control. Here God steps in and overrules the poet's "rhyme and reason," changing the crucial rhyme-word of the last stanza from "Stay" to "*Come*" (ll. 75-76), a word that invites us to come toward something beyond the poem, beyond the poet's mere rhyme-scheme to a resolution on a higher plane, to God's perfect "Home" which makes its power felt by causing the word "Come" to rhyme with it.

Such emphasis on form may seem to be mere playfulness until we realize that the poet wants us to feel the narrowness within which his reason is confined, and thus to desire something better. When, for example, in "A Wreath" he says "Give me simplicitie" (l. 9), we look in vain in the poet's (and the poem's) "crooked winding wayes" (l. 4) for the simplicity he praises; our pleasure in the poem, valid though that of course is, must be tempered with a realization of its imperfection in comparison with true simplicity, which belongs only to God. Again, in "Easter Wings" Herbert uses poetic form to move, very graphically, from a sense of man's contracted, narrow state toward the sense of expansion God brings, a winged liberation into an ideal enclosure that can counteract the narrowness of the first half of the poem.

Thus we are led beyond the poet himself to God, the ideal artist who makes "the whole frame" ("The Church-floore," l. 11), the perfect enclosure. The poetic experience finally takes us, as the poem "Prayer" (I) does at its end, beyond mere earthly things, beyond what the poet can put into words, to "something understood" (l. 14).

IV. PROSODY

COUNTERPOINT IN HERBERT

Albert McHarg Hayes

Nearly everyone has had the experience, while reading poetry, of suddenly discovering that he has not the slightest idea what the words he has been reading mean; he has been conscious of nothing but pleasant sound. The frequency with which this experience recurs in the reading of certain poets, Swinburne for example, constitutes for some a fatal defect in their work. Poetry has an almost magic power of incantation, by which it can penetrate to the most secret recesses of the human mind. And yet this power is given it only that it may communicate its meaning more fully. Incantation is not an end in itself.

All true poets of course recognize this fact and exercise strict self-discipline to make sure that sound does not obscure sense, that rime accords with reason. This control, though present even in narrative poetry, is naturally of greatest importance in what is called "poetry of ideas." There, sense is so tightly packed into a few words that the reader must be kept alert if he is to comprehend it. To ensure this alertness is a major problem of the intellectual poet, and so he is constantly inventing devices to accomplish this end. With one such device, "invented" by George Herbert, this paper is concerned.

I

Among English poets Herbert is one of the most experimental. His loving editor, George Herbert Palmer, noted this fact in 1905, but few have really absorbed it. Let me reiterate. The 127 stanzaic poems in *The Temple* represent 111 different stanza patterns. Of these 111 patterns, 11 are used twice, 1 three times, and 1 four times. The other 98 are unique in Herbert; most of them also, in English poetry. And yet they are not outlandish patterns, but the natural and often beautiful result of what seems at times systematic experimentation. Take the 29 quatrain

From *Studies in Philology*, 35 (1938), 43-60. © The University of North Carolina Press. Reprinted by permission of the publisher and the author.

patterns. Two have the rime scheme *a a b b,* the *b* line representing a refrain. The difference comes from variation in the lengths of the lines: 10 4 8 4 and 10 10 10 6. The scheme *a a b b* has three forms: 8 8 6 4, 8 8 8 8, 10 6 10 8. Three others are *a b b a:* 10 4 8 10, 10 6 10 4, 10 8 8 10. The remaining 21 are all in the common pattern *a b a b;* the variety is instructive: 4 8 8 4, 4 10 4 10, 5 5 3 5, 6 6 6 6, 6 6 8 6, 6 8 8 10, 6 10 8 10, 7 4 7 4, 7 7 7 7, 8 4 8 4, 8 6 8 6, 8 8 8 2, 8 8 8 4, 8 8 8 8, 8 8 8 10, 8 8 10 4, 8 10 10 8, 10 4 10 10, 10 8 8 6, 10 8 10 8, 10 10 10 10. This is experiment with a vengeance; but, though this is the extreme example, it is nearly equaled by the 19 variations on *a b a b c c* — another very familiar rime scheme. Although there are eccentric patterns in Herbert's repertory, some of which will be noted presently, for the most part he confined his efforts to simple variations in length of line such as would not startle the reader.[1]

The cause of this great variety in stanzas lies partly in Herbert's desire to make the outward form of each poem representative of its inner meaning. Everyone knows the pictorial appropriateness of "The Altar" (II, 121) and of "Easter Wings" (II, 335). Not so many will recall the ingenuity of "Aaron" (III, 11). This poem consists of five stanzas of five lines each — because *Aaron* contains five letters. The first two stanzas, contrasting Aaron the perfect priest with Herbert the imperfect, are exactly parallel, phrase for phrase — because of the double *a* in the name. Consider also "Trinitie Sunday" (II, 161), three stanzas of three lines each. And "Sinnes Round" (III, 143), in which the stanzas are linked by the repetition of the last line of each stanza as the first of the next, the last line of the poem being the same as the first — to symbolize the vicious circle of sin leading on to sin. In a more subtle manner, Herbert has made length of line in "The Pulley" (III, 149) and "The Collar" (III, 211) represent most aptly the turns of his thought. In the former, God is shown pouring out all his treasures on man, all except "rest"; then, fearing that if he gives all man may adore the gifts instead of the giver, he withholds this last one so that, in the end, weariness "may toss him to my breast." The motion of this process, God to man to God, resembles that of a pulley, as Herbert suggests by his stanza; one short line, three long lines, and another short one. Similarly the theme of "The Collar," the poet's chafing under God's restraint, is reinforced by the irregularity of the lines ("My lines and life are free, free as the road, Loose as the wind") and by the irregularity of the rimes. For even rime can be manipulated. Thus in "Deniall" (II, 297) the fifth line in each of the first five stanzas does not rime, in keeping with the discord between Herbert's soul and his God; the sixth and final stanza asks God to restore harmony between them "and mend my ryme" — and with these words of the request the rime is mended. In contrary manner, the last line of "Grief" (III, 323 — quoted in the next paragraph of this paper) breaks away from "measure, tune, and time" — to prove its sincerity.

To modern taste such tricks as these may seem unworthy of a great poet. Perhaps they are, and yet — remember Shakespeare's puns — they are typical of an age and, more important for my purposes, typical of a man who brought to the construction of his verse an ingenious and extremely active mind. Versification was an art upon which Herbert reflected seriously. When he first determined that "my poor Abilities in Poetry shall be all and ever consecrated to God's glory" and sent two sonnets to his mother (II, 79 and 81) affirming this purpose, his intention and practice was to use for religious purposes all the decorative devices of secular poets, to substitute love of God for love of women and thus to supply a worthier object for poetic ingenuity.

> When first my lines of heav'nly joyes made mention,
>   Such was their lustre, they did so excell,
> That I sought out quaint words and trim inventions;
>   My thoughts began to burnish, sprout and swell,
> Curling with metaphors a plain intention,
>   Decking the sense as if it were to sell.

Gradually, however, he came to see that an artificial style was incompatible with true sincerity, and told himself:

> How wide is all this long pretence!
> There is in love a sweetnesse readie penn'd;
>   Copie out onely that, and save expense.[2]

Still later, one may assume, even direct simplicity of poetic statement occasionally seemed too artificial:

> Verses, ye are too fine a thing, too wise
>   For my rough sorrows. Cease, be dumbe and mute,
> Give up your feet and running to mine eyes,
>   And keep your measures for some lover's lute,
> Whose grief allows him musick and a ryme.
> For mine excludes both measure, tune, and time.
>   Alas, My God![3]

Perhaps this denial of artifice is only a more subtle form of the thing it denies. Certainly Herbert did continue to write poetry to the end. But, trick or no trick, these lines convey sincerity — as Herbert intended they should — and they do prove the full consciousness of his poetic art.

For no student of Herbert can help feeling, beneath the simple texture of his verse, a strong and controlled intelligence directing every stroke of his pen. Clearness and exactness were his aims; simplicity, his art. No irrelevant interests must be allowed to distract the reader. Palmer has pointed out some of the metrical consequences of this determination:

To effect his purposes the most familiar foot is the best. A movement of an unusual, swift, or melodious sort might distract attention from the thought, where all the pleasure is intended to be found. Feet of three syllables are accordingly discarded. ... His working foot is the common iambic.... In this rhythm all but eleven of his poems are written, these eleven being trochaic.... Everywhere his rhythm is of extreme regularity. I know no other poet of his time so constantly exact.... In all his verse I count only a dozen irregular lines.... But, though regular, his line is far from mechanical. (I, 125-126)

In view of his intellectual aims, Herbert avoids ... the long and melodious lines prized by his predecessors.... His longest line is ten syllables, his shortest three, except in refrain. (I, 130) ... He uses about one "run-over" line to three "end stopped" in his Cambridge poems; and somewhat more, though not so many as two, in those of the Bemerton time. (I, 128)

In accordance with the largely intellectual cast of his verse, Herbert employs little vowel color. (I, 128) ... Seldom, too, does Herbert strengthen a line with alliteration.... In a poet so fond of music one suspects that this failure to appeal to the ear was not wholly due to dulness, but was part of a deliberate plan to push thought into the foreground and fix attention on harsh, intricate, and veritable experience. (I, 129)

II

Herbert's attempt to push thought into the foreground — here the "contribution" of this paper begins — led to his many experiments with stanza patterns. Like the average reader of my first paragraph he had been carried away by the music of Elizabethan poetry; like Pope he had been annoyed by the expectedness of most rimes.[4] And yet he would probably have admired the melodiousness of such lines as

> Wrong not, dear empress of my heart,
>   The merit of true passion
> With thinking that he feels no smart
>   That sues for no compassion;
> Since, if my plaints serve not to prove
>   The conquest of your beauty,
> They come not from defect of love
>   But from access of duty.

For Raleigh's purposes this easy swinging rhythm was highly effective. But, Herbert would have said, it runs too glibly to convey the impression of deep sincerity, too sweetly to express the struggles of a soul trying to reach God. Couched in such a form, the full force of Herbert's thought would have escaped the reader. For intellectual poetry of such compression as that Herbert wrote, it is necessary somehow to make the lines vibrate with a certain tension, to offer in sense and rhythm a resistance which will disturb the reader's inertia.

The glibness of the verses quoted above comes principally from the fact that the pattern of rimes, *a b a b,* coincides with the pattern of line-lengths, also *a b a b* (8 7 8 7). Change the rime pattern to *a b b a,* leaving the line-lengths unchanged, and all swing is gone from the poem:

> Wrong not the merit of true passion,
>   Dear empress of my heart,
> With thinking that he feels no smart
>   That sues for no compassion;
> Since, if my plaints serve not to prove
>   The conquest of your beauty,
> They come but from access of duty
>   Not from defect of love.

The mood is quieter now and, if the turn of thought is less graceful, perhaps it is more thoughtful. If the clash of patterns takes away some of the magic music, it permits closer examination of the actual idea. Admittedly, on examination, what Raleigh is saying proves to be quite trivial and so the poem suffers from the change. But with Herbert, a man who packed unfamiliar thoughts into the smallest compass, it is a different matter. This clash of patterns, this contrapuntal music, might prove a real aid to the reader, and so to the poem. And this is precisely Herbert's experiment — to construct the pattern of his line lengths independently of the pattern of his rimes. Thus he defeats the excessive expectation of rime by making its position unpredictable. As counterpoint in music stimulates the intellect of the listener, so in poetry it keeps the reader alert.

Although most English lyrics are written in harmony, like Raleigh's, rather than in counterpoint, there is no inevitable connection between rime pattern and length-of-line pattern. Tradition has accustomed us to the one; it might have accustomed us to the other. Breaking with tradition, then, in a surprisingly large number of poems, Herbert sought to "push thought into the foreground" by the intellectual music of a contrapuntal poetry. He probably got the idea for his experiments from

two sources, the practice of John Donne and the theory of Puttenham's
Arte of English Poesie.

First, the theorist. That Herbert knew *The Arte of English Poesie*
cannot be definitely proved; it is, however, likely. At any rate Herbert's
practice accords with Puttenham's theory. Most of the occasional
awkward lines in his poems, for example, may be explained by saying he
adheres to the theory that in English versification the line is determined
by the number of syllables rather than the number of feet.[5] Like
Puttenham also,[6] he prefers an even to an odd number of syllables, and
follows his advice[7] to construct well-knit stanzas which, by their rime
scheme, cannot fall apart.[8] Further, his use of pictorial stanza patterns
may be due to Puttenham, who praises the practice;[9] the technical name
given for the stanza of "Easter Wings" (II, 335) is "The Triquet
Displayed." But his principal debt is to Chapter XI, "Of Proportion by
Situation," in which Puttenham shows how form ("proportion") may be
given to a stanza by care in the arrangement (1) of rimes ("concords")
and (2) of lines of different lengths ("metres" or "measures"). The
chapter begins with the distinction:

> This proportion consisteth in placing euery verse in a staffe or
> ditty by such reasonable distaunces as may best serue the eare for
> delight, and also to shew the Poets art and variety of Musick. And
> the proportion is double: one by marshalling the meetres, and
> limiting their distaunces, hauing regard to the rime or concorde
> how they go and returne; another by placing euery verse, hauing a
> regard to his measure and quantitie onely, and not to his concorde,
> as to set one short meetre to three long, or foure short and two
> long, or a short measure and a long, or of diuers lengthes with
> relation one to another, which maner of *Situation*, euen without
> respect of the rime, doth alter the nature of the Poesie, and make it
> either lighter or grauer, or more merry, or mournfull, and many
> wayes passionate to the eare and hart of the hearer, seeming for
> this point that our maker by his measures and concordes of sundry
> proportions doth counterfait the harmonicall tunes of the vocall
> and instrumentall Musickes.[10]

Puttenham now proceeds to a full discussion of "concords" and to many
illustrative "proportions," some of which Herbert used. Then turning to
the second kind of "proportion by situation":

> Now touching the situation of measures, there are as manie or
> more proportions of them which I referre to the makers phantasie
> and choise, contented with two or three ocular examples and no

moe. [Five follow.] Which maner of proportion by situation of measures giueth more efficacie to the matter oftentimes then the concords them selues, and both proportions concurring together as they needes must, it is of much more beautie and force to the hearers mind.[11]

Puttenham, it will be noted, does not advocate a contrapuntal use of his two proportions; quite the contrary. But he distinguishes between them so specifically that, if Herbert used this book as his first text in the art of versification, he would certainly have had it fixed in his mind that the two proportions were separate patterns. The idea that they could be used independently of each other, possibly in conflict with each other, came from acquaintance with Donne's poems.

That Herbert knew Donne of course needs no proof. Both by family and by poetry the two were intimately associated. It is not beyond possibility that they discussed together the matters I am writing about. What, then, was Donne's practice? In the first place, his stanza forms are even more varied than Herbert's: 47 out of 49 "Songs and Sonets"[12] compared with 111 out of 127 in Herbert. As Legouis has pointed out, Donne was a real innovator in the way he combined different metres in the same stanza. "Out of forty-nine pieces, seven only are isometrical (including one in which the heptasyllabic is occasionally substituted for the octosyllabic); in eighteen, two measures are found; in sixteen, three; in eight, four. Which of his contemporaries has used so many metres in so many ways?"[13] For once the rhetorical question gets an unexpected answer. Of the 127 stanzaic poems published in *The Temple* in the same year, 1633, as Donne's *Poems*, 19 are isometrical; in 56 two measures are found; in 43, three; in 8, four; in 1 ("Easter Wings"), five. The percentages are remarkably parallel. But here the parallels cease. As noted above,[14] Herbert had great care for the coherence of his stanzas; Donne, very little. The average Herbert stanza is shorter than Donne's (see Table II at end of this paper) and it is held together by interlocking rimes. The average Donne stanza is a shapeless group of quatrains, couplets, and triplets, held together only by the thought. Legouis has advanced the most reasonable explanation of Donne's practice:

... in the first stanza of most of the *Songs and Sonets*, thought and feeling are allowed to shape their metrical mould unhampered by any convention of tradition. In the following stanzas the position is completely reversed: thought and feeling are at great pains to fit themselves into the now hardened mould. In other words the extreme of freedom becomes the extreme of slavery.[15]

The cause, then, of Donne's variety in stanza pattern was very unlike that of Herbert's, and so the younger man found in the older not a model but a precedent.[16] Also, Donne's freedom in varying line length served to confirm the precepts of Puttenham. But in one other respect Donne may have been even more influential, for, whether by accident or design, Donne did occasionally employ the contrapuntal method. Only three whole poems ("A Valediction: of my Name, in the Window," "Witchcraft by a Picture," and "A Jeat Ring Sent") can be strictly classified as contrapuntal, but many others include quatrains, especially at the beginning of the stanza, which exhibit the typical clash. For example, the opening lines of "Loves Growth":

> I scarce beleeve my love to be so pure
>   As I had thought it was,
>   Because it doth endure
> Vicissitude, and season, as the grasse.

If Herbert observed the quiet sincerity, the restrained melody, of these lines, as it is likely he would have observed, he might well have remarked to himself: "Here is the very form I've been looking for; the tune is exactly right for my ideas. I'll see what I can do with it."

Let us see what he did do. He wrote 127 stanzaic poems for *The Temple*. These I have analyzed out into seven major types, which may be described as follows:

Type 1, Harmonic Stanzas. Here the rime pattern and the length-of-line pattern reinforce each other; all lines which rime together have the same length.

> Whither, O, whither art thou fled,
>   My Lord, my Love?
> My searches are my daily bread,
>   Yet never prove.
>   "The Search," III, 219.
>   (*a b a b,* 8 4 8 4)

Type 2, Approximately Harmonic Stanzas. As the name suggests, one pair of riming lines lacks absolute harmony.

> Death, thou wast once an uncouth hideous thing,
>   Nothing but bones,
>   The sad effect of sadder grones;
> Thy mouth was open but thou couldst not sing.
>   "Death," II, 263.
>   (*a b b a,* 10 4 8 10)

Type 3, Isometrical Stanzas. All lines have the same length and so there is no line pattern.

> My God, a verse is not a crown,
> No point of honour, or gay suit,
> No hawk, or banquet, or renown,
> Nor a good sword, nor yet a lute.
>
> > "The Quidditie," II, 97.
> > (*a b a b*, 8 8 8 8)

Type 4, Approximately Contrapuntal Stanzas. One pair of riming lines possesses harmony; the rest clash.

> Peace pratler, do not lowre!
> Not a fair look but thou dost call it foul.
> Not a sweet dish but thou dost call it soure.
> Musick to thee doth howl.
> By listning to thy chatting fears
> I have both lost mine eyes and eares.
>
> > "Conscience," III, 229.
> > (*a b a b c c,* 6 10 10 6 8 8)

Type 5, Contrapuntal Stanzas. No lines which rime together have also the same number of syllables; the patterns are wholly independent of each other.

> Poore heart, lament.
> For since thy God refuseth still,
> There is some rub, some discontent,
> Which cools his will.
>
> > "The Method," III, 197.
> > (*a b a b*, 4 8 8 4)

Type 6, Off-Balance Stanzas. One line is shorter or longer than the rest.

> Sweet day, so cool, so calm, so bright,
> The bridall of the earth and skie;
> The dew shall weep thy fall to night,
> For thou must die.
>
> > "Vertue," III, 335.
> > (*a b a b*, 8 8 8 4)

Type 7, Irregular Stanzas. This is a motley group of miscellaneous patterns. I shall let that of "Aaron" (III,11) stand for the group: *a b a b b,* 6 8 10 8 6. Like many others here, this could have been classified under Type 4; the line pattern seems to have been devised, however, for symmetry rather than for clash, and so I have called it Type 7. It will be noted that if the third *b* rime were *a,* the stanza would belong to Type 2.

> Holinesse on the head,
> Light and perfections on the breast,
> Harmonious bells below, raising the dead
> To leade them unto life and rest;
> Thus are true Aarons drest.

The 127 poems are divided among these types as follows: Type 1, 26 poems; Type 2, 18; Type 3, 19; Type 4, 12; Type 5, 20; Type 6, 15; Type 7, 17.[17] Observe that half the poems (63) fall into the first three classifications, which are the normal patterns of English lyrics, and half (64) into the last four, the experimental types. One quarter belong to Types 4 and 5. Such a large number cannot be accidental. Herbert must deliberately have chosen to depart from tradition, and probably for the reasons by now familiar to the reader.

This conclusion is confirmed by the existence of several closely parallel patterns. They show the poet trying out the various possibilities. A few deserve examination. They will also serve to demonstrate the different effects produced by different types of stanzas.

In the Williams manuscript, Palmer found a poem entitled "Evensong" which does not appear in *The Temple.* It is probably an early poem, and it belongs to Type 2. The first stanza runs:

> The Day is spent, and hath his will on mee.
> I and the Sunn have runn our races.
> I went the slower, yet more paces;
> For I decay, not hee.   (III, 391)

Parallel with it, but included in *The Temple,* is "Mattens." Here the order of the lines is reversed — to make the stanza appropriate to the morning, when the day is growing:

> I cannot ope mine eyes
> But thou art ready there to catch
> My morning-soul and sacrifice;
> Then we must needs for that day make a match.
>   (II, 285)

Next, compare "The Temper" with the first "Even-song." The lines are the same but the rimes have been changed so that the stanza now belongs to Type 5:

> How should I praise thee, Lord! How should my rymes
> Gladly engrave thy love in steel,
> If what my soul doth feel sometimes,
> My soul might ever feel! (II, 315)

Finally consider the "Even-song" which Herbert included in *The Temple*. The rime scheme is the same as that of the earlier poem, but, because the short line is placed first instead of last, the poem belongs to Type 5:

> Blest be the God of love
> Who gave me eyes, and light, and power this day
> Both to be busie and to play.
> But much more blest be God above ...[18]

Since, of course, one cannot tell what order these poems were written in, one cannot speak of progress. To me the first seems the weakest stanza and the last the strongest; but they may not have been written in that order, and tastes may differ. At least one can see in these four stanzas the operation of a curious mind, one never satisfied, ever wondering whether some other combination might not be better. For those who may wish to pursue these speculations, I list some other parallel stanzas: "The Method" (III, 197; *a b a b,* 4 8 8 4) and "The Search" (III, 219; *a b a b,* 8 4 8 4); "Church-Musick" (II, 199; *a b a b,* 10 8 10 8) and "The Reprisall" (II, 293; *a b a b,* 8 10 10 8); "Judgment" (II, 271; *a a b b a,* 10 4 10 4 8) and "The Discharge" (III, 187; *a b b a a,* 10 4 10 4 8); "Affliction" (II, 339; a *b a b c c,* 10 6 10 6 10 10) and "Love" (II, 401; *a b a b c c,* 10 6 10 6 10 6); and finally "The Pilgrimage" (III, 237; *a b a b c c,* 10 4 8 8 10 4), "Praise" (III, 45; *a b a c b c,* 8 4 10 8 10 6) and "Peace" (II, 377; *a b a c b c,* 10 4 8 6 10 4). The music of the last-named poem, with a rime scheme that falls into two parts and a line scheme that falls into three, is so subtly interwoven that I cannot forbear quoting the first stanza as one last example of Herbert's contrapuntal style:

> Sweet Peace, where dost thou dwell? I humbly crave
> Let me once know.
> I sought thee in a secret cave,
> And ask'd if Peace were there.
> A hollow winde did seem to answer, No:
> Go seek elsewhere.

III

This, then, was Herbert's experiment, that, desiring to focus attention upon sense rather than sound, he constructed the line pattern of his stanzas independently of the rime pattern. At times he wove the separate strands together in such a fashion that they seem to complement each other in exactly the manner of the two melodies in a fugue. It remains to be seen whether this experiment was unique.

With this question in mind I have examined the works of many other poets and analyzed a dozen exhaustively. The results are tabulated in Table I at the end of this paper. I have found no other poet who has used Types 4 and 5 in anywhere near the proportion that Herbert has used them. Possibly Herbert's disciple Vaughan and probably his brother, Lord Herbert of Cherbury, were conscious of what they were doing in their few contrapuntal poems. The other instances I have found can well be considered accidental.[19] In every period of English literature, except the seventeenth century, an overwhelming majority of the lyrics belong to Types 1 and 3, the harmonic and isometrical patterns. But during the seventeenth century the stanza appears to have been extremely fluid; every poet felt free to invent new forms whenever he pleased. For this freedom, even among those who were not strictly his followers, the example of Donne, and perhaps of Herbert, was chiefly responsible. The variety of Donne's stanzas I have already discussed; the greater number of them, thanks to his individual method of composition, fall under Type 7. Among other seventeenth century poets, Herrick, Crashaw, Marvell, and Vaughan wrote a majority of their pieces in couplets of varying measures. But Herrick and Vaughan have also a large number of stanzaic poems in what would be a wide variety of patterns if it were not compared with Herbert's variety; the number in Types 4 and 5 is so small that accident could explain them. Traherne resembles Donne metrically: his stanzas are long and none is repeated (see Table II); they fall into every type but most frequently into Type 7. It is possible that his method of composition may have been the same as that Legouis attributes to Donne; unlike the latter, however, Traherne occasionally failed to sustain the form set up in the first stanza. But with all these men, including Donne, the variety of their stanzas represents license, not law. Their inventions are haphazard, thoughtless, unplanned. Herbert's, I hope I have shown, are the result of long reflection upon metrics and of systematic experimenting with various types of stanzas.

In writing about these experiments I have used the musical terms, harmony and counterpoint. Although the primary reason for their use is their appropriateness to the phenomena described, they have an additional significance. Herbert loved music; he played the lute, joined regularly in the activities of a singing society at Salisbury, and listened to the organ. Aubrey tells us that he set his own poems to music. And this music, which Herbert knew so well, was largely contrapuntal. In Europe at large the seventeenth century signalizes the ultimate emergence of harmonic or monophonic music into dominance over contrapuntal or polyphonic. But in English church music under James I, "the heavy harmonic style was replaced for a time by a return to the old counterpoint."[20] When it is remembered that this was also the period of the great English madrigals, it becomes apparent that music to Herbert would inevitably have implied counterpoint. If he really did write music for his lyrics, it was contrapuntal music. What more natural, then, than that the lyrics should also be contrapuntal? Strangely enough, the madrigal writers themselves used harmonic stanzas. Of the 1423 lyrics in Fellowes' collection of *English Madrigal Verse* (Oxford, 1920) only 32 or 2% belong to Type 5, while 342 belong to Type 1 and 742 to Type 3; only Morley used any number of contrapuntal stanzas, 11, and all but one of his were made up of irregular couplets. Perhaps this very disparity between words and music it was Herbert's hope to eliminate. Perhaps he hoped to write poems of which his readers might say that they were as worthy of the God they served, in their structure and melody, as was that "Church-Musick" of which Herbert wrote:

> Sweetest of sweets, I thank you! when displeasure
> > Did through my bodie wound my minde,
> You took me thence, and in your house of pleasure
> > A daintie lodging me assign'd.
>
> Now I in you without a bodie move,
> > Rising and falling with your wings.
> We both together sweetly live and love,
> > Yet say sometimes, *God help poor Kings.*
>
> Comfort, I'le die; for if you poste from me,
> > Sure I shall do so, and much more.
> But if I travell in your companie,
> > You know the way to heaven's doore. (II, 199)

The contrapuntal music of these lyrics in *The Temple* may not be judged by most readers "the way to heaven's doore." The heaven of poetry has many doors, of which this is only one. It is one, and when it is opened by a Herbert mortals below hear celestial music. To intellectual poets of the present day, experimenters in form, Herbert is saying: "Seek, and ye shall find; knock, and it shall be opened unto you."

TABLE I.

STANZAIC POEMS CLASSIFIED BY STANZA-TYPES

Poet	Total of Stanzaic Poems	Type 1	Type 2	Type 3	Type 4	Type 5	Type 6	Type 7
Sir P. Sidney	32	12	1	12			2	5
John Donne	49	4	7	7	5	2/1	3	20
Ben Jonson	24	7	2	11	/1		1	2
Robert Herrick	90	56	8	6	2	3/3	6	3/3
George Herbert	127	26	18	19	11/1	19/1	15	17
Richard Crashaw	14	5	1	5	1/1			1
Andrew Marvell	13	3		8			1	1
Henry Vaughan	80	26	15	19	8	1/1	5	5
Thomas Traherne	37	1	5	4	6/2	1/2	2	13/1
Thomas Gray	15	1	3	8			1	2
John Keats	36	17	1	12			6	
Elinor Wylie	113	51	4	49	2/1		6	

Explanations

The meaning of the types used here is explained in detail on pages 12-14 above. Under Types 4, 5, and 7, certain figures appear after a slanting line. These represent stanzas, 4 to 20 lines long, made up of couplets. These are not properly stanzas at all; variation in line-length gives them all the form they possess.

In compiling this table, I have used the following editions: *The Poems of Sir Philip Sidney* (Muses Library, London, 1922); John Donne, "Songs and Sonets" in *Complete Poetry and Selected Prose*, ed. John Hayward (Bloomsbury, 1929); *The Songs and Poems of Ben Jonson* (The Pilgrims Books, London, 1924); Robert Herrick, *The Hesperides and Noble Numbers*, ed. A. Pollard (New York and London, 1897); George Herbert, *The English Works*, ed. G. H. Palmer (Boston, 1905); Richard Crashaw, *Complete Works* (London, 1858); Andrew Marvell, *Poetical Works* ed. Bertram Dobell (London, 1903); Thomas Gray, *Poetical Works* (published with Collins, Oxford, 1917); John Keats, *Poetical Works* (Oxford, 1924); Elinor Wylie, *Collected Poems* (New York, 1932). With all these poets, except Herbert, I have eliminated from my calculations poems less than twelve lines long; these are especially numerous, of course, in Herrick and Crashaw. It will also be noted that I have not attempted completeness in either

Donne or Traherne; I have ascertained, however, that the poems here used are representative samples.

TABLE II.

POEMS CLASSIFIED BY LENGTH OF STANZAS
(Numbers at the top = lines)

Poet	2	3	4	5	6	7	8	9	10	14	Others over 10	Miscellaneous poems
Sidney		1	8	4	8/3			3	3	16/115	2/1	
Donne	1		5/2		6	4	10	10	5		7	4
Jonson	3/15		7/2		7/2	1	3		2	1		10
Herrick.....	7/165	5/6	17/28	3	18/8	2	4	1	5		3	2
Herbert	5/2	2/1	29/11	23	43/5	4	8		4	3/11		16
Crashaw....	4/42	1	1/2		6/1		2		2			7
Marvell	3/33	1	6/3		3		1					
Vaughan ...	6/86	1	13/21	2	16/1	3	12	1	4	1	7	22
Traherne ...	2/8		3	1	6	3	3	4	7		9	1
Gray	5/4		3/4		2		2		2	1	2	2
Keats	4/23		11/4		5		4	1/3	4/2	15/48	2	12
Wylie	5/12	1	30/64	5	6	2	3		1	15/34	2	3

Explanations

Single figures and figures to the left of slanting lines represent the number of distinct stanza patterns of each given stanza length. Figures to the right of slanting lines represent repetitions of stanzas previously used by the same poet. Thus 29/11 under 4 means that Herbert wrote 40 poems in quatrains, using 29 different quatrain patterns. In each case the addition of the figures to the right and left of the line gives the total written in the individual stanza length.

The column headed "Miscellaneous Poems" includes poems written in irregular stanzas, poems composed of two or more different stanzas (usually the result of a poem within a poem), and non-stanzaic poems.

SONG AND SPEECH IN THE METRICS OF GEORGE HERBERT

Alicia Ostriker

Modern critics have stressed the element of paradox in Herbert's work. Herbert is homely, as has commonly been remarked, yet he is sophisticated. He appears spontaneous, yet his poems are scrupulously well-constructed. He is unsure of his union with God, yet he is sure. He doubts himself and he does not doubt. He seems to sing, and he seems to speak. Any new technical analysis of Herbert's verse[1] should take these paradoxes, and the syntheses forged from them, into account. The present paper attempts to do so by isolating, in metrical terms, the apparently irreconcilable modes of "song" and "speech" which have been observed in Herbert by several critics, notably Joseph H. Summers;[2] by discovering what conventions they derive from and how Herbert used and changed what he learned from others; and by showing how the prosodic causes serve as instruments of an overall poetic vision in *The Temple*. It will follow the division of theory, between the poet's song and his speech, although it should be remembered that Herbert himself made no such division. His most typical work contains both elements. Together they form his style.

The singing qualities in Herbert continue the music-oriented tradition of late Elizabethan lyric, which had turned from "drab" to "golden" toward the close of the sixteenth century largely because of the prosodic influence of musical forms imported from France and Italy. Metrical composition was transformed in this period from a mere cart for thought to a vessel which might not only house nectar but itself become an object of delight. And the "heavy jog trot and monotonous fourteener verse of the sixties and seventies gave way in the last two decades of the century to a versification of subtle variety and delicacy"[3] in part because the infinite possibilities of musical cadence, not confined to a rigid succession of iambs, invited experimentation by poets. The outcome of their experiments was lyric verse full of ingenious metrical complexities, yet formally strict, with well-shaped stanza-patterns paralleling the

Reprinted from *PMLA*, 80 (1965), 62-68, by permission of the author and the publisher.

coherence of a musical theme, with rhyme "emphatic and integral to the structure of the stanza, like the cadence of a musical phrase,"[4] and with considerable attention paid to the correspondence between meter and meaning. "Your ocular proportion," wrote Puttenham, "doeth declare the nature of the audible."[5]

It is hardly surprising that Herbert was influenced by the art of the song-writers. An important precedent for composing religious poetry in the style and with the techniques of courtly song had been set by Sir Philip Sidney and the Countess of Pembroke, in their translation of the Psalms.[6] Certainly many of Herbert's song-devices could have been learned directly from the Sidneys. Moreover, music was one of his own avocations.

Some obvious results of this interest in song were his use of refrains, of refrain-like repetition or parallelism within the stanza, and of brief tag-lines which have the rhythmic, if not the literal, effect of refrain. Another lyric habit was composition in short lines, which secular lyricists had used for their lightness, and which Herbert used to denote a simple gravity. But the most significant influence of Elizabethan song on Herbert lies in the structuring of his stanza-patterns, in which one finds the most important metrical qualities cultivated by the lyricists: complexity and variety, strictness of form, and concurrence of sound with sense.

Herbert's interest in metrical complexity reveals itself in the unusual flexibility of his stanza-shapes. If we open *The Temple* at random, we are far less likely to hit upon a stanza which runs, however prettily,[7]

> I got me flowers to straw thy way;   (4)
> I got me boughs off many a tree: (4)
> But thou wast up by break of day,   (4)
> And brought'st thy sweets along with thee. (4)
>   ("Easter")

than on one which goes:

> Bright spark, shot from a brighter place,   (4)
> Where beams surround my Saviours face,   (4)
> Canst thou be any where   (3)
> So well as there?   (2)
>   ("The Starre")

Only nineteen of his 127 stanzaic pieces are, like "Easter," isometrical. Fifty-six are written in two measures; forty-three in three; eight in four; and one ("Easter Wings") in five measures. These proportions may be compared with those in Campion's first two Books of Ayres, which are: 43 isometrical poems, ten in two measures, five in three measures, and one each in four and five measures. In the Sidneyan versions of the Psalms, 90 poems are isometrical, 33 in two measures, 18 in three, one in four, and none in five. These statistics indicate that Herbert considerably advanced the Elizabethan tendency to frame verse out of lines not identical in length, but changing. His most typical cadences do not repeat, but vary, punctuate, extend, contract, and reflect one another.

Variety, however, does not mean license. Just as Herbert pruned his language for greater coherence of thought,[8] so he took care always to apply some principle of symmetry or proportion in the construction of his stanzas. A favorite pattern, for instance, is an opening of pentameter or tetrameter followed by a contraction into short lines, and concluded by another long one, as in the stanza of "Nature":

Full of rebellion, I would die,	(4)
Or fight, or travell, or denie	(4)
That thou hast ought to do with me.	(4)
O tame my heart;	(2)
It is thy highest art	(3)
To captivate strong holds to thee.	(4)

This same pattern in miniature becomes the gemlike stanza used in "Discipline":

Throw away thy rod,	(3)
Throw away thy wrath:	(3)
O my God,	(2)
Take the gentle path.	(3)

If the shape of these poems is "concave," the reverse, or convex movement, might take the form of a cross, as in "The Reprisal," "Good Friday," "Sunday," and "Sighs and Groans"; or of a gradual, stepped expansion and contraction, as in "Holy Baptism (II)," "Baptism (II)," or "Aaron." Other forms include varieties of the triangle, simple or complex alternation of shorts and longs, isometric stanzas set off by a brief tail line, and so on. It would be impossible to describe the many forms Herbert's sense for patterned structure takes in *The Temple*, but even a casual reader cannot fail to observe its existence.

Sometimes the formal pattern of the poem itself becomes a hieroglyph for its meaning. We are all familiar with the dwindling and expanding shape of "Easter Wings" and the altar shape of "The Altar." Herbert also

devised other correspondences. The stanza of "Good Friday," significantly, is cross-shaped:

O my chief good,	(2)
How shall I measure out thy bloud?	(4)
How shall I count what thee befell,	(4)
And each grief tell?	(2)

"Aaron," in addition to taking its structure from its title, with five 5-line
stanzas of which the first two exactly correspond in phrase to match the
two "A's," follows a shape which swells and diminishes like a repeated
pealing of the bell which is its central image. This shape also duplicates
the expansion and return to firmness of the thought:

Holiness on the bead,	(3)
Light and perfections on the breast,	(4)
Harmonious bells below, raising the dead	(5)
To lead them unto life and rest;	(4)
Thus are true Aarons drest.	(3)

A still more subtle conjunction of sound and sense is in "Deniall":

When my devotions could not pierce	(4)
Thy silent eares;	(2)
Then was my heart broken, as was my verse.	(5)
My breast was full of fears	(3)
And disorder.	(2)

Here, the keynotes are breaking and disorder. Phrases which should
hang together syntactically are disjoined, to express disturbance of
mind. The inversions of line 3 both stress the actual word "brŏkĕn" and
create a metrical break to suit it. "Disorder" is implied by the fact that no
two lines are rhythmically identical, since the two dimeters "Thy silĕnt
ĕars" and "Ănd dísŏrdĕr" scan disparately. Finally, the unrhymed last
lines leave a sense of incompletion, unresolved until the closing stanza in
which the poet "mends his rhyme." Remarking these consistent correspondences of tune to sense, Palmer observed that Herbert "invents for
each lyrical situation exactly the rhythmic setting which befits it."[9] But
this practice was not unique to Herbert, since all the major Elizabethan
song-writers occupied themselves with the creation of "lyrical situations" in which sound and meaning became one.
    Herbert's most interesting extension of the song style was his espousal
of "counterpointed" rhyme patterns. In most stanzaic poetry, rhymed

lines are of the same length. This produces a smoothing and soothing effect, due to the pauses of measure concurring with the sound-echo felt by the ear. But as Albert McHarg Hayes points out in a paper on Herbert's counterpoint, only one-half of Herbert's stanzaic poems follow this usage. The other half range from patterns in which one set of rhyming lines do not concur metrically, to some in which none do so. Such, for example, is the stanza of "Judgement":

Almightie Judge, how shall poore wretches brook	(5-a)
Thy dreadfull look,	(2-a)
Able a heart of iron to appall,	(5-b)
When thou shalt call	(2-b)
For ev'ry mans peculiar book?	(4-a)

This device was used on occasion by many of the song-writers. Herbert might have found it in the Sidneys' psalms, or in Jonson, who liked it when he got away from couplets. In him, however, it becomes systematic, a hallmark of his style. Statistically, the net result of his experimentation along these lines is that "the 127 stanzaic poems in *The Temple* represent 111 different stanza patterns. Of these ... 11 are used twice, 1 three times, and one four times. The other 98 are unique in Herbert; most of them also, in English poetry."[10] Such delight in prosodic variety continues the sixteenth-century lyricists' taste for novel patterns. It does not sacrifice the song-principle of formal coherence, since Herbert's construction of metric and rhyming patterns independently of each other produces an effect which in music would be called counterpoint. One hears the snare-drums of meter as a sort of basso continuo, moving and pausing; and above them, chimes of various pitches playing a pattern of their own. Finally, the device has poetic, as well as musical significance. Its psychological effect, argues Mr. Hayes, is that it serves "to make the lines vibrate with a certain tension; to offer ... a resistance which will disturb the reader's inertia"[11] and consequently make him more alert to the intellectual stimuli offered by the poet. One may suggest that in some poems the counterpoint is sensuously or emotionally, rather than intellectually, stimulating. In either case, it provides a distinct and substantial poetic satisfaction.

Some remarks remain to be made about the effects of Herbert's singing voice on his expression as a religious poet. Not all of Herbert's songs by any means illustrate his positive-thinking moods. On the contrary, some of his most delicate, intricate, sweetly-sounding poems bear titles like "Sighs and Groans," "Affliction," "Repentance," "Justice," or "Complaining." The last-named, for example, begins:

Do not beguile my heart,	(3-a)
Because thou art	(2-a)
My power and wisdome. Put me not to shame	(5-B
Because I am	(2-b)
Thy clay that weeps, thy dust that calls.	(4-c)
Thou art the Lord of Glorie;	(3-d)
The deed and storie	(2-d)
Are both thy due: but I a silly flie,	(5-e)
That live or die	(2-e)
According as the weather falls.	(4-c)

This is one of Herbert's most complex constructions: he uses four different line-lengths in a five-line stanza, and counterpoints throughout, except for rhyming the last lines of each pair of stanzas. It is also one of his most poetically effective patterns: the echoing asymmetry of the paired rhymes, the suspension of a final rhyme from stanza to stanza, and above all the languid rising and ebbing of the cadences, all suit the poem's mournfulness. And at the same time, all these effects are highly musical; and are the more so in that succeeding stanzas duplicate almost entirely the whole pattern, including the curious middle caesura and the slight accentual irregularities.

Prosody, at this point, touches directly on some of the most basic areas of intellectual and emotional appeal in Herbert's work. For one finds, with lyrics like "Complaining," that while the words cause the mind quite properly to register despair, the sound and cadence of the words cause the ear to register delight. The case is similar with such pieces as "Deniall," mentioned above, with its slight roughness and metrical break signifying the breaking of a heart. These identical irregularities appearing in successive stanzas, when taken cumulatively, do not grate but please the ear. They form a pattern of their own, and the very formation of a pattern belies the literal sense of the words. Sound creates an independent sense, and Herbert speaks to us, in this way, of his hope and wanhope, his trust and mistrust, at once.

Elizabethan lyric is full of instances in which words of woe, conjoining musically to the ear, belie themselves. Ariel's song about drowning does not frighten us; "Come away, come away death" does not afflict us; no more do Herbert's songs. Again, when a poet habitually writes verse which is complex yet coherently organized and balanced, he expresses the sense of an ordering, cohering principle in the world. This sense never left Herbert, whatever else failed him; or at any rate, it never left his poetry. He allows no looseness or harshness of structure to suggest that "the new philosophy" — or anything else — "puts all in doubt" for him. Even in his most despairing moments, his metrics lead us to expect a change for the better. His song-meters thus provide an important hint as to why he strikes us, among all religious poets, as one of the most joyful, most certain, most on intimate, friendly terms with his Lord.

Herbert does not imitate all the devices practiced by the song-writers. He does not use dactyls or anapests. He does not use more than one meter in a poem, even a combination of iambic and trochaic lines. He does not use the fourteener or alexandrine. The probable reason for these omissions is that, unlike the secular lyricists, he did not wish to be too divertingly musical, or to make a show of ingenuity. The poetic credo of his two "Jordan" poems, and his continual references to the plainness, the neatness, the simplicity of what he has to say, substantiate this. He will not be admired for technical virtuosity, but employ that virtuosity in a manner which will itself appear neat and simple, and make his ideas appear so. Thus his stanza-patterns, however much cleverness went into their making, never seem solely clever. They exist to frame his thought.

This point brings us to the other side of Herbert's prosodic technique, its air of speech. Herbert had great reason to try to convey the sense of the spoken word. Almost half his poems take the form of direct addresses to God; others address the poet's heart or conscience, a friend, fellow-worshippers, or personified abstractions like Time or Death. Some are set as dialogue, and even some of the strictly narrative or expository poems in *The Temple* suggest discussion with an interested listener. Herbert no doubt felt he could be more convincing if he seemed to be merely speaking his mind without adornment. However, it is inaccurate — if commonplace — to say that he "naturally employed with great freedom the phrases and rhythms of actual speech."[12] Despite the protestations poets may make about employing "language such as men do use," it has been astutely observed that "les grands artistes ne sont pas les transcripteurs du monde, ils en sont les rivaux."[13] When poets wish to create an illusion of speech, they produce not a replica of its phrases or rhythms, but something resembling and rivalling them, in poetry's own terms. For the early seventeenth century, these terms were supplied by the techniques of blank verse.

Dramatic blank verse and song, at the peaks of their respective developments toward the close of the sixteenth century, occupied opposite ends of the poetic spectrum. Blank verse had developed independently of music, song in partnership with it. Blank verse stemmed from rhetoric, the art of public speaking; song stemmed from the artificial language of courtship. The plays composed of blank verse were supposed to be "mirrors," "glasses," "images" of real life and character. Song rarely pretended such resemblance, but imitated, if anything, the Idea of Beauty. Hence in diction, structure, and metrics, blank verse had an obvious interest in producing the illusion of speech, where song had no such interest.

Metrically, the composition of blank verse paragraphs involved a high degree of flexibility in overriding the basic pentameter beat with freer rhythms, the effect of which was to suggest that thought itself was flowing freely, digging its channels of form at hazard as it went. This precisely opposed the effect of song, in which thought and pattern were one. If blank verse moved like a river, which might at any moment overflow its banks, cut a new stream, or go underground, song was a fountain set in a garden, which could only rise and fall gracefully in the same planned place.

Such, at any rate, was the original condition of song. At the turn of the century, however, men like Donne and Jonson invaded lyric with the emotional and rhythmic predispositions of blank verse writers. Desiring like the play-wrights to create an illusion of speech, to concentrate on immediacy, to manifest the mind as it spins and the passions as they spring, each created his own compromise between lyric formality and blank verse spontaneity. Donne's way was flamboyant. His use of stanza forms in the *Songs and Sonets* scarcely resembles the balanced compositions of earlier lyricists. Legouis, while observing Donne's "extraordinary variety of metrical schemes,"[14] notes that many of his stanzas are simply groups of "couplets or triplets following one another," and that they "nearly always lack internal concatenation or rhyme-linking."[15] His metrical irregularity was notorious, and it is significant that few of his poems were set to music. Jonson, more restrained, developed what Trimpi has analyzed as the "plain style." His coupleted verse discreetly balances between the exigencies of pentameter and the freer movement of accentual and caesural irregularity, with a modest but not overwhelming use of overflow.[16]

Donne probably provided Herbert's earliest models for the speaking lyric. In his mature work, however, Herbert achieved something very like the Jonsonian poise, in which not egoistic monologue, but dialogue — the possibility of communication between minds — is the thing sought. How he obtained this in his metrics may be seen in his treatment of the individual line: how he used, or abstained from using, the tricks of accentual variety, caesural irregularity, and overflow, common to blank verse.

The simplest and most usual means of disturbing metrical flow, for Herbert as for the blank verse writers, lay in disrupting a single foot at a time through internal inversion: the substitution of a trochee for an

iamb in the middle or end of a line. Herbert's inversions sometimes
barely produce a ripple in the verse's stream: "But since thy breath gave
me both light and shape" ("Affliction" II). More often, they are
accentuated by a tangent caesura, either splitting the inverted foot:

> His beams shall cheer my breast; and both so twine
> Till ev'n his beams sing,/ ănd my musick shine.
> ("Christmas")

or heralding it:

> My God,/ what ĭs a heart?
> ("Mattens")
> He did, he came:/ Ó mў Redeemer deare,
> After all this/ cánst thŏu be strange?
> ("Home")

Another type of single-foot disturbance consists in the substitution of
trisyllabic feet for iambs. Herbert uses this device less than Donne, and
its effect with him is often mild, due to the possibility of elision. But to
read, for example, "Th'art," in

> Who can indeare
> The praise too much? Thŏu ărt héav'ns Lidger here,
> ("The H. Scriptures")

would suppress an emphasis which Herbert apparently intended to rest
on the words "Thou art."

Although inversion and substitution do not necessarily suggest any
particular speech inflection, the fact that they make a line slightly
irregular by breaking an iambic pattern does imply the spontaneity
associated with ordinary talk. Two more specifically rhetorical devices,
however, are over- and under-accentuation of the single foot; that is,
making the foot into a spondee, which bears double stress, or skipping
over it with little or no stress. Spondees alone will lengthen a line;
dropped accents will speed it up:

> Chúrch-bélls beyond the stárres heárd, the sóul's
> Blóud;   ("The Prayer")

> Thrów ăwăy thў ród,
> Thrów ăwăy thў wráth: ("Discipline")

Used alone or together, they serve any number of rhetorical functions in
Herbert. "The Collar," for example, welds the two effects together to
produce groups of angry, impatient formations. Beyond its opening "I

struck the board, and cry'd, Nó móre," we find clusters of dropped accents and spondees throughout:

> Nót só, my heart: but there ís fruít,
> Ănd thŏu hást hánds.
> Recover all thy sígh-blówn áge
> On double pleasures: leave thy cold dispute
> Ŏf whăt is fít, ănd nót.

"The Collar" comes as close to total irregularity as Herbert ever allowed himself to venture. With its rhyme but no rhyme scheme, its unsystematically varying line-lengths, its rhythms resembling a man trying to fight his way out of a paper bag, hitting in every direction but to no purpose, the poem's total effect is Herbert's equivalent of the ranting passages which Elizabethan dramatists composed as set pieces to tickle the palate of the pit.

Herbert understates his case as often as he dramatizes it. We see the lightly-accented line used to suggest quick and casual conversation in the allegorical "Redemption," which pretends that the momentous event of the soul's search for salvation resembles the worldly search of a tenant for his absentee landord:

> Having been tenant long tŏ ă rích lórd,
> Nót thríving, Ĭ rĕsólvĕd tŏ bĕ bóld,
> And make a súit úntŏ hĭm, tŏ ăffórd
> A néw smáll-rented lease, and cancel th'old.
> Ĭn héavĕn át hĭs mánŏur Ĭ him sóught:
> They told me there, thăt hĕ wăs látelỹ góne
> Ăboŭt sŏme lánd, whích hĕ hăd déarlỹ boúght
> Lóng since ŏn éarth ...

In addition to the enjambment and the asymmetrical pauses, we see the spondees "rích lórd," "Nót thríving," "Lóng sínce," and the inverted "new smáll-rĕnted" irregularly accenting important terms, while light stresses in the first three lines suggest informal talk about something not very important. Although line 4 approaches metrical normality, succeeding lines revert to lightness. The casualness here is of course ironic, but irony is a favorite device in Herbert.

Besides accentual irregularity, the most important resemblance between Herbert's metrics and blank verse lies in his employment of enjambment and caesura. The proportion of technically enjambed (i.e. not end-punctuated) lines in Herbert — one-sixth or more in 70% of his poems, one-fourth or more in 33% — is not uncommon for stanzaic verse. But he consistently resembles blank verse in his use of genuine *syntactic* overflow, which suggests a forward motion of thought, unrestricted by the pattern of a line, and intercepted only by the cross-current of another thought:

> If that hereafter pleasure
> Cavill, and claim her part and measure
> ("Obedience")
> Christ left his grave-clothes, that we might, when grief
> Draws tears, or bloud, not want an handkerchief.
> ("The Dawning")

Overflow and careful varying of caesura, in Herbert's work as in blank verse, go together. Throughout Herbert's verse one finds lines breaking more than once, breaking in the middle of the foot, or breaking near the beginning or end of a line rather than at the center. Where enjambment is extensively used, caesura variation becomes particularly important, because these internal pauses, rather than the formal line-endings, actually determine the working rhythm of the verse. As the units between pauses stretch or contract, grow choppy or rotund, remain equivalent or disparate from each other, so follows the poetry. Thus the rhetorical movement can take precedence over the formal frame. In the opening lines of "Mattens" the parallel brief cadences, with a rocking motion which ultimately overflows, follow the rhetorical units of the initial apostrophe, the hesitant metaphors for "a heart," and the speaker's eager expansion into abstract probability:

> My God,/ what is a heart?//
> Silver,/ or gold,/ or precious stone,/
> Or starre,/ or rainbow,/ or a part
> Of all these things,/ or all of them in one?//

In more conversational poems, the units vary further. "Love Unknown," though rhymed abab throughout, consistently suggests blank verse in several ways, but especially in its use of pause:

> Deare Friend,/ sit down,/ the tale is long and sad:/
> And in my faintings I presume your love
> Will more complie then help.// A Lord I had,/
> And have,/ of whom some grounds,/ which may
> improve,/
> I hold for two lives,/ and both lives in me.//
> To him I brought a dish of fruit one day,/

> And in the middle plac'd my heart.// But he/
>   (I sigh to say)/
> Lookt on a servant,/ who did know his eye
> Better then you know me,/ or/ (which is one)/
> Then I my self.//The servant instantly
> Quitting the fruit,/ seiz'd on my heart alone,
> And threw it in a font, wherein did fall
> A stream of bloud,/ which issued from the side
> Of a great rock...

Here the units between pauses range from half a foot to over eight feet. The opening lines are uneven, with parenthetical digressions and internal full stops corresponding to changes of topic in midstream, representing the speaker's agitation as he buttonholes his auditor. Then as the speaker reaches a crisis in his narrative, he moves more swiftly. Although we cannot in fact read lines 12-15 without pausing, it is significant that Herbert uses no commas or other punctuation here. Throughout "Love Unknown" he counterpoints changing rhythms on his pentameter base. If we barely notice the rhymes in this poem, it is because the poet overrules restrictions of line with a flow of thought which shapes its own laws.

Along with the above catalogue of blank-verse irregularities which Herbert uses, must be mentioned several from which he abstains. Herbert never either truncates a line or extends it beyond its expected number of feet; he never allows a single syllable to stand for a whole foot; and he never flings his accents about with such abandon as to make his lines quite unscannable. These omissions point up the difference between Herbert's prosodic tendencies and those of Donne, who is more free in all these ways. Unlike his predecessor, Herbert did not value the rugged line for its own sake. Although he uses several different types of irregularity, he does not use them all at once to see just how irregular he can get. (Correspondingly, although his speech has considerable range, — he can plead, dispute, rejoice, grieve, narrate, converse — yet in all things he avoids extremes. For this reason, one may never grow so excited reading Herbert as reading Donne. On the other hand, Herbert offers more than Donne a sense of emotional stability, surety, control.

Summers suggests an analogy between Herbert's art of the divine poem and that of public prayer, in which the leader of a congregation, praying aloud in his own person, would attempt to kindle his hearers to similar emotions.[17] Pursuing this, one finds an apt model for Herbert's speech in his chapter on "The Parson Praying" in *The Priest to the*

Temple. This advises that the parson's "voyce is humble, his words treatable and slow; yet not so slow neither, as to let the fervency of the supplicant hang and dry between speaking, but with a grave liveliness, between fear and zeal, pausing yet pressing."[18] These recommendations of "slow, yet not so slow neither . . . pausing yet pressing" apply very well both to the tone of Herbert's poetry and to the handling of its rhythm. It is also significant that he almost invariably tempers or balances his ruggedness with some corresponding regularity. Indeed, where variation is richest, a return to metrical simplicity may be the crucial event of a Herbert poem, indicating the resolution of mental disturbance to mental calm. This observation brings us full circle to a reconsideration of the virtues of Herbert's song-structures.

As we have seen, the "song" elements in Herbert's prosody are supplied by the structure of his stanza-patterns; while the "speech" elements are given by internal rhythmic variation. Since stanza-structure and rhythmic pattern are to each other as container to thing contained, it is easy to see how they may modify one another. A graceful stanza-pattern which harmonizes discordant thoughts may also check and modulate a rough meter. Perhaps a third of the poems in *The Temple* are of this type, dominated by internal irregularities which suggest speech, but contained within a stanza form which suggests song. An equivalent number have the reverse emphasis, with conspicuous stanza-patterns dominating, but broken through by enjambment or varied by shifts in accent or caesura placement from line to line or from stanza to stanza. Finally, there is a sizeable group which seem to balance equally between song and speech, combining the strictness of stanza form with the freedom of internal variation so that neither element predominates. Within this group are some of Herbert's finest pieces, which range in tone from laments like "The Sacrifice," to buoyant lyrics like "Mattens," to a few gravely smiling statements like "Virtue," whose simplicity comes of the art which conceals art. Readers will differ, according to their habits of reading, on the precise proportions of "song" and "speech" in any given poem. The important point is that the poet's treatment of stanza and rhythm helps produce not only his mingled voices of singing and speaking, but affects every aspect of his poetic expression. Like two stones dropped in a pool, their ripples both intercept each other, and widen to touch the pool's circumference.

HERBERT'S TECHNICAL DEVELOPMENT

Mary Ellen Rickey

George Herbert's development as a craftsman has not been adequately explored by commentators.[1] In the present study I propose to show that a number of formal differences between his early and late work exist, and that these differences are sufficiently alike in kind to enable one to see a concerted direction in which his writing was moving at the time of his death. While Herbert's English verse was composed in a relatively short period of time, probably six or seven years, almost half of the poems in *The Temple* were completed by about 1629 and were recorded by an amanuensis, but corrected by Herbert himself, in a document now commonly known as the Williams manuscript.[2] About all that can be done by way of surveying Herbert's poetic development is to assess the differences between the sixty-nine "earlier" poems and the additional "later" poems which appeared in *The Temple* in 1633.

As one might expect of two bodies of verse written in close sequence by an already accomplished poet, the Williams MS group and the later poems reveal more similarities than dramatic differences. In both groups, Herbert consistently uses the iambic foot; in both, he restricts himself to a poetic line of five feet or less; in both, he appears to prefer cross-rhyme stanza forms to enclosed rhyme; he changes diction and imagery very little; he never sustains a stanza form like *abcb* in which some lines have no rhyme counterparts; he changes over-all lengths of his poems very little; and, perhaps most important, he is always careful to produce verse forms which, while strikingly original, are well ordered and well polished. Fundamental and pervasive though these common characteristics are, however, the post-1629 poems show some unmistakable signs of Herbert's developing poetic technique. Let us see some of these signs.

1. *Increasing use of figurative titles.* Ten of the Williams poems bear substantially different titles when they reappear in *The Temple*. Many of

From *JEGP,* 62 (1963), 745-60, © 1963 by the Board of Trustees of the University of Illinois. Reprinted by permission of the author and the University of Illinois Press. This article appears in a revised form in *Utmost Art: Complexity in the Verse of George Herbert* (Lexington: University of Kentucky Press, 1966), pp. 103-47 these changes significantly foreshadow the kind of heading which Herbert used more and more frequently as he matured, that is, one which not merely states the topic of a poem or summarizes it, but which itself metaphorically adds dimension to the piece. Of the ten changed titles, five fall into this category: *The Second Thanksgiving* becomes *The Reprisall, Prayer* becomes *Churchlock and key, Poetry* becomes *The Quidditie, Perfection* becomes *The Elixir*, and *The Publican* becomes *Miserie*. The title *Reprisall* points up a military metaphor in the last two stanzas of the four-stanza poem, a figure which, under the former title, goes almost unnoticed. *Churchlock and key*, for the quite general title *Prayer*, is a much more striking and particular signpost which both calls attention to the personal statement of the first two lines and raises it by implication to a more universal level:

> I know it is my sinne, which locks thine ears,
> And bindes thy hands....[3]

The change from *Poetry* to *Quidditie* probably needs little comment. The title *Elixir* works much the same as *The Reprisall*, emphasizing the figure of the last three lines of the poem:

> Nothing can be so mean,
> Which with his tincture (for thy sake)
> Will not grow bright and clean.   (p. 184)

The new title *Miserie* deepens the poem of that name by diagnosing man's condition, which he does not see to be miserable at all.

Only one other poem in the William MS, *The Pearl*, carries such a figurative title. Here, of course, Herbert characterizes his love of God as a pearl of great price, worth all of his other goods and abilities. Among the new poems in the *Temple*, however, one finds a number of similar titles: *Sighs and Grones; Home,* which indirectly names God's heaven-haven; *The Quip; Businesse; Giddinesse; The Bunch of Grapes; Mans Medley; The Method; The Familie; The Size; Artillerie; The Discharge; The Bag; The Collar; The Glimpse; Clasping of Hands; Joseph's Coat; The Pulley; The Water-Course.* In these titles, all metaphorical, one finds hints of the maturing Herbert's realization that the proper kind of title need not be a mere prediction of the language of the poem, but could function much like an additional, and highly desirable, unit of imagery.

2. *Use of more than one stanza form in a single poem.* None of the Williams MS poems is made up of more than one stanza form, except *Man, Antiphon* (II), and *Deniall*, all of which have last stanzas different

from those which have gone before; I shall consider them presently. In *The Temple*, however, one finds seven poems in which the form changes about halfway through: *Good-Friday, Easter, The H. Communion, The Church-floore, Christmas, An Offering, Vanitie* (II). Two of these, *Easter* and *Good-Friday*, are simply combinations of pairs of poems from the Williams MS. That the combinations are appropriate is evident from even a brief glance at either one of them. In *Good-Friday*, the shift from impersonal natural imagery in the first five stanzas to more orthodox theological imagery in the last three stanzas gives a heightened liturgical tone to the ending of the poem. *Easter's* three initial stanzas find Herbert resolving to purify himself adequately for the worship of the risen Christ, while the last three stanzas consist of his Easter hymn, more important after the purification of the opening passage.

If all of the two-stanza-form poems in *The Temple* were merely combinations of old poems, one could not attach much significance to them as structures. But Herbert goes through two other processes in their making. *The Temple's* version of *Christmas* represents an opening section from the Williams MS, a meditation on the season, plus a new twenty-line passage, Herbert's song to the Christchild. Similarly, *The Temple's* version of *The H. Communion* contains one section retained from Williams, and one new part — the first unit dramatizing the communicant's preparation for the sacrament, the second, his experience during the sacrament itself.

Furthermore, three double-patterned poems are entirely new. *The Church-floore,* as Summers has observed, consists of two parts, the first of which allegorizes the various parts of the floor, the second of which reveals that the real church, and so the real foundation for Christian worship, is the human heart.[4] *An Offering*, also new, begins with four stanzas (*a*5, *b*5, *c*5, *a*5, *b*5, *c*5) of examination of the nature and values of offerings; it concludes with three stanzas (*a*2, *a*2, *b*3, *c*2, *c*2, *b*3) presenting the poet himself as an oblation. And *Vanitie* (II) is composed of an initial section of pentameter couplets characterizing the foolish soul, plus a final, more metrically varied section making specific suggestions for improvement to the soul.

3. *Decreasing production of sonnets.* Proportionately, the Williams MS contains more sonnets than does the later group — ten in Williams (*The Sinner, H. Baptisme, Love* [I], *Love* [II], *H. Scriptures* [I], *H. Scriptures* [II], *Christmas-Day, Sinn, Prayer,* and *Redemption*), only five new ones in *The Temple* (*Avarice, The Holdfast, Joseph's Coat, The Sonne,* and *The Answer*). Part of the reason for Herbert's lessened

activity on sonnet-writing probably lies in the fact that he, like many other Renaissance poets, seldom attempted any notable innovations within the sonnet form. Most of the Williams sonnets (*The Sinner, H. Baptisme, Love* [I], *Love* [II], *Prayer* [I] *H. Scriptures* [I] and [II]) rhyme *ababcdcdeffegg*; the others rhyme similarly, *ababcdcdefefgg*. Each of the five additional sonnets in *The Temple* has one of these rhyme plans. Since Herbert seems to have thought of the sonnet in terms of these conventional schemes, and since his interest in variation of form was great, in all likelihood he turned from the sonnet in favor of more original stanza types.

4. *Use of different kinds of hieroglyphs.* If one conceives a hiero-glyphic poem as one the physical shape of which reinforces its actual meaning, he doubtless associates the hieroglyph primarily with *The Altar* and *Easter Wings.* These two poems, both present in the Williams MS, are the only such patterned works in Herbert. For reasons best known only to him, he chose not to delineate other physical shapes in verse, though one can imagine numerous other religious objects which might have served him equally as well — crosses and circles, for example. He did, however, write other less striking hieroglyphs, in which the external form calls attention to sense. Four of these are also in the Williams MS — *Deniall, Coloss. iii 3, Antiphon* (II) (all discussed below), and *A wreath,* which, by means of a circular rhyme pattern (*praise, give, wayes, live, straight, thee, deceit, simplicitie, live, wayes, give, praise*) and anadiplosis, materially suggests its subject.

Among the new poems in *The Temple,* Herbert has six of the semi-hieroglyphic type: *Anagram of the Virgin Marie* ("How well her name an *Army* doth present, / In whom the *Lord of Hosts* did pitch his tent"); *Dialogue, Grief, Sinnes Round,* and *Clasping of Hands* (all discussed elsewhere here); and *The Water-course,* where the shape of the last lines of the two stanzas is at least mildly suggestive of its subject:

For who can look for lesse, that loveth ⎰ Life?
                                                                              ⎱ Strife?

Who gives to man, as he sees fit, ⎰ Salvation.
                                                                 ⎱ Damnation.

                                                                              (p. 170)

Herbert's progressive use of the hieroglyph, then, is marked by his moving away from absolute physical imitation of the topic of his verse, to what might be called a "semi-hieroglyphic," in which some less conspicuous formal quality reinforces the matter of the poem.

5. *Increasing number of "contrapuntal" poems.* The so-called contrapuntal aspect of many of Herbert's poems, first observed by Hayes as an important aspect of their structural tightness, assumes new importance in the post-Williams MS group.

	WILLIAMS MS		NEW POEMS IN *THE TEMPLE*	
	CONTRAPUNTAL	HARMONIC	CONTRAPUNTAL	HARMONIC
aabb	1	2	2	0
abab	6	4	4	9
abba	1	1	2	0
ababa	0	4	0	0
aaabb	0	1	0	0
aabbb	0	0	1	0
abaab	1	1	3	0
aabba	2	0	3	2
ababcc	2	4	14	4
abbacc	0	1	1	0
aabccb	1	2	3	3
abccba	1	0	1	0
abacbc	0	0	2	1
abcabc	1	0	1	1
ababab	0	1	0	0
ababcac	1	0	3	0
ababccdd	1	0	2	0
ababcdcd	0	1	0	0
aaabcccb	0	0	0	1
aabccbdd	0	0	0	1
ababccccc	0	0	0	1
abacbddc	0	0	1	0
Totals	19 (47%)	22 (53%)	44 (64%)	23 (36%)

For reasons obviously impossible to determine, Herbert wrote progressively more poems in which rhyme patterns are countered by line-length patterns.

6. *Increasing use of longer, more elaborate stanza forms.* In the new *Temple* poems, Herbert uses more long and complex stanza forms, as is shown in the following comparison:

WILLIAMS MS		NEW *TEMPLE* POEMS	
6-line stanzas:		6-line stanzas:	
14 poems	*ababcc*	32 poems	*ababcc*
	aabbcc		*abbacc*

	aabccb		*abcbca*
	abccba		*aabccb*
	abbacc		*abacbc*
	abcabc		*abaccb*
	ababab		*abaccb*
			abcbac
			abcabc

7-line stanzas:		7-line stanzas:	
1 poem	*ababcac*	3 poems	*ababcac*
			ababbcc
			ababccb

8-line stanzas:			
2 poems	*ababccdd*	8-line stanzas:	
	ababcdcd	6 poems	*aaabcccb*
			aabccbdd
			ababccdd
			ababccccc
			abacbddc

Apparently Herbert must have grown more comfortable about using long stanzas as he discovered more and more ways of keeping them structurally unified.

7. *Increasingly careful use of feminine endings.* Before 1629, Herbert paid little attention to keeping feminine rhyme consistent or meaningful. Of the thirty-eight Williams MS poems containing some feminine endings, only one, *Coloss. iii 3,* uses weak rhyme in a sustained manner. In the thirty-seven others, masculine and feminine rhymes are combined at random. *Coloss. iii 3,* however, looks forward to the large number of new poems in *The Temple* making significant use of regular feminine rhyme, the weak endings of its first and last couplets serving to frame the hieroglyphic:

My words & thoughts do both expresse this notion,
That *Life* hath with the sun a double motion.
  The first *Is* straight, and our diurnall friend,
  The other *Hid* and doth obliquely bend.
    One life is wrapt *In* flesh, and tends to earth:
The other winds towards *Him,* whose happie birth
      Taught me to live here so, *That* still one eye
    Should aim and shoot at that which *Is* on high:
        Quitting with daily labour all *My* pleasure,
          To gain at harvest an eternall *Treasure.*   (pp. 84-85)

Among the later poems, one finds six embodying somewhat more elaborate masculine-feminine distinction. In *Sepulchre* (*a*5, *a*5, *a*5, *b*1,

$c5$, $c5$, $c5$, $b1$), Herbert emphasizes the difference in line lengths by making the a- and c-rhymes of all three stanzas masculine, the b-rhyme feminine. His technique in *Sighs and Grones* ($a2$, $b5$, $c5$, $b5$, $c5$, $a2$) is similar, though more developed. Here, also, the short lines seem more conspicuously separate by virtue of their feminine endings. Moreover, in four of the five stanzas (2-5), the short, feminine rhymes embody imperative requests on the part of the poet, while the body of the stanza consists of declarative statements about the spiritual life of the distressed man:

> O do not urge me!
> For what account can thy ill steward make?
> I have abus'd thy stock, destroy'd thy woods,
> Suckt all thy magazens: my head did ake,
> Till it found out how to consume thy goods:
> O do not scourge me! (p. 83)

Dialogue ($a4$, $b3$, $a4$, $b3$, $c4$, $c4$, $c4$, $c4$) contains all feminine b-rhymes, thereby heightening the shift in tone and rhythm between the first and last halves of each stanza, the near-ballad stanza form of the first half giving way to the more level, sustained verse of the last four lines. And *An Offering*, one of the double-patterned pieces, uses feminine rhyme; in each of the stanzas of its last section ($a2$, $a2$, $b3$, $c2$, $c2$, $b3$), the feminine a-rhymes resolve into the stronger end words of the rest of the stanza.

That Herbert came to regard feminine rhyme as expressing weakness or disorder is evident in these poems, where he usually arranges to begin a stanza with it, stating a problem, but then ends the stanza on what he considers a stronger note, firming it with masculine rhymes. In addition, other poems in both the Williams MS and *The Temple* clearly make a feminine-masculine, confused-ordered equation. *Deniall*, for example, a Williams poem, includes an unrhymed line in each of its stanzas but the last, the last line "mending the rhyme" according to the pattern $a4$, $b2$, $a5$, $b3$, $b2$. Significantly, each of the unrhymed lines dramatizes disorder not only by having no rhyme counterpart, but by ending with a feminine word.

8. *Increasing use of stanza linking.* Only two of Williams MS poems evince Herbert's skill in stanza linking through the use of nonrefrain rhyme repetition. *Easter Wings*, as everyone knows, imitates the shape of two pairs of wings. The two wing-stanzas have their likenesses pointed up not only through their bizarre common shape, but through word repetitions within the line (both stanzas use *let me, flight*, etc.), and rhyme echoes in corresponding lines (*store, same, more, become, poore,*

thee, rise, harmoniously, victories, me in the first unit, and *beginne, shame, sinne, became, thinne, thee, combine, victorie, thine, me* in the second). Another Williams MS poem, *Ode*, retitled *Antiphon* (II) in *The Temple*, contains nonrefrain stanza linking designed to reinforce the intellectual matter of the piece, the first three stanzas suggesting antiphonal singing of men and angels, the last stanza the unifying of their song. The rhyme words: (I) *love, below, above, so, friend, foe;* (2) *tend, old, end, fold, make, sold;* (3) *brake, touch, take, such, adore, crouch;* (4) *more, none, store, alone, one.*

Apparently Herbert enjoyed such conspicuous stanza linking and realized the various services which he might make it perform, for among the new poems in *The Temple* are ten containing permutations of it — *Church-floore, The Quip, Businesse, Sinnes Round, Complaining, Clasping of hands, Praise* (III), *Aaron, Dotage,* and *The Posie.* See, for example, the first section of *Church-floore*:

> Mark you the floore? that square & speckled stone,
>   Which looks so firm and strong,
>   Is *Patience*:
>
> And th'other black and grave, wherewith each one
>   Is checker'd all along,
>   *Humilitie*:
>
> The gentle rising, which on either hand
>   Leads to the Quire above,
>   Is *Confidence*:
>
> But the sweet cement, which in one sure band
>   Ties the whole frame is *Love*
>   And *Charitie*.   (pp. 66-67)

This rhyme plan, delineating as it does the subtle relationship of the four groups of lines, represents a marked development of Herbert's technique over that of even such a neat structure as *Antiphon* (II). In one sense, each of the four stanzas is parallel with the others since it names an allegorical equivalent for a part of the church floor. The first two, however, have a special relationship, since they point out kinds of stones; appropriately, then, they are bound together by the *stone-strong* and *one-along* rhymes. The same is true of stanzas three and four: they call attention to parts of the floor besides the stones, and so their *hand-above* and *band-Love* association is fitting. The *Patience-Humilitie-Confidence-Charitie* sequence of the last lines, however, provides a contrapuntal effect to what otherwise might have become a too-pat rhyme arrangement. While the first two lines of each of the stanzas lend an *aabb* shape to the section, the last lines do not sustain this relationship, but, considered separately, impart an *abab* form to the group of stanzas. Thus, Herbert avoids the monotony which might well have resulted from an overly consistent rhyme plan among such short lines.

Businesse, another relatively late poem, makes comparably elaborate use of rhyme echoes. Each of the significant meaning units treats a different topic: lines 1-14 (rhyming *play, day, one, gone, none, tears, fears, forbears, plot, hot, not, grones, bones, ones*) deal with the officious soul in relationship to its proud self; lines 15-28 (rhyming *be, thee, throne, bone, none, thee, wretchedly, fee, plot, forgot, not, thee, miserie, be*), the soul in relationship to the Incarnation; lines 29-38 (rhyming *breath, death, drosse, crosse, losse, vein, again, gain, kneels, feels*), the soul's sensitivity to both good and evil. The initial section sets forth the supreme evil of pride. After an introductory couplet, the passage is framed by rhyme repetition: *one-gone-none* in the first tercet, *grones-bones-ones* in the last. A similar, though not identical, repetition marks off the second section, which presents the supreme good of the Incarnation, the couplet's *be-thee* rhyme being complemented by the concluding tercet's *thee-miserie-be*. And the two sections are forced into particularly close parallel by their similar rhymes *one-gone-none* and *throne-bone-none* in the first tercets, *plot-hot-not* and *plot-forgot-not* in the third. The concluding section, a resolution of the disparate first passages, contains no rhyme echoes. Rather Herbert substitutes strong syntactical parallels between the two tercets within the section:

> He that loseth gold, though drosse,
> Tells to all he meets, his crosse:
> He that sinnes, hath he no losse?
>
> He that findes a silver vein,
> Thinks on it, and thinks again:
> Brings thy Saviours death no gain?   (p. 114)

The whole arrangement is managed with much cleverness. The first two sections, seemingly such opposites, are forced into forms so similar that surely every reader must notice the likeness. Then comes the concluding synthesis, the belief that the unfeeling person is incapable of being touched either by great sin or great goodness:

> Who in heart not ever kneels,
> Neither sinne nor Saviour feels.

This couplet can be emotionally realized by the reader only after he recognizes Herbert's formal paralleling of the two members of the sin-virtue dichotomy.

The other late poems employing stanza linking may be surveyed more briefly. *Praise* (III), a song lauding the marvelous complexity of God's blessings, presents a clue to the form of the poem in the first stanza, where Herbert says that he will *spin* his Lord's praise. A résumé of the rhyme-words of each stanza shows that the poem is, indeed, the product of a sort of spiritual spinning wheel, always returning to the same rhyme: (1) *praise, alone, dayes, store, grone, more*; (2) *action, flies, perfection, before, rise, more*; (3) *blow, clogs, row, doore, logs, more*; (4) *employ, all, joy, shore, call, more*; (5) *tear, eyes, there, poore, size, more*; (6) *drop, eye, top, sore, trie, more*; (7) *heart, thin, convert, store, in, more.* Then there is *The Quip*, a six-stanza piece presenting the futility of the pleasures of the world. Stanzas 2-5, which pass some of these pleasures before us in quick parade, are unified by a common last line in which the poet counters their immediate attraction — *"But thou shalt answer, Lord, for me."*

Sinnes round, the title of which predicts both the form and matter of the poem, has rhyme words which constitute a kind of round: (1) *am, ring, flame, bring, draughts, thoughts*; (2) *thoughts, Hill, faults, ill, intentions, inventions*; (3) *inventions, high, dissensions, supplie, shame, am.* *Clasping of hands* is even more nearly circular, both of its stanzas having the same rhyme words, *thine, more, mine, restore, mine, more, thine, restore, mine,* and *thine.* The four stanzas of *Complaining* are divided into two groups by the rhymes linking the first two and last two stanzas (*aabb, calls, ccdd falls, eeff grief, gghh relief*), a separation corresponding to the logical structure of the piece. *Aaron,* one of the few poems of *The Temple* dealing directly with the duties and shortcomings of the priest, heightens the important parallels of each of its five stanzas by having the rhyme words for each of them identical (*head, breast, dead, rest, drest*). And finally, *Dotage* (*a5, b5, a5, c5, b5, c3*), a catalogue of human "False glozing pleasures," dramatizes the common vainglory by ending each stanza of the poem with the same rhyme (*career-here* in the first, *clear-here* in the second, and *cleare-here* in the third).

9. *Increasingly careful use of variation.* One of the six Williams poems which Herbert decided to drop from *The Temple* is *Trinity Sunday*, his sole excursion into the realm of free verse. The pattern of the poem (*a2, a1, b2, b2, c2, c4, d3, d2, d3, e4, f2, f4, g2, g3, h2, e5, a2, h1*) causes the piece to gain tension with the elongation of the second *c*-line, then to grow with the *d*-tercet, next to mount in interest with the delay in

completing the *e*-rhyme, and finally to reach a peak with the extended length of the second *e*-line. Interesting though the experiment is, evidently Herbert did not feel that this practice of improvising rhymes and line lengths to go with the changing matter of the poem was suitable to his talent, since he discarded *Trinity Sunday* and thereafter used variation solely as a sort of poetic shorthand for disorder or laxness.

True, three other poems in the Williams collection deviate from strict stanzaic regularity, but they do so in a quite different way. *Deniall* and *Antiphon* (II), both discussed above, utilize their rhyme irregularities to express spiritual dryness and separateness, respectively. *Man*, also in the Williams collection, contains deliberate variations the function of which has not, I feel, been fully explained. The rhyme scheme here is different in nearly every stanza, but the line lengths remain constant throughout: three feet in the first line, five in the second, four in the third, four in the fourth, five in the fifth, and three in the sixth. Now, the rhyme plan which Herbert uses most frequently in six-line stanzas, and which apparently represents the norm to him, is *ababcc*. Yet in *Man*, he does not arrive at this rhyme scheme until the ninth and last stanza. The first eight have some rearranged form of this pattern: *abccba* in stanza one, *abcabc* in two, *abcbac* in three, *abacbc* in four, *aabcbc* in five, *abaccb* in six, *abbcac* in seven, and *abcabc* in eight. Apart from the resolution to the *ababcc* form at the conclusion, one more tendency is immediately noticeable — the only recurring pattern is *abcabc*, which is used in stanzas two and eight. A second look reveals one more trace of symmetry besides this sameness of the second and the second-from-last stanzas: the middle stanza is an exact inversion of the last one, the couplet coming at the beginning instead of the end. The other stanzas shift subtly in pattern, stanza two representing an inversion of the third and sixth lines of stanza one, stanza three an inversion of lines four and five of stanza two, stanza four a moving of line five of stanza three to the third position, stanza five an inversion of lines two and three of stanza four, stanza six an inversion of lines two and three as well as five and six of stanza five, stanza seven a complete inversion of stanza six, stanza eight an inversion of lines three and four as well as four and five of stanza seven, and stanza nine an inversion of lines three and four as well as four and five of stanza eight. The poem is, then, divided into two parts by means of the degree of rhyme inversion from preceding stanzas — each of stanzas two through five representing only one change, while stanzas six through nine undergo more extensive changes.

In what way, if any, do these mechanical balances stiffen the inner structure of the poem? And what is the purpose of the changing stanza form? Is it haphazardly irregular, or does Herbert use it to signal shifts of tone and subject matter? These questions can best be settled by a look at the initial thesis of *Man* and the two changes of argument in its development. The first stanza states a Biblical commonplace:

> My God, I heard this day,
> That none doth build a stately habitation,
> But he that means to dwell therein.
> What house more stately hath there been,
> Or can be, then is Man? to whose creation
> All things are in decay.   (p. 90)

The following passage gives a philosophical and largely impersonal commentary on the eminence of man. In the second stanza, one is told that "Man is ev'ry thing"; in the third, that "Man is all symmetrie"; and in the fourth, that "Nothing hath got so farre, / But Man hath caught and kept it, as his prey." In the fifth stanza, however, one notices a marked change to a more personal realization of the ministry of the universe to man:

> For us the windes do blow,
> The earth doth rest, heav'n move, and fountains flow.
> Nothing we see, but means our good,
> As our delight, or as our treasure:
> The whole is, either our cupboard of food,
> Or cabinet of pleasure.

This intimate vein continues until the last stanza but one, when Herbert prepares for his conclusion by returning to a discussion of man in general, reproaching him for his indifference to the services of the universe. In the last stanza all of the various strands are knit up: man at large is reminded of his proper place in the order of things, a place between God and the world; the poet and general man are treated as one, the personal dominating as Herbert prays for God to dwell in the house of man's body:

> Since then, my God, thou hast
> So brave a Palace built; O Dwell in it,
> That it may dwell with thee at last!
> Till then, afford us so much wit;
> That, as the world serves us, we may serve thee,
> And both thy servants be.

He has come back to the metaphor of the beginning and to some of its diction (*my God, built, dwell*), changing it from a general statement

which is second-hand knowledge to a general-personal one which he has
realized in the course of the poem. The changing stanza forms are clearly
appropriate to his exploratory mood; the link of the beginning and the
end is no mere mechanical device; the similarity of the rhyme patterns of
the fifth and last stanzas is indicative of the important affinity between
the personal tone of the second part of the poem and the personalized
generality which climaxes it; and the difference in the sort of changes
occurring in stanza patterns coincides with the shift at stanza five.

Five of the new *Temple* poems (in addition to those containing two
sustained stanza patterns) show some kind of formal variation. *Grief*
uses its one unrhymed line much as *Deniall* uses its unrhymed lines in the
first stanzas — to express discord and lack of harmony with God. In
Grief, Herbert laments the fact that his verse cannot attune him to God,
concluding,

> Give up your feet and running to mine eys,
> And keep your measures for some lovers lute,
> Whose grief allows him music and a ryme:
> For mine excludes both measure, tune, and time.
> > Alas, my God!   (p. 164)

In *Love unknown*, Herbert chronicles previous efforts to reach and
please God, following, for the most part, an *abab* pentameter design.
Three times in the course of the poem, however, he injects a note of
intensified dissonance by abbreviating lines to dimeters — all fitful little
exclamations:

> But when I thought to sleep out all these faults
> > (I sigh to speak)
> I found that some bad stuff'd the bed with thoughts,
> I would say *thorns*.   (p. 130)

Businesse, discussed above, contains three sections, the first two
identical in form, the third, a synthesis of the first two, abbreviated and
compressed.

The Temple's most famous dramatization of rebellion and disorder,
The Collar, presents problems of great complexity. In his commentary
on its structure, Summers comes very close to explaining the arrangement of rhymes:

> Although readers accustomed to Renaissance poetry might feel
> uncomfortable with the disorder of the first thirty-two lines, they
> could hardly divine the stanzaic norm which is the measure for
> that disorder until it is established simultaneously with the

submission of the rebel in the final quatrain: $10^a4^b8^a6^b$. That pattern of line lengths and rhyme does not occur until the final four lines; with those lines the elements of the pattern are arranged so as to form almost the mathematical ultimate in lack of periodicity. If we consider that the first thirty-two lines represent eight quatrains, we discover six different patterns of rhyme and seven patterns of line lengths.

It is true, I think, that the final quatrain is for Herbert a resolution of disorder, but the resolution is a commutation of a pattern faintly discernible in the first thirty-two lines but artfully obscured by some inversions of rhymes, some intrusive rhymes, and tensions between line divisions and semantic groups. Keeping in mind the possibility of disarranged *abab* patterns in the "fierce and wilde" section of the poem, let us divide it into the dialogue between the two psychological persons of the speaker. The first sixteen lines represent Herbert's rebellious self in revolt against the disciplines of religion. Lines 17 through 26 counter this outburst with a more considered, but still agitated, rationalization of the position of the clergy. The passage bounded by lines 27 and 32 is the voice of the impulsive Herbert once more, echoing his initial outburst.

The rhymes in each of these sections have natural groupings, but not the straight quatrains which Summers suggests. The first sixteen lines contain three rhyme units of five, six, and five lines each, rhyming *abcba, deadce,* and *fgfhh.* The following ten lines divide neatly into two groups rhyming *dijdji* and *gkkg.* The final speech by the irritable Herbert, lines 27-32, rhymes *lbmmlb.* There are, then, six rhyme groups before the final *abab* pattern. Let us examine these groups. The first, except for the intruding *c*-rhyme, is almost an enclosed-rhyme quatrain. The second group, *deadce,* has a certain degree of balance because of the two *d*'s and *e*'s, but this balance is blurred by the substitution of *ce* and *ea* in the last two lines. The third rhyme group, *fgfhh,* has similar balance and a similar deviation, an element of the *g*-rhyme intervening in what would otherwise be a sequence of two couplets, and thus creating an interlocking effect similar to that of the *abab* type. The fourth rhyme group, *dijdji,* shows the interlocked structure and the parallelism of the *abab* design, with some disturbance of the balance by the change of *ij* to *ji.* The fifth rhyme group is something like the first except that it is a true *abba* type with no added elements. And the last rhyme group before the conclusion, *lbmmlb,* actually crowds the edges of the *abab* form, being distinguished by the couplet in the middle. These first thirty-two lines, then, are not completely formless. They represent six clusters of rhymes which approach the final home-base rhyme pattern but which distort it enough to make the four concluding lines a true ordering of verse. While varied, however, the groups are not randomly arranged. The first five lines and lines 27-32, similar in rhyme scheme, are also parallel in diction:

> I struck the board, and cry'd, No more.
>   I will abroad.
>   What? shall I ever sigh and pine?
> My lines and life are free; free as the rode,
>   Loose as the winde, as large as store.

>   . . . .

>   Away; take heed:
>   I will abroad.
> Call in thy deaths head there: tie up thy fears. (p. 153)

Not only the rhymes, but the rhythms and short word groups of these two passages are similar. The great difference is the almost exclusive use of the imperative in the second, in imitation of the imperative which the narrator's more rational personality gives him in lines 19-26. The rhymes, then, reinforce the structure within the first thirty-two lines as well as divide this section from the final quatrain. For the mature Herbert, disorder was not attractive; and so he here only feigns a confusion which is actually well controlled. His irregularity, unlike that of the discarded *Trinity Sunday*, is a dramatic device.

A careful survey of Herbert's early and late poetry shows that his fundamental method was already well established in even the early English poems. From beginning to end, the verse shows its maker's respect for order, structural tightness, and precision of imagery. Throughout *The Temple* one senses what T. S. Eliot has called Herbert's intellectual stamina, both in the dialectic of the verses and in their structures. The small differences between the pre- and post-1629 poems, when considered as a whole, demonstrate Herbert's increasingly fine and delicate control of the adjustment of form to substance, as well as a more subtle approach to this adjustment. How more subtle? Surely one must recognize his abandoning such near-showy hieroglyphs as *The Altar* and *Easter-Wings* in favor of more restrained poems like *Sinnes round* and *Clasping of hands* as a sign of increased discipline. Similarly, his increasingly frequent use of metaphorical titles and more controlled use of variation point to his broadening vision of original ways in which he could use verse elements which initially he made count for very little. The same might be said of how he learned to use certain other techniques

— tight control of sustained feminine rhyme, stanza linking, and counterpoint of rhyme and line lengths — as purveyors of meaning. And finally, much might be said of his increasing facility in unifying stanzas of over six lines by means of elaborate rhyme patterning and unusual sequences of line lengths. His technique did not change radically. His verses did, however, become more incisive, and, while still lucid and smooth, more ideologically concentrated.

V. THE UNITY OF *THE TEMPLE*

THE UNITY OF HERBERT'S "TEMPLE"

Elizabeth Stambler

In George Herbert's own century *The Temple* was read and praised by men of all shades of Christian piety from Baxter to Crashaw. Though the poems of *Steps to The Temple* may seem to us very little like Herbert's, Crashaw implied that his poetic impulse came from *The Temple*. Vaughan, Harvey, and, later, Wesley not only acknowledged Herbert to be their spiritual mentor and modelled their books upon *The Temple*, but also, as far as they were able, constructed their individual poems in close imitation of Herbert's. Such strong effects on men of such varying religious beliefs argue a power and a meaning in *The Temple* greater than the sum of some 100 lyric poems.

Walton's *Life* seems to have fixed a paradoxical image of Herbert and of *The Temple:* on the one hand rare and fine and on the other entirely accessible as a model of conduct, both exquisitely educated and plain, both simple and subtle. The man and the book were identified, as Gerard Manley Hopkins is for many readers inextricable from his sonnets. Modern writers on Herbert continue to speculate on a myste-rious aspect of his book, a oneness both teasing and satisfying.

Eliot, more than usually gnomic, called *The Temple* 'an oeuvre to be studied entire.'[1] Recently both Louis Martz and Joseph Summers have attempted a formulation of the book's unity. Both attempts are eloquent; the Herbert legend, I think, shows itself still at work in the earnestness of both scholars' efforts, in the need both obviously feel to attempt solution of a problem. Martz finds essentially that the book as a whole reduplicates the process of meditation which he finds character-istic of many of the individual poems. The three parts of the whole, 'The Sacramental Introduction,' 'The Body of Conflicts,' and 'The Plateau of Assurance,' correspond to composition of place, analysis, and colloquy.[2] But are not the poems throughout the book as sacramental as the initial ones? Is not the whole book a 'body of conflicts?' What becomes of the 'plateau of assurance' in 'Dotage,' in 'My comforts drop and melt away

Reprinted from *Cross Currents*, 10 (1960), 251-66, by permission of the author and the publisher.

like snow' of 'The Answer,' in the pains of 'Discipline,' in the 'dreadful look' of 'Judgement,' or in the precarious exaltation of the last poem of the book, 'Love (III)'?

Summers, though in a briefer and less elaborate treatment than Martz', succeeds better by describing a less rigid unity. While warning against interpretation of *The Temple* as autobiography, he stresses the organic quality of the book: '. . . the temple as a building was a hieroglyph for the body, particularly the human body in the service of God and the divine body of Christ.'[3] He takes full note of the 'violently alternating spiritual change' characteristic of the book. He says we may 'conceive of *The Temple* as the symbolic record written by a poet, of a "typical" Christian life within the Church.'[4] He concludes,

> *The Temple* is almost a casebook of examples showing how 'Order' gives 'all things their set forms and houres.' It reflects Herbert's belief that form was that principle by which the spiritual created existence out of chaos, and Herbert assumed that that process could be rationally apprehended. Since the principle was divine and therefore universal, the understanding of the formal organization of any one object or state or action gave a clue to the understanding of the rest. The poet's duty was to perceive and to communicate God's form. In the process he would construct out of the chaos of experience and the mass of language another object which would reflect his discovery: literary form as we understand it was but a reflection of that form which was everywhere present, although often hidden to eyes that could not 'see.' It, too, in its material embodiment appealed to man's senses, and moved his affections. The rational contemplation of it should lead to an understanding of its symbolic significance.[5]

It is hard to disagree, but the remarks are too general. 'Casebook' is a cold word for *The Temple*. Summers' reader continues to ask, just what *is* the form? What *is* the 'Order?' How do the form and order of the whole differ from the form and order of the individual poems?

I do not expect here to provide any final analysis of the unity of *The Temple*; I offer only one more partial explanation, which I consider not radically in conflict with other readings but which may be used along with them in a serious reading of Herbert.

To summarize this explanation I am led to a discussion of ways in which *The Temple* as a whole resembles a volume of courtly love poetry — the *Vita Nuova*, Petrarch's *Rime, Astrophel and Stella* — as individual poems of *The Temple* resembles lyrics of the courtly love tradition. I find these resemblances in several important details and in two fairly large general themes, the theme of loss and the theme of discipline which brings the protagonist at last to a condition of purified desire.

1

The Temple, like the best of the volumes of courtly love lyrics, is unified in its protagonist. His roles of courtier, soldier, and poet resemble Dante's, Petrarch's, and Sidney's protagonists.[5a] There can be no doubt, I think, of the consistent character of Herbert's *persona:* he is one throughout the volume. The three roles are woven together in too many instances, and too consistently over the whole book, to permit the reader to suppose that the speaker of nearly every one of the poems is not the same. The character of the protagonist dominates *The Temple* as the courtly lyric protagonist dominates Dante's, Petrarch's, or Sidney's volume: the whole book consists of his emotions, responses, thoughts, and actions. Herbert's God appears in *The Temple* very much as the beloved woman appears in the courtly lyrics, characterized indirectly, via the reactions of the protagonist.

In collecting his individual poems in a volume Herbert had no model from the body of religious poetry. Only in the volumes of courtly love poetry could he have found precisely the dramatic qualities of his protagonist in individual poems and his cumulative drama over a whole volume. Far from disparaging Herbert's originality, to study the formal and dramatic analogies between *The Temple* and the courtly love volumes is, I think, to see his great skill. Not only did he turn the old form to a new use, but as we trace the traditional material through *The Temple* we come with fresh insight to many essential aspects of the tradition which had become obscured and stultified in the masses of sonnet sequences turned out in the late Renaissance. Throughout Herbert criticism it is not so much his originality which has been praised as his beautiful molding and polishing of old material; this is the view taken by Rosemond Tuve, Martz, and Summers; this is the source of the peculiar 'order' Herbert is said to exemplify. His reordering and revitalizing of the form of the courtly love volume is an entirely characteristic display of his talent, on the same principle as his utilization of Christian typologies or tracts of meditation.

2

I use the word 'form' here in an additive sense: the form of a work may be described as the sum of the work's several formal elements. (After making such a sum, of course, we may feel that the work far exceeds our addition.) One such element has been discussed above — the dramatic protagonist who dominates the work but who also serves as a mirror through which we see another (even more dominant) figure. A second formal component of both *The Temple* and the courtly love volume is the unceasing shift in the states of feeling, registering every shade of emotion from joy to despair. Summers calls this the 'symbolic record ... of a "typical" Christian life within the Church,' and so it may be, though we can scarcely ask for documentary proof. The volumes of love poems, however, do offer in a sense documentary proof that violently alternating emotions were involved with six centuries of literary analysis on the subject of love. I am more than a little in disagreement with Martz' idea that *The Temple* concludes on a 'plateau of assurance' when I say that over the entire length of Herbert's volume we find Petrarch's emotional contrarieties (merely sharpened and emphasized in Petrarch's imitation of Dante and the troubadours and handed down entire to the Petrarchan poets of the Renaissance). If there is a 'plateau of assurance' in *The Temple,* I believe it is one of only slight degree; the last poems of the book show very little more assurance than the earlier ones.

A cursory look at the sequences of emotional states in *The Temple* shows shattering grief in 'The Sinner,' 'Good Friday,' and 'The Sepulchre' followed by joyous exaltation in 'Easter'; bitter rebellion and remorse in 'Affliction (I)' and 'Repentance' followed by assurance in 'Faith'; desiccation of the spirit in 'Grace,' self-reproach for sloth in 'Praise (I),' near-mortal pain in 'Affliction (II)' followed by trust in all-providing Providence in 'Mattens' and 'Even-song.' I think a fair reading will find this kind of alternation continuing through the last poems of the volume. After 'The Flower' (which Martz considers the turning point from the 'body of conflicts' to the 'plateau of assurance') we come immediately to 'Dotage,' of which the second stanza suggests no retrospect on pain but rather the immediate experience:

> True earnest sorrows, rooted miseries,
> Anguish in grain, vexations ripe and blown,
> Sure-footed griefs, solid calamities,
> Plain demonstrations, evident and cleare,
> Fetching their proofs ev'n from the very bone;
> These are the sorrows here.

The two next poems, 'The Sonne' and 'A true Hymne,' express great joy; 'The Answer' follows with:

> My comforts drop and melt away
> like snow

as its first line. The rest of the sonnet, at least until the couplet, is enumeration of vanished comforts. 'A Dialogue-Antheme,' next, shows the Christian triumphant over death, but 'The Water-course' and 'Self-condemnation' warn of the precariousness of salvation; the beautiful miniature poem 'Bitter-sweet' is all contrarieties.

A mixture of attitudes is revealed in the poems which follow until we reach three on death. The protagonist faces his end with courage, his faith unmarred by doubt, with hope. It is *with hope*, however, and thus far from that quality which marks the end of hope, assurance. There is no blinking at the grimness of the images of death in these poems, from the 'once uncouth hideous thing' of 'Death,' through the 'noisome vapours' and 'plague and publick wo' and 'decay' where 'Man is out of order hurl'd' of 'Dooms-day,' to the 'dreadful look, / Able a heart of iron to appal' of 'Judgement.'

'Heaven' is no more free of ambiguity and complexity than the first poems of *The Temple*: the dramatic speaker Echo is carefully qualified as *not being* the pagan and mythic figure 'born among the trees and leaves,' and the poem's protagonist is shown to receive an understanding of Heaven's 'Light to the minde' and 'Light, joy, and leisure.' But the form of the poem gives us pause: Echo as teacher here continues to repeat the protagonist's own words, as by definition *Echo* must do. Is Heaven no more distant from the protagonist than this? Echo speaks last: if the protagonist spoke again would he not have to maintain the *questioning* form of his speeches throughout the poem?

I shall return later to the last poem of the volume, 'Love (III),' here noting only that its beauty results from Herbert's expression, subtle and indirect, of the protagonist's overwhelming surprise. The joy is the keener because it is undeserved and unexpected. It is sudden, another of the violently alternating emotional states which have characterized the whole volume, not a development of preceding states or poems.

The volume of love lyrics has a paradoxically double form; typically it is both lyric and narrative. If they are to remain pure lyrics, complete and self-contained each within itself, the individual poems must remain free of one another in the volume. The reader must not be able to say of the whole: this later joy cancels the emotion of the earlier poem of sorrow, or vice versa. Every poem must seem to be in the present tense, emotion conveyed directly it is experienced. Such is the formal convention of the traditional volume of love lyrics, demanded, no doubt, by the nature of the subject: love is that emotional experience most susceptible of extreme change, least susceptible of final logical analysis. Many readers have found this form inconclusive, anti-climactic, monotonous — all, in short, that militates against *form* — and when it is poorly handled I agree that it is so. I tentatively assert, however, that it was the consciously chosen form of Dante, Petrarch, and Sidney: the formal principle is that only through constant alternations, without conclusion, and with one mood presented as equal in weight and immediacy to every other mood, can the individual lyrics remain undiluted. Herbert preserves the purity of the lyric form over the whole of his volume in just this way. His poems express emotional states; in sequence those states continually contradict one another, but to none is given primacy over the others.

3

There is evidence that Herbert did consider the book a whole rather than a random collection. Hutchinson's carefully weighed conclusion that we have the poems in roughly the order Herbert wished cannot be discounted.[6] Herbert's message to Ferrar is clear: in the *volume*, considered entire, the reader would find 'a picture of the many spiritual Conflicts that have past betwixt God and my Soul ...'[7]

The poet's role in *The Temple* would lead the reader to expect evidence of other poems to present itself in any given poem; the poet's role would not be convincing on the strength of a single poem, no matter how excellent. Herbert by many subtle means establishes his poet's role as the dominant one in *The Temple*; here it is appropriate to mention his very explicit and overt references to poems outside the one at issue, quite in the spirit of that troubadour convention (which became a permanent feature of the courtly love poem) of reference to 'my songs.' 'Jordan (II),' half-way through *The Temple*, looks back on a career of poetry,

> When first my lines of heav'nly joyes
> made mention ...

'Dulnesse' also refers to poems written before this one,

> Where are my lines then? my
> approaches? views?
> Where are my window-songs?

'Providence' speaks of 'all my other hymnes'; in 'The Priesthood' Herbert puns with 'my slender compositions.'

Usually, it is true, Herbert's handling of the subject of poetry is one which points directly to the single text under our eyes, but a few clear and obvious extensions into other work such as those above cause the reader to notice more oblique references. Reading *The Temple* backward as well as forward, as the complexity of the book demands, we may interpret lines from the early poem 'The Thanksgiving' as seeming to promise a volume.

> Nay, I will read thy book, and never move
> Till I have found therein thy love,
> Thy art of love, which I'le turn back on thee ...

An Art of Love cannot be accomplished in a single lyric poem. The last line of 'Good Friday' points to a mass of work, 'And all the writings blot or burn.' The first lines of 'Praise (I)' suggest work previous to that of this particular poem,

> To write a verse or two is all the praise,
> That I can raise ...

'Deniall' exemplifies 'broken verse' in its own form, but its first stanza evokes a long career of frustration of happiness in general and of poetic composition in particular. At least the third stanza of 'The Pearl' expresses a very deep familiarity with the art of poetry,

> what love and wit
> Have done these twentie hundred yeares,
>   and more:
> I know the projects of unbridled store...

The new state of 'The Flower,' in which the protagonist can 'relish versing' pre-supposes earlier attempts when the relish was absent. 'A true Hymne,' wholly on the subject of poetry, implies the same kind of experience of a time when 'somewhat is behinde / To make his verse...' Like 'The Pearl,' 'The Forerunners' conveys intensely long and deep work with poetry's 'sweet phrases, lovely metaphors...' and 'Lovely enchanting language.' In 'The Posie,' 'invention' and 'comparisons' of past poems are dismissed, but without them there remains enough to make up a *book*:

> This on my ring,
> This by my picture, in my book
> I write ...

In 'Judgement' also there is a very concrete image of *The Temple* protagonist's own 'peculiar *book*.'

These references, the reader will have observed, extend over the whole of *The Temple*. They are not elaborate; they are not very important. They function as lightly and delicately as the love poets' mention of 'my songs,' to remind the reader of the protagonist's abiding preoccupation with poetry and of the fact that any single poem, however enchanting and engrossing, must take its place with others in the book.

4

The title of *The Temple* is a unifying one. However, we interpret it, we must regard it as symbolic. In Herbert's time, and before it, such titles for collections of lyric poems were entirely characteristic of the volumes of love poetry — *Astrophel and Stella, Amoretti, Delia, Idea.* All of these, like the *Vita Nuova*, confer a meaning upon the whole volume which the reader can obtain only obliquely, if at all, from any part. They extend the implication of the volume into the realm of the abstract, into vast and universal generalization. They make sharp contrast with the tone of most poems in the volumes, a tone which is intensely personal and private; they present a long span of time, in contrast with the transitory moment of the individual poems. The word *temple* evokes a structure, massive and public, built over a long period, for the use of many. The poems within *The Temple* are altogether personal, dealing as Herbert himself said, with the 'many spiritual Conflicts that have past betwixt God and my Soul...' Herbert should not be thought to have taken his title's abstract significance from the love poets. It is enough to see that his title functions in much the same way as the love poets' titles, and that Herbert, because of the love poets' consistent practice in naming their works, could have depended upon his audience's recognition of a symbolism involved in such a title for a collection of lyric poems. No other genre, I think, could have supplied him with this traditional convention.

5

The nature of the symbolism which these typical titles promised in such large and general terms involved nothing less than life itself. The *Vita Nuova* is archetypal; later volumes followed, sometimes crudely, sometimes skillfully, its significant outlines. The word *life* here needs much qualification: the volume is not autobiography; it is the life of its fictional protagonist as courtier, soldier, and poet dating from his experience of love. As Dante makes very clear, the life cannot be separated from the act of writing poems; the separate experiences of the life are not complete until they are rendered into poetry. Reinforced, no doubt, by the Platonism of the Renaissance, Dante's fiction of the interpenetration of poetry and life appeared with even greater clarity and intensity in Petrarch and his successors. For them the writing of a poem is rarely retrospection upon an experience; the experience occurs simultaneously with the writing of the poem. A volume then, made up of many such disparate experiences, conveys the whole of the protagonist's experience — his life.

Herbert vividly identified poetry with life in, among other poems, 'Man's Medley,' 'The Flower,' 'The Forerunners,' and 'Judgement.' But these might be random references. A record of a life must be a sustained thing; it can be convincing only if it conveys a span of time, a developed chronology. I have referred to the double form of the courtly love volumes, to the fact that they are simultaneously lyric and narrative. I have discussed Herbert's preservation of the integrity of the lyric form in *The Temple*; his individual poems are points in time, intense and independent of all other times. In Herbert, however, as in the love poets, beneath the surface we find a flow of time, an ordered chronology. Modern physics, I think, supplies an analogy: like light these poems require a double principle to explain them.

6

The poems at the beginning of *The Temple* have death as their theme. Christ's passion is agonizingly described and commented upon in every poem until the two Easter poems. But Christ's is not the only death in these poems; the protagonist himself is very vividly characterized as enduring a condition of dead matter, inert, a stone.

In 'The Altar,' a chain of demonstrative adjectives holds the key to the meaning of the poem; "this frame ... these stones ... this ALTAR" reveal the poem itself to be the subject of the poem, the altar, in a way which subsumes the other two, the heart of man and the heart of the Church. Placed at the beginning of Herbert's volume, 'The Altar' makes an identification between the poet's heart and his poem as a dedicated instrument of praise.

The next poem in the *Temple* which uses the image of the stony heart is 'The Sinner.' The 'heart' of this poem is not the metaphorical expression of an altar, but the Tablets of the Law, more intimately related to a literary purpose.

> And though my hard heart scarce
>   to thee can grone
> Remember that thou once didst
>   write in stone.

As in 'The Altar,' the desired action of God is one we have seen the poet consummate. God is asked to write; the poet has written. 'The Sepulchre' continues this line of imagery:

> And as of old the Law by heavn'ly art
> Was writ in stone; so thou, which also art
> The letter of the word, find'st no fit heart
>   To hold thee.

The protagonist in these poems calls upon God to animate the stone; the stone is the protagonist's heart and also the page of poetry. God's life-giving action, so these poems say, will manifest itself as *writing upon the stone*: God's 'art' in 'Nature' is again clearly literary art, the writing of a poem. The protagonist's heart, when it wakens, will be a poem.

This imagery is dense in the short poems at the beginning of *The Temple*; it is intensified in proximity to 'The Sacrifice,' on the great theme of universal death, and to 'The Thanksgiving.' 'Reprisall,' 'The Agonie,' 'Good Friday,' and 'Redemption,' all of which concentrate on the crucifixion. These and the stone-image poems are deeply interconnected, of course: among other implications we see two parallel deaths; the two are also reversibly related as cause and effect. (Christ dies for man; man is stricken almost to death with horror at Christ's suffering). Nowhere in *The Temple* do we find again the sense of heaviness, of inert matter, of these early poems. The stone images do recur — no theme is lost in *The Temple* — but they reappear transformed in 'The Church-floore,' 'Mattens,' 'Love Unknown,' and 'Sion.' In these later poems the stone is an element of construction, purposive, useful, a component of the living body of the Church, or an old building-block replaced by the living heart. Through linkages with still other poems Herbert's later uses of the stone image are closely associated with the images of song, *The Temple's* symbol for most intense animation in union with God.

I have said the two deaths at the beginning of the book are parallel. In a sense they are not so: comparison is impossible, the protagonist (in "The Thanksgiving,' for example) cannot conceive the full meaning of Christ's action. The protagonist's condition in these early poems is not one in which his stony deathliness succeeds a span of life; it is as though he had not known life at all. The protagonist is here metaphorically at the lowest level of the Great Chain. This is the subject, the *statement* of the early poems, the description of the protagonist's physical condition. His emotions, violently registered in the poems, do not contradict the physical image; they are locked-in, chaotic, like seething lava before the

eruption. They struggle, however, towards the light, towards love.
Christ's speeches in 'The Sacrifice' state the problem and its solution:

> I answer nothing, but with patience prove
> If stonie hearts will melt with gentle love....
>
> Why, Caesar is their onely King, not I:
> He clave the stonie rock, when they were drie;
> But surely not their hearts, as I will trie.

In almost an ironic insight the protagonist says in 'The Thanksgiving':

> Nay, I will read thy book, and never move
> Till I have found therein thy love ...

With the two Easter poems, both aubades, brilliant sunlight stirs the
stony protagonist:

> Rise heart; thy Lord is risen ...
> Who takes thee by the hand, that thou likewise
> With him mayst rise.

Movement in these two poems is more projected than actual; the
protagonist in 'Easter-Wings' exhorts himself to ascend in feeble and
tentative imitation of Christ.

'H. Baptisme (II)' emphasizes and reemphasizes the protagonist's
condition as that of childhood.

> Since, Lord, to thee
> A narrow way and little gate
> Is all the passage, on my infancie
> Thou didst lay hold, and antedate
> My faith in me.
>
> O let me still
> Write thee great God, and me a childe;
> Let me be soft and supple to thy will,
> Small to my self, to others milde,
> Behither ill.
>
> Although by stealth
> My flesh get on, yet let her sister
> My soul bid nothing, but preserve
> her wealth:
> The growth of flesh is but a blister;
> Childhood is health.

Herbert does not use many images like this initial one; it is a very graphic image of birth. In the next poem the protagonist's 'Nature' is dedicated to the 'highest art' of God.

In these first fourteen poems of *The Temple* Herbert has constructed a beautiful chain of images by which his protagonist is transformed from an inanimate object into a living being. The beauty comes, I think, from the absolute literalness of the images; the religious, philosophical, and psychological implications of the poems, of course, ramify almost indefinitely. The subject of poetry is closely involved with the image chain from stone to child; we can everywhere paraphrase the process by saying that the poem equals life. This equation is typical of the courtly love volume as are also certain features of the demonstration of change from lifelessness to life which Herbert makes in his first fourteen poems.

Several important texts for the courtly love theory of the *cor gentil* use the stone to express the precondition of love; the action of the sun, or another 'star' upon the stone gives it its 'virtu,' or frees the function of the 'virtu,' and the stone becomes a precious stone. Guinizelli's canzone 'Of the gentle Heart' for example, to which Dante defers in the *Vita Nuova*, says:

> The fire of love comes to the gentle heart
> Like as its virtue to a precious stone;
> To which no star its influence can impart
> Till it is made a pure thing by the sun ...

> Through gentle heart Love doth a track divine, —
> Like knowing like; the same
> As diamond runs through iron in the mine.[8]

The first section of Herbert's 'Easter,' of which the second part deals wholly with the 'Sunne,' says,

> ... thou likewise
> With him mayst rise:
> That, as his death calcined thee to dust,
> His life may make thee gold, and much more, just.

A courtly love volume begins, logically enough, with the lover's 'first acquaintance' with his beloved, who is the star, or indeed often the sun itself, which warms the stony heart. In the first *Temple* poems, despite the quality of parallelism of the two deaths, God and the protagonist are separated, the one isolated ('The Sacrifice' makes this very clear and poignant) in the mystery of the Passion, and the other frozen in the stone. 'H. Baptisme (I)' speaks of the 'first acquaintance' of the protagonist and God in the sacrament of baptism. The first line of the poem, incidentally, speaks of the 'dark and shadie grove' which must be avoided. Could Herbert have known of Dante's symbolic 'selva oscura,' into which light (Lucia) from Beatrice still penetrates in the *Comedy's* version of 'first acquaintance'?

I do not wish to press analogies too far. The resemblances between Herbert's images and their implications and the theory of the gentle heart are substantial; Herbert's poems are not, however, derivative. He works with such care, establishing his chains of images with such thoroughness, that it is as though he were recreating the old theory. Herbert gives a sustained and developed account of the book as the life. His protagonist comes to life in the first fourteen poems of *The Temple*, and does so by a process worked out very long before Herbert wrote. It is important, I think, to see that Herbert *could have* used another process: baptism, as the first sacrament, confers life, but it need not be construed as *producing a child*. Christ had very often before Herbert appeared in images of the sun, but there was no need to describe Him as finding the gold in a stone.

If we follow the sun images through *The Temple* we can see how Herbert advances the dramatic development of his protagonist over a sequence of poems. In 'Mattens' the stone image is beautifully stated:

> My God, what is a heart?
> Silver, or gold, or precious stone,
> Or starre, or rainbow, or a part
> Of all these things, or all of them in one?

The last stanza unites the sun with the work (of the song 'Mattens') as means for achieving union with God:

> Teach me thy love to know;
> That this new light, which now I see,
> May both the work and workman show:
> Then by a sunne-beam I will climbe
>   to thee.

Fourteen poems further on, 'The Starre' which has come from Christ the sun is asked (st. 2) to 'Take a bad lodging in my heart' and (st. 3):

> Then with thy light refine,
> And make it shine:

The result will be the protagonist's 'flight' (st. 5) to what is here described as a very courtly Heaven. The poem concludes with an image of the protagonist's *work*, his industry as of the 'laden bee,' as does 'Sunday,' next following. In 'Christmas,' five poems later, the 'sunne' (theme of the whole second section of the poem) evokes and is intertwined with the protagonist's song to express union with Christ. 'Vertue' and 'Life,' separated by five poems, both image *day* as *life*, the time for making 'musick' (st. 3) in 'Vertue' or 'a posie' (a poem) in 'Life.'

The shooting star of 'Artillerie' functions like the 'Bright spark' of 'The Starre.' It is likened to music in stanza 2. It calls into being the protagonist's own powers:

> Then we are shooters both ...
> Shunne not *my* arrows, and behold my breast.

The protagonist's 'arrows' are his arguments of this poem; the poem itself is his 'Artillerie.' In 'The Flower' God is the spring sun and also, as in 'H. Baptisme (I),' healing waters. In stanza 6 God is addressed, 'O my onely light'; this is the stanza most devoted to the subject of poetry. In 'The Sonne' Christ is elaborately:

> ... the sunnes bright starre!
> ... a fruitfull flame ...

The protagonist is concerned here not so much with joining Christ as with finding a way to express His nature; he is concerned with language:

> I like our language, as our men and coast:
> Who cannot dresse it well, want wit, not words.

Throughout these poems Christ as sun functions to release from the protagonist's heart his unique and particular virtue, his ability to write poems. In sequence the poems show a gain in strength sufficient to enable the protagonist to reach God and to express Him.

Here we may return to earlier poems in *The Temple* for insight into how that increase in strength was obtained. After the protagonist's dedication to God's 'art' in 'Nature,' several poems deal strikingly with the subject of youth. 'Sinne (I)' begins:

> Lord, with what care hast thou begirt us round!
> Parents first season us: than schoolmasters
> Deliver us to laws ...

The theme of youthful ambition is treated in 'Affliction (I),' with its imagery of the squire in training for knighthood. 'Repentance' recalls the fragility of the new life created in 'H. Baptisme (II)':

> ... Oh! gently treat
> With thy quick flow'r, thy momentarie bloom.

'Faith' has stanzas touching education:

A peasant may beleeve as much
As a great Clerk, and reach the highest stature.
Thus dost thou make proud
    knowledge bend & crouch ...

— the power of the sun as I have been discussing it, and an evocation of
the 'dark and shadie grove' of 'H. Baptisme (I)':

When creatures had no reall light
Inherent in them, thou didst make the sunne
Impute a lustre, and allow them bright;
    And in this shew, what Christ hath done.

That which before was darkned clean
With bushie groves, pricking the lookers eie,
Vanisht away, when Faith did change the scene;
    And then appear'd a glorious skie.

After this gradual and steady maturation, a further development
occurs in *The Temple's* protagonist in the two sonnets titled 'Love' and
the group of poems just following. These, 'The Temper (I),' 'Jordan (I),'
'Employment (I),' and the two 'H. Scriptures' sonnets contain a body of
more systematic, theoretical material on the subject of poetry than has
appeared before in *The Temple*. Not, I hope, to make too homely a little
drama, in these poems, after childhood, youth, and education in the
previous ones, the protagonist seriously commits himself to his vocation,
first simply the vocation of poet and perhaps in the two last poems of the
group to that of poet-priest.

The Temple, considered as a whole, symbolizes, in a peculiarly *literal*
sense, its protagonist's life. In all respects the poems remain pure lyrics,
independent of one another. Through their image linkages they supply
the sense of change and development necessary to a narrative or a
drama. In the first fourteen poems we do not *read about* the birth of a
child; that is not at all the poems' statement. Only in the images is such a
meaning carried. The images of the last poems in the book might easily, I
think, be shown to bring the life to a close. With 'The Forerunners' age
comes on; in 'Death' and the three poems following, the poet-
protagonist thinks of the last things. In *The Temple's* final poems, as
well as in its first ones, the life remains the book; experience has no form
or meaning other than the poem which expresses it.

7

In 'Good Friday' the word *measure* is structural, occupying the first three stanzas, and it is closely related to the poetic task at hand:

> O my chief good,
>> How shall I measure out thy bloud?
> How shall I count what thee befell,
>> And each grief tell?

The poem's six questions may be paraphrased as, How shall I write a poem on the subject of Good Friday? We see here partly an irony: I am so inadequate to the task of writing this poem that I am able only mechanically to *count*. But the questions and the subject are too serious to allow the measuring to be wholly ironic. The verb *to measure* is colored by its sense in 'The Agonie'; it means 'to know,' and the process of measuring, like the process of knowing, is a part of the province of poetry. In 'Good Friday,' five stanzas of measuring lead to the condition of the final section, where the state of consciousness is one of 'Sinne being gone.'

'The Sinner,' also, between 'The Agonie' and 'Good Friday,' has its counting, too, of the 'treasure in my memorie,' of 'piled vanities,' of the 'many hundredth part' of the heart. Counting in 'The Sinner,' too, is contrasted with *valid* writing, that of God upon the stony heart, the page of poetry:

'Vanitie (I)' is very similar to 'The Agonie' in listing areas of secular knowledge for the sake of contrast with the knowledge of God, but here the list is elaborately courtly. The form of the first three stanzas shows an opening image of scientific examination in terms of physical action: the astronomer 'bores,' the diver 'cuts through,' the chemist 'can devest/And strip.' The physical action is a metaphor for mastery of subject; measure *is* a crucial part of knowledge.

This knowledge is defined in the last line of 'Vanitie': it is death:

> Poore man, thou searchest round
> To finde out *death*, but missest *life* at hand.

Looking backward into the poem from this line we see its stunning irony. The conclusion of each of the first three stanzas has contained a courtly image raised to erotic intensity.

> ... he sees their dances
> And knoweth long before,
> Both their full-ey'd aspects, and secret glances.

> ... he might save his life, and also hers,
>> Who with excessive pride
> Her own destruction and his danger wears. ....

> Admitted to their bed-chamber, before
> They appear trim and drest
> To ordinarie suitors at the doore.

The sequence describes a courtship, from love glances through betrothal gift to bed-chamber, the usual process of obtaining new life. And this is called death, while life is to be found in 'love and aw' (repeating the 'strong regard and aw' of 'The Windows') of God; this life is said to be 'at hand.' It is not sophistical, I think, to ask the reader, What precisely do you have at hand?, and the answer must be, this poem. Measure has here again been the formal prelude to a state of knowledge and feeling which is beyond measure.

Often in Herbert's poems it is only when measure can be dropped from consideration that true poetry and song begin. 'The Thanksgiving' is an outstanding example:

> My musick shall find thee, and ev'ry string
> Shall have his attribute to sing;
> That all together may accord in thee,
> And prove one God, one harmonie.
> If thou shalt give me wit, it shall appeare,
> If thou hast giv'n it me, 'tis here.

Rosemund Tuve writes movingly on Herbert's musical images,[9] to see them also as little treatises on the art of poetry will only show a greater number of poems that she examines in *The Temple* to be concerned with the poet's taking on of the *humanitas Christi* — akin, of course, to the paradoxical interinvolvement of the *cor gentil*.

Miss Tuve points out that 'Easter' derives from the Easter Proper Psalm 57; its exultation surely confirms her opinion.[10] Her argument is not disparaged, however, nor is Herbert's art, when it is said that the poem is also very courtly. For David's psaltery (Psalm 57.8), Herbert substitutes the lute, the accompanying instrument of the ayre, the love song. The whole poem is concerned with music, but its third stanza is particularly interesting:

> Consort both heart and lute, and twist a song
> Pleasant and long:
> Or, since all musick is but three parts vied
> and multiplied,
> O let thy blessed Spirit bear a part,
> And make up our defects with his sweet art.

The entire image-cluster I have been discussing appears in 'The

Temper (I).' The hard substance (here of the sword, but surely also of the engraver's *stone*) is the task at hand, the poem:

> How should I praise thee, Lord!
>> how should my rymes
>> Gladly engrave thy love in steel . . .

The second stanza deals with the theme of measuring, counting, the areas of scientific knowledge of 'The Agonie' and 'Vanitie (I),' with frantic effort, physical as well as intellectual and spiritual:

> Although there were some fourtie heav'ns or more,
>> Sometimes I peere above them all;
> Sometimes I hardly reach a score,
>> Sometimes to hell I fall.

Stanza 4 contains a very clear image of the feudal champion, though there is also an evocation of Jacob's mysterious and supernatural struggle:

> Wilt thou meet arms with man, that thou dost stretch
> A crumme of dust from heav'n to hell?
> Will great God measure with a wretch?
>> Shall he thy stature spell?

God is here the measurer. The involvement of poetry and struggle, and of God and man as collaborators in poetry, the possibility that man can reach to God through a *spell* (a poetic one) — are all here.

Stanza 6 introduces music (which has been present all along, from the title, from the word 'rymes' in the first line, and from the heavenly spheres in the second and third stanzas):

> Yet take thy way; for sure thy way is best:
> Stretch or contract me, thy poore debter:
>> This is but tuning of my breast,
>> To make the musick better.

The final stanza offers, once again, an image of flight to achieve unity with God:

> Whether I flie with angels, fall with dust,
> Thy hands made both, and I am there:
> Thy power and love, my love and trust
>> Make one place ev'rywhere.

STAMBLER

8

Love in *The Temple*, as in the volumes of love poetry, is constantly expressed as that which asks the whole man and that which in the fulfillment will satisfy him. I think Herbert wrote in vain if we do not interpret his work as strongly linked with mysticism. The agonizing poignancy of poems on God's absence (those preceding 'Easter,' 'Home,' and 'Longing' are examples among many) is missed if we do not see that at other moments in *The Temple* God is present to the protagonist. The 'silk twist' is let down from heaven in 'The Pearl,' His footprint is seen in 'Dulnesse,' His touch is felt in 'Paradise' and 'Clasping of Hands,' He speaks in 'Dialogue' and 'The Collar.' The opening lines of 'The Search':

> Whither, O whither art thou fled,
> My Lord, my Love?

tend to become meaningless, as do the last lines of that poem, if we say only that Herbert is here engaging in the art of sacred parody. The title gives sensuous significance to 'The Flower':

> How fresh, O Lord, how sweet and clean
> Are thy returns ...

Lines of 'Aaron' have much more meaning in the light of other poems in *The Temple* than as the doctrinal generalization they appear to be here:

> My doctrine tun'd by Christ, (who is not dead,
> But lives in me while I do rest) ...

We fail in our reading if we think it only a pretty metaphor when we come again and again to a passage on *song*, coming after *measure* (knowledge, discipline, the work of poetry), or struggle (the work of the soldier), or after the imagery of the stone.

In the image of song, usually associated with an image of flight, the protagonist has a sense of reaching the actual presence of God. Song is not only spiritual, ethereal transcendence in Herbert; it is effortless and graceful sensuousness, of a practical efficacy beyond reason, inexplicable.

But *The Temple* protagonist is a 'short-breached man': his flight cannot be sustained. The image is to be read quite accurately: no flying thing flies continually. The form of *The Temple*, as I have already discussed it, is a persistent alternation of contrarieties. It remains so at the end.

In the love poems, I believe, it was a Platonic discipline which overcame loss.

The lover remained constant, and continued to purify his desire. It could scarcely be urged that the desire of *The Temple* protagonist was ever impure, but again a chain of images running through the book seems to demonstrate a process of purification.

I said above that 'Love (I)' and (II) mark a turning point. Both sonnets state importantly the theme of poetry — God is addressed as 'author' of the universe; the poet-protagonist reflects throughout on his own work and looks forward to redeeming the promise of 'The Altar': '... then shall our brain / All her invention on thine Altar lay.' In 'Love (II)' God is fire, the fires of judgment *and* the heat of the sun which, as in the stone-image poems, brings out the best in the protagonist:

> Immortall Heat, O let thy greater flame,
> Attract the lesser to it: let those fires,
> Which shall consume the world, first make it tame;
>
> And kindle in our hearts such true desires,
> As may consume our lusts, and make thee way.
> Then shall our hearts pant thee;
>   then shall our brain
> All her invention on thine Altar lay,
> And there in hymnes send back thy fire again:

Then a new imagery appears: very emphatic reference is made to the *eyes*.

> Our eies shall see thee ...
> All knees shall bow to thee; All wits shall rise,
> And praise him who did make and mend our eies.

It is, of course, entirely appropriate that the Christian express a longing to see God, but Herbert stresses other associations with eyes in these two poems. In context here 'mended eyes' are involved with perfected poems in a process almost duplicating that of the stone-image poems: the 'Heat' of love mends the eyes as it wakened and animated the stone, and with the same result — poetry.

Again I do not wish to rely on factitious comparisons, but Herbert's use of imagery of the eye here is much like the persistent eye-heart motif in the whole tradition of courtly love poems. There 'first acquaintance' with the beloved was at first *sight* of her. Her mysterious 'salutation' was her glance, which functioned like the sun in Guinizelli's canzone: it wakened the lover's virtu.

Very often in the love poems, however, the process of sensation proceeding to the heart was expressed as a suspenseful one. Are the eyes (considered by Aristotle and by the medieval love-poets to be the highest and noblest of the sense-organs) capable of lying? The heart in order to function *must have* evidence from the senses, but how to guarantee the heart against the eyes' betrayal? Herbert, speaking of the need to 'mend' the eyes, seems to be using the same complicated sense.

The image returns in 'The H. Scriptures':

> Ladies, look here; this is the thankfull glasse
> That mends the lookers eyes ...

The several components — star, light, life, poetry — are linked in the final couplet of 'The H. Scriptures (II)':

> Starres are poore books, & oftentimes do misse:
> This book of starres lights to eternall blisse.

as again more elaborately in 'Mattens' and 'Even-song.'

Throughout these poems the protagonist's desire is to see as God sees; the process is a reciprocal one, like that in which the stone's virtu flashes back to the star or like the process of 'The Temper (I),' where the protagonist asks for the sufferings of Christ for the sake of a purified heart and a better poem.

Looking backward in *The Temple* from 'Love (I) and (II),' we find that most often the protagonist asked God to write on the stone. This image I have shown to be akin to the love poets' attributing the poem to Love's authorship. Dante and Sidney write 'as Love dictates.' I think that the change from sun-stone to eye images in 'Love (I) and (II),' and in the whole group of poems following, marks the beginning of *The Temple* protagonist's ability to write his own poems. In 'Easter' and 'Easter-wings' the speaker's upward movement depends wholly upon God. In 'Mattens' his own work is of the essence:

> Teach me thy love to know;
> That this new light, which now I see,
> May both the work and workman show:
> Then by a sunne-beam I will climbe to thee.

In 'Whitsunday,' just after the brilliant 'light' of 'The H. Scriptures,' the poet-preacher's song invokes the flight: the previous process has been reversed. In 'Frailtie' the protagonist's comparisons between heaven and the world are visual ones; he judges in favor of heaven, but he is troubled:

> That which was dust before, doth quickly rise.
> And prick mine eyes.

The process of 'clearing the gift' of sight is a long and difficult one. 'Deniall' expresses denial of flight and song (at stanzas 5 and 6) but poetry has been written nevertheless, as it could not have been in earlier stages of *The Temple*. The shepherd sings in 'Christmas,' but a further process will make the 'musick shine.' The image ramifies in depth and complexity in 'Ungratefulnesse':

> But man is close, reserv'd and dark to thee:
> When thou demandest but a heart...

and in the sun and eye images of 'Coloss. 3.3,' or 'A face not fearing light, of 'Lent.'

A group of poems beginning with 'Gratefulnesse' stresses the theme of purification of the heart:

> Thou that hast giv'n so much to me,
> Give one thing more, a gratefull heart...
> See how thy beggar works on thee By art.

In 'Confession':

> I challenge here the brightest day,
> The clearest diamond: let them do their best,
> They shall be thick and cloudie to my breast.

In 'Giddinesse':

> Surely if each one saw anothers heart,
> There would be no commerce ...
> Lord, mend or rather make us ...

'Love unknown' elaborately reenacts the whole process; in the next poem, 'Man's medley,' the result of the purified heart is again the poem, the song. In 'An Offering' the proof of purity of heart is the song which concludes the poem.

'The Glimpse' is a restatement of the reciprocal function: the protagonist's heart received God's glimpse; in that action he was able to look briefly at God. 'The Glance' gives evidence that the protagonist's eye and heart are in right relationship; he can work alone, in long absence of God's animating look:

> But still thy sweet original joy,
> Sprung from thine eye, did work within my soul ...

The Temple's last poem, 'Love (III)' is very close in spirit to the mystical dream of the feast of love in the *Vita Nuova*. It is appropriate that 'Love (III)' should stress the image of purified eye and heart which first appeared in 'Love (I) and (II)':

> Love bade me welcome: yet my soul drew back,
>   Guiltie of dust and sinne.
> But quick-eye'd Love, observing me grow slack
>   From my first entrance in,
> Drew nearer to me, sweetly questioning,
>   If I lack'd any thing.
>
> A guest, I answer'd, worthy to be here:
>   Love said, You shall be he.
> I the unkinde, ungratefull? Ah my deare,
>   I cannot look on thee.
> Love took my hand, and smiling did reply,
>   Who made the eyes but I?
>
> Truth Lord, but I have marr'd them: let my shame
>   Go where it doth deserve.
> And know you not, says Love, who bore the blame?
>   My deare, then I will serve.
> You must sit down, sayes Love, and taste my meat:
>   So I did sit and eat.

Desire, not fulfillment, is the emotional sense of the poem; its strength is its delicate, precarious, and tentative intrusion of the human heart and senses into absolute purity. The multitude of meanings in this poem are finally embraced in one: 'Love (III)' completes the protagonist's discipline of the gentle heart.

THE STRUCTURE OF GEORGE HERBERT'S *TEMPLE*: A RECONSIDERATION

Annabel M. Endicott-Patterson

One of the more prolific symbols which Christian commentators took over from the Jewish religion was that of the Temple in Jerusalem. Some of the traditional exegesis on this building was recently brought to light in an article by J. D. Walker, who invoked it in an interpretation of George Herbert's *Temple*.[1] The division of Herbert's book into "The Church Porch," "The Church," and "The Church Militant," it was suggested, can be explained by the Hebraic Temple's tripartite division into porch, holy place, and holy of holies.[2] The purpose of my article is partly negative — to deny emphatically the structural analogy between Herbert's *Temple* and the Hebrew one; and partly positive — to provide some additional knowledge about the use of this symbol in the Renaissance, and to show that Herbert would almost certainly have been aware both of its complexities and its disadvantages.

The adoption of the Hebrew Temple by Christianity was of dubious value because the whole rationale of the building was antipathetic to Christian thought. As Joseph Hall commented, the structure of the Hebrew Temple was progressively discriminatory:

> I finde one Courte of the Temple open to the uncleane, to the uncircumcized: Within that, another, open onely to the Israelites; and of them, to the cleane; within that, yet another proper onely to the Priests and Levites. . . . The eyes of the Laitie might follow their oblations in hither, their feet might not. . . . Yet more, in the covered roomes of the Temple, there is, whither the Priests only may enter, not the Levites; there is, whither the high Priest onely may enter, not his brethren.[3]

Early Christian churches, on the other hand, whether or not for purely practical reasons, were almost democratic in structure, designed to *include* large numbers of people. Christian basilicas probably

Reprinted from *University of Toronto Quarterly*, 35 (1965), 226-37, by permission of the author and University of Toronto Press.

borrowed their form from public meeting places. And their name is pleasantly rationalized by Donne, since "the Church is not onely *Domus Dei*, but *Basilica*; not onely his house, but his Court: he doth not onely dwell there, but reigne there: which multiplies the joy of his houshold servants."[4] Also, in the holy of holies the mystery of the Presence was expressed by total darkness and hidden by a partition or veil, in Christian churches the mystery was expressed by the altar in full view at the eastern end, and often framed by brilliant mosaic on arch and apse.

Nevertheless, the image of the Temple retained its hold on the imagination as the centre of so much Old and New Testament activity, and the name came to be freely applied to the Christian Church. If we continue with the same sermon from Donne, we come upon an explanation which goes beyond fanciful etymology in its wary longing to account for this seeming contradiction in terms:

> But of all Names . . . the name of *Temple* seems to be most large and significant, as they derive it *a Tuendo*; for *Tueri* signifies both our beholding, and contemplating *God* in the Church, and it signifies Gods protecting and defending those that are his. . . . And therefore, though in the very beginning of the Primitive Church, to depart from the custome, and language, and phrase of the *Jews*, and *Gentiles*, as farre as they could, they did much abstain from this name of *Temple*. . . . Yet when . . . the Christian Church, and doctrine was established, from that time downward, all the Fathers did freely and safely call the Church the *Temple*. . . . As the Apostle had given a good patterne, how to expresse the principall holinesse of the Saints of God, he chooses to doe it, in that word, *ye are the Temples of the Holy Ghost*.

In other words, the Temple had such emotional value as a symbol of organized and housed religion, even if of the superseded religion, that it became desirable, after a period of caution, and with certain mental reservations, to use it as a metaphorical name for the Church. It was a metaphor which was capable of almost unlimited extension into the realms of analogy and typology, as we shall see.

One of the simpler patterns of analogy which developed was between the three rooms of the Temple and the three stages of Christian life. The porch, the scene of ritual purification, corresponded to Christian conversion; the holy place, or mid-temple, to religious activity within the Church; and the holy of holies to the final stage of union with God after death. As noted by Walker, this scheme appears in the writings of Joseph Hall. Hall's scheme, however, is not simple, as will appear if the whole of his exegesis is taken into account. Hall sees the holy of holies not merely as heaven, but as the heaven "into which our true high-Priest, Christ Jesus, entred once for all to make an atonement betwixt God and man."[5]

He goes on to elaborate other patterns. He observes that the proportions of the Temple were those of the human body, in that "the height was thrice the breadth, and the breadth one third of the height," referring by this tautology, apparently, to the combined *length* of holy place and holy of holies, which was sixty cubits, and their width, which was twenty cubits. And, with some sleight of hand, he declares that these are also the measurements of the Church Militant, or visible Church, since "there is a necessary inequality, without any disproportion," and of the Church Triumphant, because "it hath a length of eternity, answered with a height of perfection, and a breadth of incomprehensible glory." And he concludes with an elaborate comparison between the various articles of furniture in the Temple and the various qualities of a Christian soul.

The second pattern already noted was an analogy between the physical structures of the Temple and the universe. The various versions of this scheme suggest that the commentators started with the idea of the holy of holies as God's heaven, and then tried to extend the pattern downwards, with varying degrees of appropriateness. Apparently several of the Church Fathers held the scheme to be:

holy of holies	God's heaven
holy place	heavens (in the sense of sky)
porch	Earth[6]

Hall, however, elsewhere in the *Contemplations*, confines his analogy to three layers of heavens:

This lowest Heaven for Fowles, for Vapours, for Meteors: The second, for the Starres: The third, for thine Angels and Saints: The first is thine outward Court, open for all: The second is the body of thy covered Temple, wherein are those Candles of Heaven perpetually burning: the third is thine Holy of Holies. In the first is Tumult and Vanity: In the second Immutability & Rest: In the third, Glory and Blessednesse.[7]

Hall's analogy between the famous candelabra of the holy place and the stars of the sky provides a clue to the other traditional scheme just mentioned, in which the holy place was also compared to the sky; and we may notice that the moral implications of the hierarchy, whether the porch be compared to third heaven or earth, remain the same. We can also find a scheme which appears to combine both of these, in a commentary on Genesis by Lancelot Andrewes:

> ... for as there was in the Temple of *Salomon Sanctum &
> Sanctum Sanctorum*, so in the great Temple of the world there is
> *Coelum & Coelum Coelorum*, to answer to it. In the upper and
> higher Heavens, as was shadowed in the Temple, is the mercy Seat,
> the Altar, and the Propiciatory; but in the nether is *atrium* . . . that
> is, a division of severall Courts for Starres, Clouds, Fowls, Men,
> &c. Between the higher and the nether Heavens, as it was in the
> Temple, there is a Vail or Curtain spread . . . which doth part the
> one from the other.[8]

There are several curious points here: first, there is the delight of the Renaissance mind in the correspondence between the Latin names, *Sanctum* and *Sanctum Sanctorum, Coelum* and *Coelum Coelorum*; second, although Andrewes appears to confine himself to the two upper divisions of the Temple, when we look more closely we realize that for him the lower includes the porch and its surrounding courts, and the mention of "Men, &c." implies that the lower heavens include Earth. The division really seems to be between the visible universe, where God is revealed only through his creation, but which is nevertheless good (*Sanctum*), and an invisible heaven, where his Presence is immediate, and which is perfect.

In view of this passage, it is odd to find Andrewes elsewhere rather scornful of cosmological analogies, which he relegates to the time-wasting activities of Rabbins. The Church Fathers, he asserts, "bestowed their time and travaile more to the point" in working out a different analogy, that between the Temple and Christ.[9] This was, of course, first suggested by Christ himself when he promised metaphorically to destroy the temple of his body and raise it again in three days (John 2:19). Andrewes devotes a whole sermon to this text, and since it was one of the *XCVI Sermons* first published in 1629, it would have been available to Herbert, just entering his ministry, should he have wished to learn from the sermons of others.

Andrewes conveniently subdivides this exegesis into four main branches: "1. Whither you looke to the composition or parts of it. 2. Or to the furniture, and *vessells* of it. 3. Or, to what was *done in it*. 4. Or, to what was *done to it*." And although he proposes, for the sake of brevity, to confine himself to the fourth, he manages to work in a good deal of information belonging to Sections 1 and 2 under the appearance of keeping to his text. Thus the two tables of the Law, which were broken but remade, are "the type of the true treasures of *Wisedome* and *Knowledge* hid in Him," and the vessel of manna is a "perfect resemblane."

> The *Urna,* or the vessell being made of *earth,* so *earthly*; The *Manna,* the contents of it, being from *heaven,* so heavenly: The Manna (we know) would not keepe past *two daies* at the most, there is *Solvite*: but, being putt into the *Urna,* the third day it came againe to it selfe, and kept in the *Pott* without putrifying ever after; there is *Exitabo.*[10]

His "looke to the composition or parts" of the Temple is somewhat primitive, although combined with a sophisticated conceit that the nailing of Christ's body paradoxically constituted his *un*building:

> The *roofe* ... (His *head*) loosed with *thornes*: the *foundation* (His *feet*) with *nayles.* The *side Isles* (as it were) His *hands both* likewise. And his *bodie,* as the *bodie of the Temple,* and *His heart* in the midst of his *bodie,* as the *Sanctum Sanctorum,* with the *Speare: Loosed,* all.[11]

Images of the Temple also appear from time to time in Donne's sermons, which would not have been available to Herbert in print, though he may have availed himself of the older man's knowledge in private. Donne's influence was obviously strong, in Herbert's poetry and perhaps also in his life. F. W. Hutchinson believes that "we may assume that Donne, as well as Lady Danvers, confirmed Herbert in his resolution [to take orders].[12] It is therefore highly probable that Herbert's concept of the Temple derives at least in part from Donne, with whom he almost certainly discussed his own poetic plans.

Donne, like Andrewes, seems to prefer a double, rather than a triple scheme of analogy. He does not concern himself with the cosmos, but concentrates on the structure of Christian history, thus:

> ... this world to the righteous is *Atrium templi,* and heaven is that Temple it selfe, the Militant Church is the porch, the Triumphant, is the *Sanctum Sanctorum,* this Church and that Church are all under one roofe, Christ Jesus."[13]

And again:

> Here in the *militant Church,* you stand, but you stand in the *porch,* there in the *triumphant,* you shall stand *in Sancto sanctorum,* in the *Quire* and the *Altar.*[14]

Or, more intricately:

> The blood of the sacrifices was brought by the high priest, *in
> sanctum sanctorum* ... ; but it was brought but once ... in the feast
> of expiation; but in the other parts of the Temple, it was sprinkled
> every day. The blood of the Crosse of Christ Jesus hath had his
> effect *in sancto sanctorum*, even in the highest heavens, in
> supplying their places that fell. . . . In the other parts of the Temple
> it is to be sprinkled daily. Here, in the militant Church upon earth,
> there is still a reconciliation to be made.[15]

Like Andrewes, Donne is concentrating on a two-fold division of the
Temple, in order to clarify the contrast between partial good and
perfection. Only, where Andrewes achieves simplicity (if not clarity) by
fusing the holy place and the porch, Donne achieves it, in the first two
passages quoted, by fusing the holy place and the holy of holies. Indeed,
he appears to be thinking of a temple already so modified by its
Christian context that the veil is down. The possibility of standing
simultaneously in the holy of holies and "in the Quire and the Altar"
certainly makes architectural identification with the Hebrew Temple
rather difficult.

Finally, Herbert would have been able to gather much of the
traditional typology of the Temple without recourse to the Church
Fathers at all, simply by referring to the "Second Week" of Sylvester's
translation of Du Bartas, which was in print by 1598, and which Herbert
would surely have read. Here the poet praises Solomon for having
architecturally reproduced the "Worlds Idea," which

> Was sever'd in a Three-fould divers Frame,
> And God Almighty rightly did Ordain
> One all Divine, one Heav'nly, one Terrene,
> Decking with Vertues one, with Stars another,
> With Flowrs, & Fruits, & Beasts, & Birds, the other.[16]

The moral hierarchy is also explicit; for although the poet is concentrating on the decorative, rather than the discordant aspects of Earth, it
nevertheless corresponds to the porch, "The Vulgars Ile, the World of
Elements." The holy place, by contrast, is inhabited by "Sun-bright
Levits," corresponding, presumably, to the stars in other schemes. And
the holy of holies is inhabited by none

> But God, the Cherubins, and (once a year)
> The *sacred Figure* of Perfection dear,

> Of God's eternall Son (Sins sin-lesse check)
> The everlasting true MELCHISEDEC.

We have already noticed both Hall and Donne alluding to this scheme, or some version of it, in their references to Christ the High Priest. But Du Bartas has a further elaboration still. He observes that Solomon has built, in words as well as in stone, in a three-fold pattern. The Book of Proverbs is compared to the porch because "it gives us Oeconomick Lawes. / Rules Politick, and private civill Sawes." Ecclesiastes can be compared to the holy place, because it is an intermediate stage between Earth and Heaven and, "all the World proclaiming *Vain of Vains*," draws us away from one and prepares us for the other. And finally, of course, the Song of Songs corresponds to the holy of holies, in that it celebrates "in *Mysterious* Verse ... CHRIST'S and his CHURCHES Epithalamy." Once again, it seems likely that this scheme could have developed downwards, so to speak, from the allegorical interpretation of the *Carmen Carminum*, by which it was easily linked to the *Sanctum Sanctorum*. It would have been a natural desire to give the rest of Solomon's canon the same kind of significance.

These references, collected from rather obvious places, imply that the image of the Temple was indeed one of the commonplaces of at least the theologically-trained mind, and that it would indeed have been strange if Herbert had framed his *Temple* in complete ignorance of the tradition. But what these quotations also show is that the tradition itself was by no means simple, and allowed much scope for individuality. In at least one writer whom Herbert knew well, Donne, there seems to be an understanding that the name and features of the Hebrew Temple should only be applied to the Church with caution and adaptation. The question we now have to consider is just how much of the *Hebraic* nature of the Temple could be implied by Herbert's use of the name.

If we consider first the porch (noting that it is a "*Church* Porch") there can be no doubt that Walker is right in regarding this as a poem of purification and preparation. However, the title "Perirrhanterium" and the reference to sprinkling do not necessarily imply anything other than baptism. Nor is it easy to accept the statement that "the Hebraic ritual of vesting with holy garments and sprinkling with blood are implied in the moral instructions" to beware of lust, alcohol, and so forth.[17] These precepts sound like nothing so much as the Book of Proverbs as it might have been brought up to date by Francis Bacon. Bacon himself is constantly quoting Solomon in the *Essays*, and the aphorisms of "The Church Porch" have much in common with both. Herbert's advice to the returning traveller, for example (st. 61) —

> Keep all thy native good, and naturalize
> All forrain of that name; but scorn their ill:
> Embrace their activenesse, not vanities —

bears close relation to Bacon's essay "Of Travel":

> Let his travel appear rather in his discourse than in his apparel
> or gesture ... and let it appear that he doth not change his country
> manners for those of foreign parts; but only prick in some flowers
> of that he hath learned abroad into the customs of his own
> country.

Or, for a closer comparison still, we may set together stanzas 50 and 51
of "The Church Porch" and part of Bacon's essay "Of Discourse."
According to Bacon:

> The honourable part of talk is to give the occasion; and again to
> moderate and pass to somewhat else; for then a man leads the
> dance.... He that questioneth much, shall learn much: but
> especially if he apply his questions to the skill of the persons whom
> he asketh; for he shall give them occasion to please themselves in
> speaking, and himself shall continually gather knowledge....And
> let him be sure to leave other men their turns to speak.

Herbert advises his novitiate to "Entice all neatly to what they know
best" if he wishes to please and be pleased. And having, it seems, a rather
more pugnacious idea of the art of conversation than does Bacon, he
continues:

> If thou be Master-gunner, spend not all
> That thou canst speak, at once; but husband it,
> And give men turns of speech: do not forestall
> By lavishnesse thine own, and others wit,
> As if thou mad'st thy will. A civil guest
> Will no more talk all, then eat all the feast.

The introduction of these parallels, striking as they are, is not intended
to show that Herbert was versifying sections of Bacon's *Essays*.[18] It is
intended to show that the tone of this poem is not that of "priest-making
ritual" but of practical advice. If this section is to relate at all to
traditional interpretations of the Temple Porch, it seems closest to that
part of the tradition represented by Du Bartas, providing as it does for
the young and callow "Rules politicke, and private civill Sawes."

However, it would be possible to explain the poem, including the warning over the lintel of the door, without reference to the Hebrew Temple at all. In early Christian churches there was also a porch, or narthex, at the western end, reserved for, among others, the cate-chumens, those trainee converts who were not yet baptized or allowed to take part in the eucharist.[19] The porch was also used for some secular functions, such as the first part of marriage ceremonies, as witness Chaucer's Wife of Bath and her five "Housbondes at chirche dore,"[20] and this practice survived into the sixteenth century. And if the type of instruction given in "The Church Porch" still seems too secular for the kind of training we might expect a catechumen to receive, the explana-tion may be that Herbert is here making use of an earlier didactic poem as neatly as he can.

If we now enter Herbert's "Church," expecting to find in it some obvious resemblances to the holy place, we shall be disappointed. In contrast to Hall, for example, we do not find Herbert alluding, either in his poems or in their titles, to the famous golden candelabra, or the tables of shew-bread.[21] Instead, the building has a chequered stone floor sloping gently to the Quire ("The Church-floore"), stained glass ("The Windows") and heraldic "Church-monuments" of "Jeat and Marble." In this building are celebrated "Holy Communion" and "Holy Baptism," "Mattens" and "Even-song," the latter two presumably accompanied by "Church-Musick." It is the kind of building of which Herbert writes in *A Priest to the Temple* that:

> The Countrey Parson hath a speciall care of his Church, that all things there be decent, and befitting his Name by which it is called. Therefore first he takes order, that all things be in good repair; as walls plaistered, windows glazed, floore paved, seats whole, firm, and uniform, expecially that the Pulpit, and Desk, and Com-munion Table, and Font be as they ought, for those great duties that are performed in them [246].

We also find Herbert praising "The British Church" for her achieve-ment of the golden mean in ritual, "Neither too mean, nor yet too gay," and in "The Holy Communion" he rejoices that:

> Not in rich furniture, or fine array,
> Nor in a wedge of gold,
> Thou, who for me was sold,
> To me dost now thy self convey.

Moreover, in "Sion," where Herbert defines his concept of the inward temple of the soul, he does so in terms of a *rejection* of the Temple of Solomon:[22]

> Lord, with what glorie wast thou serv'd of old,
> When Solomons temple stood and flourished!
> Where most things were of purest gold;
>
>   .   .   .
>
> Yet all this glorie, all this pomp and state
> Did not affect thee much, was not thy aim
>
>   .   .   .
>
> All Solomons sea of brasse and world of stone
> Is not so deare to thee as one good grone
>
>   .   .   .
>
> And truly brasse and stones are heavie things,
> Tombes for the dead, not temples fit for thee:
> But grones are quick, and full of wings,
> And all their motions upward be.

In fact, the only object that Herbert's "Church" has in common with the holy place is the altar, and there is no need to identify this with the Hebrew golden altar of incense, just as there is no need for any elaborate explanation of the placing of "The Altar" as the first poem in "The Church." There is no obvious architectural order of precedence to the poems in "The Church," and "The Altar" (at the head of a group of Passion poems) comes naturally first by virtue of its primary importance.

If we turn now to "The Church Militant," we are asked to believe that it forms the highest step in an ascending scale, that it corresponds to the holy of holies, and hence, as in any of the typologies mentioned, to God's heaven. The evidence given for this is as follows: first, Herbert identifies the Cross as the Ark of the New Covenant, and thus the poem can be seen as an account of the travels of this new Ark; and secondly, the poem must correspond to God's heaven because here "the point of view is that of an omniscient being who in one glance perceives the sweep of human history. This is God's mode of awareness...."[23] These are both interesting comments, but not, I submit, sufficient evidence to permit us to identify "The Church Militant" with the Hebrew holy of holies, especially when there is other evidence that seems to point the opposite way.

To begin with, as Hutchinson points out, it is by no means clear that the poem is organically related to the rest of *The Temple* at all. It "stands apart in both MSS from the lyrical poems which have *Finis* at the end of the section called 'The Church'. All the internal evidence points to an early date for the inception."[24] Also, after the early metaphysical correlation between Noah's Ark, the Ark of the Covenant and the Cross, none are mentioned again. After the first thirty lines, the emphasis of the poem is not on the spreading of the Gospel, the positive operation of the new Ark, but on the gradual corruption of the Church, and the progress of her travelling companion, Sin. Indeed, Herbert says gloomily that

> The latter Church is to the first a debter.
> The second Temple could not reach the first:
> And the late reformation never durst
> Compare with ancient times and purer yeares....
> Nay, it shall ev'ry yeare decrease and fade;
> Till such a darknesse do the world invade
> At Christ's last coming, as his first did finde.

Now, however much the typology of the holy of holies varied according to the purposes and predilections of the individual commentators, there is one quality which is constantly stressed — perfection. For Hall, its glory and blessedness are contrasted with the "Tumult and Vanity" of the Earth, the porch. For Andrewes it symbolizes the heart of Christ. For Hall, Donne, and Du Bartas, it is the place where Christ the High Priest "entred once for all" to make the perfect atonement. And for Du Bartas it corresponds to the epithalamion of Christ and his Church, expressed in the imagery of the Song of Songs. None of this symbolism is used or alluded to in "The Church Militant," except that in the opening section of the poem we are told that long ago, in her earliest beginnings, the Church *was* a fit Spouse:

> Trimme as the light, sweet as the laden boughs
> Of Noahs shady vine, chaste as the dove.

But she soon loses her chastity, and the poem ends not with a marriage, or even the promise of one, but with the threat of judgment. It is inconceivable that Herbert should have departed so far from traditional interpretations as to identify the holy of holies with a poem which is a satire on the corruption of the Church on earth.

Finally, it is inconceivable that Herbert should have called his holy of holies "The Church Militant" instead of "The Church Triumphant." When we think back to the careful and emphatic contrasts worked out by Donne between the partial and the complete, this world and that, the here and the hereafter — "Here in the *militant Church,* you stand in the *porch,* there in the *triumphant,* you shall stand *in sancto sanctorum*" — we realize that Herbert could never have intended such a reversal of terms. It would seem wiser not to force the third poem into the structure of *The Temple,* but to see it simply as earlier work included there for convenience. Alternatively one can satisfy the need for pattern by seeing a threefold structure of didactic, lyrical, and satirical poems.

If this is a more correct explanation of "The Church Militant," it
follows that Herbert, like Donne, is using only two architectural
divisions, not three. Once past the porch, "All equall are within the
churches gate."[25] This kind of Temple, in which there is no veil dividing
man from his God, is a much more suitable controlling metaphor for the
poet who could write an unusually virulent little Latin poem on the
"Velum scissum".[26]

> Frustra, Verpe, tumes, propola cultûs,
> Et Templi parasite; namque velum
> Diffissum reserat Deum latentem,
> Et pomoeria terminosque sanctos
> Non urbem facit unicam, sed Orbem.
> Et pro pectoribus recenset aras....

(In vain you swell with pride, O circumcised, huckster of ritual, parasite
of the Temple; for the cloven veil reveals the hidden God, and the
boundaries and the sacred limits. He does not merely unify a city, but the
whole world; and numbers his altars according to human hearts.) It is a
more suitable controlling metaphor for a collection of some of the most
intimate religious poems we have, and which ends with the invitation to
priest and layman alike:

> You must sit down, sayes Love, and taste my meat.

TIME AND *THE TEMPLE*

Stanley Stewart

In showing the influence of the meditation on the form of *The Temple* (1633), Professor Louis Martz draws attention to an interesting question in Herbert criticism, i.e., to what extent is *The Temple* (like a sonnet sequence) a patterned work of art of some length, made up of short poems, most of which manifest a structural integrity of their own?[1] Closely related to this question is another concerning that minority of Herbert poems which do not exhibit a firm integrity, but instead appear weak when considered apart from *The Temple*. Martz suggests the inappropriateness of evaluating certain poems without giving full consideration to their function in *The Temple*. In the case of "The Church-porch," this argument is especially significant. For in spite of the recent surge of interest in Herbert's work generally, this long poem continues to meet with critical indifference. Stiffly proverbial in language, didactic in intent, "The Church-porch" lacks the intensity of the Herbert lyrics so admired by critics. Concerned with precepts for the conduct of the moral life, "The Church-porch" treats of the "preparation for spiritual communion in prayer and meditation" which "The Sacrifice" and its succeeding liturgical pieces represent (Martz, p. 290). Thus, according to Martz, the lack of intensity in "Church-porch" is appropriate to the function of the poem within the larger context of *The Temple*; the critic must revalue the work with a full awareness of this function.

By arguing that the unity of *The Temple* depends on its appropriate structural relations, Professor Martz directs the critic's attention to "Church Militant" no less than to "Church-porch." Yet the former poem, the third part of Herbert's "tripartite arrangement," Martz finds weakly conjoined to the preceding sections:

> Certainly the first two parts are much more closely related than the last two. And certainly the "Church Militant," in many respects, may seem to represent a rather desperate effort to salvage, if only by way of appendix, a very early poem. (p. 289)

Reprinted from *SEL*, 6 (1966), 97-110, by permission of the author and William Marsh Rice University.

Since Martz does not return to "Church Militant" (his main concern is with the meditative structure of "The Church"), we are left with the question of the way in which this long poem fits into the sequence of *The Temple*, if indeed it fits into it at all.

Recently, John David Walker offered a possible answer to this question by suggesting that the structure of *The Temple* was analogous to "the architectural structure of the Hebraic temple," and that as such it was basically a "unified spatial structure."[2] This argument is not altogether satisfying, for it leads us to expect the third part of *The Temple*, as Herbert's analogue to "the Hebraic holy of holies," to carry through this "spatial structure," which it clearly does not do. In fact, Professor Martz's term "appendix" (if I may use the term in a somewhat different sense from that implied by Martz) more accurately describes the relation of "Church Militant" to "The Church" and "Church-porch." "Church Militant" follows "The Church" in time, though not in space; the transition between the two poems does not have, as comparison with the Hebrew temple suggests, a spatial aspect, and thus it differs from the earlier transition in kind.

I

As both Walker and Martz have pointed out, the transition between parts one and two of *The Temple* depends largely on the repetition of an analogy developed in "Church-porch" between space and time. "Super-liminare," placed between "Church-porch" and "The Church," reiterates the architectural pattern seen in the title and subtitle ("Perirrhanterium") of the first poem, thereby amplifying the theme of time's movement. Just as the pilgrim moves in space from the exterior into the main sanctuary of the Church, the soul moves in time from an earlier state of unpreparedness to a later one of preparedness. Herbert intends the sequence as a hieroglyphic of time's passage. The soul moves in time in the same way as the Temple — the highest achievement of the divine Architect (and on another level, of the poet too) — unfolds in time. The pilgrim enters the Church improved, but merely improved, by the moral (and therefore natural) crossing of "Church-porch." The passage of time has brought with it the awareness of his great need:

> A HEART alone
> Is such a stone
> As nothing but
> Thy pow'r doth cut.[3]

The altar's shape is the visual impression of God's power to "cut" the hard rock of man's will. Herbert returns to this figure, or to one like it again and again ("Nature," "Even-song," "The Priesthood"). They emphasize Herbert's theme of spiritual metamorphosis, which does not take place spontaneously, but results from the struggle between man's nature and divine Will ("Nature"). The outlines of this struggle bear the traces of divine artistry, but because of the limits of his perspective, man often fails to perceive it. Mistaking gratitude for submission to God's Will ("The Agonie," "The Crosse"), man tries to match the love-gift of the Sacrifice, and so to compete with his Creator. Always outstripped ("The Reprisall"), he learns, only after *"many spiritual Conflicts ... have past,"*[4] to humble his will before God's. The larger movements in "The Church" reflect the recursive quality of this struggle: time passes and man seems to experience the same conflict over and over. Yet that apparent sameness denies the one necessary condition of the Christian life. Change, though imperceptible at times, is inescapable. In this respect, like time, it is a limiting aspect of existence. The dramatic sense of this limitation imposed by time and change is, perhaps, the dominant theme of "The Church."

Like many of his Calvinist brethren, Herbert believed that the knowledge of this connection between time and change underlay man's anxiety, giving rise to despair. The universe around him and within him was in constant motion. The sense of duration haunted man, for ultimately duration was only another word for change, which was, in turn, a synonym for death. The idea of time, or the emblems with which that idea was connected, unfolded a sequence of mental equations, which prompted the awareness of the omnipresence of death. In the logic of these associations we find an important source of intensity in many of Herbert's finest poems. "The Flower" is a case in point.

At first glance, "The Flower" (pp. 165-167) is a poem of thanksgiving; the speaker senses in the present moment of God's blessing the tokens of spiritual rebirth: "How fresh, O Lord, how sweet and clean/Are thy returns! ev'n as the flowers in spring...." But underneath this gratitude lies a bitter memory of "late-past frosts." And since the past is the mirror of a potential future, it exercises a disturbing influence on the present. Just as winter passes, it returns, often with precipitous speed. For this reason, the speaker's recollection is rooted in anxiety:

> But while I grow in a straight line,
> Still upwards bent, as if heav'n were mine own,
> Thy anger comes, and I decline:
> What frost to that? what pole is not the zone
> Where all things burn,

> When thou dost turn,
> And the least frown of thine is shown?

The moment of assurance dissolves into an awful sense of the instability of spirit to which even the Elect are exposed. The figure of a winter tempest (the Creator's imagined frown) represents the ultimate danger of the Christian life: submission to despair. Any change in the surroundings might prompt a doubt; illness (the Bemerton years) might be a sign of God's displeasure and impending wrath.[5] For the sensitive Calvinist the pendulum swing in human consciousness between assurance and despair becomes the overriding norm of the Christian life: "These are thy wonders, Lord of power,/ Killing and quickning, bringing down to hell/And up to heaven in an houre."

As in spiritual autobiography, Herbert uses the flower image as a hieroglyphic of man's life: "And now in age I bud again,/After so many deaths I live and write." The winter-death of despair recurs because, at any given moment, man's life is neither understood nor fully seen. Anxiously absorbed in the moment (because aware of what the future may hold), he fails to discern the emerging design in life. Still, God's secrets are revealed to the proper reader in his Book of Creatures. The flower shadows forth the mystery of the Christian life, which man grasps only in hints and starts:

> Who would have thought my shrivel'd heart
> Could have recover'd greennesse? It was gone
> Quite under ground; as flowers depart
> To see their mother-root, when they have blown;
> Where they together
> All the hard weather,
> Dead to the world, keep house unknown.

Here, of course, is the mystery of the Incarnation, of man's death in life and life in death. The flower recedes, yet lives on, unaware both of its own life and of the source of that life. Though despair seems to overwhelm the spirit, the house of the Elect is sustained by the power of God's love. Despair is a quality imposed on man's experience because of his existence in time. He cannot see what time will unfold; at one moment it seems that the flower is dead, at another, not. But from yet another point of view, nothing has changed. There is a sense in which time is an illusion.[6]

For the same reason, there is a sense in which death also is illusory. Such a view may seem to contradict the point of Herbert's poem, but that contradiction is only apparent. It is true that in some cases the

flower is a figure of death: it is used that way in Herbert's "Life." But
even here the title gives the irony away; by reminding him of death the
"posie" summons man to renewed spiritual vigor. Time may beckon to
the flowers, but his intended audience is man, whom he wishes to lead to
a proper understanding of the present experience. That experience is, in
miniature, the whole of life, for it is a confrontation with Time
incarnate:

> My hand was next to them, and then my heart:
> I took, without more thinking, in good part
> Times gentle admonition:
> Who did so sweetly deaths sad taste convey,
> Making my minde to smell my fatal day;
> Yet sugring the suspicion.   (p. 94)

"Times gentle admonition" concerns the value of what time remains in
life. Duration itself is of little importance; what matters is the quality of
time spent. The meaning is that man must properly respond to Time's
implied imperative. Just so in "The Flower":

> These are thy wonders, Lord of love,
> To make us see we are but flowers that glide:
> Which when we once can finde and prove,
> Thou hast a garden for us, where to bide.

Just as in "Life" Time made man aware of the imminence of death, so in
"The Flower" the Almighty "makes" him aware of time's swift passage.
In this light, the experiences which had seemed so like rehearsals of
death are recognized as the source of eternal life. Man's limited point of
view had restrained him from seeing that the "Lord of power" and the
"Lord of love" were one. Moreover, the contrast between assurance and
despair which had made life seem like an endless hurtling between hell
and heaven was simply the means by which God taught man the lesson
of his mortality. When he learned that, he found peace. Ultimately, man
was placed in time to make this simple choice: to accept the limits
imposed by time ("To make us see we are but flowers that glide"), or to
aim beyond them. Scripture described the consequences of the latter
choice:

> Who would be more
> Swelling through store,
> Forfeit their Paradise by their pride.

As the last stanza of "The Flower" suggests, just as time and death are
illusory, so, finally, is change itself. The speaker's prayer, "O that I once

past changing were,/ Fast in thy Paradise, where no flower can wither,"
had been answered eons before it was made. Indeed, at another time, the
pilgrim seems to know this, for he gives thanks for his inclusion in
"Paradise": "I Blesse thee, Lord, because I GROW/ Among thy trees
..." (p. 132). There was a medieval tradition, perpetuated in the
literature and iconography of the seventeenth century, which identified
the "Paradise" of the Church with *hortus conclusus*. The relevant text is
from the Song of Songs: "A garden inclosed is my sister, my spouse; a
spring shut up, a fountain sealed." In the literature and art of the Middle
Ages and the Renaissance, the garden wall referred to the protection of
the Church through the dispensation of Grace. Perhaps Herbert has this
tradition in mind when he writes:

> What open force, or hidden CHARM
> Can blast my fruit, or bring me HARM,
> While the inclosure is thine ARM?

By representing the division between nature and Grace, the wall pointed
up the distinction between the time-bound and the timeless. The mystery
of the Christian experience was that, though in time, man existed
outside of time, for he was born of the spirit as well as of the flesh.

Insofar as he was a creature of time, man must die. And as the
sequence of Christian holidays in "The Church" suggests, man's year on
earth passed swiftly.[7] Yet while it passed man could, like the flower,
recapitulate the wonder of Christ's death and transfiguration. To the
Christian, time was no enemy, but rather, as comparison between
Herbert's "Time" and a poem like Aurelian Townshend's "A Dialogue
Betwixt Time and a Pilgrime" will show, time was the dresser of God's
timeless garden.[8] The sacramental interpretation of the Incarnation
placed man's every experience in relation to the timeless. That is why in
Herbert's "Time" (pp. 122-123) the figure of Time is reduced from the
aggressive deliverer of homilies and poser of riddles seen in such poems
as Townshend's "Dialogue" to a conciliatory figure — from an "execu-
tioner at best" to a "gard'ner." For, as Herbert writes in "Paradise," each
moment is the beginning as well as the end of time. With respect to
Christian truth, the prolongation of life becomes the scourge of the soul
("Time"): "For to me to live is Christ, and to die is gain"(Phil. 1:21).

It seems to me that now the full richness of Martz's remarks
concerning the closing sequence in "The Church" may be seen. The soul
has entered time, passed through "this school" of the Church, and
learned of its sordid origins and humble destiny: "Comparing dust with
dust, and earth with earth" ("Church-monuments"). Having properly

applied the meaning of his encounter with time, he knows that the body
is an hourglass, measuring out the sands of itself:

> Deare flesh, while I do pray, learn here thy stemme
> And true descent: that when thou shalt grow fat,
>
> And wanton in thy cravings, thou mayst know,
> That flesh is but the glasse, which holds the dust
> That measures all our time; which also shall
> Be crumbled into dust. Mark here below
> How tame these ashes are, how free from lust,
> That thou mayst fit thy self against thy fall. (p. 65)

Beginning with "The Forerunners," we may trace the approach of
Death. "The Rose" is a reminder that true pleasures wait upon that final
union, which is now but moments off.[9] Except for reiteration of that
theme in "Discipline," the sequence ("The Invitation" and "The Banquet")
heralds the end of time. "The Posie," with its delicate emphasis on God's
mercy, is juxtaposed against the final recurrence of doubt ("A Parodie")
before "Death."

In four poems on "the last things" we may follow the soul's pilgrimage
beyond death: "Doomsday," "Judgement," "Heaven," "Love III." The
last poem in "The Church," "Love III," completes the pattern begun in
"The Invitation" and "Banquet." The soul, having passed through time,
succumbs at last to the overpowering love of God, and is seated at the
banquet table in the Heavenly City. One is tempted to say in this context
that even the "*FINIS*" is part of Herbert's poetic design, for the odyssey
of the soul, and so the passage of the Church through time as seen from
the individual's point of view, has ended.

II

We are now in a position to consider the function of "Church
Militant" in *The Temple*. As with "Church-porch," the placement of this
poem is a hieroglyphic of a temporal relation. The absence of intensity in
"Church Militant," like that in "Church-porch," cannot be detached
from the function of the poem within the larger structure. The voice in
"Church Militant" does not sound with the wonderfully intense tones of
a soul in agony precisely because it belongs to one who exists apart from
time; and time is the defining feature of a world in which change and
anxiety exist. The speaker in "Church Militant" sees the world with the
vision of one in a state outside of life, a state which was achieved by the
proper redemption of time in life. "Church Militant" is an apocalyptic

poem; its tone is detached and austere because its speaker sees the past, the present, and the future with equal clarity.

"Church Militant" is set off from "The Church" in such a way as to suggest a deliberate "distancing" of the two sections. The reason for this is simple: the present transition differs from the earlier one in kind. Most obviously, the spatial analogy seen in the movement from "Church-porch" beneath "Superliminare" to "The Church" has no counterpart between "The Church" and "Church Militant" because the separation between the latter sections is a final one ("*FINIS*"). It is not a movement from one time and place to another, but from time to the timeless. Space has no part in such a movement. The way has been laid for the recognition of an entirely new dimension in *The Temple*; "Church Militant" is a poem concerned, not with the struggle of the soul in time, but with the movement of the Church throughout all time.

Critics have noted the similarity in structure and content between "Church Militant" and Donne's "First Anniuersary."[10] Both poems deal with the passage of time; both are divided into parts by a refrain. Donne's poem treats of history in the natural sense; it pictures the progressive separation of man and nature from their prelapsarian state. During this "progress" the universe has decayed. Herbert's poem, on the other hand, interprets history through the use of three allegorical figures: the Church, Religion, and Sin. Time is traced in the movements of the Sun, which are followed by the Church. In "The Church," the time of life was seen as the passing of one year; in "Church Militant," all of time is seen as the passing of one day: ". . . one day is with the Lord as a thousand years, and a thousand years as one day."

The long day of history is divided into epochs by a refrain: "*How deare to me, O God, thy counsels are!/ Why may with thee compare?*" An intuitive reading of this passage might go something like this:

> I praise thee, Oh Lord, for the sustaining value of thy Word, with
> its promises; You are incomparable, supreme.

Such a paraphrase would be true to the tone of the refrain, and this is important, for it is here that Herbert makes his meditative intention clear. For his refrain, Herbert returns to the Psalms, and to one in particular, which, as one commentator expressed it, was "*A meditation of the omnipresence of God, and a prayer that we may alwaies walk in his sight.*"[11] But the above paraphrase leaves the figure of God's "counsels" unexplained. For to call God's "counsels" promises is to make only an educated guess. Actually, the refrain is a pastiche of lines from verses in Psalms 89 and 139, respectively:

For who in heaven can be compared unto the LORD? who among the sons of the mighty can be likened unto the LORD? (6)

How precious also are thy thoughts unto me, O God: how great is the summe of them? (17)

Why did Herbert select lines from these two Psalms, and from these two verses in particular, for his refrain?

An answer to this question may help explain Herbert's purpose in making "Church Militant" part of *The Temple*, and having decided that, in placing the poem last, rather than first or second, in the sequence. The question hinges partly on the reason Herbert linked the two verses. Unfortunately, Herbert did not write a commentary on the Psalms. But as a clergyman and poet who loved and paraphrased the Psalms, he had no doubt read many of the popular expositions. He may have believed with one of his contemporaries that the 89th Psalm expressed the Prophet's gratitude for "the goodnes of God ... For his testament and couenant, that he had made between him and his elect by Iesus Christ the sonne of Dauid.'[12] Similarly, much of Herbert's poem might appear to be about "the great ruin and desolation of the kingdom of Dauid, so that the outward appearance of the promes was broken ...." The corruption of the Church gave even the faithful reason to wonder at God's design. What, after all, was the meaning of a world in which the Church was overrun by Sin, and in which darkness was always but one step behind the light?

According to Calvin's exposition, Psalm 89 advanced an eloquent answer to this question, for here King David (or *"whosoeuer he was that was the author of this Psalme") commendeth in generall the power of GOD, whiche is seene in the whole gouernaunce of the world."*[13] The verse paraphrased by Herbert (and rendered by Calvin, "For who shall be equall to the Lorde in the Cloudes, or bee like too [sic] the Lorde among the sonnes of the Gods") meant that "god reigneth alonly soueraign" in the heavens, and thus, "that god doth actually dispose whatsoeuer is done in heauen and earth. For it were against reason, that the heauens beeying created by God, should now be rolled by fortune: and that things should be mingled vpon earth, either at the pleasure of men, or by chaunce æ casualty."[14] This passage from the Psalms was meant as a rejoinder to any doubts raised with respect to the direction of any particular in nature. All movements in space and time were perfectly guided, their ends known and ordained by an omniscient, omnipotent Creator. As we read in Ainsworth's *Annotations*, in Psalm 139 *"David praiseth God for his all-seeing providence ...."*[15]

If, as I believe, Herbert's refrain alludes to the idea of Providence,

then, as the history of the Church unfolds, the speaker reminds himself
at intervals of the orderliness of God's plan in creation. The lines treat of
God's infinite "wisdom in ye creatio of ma."[16] In this way the refrain
does more than simply invoke a meditative tone; it places the past
struggles of the soul in time (as pictured in "The Church") in a wider and
final perspective. Pain, despair — the aspects of evil in human experience
— are simply tokens of the limits of human life, images of the time-
bound. Because they exist only in the illusory domain of time, they lack
substance. For all that is real endures, and that is what accords with
God's Will. This had been Herbert's theme in "The Church," and so it
remains in "Church Militant":

> Almightie Lord, who from thy glorious throne
> Seest and rulest all things ev'n as one:
> The smallest ant or atome knows thy power,
> Known also to each minute of an houre:
> Much more do Common-weals acknowledge thee,
> And wrap their policies in thy decree,
> Complying with thy counsels, doing nought
> Which doth not meet with an eternall thought. (p. 190)

God's "counsels" and his "eternall thought" are the same as His
"decree." Here in the opening lines of "Church Militant" Herbert states
his major theme of Providence. Throughout the poem the progress of
the minutes, hours, years, and ages which make up history unfolds, and
in its entirety proves what is "Known also to each minute of an houre."
At every moment, and throughout all time, the world is ordered by
God's love.

Here and throughout "Church Militant" the emphasis is on God's
Providence as seen in His creation. While it is true that Sin pursues the
Church from the beginning of time:

> Much about one and the same time and place
> Both where and when the Church began her race,
> Sinne did set out of Eastern *Babylon*.
> And travell'd westward also ... (pp. 192-193),

in the final analysis Sin lacks substance ("Sinne"). Like the darkness
which would overtake the world before the dawn of eternal day, Sin and
Death were the specters of time. In God's mind, however, every instant
and the sum of all instants aimed at a single moment:

> Nay, it shall ev'ry yeare decrease and fade;
> Till such a darknesse do the world invade
> At Christs last coming, as his first did finde. (p. 196)

All of time past aimed at time present: all of time present aimed at time future, and the sun moved steadily westward as the day of creation ran its course. Everything was planned; all was proportion and design. Indeed, the perfection of God's plan was nowhere better revealed than in the paradox of time. For as the sun runs west, it comes east. As time fulfills its cyclic, self-destructive pattern, the Church moves toward the dawn of that wedding envisaged by St. John:

> Thus also Sinne and Darknesse follow still
> The Church and Sunne with all their power and skill.
> But as the Sunne still goes both west and east;
> So also did the Church by going west
> Still eastward go; because it drew more neare
> To time and place, where judgement shall appeare.
> *How deare to me, O God, thy counsels are!*
> *Who may with thee compare?* (p. 198)

Now Herbert's speaker clearly sees what he could not see in life, when time appeared as a solely linear phenomenon: as long as time existed there would be physical motion and spiritual unrest. But every movement expressed God's unchanging Will. Just as the pain of human life was part of a larger design, the trials and tribulations of the Church must also be seen in perspective. Only a part of that perspective was available to man in time. It is true that "Church Militant" seems like an "appendix" to *The Temple*, but as such it is the appropriate denouement of a larger poetic whole. The speaker of "Church Militant," who views creation in the fulness of time, is able to pronounce (after a short "L'Envoy") a second, final, and soul satisfying "*FINIS.*" For now the whole of God's design lies open to his view.

THE UNITY OF GEORGE HERBERT'S
THE TEMPLE: A RECONSIDERATION

Valerie Carnes

The structure of George Herbert's *The Temple* has been the subject of considerable critical controversy. Scholarly opinion has run the gamut from articles purporting to have discovered an irrefutable principle of organization to those works which write off the whole collection as an anthology of religious verse, interesting enough for its individual poems, but lacking overall thematic and structural unity. For example, in *A Reading of George Herbert* [1] Rosemond Tuve attempts to establish the relationship between Herbert's poems and an elaborate and rather diffuse system of traditional and publicly-known correspondences and analogies on which medieval and Renaissance popular theology was based, while Rosemary Freeman's *English Emblem Books* [2] elaborates Miss Tuve's suggestions as she studies the "almost wholly visual" nature of Herbert's imagery in its obvious indebtedness to Quarles' *Emblemes* and other similar books. A somewhat more tenable thesis on the subject is developed in Joseph H. Summers' *George Herbert: His Religion and Art*, [3] a reconsideration of *The Temple* as Herbert's own attempt to imitate the supreme unity and order of God's creations.

In addition to these three main sources, at least two periodical articles treat the question of unifying factors in *The Temple;* Elizabeth Stambler's "The Unity of Herbert's 'Temple,'" [4] and John David Walker's "The Architectonics of George Herbert's *The Temple*." [5] Miss Stambler finds the collection held together by its resemblance to volumes of courtly love poetry, such as *La Vita Nuova*, Petrarch's *Rima* or perhaps *Astrophel and Stella*. The themes of loss and discipline, leading at last to purified desire, serve as a link between secular and sacred traditions. Further points of similarity are the consistent *persona* of the poet, God characterized as a woman, and the eye-heart motif. Walker's explication, which is a bit more flexible and convincing, suggests a threefold structure for the collection, consisting of architectural, cosmological

From *ELH,* 35 (1968), 505-26. © Copyright 1968 by The Johns Hopkins University Press. Reprinted by permission of the author and The Johns Hopkins University Press.

and psychological analogies which are carried throughout the whole work. The integration of the three strands, he suggests, comes in "The Church Militant" where the point of view is neither simply human nor simply divine, but is rather that of the soul united with its God and thus able to see perfectly past, present and future as one time.

This tripartite scheme is an interesting one, but proves itself at many points inadequate for a full-scale analysis of *The Temple*. Walker's thesis suggests, for example, that the poem is a linear progression from one level of religious experience directly to another and higher one — from "The Church Porch" straight to "The Church" itself and hence to the "omniscient" vision of "The Church Militant." Unfortunately, the matter is not quite so simple as Walker's article would lead us to believe. Although there is an overall progression to be noted in the poet's shift from the didacticism of the earlier pieces to the apocalyptic mood of "L'Envoy," within the general pattern of the progression there are numerous alternations, numerous shifts in mood and tone, resolutions temporarily reached and equally temporary reversions back to the old questionings and rebellions. Therefore it is to the text itself that we must turn for a clue to the intended source of unity within the poems which comprise this extraordinary work.

Perhaps the best key to Herbert's intended principle of unity in *The Temple* is to be found in the title of the book itself. Throughout the various poems, the physical temple itself remains the collection's presiding metaphor, existing simultaneously as the Hebraic tabernacle, the Christian church universal, the physical church of Herbert's own day, the human heart, and finally, the poems themselves as God's dwelling place. In a very real sense the temple itself is the collection's presiding metaphor, suggestive of a fusion of words, music, sermons, the immobile drama of statues, paintings, and images, and the living drama of the liturgy and the religious theater. All of these subordinate figures of speech have one thing in common: they all are earthly symbols of God, concrete images which point to a higher metaphysical reality. The whole book is, in fact, a poetic exposition of the nature of symbolic perception. Herbert's subject is not only God, both as Incarnation and as abstraction, and His meaning to man, but also meaning in general; not only *what* the focal symbols mean, but also how they gain their significance. In view of this fact, then, it is not surprising that the analogy between man's religious and aesthetic activity emerges as a predominant theme in *The Temple*. The artistic dimension of the poem is neither secondary nor peripheral; it is precisely the dimension in which the collection's chief drama is enacted, and through which Herbert's sense of the correspondence between human creativity and human conduct reaches its most thorough and complex expression.

This reading of *The Temple* as an analogy between man's religious and aesthetic activities can be supported by textual evidence within the poems themselves. "Sion," for example, suggests that the Biblical temple from which Herbert's poem borrows its title was not ony a place of worship; it was also an artistic construct, designed for the double goal of pleasing both man and God:

> Lord, with what glorie wast thou serv'd of old,
> When Solomons temple stood and flourished!
>   Where most things were of purest gold;
>   The wood was all embellished
> With flowers and carvings, mysticall and rare:
> All show'd the builders, crav'd the seers care. (ll. 1-6)

An even more specific analogy is established between religion and literary endeavor in the numerous poems which represent God as Logos and as Author — an image which controls "The Altar" and also informs numerous other poems, including "Good Friday," "Jesu," and "Sepulchre." Man's heart is an altar erected to the glory of God, but ironically, its stone composition contributes to its hardness past redemption. Only the authorial activity of God, who alone is capable of writing on the hard stone, revivifies the dead material and makes it pliable again. Herbert sees in God the word, the Logos, the essence of which ideally should be apprehended directly and immediately with no intervening steps. Thus he states in "The Flower," "Thy word is all, if we could spell" (l. 21). That "if" is a large one, however, and is not easily overlooked. Although direct communication between man and God might have been possible in "the days when thou didst lodge with Lot" ("Decay," l. 1), man cannot now perceive Divinity on its own terms. God must reveal His infinity to man in finite forms — images, symbols, types, hieroglyphs — which can serve as the basis for a higher form of apprehension. Thus in "The Agonie" "who would know Sinne" (l. 7) must find it imaged forth in the Christ of Mt. Olivet, while "who knows not Love" (l. 13) is advised to seek its visual representation in the flowing blood of the crucified Savior and hence, by extension, in the sacrament of the Eucharist.

It is important that we remind ourselves that for the seventeenth century this image of God as author was more than an interesting figure of speech. Although angels (and perhaps prelapsarian man) might be capable of the direct perception of timeless essences, in the words of Thomas Aquinas, "To know God, man, in his condition after the Fall, needs a medium, which is like a mirror in which appears the image of

God, for it is necessary that we arrive at the invisible things of Him from the things that are made, according to Romans I."[6] It is from Aquinas' view of the matter, perhaps, that the medieval mind conceived the image of the book of nature, the book of life, and the Scriptures as God's writings — an idea which persisted into the Renaissance and later. Only ten years before the publication of Herbert's *Temple* John Donne had written:

> My God, my God, thou art a direct God, may I not say a literal God, a God that wouldst be understood literally and according to the plain sense of all that thou sayest? but thou art also ... a figurative, a metaphorical God too; a God in whose words there is such a height of figures, such voyages, such peregrinations to fetch remote and precious metaphors, such extensions, such spreadings, such curtains of allegories, such third heavens of hyperboles, so harmonious elocutions, so retired and so reserved expressions, so commanding persuasions, so persuading commandments, such sinews even in thy milk, and such things in thy words as all profane authors seem of the seed of the serpent that creeps, thou art the Dove that flies. . . . Neither art thou thus a figurative, a metaphoricall God in the word only, but in thy works too. The style of thy works, the phrase of thine actions, is metaphorical. The institution of thy whole worship in the old law was a continual allegory; types and figures overspread all, and figures flowed into figures, and poured themselves out into further figures; circumcision carried a figure of baptism, and baptism carries a figure of that purity which we shall have in perfection in the new Jerusalem. Neither didst thou speak and work in this language only in the time of thy prophets; but since thou spokest in thy Son it is so too. How often, how much more often, doth thy Son call himself a way, and a light, and a fate, and a wine, and bread, than the Son of God, or of man? How much oftener doth he exhibit a metaphorical Christ, than a real, a literal? This hath occasioned thine ancient servants, whose delight it was to write after thy copy, to proceed the same way in their expositions of the Scriptures, and in their composing both of public liturgies and of private prayers to thee, to make their accesses to thee in such a kind of language as thou wast pleased to speak to them, in a figurative, in a metaphorical language ....[7]

Thus the symbolic method of expression emerges as the way of Divine manifestation which man is to imitate. Behind *The Temple* lies a certain analogical cast of mind that could conceive God simultaneously as Author and Logos, as Great Artificer and as Supreme Beauty. The theory of art implicit in the work as a whole assumes the form of a cycle of which God is both origin and end; the Divine Logos is allowed to descend earthward in visual or imagistic form and to re-ascend in verbal form as the poet's own song of praise. The nature of this cycle is well defined in this passage from Samuel Mather's introduction to Stone's *A Congregational Church is a Catholike Visible Church:*

> All the Arts are nothing else but the beams and rays of the Wisdom of the *first Being* in the Creatures, shining, and reflecting thence, upon the glass of man's understanding; and as from *Him* they come, so to him they tend: the circle of Arts is a *Deo ad Deum.* Hence there is an affinity and kindred of Arts (*omnes Artes vinculo & cognatione quadem inter se continentur*: Cicer. pro. Arch. Poet.) which is according to the reference and subordination of their particular ends, to the utmost and last end: One makes use of another, one serves to another, till they all reach and return to Him, as Rivers to the Sea, whence they flow.[8]

This religious-aesthetic cycle serves as a structural basis for the entire group of poems, each section of which represents one phase of the cycle. These three stages we may somewhat arbitrarily designate as 1) descent of the sacred Word in visual images, often with an allegorical or didactic meaning, which man must learn to recognize and interpret; 2) verbal re-expression of the sacred Word through the secular word, particularly the words of poems and prayers; and 3) reunion of secular word with sacred Word. *The Temple* clearly is motivated by the religious impulse and always returns to that focal point. But the interim between the Dedication and "The Church Militant" is a long one, capable of encompassing almost every quality and degree of religious experience known to mankind, and these various degrees of experience are suggested not only by the subject matter of the three sections, but also by the various distinctive levels of discourse. Let us see how this is true.

The frankly didactic, often sermonizing tone of "The Church Porch" may have prevented this section's receiving its due share of critical attention. Yet its existence may be justified simply in terms of its use as a symbolic gathering-place for the imaginary congregation before services — a function which, as Mr. Walker has noted in his explication of the poem, corresponds to the court of the old Hebraic temple. An even stronger case for the appropriateness of this section, however, can be made in terms of the *Deo ad Deum* cycle just described, as the first four lines of the Dedication suggest:

> Lord, my first fruits present themselves to thee;

> Yet not mine neither, for from thee they came,
> And must return. Accept of them and me,
> And make us strive, who shall sing best thy name.
>
> (ll. 1-4)

Once the Logos has descended to earth in symbolic form — that is, through nature, conceived by Herbert, as by Donne and other seventeenth-century writers as radically figurative, the Scriptures, and the Incarnation of Christ — man's task is to learn to recognize, to read and hence to interpet these visual signs which were placed on earth for his benefit. And in order to do so, he needs instruction at the hands of the priest who, as type and symbol of Christ, is obligated to follow "that which Christ did, and after His manner, both for Doctrines and for Life."[9] As Summers notes, the poet's verses here metaphorically become both wreaths for the Altar of God and fruits of edification for others on earth, communicating to them the fitness of symbolic forms and inflaming them with the desire to follow "the beautie of holinesse." Just as Christ revealed Himself to man in parables and miracles, so the poet-preacher must work in a similarly symbolic method in order to make present to his readers and hearers the religious reality of which he is aware. First, however, he must instruct his flock in the reading of God's symbolic method of signs working outward from the known to the unknown, from the natural to the supernatural, from the domestic to the Divine. Thus the section begins with its first poem proclaiming itself the work of a verser who, following Horace's notion that the poet should "inform or delight, or ... combine together, in what he says, both pleasure and applicability to life,"[10] may "chance"

> Rhyme thee to good, and make a bait of pleasure.
> A verse may find him, who a sermon flies,
> And turn delight into a sacrifice.
> ("The Church Porch," I, ll. 3-6)

The perspective throughout this section clearly is that of the preacher or the didactic poet, who has taken upon himself the task of discovering and explicating the visual symbols through which Divinity manifests itself. Thus much of the language is discursive in nature; symbols are infrequent, and the few metaphors used are directed almost entirely toward an understanding of the rituals which God has instituted as outward signs of inward states. Thus lust is discouraged because it blots "the lesson" written in blood on the soul of man through the sacrament of baptism, while incontinence is denounced as a violation of the sacrament of holy matrimony.

It would be an obvious critical oversimplification, however, to say that all of the language in "The Church Porch" is pure discursive statement. Although many of the so-called "poems" are little more than assertive prose cast in verse and directed toward the teaching of a moral lesson, the predominant mode of discourse is that of simple image — an elemental form of metaphor which, although strong in sensuous appeal, gives the reader little or no sense of a higher abstraction. Something of the theory behind Herbert's use of image in this section is suggested by the following passage from *The Countrey Parson or, A Priest to the Temple*:

> Doubtlesse the Holy Scripture intends thus much, when it con-descends to the naming of a plough, a hatchet, a bushell, leaven, boyes piping and dancing; shewing that things of ordinary use are not only to serve in the way of drudgery, but to be washed, and cleansed, and serve for lights even of Heavenly Truths.[11]

One of the most memorable features of this prose work is Herbert's unusual awareness of the need to match the mode of discourse to the level of sophistication of the audience. Thus it is no accident that the figures in "The Church Porch" are elemental, realistic, "earthy," domestic, all of a sort calcualted to appeal to the simple parishioners who might gather each week on the church porch. By their appeal to the known and familiar, these figures seek to increase the average parish-ioner's or reader's awareness of the practical applications of religion to daily social and domestic life. Many of these images are quite literally rooted in the earth — for example, the figure of the human soul as a "poore clod of earth" ("The Church Porch," IX, l. 6) which not infrequently dares to defy "the spacious sky" ("The Church Porch," IX, l. 6), or the recurrent image of man as a beast, "impal'd" ("The Church Porch," IV, l. 3) by God's precepts. Other analogies are drawn from domestic life, like the priest's diatribe against obscenity and needless oaths that ends with the words, "He pares his apple, that will cleanly feed" ("The Church Porch," XI, l. 4).

As "The Church Porch" progresses, the images, like the precepts to which they point, become increasingly sophisticated and more strikingly original. Many poems which begin on a note of pure didacticism ("Play not for gain, but sport," "The Church Porch," XXXIII, l. 1) end with an image vivid and memorable enough to rival some of those in the subsequent sections of the book ("Onely a herauld, who that way doth passe,/ Finds his crackt name at length in the church-glasse," "The Church Porch," XXXIII, ll. 5-6). The images, then, become progressively less visually oriented and more abstract in nature — a progression which is suggested by one of the last poems in the series:

> In time of service seal up both thine eies,
> And send them to thine heart; that spying sinne,
> They may weep out the stains by them did rise:
> Those doores being shut, all by the eare comes in.
> ("The Church Porch," LXX, ll. 1-4)

Here the reader cannot help being reminded of Donne's pronouncement that while the eye is the Devil's doorway, the ear is the gateway to God. Certainly "The Church Porch" follows in this auditorially oriented tradition. If we consider the collection as a series of instructions to the worshipper about to be inducted into the Church proper, it is only natural that the collection should progress as it does from the visual image built around moral analogies drawn from nature and daily life to an auditory phase of understanding. The parishioner thus is led by slow and easy degrees from one level, one mode of cognition and perception to another and more abstract one. Further, this imaginary parishioner is encouraged to turn from the purely sensuous visual object as a medium of religious experience toward the more verbally oriented mode of understanding suggested by the poems in "The Church"; to make the imaginative leap required to move from the known image with clearly allegorical and didactic intent to the less familiar, more ambiguous symbol. Indeed, many poems in "The Church Porch" contain clearly metaphorical statements, including "O crumble not away thy souls fair heap" ("The Church Porch," XII, l. 4), "The stormie working soule spits lies and froth" (XIII, l. 4), and "God gave thy soul brave wings" (XIV, l. 2) which clearly anticipate the more flexible and hence more "symbolic" images that inform later poems. Another such anticipation of the Church proper is found in Herbert's favorite analogy between the physical temple and the human heart, introduced in the lines, "Christ purg'd his temple; so must thou thy heart" ("The Church Porch," LXXII, l. 3). Just as the temple is to be ornamented and simplified at the appropriate seasons, so man is cautioned to "dresse and undresse thy soul; mark the decay,/ And growth of it" ("The Church Porch," LXXVI, ll. 3-4). "Superliminaire" effects a further transition from the sermonizing of the "Church Porch" to the more sophisticated level of discourse in "The Church" itself. Here Herbert clearly suggests that the didacticism and the "former precepts" ("Superliminaire," line 1) of the earlier section have "sprinkled and taught" (l. 2) and thus have served the purpose of instruction before baptism and subsequent admission into the church itself. Mary Ellen Rickey in her *Utmost Art* has demonstrated that the Greek term "Perrihanterium," the subtitle affixed to "The Church Porch," denotes a sprinkling brush used for preceremonial cleansing. As Miss Rickey comments, Herbert's

> instrument of cleansing is the collection of ethical injunctions compressed in "The Church Porch," which, if followed by his fictional visitor, would enable him through his own efforts to achieve chastity, sobriety, frugality of diet, truthfulness, industry, modesty, humility, cleanliness, and generosity to the poor. These are the qualities which, actually practiced by the Christian, prepare him for entering the Church proper, and which, by implication, transcend the ancient's passive acceptance of preliturgical sprinkling.[12]

The subject thus edified is invited to come and taste "the churches mysticall repast" (l. 4) — a prefiguration of the sacrament of Holy Communion which points to the increasingly symbolic nature of the subsequent section.

The right reading of the visual analogues in the Books of Nature and of the creatures, then, emerges as the major concern of "The Church Porch." Interpretation, however, is only one stage in the cycle which *The Temple* embodies; a second and even more important phase of human activity, both religious and aesthetic, is the re-expression of the sacred Word, which God has rendered down to man in visual form, through the secular word. Read in this way, man's creation of poetic praise functions as living proof and acknowledgement of his right reading and interpretation of those visual signs placed on earth for his benefit. It is no coincidence that Herbert in this section expresses his conception of the art-religion analogy through the consistent *persona* of the poet whose aesthetics are presented in both their theoretical and practical aspects — both by explicit references to his theories of poetry and other arts, and to the process of aesthetic creativity in general, as well as by the highly symbolic forms and language which he employs. It is not surprising, therefore, to discover that well over 100 of the some 170 poems which comprise "The Church" are concerned with art in general and methods of symbolic perception in particular, while many of the others contain explicit statements on the matter. Numerous poems in the first category, however, do less toward formulating a specific aesthetics than toward simply establishing and illuminating the intimate relationship among the various art forms. For example, analogies with the drama come naturally to the pen of this poet-priest with his intense awareness of the dramatic potentialities of the Christian message — an awareness which doubtless grew out of his intimate knowledge of the liturgy and the Sacraments of the Church, suggested by such poems as "H. Baptisme," "The H. Communion," "Confession," and "The Priesthood." This sense of the effectiveness of dramatic form as a medium for communicating religious reality is reflected not only in the content but also in the form of many poems in "The Church." Herbert's favorite poetic form, in fact, appears to be the dramatic colloquy — either one-sided conversation that posits an imaginary listener, human or divine, an argument between the two halves of a divided soul, or a dialogue between the poet and his God. Thus we have poems like "Heaven," conceived as a dialogue between the poet and Echo, or "Antiphon II," which like its companion piece is a dialogue between solo voice and chorus about the verbal praise of God. And what is articulated in these dialogues is a comprehensive view of human life in an ideal extension of its latent possibilities. While the vision may be formulated in the orderly language of quasi-rational thought, as was the case in "The Church Porch," it also takes form in a recurring pattern of images which, taken together, form an assumed dramatic design for the representative life. Man's proper role according to Herbert was to act in every instance out of an entire communion with God; whatever he did of and for himself alone was sinful. And significantly, the way of artistic endeavor is for Herbert an integral part of this pattern for the ideal life.

Even more crucial to this design than the dramatic analogy is the relationship between music and poetry, here conceived as an exceptionally intimate one. The poem entitled "Christmas," for example, contains a promise of continued artistic endeavor on the part of the poet "Till ev'n his beams sing, and my musick shine" ("Christmas," l. 34) — a skillful interchange of the attributes of the two arts which strongly suggests their essential identity. If, as "The Church Porch" seems to indicate, the essence of divinity is made manifest to man through the medium of sight, it is through the medium of sound that the fallen visual image is re-elevated and returned to its original source. Significantly enough, the two chief means by which the re-ascent of this image is accomplished are prayer and, on a slightly higher level, the poet's hymns of praise. Music and poetry, both separately and together, are exalted above visual media which are portrayed as limited modes of communication, subject to the effects of the spiritual blindness that plagues even the best of men. In contrast to this motif of blindness, around the song-poem equation centers a whole symbolic cluster composed of the soaring motion of flight and the heat and light of God and thus corresponding to the "trinitie of light,/ Motion, and heat" to which Herbert refers in "The Starre" (ll. 17-18).

It is, however, not music but poetry which is most exalted in "The Church" — perhaps because, as Northrop Frye has observed, a literary construct combines all the arts in "the flow of sounds approximating music on one side, and an integrated pattern of imagery approximating the pictorial on the other."[13] Poetry, then, not only appears in this section as the aesthetic "norm"; it frequently is raised to the level of actual religious imperative. The poet's obligation to reflect in his verses a reality which is essentially spiritual in nature introduces, in turn, the whole question of the relationship between appearance and reality and the related aesthetic problem of the relative merits of beauty and truth — concerns both of which are debated back and forth at some length in numerous poems, including "Love I," "Jordan I and II," and "The Forerunners." "Jordan I" begins with a lament:

> Who sayes that fictions onely and false hair
> Become a verse? Is there in truth no beautie?
> Is all good structure in a winding stair?
> May no lines passe, except they do their dutie
> Not to a true, but a painted chair?   (ll. 1-5)

Throughout this section Herbert's view of the appearance-reality relationship appears to adhere rather closely to the classical Christian conviction that religious reality embraces or is manifest in all genuine reality — a concept which in the twentieth century has served as the basis not only for Mircea Eliade's identification of the real and the sacred, but also for Paul Tillich's assertion that religious symbols open up for a man a transcendent reality evident in all human experience. The conventional lyric, Herbert argues in "Jordan I," is a false representation, a false equation of appearance and actuality. Only the religious lyric can adequately represent for Herbert the true relationship between these two dimensions. Although "Jordan II," seems to move closer to a solution of the poet's dilemma in the lines,

> But while I bustled, I might heare a friend
> Whisper, How wide is all this long pretence!
> There is in love a sweetnesse readie-penn'd,
> Copie out onely that, and save expense,   (ll. 15-19)

the final resolution of the question is reserved for "The Forerunners" where Herbert concludes that God is not only Supreme Artificer but also Absolute Beauty which must be re-united with the poet's own re-expression of it:

> True beautie dwells on high: ours is a flame
> But borrow'd thence to light us thither.
> Beautie and beauteous words should go together.
> (ll. 28-30)

As we move from the theoretical to the practical aspects of Herbert's art-religion analogy, the poem which most immediately engages our attention is "Coloss. 3":

> My words and thoughts do both expresse this notion,
> That Life hath with the sun a double motion.
> The first is straight, and our diurnall friend,
> The other hid and doth obliquely bend.
> One life is wrapt in flesh and tends to earth:
> The other winds towards Him, whose happie birth
> Taught me to live here so that still one eye
> Should aim and shoot at that which is on high.
>
> (ll. 1-8)

Although all things in *The Temple* originate with God and must return to Him, yet within the larger cycle leading to this predetermined end there are vacillations, alternations, the "double motion" of the soul that yearns simultaneously for heaven and earth. The religious poet is well suited to be the representative *par excellence* of these psychological shiftings. Although the nature of his subject inevitably fixes his aspirations on divine things, by the very nature of his craft he is chained to the earthly sphere of activity — he is "a man speaking to men," to borrow Wordsworth's famous phrase, and thus must employ words, the medium of terrestial communication, to convey a celestial message. This disparity between form and content requires the double consciousness of the artist and religious mystic, himself in motion from the actual to the potential and ideal, whose re-expressions of the Logos are capable of reconciling this double thrust of material and spiritual. It is no coincidence, then, that the incessant activity produced by the double motion of the poet and his verses is one of the major motifs of the verses in "The Church," including "The Water Course," with its dual channels of action, both literal and symbolic; "The Search"; "The Flower"; and "Man," which defines the position of the human being in terms of this rise-fall motion: "All things unto our flesh are kinde,/ In their descent and being; to our minde,/ In their ascent and cause" (ll. 34-6). It is interesting to note that all of these poems have both religious and artistic implications. Besides suggesting the natural dialectic of creation, day and night, sleep and waking, summer and winter, and the religious cycles of Fall and Redemption, sin and spiritual rebirth, death and resurrection, they also call to mind the journey of the symbolic mode of perception *de sursum descendens* — from a God whom Herbert, like Donne, obviously conceived as visually "metaphorical," to re-ascend verbally as the poet's own song of praise. The poet, then, is not the maker of metaphors as a twentieth century critic might be tempted to say; rather, his task is to discover and correctly interpret the visual symbols already present in nature, in the Scriptures, in the Incarnation of Christ, to re-express them in verbal form, and to re-address them to their original source.

It is important to note that this designation of "symbol" as the predominant level of discourse in "The Church" makes use of the terms "symbol" and "symbolic" in the broadest possible sense, of any concretion which points us toward a corresponding abstraction. Such a definition would also include numerous subordinate groupings, such as allegory and poetic emblem. Actually, however, both of these categories of discourse conform in most details to the description of the symbolic mode suggested above. For example, the emblematic representation of some concrete figure or situation cannot be understood without the aid of the more abstract and symbolic word and explanation. Turning to the allegorical mode, we find that the chief distinction between this type of discourse and the "pure" symbol is one of degree rather than of kind. Both embody an object-thought relationship which in the case of the allegory is fixed by convention and is arbitrary in the case of the symbol. The distinction between image and symbol is, fortunately, a bit less complicated. As we have noted, the distinguishing characteristic of the symbol is this double perspective of the verbal structure and the phenomena to which it is related. Thus while in "The Church Porch" the images were represented as subordinate to the reality they purported to mirror, in "The Church" the image-making faculty becomes an entity in its own right, coping with material creation and rivaling it, almost triumphing over it. In contrast to the earthbound images of "The Church Porch," the figures of speech in "The Church" always are struggling, both literally and metaphorically, to take flight and rise toward the higher reality they mirror.

For Herbert's purposes, then, the fall-flight imagery of physical motion assumes great importance as a metaphor both for the poet's religious and aesthetic activities. The double motion mentioned in "Coloss. 3.3" and similar verses suggests one of the more obvious features of the symbolic consciousness — its ability to point simultaneously toward a concretion and toward its corresponding abstraction. It is for this reason that within each poem there is a double pull of the images which, like the soul of their poet, look both earthward and heavenward — a movement which is strongly suggestive of verses like "The Collar." In this poem Herbert employs such words as "cordial fruit," "corn," "bayes," "garlands gay," and "harvest" in a context which is ostensibly religious but is actually secular, almost pagan. The words, obviously derived from the sacrament of the Eucharist, are carefully placed in a deceptively theological setting and left to make their accustomed impact on the reader. The irony of the situation lies in the fact that the poet's mature understanding of the specifically religious significance of these words was an act of cognition in retrospect only. Thus the dual thrust of the poet's symbolic consciousness is here turned back upon itself with highly ironic effect.

Other poems in the collection also partake of this same ambiguity, this same "double motion" of sacred and secular, with a continual overflow of images from one level to the next, especially in those poems where the poet assumes the *persona* of Christ. We already have noted the image of the human heart, the perversity of which is emphasized as an ironic contrast to the relative pliability of natural stone. Similarly, the image of the garden vacillates between post-lapsarian Eden and the celestial Garden of Paradise so that the figure becomes at last an ambiguous symbol, "the fruit of this, the next worlds bud" ("Sunday," l. 2). A similar impingement of sacred and secular worlds upon one another appears in "Agonie," which states that "Love is that liquor sweet and most divine,/ Which my God feels as bloud; but I, as wine" (ll. 17-18). In these three examples, as in "The Collar," the ambiguity of the symbol results in the deliberate irony and paradox which in *The Temple* seems a natural concomitant of highly figurative language.

Throughout "The Church," then, we have seen that the poet strives continually and with varying degrees of success to unite, through artistic re-expression of God's symbolic method, form and content, knower and known, soul and God, object and word, fallen image and soaring song. Herbert obviously found that the curious bipolar unity, the paradoxical order based on conflict which emerges as a major ramification of the "double motion" theme in this section was insufficient to express his vision of the world. As the collection progresses, however, it becomes abundantly clear that such a union cannot take place in the realm of terrestial things. Hence all of the poems in "The Church" suggest, either explicitly or implicitly, the need for a point of view, a level of discourse more comprehensive, more all-inclusive, than any thus far discovered. And it is precisely such a point of view that is attained in the poem's final section, "The Church Militant."

The final stage of the cycle embodied in *The Temple* is represented by

"The Church Militant," a section which proves to be especially significant for our purposes, tying together as it does many of the predominant
motifs of the previous sections and placing them in their proper
perspectives. Not the least important of all these motifs is the art-
religion analogy which is explicitly identified as a major concern of the
entire collection. As the poet views from his celestial vantage-point the
entire panorama of human history, he observes the relationship between
the Church and the arts in all its various phrases. First of all, "Religion
thence fled into Greece, where arts/ Gave her the highest place in all
mens hearts" (ll. 49-50). So too in Germany the dual effort of religion
and art made that country "the churches festivall" (l. 82). The poet then
seizes upon this opportunity to set forth some of his own theories
concerning the exact relationship between Church and Arts, the
sequence in which they function, and their ultimate effects;

> That as before Empire and Arts made way,
> (For no lesse Harbingers would serve then they)
> So they still, and point us out the place
> Where first the Church should raise her down-cast face.
> Strength levels grounds, Art makes a garden there;
> Then shoures Religion, and makes all to bear.
>
> (ll. 83-8)

Finally lines 262-4 relate the whole religion-art analogy to the larger
cycle of human history:

> And where of old the Empire and the arts
> Usher'd the Gospel ever in mens hearts.
> Spain hath done one; when Arts perform the other,
> The church shall come, and Sinne the church shall
> smother.

This total identification of art and religion points to the section's
predominant metaphor of unity and reconciliation. Appropriately
enough, the poem begins with the invocation, "Almightie Love, who
from thy glorious throne/ Seest and rulest all things ev'n as one" (ll. 1-2).
The reference in line 9 to the Church as "Spouse" of God suggests a
further identification of the temple, both physical and ideal, with the
Divinity it reflects. And in the course of the poem the solitary voice of
the individual poet and his work expands into the presence of the all-
inclusive Word with which he and his work have at last achieved union.
    Perhaps the most interesting problem presented by "The Church
Militant" is that of defining the exact nature of its language. We already

have seen that Herbert finds both simple visual image and the more complex poetic symbol inadequate to express the vision of unity toward which his verses continually aspire. In his chapter on the symbolic mode in ' *The Anatomy of Criticism* Northrop Frye agrees that symbolic expression of the kind encountered in "The Church" is not the highest level of metaphorical discourse. If we proceed beyond image and symbol, says Frye, we encounter "myth," a third phase of language capable of expressing a more comprehensive view of things.

> One step further, and the poem appears as a microcosm of all literature, an individual manifestation of the total order of words. Anagogically, then, the symbol is a monad, all symbols being united in a single infinite and eternal verbal symbol which is, as *dianoia*, the Logos, and as *mythos*, total creative activity.[14].

Frye's description of this symbol-as-monad in terms of the Logos and of total creative activity suggests the closest sort of relationship between the language of mythic expression and the structural and linguistic level of "The Church Militant." Further support for this reading of the last section as the seventeenth-century equivalent of the contemporary term "myth" is added by Frye's suggestion that this state of language finds its ultimate expression in Christ, "the young dying god who is eternally alive, ... the head and body of the Church, the good Shepherd whose pastoral world sees no winter."[15]

Walker's article describes the point of view of "The Church Militant" with the following passage from John Preston's *Life Eternal or, a Treatise of the Knowledge of the Divine Essence and Attributes* (1633).

> A thousand yeares in his sight are but as yesterday, when it is past: that is, a thousand yeares that are to come, they are to him as past, are (as it were) present to him ... to him all things are present. As he that stands upon an high mountaine, and lookes downe (it is a simile that the schoolemen often use;) though to the passenger that goes by, some are before, some behinde, yet to him they are all present. So though one generation passeth and another cometh; yet to God, that inhabits and stands upon eternity, they are the same, they are present, there is no difference.[16]

It is interesting to compare this statement on the method of Divine perception with Ernst Cassirer's definition of the term "myth." Like the seventeenth-century Preston, the contemporary philosopher finds the treatment of the temporal dimension to be one of the most useful criteria for distinguishing true mythic discourse from the merely symbolic.

Mythical thinking, says Cassirer,

> comes to rest in the immediate experience; the sensible present is
> so great that everything else dwindles before it. For a person whose
> apprehension is under the spell of this mythico-religious attitude,
> it is as though the whole world were simply annihilated; the
> immediate content, whatever it be that commands his religious
> interest so completely fills his consciousness that nothing else can
> exist beside and apart from it. The ego in spending all its energy on
> this single object, lives in it, loses itself in it . . . This focusing of all
> forces on a single point is the prerequisite for all mythical thinking
> and mythical formulation.[17]

For the student of Herbert the statements of both Preston and
Cassirer are immediately suggestive of the apocalyptic mood and tone of
"The Church Militant." One of the predominant images of "The
Church" was that of the human soul tortured "in the space/ Betwixt this
world and that of grace" ("Affliction IV," ll. 5-6), torn between the two
realms of flesh and spirit, unable to move decisively in one direction or
the other. "The Church Militant," however, transports the poet "beyond
the anxious middle where we have our being"[18] to the vantage point of
Divinity where all things may be viewed *sub specie aeternitatis,* with
celestial detachment and more than a touch of humor. As the poem
traces the progress of religion from the east, "like a pilgrime, westward
bent" (l. 28), temporal and spatial barriers are eradicated and ancient
Greece and Rome, Plato, and Aristotle, Alexander the Great and
Constantine exist in comfortable juxtaposition with Solomon, Abraham, and Moses. Although the religion of the present day is tried and
found wanting ("The second temple could not reach the first./ And the
later reformation never durst/ Compare with ancient times and purer
years," ll. 226-8), its merits are justly praised and its future success
predicted ("Religion stands on tip-toe in our land,/ Readie to passe to
oure American strand," ll. 236-7). Past, present, and future no longer
exist except as all time exists, within one specious present which reminds
one of Donne's characteristic temporal compression, although with a
totally religious rather than amatory or sexual connotation.

Clearly, then, "The Church Militant" represents the point toward
which the entire course of *The Temple* has tended. The poem, like the
"Churche and Sunne," comes full circle with the italicized lines at the
end of the "L'Envoy," "Blessed be God alone/ Thrice blessed Three in
One," suggesting not only the traditional trinitarian concept of God, but
also the fact that the three divisions of the poem, the three stages of the
cycle with their corresponding levels of discourse, all are united in the

"single infinite and eternal verbal symbol" of God. The total pattern of life has been viewed with reference to God as its center. Reality has been affirmed in terms of this one great symbol: since time has ceased to be, there are no more analogies to be drawn, no poetic tensions to be resolved, no new metaphors to be discovered. Thus *The Temple* returns to God, its origin and end, its present reality and the process that unifies all contradicitons into final communal vision.

We have seen, then, that the unity of Herbert's *The Temple* centers in an aesthetic cycle which corresponds not only to the individual religious experience, but also is paralleled by the universal Christian drama of Fall, redemption, and final reconciliation of soul and God. One additional parallel might also be drawn between the artistic cycle and the ritual of the Mass as it moves through the three phases of consecration, sacrifice, and communion. Within the book itself the three-part physical structure follows the triple process of recognition of the sacred Word as it descends in visual form; re-expression through the secular word, and reunion of secular word with sacred Word, the *persona* of preacher, poet, and redeemed soul, and, finally, the three levels of discourse — simple image with didactic intent, symbol, and mythic expression. This reading of *The Temple* carries with it many critical implications, several of which should at least be mentioned.

First of all, a reconsideration of the poem in terms of the unifying principles just described suggests that for Herbert, religion was vital rather than static or mechanical; that it was a matter of creative becoming rather than of inert being. The imagery of flight is paralleled by the poem's movement toward increasingly higher levels of discourse, from discursive statement and images directed toward moral instruction through symbolic representation and hence toward the literal and metaphorical unity possible only in "mythic" expression transcending the artificial boundaries of time and space. Although a Herbert poem may refer to a completed act of perception, more often it re-enacts that act and thus is less a description of reality than a realization. For it is only in the process of artistic recollection and re-creation that the full import of a religious experience may be grasped in its totality. Herbert implies that since the "real" (that is, the religious) world is known in symbolic form, to know is to symbolize in one form or another.

Although for Herbert an integral act of knowledge is a very vivid and immediate possibility, part of the irony of *The Temple* lies in the fact that this act of knowledge must of necessity come in the celestial regions rather than upon earth. Only there can man find the essence of the religious experience at the level of unadulterated cognition; only then can he know as angels know, directly and without the intervening stages of discursive statement, image, and symbol. However, in Herbert's *Temple*, as in Donne's *Devotions Upon Emergent Occasions*, the memory, understanding, and will, when directed toward their proper goal, enter directly into what they love, thus becoming in themselves *Sapientia Creata*, the image of the increate Wisdom of God. And this process is itself a symbolic action, cyclical in nature, whereby the poem assumes the role of aesthetic sacrifice proffered back to God as living proof and acknowledgement of the pervasiveness of His influence. Salvation, then, may be represented in terms of the completed aesthetic cycle; only through following the three stages of recognition, re-expression and reunion can the direct perception of God lost in the Fall be restored. If, as Emerson once suggested, the Fall of Man consisted in the separation of the knower and known, then the aesthetic experience traced in *The Temple* might be considered as a trope for the Redemption — a secular "epiphany" which draws progressively closer to the sacred. Herbert, with his intense sensitivity to both artistic and moral questions, could not accept art on Puritan terms as a mere metaphor for redemption nor could he wholly subscribe to the romantic avowal that salvation is only a trope for art. For him the whole problem assumed the form of an analogy amounting at times to an equivalence.

Support for such a reading of aesthetic creation as a metaphor for spiritual redemption may be found in numerous poems, including "The Flower," which establishes a threefold relationship between poetic activity, natural regeneration and spiritual rebirth in the lines, "And now in age I bud again,/ After so many deaths I live and write;/ I once more smell the dew and rain, /And relish versing" (ll. 36-9). Similarly, the line from "Easter Wings," "Then shall the fall further the flight in me" (l. 10), carries an implication of an aesthetic, if not theological, *felix culpa*: the process by which the image of God must fall earthward in visual form in order to rise as the poet's song which is second only to the Logos itself as a source of enlightenment. The poet's verses, "crooked winding wayes" ("A Wreath," l. 4) that they are, at last form "a wreathed garland ... a crown of praise" (ll. 1. 2), the elevation of which virtually assures their maker's ascent to a heaven represented by the metaphor of sound rather than of sight. For it is only through the poem itself that man may find "the art/ To turn his double pains to double praise" ("Mans Medley," ll. 35-6), and thus to achieve the communal vision of the poet reunited with the Supreme Author, the eternal Song, "the Word that contains all poetry."[19]

THE VOICE OF GEORGE HERBERT'S "THE CHURCH"

Heather Asals

Louis Martz has said, "Sidney's translation of the Psalms (1-43) represents, I believe, the closest approximation to the poetry of Herbert's *Temple* that can be found anywhere in preceding English poetry."[1] Somewhat similarly, I want to suggest that the Christian commentaries on the Psalms represent, I believe, the most profound influence on *The Temple* that can be found anywhere. Certainly, there is no question that *The Temple* is filled with echoes from the Psalms,[2] but critics have sensed for some time that the relationship between *The Temple* and the Psalms extends beyond the explicit verbal echoes. Ralph Waldo Emerson calls Herbert "the beautiful psalmist of the seventeenth century";[3] Harold Fisch says that "Herbert's poetry has its roots deep in the Psalter, and its simplicity is that of the Psalmist";[4] Margaret Bottrall speaks of the influence of the Psalms on Herbert's poetry;[5] and Bernard Kneiger points out that Herbert's poetry, like the Psalms, contains the " 'quiet' imagery of commerce (as well as the plant and tree imagery)."[6] But no one has yet turned to the various pre-1633 commentaries on the Psalms to discover the reverberations of meaning in the various lines and verses which Herbert uses as well as the reasons that his poetry is so thoroughly immersed in the Psalter.

The commonplace Renaissance notion of the Psalms as poetry was, without doubt, conducive to any poet's and especially a religious poet's modelling his poetry on that of the Psalms. Defending his definition of the poet as *Vates*, Sidney asks,

> And may not I presume a little further, to shewe the reasonable-nesse of this word *Vatis*? And say that the holy *Davids* Psalmes are a divine *Poeme*? If I do, I shal not do it without the testimonie of great learned men, both auncient and moderne. But even the name of Psalmes wil speake for me, which, being interpreted, is nothing

From *ELH*, 36 (1969), 511-28. © Copyright 1969 by The Johns Hopkins University Press. Reprinted by permission of the author and The Johns Hopkins University Press.

but Songs: then that it is fully written in meeter, as all learned *Hebritians* agree, although the rules be not yet fully found. Lastly and principally, his handling his prophecie, which is meerely Poeticall. For what else is the awaking his musical Instruments; the often and free chaunging of persons; his notable *Prosopopeias*, when he maketh you as it were see God comming in his majestie; his telling of the beasts joyfulnesse, and hils leaping, but a heavenly poesie, wherin almost hee sheweth himselfe a passionate lover of that unspeakable and everlasting bewtie, to be seene by the eyes of the mind, onely cleared by fayth?[7]

Puttenham, too, defends poetry by pointing out that the Psalms are poetry — "It can not bee therefore that anie scorne or indignitie should iustly be offred to so noble, profitable, ancient and diuine a science as Poesie is."[8] In fact, not only was the dignity of poetry and the poet justified by its precedent in the Psalms, but also a new kind of poetry was being modelled on its precedent in the Psalms: in the many metrical translations of the Psalms which were being done in France and England in Herbert's time and shortly before there was, as both Hallett Smith and Lily B. Campbell have suggested, "a concerted movement to displace the new love poetry and the newly popularized pagan literature by a new poetry founded on the Bible."[9]

Aside from the fact that the Psalms were written in Hebrew as poetry and were, therefore, in form well suited to be the foundation of the new religious poetry, the Psalms were also in content well suited to be the foundation of that new poetry. As George Wither puts it in his *A Preparation to the Psalter*, the Psalms were considered to be "an *Epitome* of the whole volume of Gods word,"[10] and they were intended to show "how we being deformed in *Adam*, are to be reformed in *Christ*, and to deliver vnto us the present meanes of our Saluation."[11] Since the Psalms, more than any other book in the Bible, were thought of as mirroring the inner life of every individual, deformed in Adam and reformed in Christ, the Psalms were, of course, a particularly appropriate model for the religious lyric. In the preface to his commentary on the Psalms, John Calvin distinguishes the Psalms from the rest of the Bible by what we would call their lyric quality; he calls them " 'An Anatomy of all the Parts of the Soul' " — "Reliqua Scriptura continet, quae Deus servis suis mandata iniunxit ad nos perferenda. Hic vero Prophetae ipsi cum Deo loquentes, quia interiores omnes sensus retegunt, quemque nostrum vocant aut trahunt ad proprium sui examen, ne quid ex tot infirmitatibus, quibus sumus obnoxii, totque vitiis, quibus sumus referti, occultum maneat."[12]

The historical conditions, however — the tendency to justify the writing of poetry by the existence of the Psalms, the tendency to think that the Psalms were a mirror of the inner life of every man — served only as a catalyst in producing the major accomplishment in the use of the Psalms in *The Temple*. The identification which Herbert makes between his own poetic voice and that of the Psalmist is not ornamental but functional and accumulates throughout *The Temple* profound significance. By echoing the voice of the Psalmist, Herbert expands the dimensions of the "I" of his poetry. Perhaps, however, one should look first at the few explicit clues which Herbert gives us about the identity of the speaker of his poetry. On the title page itself Herbert tells us who the speaker in *The Temple* is: "In his Temple doth every man speak of his honour." Once one begins to entertain the possibility that the "I" of *The Temple* incorporates the voice of *every man*, still more evidence presents itself. Consider the various "I's" which one encounters even within "The Church": the "I" of "The Sacrifice" is obviously the voice of Christ; the "I" of "The 23d Psalme" is clearly the voice of David; and the "I" of "A Dialogue-Antheme" is the voice of one whom Herbert labels "*Christian*." One finds an explanation of the kind of thing Herbert is doing in the Christian commentaries on the Psalms — especially Augustine's. Moreover, one also discovers there the way in which Herbert must have found all the "I's," all the voices, capable of being thought of as one "I" and united as the voice of one man.

Although Hutchinson notes some of the echoes from the Psalms in "The Sacrifice," he does not mention the most significant echo of all nor the extensive use of the prophecies of Ps. 22 in the poem. Christ cries out from the Cross in "The Sacrifice,"

> But, *O my God, my God*! why leav'st thou me,
> The sonne, in whom thou dost delight to be?
> *My God, my God* —.[13]

The words follow, of course, the account in Mark 15: 34 — "And at the ninth hour Jesus cried with a loud voice.... My God, my God, why hast thou forsaken me?" Far more important, however, to understanding the meaning of Herbert's incorporating "The Sacrifice" in *The Temple* is the fact that just these words are found in Ps. 22: 1 — "My God, my God, look upon me; why hast thou forsaken me? and art so far from my health, and from the words of my complaint?" The parallel between the words of the Psalmist and the words of Christ on the Cross is hardly an isolated coincidence; as Augustine says, "vix est ut in Psalmis invenias voces, nisi Christi et Ecclesiae, aut Christi tantum, aut Ecclesiae tantum."[14] In fact, Christ's more elaborate complaint in "The Sacrifice,"

that God used to delight to be "in" him, resembles more closely the
complaint of the Psalmist, that God is "far from" him, than it does the
actual account in Mark. Of utmost importance is Augustine's interpretation of the exact nature of the speaker of these words in the Psalms:

> sua ipse Dominus Jesus Christus loquitur. . . . Dicuntur autem ista
> ex persona crucifixi: nam de capite psalmi hujus sunt verba quae
> ipse clamavit cum in cruce penderet, personam etiam servans
> veteris hominis, cujus mortalitatem portavit. Nam vetus homo
> noster confixus est cruci cum illo. . . . *Deus, Deus meus, respice*
> *me, quaere me dereliquisti longe a salute mea*? longe factus a salute
> mea; quoniam longe est a peccatoribus salus. *Verba delictorum*
> *meorum*: nam haec verba sunt non justitiae, sed delictorum
> meorum. Vetus enim homo confixus cruci loquitur; etiam causam
> ignorans quare eum dereliquerit Deus.[15]

Explaining still further elsewhere the identity of the "old man" who cries
in the Psalm from the Cross, Augustine describes Christ, "Transfigurans
enim nos in id quod dicebat, et in corpus suum (quia et nos sumus corpus
ejus, ille caput nostrum), vocem de cruce non dixit suam, sed nostram."[16]
Moreover, when the words occur again in Ps. 38:21, Augustine turns the
meaning of the cry into a moral for all Christians: "*Ne derelinquas me,*
Dominus Deus meus, ne discesseris a me. Dicamus in illo, dicamus per
illum . . . et dicamus, *Ne derelinquas me* . . . . quia desiderando cum et
passionem ejus imitando renovamur."[17] It is not surprising, then, to find
the speaker of "The Thanksgiving," echoing the words of "The Sacrifice,"
speaking in and speaking through the voice of "The Sacrifice": "*My*
God, my God, why dost thou part from me?" By repeating the words of
His Body, the speaker is transferred in a figure to that Body, the Church,
for whom Christ is the Head.

The voice heard throughout the Psalms, as well as the voice from the
Cross, is the voice of Christ's Body, of his mortality: "Ergo quia ex
semine David, non secundum divinitatem, qua Creator est ipsius David,
sed secundum carnem . . . corporis ejus vocem audi, et esto in corpore
ejus."[18] However, as Augustine also reminds us, the Church is Christ's
Body: "*Deus meus . . . quare me dereliquisti*? Quare dicitur, nisi quia nos
ibi eramus, nisi quia corpus Christi Ecclesia."[19] Thus, the voice of Christ
in "The Sacrifice" is properly in the voice of His Body, which is the voice
of the group of poems which Herbert calls "The Church." As Christ is
the Head of the Body, Christ's voice begins the voice of "The Church."
In fact, the "I" who complains from the Cross and the "I" who speaks
throughout the rest of "The Church" are one: "Se dixit sponsum, se
sponsam. . . . Si duo in carne una, cur non duo in voce una? Loquatur

ergo Christus, quia in Christo loquitur Ecclesia, et in Ecclesia loquitur
Christus."[20] Although apparently distinct and separate, the various
voices heard throughout "The Church," all voices of Christ's Body, are
the voices of one man — all the "I's" are one "I": "omnis homo in Christo
unus homo est, et unitas Christianorum unus homo."[21] At the same
time, however, the "I" which speaks throughout "The Church" is the
voice of Christ; Augustine remarks, commenting on Ps. 75, "Audite
jam verba Christi. Nam quasi non ejus verba videbantur, *Confitebimur
tibi, Deus: confitebimur tibi, et invocabimus nomen tuum....* Sive
autem caput loquatur, sive membra loquantur, Christus loquitur:
loquitur ex persona corporis.... *Sacramentum hoc magnum est; ego,*
inquit, *dico, in Christo et in Ecclesia....* audiamus eum, et in eo nos
quoque loquamur."[22] Like the speaker in "Aaron," all the members of
Christ's Body find their voices in the Head:

> Christ is my onely head,
> My alone onely heart and breast,
> My onely musick, striking me ev'n dead;
> That to the old man I may rest,
> And be in him new drest.

The dimensions of the "I" of "The Church," then, are as large as the
dimensions of the "I" of the Psalms. Herbert tells us himself that he who
speaks in *The Temple* is *every man*, and, similarly, John Donne says that
the Psalms "minister Instruction, and satisfaction, to every man, in
every emergency and occasion. *David* was not onely a cleare Prophet of
Christ himselfe, but a Prophet of every particular Christian; he foretels
what I, what any shall doe, and suffer, and say."[23] The conception of the
"I" of "The Church" as the voice of the One Man who is every man
explains the frequent shifts of point of view which the poet makes, even
within one poem, between the first person, "I", and the third person,
"Man": "To write a verse or two is all the praise,/ That I can raise:/ ...
Man is all weaknesse" and "Oh foolish man! .../ A sick toss'd vessel,
dashing on each thing;/ Nay, his own shelf: / My God, I mean my self."
Moreover, the plural identity of the speaker in "The Church" is
probably responsible for the preponderance of the relative pronoun,
"who" as the subject of the sentence: "Who goes to bed and does not
pray,/ Maketh two nights to ev'ry day," "Who sweeps a room, as for thy
laws,/ Makes that and th'action fine," and the words on the "Superliminare" of "The Church" itself —

> Thou, whom the former precepts have
> Sprinkled and taught, how to behave

Thy self in church; approach, and taste
The churches mysticall repast.

All who relate to the description which follows the relative pronoun are
the subject of the statement in "The Church." Each Christian finds the
chronicle of his own life in the narrative told by the "I" of "The Church":
"I did towards Canaan draw; but now I am/ Brought back to the Red
Sea, the sea of shame./ ... So now each Christian hath his journeys
spann'd." The "Christians destinie" is written as "my life"; however, "my
life" is the life of "The Church," which is the Body of Christ — "Thy life
is Gods.../ God did make/ Thy business his, and in thy life partake."

II

After "The Sacrifice," in "The Thanksgiving," the poet asks, "Shall I
be scourged, flouted, boxed, sold?" At first glance the question seems to
be, in effect, a statement that there is no way for the Christian to thank
Christ for His Sacrifice, for there is no way in which he can repay so
great a sacrifice. However, the language of the speaker, his choice of the
word, "scourged," particularly, reveals that he himself is aware that his
question is a naive question. His words reverberate with a deeply ironic
echo from Ps. 38, which Augustine interprets as follows: "*in flagella
paratus sum*; quia mihi haereditas praeparatur. Non vis flagellum, non
tibi datur haereditas. Omnis enim filius necesse est ut flagelletur. Usque
adeo omnis flagellatur, ut nec illi pepercerit qui peccatum non habuit."[24]
There should be no such question from the Church, for *every son* must
be scourged. Throughout *The Temple*, and especially in the five
"Affliction" poems, one sees the speaker dramatising his growth to a
mature understanding and acceptance of the nature of suffering;
furthermore, one sees the speaker, through his questioning, gradually
falling into line with the position of the Psalmist, or rather what was
considered by the Christian commentators to be the position of the
Psalmist, on the meaning of affliction.

The afflictions of the Psalmist are universally thought to be by the
Christian commentators prophecies of the sufferings of Christ. But also,
as Augustine interprets the prophecies, "Passiones itaque Christi non in
solo Christo; imo passiones Christi nonnisi in Christo. Si enim Christum
intelligas caput et corpus, passiones Christi nonnisi in Christo ....
tantum pateris, quantum ex passionibus tuis inferendum erat universae
passion Christi, qui passus est in capite nostro, et patitur in membris
suis, id est in nobis ipsis."[25] The sufferings of the Church, then, are a part
of the sufferings of Christ — Christ is still suffering in the members of
His Body. Thus, Augustine pleads that the Church attend to the voice of

Ps. 35: "Ergo vocem ejus audiamus, nunc corporis, nunc capitis. Est enim psalmus iste invocans Deum contra inimicos in tribulationibus hujus saeculi: et utique ipse est Christus, tribulato tunc capite, tribulato nunc corpore."[26] Similarly, as the speaker of "The Reprisall" to "The Thanksgiving" reconsiders it, "by thy death I die for thee"; and as the speaker of "Confession" observes, "Gods afflictions" come "into man."

Most important to understanding the significance of the Psalms in *The Temple* is the fact that the Psalms were thought to be God's gift to the Church, giving it means of articulating its sufferings in this world:

> Dominus ergo misericors, nos miseri: misericors loqui dignatus miseris, dignatur etiam uti in ipsis voce miserorum. Ita utrumque verum est, et nostram esse vocem, et nostram non esse; et Spiritus Dei esse vocem, et ipsius non esse. Spiritus Dei vox est, quia ista nisi illo inspirante non diceremus: ipsius autem non est, quia ille nec miser est, nec laborat. Istae autem voces miserorum et laborantium sunt. Rursus nostrae sunt, quia voces sunt indicantes miseriam nostram: item non sunt nostrae, quia ex dono ejus vel gemere meremur.[27]

When the voice of "The Church" cries, sighs, and groans, it does so through the voice of the humanity which Christ "put on" in the speaker of the Psalms. Moreover, as the voice of the Church is one with the voice of Christ, so also are the complaints of the Church one with the complaints of Christ. Augustine explains, "*Ego ad Dominum exclamavi. Corpus Christi et unitas Christi in angore, in taedio, in molestia, in conturbatione exercitationis suae; ille unus homo, in uno corpore posita unitas, cum taederet animam ejus exclamans a finibus terrae.*"[28] Small wonder is it, then, to find the speaker of "Ephes. 4.30" saying,

> Almightie God doth grieve, he puts on sense:
> I sinne not to my grief alone,
> But to my Gods too; he doth grone.

Indeed, surely these lines from "Ephes. 4.30" are some indication of the similarity between the nature of the suffering of the Psalmist and the nature of the suffering expressed in "The Church."

The drama of the relationship between the individual and the Church centers around the struggle of each to recognise his own voice for what it is, the voice of "The Church." The development of "The Church" dramatizes the gradual acknowledgment by the speakers in "The Church" of the fact that the real speaker in all the poems is the voice of "The Church." As Augustine suggests about that moment of truth, "quando voces nostras agnoscimus, sine affectu agnoscere non possumus."[29] Until the various (and yet one) speakers in "The Church" acknowledge their own words to be the words of the suffering Body of Christ, the poetry is filled with profound ironies created by parallels and discrepancies between it and the poetry of the Psalms. In the five "Affliction" poems the speaker, who is ultimately to be the voice of "The Church," dramatizes his steady advance toward becoming a member of and spokesman for the suffering Body of Christ. As the Psalmist in Ps. 84 exclaims, "O how amiable are thy dwellings, thou Lord of hosts!," the speaker of "Affliction I" tells of the time when "I looked on thy furniture so fine,/ And made it fine to me:/ Thy glorious houshold-stuffe did me entwine." Shedding great light on "Affliction I," Augustine interprets Ps. 84:

> Uva certe pendet in vitibus, et oliva in arboribus ... et quamdiu pendent in fruticibus suis, tanquam libero aere perfruuntur.... Sic sunt homines quos praedestinavit Deus ante saecula conformes fieri imaginis unigeniti Filii sui, qui praecipue in passione magnus botrus expressus est. Hujusmodi ergo homines antequam accedant ad servitutem Dei, fruuntur in saeculo tanquam deliciosa libertate, velut uvae aut olivae pendentes ... accedens quisque ad servitutem Dei, ad torcularia se venisse cognoscat; contribulabitur, con-er tertur, comprimetur; non ut in hoc saeculo pereat, sed ut in apothecas Dei defluat.[30]

It is important that the speaker of "Affliction I" uses the past tense while describing the time of "milk and sweetnesses" — he *looked* on the furniture so fine. He has already gone beyond the point where he was allured by enjoyment, beyond the point where he was drawing only near the service of God, and, thus, he has already reconsidered the nature of the service: "I thought the service brave" but "I will change the service." By the time of the poem — "Now I am here" — he has already entered into the winepresses of "Affliction," which are the winepresses of "The Church" — "torcularia nominantur Ecclesia Dei hujus temporis":[31]

> Consuming agues dwell in ev'ry vein,
>   And tune my breath to grones.

Presenting himself as still unaware of the full implications of being a member of Christ's Body, in "Affliction II" the speaker, echoing the Psalms ironically, defines by contrast the degree of his own self-knowledge. Of use here is Augustine's elaboration of Ps. 86: 3 ("Be merciful unto me, O Lord; for I will call daily upon thee"): "*Miserere mei, Domine, quoniam ad te clamavi tota die*: non una die. *Tota die*, omni tempore intellige: ex quo corpus Christi gemit in pressuris, usque in finem saeculi quo transeunt pressurae, gemit iste homo, et clamat ad Deum; et unusquisque nostrum proportione habet clamorem suum in toto isto corpore."[32] This, however, is not yet the realization of the speaker of "Affliction II": "Kill me not ev'ry day." Importantly, the speaker at this point of the spiritual journey, revealing how far he is from awareness of his own voice as the voice of "The Church," as the voice of both Head and Body, distinguishes his own afflictions from the sufferings of Christ: "thy one death for me/ Is more then all my deaths can be." Moreover, as the ironic echo from the Psalms suggests ("Kill me not ev'ry day"), the speaker is, on the other hand, wholly aware intellectually of the relationship that should exist between his own tribulations and those of Christ, but he is not yet convinced emotionally — "sine affectu agnoscere non possumus" — that he believes Christ's cries to be his own: "Thou art my grief alone,/ Thou Lord conceal it not."

In "Affliction III" finally the speaker comes to know fully the voice of his own sufferings to be the voice of the Church suffering, the voice of Christ still suffering:

> My heart did heave, and there came forth, *O God!*
> By that I knew that thou wast in the grief,
> To guide and govern it to my relief.

In fact, it is for the first time in "Affliction III" that a voice is given to the speaker's suffering and that he is able to cry out in suffering. Augustine explains a line in Ps. 3, "*Voce mea ad Dominum clamavi; id est, non corporis voce, quae cum strepitu verberati aeris promitur; sed voce cordis, quae hominibus silet, Deo autem sicut clamor sonat,*"[33] and, similarly, Herbert specifies, "My heart did heave." Interestingly, the poem is in the past tense — it is not and cannot be written at the moment when the heart speaks, for the voice of the heart is not the sound of the reverberation of air. One might wonder why the particular words, "*O God!*," convince the speaker that God is "in" his grief; but clearly the cry, "*O God!*," is a refrain of the cry of 'The Sacrifice," the cry of Christ's suffering humanity, the cry of the Psalms: "*O my God, my God!*" By God's words the speaker knows that his sorrows are Christ's sorrows and that the afflictions of the individual are the afflictions of "The Church":

> Thy life on earth was grief, and thou art still
> Constant unto it, making it to be
> A point of honour, now to grieve in me,
> And in thy members suffer ill.

Whatever perspective can be given to suffering as the speaker in

"Affliction III" looks back on it as if it were past, whenever the voice speaks in the present, as in "Affliction IV," it speaks from the midst of affliction, for all "The Church" is for the present in the time of its affliction: "Christ prayed in his affliction, and yet prayed againe, that which was *Davids* case and is ours, was his case too, he was heard, but not at the first prayinge .... the Father was allwayes with him, and is with us, but our deliuerance is in his time, and not in ours."[34] As "The Church" speaks in the present it sees without perspective only the apparently unceasing tortures of the temporal world — "My thoughts are all a case of knives,/ .... All my attendants are at strife" — and, thus, it thinks, like David and like the humanity of Christ, that it is not heard, not heard at its first praying nor until the final time of deliverance: "Wherefore I crie, and crie again." Issuing from the speaker who has already claimed that God guides and governs him to relief, the commands — "Lord, hunt me not,/ .... Oh help, my God! let not their plot kill them and me" — must be of the same nature as the Psalmist's imperatives, which Augustine interprets as follows: "non enim optat ut eveniat, sed cernit quid eventurum sit."[35] What seems to men in the present to be the speaker's request that his state be other than it is remains in the eyes of God and from the perspective of eternity but a figure of speech prophesying that his state will be other than it is. Moreover, the speaker's promise that he will sing when God removes him from his afflictions —

> Then shall those powers, which work for grief,
> Enter thy pay,
> And day by day
> Labour thy praise, and my relief —

achieves particular force in light of Jerome's interpretation of the Psalmist's promise that he will sing: "Quam pulchre non dixit, canto, sed *cantabo*. In futura repromisit: in praesenti enim scit certamen esse, non canticum. Non quam cantat exercitus, nisi quando vicerit. Ergo quoniam in praesenti pugno, non mihi vacat cantare. Cum vicero, tunc cantabo."[36] As the cries which are uttered from the depths of suffering must go without answer, must be repeated, until the end of the temporal world, so also the speaker's enthusiasm and promise to sing cannot be fulfilled in this world: "Then shall."

While the speaker pleads in "Affliction IV," however, he dramatizes no real awareness that he uses only figures of speech, that when he commands and uses the future tense he speaks not literally of some time and fulfillment in the temporal world. The voice of "Affliction V," on the other hand, is the voice of a speaker who is far more aware of the relationship between past, present, and future, between suffering and relief, between the figure and the fulfillment, than any of the other "Affliction" speakers. Significantly, after the first stanza of the poem the speaker moves from the first person singular to the first person plural and uses the first person plural for the rest of the poem — he speaks with the knowledge that it is not only his own situation but also the condition of us all which is responsible for affliction, the condition which "was and is." In short, he grows into the awareness that his voice is the voice of all other "I's," all other first persons, all other speakers in "The Church," and that by necessity there is no hope that the temporal existence of all the members of "The Church" can be other than it is: "Affliction then is ours." The history which the speaker of "Affliction I" told in terms of the subject "I" — "What pleasures could I want, whose King I served,/ . . . . But with my yeares sorrow did twist and grow" — becomes the history which the speaker of "Affliction V" tells with the subject "we":

> At first we liv'd in pleasure;
> Thine own delights thou didst to us impart:
> When we grew wanton, thou didst use displeasure
> To make us thine.

The speaker demonstrates his acceptance of the fact that suffering has and will always characterize the present as well as his remembrance of who it is in us who is still suffering: "As we at first did board with thee,/ Now thou wouldst taste our miserie." Affliction, then, is the condition under which "The Church" exists in the temporal world; "The Church" in the temporal world, however, is but a "floting Ark" waiting for the deluge to subside, for eternity to come, and the speaker, who is "The Church," the One speaker who includes all the members, all the speakers in "The Church," need not fret about the present, which it must know is without any ultimate reality and which will shortly pass away.

III

Only Robert Ellrodt has remarked at any length about the peculiar nature of Herbert's use of verb tense in his poetry;[37] however, the interpretations of the Psalmist's use of tense shed a clarifying light on what Herbert must be doing in using tense the way he does, and they open the possibility that we must think of his use of tense not as a device to inform the reader about the relative time of an event but, like the use of the imperative, as a figure of speech. Moreover, as one might expect, the nature of the speaker's view of time is inextricably connected with the nature of his attitude toward suffering. As John Donne demon-

strates to us, it was well known in the seventeenth century that the
Psalmist does not use the present tense: "In Hebrew there is no Present
tense; In that language wherein God spake, it could not be said, *The
upright in heart, are praised*; Many times they are not. But God speaks
in the future."[38] Chomsky verifies, "The Present tense is generally
expressed in biblical Hebrew by an adjectival form. No special form for
it exists in Hebrew. Actually, to quote the medieval grammarian Ibn
Janah, the present is merely an assumption; it has no reality. It is merely,
he maintains, a line of demarkation between past and future."[39] About
the semitic languages in general he observes, "The tense-idea in these
languages is related not to *time*, but to the *kind* of action. The difference
in tense is determined by whether the action, in the mind of the speaker,
is completed or uncompleted."[40] So too in Herbert's poetry, I think, one
can look at tense as related to the kind of action. In addition, one can
understand through "that language wherein God spake" that the
suffering of the present is so illusory that it cannot find linguistic
formulation in His language; the Church's "life is God's" and its "time to
come is gone," but the present is its 'part and fee."

Turning to "Love III," one finds that the poem is written not in the
present tense nor in the future tense — as one might expect from the fact
that the poem is a dramatization of the soul's final reconciliation with
God — but in the past tense. The Psalmist also, however, uses the same
device of speaking of things which have not yet come to pass as if they
already were fulfilled; George Wither explains,

> And that might be for some of these reasons: First, to signifie vnto
> the world, the certaintie of that which he deliuered and foretold....
> Secondly, it might be, the Prophet spake as in the person of the
> holy Spirit. For, although the mysteries of the Gospell, of which
> the *Psalmes* treat, were not then fulfilled in act, in respect to vs to
> whom they were to be maninfested in *Time*: yet in regard to God,
> with whom all *Times* are present, they might be properly enough
> mentioned as things alreadie effected.... Another reason may yet
> be added, and that is this; it might be *Dauid* foresaw in spirit, that
> after the *Messias* was come, we of the latter Ages should (as now
> we doe) sing these Psalms and holy Mysteries in the Christian
> Church; rather Historically then Prophetically.... Therefore we
> sing them partly in *Commemoration* of the Prophecies, and partly
> with praise and heartie thankesgiuing to God, that those Proph-
> ecies are fulfilled and changed into Histories.[41]

Similarly, Wither says elsewhere of the Psalms, "For, most things,
which God is said in this booke, to *have done* for his people, or against

his enemies; he *now doth, & will doe hereafter*. That, also, which he *will doe*, he may be said to *do now*, to *have done heretofore*; because, all time is *present* with God."[42] As the speaker moves in "Love III" from the future tense — "You shall be he" — to the past tense — "So I did sit and eat" — the Psalmist too moves freely between the use of the past and the future; Augustine remarks on Ps. 3, "*Et exsurrexi, quoniam Dominus suscipiet me*. Hoc magis animadvertendum est, quem admodum in una sententia et praeteriti temporis verbum posuit, et futuri . . . . in prophetia bene miscentur futura praeteritis, quo utrumque significatur: quia ea quae ventura prophetantur, secundum tempus futura sunt; secundum scientiam vero prophetantium, jam pro factis habenda."[43] Clearly, then, the speaker's use of the past tense in "Love III" is meant to be seen as a figure of speech declaring the fact that the reconciliation of "The Church" with God in God's time is as sure as done. The past tense designates that in God's time the action has already been completed and that the apparent present separation of "The Church" from God is as unreal as the present itself.

Using the past tense, the speaker of "Praise II" thanks God:

> Thou hast granted my request,
> Thou hast heard me:
> Thou didst note my working breast,
> Thou hast spar'd me.

In a later poem, however, in "Longing," the speaker suggests by using the imperative that, on the contrary, he is still to be heard: "Consider, Lord; Lord, bow thine eare,/ And heare!/ . . . . Lord heare! *Shall he that made the eare,/ Not heare?*" The solution to the apparent chronological contradiction rests in the nature of Herbert's use of tense and in recalling the dimensions of the voice of "The Church" and the fact that the experiences related in "The Church" are the experiences of all its members throughout all time. Donne explains the same kind of temporal incongruity found in the voice of the Psalmist: "*The Lord hath heard my supplication, the Lord will heare my prayer*; upon no premises doth any conclusion follow, so logically, so sincerely, so powerfully, so imperiously, so undeniably, as upon this, *The Lord hath, and therefore the Lord will*."[44] As can be seen from the different attitudes of "The Glimpse" and "The Glance," the more mature speaker is the one who knows that God has promised the future by the past. Although the speaker in "The Glimpse" complains about the loss of things past,

> Whither away delight?
> Thou cam'st but now; wilt thou so soon depart,
> And give me up to night?,

the speaker of "The Glance" holds hope through the past: "If thy first glance so powerfull be,/ ... What wonders shall we feel, when we shall see/ Thy full-ey'd love!"

The cries and commands, therefore, of both "The Church" and the Psalmist for God to hear are evidence not of God's but of man's infirmity as well as the illusion under which the Church exists in the temporal world — God has already heard. In "The Sinner" the speaker concludes, "Yet Lord, restore thine image, heare my call:/ And though my hard heart scarce to thee can grone,/ Remember that thou once didst write in stone." On the other hand, the speaker begins the poem by suggesting that it is not God but he himself who has difficulty in remembering: "Lord how I am all ague, when I seek/ What I have treasur'd in my memorie!" Resolving the difficulty about how God is said to be at fault for not remembering — "Remember that thou" — Augustine explicates Ps. 9, "*Memoratus est* autem, nemo ita positum putet, quasi oblivio cadat in Deum; sed quia post longum tempus futurum est judicium, secundum affectum infirmorum hominum positum est, qui quasi oblitum Deum putant, quia non tam cito facit quam ipsi volunt."[45] Moreover, illustrating the way in which man projects onto God the art or the lack of memory, Donne says, "The art of *salvation*, is but the art of *memory*. When God gave his people the *Law*, he proposed nothing to them, but by that way, to their memory; *I am the Lord your God, which brought you out of the Land of Egypt*; Remember but that. And when we expresse Gods mercy to us, we attribute but that faculty to God, that he *remembers us; Lord, what is man that thou art mindfull of him*? And when God works so upon us, as that *He makes his wonderfull works to be had in remembrance*, it is as great a mercy, as the very doing of those wonderful works was before."[46] Thus, like the speaker's requests that God hear, the speaker's pleas that God remember are not ultimately requests but figures expressing the condition of "The Church" in this world.

Since the time dimensions in which the experience of "The Church" takes place are of such large proportions, the afflictions of "The Church," in the temporal world are equally great — though of small proportions in terms of eternity. The complaint of "The Church," the "Longing" of the Church, is indeed endless for the duration of the temporal world: "To thee my cries,/ To thee my grones,/ To thee my sighs, my tears ascend:/ No end?" The situation of "The Church" in the temporal world has been, is, and will always be, one of waiting: "Thou tarriest, while I die,/ And fall to nothing," and "my heart is sick,/ While thou dost ever, ever stay:/ Thy long deferrings wound me to the quick,/ My spirit gaspeth night and day" — "I in broken pay/ Die over each houre of Methusalems stay." I think that this understanding of the temporal dimensions of the voice of "The Church" permits a greater appreciation of the aesthetics of the complaint of "The Church." Yet the temporal world is a world of "disorder'd clocks" which will be adjusted at the end of time: "Mans joy and pleasure/ Rather hereafter, then in present, is." At the end of time the fruit will not follow but precede the bud — "O day most calm, most bright,/ The fruit of this, the next worlds bud." When the figure of time is fulfilled, when "The Church" is no longer "in present," it will be heir to "th'Isle of spices."

THE POET AS CASUIST: HERBERT'S "CHURCH-PORCH"

Sheridan D. Blau

Nearly the whole of George Herbert's poetic work is collected under the single title given it in its first published edition in 1633, *The Temple: Sacred Poems and Private Ejaculations*. That volume and its two manuscript versions were divided into three sections, the first headed "The Church-Porch," the middle and largest section called "The Church" and the last, "The Church Militant." Most readers who know Herbert probably know him as the poet of the large middle group of poems collected under the heading "The Church," for it is here that we find all of the witty and passionate devotional lyrics upon which Herbert's poetic reputation rests.

The last section of *The Temple*, a poetically undistinguished account in heroic couplets of the history of the church, discontinues the architectural metaphor of *The Temple*, "The Church-Porch" and "The Church," and its poetic and conceptual relationship to the poems with which it appears remains problematic. This is not the case, however, with "The Church-Porch," whose title identifies it as some sort of prologue to the body of devotional poems which follow it but to which its flat, sententious verses bear little poetic resemblance.

Yet to speak of "The Church-Porch" as a prologue does little to describe its precise relationship to "The Church" except by way of substituting one sort of metaphor for another. Nor does it account for the important differences in style and moral tone that distinguish the verses of "The Church-Porch" from the poems which they precede. We may begin to find some solutions to these two critical problems, however, by addressing ourselves to the question of the cultural provenience of "The Church-Porch"; for such an inquiry should tell us just what intellectual and literary traditions inform its verses, that is, give rise to their stylistic and moral peculiarities. It may also show us more precisely what relationship obtains between the stanzas of "The Church-Porch" and the larger body of poems that make up "The Church."

Reprinted from *Genre*, 4 (1971), 142-52, by permission of the author and the publisher.

"The Church-Porch" is made of a series of moral exhortations arranged in seventy-seven decasyllabic six-line stanzas. Austin Warren has said that it contains such homely maxims as might well have been versified in neo-classical couplets and that its aphorisms are the sort that "have passed into the treasury of common sense."[1]

It is true that many of the lines of "The Church-Porch" echo sentiments similar to those recorded in a collection of aphorisms attributed to Herbert called *Outlandish Proverbs*,[2] and that many lines are borrowed from classical and commonplace wisdom; but this is not to say that "The Church-Porch" contains no specifically Christian or ecclesiastical burden. Professor Warren himself has observed that "The Church-Porch" constitutes a humanistic preparation for Christian devotion, and Professor Louis Martz has found it to be directly in the tradition of Catholic meditation as a "versified elaboration of the methods of preparation for Communion" as advised by Thomas a Kempis' *Imitation of Christ*.[3]

That "The Church-Porch" is something of a preparation for participation in the sacrament of the Lord's Supper seems evident from the first of the two quatrains which appear between it and "The Church" proper under the heading "Superliminare":

> Thou whom the former precepts have
> Sprinkled and taught, how to behave
> Thyself in church; approach, and taste
> The churches mysticall repast.

Yet to associate "The Church-Porch" as Martz does with Book IV, chapter vii of the *Imitatio Christi* is to confuse the sociology of Herbert's document and to identify the second person of the stanzas with the same second person of the *Imitatio*, who in the passages Martz quotes is the priest and not as in "The Church-Porch," the parishioner. The confusion here is important, for Martz is suggesting that "The Church-Porch" is the priest's preparation for the extended act of mental communion which he claims occurs in the poems of "The Church" and he therefore holsters his thesis by identifying the person addressed in the earlier stanzas with the exercitant of "The Church."

However, when we look at the context in the *Imitatio* of the most important passage Martz quotes as a parallel and source for Herbert's intentions in "The Church-Porch," we find that the priest whom Christ addresses in the *Imitatio* who is about not only to receive but to consecrate and administer the communion sacrament is not at all like the "sweet youth" whom the priest speaking in "The Church-Porch" addresses. More importantly, what the *Imitatio* advises the priest who will be communicant to do for himself is far different from the didacticism of Herbert's stanzas of instruction for his parishioner.[4]

In the *Imitatio*, the priest is advised to engage in an act of introspection which is familiarly used by exercitants of meditational devotion. He is to examine diligently and make clear his conscience by true contrition and confession. The stanzas of "The Church-Porch," however, neither constitute nor advise any such act of contrition or confession. On the contrary, they simply offer sound advice to a young man on how to avoid sin, how to conduct himself at home and abroad in his daily activities, and finally how to behave himself in church. It would seem therefore that we must look not to the practice of mental communion, but elsewhere to discover the tradition that informs Herbert's "Church-Porch" and locates its function in *The Temple*.

The place of "The Church-Porch" within the precinct of Herbert's poetic temple is probably indicated by the threefold division of the sins or faults against which the speaker warns the youth. These are sins related to individual conduct (stanzas 1-34), sins related to social behavior (stanzas 35-62), and sins related to religious duties (stanzas 63-77).[5] What these categories and the general tenor of the verses in "The Church-Porch" might suggest to someone familiar with seventeenth-century pastoral practice is the enormously important seventeenth-century Protestant concern with case-divinity or casuistry. In fact, William Perkins, the Elizabethan divine who is usually regarded as the first Anglican casuist,[6] divided case-divinity into three categories or questions which correspond precisely to the three areas of Herbert's concern in "The Church-Porch." These are, according to Perkins: "those that do concern man as he is considered apart by himself, without respect to another; some again concern man as he stands in the first relation, namely to God; and some as he stands in the second relation to man."[7]

The development of casuistry or case-divinity as a principal concern of the English church was in part a response to the serious moral distress and dislocation which attended the loss of the religious discipline that the unreformed church had exerted through the confessional and canon law. The need for a new moral guide was expressed by Francis Bacon in 1589 when he criticized Anglican preachers because "the word (the bread of life) they toss up and down, they break it not. They draw not their directions down *ad casus conscientiae*; that a man may be warranted in his particular actions whether they be lawful or not."[8] It was, however, mainly under the influence of Perkins, who by the seventeenth century was regarded as an authority inferior only to Hooker and Calvin,[9] that casuistry, that is, a concern with practical rules of conduct in varying particular circumstances, came to occupy a place of first importance for many of the most prominent seventeenth-century divines. King Charles I himself conducted and encouraged the study of casuistry, and for such diverse theologians as Richard Baxter, William Ames, Thomas Fuller, and the Bishops Hall, Sanderson, and Taylor practical divinity took precedence over the controversies of theoretical theology.[10]

In many respects, "The Church-Porch" seems to be a work closely related to a pastor's function as casuist, for Herbert's purpose in his seventy-seven stanzas was like that of the leading practitioners of practical divinity: to define holiness in conduct rather than in belief. In his treatise on the pastoral office, *A Priest to the Temple, Or The Country Parson His Character, And Rule of Holy Life*, Herbert indicated his high regard for this branch of divinity:

> The parson greatly esteems also of cases of conscience, wherein he is much versed. And indeed, herein is the greatest ability of a Parson to lead his people exactly in the wayes of Truth, so that they neither decline to the right hand, nor to the left. Neither let any think this a slight thing. For every one hath not digested, when it is a sin to take something for money lent, or when not; when it is a fault to discover another's fault, or when not; when the affections of the soul in desiring increase of means, or honour, be a sin of covetousness or ambition, and when not; when the appetites of the body in eating, drinking, sleep, and the pleasures that come with sleep, be sins of gluttony, drunkenness, sloath, lust, and when not, and so in many circumstances of actions. Now if a shepherd know not which grass will bane, or which not, how is he fit to be a shepherd? Wherefore the Parson hath thoroughly canvassed all the particulars of humane actions, at least those which he observes are most incident to his Parish.[11]

In another chapter of this treatise Herbert surveyed some of the most typical cases of conscience and offered brief solutions of the sort we also find in "The Church-Porch":

> A man may be both Covetous and Intemperate, and yet hear sermons against both, and himself condemn both in good ernest; and the reason hereof is, because the nature of these vices being not evidently discussed, or known commonly, the beginnings of them are not easily observable ... because of the suddain passing from that which was just now lawful, to that which is presently unlawful, even in one continued action. So a man dining, eats at

first lawfully, but proceeding on, comes to do unlawfully ... so a
man storing up money for his necessary provisions, both in present
for his family, and in future for his children, hardly perceives when
his storing becomes unlawful: yet is there a period for his storing,
and a point or center, when his storing which was even now good,
passeth from good to bad.[12]

It is with just such matters that Herbert is concerned in much of "The
Church-Porch" as may be seen in this selection of stanzas:

> Be thriftie, but not covetous: therefore give
> Thy need, thine honour, and thy friend his due.
> Never was scraper brave man. Get to live;
> Then live, and use it: els, it is not true
>> That thou hast gotten. Surely use alone
>> Makes money not a contemtible stone.   (stanza 26)

> Never exceed thy income. Youth may make
> Ev'n with the yeare; but age, if it will hit,
> Shoots a bow short, and lessens still his stake,
> As the day lessens, and his life with it.
>> Thy children, kindred, friends, upon thee call;
>> Before thy journey fairly part with all.   (stanza 27)

> Yet in thy thriving still misdoubt some evil;
> Lest gaining gain on thee, and make thee dimme
> To all things els. Wealth is the conjurers devil;
> Whom when he thinks he hath, the devil hath him.
>> Gold thou mayst safely touch; but if it stick
>> Unto thy hands, it woundeth to the quick.   (stanza 28)

> Thy friend put in thy bosome: wear his eies
> Still in thy heart, that he may see what's there.
> If cause require, thou art his sacrifice;
> Thy drops of bloud must pay down all his fear:
>> But love is lost, the way of friendship's gone,
>> Though *David* had his *Jonathan, Christ* his *John.*
>>> (stanza 46)

> Yet he not surety, if thou be a father.
> Love is a personall debt. I cannot give
> My childrens right, nor ought he take it: rather
> Both friends should die, then hinder them to live.
>> Fathers first enter bonds to natures ends;
>> And are her sureties, ere they are a friends.
>>> (stanza 47)

These stanzas represent attempts to solve legitimate cases of con-science and very much resemble the work of a pastor who is engaging in typical seventeenth-century Protestant casuistry. In stanza 26, the casuist tries to discriminate between thrift and covetousness. One should be thrifty, he says, but not at the expense of one's needs or honour or friends; for money is not contemptible only when it is used. Yet, the casuist advises in stanza 27, be careful not to exceed your income, or spend your entire substance in youth, for in your age your friends and family may require aid and are entitled to some inheritance. However, stanza 28 proceeds, in acquiring wealth be careful not to become devoted solely to its acquisition: "Gold thou mayst safely touch; but if it stick / Unto thy hands, it woundeth to the quick."

Stanzas 46 and 47 deal with another problem of conscience, the respective obligations that a man owes to his friends and his children. A man should open his heart to his friend, advises the priest in stanza 46, and should be prepared to make sacrifices for him. Yet, stanza 47 asserts, a father may not be his friend's surety, and thereby risk the inheritance of his children; nor should a friend accept such a surety. A man's obligations to his children take precedence over his obligations to his friends.

Like all works of seventeenth-century Protestant casuistry, Herbert's "Church-Porch" is directed not to the polluted but to the perplexed, and it serves as a living guide to the everyday questions of what is right and lawful in particular actions.

The gnomic style of "The Church-Porch" which connects it with the *Outlandish Proverbs* and commonplace wisdom also connects Herbert's work with the casuistical tradition and Herbert's own homiletic practice. To begin with, the writings of the English casuists were frequently aphoristic and often prepared expressly for reading in a family circle or as sermons to be delivered from the pulpit. Commonly in the seven-teenth century was case-divinity the subject of a preacher's sermon.[13] Though none of Herbert's own sermons are extant, the only seventeenth-century account we have of Herbert's pulpit oratory informs us that in his first sermon as Rector of Bemerton he "gave his parishioners many necessary, holy, safe rules for the discharge of a good conscience, both to God and man."[14] That Herbert's first sermon was casuistical in sub-stance therefore seems clear, but Walton, who is the source of this account, also reports the curious fact that although Herbert delivered the sermon "after a most florid manner; both with great learning and eloquence," he nonetheless concluded by promising his auditory that in the future "his language and expression should be more plain and practical."[15] This is surely a strange report. It is difficult to imagine any minister, in particular one with Herbert's scrupulous sense of propriety, preaching an entire sermon in a style which at his conclusion he must forswear.

One plausible explanation for Walton's implausible description of the style of Herbert's first sermon may be that Walton is transmitting a composite account of the sermon based first on what informants must have assumed about the preaching of a man who had been Lecturer in Rhetoric and Orator of Cambridge University, and then on what Walton himself, writing in the late 1660's, knew of Herbert's advice to the country parson on preaching. Herbert's handbook for the rural minister, *A Priest to the Temple*, was first printed in 1652 with a preface by Barnabas Oley from which Walton avers he borrowed "some of those truths" that he relates in his "Life of Herbert." One chapter of *A Priest to the Temple* is called "The Parson Preaching," and if Herbert followed his own advice in this chapter as much as we know him to have followed it in most other parts of his treatise, we have here a fairly accurate account of Herbert's own pulpit practice. For the country parson, at any rate, Herbert advocates a style that is "not witty, or learned, or eloquent, but holy," and he urges a form of discourse that derives much of its power from, among other things, the particularities of case divinity and the memorability of aphorisms:

> When he preacheth, he procures attention by all possible art, both by earnestness of speech, it being naturall to men to think, that where is much earnestness, there is somewhat worth hearing; and by a diligent, and busy cast of his eye on his auditors, with letting them know, that he observes who marks, and who not; and with particularizing of his speech now to the younger sort, then to the elder, now to the poor, and now to the rich. This is for you, and This is for you; for particulars ever touch, and awake more than generals ... Sometimes he tells them stories, and sayings of others, according as his text invites him; for them also men heed, and remember better then exhortations; which though earnest, yet often dy with the Sermon, especially with Countrey people.[16]

From such statements we can probably conclude with Walton that Herbert's own sermons, at least after his first one, must have shared a good deal with the plain aphoristic style and practical wisdom of "The Church-Porch."

Finally, when we consider that the opening section of *The Temple* is followed by the "sacred prayers and private ejaculations" of "The Church," we may do well to take seriously two very suggestive lines from one of the last stanzas of "The Church-Porch":

> Resort to sermons, but to prayers most:
> Praying's the end of preaching.

These lines might well suggest that Herbert thought of "The Church-Porch" as a sort of sermon based on practical divinity or casuistry and that its purpose, like that of all sermons, was to prepare its auditors for the prayers of "The Church." Those prayers, beginning as they do at "The Altar" and concluding at the communion table represented in the final poem of "The Church" would seem to constitute the sort of sacramental ritual which the Communion Service of the Anglican prayerbook referred to in Herbert's day, as it does now, as a "Sacrifice of prayse and thanks geving."[17] It is certainly this sort of sacrifice that the poet-priest of *The Temple* has in mind when in the opening stanza of "The Church-Porch" he tells the sweet youth:

> Hearken unto a Verser, who may chance
> Rhyme thee to good, and make a bait of pleasure.
> A verse may find him, who a sermon flies,
> And turn delight into a sacrifice.

THE WILLIAMS MANUSCRIPT AND *THE TEMPLE*

Amy Charles

The unpretentious manuscript volume in which three and a half centuries ago George Herbert set forth his poetic first fruits is probably more important as a measure of Herbert's development than the more famous Bodleian manuscript.[1] Although it includes fewer than half the poems in *The Temple*, the Williams manuscript is important for its earlier versions of many poems, the general three-part division, a scheme of order for the lyrics in "The Church," and Herbert's subsequent retention or rejection of some of its features.

It is not surprising that *W*, known to editors of Herbert from Grosart on, should have received only passing notice, usually for some point about text rather than for the light it can shed on the arrangement of the poems. For one thing, the alphabetical table of contents in general use in editions of *The Temple* since 1633 affords no sense of order for the whole work, and only in recent years has the existence of a specific plan been considered significant. Early in this century Professor George Herbert Palmer, who must always be accounted one of the great students of Herbert, so completely misunderstood Herbert's arrangement that he printed all of the English verse in what he thought the most likely chronological order, although he thereby conveyed the impression of a spiritual life ending in discontent and defeat rather than the joy Herbert intended; and even the late Professor Helen White, who generally served Herbert well, could see only clusters of poems that formed "beads of verse" in a "partial order."[2] Critics misled by the title have attempted to find parallels in classical or Biblical architecture, despite the likelihood that Nicholas Ferrar, not Herbert, was responsible for the choice of title. The only way to comprehend the plan of *The Temple* is to examine the order given it by its author, as Professor Louis Martz did so ably in *The Poetry of Meditation* (1954). A comparison of

Reprinted from *RenP* (for 1971), (1972), pp. 59-77, by permission of the author and the publisher.

the two manuscripts establishes that Herbert planned his final arrangement with great care and subtlety.

I very much doubt that anyone can now discern the precise reasons for the order of the poems in *The Temple* because, for one thing, they were not precise, but personal, intuitive, and allusive. The general concept is clear, but only Herbert himself could describe fully the details of his plan. But whatever those details, it is beyond question that the same basic order prevails in *W* and in *B* and that in both volumes the soul moves haltingly but surely to the final triumph of joy in "Love." In *B* the pattern is infinitely more subtle and complex, the basic order established in *W* obscured by the greater length; but the order of *W* continues to provide the ground upon which the later variations are played.

The comparative table of contents of the two manuscripts, with the edition of 1633 following the order of *B* except for No. 52, shows how the *W* poems are distributed in *B* and the first edition and provides also the basis for relevant schematic analysis.

Bodleian MS Tanner 307 and 1633 edition		Jones MS B 62	
[0.]	The Dedication	[0.]	The Dedication
1.	The Church-porch (sub-title: *Perirrhanterium*)	1.	The Church-porch
2.	Superliminare	2.	Perirranterium
		3.	Superliminare
3.	The Altar	4.	The Altar
4.	The Sacrifice	5.	The Sacrifice
5.	The Thanksgiving	6.	The Thanks-giving
6.	The Reprisall	7.	The Second Thanks-giving
7.	The Agonie		
8.	The Sinner	11.	The Sinner
9.	Good Friday	10.	Good Friday
		8.	The Passion (I)
10.	Redemption	9.	The Passion (II)
11.	Sepulchre		
12.	Easter	12.	Easter (I)
		13.	Easter (II)
13.	Easter-wings	14.	Easter-wings
14.	H. Baptisme (I)	15.	H. Baptisme (I)
15.	H. Baptisme (II)	16.	H. Baptisme (II)
16.	Nature	34.	Nature
17.	Sinne (I)	61.	Sinn
18.	Affliction (I)	43.	Affliction (I)
19.	Repentance	32.	Repentance

20.	Faith	56.	Faith	
21.	Prayer (I)	22.	Prayer (I)	
22.	The H. Communion	{	....	
		{23.	Prayer (II)	
23.	Antiphon (I)			
24.	Love I. and II.	17.	Love 1. & 2.	
25.	The Temper (I)	20.	The Christian Temper (I)	
26.	The Temper (II)	21.	The Christian Temper (II)	
27.	Jordan (I)	46.	Jordan	
28.	Employment (I)	25.	Imploiment (I)	
29.	The H. Scriptures I. and II.	27.	The H. Scriptures 1. and 2.	
30.	Whitsunday	26.	Whitsunday	
31.	Grace	35.	Grace	
32.	Praise (I)	33.	Praise	
33.	Affliction (II)			
34.	Mattens	36.	Mattens	
35.	Sinne (II)	29.	Sinn (I)	
36.	Even-song			
37.	Church-monuments	39.	Church-Monuments	
38.	Church-musick	19.	Church-Musick	

52. Ana {MARY / ARMY} gram
(in this order in the Bodleian
manuscript only)

39.	Church-lock and key	24.	Prayer (III)	
40.	The Church-floore			
41.	The Windows			
42.	Trinitie Sunday	30.	Trinity Sunday (I)	
43.	Content	41.	Content	
44.	The Quidditie	42.	Poetry	
45.	Humilitie	44.	Humility	
46.	Frailtie	40.	ffrailty	
47.	Constancie			
48.	Affliction (III)			
49.	The Starre			
50.	Sunday	45.	Sunday	
51.	Avarice			

52. Ana {MARY / ARMY} gram

53.	To all Angels and Saints	51.	To All Angels and Saints	
54.	Employment (II)	49.	Imploiment (II)	
55.	Deniall	47.	Deniall	

56. Christmas	{ 38.	Christmas-day
	{	
57. Ungratefulnesse	48.	Ungratfulnes
58. Sighs and Grones		
59. The World	54.	The World
60. Coloss. 3. 3.	55.	Coloss. 3. 3.
61. Vanitie (I)		
62. Lent	57.	Lent
63. Vertue		
64. The Pearl	52.	The Pearle
65. Affliction (IV)	53.	Tentation
66. Man	58.	Man
67. Antiphon (II)	59.	Ode
68. Unkindnesse	63.	Unkindnes
69. Life		
70. Submission		
71. Justice (I)		
72. Charms and Knots	62.	Charmes and Knots
73. Affliction (V)	60.	Affliction (II)
74. Mortification	64.	Mortification
75. Decay		
76. Miserie	65.	The Publican
77. Jordan (II)		
78. Prayer (II)	68.	Invention
79. Obedience	66.	Prayer (IV)
80. Conscience	67.	Obedience
81. Sion		
82. Home		
83. The British Church		
84. The Quip		
85. Vanitie (II)		
86. The Dawning		
87. JESU		
88. Businesse		
89. Dialogue		
90. Dulnesse		
91. Love-joy		
92. Providence		
93. Hope		
94. Sinnes round		
95. Time		
96. Gratefulnesse		

97.   Peace
98.   Confession
99.   Giddinesse
100. The Bunch of Grapes
101. Love unknown
102. Mans medley
103. The Storm
104. Paradise
105. The Method
106. Divinitie
107. Ephes. 4. 30
108. The Familie
109. The Size
110. Artillerie
111. Church-rents and schismes
112. Justice (II)
113. The Pilgrimage
114. The Holdfast
115. Complaining
116. The Discharge
117. Praise (II)
118. An Offering
119. Longing
120. The Bag
121. The Jews
122. The Collar
123. The Glimpse
124. Assurance
125. The Call
126. Clasping of hands
127. Praise (III)
128. Josephs coat
129. The Pulley
130. The Priesthood
131. The Search
132. Grief
133. The Crosse
134. The Flower
135. Dotage
136. The Sonne
137. A true Hymne
138. The Answer

139. A Dialogue-Antheme
140. The Water-course
141. Self-condemnation
142. Bitter-sweet
143. The Glance
144. The 23d Psalme
145. Marie Magdalene
146. Aaron
147. The Odour
148. The Foil
149. The Forerunners
150. The Rose
151. Discipline
152. The Invitation
153. The Banquet
154. The Posie
155. A Parodie
156. The Elixir   69. Perfection
157. A Wreath   50. A Wreath
158. Death   72. Death
159. Dooms-day   73. Dooms-day
160. Judgement   74. Iudgment
161. Heaven   75. Heaven
162. Love (III)   76. Love (IV)
163. The Church Militant   77. The Church Militant
[164.] L'Envoy   [78.] L'Envoy
                              18. The H. Communion
                              28. Love (III)
                              31. Trinity Sunday (II)
                              37. Euen-song
                              70. The Knell
                              71. Perseverance

Clearly, then, *W* is the "skeletal version"[3] Mrs. Rindler saw — but more: a sturdy and serviceable framework that would be greatly expanded and undergo small but significant internal rearrangements, would be revised but not replaced, a framework with its beginning and its end firmly fixed. There was no doubt in Herbert's mind of the point of inception or the goal of triumphant conclusion: what he was to deal with in the expansion and re-ordering of the original of *B* was what might be termed the fallacy of the undivided middle — or, to be more accurate, the insufficiently explored middle.

The order of *W* is obviously simpler and more literal than that of its successor, less imaginative and less subtle in its more direct approach, its linkings and pairings of poems, and its progression from the acknowledgment of God's love in sacrifice to the full knowledge of joy and the final acceptance of God's love in sacrifice. What Herbert perhaps learned during the years between the preparation of the two manuscripts is that the Christian's road is not one of immediate achievement, of unexceptional joy, or even of steady progress: eventual achievement, ultimate joy, yes — the final comprehension. (And perhaps this was what Herbert meant in the words Walton represents him as saying: "*before I could submit myself to the will of* Jesus my Master, *in whose service I have now found perfect freedom.*") The poems Herbert moved forward in the arrangement, the new ones he inserted among the first sixty-seven poems in *W*, the minor rearrangements in the *W* poems, and the addition of the entire new group of seventy-six poems between "Obedience" and "The Elixir" all support this view. As he made his revision, which Professor Martz has described as "changing his style from the 'winding' of wit to a witty simplicity,"[4] he also came to his poetic maturity.

When *W* was revised and became the basis of *B*, the original plan was retained as the foundation of a volume re-ordered, expanded, corrected, and refined. At many points in the earlier version Herbert brought about small changes in order or combined or expanded existing poems, but the schematic representation of the new order demonstrates that the basic plan was retained, with slight but significant variations.

A Schematic Representation
of the Order of THE TEMPLE (1633)

0-7; *The Agonie*; 11-10, 8-9; *Sepulchre*; 12-16; 34, 61, 43, 32, 56, 22; *The H. Communion*-23, *Antiphon*; 17, 20-21, 46, 25-27-26; *Affliction* (II); 36, 29; *Even-song*; 39, 19, 24; *The Church-floore, The Windows*; 30, 41-42-44-40; *Constancie, Affliction* (III), *The Starre*; 45; *Avarice, Anagram*; 51-49-47-(38), 48; *Sighes and Grones*; 54-55; *Vanitie* (I); 57; *Vertue*; 52-53, 58-59, 63; *Life, Submission, Justice* (I); 62-60-64; *Decay*; 65-68-66-67; seventy-six new poems; 69, 50, 72-78.

Of the first sixteen poems in *W*, for example, we see that Nos. 0-7 remained firmly in place, but Herbert added "The Agonie," re-ordered Nos. 11-10 and 8-9, then added "Sepulchre" before proceeding with Nos. 12-16. Each one of these minor rearrangements is worth exploring for what it tells us of Herbert's expanding concept of the order — as, indeed, are all the changes in order throughout the revised volume.

Immediately following this "sacramental introduction" (to use Professor Martz's term) Herbert has made a most significant change in order in creating a new group of five poems: Nos. 34, 61, 43, 32, 56 — or, to give them their titles, "Nature," "Sinne" (I), "Affliction" (I), "Repentance," and "Faith." These poems have been moved far from their original positions and made to form a new cluster of thought at a critical point in the order. This change in order is Herbert's most dramatic.

This group of poems, with the two entitled "Prayer" (the second with addition) and the new "Antiphon" break the original progression in *W* from the two poems called "H. Baptisme" to the double sonnet "Love." But the progression from baptism to the immediate recognition of divine love comes too quickly (perhaps too patly?), and the milder second thoughts of "The Christian Temper" that follow "Love" are insufficient to delineate the difficulties of the Christian's way. In the new order the simplicity and control of "Childhood is health" immediately give way to "Full of rebellion, I would die... O tame my heart," to be succeeded by "Sinne" (I), the remarkable companion-piece to "Prayer" (I), four poems away. (The introduction of "Sinne" (I) at this point serves also to emphasize a theme already proposed in "The Agonie" and "The Sinner" that will recur many times. Herbert states explicitly in "The Agonie" the necessity for measuring "two vast, spacious things... Sinne and Love.") "Affliction" (I), with the biographical implications not found elsewhere, then introduces the most recurrent theme that Herbert chose to give a name, and this new position, which moves it up about a third of the extent of "The Church," focuses attention on the importance of the theme to Herbert, just as its paradoxical conclusion asserts his desire for integrity in his relationship with God — no easy and empty acceptance, no succumbing without knowing the terms. Like Job, Herbert maintains his own ways; and, as with Job, when the full realization of God's way is borne in upon him, he accedes so completely and so effortlessly that the earlier struggle and agonized questioning become days lived in another life. The placement of this poem is essential to the opening of new ways of understanding God's continuing search for man and man's persistent and willful misunderstanding of God's love.

In this sequence of five poems, we find a method characteristic of the development of *The Temple*, a cluster of poems on a theme that comes to at least a partial resolution. "Repentance" admits some of the benefits of affliction (even though the upward-tending ll. 28-29 of the *W* version are replaced by downward-dropping lines in the revision), and "Faith" comforts with the thought that "grace fills up uneven nature" — nature, with which this sequence opened. Such a group of poems is often succeeded by a poem of prayer or of praise that rounds off this small segment but does not form the final resolution until the group of poems beginning with "The Elixir" that resolves all conflicts in the ultimate acceptance in "Love" (III).

Related imagery, related forms, related themes all suggest such sequences, and open new ways of fathoming the richness of *The Temple*. Poems known separately yield new interpretations when they are linked or echoed or otherwise drawn into a sequence, or several sequences. The imagery of Communion that Professor Martz has discussed with insight and understanding is so pervasive as to bewilder, allusive and elusive, constantly suggesting new relationships and interpretations. Recurrent single images (of dust or of the heart, for example) combine in unexpected ways: sin turns flesh to stone in "Prayer" (II); in "Nature" the heart becomes a stone to hide the poet's dust. A single linking, like that in which "Lent" points to "Love" (III) in the figure of taking repast and banqueting the soul, enlarges and deepens when the reader finds it also in "Affliction" (V) and "The Banquet" and may discern relationships also with "The Call" and "The Invitation." From "Affliction" (V) one may profitably examine the parts played by both joy and grief in numerous other poems. One can trace a Christmas sequence in "The Starre," "Sunday," "Anagram of the Virgin Marie," "To All Angels and Saints," "Christmas," "The Incarnation," and "Coloss. 3. 3.," with Herbert's reactions interspersed in "Deniall," "Ungratefulnesse," "Sighes and Grones," "The World," and "Vanitie" (I). Another sequence is based in "Longing," "The Collar," "The Glimpse," "The Call," "The Priesthood," "The Answer," "A Dialogue-Antheme," "The Glance," and then an upward movement to the Last Things. Still another sort of linking occurs in Herbert's use of musical imagery which, though it does not usually develop specific sequences, links, unifies, and enriches many of the poems.[5]

In contrast with these varied and suggestive means of linking poems, developed so extensively in Herbert's revision, the linkings in *W* are apt to be much less imaginative and flexible. Both the pairing of poems with the same title and the device of placing related poems on facing or succeeding pages urge a sole order and interpretation, hamper the free-ranging imagination, and create the impression that both poems and poet were far too literal and stationary. The conflicts he described in the *W* poems may have been real to Herbert, but here they are far less alive and convincing than they become in the later version, where Herbert works as steadily toward his goal as in *W*, but strengthens the musculature of the whole through continuous flexing and movement.

If we count seventy-seven poems in the body of *W* (omitting "The

Dedication" and "L'Envoy"), we shall find that perfect number reduced to seventy-one in *The Temple*, with sixty of the remaining poems staying in or close to their original positions, some with revision, addition, or combination, and some without significant change. Twenty new poems are interspersed (with one exception, singly or in pairs) through the portion before "Obedience" (now No. 79) and seventy-six after it. (The latter large group raises the possibility that Herbert had not completed his revision beyond this point, but had decided that his conclusion would remain unchanged, and that Nicholas Ferrar then had this unarticulated group of poems added at this point when the fair copy was made at Little Gidding; but the group is articulated, and to me the possibility of its having been added in such a way is most unlikely.) The addition of these seventy-six poems between "Obedience" and the poem now known as "The Elixir" constitutes the most noticeable difference between the two manuscripts.

"Perfection," the title by which "The Elixir" was originally known, seems to me the key to the reason for this expansion. In preparing his revision, Herbert removed the intervening poem that apparently at one stage of his thought had served as an adequate bridge between the "perfections" and "actions" of "Obedience" and the perfecting clause "for thy sake" in all his actions in "Perfection." "Invention," with its "sweetnesse readie penn'd," may have seemed too ready and accessible a bridge to represent sufficiently the Christian way of life; yet with its new title of "Jordan" (II), its new position (No. 77), and its more witty conclusion, it becomes a climactic poem, at least for this section, and is followed, as so many other such poems are followed, by prayer or song — here, "Prayer" (II).

At the other end of this long interpolation, Herbert omitted the two *W* poems that had followed "Perfection," possibly because "The Knell" marked a rapid descent from the exaltation of the new concluding stanza of "The Elixir"; and both it and "Perseverance," with its implied duration,[6] would break the pace and tone and interrupt the progression toward the final resolution in joy. In the new order "A Wreath," perhaps turned to gold, is moved from its earlier position to replace these two *W* poems, and the series continues with the remaining poems of *W*, which treat the most joyous of the Last Things, the whole culminating in the final surrender to divine love in Herbert's adaptation of Luke 12: 37[7] in "Love" (III), when the poet sits and eats at the board he had struck in "The Collar."

The three single poems from *W* placed at some distance from their original positions should be especially noted. "Christmas-day" is moved back and expanded to give focus to the sequence of poems related to

Christmas. "A Wreath," moved almost to the end of the volume, is no longer an example of "Imploiment," but a type of the stone that turns all to gold. "Jordan" (I) is moved forward by nearly twenty places to form a new link with "Employment" (I) and to prepare the way for Herbert's songs in "Whitsunday" and "Praise" (I).

Even an experienced reader trying to determine the pattern of *The Temple* must divine and catch the sense at two or more removes. The final arrangement is infinitely more complex and subtle than that of the early manuscript, because the reader must discern and follow several orders at one time: the physical order in which he follows the poet through the preparatory stages into the church; a generally chronological arrangement leading from Holy Week and Easter through Whitsun and Christmas back through Lent; a theological arrangement leading from sin to salvation; and, most important, the spiritual arrangement in which the soul grows in knowledge and understanding of God's love toward man, undergoes trials and discouragements, and is drawn gradually, sometimes haltingly, but inexorably from the point of knowing in part to the point where it might have proclaimed triumphantly, "I know even as also I am known." Instead, Herbert surrenders quietly to divine love in the powerful understatement of "So I did sit and eat." This spiritual arrangement, evolved from the poet's agony and realization and uncompromising honesty, broadens to a universality that can include Richard Crashaw, Richard Baxter, John Wesley, Samuel Taylor Coleridge, and Aldous Huxley (and countless others), because in revising and expanding the early version of his poems, Herbert transcended his own spiritual conflicts and spanned the journeys of each Christian.

* * *

Essential as the earlier manuscript of Herbert's poems is for what it shows of his concept of general plan, however, its earlier versions of many poems and titles and the revisions Herbert made between *W* and the original of *B* provide invaluable evidence of his development as a poet. Although the footnotes in the Hutchinson edition record all significant variant readings (but not *all* variants), the forthcoming facsimile edition of *W* to be published by the Renaissance English Text Society will afford the opportunity to see this volume as its author saw it when it was completed.

For detailed consideration of all the poems in *W*, including those subsequently omitted, one should examine the unpublished dissertation of the late Professor Phyllis Berla Rindler of Southern Methodist University, "George Herbert's *Temple* in the Early Manuscript" (Yale

University, 1960). The poem in which we observe most fully the method of Herbert's revisions, the "Perfection" that was transformed to "The Elixir," has been treated in exemplary fashion by Professor White in *The Metaphysical Poets.*

One of the most rewarding approaches to *W* is to consider what Herbert later changed and what he chose not to change: in no other way can the reader learn how Herbert's skill in diction, sense of control, imagery, and poetic technique matured. Comparing *W* poems with the versions finally printed may also help to formulate some impressions about points of order or of dating.

The Temple grew by accretion; and within the limits of *W* we may trace some of its processes of growth. We are dealing, after all, with a mature work of literature that passed through four stages: the period of writing and revision that preceded the preparation of *W*; the period during which this manuscript was Herbert's main poetic concern and he revised some of the poems; the period during which he composed many other poems and incorporated them into the basic order he had already devised, along with further revision of some poems in *W* and the decision to omit six entirely; and the preparation of the manuscript from which *B* was copied.[8] The necessity for making a fair copy at Little Gidding after Nicholas Ferrar received the text from the hands of Edmund Duncon lends substance to Mrs. Rindler's suggestion that Ferrar received at least some parts of the manuscript as a sheaf of loose papers.[9].

The sole change in order between *B* and the first edition of *The Temple*, moving the "Anagram of the Virgin Marie" from its original position preceding "Church-lock and key" to its new position just before "To All Angels and Saints," may have resulted from someone's failure to cancel it in its original position when its link to the succeeding poem was dropped. The *W* version of the poem (called "Prayer") includes the original second stanza, which must have been cancelled in the original of *B*, referring to "Armies of blessings." (An alternative explanation, almost too base to mention, is that in the position it occupies in *B*, the printer would not have had space enough in the edition of 1633 for the title, the leading out, the two lines of text, the signature, and the catchword.) It is unlikely that an editor so perceptive and conscientious as Ferrar, who declared that *"the whole Book was such a harmony of holy passions, as would enrich the World* with pleasure and piety,"[10] would have made any change without direction from Herbert's manuscript.

The first noticeable addition in *B* is the title *The Temple*, with its accompanying epigraph, probably in the hand of Nicholas Ferrar. *W* has no title, and probably never had a title. (The only leaves removed, in the middle of the first gathering, may possibly have included a title page; the renumbering of fol. 1 shows that the original first numbered leaf was rejected, for whatever reason.) Although Herbert uses the word "temple" in five *Temple* poems (and it appears in the doubtful poem "The Convert"), in none of them is his use noteworthy, and only in "Sion" does he make particular use of the term, though even here he rejects architecture in favor of a responsive heart. Nowhere is there evidence that he pointed the usage toward a title for the entire work (or even of a single poem). The epigraph included on the title page of *B* is not the one most usually associated with the figure of the temple. Much more likely as first, indeed automatic, association (and most apt to the theme of *The Temple*) is the passage in I Corinthians 6: 19-20:

> What? know ye not that your body is the temple of the Holy Ghost which is in you, which ye have of God, and ye are not your own?

> For ye are bought with a price: therefore glorify God in your body, and in your spirit, which are God's.

At this point one of Walton's uses of the word "now" should be considered, in the continuation of the familiar passage about Herbert's sending his book to Nicholas Ferrar: "Thus meanly did this humble man think of this excellent Book, which now bears the name of *The TEMPLE*."[11] Again, though we must be wary of basing too much on the exact words of this devoted biographer, we must not ignore the strong implication that this excellent book had not always borne the name of *The Temple*; and no one now living can say how the sub-title originated, although two of Herbert's imitators continued it.

Yet not all of Herbert's readers accepted this grand title. Among those who referred to Herbert's book as *The Church* was the Reverend John Polwhele (or Polwheile) of Tremorgan, who also had some connection with the diocese of Lincoln. In a collection of his poems acquired by the Bodleian in 1947, a series of Latin and English occasional verses dating from 1649 to 1662, we find "On Mr. Herberts Devine poeme the Church. Jo. Polw: post mortem author mestris posuit":

> Haile Sacred Architect
> Thou doest a glorious Temple raise
> Skil ecchoinge his praise,
> Who taught thy genius thus to florish It
> Wth curious grauings of a Peircinge witt.

Statelye thy Pillars bee,
Westwarde the Crosse, the Quier, and
Thine Alter Eastward stande,
Where Is Most Catholique Conformitie
Wth out a Nose-Twange spoylinge harmonie.

Resolue to sinne noe more,
From hence a penitent sigh, & groane
Cann flintye heartes vnstone;
And blowe them to their happye porte heauen's doore,
Where Herberts Angells: Flow on a way before.[12]

Between the two manuscripts the titles of several poems were changed
and one modified. Some of these changes emphasize specifically musical
terms. In *W* the two poems called "The Christian Temper" might well
refer to a Christian's mood or temperament, but when Herbert modifies
the titles to "The Temper," he stresses the musical interpretation,
particularly in the first poem with its figure of tuning the breast to
improve the music. The change from "Ode" to "Antiphon" (II) again
uses a more specific term drawn from music. Perhaps the most
interesting of these revisions is that from "The Second Thanks-giving"
to "The Reprisall" (which on first consideration might convey an
infelicitous meaning of getting at someone or something a second time).
The musical term *reprise* or *ripresa* had not yet developed the meaning
of "recapitulation" that it would acquire after the development of the
sonata form, but it had already been in use for several centuries and at
this time referred to a repeat, a refrain, or a cadence.[13] Here also it
echoes the lines of "The Thanks-giving": "My musick shall finde thee,
and ev'ry string/ Shall have his attribute to sing ..."

With two exceptions the other changes in title bring an idea into
sharper focus or set up an image. Herbert exchanges one quality for
another when "Tentation" becomes "Affliction" (IV), but moves from a
specific to a more general application when he replaces "The Publican"
with "Miserie." The real subject of "The Publican" is not the pariah, but
Man, foolish, imperfect, and perverse. Herbert rejects the specific title
for one better suited, result rather than cause, and thus adds to his store
of the varied reactions of human beings to circumstance.

The usual effect in these new titles is to give greater significance: "The
H. Communion" is directed toward the sacrament rather than toward
the less clearly defined "Prayer"; another poem of the same name
becomes "Church-lock and key" to emphasize man's perversity. In the

remaining four, the poems now known as "Redemption," "The Quid-ditie," "Jordan" (II), and "The Elixir," we see another device of Herbert's developing. Each title represents a symbolic or an operative principle, and examining the significance of the title discovers another meaning — one that heightens or intensifies understanding, sometimes brings the meaning of the entire poem into focus. "The Quidditie" verges on paradox in its puzzling over the nature of Herbert's gift of poetry addressed to God; "Redemption" clarifies the theme of the entire poem; "Jordan"(II), whatever the figurative crossing or washing meant to Herbert, stresses that love has already penned a sweetness and that his own efforts are superfluous;[14] and the famous figure of "The Elixir" intensifies the point of what had originally been a poem less notable for form and succinctness.

Mrs. Rindler has discussed at some length the six *W* poems not included in *B*.[15] Herbert showed keen critical instinct in his choices. On the whole, the content is treated adequately in other poems, although a combination of reasons may have led to their rejection. Herbert sacrifices an effective contrast of line length reflecting the increasing and declining rays of the sun in "Mattens" and "Euen-song"; and even the best of the poems, the almost unbearably poignant "Perseverance," finds no place in the sweep of the final upward movement.

Another sort of change affords further evidence of Herbert's develop-ment in poetic judgment. In several poems youthful excess of language is subtly brought under control. Some changes occurred in revisions of *W* itself ("garland" to "posie" in stanza 6 of "To All Angels and Saints"; "these twenty hundred years" in "The Pearle" to "many hundred"), and extreme expressions continue to be toned down in *B* ("King of all Grief" in "The Thanks-giving" to "O King of grief!"). The spinning but fatal spider of "Praise" (I) is changed to bees that sting, yet labor to accomplish their work. Conversely, the "millions" of surprises in "Sinne" remain to mark the early origin and Herbert's undiminished sense of the infinite.

In reading *W*, it is as important to notice what remains constant as to account for the host of minor changes and revisions and to evaluate the significance of the major ones. One point of importance about this manuscript is that its verse forms (which do not change when they are transferred to the later manuscript) afford a tremendous range of metrical variation. Although Herbert generally uses the iambus, *The Temple* includes twelve poems in trochaic meter, among them some of his best lyrics; three of the twelve are found in *W* ("Ode," "Dooms-day," and "L'Envoy") along with "ffrailty," a poem in iambic meter that (like

"Deniall") uses one trochaic line in each stanza. The nine new trochaic poems in *B* all occur within the large group added between "Obedience" and "The Elixir," a circumstance suggesting that the experiments with the trochee are among Herbert's later poems and that this whole group was the latest he composed. That most of these poems are not only lyric, but much like stanzas to be set to music, raises the possibility that the trochee may have been intended to suit them to musical measure and that these may have been poems Herbert himself set to music and sang.

Ten of Herbert's fifteen sonnets (not counting the two printed by Walton) are included in *W*, all Shakespearean in the octave, with eight using EFFE in the third quatrain and only two, "Christmas-day" and "Sinn," using the expected EFEF pattern. (Four of the five sonnets added in *B* follow the EFEF pattern, "The Sonne" being the exception; but nothing in content or technique shows conclusively that they are "later" poems. Both New Year's sonnets quoted by Walton follow the EFFE pattern.)

Couplet rhyme is used in four poems: one in four-stress, two in five-stress, and one in five-four alternating. Three poems in unique forms were retained in the revision ("The Altar," "Easter-wings," and "A Wreath"), but the second "Trinity Sunday," a *durchkomponiert* experiment, was omitted.

Of the remaining forms one is used three times, five twice, and forty-seven but once (including five omitted from later versions). The stanza in which the number of feet remains constant is rare; typically Herbert uses two or even three line lengths in a stanza. In "Iudgment" he uses a separate rhythmic pattern for the opening stanza.

The skill in handling meter and rhyme that would be shown most extensively in the rich complexity of "The Collar" may be discerned in several *W* poems: in the variant rhyme pattern in the final stanza of "Prayer" (II) and the fourth stanza of "Sunday," in the eight patterns of rhyme in the nine stanzas of "Man" that echo his "symmetrie" and "proportions," or in the mended rhyme that finally comes right in "Deniall."[16]

One of the most important conclusions to be drawn from a study of *W* is that Herbert's technical skill had already matured at the time this volume was compiled. The variety in form and in rhyme and the revisions that reflect a tightening of concept, strengthened diction, and greater sense of the poet's confidence in handling his materials demonstrate amply that at this stage Herbert was already an accomplished poet. That he would become a greater poet no one can now question; but had we no English poems but those in *W*, Herbert would be recognized today as a lesser, but still important devotional poet. The little calf-bound volume preserved in Dr. Williams's Library in London is therefore a milestone marking Herbert's accomplishment up to that point and providing the measure for assessing his further development.

VI. INDIVIDUAL POEMS

ON HERBERT'S "SACRIFICE"

Rosemond Tuve

A few years since, William Empson[1] gave some nine pages to a treatment of George Herbert's long poem "The Sacrifice," as an example of the seventh of his *Seven Types of Ambiguity*. These pages, through brilliant exposition of meanings overt and hidden, bring a reader closer to the heart and core of a beautiful poem than much criticism of Herbert between his day and our own has been able to do. They also demonstrate certain undeniable virtues of modern criticism, and the skillful use of its most typical instruments, especially of those provided for a critic's use by various developments of modern psychology. Nevertheless, a reader familiar with the traditions out of which this poem sprang will find Empson's reading inadequate. This essay is concerned to supply these felt deficiencies of interpretation; it is as much concerned — and here the consideration touches most of us, certainly not Mr. Empson alone — to examine the problems which are raised by the modern critic's use of certain favored instruments or methods and by his ignoring of various others.

The type of ambiguity which "The Sacrifice" is said to exemplify is that type wherein two opposite meanings are defined by the context, "so that the total effect is to show a fundamental division in the writer's mind." Empson speaks of the poem as an example "where the contradictory impulses that are held in equilibrium by the doctrine of atonement may be seen in a luminous juxtaposition" and analyzes various stanzas to demonstrate how "only the speed, isolation, and compactness *of Herbert's method* could handle in this way impulses of such reach and complexity" (my italics).

To my mind also this is a great and an original poem. But in point of fact it offers an interesting study in what one can possibly mean by

Reprinted from *KR*, 12 (1950), 51-75, by permission of the author's executor, Mr. Richard L. Tuve. An expanded version of this essay appeared in *A Reading of George Herbert* (Chicago: University of Chicago Press; London: Faber and Faber; Toronto: W. J. Gage & Co., 1952), pp. 19-99.

"originality," for its basic invention or structural situation, the sequence of ironies upon which it is built, the occurrence, setting and application of the refrain which binds it together, the very collocation of antitheses which make up the poem, are none of them Herbert's.

Herbert's poem belongs with two interlinked groups, both well-known, of medieval lyrics; both groups belong as does his poem to a larger group, the Complaints of Christ to his People, and all apparently have their spring in the liturgical offices of Holy Week, most obviously (for one group) in the *Improperia* or Reproaches of Good Friday.[2] The earlier lyrics in the tradition of which Herbert's is a part make use as he probably does of the sequence of responsories for matins of Maundy Thursday, Good Friday and Holy Saturday. This sequence had made traditional, in music and in vernacular lyric, the application Herbert makes of the *O vos omnes qui transitis:* "O all ye who passe by, behold and see ... Was ever grief like mine?" Some of the loveliest polyphonic music of the late 16th and early 17th Centuries — some perhaps which moved him most on those twice-a-week journeys to Salisbury Cathedral when Walton tells us he "would usually sing and play his part at an appointed private Music-meeting" — was written for these liturgical uses, and preserves in a form more moving than any other those ironic contrasts which the liturgy, not Herbert, had put into Christ's mouth.

I do not know whether it makes an extreme difference to what Empson most wished to bring out that the "method" is not "Herbert's method," that the luminous juxtaposition is equally not his. It may. He says of Herbert's poem that "the various sets of conflicts in the Christian doctrine of the Sacrifice are stated with an assured and easy simplicity, a reliable and unassuming grandeur, extraordinary in any material, but *unique as achieved by successive fireworks of contradiction, and a mind jumping like a flea.*" When we realize that the assured simplicity and the unassuming grandeur had accompanied the statement of these conflicts for some hundreds of years, the word "unique" pulls us up with some sharpness, for of course successive fireworks of contradiction very like these had been set off in public and to all men's eyes and ears for generations, and Herbert's mind makes its jumps under the very precise guidance of those selectors of lections, responses and antiphons for Holy Week who had made the jumps before him. But there are two points here, and they are interesting for the theory of criticism.

The first is this point of dependence. The ironies in Herbert's poem are no less marvellous for speed and compactness because they were found by others; the tone is no less fitting because it is not strange but is precisely the tone of the "Reproaches" and of sundry medieval lyrics; we must note and praise these excellences quite aside from any knowledge of their being conventions rather than inventions of this poet. But can we construct notions of what *is* "Herbert's method" while regarding such knowledge as impertinent? (To the *act* of decision concerning aesthetic value the knowledge seems to me impertinent. Nevertheless, it assists — and sometimes even provides — the state of awareness whence such decisions arise.) Do we somehow phrase our criticism differently, when we realize that the "achievement" by which "all these references are brought together," as Empson asserts, and "kept in their frame, of monotonous and rather naive pathos," happens not to be Herbert's achievement? and that the same "rarefied intensity of feeling" characterizes many moving and beautiful Middle English poems which use this same frame? The danger may enter especially when we imperceptibly move from remarks about the poem to remarks about the poet's style or achievement; but *if we think we can avoid so moving,* I believe we deceive ourselves. How can we know the dancer from the dance? It may be that criticism of "the poem as poem" requires a division between creation and creator which is not possible because of the nature of "meaning" in language. It is time we recognize this impossibility if it exists. It may be, also, that we have no choice but to keep trying to do this impossible thing. But then we had best be openminded rather than arrogant about relating a poem's genesis to its meaning.

But there is another and more teasing point. Language is a social phenomenon and no man's private oyster, so that there is such a thing as misreading; and meanings have histories, and shrink as well as spread, so that there is such a thing as ignorance of one's misreadings. Hence it is that — little as modern criticism cares to acknowledge it — meanings of elements or motifs in poems, like meanings of single words, are clarified by knowledge those elements have carried before the poem was written and, as we think, "outside" it. For much that is "outside" a poem to us was well inside it to our forefathers, and still is to some readers.

I speak here rather of our typical modern presuppositions than of Empson, but, for an example, there are various cases in which his readings are pretty well ruled out by such knowledge. Christ says in Herbert's poem (121):

> Why, Caesar in their onely King, not I:
> He clave the stonie rock, when they were drie;
> But surely not their hearts, as I well trie:
> Was ever grief like mine?

Empson thinks of this as Christ identifying "Caesar with Moses as the chosen leader of Israel" in the bitterness of his "apology" or "defence." But it is next to impossible to think of it thus if one is conscious of the liturgical and patristic identification of Moses with Christ, of the legendary and iconographical identification of Moses' rod with the wood of the cross, and if there rings in one's ears the sorrowful but accusatory contrast of the Good Friday Reproaches:

> I gave thee to drink wholesome water [*aqua salutis*] from the rock:
>   and thou hast given me gall and vinegar.
> *O my people,*[3] what have I done to thee? or in what have I afflicted
>   thee?

"Cleaving the stony rock" is far more than a mere allusion to Moses the chosen leader. No cleric of the 17th Century, as liturgically literate as George Herbert, and brought up on typology, could mention this act of Moses without thinking both of the water from the side of Christ, the living rock (as in Herbert, 170), and of the mystical regenerative power of water (so stressed, for example, in the services for Easter Even). The connections ultimately of course are with the culture-hero who gave his people life-giving water in the wilderness of the dry rock, the land waste through guilt; and the primitive depth of such meanings would be in some sort present to a 17th Century Christian who read, "I, Christ, gave thee to drink of the healing water, I am all Saviors, and Moses was I. *Caesar* your King and regenerator! Alas, he cannot cleave those hearts of stone which make you scourge me, those hearts which I as just judge must sometime punish — was ever grief like mine?" This is a terrible and damning irony rather than Empson's "I am not a political agitator."

Whole stanzas of Herbert's poem gain their compressed force from that acceptance of Moses as a type of Christ which is a commonplace of iconography, of commentary, and of other Holy Week offices as well as of the *Improperia*. The terror in his lines depends from our realizing the enormity of an error which confuses the Caesars of the world with the eternal regenerative King, and from our perceiving the fearful ineluctable connection between this error and Christ's kingly function as Judge.

> They buffet him, and box him as they list,
> Who grasps the earth and heaven with his fist,
> And never yet, whom he would punish, miss'd:
>   Was ever grief like mine?

The combination of irony and pity with inescapably just judgment makes for a "concentration" yet more "powerful" than that which Empson remarked. And the identification of Christ with Moses (the force of this word is intended; this is metaphor, not example) was common to all the materials Herbert echoes; the identification was assuredly in the author's mind, if that makes any odds to our reading. If it does not make any odds, I submit that we are stubborn readers, cutting off our noses to save face. Better even to be accused of the Intentional Fallacy than thus to accede to "Wisdom at one entrance quite shut out."

Again, one of Herbert's most striking antitheses reads:

> *O all ye who passe by, behold and see;*
> Man stole the fruit, but I must climbe the tree;
> The tree of life to all, but onely me:
>   Was ever grief like mine?

I shall presently treat this stanza in considerable detail for another reason, but one question it brings up is relevant here. "He climbs the tree to repay what was stolen, as if he was putting the apple back," says Empson, later commenting that this makes Christ smaller, more childlike, than Eve, who could reach the apple without climbing; "but the *phrase in itself implies rather* that he is doing the stealing." Does it imply this? Perhaps a critic has to decide whether or not it makes any difference to us that it could not have implied this to Herbert (insofar as there is certainly in mortal affairs), that the phrase about climbing the tree (ascending the cross) is the veriest commonplace, and that the antithetical pairing of the two trees is used with meanings that would be yet more proper to Herbert's poem, in antiphon and *communio,* in sequence and in vernacular lyric, in the oft-published Meditations on the Passion of pseudo-Augustine, in apocryphal gospel and *Golden Legend,* in the *Crux benedicta* and the *Crux fidelis,* in all those liturgical materials which the remainder of his poem echoes so persistently. Actually, there is no such thing as "the phrase in itself." The locution marks a modern critical error, and philology should have taught us all to be wary of it. "The son stealing from his father's orchard is a symbol of incest," says Empson; "Jesus seems a child in this metaphor." But to whom? Perhaps it is the answer to this last question which every critic has a responsibility to make clear. It is not possible to read the many, many uses of this liturgically common contrast and think that Jesus seems a child or an apple-stealer in them — if words, tone, context, can convey anything at all trustworthy to us ever; nor is it possible to then read Herbert and feel that his use differs from these others in words or tone or context. This reservation seems to me relevant to one's way of reading the poem, certainly to a study of what *"Herbert* deals with" (Empson) in it.

On the other hand, the reservation does not seem relevant if a critic merely wishes to discover what a poem can mean to him, can become under his hands. This is a valuable activity, and it is only too bad that it is generally accompanied by implications that this meaning is "the meaning," and that one may praise the (original) author for it. One should praise rather the critic, who is the author of another and different poem — and why should he not be? The more good poems in the world the better. But he should acknowledge his paternity. I do not take up the problem (very clear in strictures on Spenser) offered by the fact that we are oftener asked to condemn these out-of-wedlock late-born waifs. And their long-dead supposed "fathers" too. A horrid hent.

I shall not venture further in the rest of this essay into the question of what-the-poem- "really" -means; there is a bog of subjectivity just to one side in the darkness, and I should rather leave the skirting of it to others. I am frankly interested in what Herbert meant. The reasons for this interest are neither psychological nor historical; the chief one is that I have learned to trust Herbert's aesthetic judgment. "The Sacrifice" is a beautiful poem, read in any of the ways I have tried to read it. But read by the illumination of the tradition in which it was conceived it takes on a richness, a depth, complexity and moving power which I am loath to go without just because I do not know the things Herbert knew until I study them out.

Two well-known poetic and liturgical traditions, joined before Herbert joined them, meet to make the initial "invention" without which there would be no poem. The first, the extra-scriptural Monologue or Complaint of Christ (of which one type is the O-all-ye-who-pass-by poems), which provides the formal basis and thence exerts much influence upon the tone, became a poetic convention as early as we have extant religious lyrics in English. The medieval lyrics in this kind are often very lovely (especially metrically), and the element of wry contrast often goes to the length of compressed "witty" antitheses, conceits and turns of speech. Herbert's supposedly Metaphysical harshness or irony in the diction is quite native to the tradition.

The ironies are much sharper, the antitheses much neater, and the double meanings emphasized by Herbert more clear and terrible, in the second, more narrow and definite tradition — that of the *Improperia*. The liturgical tradition entered medieval vernacular lyric to produce some of the most beautiful of Middle English poems — laconic, powerful, and terse with the under-statements borrowed from the liturgical text. The portion of the Good Friday office which most interests us consists of a series of brief and sardonic contrasts, separated by *Popule meus* and sung by two cantors (as it were the words of Christ), to each of which the deacons or choir respond with the Trisagion, or three-fold Sanctus in Greek. For example:

O my people ...
Because I led thee through the wilderness forty years, and I fed thee with manna, and brought thee into a land sufficiently good, thou hast prepared a cross for thy Saviour.

Agyos O Theos, Agyos Iskyros, etc.

What could I have done more unto thee that I have not done? I planted thee indeed, O my vineyard, with fair fruit, and thou art become very bitter unto me; for thou gavest me to drink in my thirst vinegar mingled with gall, and piercedst thy Saviour's side with a spear.

Agyos O Theos, Agyos Iskyros, etc.
(*Sarum Missal in English,* tr. F. E. Warren, I, 258)

In the laconic contrasts of Herbert's Reproaches of Christ, as in those of the medieval lyrics, sound the echoes of the Reproaches sung during many centuries of Good Fridays:

> They gave me vineger mingled with gall,
> But more with malice: yet, when they did call,
> With Manna, Angels food, I fed them all:
> Was ever grief like mine?
>
> Then on my head a crown of thorns I wear:
> For these are all the grapes *Sion* doth bear,
> Though I my vine planted and watred there:
> Was ever grief like mine?

(Herbert, 237, 161)

> Fourti wenter i sente the
> angeles mete fro heuene;
> & thu heng me on rode tre,
> & greddist with loud steuene.(Cried out; voice)
>
> Heilsum water i sente the
> out of the harde ston;
> & eysil & galle thu sentist me,
> other gef thu me non.
>
> In bem of cloude ich ladde the;
> And to pylate thou ledest me.
> My volk, what habbe y do the? (*Popule meus*)

Wythe aungeles mete ich uedde the;   (fed)
And thou bufetest and scourgest me.
    My volk, what habbe y do the?

Of the ston ich dronk to the;
And thou wyth galle drincst to me.
    My volk, what habbe y do the? ...

Ich gaf the croune of kynedom;
And thou my gyfst a croune of thorn ....
                (Nos. 72 and 15 from Carleton Brown's
                Relig. Lyrics, xiv. c.; sp. modernized)

With so few and so little of any of these texts before our eyes, I shall
not pause now to demonstrate how a similarity of formal basis, initial
situation, and thence of poetic feeling has produced a similarity of tone
in the liturgical, the medieval and the Herbert "reproaches," written
though they were centuries apart and showing plenty of verbal inde-
pendence. It would be especially tempting to remark the Yeats-like,
ritualistic, modal changes in an identical refrain when it occurs in
differing contexts (an effect found in various medieval poems as well as
in Herbert's). Or to demonstrate the effect of the basic structure
provided by the liturgical text — flat, unelaborated statements of
antitheses generally found from one like verb or noun. Or to study the
curious mingling of hardness with pathos, metrically conveyed, in the
Herbert and the Middle English poems (quite independently of course).
One more general point should be made.

The tension of ambiguities and serried meanings which Empson has
commented on is precisely what Herbert owes to the tradition, and it is
our appreciation of these which is deepened by a knowledge of what he
built upon. Herbert's poem is full of minute shocks, of unexpected
connections, sudden recoils in the emotion described or produced —
and it is this temper or tone, along with the ironic contrasts which
usually bring the shock to bear, which he inherited. His is not the Christ
we know in Luke's or Matthew's straightforward narrative — but He *is*
the Christ of the liturgy of Holy Week. The importance of the sacrificial
idea with its reach into primitive levels of feeling, the almost savage
implications of impending retribution, the profound doublenesses of
meaning which will not yield to a reconciliation except at the heart of the
Mystery — these are what Herbert found ready to his hand. For the
most part, these inhere in no single statement in the liturgical text
proper, any more than they do in Herbert, but if one wishes to analyze

latent ambiguities, there is quite enough to occupy one in the *because (quia),* and the merged identities, of

> Because I brought thee up out of the land of Egypt, thou hast prepared a cross for thy Savior.
> Because I led thee ...., and I fed thee with manna, ... thou hast prepared a cross for thy Saviour.
> Before thee I opened the sea, and thou hast opened my side with a spear.
> O my people, what have I done to thee ....

And Herbert's double meanings in the ambiguous "Was ever grief like mine" toll forth the same fearful accusation as the *parasti crucem Salvatori tuo...parasti crucem Salvatori tuo... Popule meus...* of Christ's Good Friday indictment of man, wedding the questions of the apocryphal IV Esdras of the Old Testament to the Passion of the New.

Although it is my judgment that conscious borrowing is involved, I am concerned mostly with the relation between a given 17th Century religious poem and a very widely diffused tradition, and with the problems which such relations raise for criticism. One problem is that of our ignorance. What kind of readers do we make, whom circumstances have intervened to make ignorant of what every literate man once knew? I should like to speak out for willingness to repair our ignorances, despite the current fear (not least current among American "academic" critics) that we may somehow substitute knowledge about poem and author for response to poetry. This substitution, which I admit to be deplorable, is far less frequent than the losses we sustain by the absurd modern necessity to avoid seeming scholarly, in case criticism is one's end — for fear not that The People, but that The Critics, will hastily pull down the blinds and declare that one can only read the poem in the dark. Very many kinds and ways of reading are justifiable, but more good poems will have a chance for continued life when we realize once again (and here the critic mentioned is not one of the villains) that the criticism of poems of past centuries is as much in need of scholarship as if they had been written by Eliot or Yeats.

When the case is, like the present one, that of the understanding of a language of symbols, much depends certainly on how widely diffused any given tradition once was. I have been speaking as if this tradition, in its branching forms, were only to be met with in the Sarum Missal and in collections of medieval lyrics. This of course is not true. It found its way into the drama of the guilds; more than once Christ utters the "dolorous complaint" of an O-all-ye-who-pass-by poem. It is found in sermons; a powerful variant is the accusing Christ of the Judgment Day, his "complaint" a series of brittle contrasts. Even now, music is the route by which many persons unfamiliar wih the liturgy have become entirely familiar with the *Improperia* tradition; Palestrina's beautiful Reproaches have been sung every Good Friday since the 1560's and '70's in the Sistine chapel, and one can hear Victoria's any year; there are beautiful settings for the Holy Week responsories (*Was ever grief like mine* comes from one, another is the *Vinea mea electa, ego te plantavi*). The tradition was carried and spread in Latin hymns; anyone who likes may read in Dreves' *Analecta*, xxxi, 58, an address of Christ's to man which begins like Herbert's *O vos omnes, qui transitis*, which elaborates on the outcast-God concept and stresses at once the outrageousness and the necessity of the *rex immensus ... in crucem extensus, pro peccatis populi*. More famous hymns like those of Prudentius or Venantius Fortunatus (showing connections we could notice) were read as part of the corpus of Christian Latin poetry for their literary worth; the vast anonymous literature of Latin and vernacular treatments of the Passion, legendary amplifications, iconography, all fed into the stream of devotional literature endlessly reprinted in the 17th Century (Jeremiah's lament — *O vos omnes* — appears iconographically as a type of Christ's in hundreds of *Horae*; iconography and the commentaries which produce it are responsible for and enrich with further meaning Herbert's parallel (247), between the Side-wounding and sinful Eve's creation, which no doubt many readers have seen as peculiarly an instance of Metaphysical wit). There are connections with the Protestantized and much translated Meditations ascribed to Augustine, and with Anselm's and Bernard's; and of course not all medieval lyrics remained unprinted, and 17th Century men owned and read manuscripts.

Liturgically connected, the *O vos omnes* and the *Improperia* (from both which traditions Herbert draws) became joined in lyrics, in Rolle's Meditation on the Passion, in popular treatises like the *Cursor Mundi*. Latin tags from the *Popule meus* turn up even in Christmas carols; an *O vos omnes* poem appears as a wall inscription. Various motifs of the tradition appear in all sorts of places, from two Monologues of Christ ascribed to Skelton to the several extended uses by Lydgate. And any of the motifs within it carries over the use of the weighted, biting oppositions we have noticed, the typical conceits and the characteristic tone.

In sum, all the channels I have mentioned serve to keep the continuity unbroken at least as late as Herbert, and especially for a man who, as Walton tells us, was so interested in liturgy that he would explain to his parishioners how certain collects, responsories, canticles and lections had come to occupy their places. He could not have got far in his explanation without familiarity with the Sarum Missal and Breviary, as anyone knows who has looked into the history of the Anglican prayer book. Nor should we forget Herbert's close connections with the Ferrars of Little Gidding; the remembrance of two other famous poets interested in Little Gidding — Crashaw and T. S. Eliot — will suggest to us that such a connection is not impertinent when we are considering Herbert's liturgical and "Catholic" preoccupations, and the full weight of some of his traditional images.

It should be obvious from all this that the notion of a monologue spoken by Christ, the notion of what such a monologue should contain, the symbolically used Old Testament refrain, the special mingling of contradictory emotions in the speaker, and the general poetic tone of the whole, were traditional for many generations before Herbert used them. Even more striking, if less fundamental, are the numerous relations between the traditional materials and the specific choices of detail found in the Herbert poem.

For the secret of the power of this poem lies in the density of the serried layers of suggested concepts and emotions, in the frequently almost shocking juxtaposition of these emotions, and in the resulting variety and constant movement of the tone, from pitying to condemnatory, from tender to intellectually incisive, from brash to gravely meditative, from the accents of the quiet sufferer of others' actions to those of the omnipotent ruler of the universe. These qualities result from the fact that the poem is built upon various types of contrasts, most of them ironic in nature. Both the contrasts and the ironies were inherited, and a demonstration of the relations between Herbert's specific details, phrasings, and tone and those of the liturgy and related symbolic materials is here in order. That I must omit from this short sketch, but it is quite provable that all the types of ironic contrast or understatement upon which Herbert's poem is constructed and which give it that ambiguity, density and ambivalence of tone that we think of as so especially "Metaphysical," are either explicit in the tradition, or implicit in the deliberate juxtaposition of concepts and images in the liturgy of what Herbert himself calls in his poem "this great week" (59). His own words show his consciousness that he is writing a Holy Week poem; that we are less conscious of its alignments with ritual and with other poetry of the same category results rather from our ignorance than from any lack of care on his part to use those alignments in order to make his poem richer, more suggestive and more clear.

Clearest and most explicit of any of the types of antithesis which are found both in Herbert and in the liturgy are those which directly pose the shocking contrast between man's actions toward God and God's actions toward man. We have encountered one group of these already: man stole the fruit, but Christ pays the penalty of a thief's death on the Cross; "They give me vineger mingled with gall ... yet ... With Manna, Angels food, I fed them all"; Christ planted his vine in Sion, but the crown of thorns he wears are all the grapes it bears; he (not Caesar) clave the stony rock when they were dry, while they strike his head, the rock whence the store of blessings issues evermore; each one of his people doth him brave, yet without him each one "Had to this day been an Egyptian slave." Most of those I have had space to refer to are stated with the same flatness, the same grossly and shamingly self-evident absurdity, in the *Improperia*. But more than that, each such contrast (and several unmentioned here) is thematically rather than singly used in Herbert's poem — just as in the liturgy of Holy Week. In both, the "robbery" motive, the vine conceit, the rock gushing forth saving water, the Red Sea of the two-fold salvation, and various others, appear and reappear as do musical phrases in a composition.

Leaving to one side the various other thematic conceits, and all demonstration of the echoing depths, magnitude and power caught and held in Herbert's metaphors for any reader trained by tradition (as we are not) to receive all their latent suggestions, I shall instead take up one single image crucial in Empson's discussion, in order to consider a certain important matter.

This image, already once quoted, is climactic in Herbert's design, and forms the climax in Empson's critique of the poem:

> *O all ye who passe by, behold and see*;
> Man stole the fruit, but I must climbe the tree;
> The tree of life to all, but onely me:
> > Was ever grief like mine?
>
> Lo, here I hang, charg'd with a world of sinne....

To shape an antithesis from these two "trees" is startling to us — "odd," to use one of Empson's words. It is profitable first to recognize the extent to which "Herbert's method" is a convention in treatments of the Passion — this method of poignant but wittily sharp antithesis, of act set against act in the neat ironic balance of phrase with phrase. In one of the most popular, most translated and reprinted of devotional books, the Meditations ascribed to Augustine, a page and more is given (ch. 7) to a series of powerful contrasts of which these are typical:

> I am delighted in eating, and thou are tormented on the tree of thy Passion. I abound with pleasures, and thou art pierced with nails. I taste the sweetness of the apple, and thou the bitterness of the gall.

My mother Eve doth laugh with me and thy mother the Virgin doth lament with thee.... (etc. etc.)

Translations differ somewhat, but in all versions the unrelieved beating of phrase upon phrase carries the same tone. One has but to glance at the *Short Title Catalogue* to see how far from "odd" must have been this motif to men of Herbert's time; these materials had extreme popularity, were Protestantized, re-Catholicized, appeared in one collection after another (1581, 1591, 1600, 1604, 1621, 1624, etc.). Liturgically more common is the use of the tree alone to point up the relation between Adam's act and Christ's: "By a tree we were enslaved; and by the holy Cross we have been set free: the fruit of a tree beguiled us; the Son of God redeemed us, alleluja." Sung in this form and others almost innumerable times a year, it is no wonder that the parallel of tree with tree became firmly imbedded as a convention, to be echoed in many a legend and poem I have no space to quote. It got early into iconography, and was part of the very tissue of men's thinking about the Tree of the Cross.

Some of the liturgical forms of this antithesis emphasize an element common in lyrics — the notion of pre-ordained necessity:

Who hast established the salvation of mankind by the wood of the cross, *that so* whence death arose, from thence life might arise again, and that he who *by a tree had gained a victory* might *by a tree be also overcome.*

This makes concrete an idea which is important, typical, and far more likely to be behind Herbert's *must* (climb the tree) than is some chance fancy that Christ was not so tall as Eve. The connection of the first tree with that "tree of life" which Christ must climb as part of a divine necessity, ordered before the beginning of time, is equally clear in the well-known hymn of Venantius Fortunatus, the *Pange lingua gloriosi*:

> When he fell on death by tasting
> Fruit of the forbidden tree:
> Then another tree was chosen
> Which the world from death should free.
> Thus the scheme of our salvation
> Was of old in order laid....

That Herbert did not know Fortunatus as a great Christian Latin poet would be hard to believe. At any rate, Herbert's "I must climbe the tree" carries something of the same philosophically important inevitability.

I should think it clear then, that the use of sharp antitheses ironically paralleling the tree of death with the tree of life is no novelty of a latter-day Metaphysical poet, and that a considerable naivete is required of us as readers if we are to think that Herbert's particular phrasing of the convention makes us see Jesus as the son of the house, climbing in the orchard. There is nevertheless a further witty oddity in the lines, a shock in the hint of actual *identification* of the tree of sin with the tree of redemption, that makes a modern mind fly at once to those symbols of psychological analysis which we think might help to explain Herbert's hidden and perhaps unrealized meaning. But we must not on this account think that the same oddity was felt either by the writer or by his contemporary readers, or is really part of the poem unless our ignorances are part of it (a theory which would extend a good many poems beyond all reasonable compass). I think it can be shown that this at first surprising and contradictory antithesis-identification of the two trees is thematically related to Herbert's idea of the Atonement, and had been felt to be so related by innumerable writers of poems or meditations or other treatments of the Passion, for centuries.[4]

The images which carry this parallelism are often more shocking and more ambiguous than Herbert's. Empson speaks with considerable insight of Christ climbing the tree "as if he was putting the apple back"; although the tradition in a sense carries this meaning, it would be too loose and careless an image to suit earlier minds, too incapable of conceptual reverberations. A more daring recurrent image, for a profounder but related conception, is the image of Christ *as* the fruit. *Tam nova poma*, says Venantius Fortunatus' famous *Crux benedicta*. "O Tree of sweetness and glory,/ Bearing such new-found fruit 'midst the green wreaths of thy boughs." It behooved that God's son were made an apple and hung with nails on the dry tree, says Caxton's version of Guillaume de Deguileville's *Pilgrimage of the Soul.*

Like all symbols, this one — while eluding conceptual statement — is capable of almost infinite variations, opening up varied but equally "true" conceptual nuances. The god as the fruit eaten of his people appears in a use of the conceit in the *Cursor Mundi*, tracing the tree of the Cross from its origin in the Garden. In one poem the Cross itself utters the same image; "One fruit for another," it says, a laconic statement of the mystery which all these images are concerned to convey:

> Whon Adam, Godes biddyng brak,
> He bot a bite that made us blak,   (bit a bite)

> Til fruit weore tied on treo with tak;   (nail)
>   O fruit for another.
> (Early Eng. Text Soc. 117, p. 623)

In another lyric a different way of phrasing the mysterious connection between man who sinned, and God-Man who redeemed, shows another characteristic of the operation of symbols; the concrete particular used can undergo a metamorphosis under our very eyes:

> The same mouth that the appyl gnewe,   (gnawed)
> In that mouth the holy cross grewe,
> Wheron I dyed for youre gylt;
> Thurgh the herte and thurgh the mylt   (spleen)
> I hadde the poynt, and ye the hylt....
>
> Ye botten an appyl that thirled my brest.
> (bit an apple that pierced)
> (EETS 124, p. 41)

All these poems belong to a mode of writing wherein there is nothing strange whatsoever in a body which is both fruit and vine, in an earthly rood-tree grown out of an apple of Paradise, in an apple which is a sword held in the hand of him who ate it. Symbolical writing (including Herbert's) is confusing only when we read symbol as picture, when we allow the concrete particulars of garden and tree to carry us, by connotation, into alien contexts dependent on our individual fancies. There is an element of the irrevocable in symbols; they have meanings, and limitations of meaning, by virtue of a kind of social compact, and are not ours to do as we like with; it will not serve to read them as if they were images in Keats.

Empson is interested to find Christ seeming a child. But indeed there is a medieval image of Christ as a swaddling-clothed babe — *in* the tree whence Adam took the apple, as Seth catches a glimpse of it when he goes to seek for that oil of mercy which he has been told may cure his father Adam of his mortal sickness. Other forms of the legend of the holy rood convey similar relations and meanings in different ways; Seth is given three pips from the apple to place under Adam's tongue, thence they grow into those rods which Moses used and into, finally, the tree which is used for the Crucifixion; Solomon sits under the tree to learn wisdom, and it has a marble stone with gold letters saying that man shall see God himself reign in this tree, but none understands that this will be Christ upon his cross: "that tree was death, this shall be life, and written it is ... that it came out of that pip that wretched Adam fell from ... for so began the cross of Jesus Christ." Seth is told, but does not understand it, that Adam shall not have the oil of mercy for 5005 years; the prophecy is fulfilled in the Harrowing of Hell, when Christ, having died upon the tree which grew from Adam's grave, cures Adam at last from his mortal wound. "Man stole the fruit, but I must climbe the tree."

I have lumped into a paragraph the chief elements in a legend that has similar purport in all its many shapes — for of course we have it in Latin, in Old French, in Middle English prose and verse, in lectionaries, treatises, poems, in the Golden Legend, in the Gospel of Nicodemus. I do not think it matters that there is no babe in the Nicodemus version for example, or that care is seldom taken to make clear whether there were two trees in paradise or only one. That the "fruit" whence springs life, love, abundance, freedom from guilt, should hang where hung the fruit whence sprang sin and death, is a profound statement. That the tree of life is both antithetical to *and* identical with the tree of death is a similar statement. Both are very common.

We need not think of Herbert as knowing these especial images (though how he could have escaped reading Venatius Fortunatus and the Golden Legend and the Gospel of Nicodemus I do not see); nor need we even attend to the differences in them; they all spring out of the same understanding. Christ is the fruit, he is the oil of compassion from the tree of life, he is the babe, he is the king reigning from the tree, he is the life which makes it burgeon, he is Sapientia itself, and the tree is the knowledge of good and evil, and when they ate of it they should be as Gods — all these are ways of saying the unsayable connection between the doing of the sin and the undoing of it, and that there is paradox and mystery at the heart of the whole conception Herbert knew and his predecessors knew.

"The Christ becomes guilty" (Empson) is the burden and the mystery not only of image after image throughout this whole poem, but of countless other images and other poems, and in order to catch that meaning we do not need to introduce as in any sense part of "Herbert's method" the mentioned interpretations, and hence of *this image* as pointing to the supreme incestuous sin. All these rabbits roll out of one small hat — the interpretations put upon "climb" and "must." One cannot but suspect that these fancies do not have as their end the *understanding* to which they are alleged to lead, but rather the desire to detect a particular *image* in the poem; that Christ *must* climb in order that we moderns may convict him of the primal incest, and that it is not Herbert's truth of insight or poetic mastery, but his modernity, which we are to be most excited at discovering. For it is not meanings (they were already plainly visible) but *the precise images* of modern analysis that we are asked to pursue — even at the cost of thinking that a sensitive poet could write, "Man stole the fruit, but I must climb and steal it for him," or the equally vapid "Man stole the fruit, but *I* must *climb* to steal it."

There are two illegalities here, and both constitute dangers but not inescapable concomitants of a new and otherwise useful method of literary criticism. The first is simple: the reading of a poem is not assisted by intimating that it somehow "means" all the connoted situations with which chance allows us to endow the author's words. The second is more important and more subtle: whereas it is legitimate to look for and enjoy similarities between the meanings an earlier author opens up, with his instruments, in his myths, and the meanings our new psychological instruments open up for us, it is illegitimate to look willy-nilly for our instruments, and for all else they open to us, in what he wrote. There is truth at the heart of all myths that men have found powerful; we should be content that psychology has taught us to perceive how like each other these truths turn out to be, and not insist that every man who has seen them must somehow, unwittingly, have been taking a look through our spectacles — and that therefore what he wrote somehow "means" whatever else we can now see through those spectacles, had he but had wit enough to know it.

Psychology has also taught us that there are reasons, deep below the conscious level *why* certain ancient symbols took the shape they took. This is interesting too, but it is interesting as psychology or sociology; it is not a literary fact. For these reasons are primarily concerned not with the utilizable meaning, but with the psychological spring, of images, and with the sociological uniformities which made certain concretions widely usable with symbolic force. Origins are relevant to criticism only if they illuminate meaning and thus deepen feeling (or whatever term we wish to use for aesthetic response). This essay has been concerned to uncover origins (in a restricted sense: *available traditional* meanings), but origins which help to explain what meanings there is considerable evidence for thinking a poem actually carried, quite consciously, for one of its greatest readers — the author. It is my belief that that should help the rest of us. But that all origins, far back in the first dawn of time, are *per se* relevant to criticism it is a pedantry to claim.

I have called these two ways of using psychological data to interpret poems written long before those data were dreamt of "illegalities" because each of the two has something other than the poem's meaning, honestly and humbly sought, as object. In additon to the method's undoubted usefulness in explaining those myriad puzzles where earlier authors have seen something of what Freudian psychology sees, before Freud saw it, there is one further help it can give. It can re-awaken our sense of the truth in ancient myths and alien images by showing us how we stare into the same mysteries in our own myths and our own images, so that we may take a living meaning from an old poem. It is because this is not the end result even of some of Empson's applications of this method that I quarrel with his rewriting of Herbert. It is one thing to re-interpret the old in ways which let its truth come through to us, to read Christ into the Fourth Eclogue or see Venus as a starry influence, and surely quite another to find a Prometheus and an Oedipus in a poem for the fun of finding modern intellectual counters. And equally surely it would be hard to find a modern reader who suddenly felt the true importance and overwhelmingness of the guilt he has been freed from because for the first time he could relate it to something which *does* move him — the sin of incest.

The reason why such discoveries (or pursuits, rather) do not affect our feelings, but rather interest and amuse, is not far to seek. It lies in the fact I have already noted, that the unexpressed antecedents of an image, or even the subconscious reasons for its formation, simply are not the meaning of that image. It has often taken on through centuries of use such layers upon layers of consciously apprehended significance, which gives richness and moving power to its use in poetry, that we feel far more loss than gain when its possible primeval meaning, or its subconscious base, is substituted for these. What this substitution does is remove the image from the domain of metaphor; a psychological datum, like an historical one, may explain and rationalize a metaphor — but a poet is not trying to show how his metaphors came to be, he is using them to think with. It is a long time since incest as the actual, the committed, primal crime has seemed as shocking and as important to a thinking man as does the total philosophical problem involved in the presence of evil in the world, its cause, and its remedy. When we have thinned down the symbol to its possible first shape, or base, we have straightway to "translate" that incest-image too, before we can feel it; and it is a question whether Herbert's own traditional symbols, unrefurbished, do not come through to us with more power. Provided, of course, that we still have the slightest interest in the subject of the poem. Nothing we can do to this poem can prevent it from being a poem about man seen as guilty of wrong-doing; if we no longer see this as a problem, then presumably we may as well treat the poem as a mine for extracting anthropological and psychological data, and salvage at least that.

I must end with something of an apology, and something of a hope. In spite of the corrections I have wished to make in it, Empson's reading of Herbert's "Sacrifice" yet reached depths of meaning which are not only truly "in the poem" (in every reasonable sense of those words) but also which were seemingly missed by the many generations of critics who have been content to ignore it. This outright addition to our understanding seemed to me to result from one habitual — and invaluable — manner of proceeding: this critic sank himself into the images as into the pit, tried every conceivable path into their meaning. He has recognized an incontrovertible fact, and I too wish hereby to recognize it: that it is of the nature of metaphors to be infinitely suggestive, and that "what do they mean" is an inquiry that cannot possibly ever be finished. This has its troublesome side, but it is the basis for poetry's claim to be a mode of knowing truth.

It is because this newly emphasized method of getting at the meaning of poetry is so fundamentally trustworthy a method that I have been at pains to criticize parts of Empson's application of it so rigorously. I have said sharp things of it, and I apologize for the sharpness, which was a rhetorical device on my part, but I do not apologize for the things. The usefulness of this favorite present-day emphasis in criticism, resuscitated after some four or five hundred years and given a new slant, will depend upon whether we deify what we have found, determined to have no other gods but it, or, as we might do, add it — a useful but humanly fallible tool — to the tools we have got from those who preceded us.

The tools they passed on to us — especially the tool, *quite as insufficient* used alone, of accurate methods for determing possible meanings in poems to their authors or their first publics — are precisely those which can show up our new errors, and excesses, and illegitimacies, and pedantries, for what they are. But we shall probably be no less single in our devotion to a new critical religion than our fathers. The modern pedantry of valuing a poem because it has "all the Freudian stuff, what fun,"[5] so like the pedantry of "intellectual climate," or like the one before that, "author's development," or like any of the ones before those, will seem quite honestly the way to enjoy the poem. We shall do a braver thing than all the Worthies did if we escape adding to this another modern critical attitude which will turn mere incompleteness into real arrogance — the attitude that our reading is somehow likeliest to be the true one, "better" than the author knew — not even just "better for us." This can be, no doubt.

Perhaps any critical advance is accompanied by this single-mindedness. Perhaps this is the best that can be done. We shall not be the first critical generation to be enamored by our own limitations. I do not know any reason in nature for it except the usual one.

HERBERT'S *THE COLLAR* RE-READ

Jeffrey Hart

The Collar

I struck the board, and cry'd, No more.
          I will abroad.
What? shall I ever sigh and pine?
My lines and life are free; free as the rode,
     Loose as the winde, as large as store.
          Shall I be still in suit?
     Have I no harvest but a thorn
     To let me bloud, and not restore
What have I lost with cordiall fruit?
          Sure there was wine
Before my sighs did drie it: there was corn
     Before my tears did drown it.
Is the yeare onely lost to me?
          Have I no bayes to crown it?
No flowers, no garlands gay? all blasted?
          All wasted?
Not so, my heart: but there is fruit,
          And thou hast hands.
Recover all thy sigh-blown age
On double pleasures: leave thy cold dispute
Of what is fit, and not. Forsake thy cage,
          Thy rope of sands,
Which pettie thoughts have made, and made to thee
     Good cable, to enforce and draw,
          And be thy law
     While thou didst wink and wouldst not see,

Reprinted from *BUSE*, 5 (1961), 65-73, by permission of the author and the Trustees of Boston University.

Away; take heed:
I will abroad.
Call in thy deaths head there: tie up thy fears.
He that forbears
To suit and serve his need,
Deserves his load.
But as I rav'd and grew more fierce and wilde
At every word,
Me thoughts I heard one calling, *Child!*
And I reply'd, *My Lord.*

According to the interpretations usually offered, *The Collar* describes the struggle between discipline and pleasure, between the duties of a clergyman and the satisfctions to be derived from the natural life, or, as Joseph Summers puts it, the struggle between God's will and the speaker's rebellious Heart.[1] But to leave the matter here is to miss, I think, the full import of the poem. Properly read — read, that is, in the context of Herbert's other poems, and with reference to the tradition which informs his imagery with meaning — the poem gains in complexity and power. It may be seen to represent in psychological terms the events of the Christian moral drama — the Fall, the Atonement, and the Redemption. It is certainly true that the speaker, under the influence of the Heart, rebels against discipline. But in reaching for the "fruit," as did Adam, he simultaneously reaches for the supernatural fruit, the fruit of the Cross. Paradoxically, the "natural" imagery of the poem, the fruit and wine and corn, in pursuit of which the speaker rebels, is also the imagery traditionally associated with the Eucharist. Therefore we may describe the moral events of the poem in this way: just as the moral disorder entailed by the rebellion of Adam and Eve was overcome by Christ's sacrifice, so the moral disorder of the speaker's rebellion is to be finally overcome by the sacrament of the Eucharist. Part of the brilliance of the poem lies in the fact that it expresses rebellion and atonement in the same vocabulary, and by so doing epitomizes its central idea: that rebellion necessarily entails, because of God's justice and mercy, atonement.

Joseph Summers has described very well the structure of the poem. It is divided into four sections of argument. First the speaker, under the influence of the Heart, complains; then the Will answers that there is "fruit" if the Heart will seek it; next, the Heart repeats its complaint and its rebellious intention; and finally there is the resolution.[2] But if we look closely at the imagery the precise nature of the resolution becomes clear. We see, furthermore, that both Heart and Will are the unconscious instruments of God's will, and that His intention, latent from the start, gradually becomes manifest. Lines 6-12 contain the unmistakable references:

> Shall I be still in suit?
> Have I no harvest but a thorn
> To let me bloud, and not restore
> What I have lost with cordiall fruit?
> Sure there was wine
> Before my sighs did drie it: there was corn
> Before my tears did drown it.

"Suit" in line 6 suggests a petitioner. The speaker, as if in a court of law, seeks something which as yet is not forthcoming. The word also carries the sense of enforced attendance, the attitude of a courtier who has little to hope for. But as one analyzes the poem and becomes aware of its full implication, one realizes that the important word in this line is not "suit" but "still." The speaker is not a litigant in an earthly court, and he is not in suit before a secular prince: his suit is before a supernatural king, and is to be decided according to transcendent laws. He should, in other words, be *still*, although he does not know it; and at the end of the poem we are indeed aware of a kind of stillness: the speaker no longer needs all those words. In the next six lines we encounter a series of references which would have presented no difficulties to Herbert's contemporaries. The speaker's suit yields him a harvest only of thorn. I do not wish to insist upon a minor point, since the poem is clearly theological in its bearing, but I cannot suppose that the mixing of metaphors here, the legal and courtly suit entailing the unfortunate agricultural harvest, is entirely without social meaning. But however this may be, we are told that the speaker's harvest yields only "a thorn" which makes him bleed. At the moment of his rebellion, the speaker understands his words in some such sense as this: my discipline is painful, in blocking the satisfaction of my desires it makes me bleed and sigh, and, to make matters worse, it brings no reward. However, the words he uses have an alternative signification. The thorn suggests the imperfections introduced into the world by the Fall, the damaging of the *rosa sine spina* of paradise. Such an association for "thorn" was commonplace. Bishop Bayly, for example, referred to "thornes, the first fruits of the curse," in his *Practice of Pietie* (1613), and Milton points out in *Paradise Lost* that Eden before the Fall boasted "Flow'rs of all hue, and without Thorn the Rose." Thus the thorn, which in its primary meaning in the poem signifies the discomforts the speaker experiences when his desires conflict with his discipline, also suggests the results of the Fall. Just as Adam, rebelling against the original "discipline" of Eden, introduced thorns into Eden, so the speaker, rebelling against *his* discipline, finds a thorn rather than fruit. But, and here is the third signification of "thorn," the thorn is not only the result of the sin of rebellion but also is associated with the means of its redemption. The speaker's harvest, the thorns which make him bleed, though at present bringing only pain, foreshadow the mode of his redemption: they are also the thorns of Christ's crown. To summarize: the speaker is linked in his rebellion with Adam, and like him he longs for "fruit"; his longing and rebellion lead to "thorns"; but, as in the case of Adam, the means of recovery is implicit in the act. The thorns are the thorns of Eden after the Fall, they are the thorns of the speaker's pain, and they are the thorns of Christ's crown, the symbol of *His* pain and therefore of the means of man's redemption.

The speaker is not aware of all this, however, at the moment the thoughts described in these lines occur. The full meaning of his rebellion, as defined by the *double entendres*, does not become clear to him until the end of the poem. In lines 8 and 9 he says merely that there is no relief for him, that his harvest is only of thorn. He is not aware, though we *are*, of the irony present in "only" — *only* Christ's crown. As far as the speaker is aware at this moment, he has no harvest which will "restore | What I have lost with cordiall fruit."

To Herbert's contemporaries the pun involved in "cordiall" would have been a routine matter: *cor, cordis.* "Cordiall" therefore alludes to that which comes from the heart, or blood. But what of "fruit"? "Cordiall fruit," the restorative fruit for which the speaker longs, is thus "bloody fruit." This would not have been a difficult allusion for a seventeenth-century reader to unravel. The Fall occurred when fruit was plucked from the forbidden tree. Because this theft introduced death into the world, the fruit Adam stole might plausibly be described as bloody. But Christ was the fruit which grew on a later tree. As Thomas Middleton put it, "The tree of Good and Evil brought forth an apple to cast us all away, and the Tree of Shame bare a fruit to save us all forever." Even a carol can count on an understanding of the conceit, and begins, "An earthly tree a heavenly fruit it bare."[3] Christ's body and blood thus constitute one meaning of the bloody fruit, or "cordiall fruit," of the poem. It is "cordiall fruit" in this sense that atones for man's rebellion, either the original rebellion of Adam or the rebellions which occur in every self much as they occur in the case of the speaker in *The Collar.*

The next three lines are fraught with implication, and, furthermore, elaborate upon the theme of the Eucharistic sacrifice.

> Sure there was wine
> Before my sighs did drie it: there was corn
> Before my tears did drown it.

Let us consider the possibilities present here. Wine and corn can represent natural food and drink, can represent the pleasures of eating which the speaker has denied himself because of his ascetic discipline. Considered in this way, they are the natural pleasures he longs for, objects of desire comparable to "fruit." But wine and corn (wheat) are also, of course, the elements of the Eucharist, wine and bread. At first the speaker seems to be saying that he desires the natural pleasures, the pleasures from which he has been cut off by discipline. But he is simultaneously saying that his tears and sighs are the manifestation of his need for the restorative, reordering powers of the sacrament. To put it another way: he *thinks* he desires natural pleasure, but the real object of his desire is supernatural, the cordial fruit of the Eucharist. Here, as in Dante, the true object of desire is not the earthly and the mutable, but the eternal. The implication is also present here that the speaker's tears and sighs have damaged the wine and corn. This may mean that the rigors of the speaker's discipline have denied him sensuous pleasure. But it can also mean that it is the speaker's emotional turmoil that has cut him off from an awareness of the restorative powers of the sacrament.

Now that we have identified the controlling imagery of the poem as Eucharistic, we can give certain details a fuller explication than they have yet received. According to Hutchinson, the "collar was in common use to express discipline, and 'to slip the collar' was often used figuratively. Preachers would use the word *collar* of the restraint imposed by conscience."[4] The speaker, it is clear, thinks of himself as a kind of prisoner, and like a prisoner he wishes to free himself from the restraints that have been imposed upon him. The "collar" of his discipline punishes him much as a criminal is punished by having to wear a real collar. The meaning of the comparison implicit in the title, between the speaker who is suffering amid tears and sighs and a criminal anxious to "slip the collar" of his punishment, was not unusual. For man, the descendant of Adam, was in fact guilty of a robbery, and was a "prisoner" because of it. As Herbert put it in *The Sacrifice*, where Christ Himself is the speaker, "Man stole the fruit, but I must climb the tree." The rebellion of the speaker in *The Collar* is a version of Adam's rebellion, or theft, and must be redressed in the same way.

It may be that the "board" in line I is Christ's table, the Communion table. The speaker, under the influence of the rebellious Heart, turns from the Communion table and entertains the possibility of gaining a

kind of freedom through rebellion. He asserts argumentatively that in
fact he *is* free, that in effect he has not fallen: "I will abroad ... My lines
and life are free; free as the rode, | Loose as the winde, as large as store."
Entertaining the notion of his own guiltlessness, supposing that his life,
"as large as store," need not be "restored," he proceeds to re-enact
psychologically the events of the Fall. He has only to stretch forth his
hand to pluck the fruit, he tells himself: "there is fruit, | and thou hast
hands." The irony implicit here is that, reaching for one fruit, as Adam
did, he will simultaneously reach for the other fruit, the cordial fruit
which grew on the Cross. Rebellion sets in motion, unknown to the
rebel, the process which leads to atonement, and at the very moment of
his psychological rebellion the speaker sets forth implications which
define the mode of his redemption. The series of questions beginning in
line 13 admit of the answer "no" in two different senses.

> Is the yeare onely lost to me?
> Have I no bayes to crown it?
> No flowers, no garlands gay? all blasted?
> All wasted?

The rebellious Heart intends these to be rhetorical questions, expects the
obvious answer that, no, the speaker has hands and may reach for the
fruit. But the fruit here, as we have seen, is not only the fruit which is the
object of rebellion but also is the fruit of the Cross, the "cordiall fruit" of
the Eucharist. Therefore another answer suggests itself: no, the speaker
has hands and may reach for the chalice. Thus, lines 17-18 can be read in
two different ways. They can represent *agreement* with the Heart, the
assent of the Will, now corrupted, to the Heart's rebellious argument.
Or, they can suggest the truth at which the speaker eventually will arrive.
The phrase "thou hast hands," therefore, signifies not only the hands
which can rebelliously reach for the fruit, or the hands which *might*
reach for the chalice, but the hands which *were* nailed to the Cross.
Similarly, in view of the pun on "cordiall," the word "heart" in line 17
may also be identified with Christ. Christ is, in a sense, the speaker's
"real" heart. These double meanings, themselves a kind of transubstantiation, the interpretation of two realms, anticipate the conclusion
of the poem, in which the speaker and Christ are united analogically,
both being "children" of God.

In addition, a third category of reference may be discerned here. The
poem is also about the writing of poetry. The imagery of the questions
just dealt with — bays, flowers, garlands — traditionally has been
associated with poetry, as it is, for example, in *Lycidas* and in Carew's
An Elegy upon the Death of the Dean of Paul's, Dr. John Donne.

Herbert's use of such imagery here thus suggests a connection between loss of poetic power and the speaker's separation from the restorative powers of the Eucharist. The Eucharist, indeed, linking as it did two disparate realms, may be seen to have been the perfect symbol for the metaphysical conceit. Furthermore, if we do consider the flower imagery here to be associated with poetry, we may see that the rebellious Heart is longing for the *wrong* kind of poetry. In *Jordan*, we recall, Herbert rejected the pastoral mode, among others, as "false," and asserted that in plainly saying "My God, My King" he was expressing truth directly. In a similar way, the pastoral imagery employed by the rebellious Heart in *The Collar* is to be replaced by the "plain" truth of the last line.

The implication is also present in *The Collar* that the *form* of poetry is a kind of analogue of the order epitomized by the Eucharist. When the poet's "lines are free," that is, when his rhetoric escapes from poetic form, he has no bays and garlands, or poems, to crown the year. The rebellious Heart, ironically enough, does not see that even "false" poetry, pastoral poetry, requires the order of poetic form, does not see that rebellion against order is ultimately destructive even of inferior poetry. Helen White has pointed out that after these lines about garlands and bays the imagery becomes more vulgar as the emotion expressed grows "more fierce and wilde."[5] At the end of the poem, when the speaker's impulse toward rebellion has been overcome and he has recovered his sense of his relation to God, his lines begin to lose their "freedom," and poetic order returns along with moral and theological order.

In lines 19-34, the Heart goes on with its counsel of rebellion, oblivious to the implications we have found in lines 17-18. The Heart urges the poet-priest to seek "double pleasures," to regard the law (which, ironically, is operating silently in the very vocabulary of the poem) as a "rope of sands." "Leave thy cold dispute| Of what is fit, and not," the Heart urges. These lines are illuminated by Herbert's remark in *A Priest to the Temple* that "Contentiousnesse in a feast of Charity is more scandal than any posture."[6] Such "dispute" as, according to the Heart, the poet-priest has been engaged in is alien to the spirit of the sacrament. Perhaps, then, we can read these lines as suggesting that it has been "cold dispute" which has, at least in part, caused the poet-priest to lose his sense of the power of the Eucharist, a sense recovered by the "childlike" consciousness of the poem's conclusion (cf. "Unless you become like children. . .," *Matthew* 18:3-4). At any rate, in lines 19-34 the Heart urges rebellion in peremptory terms. A chief result of the Fall, mortality, should not be feared: "Call in thy death's head there." But double meanings here, as previously, provide an undercurrent of ironic commentary on the Heart's speech. "He that forbears| To suit and serve his need, | Deserves his load" seems at first merely to justify rebellion. But looked at again, "suit" takes on the color of "Shall I be still in suit" (line 6), and the lines may be read as suggesting: "he that does not seek redemption deserves the burden of his sin."

Yet even as the speaker, under the influence of the rebellious Heart, raves and grows more wild, the ironies of the earlier lines are asserting themselves for his benefit. The line endings, we notice, reflect a gathering of order. Starting with line 27, earlier random endings are succeeded by a steady pattern of assonances (heed/abroad, fears/forebears, need/load, wilde/word, Child/Lord). And this re-assertion of pattern is heralded by the unsubtle *abba* rhyme of thee/draw/law/see, which brings to an abrupt end the chaotic rhyming of the first half of the poem. As Joseph Summers has summarized the function of form in this poem: "until the final four lines, the poem dramatizes expertly and convincingly the revolt of the heart, and its imitation of colloquial speech almost convinces us of the justice of the cause. But the disorder of the poem provides a constant implicit criticism, and with the final lines we recognize that *The Collar* is a narrative in the past tense: the message of the present concerns the necessity of order."[7]

We may now see what law obtains at the supernatural court in which the speaker, unawares, was "in suit." The re-establishment of order follows upon, is entailed by, rebellion. The speaker began by asserting the validity of rebellion. He then identified himself with Adam, imagined himself reaching for the fruit that brought about man's Fall. But the law remained in operation: the hands that reach for the fruit of rebellion reach also, unknown to the speaker when he is under the influence of the Heart, for Christ, reach for the chalice ("cordiall fruit," "corn," "wine") which, such is God's power, restores the speaker to his proper relationship to God. Line 34, indeed, admits of two interpretations. The speaker grows more fierce and wild "at every word"; but, also, "at every word" in the poem he now hears the voice of God: "Me thoughts I heard one calling, *Child!* | And I reply'd, *My Lord.*" The speaker's heart, previously united with Christ by means of *double entendre*, is now united with Him in a relationship which is part of the speaker's awareness: both Christ and His surrogate, the Priest who administers the Eucharist, are children of God. The moral hierarchy, epitomized in the hierarchy of father and son, and of Father and Son, has been restored.

GEORGE HERBERT'S "EASTER-WINGS"

C. C. Brown and W. P. Ingoldsby

In this century George Herbert's pattern poem "Easter-Wings" has been recognized as quite a good poem, despite the early prejudice about the childishness of writing a poem to such a stanzaic shape at all. But of course the winged shape of the two stanzas of this poem in *The Temple* was not used arbitrarily by the poet. The poem will not yield its meaning unless one reads the visual shape as part of its carefully controlled symbolic language. Joan Bennett has written of the effect of the declining and growing of the lines of the poem as being expressive as an "image" of "the rise and fall of the lark's song and flight."[1] The purpose of this article is to show that Herbert's initial image of the wings, embodied in the shape of the stanzas, is more complex and exacting than is the homely image of larks. By calling the poem a "visual hieroglyph,"[2] J. H. Summers has suggested a more adequate approach, recognizing that it is around the symbolism of the wings themselves that we are intended to meditate. And there can be no doubt that when he thought of composing a poem in this shape, Herbert remembered precedents for doing so and that he thought about these precedents, in which wings already carried symbolic meanings. As we shall see, the general shape of his stanzas is Greek, the precise dimensions Hebrew, so that in writing "Easter-Wings" Herbert opened for himself the problem of defining an attitude toward the pagan and Hebraic sources from which the wings drew some of their meaning. A second purpose of this article is to suggest that Herbert's precise practice in "Easter-Wings," where he controls these associations within the context of a celebration of Easter, may serve to typify the kind of integrity he always sought for his Christian art.

Prior to a discussion of the poem it is relevant to know that the stanzaic shape of wings seems to have been most familiar to poets of the Renaissance from verses attributed to Simmias Rhodius in what is now

Reprinted from *HLQ*, 35 (1972), 131-42, by permission of the authors and the publisher.

called *The Greek Anthology*. This poem was set out in the shape of a
single pair of wings. It had been anthologized several times by the time
Herbert wrote; it appeared for example in the well-known anthologies
of J. Crespin *(Vetustissimorum Authorum . . . Poemata quae Supersunt,*
Geneva, 1569) and of J. J. Scaliger *(Theocriti . . . Moschi, Bionis, Simmii*
Opera quae Exstant, Heidelberg, 1596). Both books went through
several editions. Simmias' verses are spoken by Eros, the unifying
cosmic power who succeeded to Chaos in the ordering of the universe;
he is the philosophic Love of the mythology of the old cosmogonies and
of Plato's *Symposium* (178 b). I may look a little fellow, he says in the
poem, but I am really one of the oldest of the gods, my cheeks are bushy
with hair.[3]

Of Simmias' wing-shaped poem as it was printed in Renaissance
anthologies Herbert would almost certainly have been aware. It is
difficult to determine how many wing-shaped poems were written in the
Renaissance in imitation of Simmias and how many of these Herbert
might have known and imitated. We have not found any which suggest
themselves as sources for "Easter-Wings." It seems probable that it was
Simmias' poem itself that Herbert remembered when he decided to
compose a poem in this shape.[4] This may be corroborated by the fact
that Herbert's poem, like that of Simmias, exploits the Platonic myth of
the winged god, except that in Herbert's poem the figure of Eros has
been metamorphosed, or has entirely vanished, into a figure for Christ.

Perhaps one may also preface a discussion of "Easter-Wings" by
pointing immediately to the obvious contrast in tone and subject matter
between the enigmatic speech of the Eros of the Greek poem and the
Christian celebration of the angels' wings of Herbert's poem. The wings
of *erotes,* the chubby boys that poets and painters delighted to
mythologize, are not the wings of Herbert's poem. This is not to say
much about the significance of Herbert's poem, perhaps, except to make
the important initial point that many other Christian poets in the
Renaissance happily accommodated the figures of "loves" themselves to
the Love of the Divine in less plain Christian poems. One may think, for
example, of the angel in *The Faerie Queene,* the "faire young man, / Of
wondrous beautie, and of freshest yeares" with "snowy front curled with
golden heares" who had "two sharpe winged sheares, / Decked with
diverse plumes, like painted Jayes" and was, predictably, "Like as
CUPIDO on IDAEAN hill" (II.viii.5-6). Or of the "thousand" and "ten
thousand" *putti* who flutter into Giles Fletcher's *Christ's Victory in*
Heaven (st. 46) and *Christ's Victory on Earth* (st. 2). Such conflations of
cupids, cherubim, and angels are commonplace in Christian poetry of
the Renaissance.[5] Instead Herbert's wings are more simply, more

deliberately Hebraic in origin — messianic, in fact. Yet of the humanistic basis of his art there can be no doubt, and in the working out of this
visual hieroglyph he relies on one of the most familiarly repeated of all
metaphors of Plato, the metaphor of the winged soul. So, too, even in
the homely precepts of "The Church Porch" (xiv.2) he had taught: "God
gave thy soul brave wings." What is at issue in "Easter-Wings," as in
many poems in "The Church," is how the learned artist, who is fully
aware of the range of poetic mythology available to the Christian
humanist, may find an art tactful enough, and free enough of an idolatry
of art, to answer his own sense of the simple language of God, which is
said to be for all men. The number and the range of Herbert's allusions
to such learned symbolism is sometimes understated. He does not limit
himself exclusively to the images of everyday and to those of the biblical
tradition. That critics should sometimes think his language is limited or
homely in this sense is largely the result of Herbert's own care, by which
he tried to ensure that all the images of his art should be in dedicated
service not to the glory of themselves but to Christ.

"Easter-Wings" comes in the section of "The Church" concerned with
Holy Week. Its immediate context may be gathered from the preceding
poem, "Easter":

> The Sunne arising in the East
> Though he give light, & th'East perfume;
> If they should offer to contest
> With thy arising, they presume.

The expected Easter metaphors of sun, dawn, day, and rising are
common to both poems. Already in "Easter" man is set against the
unattainable example of Christ in the task of imitating His "arising."
The gentle metaphorical pun is also common to both poems: Christ as
sun rises to herald the new "day," which is His era; but Christ's victory
over death was also His rising from the dead. Then again "Easter" had
begun:

> Rise heart: thy Lord is risen. Sing his praise
> Without delayes,
> Who takes thee by the hand, that thou likewise
> With him mayst rise.

In "Easter" the heart was awakened in song; in "Easter-Wings" the heart
tries to rise with Christ, to "feel this day thy victories." The metaphor of
rising is exploited in visual fashion as ascending flight, the poet wishing
to imitate the lark, which familiarly provides a figure for the hymning

poet, flying above the base earth to greet the dayspring "harmoniously." But the text that stands most clearly and centrally behind "Easter-Wings" is the messianic text at the very end of the Old Testament (Malachi iv.2): "But unto you that fear my name shall the Sun of righteousness arise with healing in his wings; and ye shall go forth, and grow up as calves of the stall." The wings of Malachi may be supported in Isaiah xl.31: "But they that wait upon the Lord shall renew their strength; they shall mount up with wings as eagles." In Luke i.78-79 the prophecy of Malachi is fulfilled: "Through the tender mercy of our God; whereby the day-spring from on high hath visited us, / To give light to them that sit in darkness and in the shadow of death." Although the "wings" of Malachi were often explained by commentators as the rays of the sun,[6] Herbert wants wings for wings; presumably the "imping" of his wings upon Christ's has its origin in the concept of "healing" in Malachi. But the most familiar myth about wings and the state of their fledgedness is of course not Christian at all, although it was often Christianized: it is the myth of Plato in the *Phaedrus*. There the plumage of the soul is fostered and increased by beauty, wisdom, virtue, and the like, and destroyed by deformity and vice. In this famous passage (246-257) Plato had also associated the moral state of the immortal soul with the myth of the winged god, Eros (Love), who is also Peteros (Flyer).

In the context of the Platonic myth we may see, in a fairly obvious way, how Herbert has made rhetorical use of the symbolic shape of his stanzas. In the shortening of the lines toward the center of each stanza is figured fall and decay: the corresponding lengthening of the lines figures redemptive arising, spiritual growth. In wishing to "imp" his wing upon the wing of Christ the poet wishes to repair his own decayed wing to full plumage by grafting into it feathers from the perfect wing of the Messiah. Metaphors of engrafting are not uncommon as illustrations of grace: Milton's God tells the Son that man shall "live in thee transplanted, and from thee / Receive new life" (*PL* III.293-294). The extended conceit embodied in the shape of the stanzas elaborates the "healing" of Malachi. The poem is shaped in ritual celebration of Easter, but the precise terms of the visual metaphor as it is exploited in both stanzas suggest exactly the fiction of the Platonic myth.

Both stanzas follow this general procedure of decay and growth, the metrical movement easily accommodated to it. More precisely, however, the first stanza enacts the fall of mankind, the second the degenerate course of the poet's own life. Mankind was created in the Garden "in wealth and store" but fell "foolishly," adding steadily thereafter to its own degeneration through sin. Herbert, beginning his life already a fallen man, shared the general "sorrow" of all mankind, then continued also to add daily to his own stock of sin, until with this affliction he became "most thinne." The second halves of both stanzas are really prayers from the poet to Christ, asking to be able to rise with Him at Easter. In the first stanza the poet asks to rise as the larks "And sing this day thy victories"; allowed this, he will play out the doctrinal paradox of the fortunate fall. In the second stanza the verbs, given exact weight in the metrical movement, change from "rise" and "sing" to "combine" and "feel." The change indicates the shift from the state of mankind treated generally, in the first part of the first stanza, to the state of the individual realized individually, in the first part of the second. He works toward a fuller apprehension of his own state seen against the pattern and sacrifice of Christ. Here, as in many poems, Herbert will not let his art resolve itself until the heart is engaged in a felt understanding. The model of the poet rising, as the lark does, in a greeting hymn has been emotionally deepened into the model of the poet superimposing himself more totally upon the example of Christ: "With thee / Let me combine/And feel" is tactual, body almost felt upon body as wing is imped upon wing. In the masculine control of Herbert's rhetoric his plain verbs, like his tenses (here past against present against future), show an exactitude of purpose.

In the fiction of the Platonic myth, as it is symbolized visually in the lengths of the lines, the redemptive meaning of Easter has been conveyed. Moreover a symmetrical patterning has emphasized the meaning, the "decaying" half of each stanza being set off against the "rising" or "combining" half and one stanza of wings paired off against the other, the same yet different. It is a rhetoric of counterpoise. Yet if the hieroglyphic shape of the poem disciplined the poet into a static pattern of resolution, all oppositions contained by the whole, then it did not produce a bland ritual only. Confronting "this day"[7] the fact of Christ's perfect redemptive act, the poet is moved to invite his own heart to feel the perfection of Christ and hence, humbly, his own imperfection. There are many poems to come in "The Church" before the delicate assurance and shy relief of "Love" III, followed by the Gloria.

At this stage it is helpful to look at the setting out of the poem on the printed page. In all early printed editions the stanzas were printed vertically. Each pair of wings occupied a page, so that the two stanzas stood side by side in the opened book, each stanza suggesting the shape of an angel's wings. We feel quite sure that this typographical arrangement is the most appropriate to the meaning of the poem: the resemblance to angels ought to be as close as possible.[8] In Hutchinson's Oxford edition the lines are printed horizontally. This makes straightforward reading easier, but does tend to obscure the important shape of the stanzas — all the more so since the lines have also been printed as it were about a central vertical axis, so that they decrease and increase equally on each side of the page. More realistically, at least to the conventions, the early printed editions show the upper edges of the angels' wings to be less steeply inclined than the lower edges.

This shape that Herbert's early printers adopted was a familiar one, for Simmias' Greek poem seems to have appeared in this fashion in Renaissance anthologies. As they appear superficially on the printed page, the only differences between the Greek poem and the English are these: Simmias' poem had six lines in each wing and consisted of Eros' single pair of wings; Herbert's poem had five lines only in each wing and consisted of two pairs of wings, the wings of two angels. The difference in size and number, between the stanzas of the two poems, may seem insignificantly mechanical, but in fact it may be that it does express the specific intention of Herbert's Christian art. It cannot of course be proved that Herbert wrote "Easter-Wings" with the details of the Greek firmly in his mind's eye. But the size as well as the shape of Herbert's stanzas does seem to be significant, because it appears to assert in itself that he intended Hebrew origins for his hieroglyph rather than Greek origins to suggest themselves primarily to the mind of the reader. Again, nothing can be proved from the bare fact that Herbert's poem happens to be of different size from that of Simmias (even supposing that he had the Greek in mind), but there can be no doubt that there are easy associations to be made between the size of Herbert's angel-wings in *The Temple* and the size of the cherubim in Solomon's temple, set out so exactly in I Kings vi.23-27:

And within the oracle he made two cherubims of olive-tree, each ten cubits high.

And five cubits was the one wing of the cherub, and five cubits the other wing of the cherub; from the uttermost part of the one wing to the uttermost part of the other were ten cubits.

And the other cherub was ten cubits: both the cherubims were of one measure and one size.

The height of the one cherub was ten cubits, and so was it of the other cherub.

And he set the cherubims within the inner house: and they stretched forth the wings of the cherubims, so that the wing of the one touched the one wall, and the wing of the other cherub touched the other wall; and their wings touched one another in the midst of the house.

Hence, perhaps, Herbert's double pair of angel-wings. The two cherubim — who were usually taken as a kind of angel, appearing in the shape of young men with wings — recur throughout the Old Testament. Two cherubim guard the Garden after the Fall (Genesis. iii.24); in the tabernacle two cherubim were made of gold and placed at either side of the mercy seat, their wings extending over it, their faces "seatward" (Exodus xxxvii.7-9); in Solomon's temple the symbolism was repeated on a larger scale, to the measurements cited above. The presence of God is often characterized "between the cherubim." To turn to the New Testament, the "angels" of I Peter i.12, who desire to look into the revelation of Christ, were associated with the type of the cherubim, who were supposed also to have desired to look into the mystery of the mercy seat. And two of the Evangelists place two angels at the sepulcher of the risen Christ. Herbert gave his wings each a span of five lines (five cubits), making a total of ten for each identical angel; and he gave as the "height" of each angel ten cubits also, since each of the longest lines of the poem has ten syllables.

If the measurements of Herbert's wings are determinedly Hebraic, then the significance of his Old Testament types is, as we should expect, determinedly Christian. He does not seem to take up precise symbolic meanings of the cherubim in particular. Rather he avoids what was something of an exegetical problem by exploiting the generic association of cherub with angel, which allows him the reference to Christ he needs. In the most common reading of the cherubim, particularly since Augustine (*On the Psalms* 79[2]), they signify fullness of knowledge, contemplating the mercy seat, which is in itself a figure for Christ, the Propitiary. But in "Easter-Wings" Christ himself, like cherub and angel (and soul and lark), has wings.[9] Christ is, as it were, perfect angel: "And I saw another mighty angel come down from heaven, clothed with a cloud: and a rainbow was upon his head, and his face was as it were the sun, and his feet as pillars of fire" (Rev. x.1). Malachi had prophesied the coming of the Son as sun with healing in his wings; Luke had written of the dayspring from on high as in fulfillment of that prophecy with regard to the first coming of the Messiah; St. John, in this passage, was supposed to figure the Second Coming, again in metaphors of sun and winged creature. That Christ could be figured in the form of an angel was universally recognized: he is sometimes termed the angel of the covenant.

By beginning with the shape of angels, who are created beings intermediary between God and man, moving between heaven and earth, Herbert has embraced within this "hieroglyph" both the perfection of Christ and the imperfection of man. For according to the predominant conceit of the poem there may be supposed to exist a hierarchy of beings with wings. From angel he may move up to Christ, clothed in the splendor of light, or downward to man and to himself, whose wings are weak. The wings of Christ may be said to have borne Him down in mercy and love: the larks (smaller than eagles) of the first stanza fly up to greet Christ in praise. But merely to observe or even to praise the rising of Christ is not enough. By feeling the example of Christ and by imitating the angelic flight himself, the poet must come closer to that pattern. For this he asks the infusion of grace.

The intellectual control which Herbert exercised over the scope of his figurative language in "Easter-Wings" is not untypical of the control which he displays in many other poems in "The Church." When he wrote a pattern poem he did not intend to make a poem essentially different in kind from the other poems of this section of *The Temple*. (Neither did he with "The Altar": the shape of the altar is in fact the first introductory image of sacrifice greeting the eyes of the reader as he enters "The Church.") The visual hieroglyph, as Summers has called it, was just one figure suitable to his purpose, one aspect of the symbolic language through which the individual may come to understand and share "the churches mysticall repast" ("Superliminare"). The precise practice of the poet in "Easter-wings," where all the images are so restrained and tightly bound within the primary messianic context, illustrates an integrity and a control over a symbolic language such as few poets have achieved, or have perhaps wished to achieve. It has been seen that this poem calls up quite a large range of commonplace metaphorical figures, playing out the terms of a well-known Platonic myth and measuring the two stanzas by the measurements of the wings of the cherubim, a familiar Old Testament type from the glorious art of Solomon's temple. Both Platonic metaphor and Old Testament type had in themselves become capable of elaborate development, in terms of the commonplace uses later poetic and exegetical traditions had made of them. But Herbert used the Platonic metaphor strictly to illustrate fall and redemption, and he seems to have wanted the wings of the cherubim only in so far as angels in general may figure Christ, against the pattern of whose love he tests his own heart and to whose service he humbly refers his art. His symbolism shows a singlemindedness, a purity of intent: the poet seems to have denied himself the enjoyment of more than a moment's indulgence in the beauties of the language of his art for its own sake. He employed a poetic mythology in the same way in which he seems to have viewed the rites of the church: they were beautiful so long as they were just. And they were just in so far as they did not distract attention toward the indulgent contemplation of themselves.

Everywhere in his verse, from the early sonnets to his mother, Herbert debates what language of art may be appropriate for the poet addressing God, or himself in the presence of God. Another poem which alludes to the symbolic decorations of Solomon's temple makes overt statements about the significance to the servant of Christ of such elaborate artistic offerings as were in the Hebrew temple:

> Lord, with what glorie wast thou serv'd of old,
> When Solomons temple stood and flourished!
> Where most things were of purest gold
> The wood was all embellished
> With flowers and carvings, mysticall and rare:
> All show'd the builders, crav'd the seers care.

But, as "Sion" makes clear, the poet-priest of the Christian era moves from the glorious outward architecture of such as the Hebrew temple to the fallen temple of the self, to the soul, and to the heart:

> And now thy Architecture meets with sinne;
> For all thy frame and fabric is within.
> There thou art struggling with a peevish heart.

"Easter-Wings," like many other poems, shows as the principal subject of the Christian poet the relationship of the heart to Christ, the reciprocal sacrifice of love. As far as such "mysticall" offerings of art as those of the temple are concerned, and with these we may associate the images of the "temple" of any Christian poet, the implication is that they are vain, or may be distracting, unless they come from the humble service of the heart: "But grones are quick, and full of wings, / And all their motions upward be." The danger of a glorious art may be seen in this to approach that of idolatry, of glorying too much in created things which are between God and man.

Better than this idolatry of art is therefore an art-less plainness. "Shepherds are honest people, let them sing." In "Jordan" (I) this determination not to glory in the intervening images of art is broadened into a criticism of the whole allegorical method (not merely "Spenserian" but broadly Augustinian)[10] which had belonged to Christian humanism: "Must all be vail'd, while he that reades, divines, / Catching the sense at two removes?" Despite the pious but consciously naïve wish that poetry may plainly portray the truth — "Is there in truth no beautie?" — Herbert knew that the Bible employed "signs" in parts and that the book of nature had also been seen as the symbolic language of God to fallen man, following the influential words of "the apostle of the Gentiles": "For the invisible things of him from the creation of the world are clearly seen, being understood by the things that are made, even his eternal

power and godhead" (Romans i.20). The Christian artist often saw his
art as an imitation of that symbolic manner, trying to picture the
invisible reality by means of the visible symbols of the world, the
hieroglyphs of creation; so that it was often said that fallen man cannot
be supposed to view the throne of God without a veil. The mystic poet
often claimed to use his art as a "veil" (to take up Herbert's familiar
image from "Jordan"), through which the brightness of God may be
glimpsed.[11]

Nevertheless "Jordan" does not determine the final answer to the
problem of finding an appropriate art. It merely shows the poet making
the dramatic gesture of renunciation, of opting out of the vainglorious
competition with other poets which encouraged the making of more
intricate, more elaborately delicate "fictions" or "winding stairs" in
which to figure out the truth. But what the poet offers in fact throughout
"The Church" is not the impossibility of a fictionless verse — rather a
verse in which the fictions are tightly subordinated to the service of his
art to Christ. The poet who dwells too long upon his created images, as if
they were, in Herbert's ironic phrase, "mysticall and rare," is in danger
of forgetting that such images are no more than the "outward and visible
signs" of an "inward and spiritual grace." The poet's images, like the
sacramental water, bread, and wine to which these phrases from the
Anglican catechism refer, are not themselves "mysticall"; but they
preserve the memory of what are called divine mysteries.

The "fictions" of "The Church" are therefore to be approached by the
reader in a way similar to that in which the communicant may approach
the sacraments, with the reverence and preparation due to an understanding of the significance conveyed through, but not in, the tangible
images used in the symbolic act. Thus despite the ironic humor with
which he referred to the symbols of Solomon's temple as "mysticall and
rare," Herbert asks the reader to approach "The Church" out of "The
Church-Porch" as if he were preparing for something "mysticall" in this
section of the book:

> Thou, whom the former precepts have
> Sprinkled and taught, how to behave
> Thy self in church; approach, and taste
> The churches mysticall repast. ("Superliminare")

Here the initial figure is again pre-Christian, alluding to pagan sacrificial rites. "Perirranterium," the title given in the Williams manuscript to
this quatrain rather than as subtitle to "The Church-Porch" itself, recalls
the lustral sprinkling by priests in the Greek mysteries. So a certain sense

of initiation is required for the right reading of the poems of "The Church." But the voice of the poet is not only that of the initiated priest protecting the hidden wisdom from the approach of the impure — "Avoid prophaneness, come not here" — but also that of the pastor to his flock, concerned with the openness of the dispensation of grace. Just as he discourages any cult of the fictions of art, because such an art may intervene as a distraction between God and man, so too he discourages any sense of a protective Hellenic cult of mystery.[12] The figure of the Greek mysteries is immediately modified by the homely language as to a child: "how to behave / Thy self in church." And this tone is appropriate because what he intends through the figure of the Greek rites is the progress of the "child," the new member of the community of the church, by way of the enactment of the two sacraments that Anglican doctrine held "as generally necessary to salvation": baptism and the celebration of the Lord's Supper. By the proverbial wisdom of "The Church-Porch" the reader has, as it were, been baptized and catechized, "sprinkled and taught," so that he may share in the communion of Christ. Entering "The Church" the reader becomes, therefore, one of the "very members incorporate in the mysticall body of thy Son, which is the blessed company of all faithful people"; and leaving "The Church" with the very last poem, "Love" (III), the reader sees the taking of the bread — "So I did sit and eat," followed by the Gloria. By the second quatrain of "Superliminare" Herbert makes it clear once again that the emphasis of his language is not, and will not be, upon any Hellenic cult of mystery, as it was not upon any intrusive art. The only qualification his readers need, if they are to benefit from his published record, is a pure heart, or even, less exclusively, the intention to be pure — "that which groneth to be so." To the art of the church, or of "The Church," no other initiation is required. The resonance of his symbolic language is again controlled by the simplicity of heart; and the sense of the mysteries of initiation, as both his art and the communion of the church are approached, is softened by the plain language of the shepherd. The imitation of Christ, it would seem, begins with the humble particularities of obedience, and the poetic language of the Christian pastor is controlled also by such a sense of service.

Few critics are likely to welcome the sight of an intellect working so devotedly as the slave of a framework of belief. It is not likely to produce poetry that conforms to ideas of an exploratory/creative method. The modern student is more likely to have been asked to approach *The Temple* by way of such gestures of dramatic revolt and "metaphysical" habits as the famous opening of "The Collar": "I struck the board, and

cry'd, No more. / I will abroad." But that poem also ends with the
service of a child: "Me thoughts I heard one calling, CHILDE: / And I
reply'd MY LORD." Perhaps it is because they are conscious of how
clearly Herbert insists on a childlike service to Christ as the simple basis
of his art that critics sometimes find it difficult not to patronize him for
"certain childlike qualities of mind."[13] And such a poem as "Easter-
Wings" may seem superficially to take a certain childlike enjoyment in
playing with formal patterns. "Herbert's poetry, despite his aristocratic
birth and breeding and his considerable learning, leaves the impression
of an unsophisticated mind": Joan Bennett made this remark immediately after discussing "Easter-Wings." But the danger of such remarks is
to forget the intellectual rigor which produced the integrity of his art, the
struggle of a mind of very sophisticated awareness which managed to
produce, through the images of art, such a childlike service in his art. It is
the intelligent sophistication of *The Temple* that has been challenging
for some years past, and it is still likely to challenge our understanding
for some years to come.

"LORD, IN THEE THE *BEAUTY* LIES IN THE *DISCOVERY*": "LOVE UNKNOWN" AND READING HERBERT

Ira Clark

Although Rosemond Tuve's brilliant *Reading of George Herbert* through biblical typology (Old Testament prefigures of Christian salvation) is universally acknowledged, most recent critical approaches to that country parson's poetry circumvent typology.[1] Yet such illuminating readings of Herbert's poems as emblems, meditations, allegorical dramas, religio-aesthetic rituals, re-inventions, and self-destructions seem to derive from Herbert's typological orientation.[2] Moreover, they seem to converge on an extended critical paradigm of Herbert as a radically typological lyricist, whose poems are structured on personal neotypology.

In much of *The Church* we read a persona who in contention against or in search of God discovers that he himself is a contemporary neotype of Christ akin to Old Testament types of Christ. Herbert places his persona in legal Old Testament typological situations with traditional allusions, diction, and imagery; during the dramatic lyric the persona senses implications of New Testament redemption through Christ, as God's primal and Herbert's imitative prophecy inevitably fulfills itself. The persona discovers the beauty of God through situations Herbert has devised out of Christian recovery of types; the reader reads through Herbert's persona and typological settings to rediscover the beauty of God.[3]

A superb vehicle by which to examine Herbert as a neotypological lyricist is "Love Unknown" since it figures in most major models for reading Herbert and because it bares complex patterns Herbert usually concealed. "Love Unknown" is a straightforward if fantasized dialogue. A persona reports to an unknown Friend a series of confrontations with

From *ELH*, 39 (1972), 560-84. © Copyright 1972 by The Johns Hopkins University Press. Reprinted by permission of the author and The Johns Hopkins University Press.

his landlord, God. During each he had tried to please the landlord only to be painfully thwarted: when he brought his landlord a dish of fruit centered by his heart, like Cain's his offering was ignored and his heart scoured; when he presented a sheep, unlike Abel's his sacrifice was ignored and his heart scalded; when he tried to recuperate and begin anew, like Job's or Christ's disciples during the bloody sweat his rest was haunted.[4] At the close of each pathetic description the Friend laconically points to the persona's failure to recognize redemption by the landlord. Finally the Friend explains:

> For ought I heare, your Master shows to you
> More favour then you wot of. Mark the end.
> The Font did onely, what was old, renew:
> The Caldron suppled, what was grown too hard:
> The Thorns did quicken, what was grown too dull:
> All did but strive to mend, what you had marr'd.[5]

But does the Friend's summation teach readers anything we did not already know? Is his explicit concluding moral not a lesson for the persona but for us a reconfirmation of God's salvation realized from the typological imagery and the neotypological situations of the persona?

I

"Love Unknown" is permeated by more eucharistic imagery than the acclaimed depictions of the font of blood streaming from the great rock (11-18) and the sacramental meal (40-45), but others are more obscurely typological. Its persona is analogous to the one in "The Bunch of Grapes" who mourns his seemingly irredeemable situations, which rightly understood are Old Testament types saved by the antitypical New Covenant; Israel's crossing of the Red Sea and trekking through Sinai to escape Egypt and return to the Promised Land is a type absorbed into salvation and the eucharist.[6]

We read "Love Unknown" through typological situations and images in the company of a host of Herbert lyrics whose typological skeletons affirm the replacement of the old covenant of justice by the new covenant of mercy.[7] As Francis Roberts explains in his popular *Clavis Bibliorum*, reading typologically requires seeing the Old Testament through the lens of the New by realizing that the Old forecasts the New, *"That Jesus Christ our Mediatour, and the salvation of sinners by him, is the very substance, marrow, soule, and Scope of the whole Scriptures. ... Still remember how Jesus Christ is revealed in Scripture, gradually in*

Promises and Covenants, till the noon day of the Gospell shined most clearly."[8] Herbert's own "The H. Scriptures. II" avows that our predestinations are written not in the stars but in the determination of eternal salvation for Christians found in the Old and New Testaments:

> This verse marks that, and both do make a motion
> Unto a third, that ten leaves off doth lie:
> Then as dispersed herbs do watch a potion,
> These three make up some Christians destinie:
> Such are thy secrets, which my life makes good,
>   And comments on thee: for in ev'ry thing
>   Thy words do finde me out, & parallels bring,
> And in another make me understood.   (5-12)

But if typological exegesis of the Bible forms the contextual constellation, "The H. Scriptures. II" further implies that the only astrology is to read the single star of Herbert's neotypology. For it is through the book of the soul that we gain our most immediate apprehensions of the confirmed revelation of widely separated biblical passages; what intimately unites Old and New Testament is Christ's salvation of the persona.[9]

Reading neotypologically through the situations of Herbert's persona is precisely like reading an Old Testament type — except that the neotype is contemporaneous with the reader, who recognizes the persona's placement in an Old Testament context. Such a reading is established in "Faith." The poem opens as the persona's sense of blind law and his hunger after God's will are absorbed by his faith in Christ's appeasement of justice and his partaking of the eucharist; it continues as the persona applies the typological prediction of Christ in the sentencing of the serpent in Genesis; it climaxes as sin and death for mankind in the old Adam are removed by faith in the birth of the new:

> Faith makes me any thing, or all
>   That I beleeve is in the sacred storie:
>   And where sinne placeth me in Adams fall,
>   Faith sets me higher in his glorie.
>
> If I go lower in the book,
>   What can be lower then the common manger?
>   Faith puts me there with him, who sweetly took
>   Our flesh and frailtie, death and danger.   (17-24)

The last stanzas apply the typological salvation by faith to the neotypological everyman, whose darkness is perfected by light and grace imputed him in order that the sun/Son be revealed and read in him:

> When creatures had no reall light
> Inherent in them, thou didst make the sunne
> Impute a lustre, and allow them bright;
> And in this shew, what Christ hath done.   (33-36)

The process described in "Faith" is precisely the method by which we read the imagery in the uncomprehending self-examinations of the persona of "Love Unknown."

Herbert masters the heritage of typological lyrics, which follow exegetical accretions to *Psalms* in embodying the predicament and fulfilment of everyman in deformation in Adam and reformation in Christ.[10] "Love Unknown" does not resemble Greene's song of the shepherd to his love so much as it does Southwell's meld of Petrarchan convention with typological imagery in "The Burning Babe."[11] In "The Burning Babe" Christ's breast is the furnace of affliction which tempers, his fuel the thorns which enliven, his bath the font which cleanses, Herbert's heart. Out of the typological heritage Herbert created the neotypological Christian Psalmist of "Love Unknown" who renders a new version of the fifty-first Psalm.[12] Herbert follows both of David's movements. He follows as David begs that God purify his heart: "Purge me with hyssop, and I shall be clean: wash me, and I shall be whiter than snow.... Create in me a clean heart, O God." Then he follows as David realizes that a contrite heart prepared for purgation is the sole sacrifice acceptable to God: "The sacrifices of God *are* a broken spirit: a broken and a contrite heart, O God, thou will not despise."

"Love Unknown" is still more the creation of the fifty-first Psalm's residence in the New Testament since man is incapable of making the sacrifice necessary for redemption. Both Protestant and Catholic commentaries, particularly in notes to the fourth, seventh, and ninth verses, establish human inheritance of Adam's original sin and everyman's purgation by the blood of Christ, the second Adam.[13] This reading was disseminated in popular biblical aids, such as Henry Ainsworth's frequently reprinted *Annotations*. Ainsworth demonstrates the Psalmists's forecast in prohibitions of the convenant of law which make way for the covenant of grace in salvation:

He applieth the washings used in the Law, (*Lev.* 11. *25. 32. Exod.* 19. 10. *Num.* 19. 19) to the spirituall washing from sinne in the bloud of Christ, *Rev.* 7. 14. I *Joh.* 1. 7 .... [Sprinkling and cleansing] was the last part of the purification of the uncleane, here used to signifie the ful cleansing from sinne by the bloud of Christ, *Heb*. 9. 13. 14.[14]

Interpreters thus divert the impetus of the Psalm in two directions: the first is the contrite self-sacrifice of the penitent believer; its vector is absorbed into the second, the sacrifice of Christ who purifies and saves all believers. The dual movement of law to grace in the typological exegesis of the fifty-first Psalm requires a similar dual response in readers and creates the dual movement of the emblems in "Love Unknown." The persona must recognize his own failing and need for self-sacrifice; in the process he must realize his contrition is justified solely by Christ's sacrifice, granted him by the grace of belief.

The first scene described by the persona of "Love Unknown" clearly sets the speaker in an Old Testament typological situation and thus establishes terms. The persona offers his landlord a dish of fruit; but the landlord's servant, realizing that the offerer must be the offering, seizes the persona's heart. As in the Psalm, what is acceptable is a heart painfully cleansed by that dipping, dying, washing, and wringing which extort tears of contrition. Herbert's reiterations of painful, tearful purgations culminate in the advice of "The Water-course":

> But rather turn the pipe and waters course
> To serve thy sinnes, and furnish thee with store
> Of sov'raigne tears, springing from true remorse:
> That so in purenesse thou mayst him adore,
>
> Who gives to man, as he sees fit, $\begin{cases} \text{Salvation} \\ \text{Damnation.} \end{cases}$ (6-10)[15]

From his limited perspective, the persona sees himself under the extortion of law. With the Friend we recognize salvation in the ceremonial font where the persona's heart is washed in blood streaming from the side of a great rock. For the rock refers to the one Moses struck to receive the waters of Meribah and thus relieve the chosen people of drouth in Sinai. Paul's exegesis established the rock of Horeb as a type of Christ: "They drank of that spiritual Rock that followed them: and that Rock was Christ" (I Cor. 10:4). Catholic and Protestant commentators had long expropriated the hint to explain that the flow of water and blood from Christ's side (John 19:34) signified baptism and the eucharist and even the decorative borders of Elizabeth's prayerbook broadcast the type.[16] It is as difficult to miss salvation in the persona's description as it is in Christ's complaint in "The Sacrifice": "They strike my head, the rock from whence all store/Of heav'nly blessings issue evermore" (170-71).[17]

CLARK

Herbert frequently acknowledges both the necessity and the availability of Christ's cleansing beyond that legal purgation the servant
exacts from the persona of "Love Unknown." A central confession is
"Ephes. 4. 30.":

> Then weep mine eyes, the God of love doth grieve:
> > Weep foolish heart,
> > And weeping live:
>
> . . . .
>
> Yet if I wail not still, since still to wail
> > Nature denies;
> > And flesh would fail,
> If my deserts were masters of mine eyes:
> > Lord, pardon, for thy Sonne makes good
> > My want of tears with store of bloud.   (7-9, 31-36)[18]

The bridge from the first to the second emblem in "Love Unknown" is
supplied by this imagistic interpretation sanctioned by the paradox of
"Marie Magdalene," popularly acknowledged in the Renaissance as the
woman who anointed Christ's feet (Luke 7:36-50). In attempting the
impossible task of washing the feet of the undefiled Christ with her tears
she washed her own multitudinous sins. The persona of "Love
Unknown" must learn what we recognize, that by her tears "in washing
one, she washed both" (18).

The central scene described by the persona of "Love Unknown" sets
the most complex typological situation. After his heart has healed, the
sight of a huge furnace with a boiling caldron stirs the persona to offer
his landlord a sacrificial lamb; but the servant hurls the offerer's heart
into the pan. First with Donne in "Batter My Heart" the persona must
acknowledge personal responsibility for sin and the necessity of painful
purification; then with Southwell in "The Burning Babe" he must
acknowledge Christ as the ultimate furnace of purification.[19]

The anguished persona of "Love Unknown" fails to recognize the
purification his heart is undergoing. Since he views God as arbitrary he
fails to recognize much less pray for the descent of God's purgative fire
as Herbert does to open "Love II":

> Immortall Heat, O let thy greater flame
> > Attract the lesser to it: let those fires,
> > Which shall consume the world, first make it tame;
> And kindle in our hearts such true desires,
> As may consume our lusts, and make thee way.[20]

The persona of "Love Unknown" feels cast into that formulaic hell, the "iron furnace of Egypt" from which God delivers his chosen (as in Deut. 4:20; I Kings 8:51; Jer. 11:4). Even more debilitating is his sense of having been found wanting. He identifies with the harsh vision of Ezekiel who sees in the furnace of Jerusalem not ore but castoff slag:

> Son of man, the house of Israel is to me become dross: all they *are* brass, and tin, and iron, and lead, in the midst of the furnace; they are *even* the dross of silver. Therefore thus saith the Lord God; Because ye are all become dross, behold, therefore I will gather you into the midst of Jerusalem. *As* they gather silver, and brass, and iron, and lead, and tin, into the midst of the furnace, to blow the fire upon it, to melt *it;* so will I gather *you* in mine anger and in my fury, and I will leave *you there,* and melt you. (22:18-20).

The persona senses this furnace of destruction to which Jesus condemns those he rejects (Matt. 13: 41-42, 49-50) rather than the Isaiahan purificatory furnace of affliction: "Behold, I have refined thee, but not with silver; I have chosen thee in the furnace of affliction" (48:10). Although Catholic and Protestant commentators recognized difficulty over whether the elect are purified in a silver furnace, in silver, or like silver, most pick the simile and claim that the dross of sin is smelted out of the chosen. Several Catholics cited by Lapide further consider the purgation a reference to Christ's grace absorbing legal condemnation.

The scalding of the heart in the pan recalls the seething of flesh in the caldron, which often forecasts the removal of the old law by the new covenant in the eucharist. The primary thrust is toward soaring beyond flesh pots into spiritual realms, a reading of Ezekiel's visions opening the eleventh and twenty-fourth chapters shared by Catholic and Protestant commentators. The Westminster Assembly annotators describe a choice in the twenty-fourth chapter. The pot can be either softening and saving or punitive and annihilating, depending on the nature of the flesh:

> The pot is Jerusalem; the flesh and fat pieces, are the chief, the richest, and the noblest that are in her; the fire are Gods judgments, by which he would have humbled, and mollified his peoples hearts, to bring them to repentance; but that having taken no effect, by reason of their obstinate rebellion, he would convert those Judgments, into a total consumption.[21]

While the persona of "Love Unknown" senses the latter, Lapide's commentators point to hope beyond that of the Presbyterians. Not only does the passage demand penitential purgation, it alludes as well to the 'Moab olla spei meae" of the fifty-ninth (sixtieth) Psalm. The line is a figurative call for the victim, Christ, to deliver the flesh, men, from the pot of hell unto the spirit: "id est, Tuth Moabitis est progenies mea quam spe concepi, nam illa pariet Christum."

More indicative is allusion to the pots of the feast of tabernacles in Zechariah's apocalyptic separation of believers:

> In that day shall there be upon the bells of the horses, HOLINESS UNTO THE LORD; and the pots in the Lord's house shall be like the bowls before the altar. Yea, every pot in Jerusalem and in Judah shall be holiness unto the LORD of hosts: and all they that sacrifice shall come and take of them, and seethe therein.
>
> (14:20-21)

Lapide's commentators explain both the mortification of the body and the parabolic type of the eucharistic sacrifice of Christ, who renders mortification efficacious. Seething in the bowl are flesh sacrifices which combine the smell of incense, the libation of wine, and the blood of the victim. These foreshadow the eucharistic sacrifice of Christ's aroma, flesh, and blood, which supplants legal exaction and purifies the gold and silver drawn from the pots of Egypt, "in quibus vel sacrificatur caro & sanguis Agni immaculati Christi Domini, vel aliquod ministerium huic sacrificio exhibetur." Such is the model for mortification and penance in acceptance of Christ's charity:

> Fit ex lebete phiala,
> In vas translata gloriæ,
> Ex vase contumeliæ.

This verse from Mary Magdalene's song of *ecclesia* is explicated by Lapide's Counter-reformation exegetes. The blood and flesh of Christians seething in the caldron of mortification are transmuted into sweet spirits rising to God from the eucharistic golden vessel: "Sic enim Magdalena, quae peccatrix erat lebes ignominiae, pœnitens facta est phiala gloriæ." The latter foot of an interpretative bridge from the first to the second emblem in "Love Unknown" is supplied by Mary Magdalene's exegesis of imagery. By her interpretation we read in the near-sighted persona both that his purgation is legally necessary to make him a contrite offering and that his sacrifice is valuable only by absorption into Christ's. Mary Magdalene's association with the disciples also links the final emblem of "Love Unknown."

The final scene described by the persona of "Love Unknown," like the first, sets its typological situation simply; its impact is compounded, however, by issuance directly from the New Testament. When he has escaped the persona retreats home in order to recover from the exhausting affliction he takes as rejection; there he discovers thorns of thought which torment him into watchfulness. He is forced to follow Paul's exhortation by remaining alert to salvation: "Let us not sleep, as *do* others; but let us watch and be sober" (I Thess. 5:6).

The persona's desire is analogous to the disciples thrice succumbing to naps despite reawakenings and requests for vigilance during Christ's bloody sweat at Gethsemane (Matt. 26:36-46; Mark 14:32-42; Luke 22:39-46).[22] Three lessons were universally derived from the episode: first, made especially of the clergy in times of trial, is the demand for vigilance against God's enemies; second is the inevitable failure of humanity to withstand satanic duress which stupefies the flesh; last is the necessity for and the availability of Christ to waken men and to withstand for them the afflictions of sin.

The typological significance of salvation rests in Christ's thorns both punishing the persona under law and alerting him under grace. Even though the persona recognizes only sacrifice the thorns signify salvation by Christ as does the juxtaposition of men's failures ("thorny all their crowns" [178]) and Christ's recovery ("on my head a crown of thorns I wear" [161] in "The Sacrifice."[23] In *Moses Unvailed* William Guild follows a host of commentators in pointing out that the thorns which grew from the old Adam's sin are replanted and redeemed in the new Adam's forehead: "Thornes were made a curse to the one, *Gen.* 3. 17. *So were they made a crowne to the other, Mat.* 27. 29."[24]

Each emblem of "Love Unknown" alludes to an Old Testament type signifying first, that each believer is legally required to sacrifice his contrite heart to God and next, that his action fails unless Christ's loving sacrifice absorbs his. The persona of "Love Unknown" understands neither, unable in his sense of God's arbitrariness to feel more than anguish. We, however, read the Christian typology of the emblems through the persona to discover both his self-offering and his salvation.

II

As we read "Love Unknown" through typological situations and images we also read it in the more immediate context of the image matrix of *The Temple*, one intimately related to typological imagery.[25] A central image cluster coheres about the notion of reading the personae of Herbert's lyrics as texts revealing God. The texts are those of Herbert's three callings — everyman, poet, and priest. By God's grace everyman can see God in himself, for God is "The Elixir" who transforms us into his own image:

> A man that looks on glasse,
> On it may stay his eye;
> Or if he pleaseth, through it passe,
> And then the heav'n espie.   (9-12)

The poet especially heeds God's calling, since man's duty is to praise God. In "Providence" Herbert declares that man supplies words and hymns for the concerted acts of praise by dumb creatures:

> Of all the creatures both in sea and land
> Onely to Man thou hast made known thy wayes,
> And put the penne alone into his hand,
> And made him Secretarie of thy praise.   (5-8)[26]

But the poet's prayer for a calling further requests that he be "A true Hymne," "*Loved*" penned by God. The poet as performer becomes the interpreter of the text of himself. While regathering the shards of heart shattered by affliction, the persona of "Jesu" parses his own mystery in a new, dual way:

> When I had got these parcels, instantly
> I sat me down to spell them, and perceived
> That to my broken heart he was *I ease you*,
> And to my whole is *JESU*.   (7-10)

The priest's special role parallels the poet's; he, too, is God's amanuensis creating and interpreting the text of himself. To open the thirty-third chapter of *A Priest to the Temple* Herbert declares that "The Countrey Parson's Library is a holy Life." In the advice of "Perirrhanterium" Herbert takes comfort in God's conveying revelation perfectly through mundane vessels:

> Judge not the preacher; for he is thy Judge:
> If thou mislike him, thou conceiv'st him not.
> God calleth preaching folly. Do not grudge
> To pick out treasures from an earthen pot.   (427-30)[27]

Herbert is drawing on Paul's self-justification through an ancient metaphor:

For we preach not ourselves, but Christ Jesus the Lord; and ourselves your servants for Jesus' sake. For God, who commanded the light to shine out of darkness, hath shined in our hearts, to *give* the light of the knowledge of the glory of God in the face of Jesus Christ. But we have this treasure in earthen vessels, that the excellency of the power may be of God, and not of us.

(II Cor. 4:5-7)

Herbert furthers the principle that by the merciful sacrifice of Christ God effects his designs through priests. Not only can the Old Testament typological priest, "Aaron" in bejeweled and brilliant glory, raise the dead to harmonious chimes but also Aaron's neotypological analogue, in defective darkness and discordant passion, can bring sinners to regeneration. Each is capable because he is perfected in Christ, the antitypical redeemer and head of the frail-bodied church:

> Christ is my onely head,
> My alone onely heart and breast,
> My onely musick, striking me ev'n dead;
> That to the old man I may rest,
> And be in him new drest.
> So holy in my head,
> Perfect and light in my deare breast,
> My doctrine tun'd by Christ, (who is not dead,
> But lives in me while I do rest)
> Come people; Aaron's drest.

(16-25)

Poet and priest as self-creative and interpretive instruments perfected by Christ are subsumed in "The Windows," a text analogous on a personal level to "Faith" on a neotypological. The persona asks God how a priest can preach the holy word since, like stained glass, he is leaded into place. Self-revelation through Christ answers that both window and poet/priest are glorified into transcendence by the grace of God in the light of the Son/sun shining through the life of one and the colored glass of the other. Christ's illumination perfects the thinnest and most wan portrait or life to move the souls of beholders. The persona is text and interpreter to the degree God is seen through him.

The image cluster most pertinent to reading "Love Unknown" coagulates around the persona's heart, variously God's offering, text, and dwelling in *The Temple*. Commentary on the first is provided by "An Offering," wherein a single repentant heart prepares for the eucharist which will rectify its failings.[28] The threefold reception of the persona's heart for preparative contrition signifying justification by faith establishes the heart as the sole offering acceptable to God. The metaphor is included in reading the fifty-first Psalm through the New Testament.

The second metaphor for the heart, one central to "Love Unknown," is a text already or yet to be written by the hand of God. In "Good

Friday" Herbert is concerned with how to calculate Christ's grief. Having discarded as inadequate the number of Christ's foes, stars, fall leaves, he first considers counting the hours of his own life eternally redeemed by the sun of Christ's suffering, then considers counting his own multitudinous sins with their multiplying sorrows repaired by Christ. Finally he hits upon calculating by his heart blood regenerated by Christ's sacrifice:

> Since bloud is fittest, Lord, to write
> Thy sorrows in, and bloudie fight;
> My heart hath store, write there, where in
> One box doth lie both ink and sinne.   (21—24)

By thus calculating Christ's sacrifice the persona hopes to scour sins from his heart so grace with its writing intact can inhabit it.[29] That heart the Friend in "Love Unknown" reads as foul until cleansed, hard until tempered, dull until regenerated is in preparation for the New Testament engraving which displaces the stone decalogue: "Ye are our epistle written in our hearts, known and read of all men: *Forasmuch as ye are* manifestly declared to be the epistle of Christ ministered by us, written not with ink, but with the Spirit of the living God; not in tables of stone, but in fleshy tables of the heart" (II Cor. 3:2-3). Again the terms are finally typological.

The third metaphor for the heart, Christ's special dwelling, belongs to Paul's request "That Christ may dwell in your hearts by faith" (Ephes. 3:17). The clearest commentary for Christ having the key to the persona's quarters is in the chill, flint "Sepulchre" of the hearts Herbert chastises for rejecting Christ while lodging sins. Despite their metaphorically stoning Christ, as the persona of "Love Unknown" would keep him out, Christ persists in making hearts fit habitations:

> Yet do we still persist as we began,
> And so should perish, but that nothing can,
> Though it be cold, hard, foul, from loving man
>   Withhold thee   (21-24)[30]

All three metaphors for the heart return to the crucial message that the persona of "Love Unknown" must offer his contrite heart to be acted upon by Christ's regeneration. Such is the impact of "The Altar." God's hand gathered together broken pieces of heart (a shattered offering, a scattered text, a demolished house) to sanctify in Christ's sacrifice. In "Love Unknown" the Lord prepares the heart by cleansing it from the pollution revealed by law as in "H. Baptisme (I)," softening it from the hardness of a Pharaoh as in "Grace," quickening it from Pauline

"Dulnesse," mending its mortal flaws as the rhyme reparation in "Deniall."

God's actions on the persona's heart in "Love Unknown" are profitably read in *The Church* context of contracts between man and God. The image of Herbert's persona as ground leased from God, tilled by man, and nurtured by charity, is frequent throughout *The Church*.[31] Usually a persona bemoans first the obligations of his contract, later his failure to discharge them. The obligations are more critical as the failure, granted original sin, is a condition of existence. "Redemption" sets the pattern. A tenant, dissatisfied with his old lease, seeks the landlord; failing to find in heaven the incarnate lord repossessing earth, the tenant searches the world; at last he finds the Lord during crucifixion and learns of the new lease. The tenant's suit is granted on his request which signifies his justification by faith. The text for "Redemption" is Paul's description of Christ's forgiveness and resurrection of Christians by "blotting out the handwriting of ordinances that was against us, which was contrary to us, and took it out of the way, nailing it to his cross" (Col. 2:14).

Revelation to the persona and reassurance of the reader that our search for the new compact of redemption overrides human short-comings and failure is surprising. Even more surprising and reassuring, however, is the revelation that the landlord plays the tenant as well. It is he who abides by the agreement, pays the penalty of death for man's original sin, and continues to stand supreme ally for each Christian. In "Assurance" a persona attacked by doubts laments that either his compact with God was false from inception or he has been deceived since. Worst, he must plead guilty to foes' charges of failure and sin. Only after recital does he recognize that the Lord has not only formed the league, the Lord has also assumed the persona's part:

> But thou art my desert:
> And in this league, which now my foes invade,
> Thou art not onely to perform thy part,
> But also mine; as when the league was made
>   Thou didst at once thy self indite,
>   And hold my hand, while I did write.   (25-30)[32]

God, in Christ taking on the human part of the tenant in addition to the deity of the landlord, has absorbed Old Testament legality in New Testament grace.[33]

Throughout his poetry Herbert utilizes the terminology of the landlord's assumption of the debts of the tenant, of Christ's paying our scores with his scourging, to emphasize Christ's sacrifice for mankind.

The expression of Christ's expenditure of sacrificial blood for our sins as a business arrangement requires no elaboration.[34] But the reflection of the neotypological mode of Herbert's lyrics in their legalistic, commercial diction and imagery deserves notice.

Three references in "Love Unknown," the first and last framing the persona's tale, establish the centrality of contractual terminology. As the poem opens the persona is telling a Friend about his ambiguous lease: "A Lord I had,/And have, of whom some grounds, which may improve,/I hold for two lives, and both lives in me" (3-5). The pun on grounds alludes to two crucial ideas. The heart is land leased from God and tilled by both the Christian and his God for two lives, the Christian's duration here and hereafter and his responsibility for gaining the hereafter. "Of whom some grounds, which may improve" additionally implies that God's contract is conditional upon actions of the tenant; but the persona does not seem to understand what the conditions entail. In the second reference the persona admits to inevitable failure to meet the terms of the lease. At the same time, however, he glibly admits that the contract is to be resolved in mercy and grace: "I did and do commit/ Many a fault more then my lease will bear;/Yet still askt pardon, and was not deni'd" (19-21). The final framing reference punningly twists legal into commercial diction, as the persona begins to grasp the terms of the contract just before the Friend reveals them: "But all my scores were by another paid,/Who took the debt upon him" (60-61). As in reading Old Testament typology the persona reveals in himself both his inability to repay the debts of sin and his grateful acceptance of Christ's reimbursement. He must also realize the price Christ pays; he must understand the pun on scourging which accompanies Christ's removal of our "scores." This legalistic commercial reading of "Love Unknown," founded on the terrain of *The Temple*, returns to the paradigmatic reading of Herbert. During the course of the poem the persona learns and we relearn God's grace in the new covenant replacing the old.

III

As we read "Love Unknown" in the contexts of Herbert's neotypological lyrics and *The Temple's* matrix of related image clusters, at its subtlest we read it through its own dramatic, rhetorical, and linguistic structures. These creations of the master poet are also intimately related to his innovative and inclusive neotypological structure. Herbert's punning on "grounds" early and "scores" late in "Love Unknown," thereby hinting at subordinate structures based on types, is reinforced by other morally significant puns. The wringing of the heart that "enforceth tears" (18) refers not only to extorting by force but also to strengthing in morality and the "tender" of the heart (33) refers not only to the persona's offering but also to God's softening.

Indirections opening "Love Unknown" create an aura of ambiguity about the persona who knows of salvation by rote but does not understand it. Having invited the Friend to sit down to hear his plight the persona adds:

> And in my faintings I presume your love
> Will more complie then help. (2-3)

The sentence says the persona anticipates that the Friend's love will be more polite concern than genuine comfort. "I presume your love," however, retains a forceful ambiguity since it forms a complete sub-sentence, its stop supported by the conclusion of the verse line. This ambiguity strikes to the center of the poem, for the persona's failure is presumption of God's love. Taking God's love for granted denies his necessary part in receiving God's love. In order to present his contrite heart in an act of faith which justifies he must first discover God's beauty. Herbert has alerted us to the crux not only of this but also of many of his poems.

"Love Unknown" belongs to that set described as double fictions.[35] These take the form of a dramatic dialogue/agon during which the persona carries on a vociferous argument against God only to further his realization of total dependence on and gratitude for God's saving sacrifice. Most often, as in the well-known "The Collar," the rebellious combat against God is carried on in multiple typological puns.[36] In "Sion," for example, God's living, threadbare, New Testament temple in the heart replaces the moribund splendor and glory of Solomon's Old Testament temple:

> There thou art struggling with a peevish heart,
> Which sometimes crosseth thee, thou sometimes it:
> The fight is hard on either part.
> Great God doth fight, he doth submit.
> All Solomons sea of brasse and world of stone
> Is not so deare to thee as one good grone. (13-18)

The personae of these poems come to defeat at God's hands in order to achieve their paradoxical victory — surrender to God in Christ's passion as in "The Reprisall":

> Couldst thou not griefs said conquests me allow,
> But in all vict'ries overthrow me?

> Yet by confession will I come
> Into thy conquest: though I can do nought
> Against thee, in thee I will overcome
>   The man, who once against thee fought.   (11-16)

Surrender of a contrite heart is the landlord's requirement of the persona in "Love Unknown," a final recognition of the persona's opening unintentional pun on "faintings" — both his dejected swoons and his feints, mock blows, countered by God.

Herbert's dialogue / agon in which God (or the Friend) corrects the rebellious persona in order to save him seems to be carried on in a probe and expansion of *metanoia* or *correctio,* the rhetorical figure of "making straight" or "setting right." In *The Arte of English Poesie* George Puttenham describes the figure in terms important for understanding the set of corrective dramatic poems "Love Unknown" belongs to:

> Otherwhiles we speake and be sorry for it, as if we had not wel spoken, so that we seeme to call in our word againe, and to put in another fitter for the purpose: for which respects the Greekes called this manner of speech the figure of repentance: then for that vpon repentance commonly followes amendment, the Latins called it the figure of correction, in that the speaker seemeth to reforme that which was said amisse. I following the Greeke originall, choose to call him the penitent, or repentant.[37]

It is critically significant that Puttenham returns to the primary Greek meaning of the figure — *the repentant.* For *the repentant* emphasizes imitation, as most rhetorical figures must initially have been thought to be reflections, of a psychic state in the speaker. Furthermore, this particular psychic condition contains a serious pun on a sacred human condition. In describing a rhetorical figure Puttenham is more importantly discussing a crucial event for the Christian psyche; he emphasizes that *the repentant* reflects the anguish attending recognition of a sin as well as the corrective revelatory afterthought. Herbert's expansion and deepening, extension and probe, of *the repentant* expresses the persona's discovery of God's New Testament in his personal formation in an Old Testament type when he learns from afflictions to repent and thus instigate the redemptive pattern of justification by faith.

Correction and repentance in the typological and neotypological settings, imagery, and diction of "Love Unknown" form a core. But Herbert's syntactic patterns compel us to discover how God disabuses the persona of presumption. Each of the three scenes the persona describes follows a single structure: as he prepared or began to do something for his landlord he was intercepted or thwarted. The syntax of "I ... But he" forming each emblem precisely mirrors the emblem: "I brought a dish of fruit ... But he / ... Lookt on a servant"; more separated, "I went / To fetch a sacrifice ... But ... the man, / ... slipt his hand"; yet more subtly, "But when I thought to sleep out all these faults / ... I found." The concluding discovery is no accident.

The Herbert repentant is even more germane to the dialogue between the persona and the Friend. In the course of the discussion just when the persona is striving hardest to gain understanding and sympathy he is mildly rebuked for misrepresentation by the Friend; as he is corrected for wilfulness so is he made repentant for self-pity. The initial impression of the persona is that of anguish over God's repeated reprimands. He himself forewarns that his story is sad. Relating each scene he interrupts the flow of frequently run-on iambic pentameters by gulping out a monosyllabic dimeter lament/refrain:

> (I sigh to say)
> (I sigh to tell)
> (I sigh to speak)

The persona's pain drives him to seek sympathy for what he takes to be a predicament. Frequently it takes the form of interpolated relative clauses colloquially modified and expanded: he tells of the grounds "which may improve" (4), the sacrifice "which I did thus present" (31), the hope of rekindling God's love "which I did fear grew cold" (32). Each is more an attempt to beg sympathy than to explain his position. None, however, is so obvious as his appeals to the Friend to understand. The mode is dramatic in the parenthetical relative clause at the climactic moment in the first scene when he makes the hyperbolic claim about the Friend's knowledge: the servant who casts the persona's heart into the font, knows God's eye "Better then you know me, or (which is one) / Then I my self" (10-11). Just later he claims capability to understand his impasse with God (though he fathoms no method) and to compel the Friend's support: "I well remember all, / And have good cause" (15-16). At the climax of the second scene the persona cries out to demand that the Friend commiserate when the servant casts his heart into the caldron: "My heart, that brought it (do you understand?) / The offerers heart" (36-37). In the final episode when he cannot rest for thorns of thought he exasperatedly laments and presumptuously claims to understand what he clearly does not:

> Deare, could my heart not break,
> When with my pleasures ev'n my rest was gone?
> Full well I understood, who had been there. (52-54)

The Friend is a teacher who corrects each misinterpretation as he reads contrition and salvation in typological situations:

> *Your heart was foul, I fear.*
> *Your heart was hard, I fear.*
> *Your heart was dull, I fear.*

The friend's three monosyllabic formulaic corrections concluding lines forcefully answer the persona's laments and teach him to reappraise his situation. The Friend denies the arbitrariness of the landlord and blames the persona. The pattern established in the persona's interpretation followed by the Friend's corrections, as well as the pattern of the scenes themselves, creates penitential movement.

The Herbert repentant extends beyond the persona's plea for sympathy and the Friend's establishment of true fault and proper penance. The persona concludes each scene with a formula integral to his developing understanding. He begins each summation with an admission of guilt in the "indeed" which leads to a "but" counterclaim of license in another analogue of Christ's encompassing and restoring types. Even though his theology is immaculate, the persona fails to genuinely understand what he says. So at first he remains presumptuously complacent. To the Friend's first charge he responds disarmingly that God forgives contractual failure:

> Indeed 'tis true. I did and do commit
> Many a fault more then my lease will bear;
> Yet still askt pardon, and was not deni'd.   (19-21)

To the last he replies comfortably that Christ redeems his debt: "Indeed a slack and sleepie state of minde / Did oft possesse me. ... But all my scores were by another paid" (57-60). To the central charge that his hard heart must be softened to demonstrate the faith which justifies his salvation, he answers with almost blasphemous complacency:

> Indeed it's true. I found a callous matter
> Began to spread and to expatiate there:
> But with a richer drug then scalding water
> I bath'd it often, ev'n with holy bloud.   (38-41)

Although the answer is couched in eucharistic terms, it fails to note that without heartfelt contrition the eucharist lacks efficacy. Since God's grace is operative despite hard-headed if not hard-hearted recalcitrance to read and enact penitential neotypology, the persona is blessed in his ignorance. He is forced out of presumption and into penance — a spiritual task achieved through the syntactical and rhetorical pattern of the poem.

The overall structure of "Love Unknown" is formed on the Herbert repentant; its first sixty-one lines are given to the persona's blind reading of supposedly unwarranted punishment, the last ten to the Friend's revelatory correction placing proper blame, initiating penance, and establishing salvation. The Friend first counters with a single line each drawn-out emblem and excuse; his subordinate relative clauses (the three "whats") demolish the persona's extensive explanatory beggings. Then he succinctly concludes.

Because the Herbert repentant creates the proper effect on the persona, it forms a new correction, a reformation by which temporal types and neotypes are joined to the eternal antitype. The persona begins both his story ("A Lord I had, / And have" [3-4]) and his first self-justification ("I did and do commit" [19]) with temporal corrections. The movement expands through "Love Unknown" with each correction: the persona begins to sense exaction of penance as he still feels the wringing of his heart ("the very wringing yet / Enforceth tears" [17-18]); then he claims perpetual applications for and grants of God's pardon ("Yet still askt pardon, and was not deni'd" [21]). In explaining the eucharist the persona notes that a friend enters the wine *for good*, both for virtue and for ever. And in explaining the redemption he implies recovery of debts to come as well as those already made good. The Friend's concluding revelatory correction envelops to redeem and eternize the persona's past tense recollection in God's ever-present concern:

> For ought I heare, your Master shows to you
> More favour then you wot of ....
>
> ....
>
> Wherefore be cheer'd and praise him to the full
> Each day, each houre, each moment of the week,
> Who fain would have you be new, tender, quick.

IV

Revelation provides the sole way the persona can reform his readings to show his neotypical status and recognize God's exaction of his penance, just as only revelation of grace in the Gospel makes possible typological exegesis of Old Testament legalism. The Friend's terse corrections throughout "Love Unknown" cumulatively reveal the persona's exegetical shortcomings and lead him to understand. Finally the Friend reveals straightforwardly the types of the three emblematic scenes in a message reminiscent of those miraculously closing several Herbert poems.[38]

In addition to the echo of revelation in "Love Unknown" visionary reflection appears in the Friend's remark that the landlord "shows" favor and his command that the persona *"Mark the end."* The statement belongs to the host of acknowledgments in *The Temple* recalling Christ's miraculous cures of the physically and spiritually blind in John.[39] The aptest text is "The H. Scriptures. I":

> This is the thankfull glasse,
> That mends the lookers eyes: this is the well
> That washes what it shows.   (8-10)

The dual reference to I Corinthians 13:12 ("For now we see through a glass, darkly; but then face to face") and to Johannine symbols of Christ as a well of purgation and a restorer of sight helps the explication. We read the revelatory reflection of God in several Gospels granted us by Christ — in Christ himself, in the document itself, and in us ourselves.

"Love Unknown" ultimately achieves the vision granted by the only Friend who can grant such miracles, Christ himself.[40] The reference is clear partly because Christ, who knows the persona infinitely well, reveals him and partly because Christ, who slips into the eucharistic chalice for good (43), is the only friend identified in the poem. But the reference is clear mainly because it belongs with other references Herbert makes to Christ, his "Friend." The Friend who tells all to conclude "Love Unknown" is the same Friend who tells the persona to copy out charity inside himself to conclude "Jordan (II)"; the Friend who chastens the persona is the same Friend who prunes away sins in "Paradise" (13); the Friend who interprets the contract to the persona is the same Friend who carries messages to the landlord in "The Bag" (36-39); the Friend who steals into the sacred wine is the same Friend who writes "Sunday" with his blood (3-4) and dispatches grace in "The H. Communion." The Friend in "Love Unknown" proves to be the friend beyond all other friends who, recrucified by the "Unkindnesse" of the complacently presumptuous, still saves them.

"Love Unknown" teaches its persona to interpret himself as a new type of Christ in precisely the same situation as Old Testament types of Christ who are fulfilled and redeemed in him. The persona is compelled to correct his notions and to do penance for complacent presumption of salvation without the sense of what is endured in redeeming sins under law. He learns corrective penance under the tutelage of Christ who, as in "The Holdfast," grants even the capacity of faith which justifies because of atonement. Paradoxically one becomes more his own individual by being Christ's:

> But to have nought is ours, not to confesse
> That we have nought. I stood amaz'd at this,
> Much troubled, till I heard a friend expresse,
> That all things were more ours by being his.
> What Adam had, and forfeited for all,
> Christ keepeth now, who cannot fail or fall.   (9-14)

All partake of Adam's original sin; those who partake of Christ and salvation are true everymen, either Old Testament or contemporary types whose existence and fulfilment rest in Christ.

Herbert would teach the reader of "Love Unknown," as he would the reader of most of his best-known poems, to know God's love by reading the contemporary neotype just as we do the Old Testament type, as an independent being ultimately and everlastingly meaningful solely through the lens of the New Testament Christ, by reading the law under which men suffer as the grace within which men are saved. Herbert teaches us to read typologically through the persona inside three principal contexts — his neotypological situations, emblems, and diction; his symbolic matrices in *The Church;* his local poetic structure, exemplifying the Herbert repentant correction. All three emanate from the radical typological orientation of his lyrics, which reflect the persona's discovery of redemption in Christ by offering his contrite heart to God and stimulate the reader's rediscovery of the beauty of God through the neotypological persona: "Lord, in thee / The *beauty* lies in the *discovery*."

GEORGE HERBERT'S "THE SONNE": IN DEFENSE OF THE ENGLISH LANGUAGE

Frederick von Ende

George Herbert's sonnet, "The Sonne," although ostensibly religious through its inclusion in *The Temple*, is in effect a nationalistic defense of the adequacy of the English language at a time when concern over language was great in England and on the Continent. Trained and skilled in the art of oratory, Herbert employed a compact and concentrated form of the classical oration to prove that English is not inferior to other tongues. His proof lies in the *sun-son* homonym, a traditional image in Christian literature and a conventional pun in English poetry. The first three lines approximate the *exordium* and *narratio* of the oration; the fourth line is the *propositio*. Lines five and six indicate the direction of the defense, thus serving as the *partitio*. Lines seven through ten, the *confirmatio,* are an assimilation of the multitude of meanings to be found in the *sun-son* word sound. The last four lines are the *peroratio,* applying the combined meanings of *sun-son* to the Son of God and in so doing suggesting that any language which could say so much about both the humility and the glory of Christ in a single word could hardly be judged inadequate.

The poetry of George Herbert is the product of a combined verbal dexterity and religious devotion, the issue of an orator turned divine. One of the many poems of *The Temple* which proved that the union was fruitful is "The Sonne." "The Sonne" is a sonnet built upon a pun on the words *son* and *sun*; the basic play-on-words is developed through the various connotations which the two words have in combination to climax in the concluding couplet with the image of Christ as both the Son and the Sun of Man. But the poem is more than just another religious lyric honoring Christ; it is an assertion and a demonstration, in a concentrated classical oration form, of the capacity and the adequacy

Reprinted from *SEL*, 12 (1972), 173-82, by permission of the author and the William Marsh Rice University.

of the English tongue for glorifying the Son of God. "The Sonne" is, in effect, a defense of the English language.[1]

Neither the pun nor the resultant image is original with the parson of Bemerton; both devices were current in the poetry, especially the religious poetry, of seventeenth-century England. The use of the sun as an image or symbol of Christ is concurrent with the development of Christian poetry and was in frequent use long before Christianity was introduced into England. The origin of the sun symbol in Christian writing may well have been the prophecy of the Messiah in Malachi 4:2: "But unto you that fear my name shall the Sun of Righteousness arise with healing in his wings," or perhaps in any number of other sun-Christ metaphors to be found in the Bible. On the other hand, it may have been borrowed from the established imagery of classical mythology. Whatever its origin, however, the sun became one of the most widely-used symbols for Christ in the Christian tradition, appearing not only in the Bible but in prayer books, in liturgies, in hymns, and in poems as well. The most common use of the sun as a symbol for the Son of God has been in poems or hymns written in celebration of the two great Christian feasts, Christmas and Easter. Prudentius, a Spaniard composing Latin hymns in the fourth century, employed the sun as a figure for Christ in a Christmas song; and Sedulius Scotus, an Irishman writing at Liege in the ninth century, described the Resurrection of Christ as the sun rising at dawn. The image of Christ arising on Easter as a new dawn became an increasingly popular metaphor in the poetry of Renaissance England. The poetry of John Donne, probably the greatest single (mortal) influence on Herbert, has several instances of sun imagery symbolizing Christ, the most important, perhaps, being in "Good Friday, 1613. Riding Westward." When Herbert wrote "The Sonne," the image was traditional.

The play on the words *son* and *sun,* primarily an English possibility, was also conventional by the early 1630's (when Herbert wrote *The Temple*). An early example of the pun in English occurs in a quatrain known to have been written before 1240; the anonymous poet employed the play-on-words then in much the same manner as his Renaissance counterparts were to do nearly four centuries later:

> Nou goth sonne under wode;
> Me rewes, Marie, bi faire rode.
> Nou goth sonne under tre;
> Me rewes, Marie, bi sone and be.

In the Renaissance, poems making use of the *son-sun* homonym became quite common; Shakespeare, the Fletchers, Donne, even the young

Milton — all had found a place for the pun before Herbert wrote his sonnet.

It may seem strange that Herbert, a poet with a sensibility capable of producing such unusual and unique poems as "Easter Wings" and "The Pulley," would build a sonnet upon so traditional an image and so conventional a pun; and yet, the primary importance of this poem seems to lie in the fact that he did just that. Unlike the other poems of *The Temple*, the purpose of "The Sonne" was not to find a new and original way of expressing religious devotion; rather, the aim was to indicate and demonstrate the inherent qualities of the language which the poet used to express that devotion. Herbert accomplished this end by employing those aspects of the language which were traditional and conventional and, therefore, representative. It remains to be seen, then, just how Herbert used these elements to defend his native tongue.

The sonnet divides naturally into four sections, there being four periods or full sentences in the poem. Herbert advances his argument for the essential greatness of the English language through the progession of these four sentences. The arrangement of the poem seems to follow approximately the plan of the classical oration, each of the sentences functioning as one or more of the parts of that established form of persuasion and defense. That the form of "The Sonne" may have been governed, or at the very least, strongly influenced by the classical oration pattern of development is not out of the question by any means, even though the poem is only a sonnet, usually a simple lyric form; if Herbert sought to argue the sufficiency of the English language, as seems most clear, the classical oration provided a logical and formal means to that end. Indeed, it would have been difficult for Herbert *not* to have adopted the oration plan in his poem: like all other schoolboys of his day, Herbert had been trained in the use of the oration form from grammar-school through the university; beyond this instruction were the years when he had actively filled the post of University Orator at Cambridge. The extensiveness of this rhetorical training created what Father Walter Ong has called "the omnipresence of the oratorical frame of mind"[2]; Herbert's education had taught him to employ the oration form "automatically" whenever an issue called for defense or persuasion. This training had influence far beyond pure oratory as well. As Father Ong points out, "It is somewhat surprising ... to note how far oratory infiltrated genres which we consider nonoratorical .... Treatises such as Sidney's *Defense of Poesie,* together with essays, letters, the prefaces, and dedicatory pieces with which the age abounds, as well as epic and lyric poetry are all organized in oratorical form probably more often than not."[3] Thus, the classical oration form in Herbert's sonnet in defense of English is even to be expected — not just possible but probable.

If we assume the presence of the oration plan, conscious or unconscious, then the first four lines of the poem, the first full sentence, approximate the introductory elements: the *exordium*, the *narratio*, and the *propositio*. These four lines introduce the subject, set the tone of the poem and give it an aura of immediacy, place the poem against a background of current controversy, and conclude with a statement of the author's attitude and position:

> Let forrain nations of their language boast,
> What fine variety each tongue affords:
> I like our language, as our men and coast:
> Who cannot dresse it well, want wit, not words.[4]

The first three lines of this quatrain are a combined *exordium* and *narratio*. As an *exordium* these lines indicate, first of all, the general subject of the poem, the adequacy of languages, and establish the author's stance in the controversy then current over which language is best. The author's attitude in this argument, indeed the tone of the whole poem, is one of intense nationalistic pride. The third line suggests that the poem is, in effect, a defense of everything English, though a defense of the English language in particular. These lines belie the misconception still current in the first decade of this century that Herbert was a saintly country parson quietly ministering to the spiritual needs of the rustics in his parish. To be sure, Herbert was a country parson, but he was also an Englishman, and it is as an Englishman that he stands in this poem, ready to defend his English language. As T. S. Eliot has written, "We are not to presume ... that George Herbert was naturally of a meek and mild disposition. He was on the contrary, somewhat haughty; proud of his descent and social position. ..."[5] The opening sentence of "The Sonne" reveals the spirit which had earlier directed Herbert toward a life of public service in the court of James prior to the death of that king. The poet of the first quatrain is not Herbert the parson of Bemerton, but Herbert the son of a noble British family, Herbert the orator in defense of his native tongue.

As a *narratio* the opening lines place the poem in the midst of a controversy. The situation implied and the attitude displayed in these lines seem to be the result of two great influences — the intellectual revival of the Renaissance and the national advances of Elizabethan England. One of the developments of the humanistic pursuits of the

Renaissance was an interest in language; Renaissance scholars had become intensely interested in their own means of communication. This concern for language produced definite results on the Continent: within five years of the writing of "The Sonne," the Académie Française was founded by Cardinal Richelieu to function primarily as a regulatory body over French language and literature. The founding of an institution concerned with language seems highly indicative of the interest in language during the first half of the seventeenth century. That the same spirit and concern was current in England has been very adequately shown by Richard Foster Jones in *The Triumph of the English Language*. The results in England, however, were not so concrete. As Harry Levin points out, "James's death, plus the troubled accession of Charles, halted a plan for founding an English Academy, along the lines that would soon control the Académie Française."[6]

Another result of the interest in language was a tendency to compare the values of various languages; the English tongue was compared to both the classical languages and contemporary tongues.[7] Although it would be difficult to pinpoint an exact source for Herbert's opening statement, it seems obvious that he is answering a charge, general or specific, that English lacked the variety of some of the other, probably continental, languages. And no Englishman of the seventeenth century, spurred on and supported by the great advancements made by England during the reigns of Elizabeth and James, would allow his native tongue to be disparaged by comparison with some foreign language without standing to its defense. Thus, George Herbert stands to defend the English language, and in the final line of the opening quatrain asserts that English is entirely adequate to any task; any inability, any inadequacy lies with the speaker, not with the language. The *propositio* of this fourteen-line oration, then, is the statement that English is a fully adequate language.

The next two lines of "The Sonne" are the *partitio* or the *divisio* of the oration. Since he is limited in his defense of English by the length and space of the sonnet form, Herbert proves the truth of his general proposition by concentrating on a single, representative example:

> How neatly doe we give one only name
> To parents issue and the sunnes bright starre!

In this emphatic exclamation, Herbert asserts the truth of his statement by saying, in effect, that the adequacy of English can hardly be questioned when one word, or one word-sound, carries so many cumulative connotations. He has narrowed the scope of his argument and then rests his defense on a single point.

Lines seven through ten are the *confirmatio* of the classical oration; they show *why* the *son-sun* homonym is proof of the sufficiency of English:

> A sonne is light and fruit; a fruitful flame
> Chasing the fathers dimnesse, carri'd farre
> From the first man in th' East, to fresh and new
> Western discov'ries of posteritie.

Within these four lines Herbert has assimilated, synthesized, and concentrated centuries of Christian imagery and scientific knowledge. By combining the two words *son* and *sun* into a single word, Herbert has imbued the quatrain with a myriad of ambiguities, with many double meanings both of which are true. There are also two levels of meaning or interpretation in these lines — the literal interpretation and the anagogical meaning (if that term may be borrowed from allegorical interpretation) which centers on the Son of God.

The first figure in the verse paragraph is a play-on-words: the *sun* is light and a *son* in the fruit of his parents. A *son* is also light, however, in that he carries on the light of life of his father's house. Thus, as the light of life begins to dim in a man as he nears death, that light is picked up by the son and carried forward in much the same manner as the torch was passed from one runner to the next in the ancient Olympic games. The initial pun then melts into the second image, a paradox: "a fruitful flame." Although a flame is usually more destructive than fruitful, the unique flame of the *sun* is fruitful because it engenders life in the earth, a concept dealt with in a number of Renaissance works including Milton's *Paradise Lost*. The rest of this paragraph combines the westward movement of the sun with the historical concept of the westward migration of mankind from the first man in the East, Adam in Paradise, to the then numerous discoveries in the West, particularly the expansion into the Americas. The sun does seem to follow a path from east to west, and the son, representing the continuance of mankind, did seem to move westward from the cradle of man in the east toward the ever-receding horizon in the west. Although expressed in figurative and ambiguous language, the meaning in these lines may be said to be literal in that they do characterize the daily and eternal action of the sun and the role of the son in the procession of life.

And when these lines are interpreted as descriptive of Christ, they take on even greater and fuller significance. The use of the sun as an image or symbol for the Son of God permeates the lines and controls their movement. When interpreted on the anagogical level, these lines are based on a contrast between Adam, the first man, and Christ, the second

Adam. Here Herbert draws on a vast storehouse of Christian tradition. Christ, as the Son of God, is light because of his association with the sun in Christian imagery and because of his connection with the accommodating light imagery used to delineate God in the Bible and in the writings of the Fathers of the Church. Indeed, Christ had called himself *light* several times in the Scriptures: "I am the light of the world: he that followeth me shall not walk in darkness, but shall have the light of life" (John 8:12). The Son is light.

The image of the Son as fruit is more involved. Adam's fall, "the fathers dimnesse," was a result of Adam's having eaten of the fruit of the Tree of Knowledge. The punishment for this act, or the "fruit" of the Tree of Knowledge, was death to all mankind. Christ, the Son of God, the "second Adam," then countered Adam's sin by dying on another tree, the cross, and became by this act the fruit of the Tree of Life. Herbert had employed this image of Christ on the Tree of Life in another, better-known poem, "The Sacrifice":

> *O all ye who passe by, behold and see;*
> Man stole the fruit, but I must climbe the tree;
> The tree of life to all, but onely me:
> Was ever grief like mine?
> (ll. 201-204)[8]

William Empson has interpreted these lines from "The Sacrifice" as a picture of Christ as a guilty little boy climbing the tree to replace the fruit which he as man stole from his father's orchard, thus becoming both "scapegoat and tragic hero."[9] The concept of Christ's "replacing" the stolen fruit is plausible, for the Passion is Christ's voluntary sacrifice of himself to atone for the sins of man; Empson's picture of Christ as a guilty little boy, however, misses the willingness of the Son to undergo the Passion, to rise upon the cross freely, to become himself the fruit of this tree. Rosemond Tuve also equates the cross with the Tree of Knowledge by recalling the tradition that the cross was made of the wood of the forbidden tree.[10] Both of these ideas and all of the traditions that related the Tree of Knowledge with the Tree of Life, the cross, are behind Herbert's description of the Son as fruit in "The Sonne." Perhaps there is also a hint here of the concept expressed in the Middle English alliterative poem, *Pearl*, which states that a seed must die and be buried in the ground before it can come back to life, grow, and bear fruit.[11] Christ died, fell from the tree, was buried, and rose again as the fruit of the Tree of Life.

The rest of the lines are almost self-explanatory. The risen Christ, like the sun at dawn, has driven away the darkness of eternal damnation caused by the fall of Adam, the first father. And also like the sun, the light of Christianity, the fruit of Christ's redeeming act, has spread westward from the East across Europe to England and beyond, chasing the dimness of paganism.

A good case might be made to show that "The Sonne" is an Easter poem as well as a defense of the language. One of the most common uses of sun imagery in Christian poetry is in the description of the Resurrection. Furthermore, in regard to the fruit image, the Book of Common Prayer of the Church of England substitutes the following passage for one of the usual psalms in the Easter service: "Christ is risen again the first fruits of them that sleep. For seeing that by man came death, by man also cometh the resurrection of the dead. For as by Adam all men do die: so by Christ all men shall be restored to life."[12] As a minister, Herbert would have been more than familiar with the light and fruit images used to delineate Christ; he may, therefore, have written his sonnet in connection with the Easter season. This possibility, however, does not detract from the poem's essential defense of the English language.

As all of George Herbert's poetry does, "The Sonne" turns to the glory of God and Christ in the concluding verse paragraph, the *peroratio*:

> So in one word our Lords humilitie
> We turn upon him in a sense most true:
>> For what Christ once in humblenesse began,
>> We him in glorie call, *The Sonne of Man.*

Having explored the many possibilities of meaning concentrated in the *son-sun* homonym, Herbert concludes his short oration with a paradoxical pun. As stated in the final couplet, Christ is both the *Son* and the *Sun* of man. His humility, his willingness to be the *Son* of Man, has become his glory, the concept that he has become the *Sun* of Man. Christ is both the fruit and the light of mankind. By applying the pun to the Son of God, Herbert has given the final proof of the adequacy, perhaps even the virtuosity, of the English language, and this concludes his defense. He has turned a criticism, the lack of variety, into a virtue; when a language has a single word that expresses both the humility and the glory of Christ, what more can it need. No further proof is needed.

"The Sonne" is, in the final analysis, a typical Herbert poem. It employs a conventional pun and a traditional image, but it employs them for a particular reason, to defend the English language. The arrangement of the sonnet according to the plan of the classical oration indicates that the defense was conscious and formal. In "The Sonne," as in the more curious pattern poems, Herbert applied form to content to achieve the desired effect.

GEORGE HERBERT'S "REDEMPTION"

Virginia R. Mollenkott

Although the sonnet "Redemption" is one of George Herbert's most brilliant and often-anthologized lyrics, several recent books have provided such conflicting readings that a close re-examination seems necessary. Is the speaker of the sonnet "self-seeking," mean-spirited, so concerned with business that he is "incapable of comprehending God's design," as John R. Mulder has claimed?[1] Is he a "humble" but "slow-witted petitioner of God," as Arnold Stein sees him?[2] Or is he neither of these?

> Having been tenant long to a rich Lord,
>> Not thriving, I resolved to be bold,
>> And make a suit to him, to afford
> A new small-rented lease, and cancell th'old.
> In heaven at his manour I him sought:
>> They told me there, that he was lately gone
>> About some land, which he had dearly bought
> Long since on earth, to take possession.
> I straight return'd, and knowing his great birth,
>> Sought him accordingly in great resorts;
>> In cities, theatres, gardens, parks, and courts:
> At length I heard a ragged noise and mirth
>> Of theeves and murderers: there I him espied,
>> Who straight, *Your suit is granted*, said, & died.[3]

Clearly it is important to establish the precise identity and nature of the speaker, the tenant who was "not thriving" under his old lease and who sought in Heaven for a "new small-rented lease." He cannot be the typical Christian, nor can he be Herbert himself, for this speaker had been tenant long before the incarnation and death of Christ, the rich landlord. The adjectives *new* and *old* in line 4 supply the answer: the tenant is the spiritual nature of Everyman, not thriving under the Old

Reprinted from *ELN*, 10 (1973), 262-67, by permission of the author and the publisher.

Testament covenant and finally seeking a New Testament one, with the smaller rent of grace taking the place of the old lease of the law. As St. Paul put it, "That no man is justified by the law in the sight of God, *it is* evident: for, The just shall live by faith. And the law is not of faith. . . . Christ hath redeemed us from the curse of the law, being made a curse for us. . . . Wherefore the law was our schoolmaster *to bring us* unto Christ, that we might be justified by faith" (Gal. 3:11-13, 24, KJV).

As Mulder points out, the diction of the sonnet is legalistic in accord with the meaning of the Latin *redimere*, "to buy back." Does this legalistic diction indicate that the spirit of Everyman is so "pre-occupied with buying and selling" that it is totally unworthy of Christ's sacrifice?[4] The unworthiness of man to receive God's gracious gifts is certainly a basic theme in Herbert; but is it treated *here*? Once we recognize that the sonnet is an allegory of the transition from Old Testament to New Testament, from the covenant of the law to the covenant of grace, and therefore that "not thriving" and seeking a better lease are references not to literal business but to an active concern for being acceptable in the eyes of God, such an interpretation becomes impossible. Humanity is not here presented as callously materialistic, but rather as being concerned enough with its inability to obey the law that it prays for some new and feasible means of settling its account with the landlord.

In his epistle, St. James explores the hopeless plight of mankind under the old lease of the law: "whosoever shall keep the whole law, and yet offend in one *point*, he is guilty of all" (2:10). Herbert's narrator is sensitive enough to know that he cannot achieve perfection in the sight of a holy God. Perhaps he also intuits Christ's own interpretation of keeping the law: "Ye have heard that it was said by them of old time, thou shalt not commit adultery: but I say unto you, That whosoever looketh on a woman to lust after her hath committed adultery with her already in his heart" (Matt. 5:28). The intent can only be to demonstrate the futility of trying to meet the terms of the old lease. The fact that the narrator knows he is "not thriving" therefore indicates the very opposite of materialism — namely, a God-awareness and a spiritual concern. He is sufficiently desperate that he resolves "to be bold" by throwing himself on the mercies of the landlord, seeking for grace (unmerited favor). Herbert himself wrote often of man's need for grace because of his inability to release himself from the shackles of his own depravity: "I can no more free my selfe from actuall sinnes after Baptisme, then I could of Originall before, and without Baptisme. The exemption from both, is by the Grace of God."[5]

Mulder claims that because the speaker "views God as a rich lord, like himself preoccupied with buying and selling," he "Of course . . . seeks

Christ in the wrong places" (p. 77). But again, if we focus on the fact that this poem is an allegory concerning the exchange of the Old Testament for the New, as both Stein and Mulder agree it is, there is no censure involved in Everyman's view of God as a rich lord. The legalistic and business imagery is only that — imagery — and is intended to point us to the real drama of God's relationship to man: He had "dearly bought" the world long ago, by the act of creation, and because of the Fall must now "take possession" by buying the world back — redeeming it — on the cross. The imagery is time-honored, for St. Paul reminded the first-century Corinthian Christians that they were "bought with a price: therefore glorify God in your body, and in your spirit, which are God's" (1 Cor. 6:20; cf. 7:23). And the author of Hebrews uses legalistic and business imagery in a context identical to Herbert's: "he [Christ] is the mediator of the new testament, that by means of death, for the redemption of the transgressions that were under the first testament, they which are called might receive the promise of eternal inheritance" (9.15). Herbert's narrator views God as a rich lord only because in the terms of the allegory He is exactly that.

It is true that Everyman seeks for Christ in all the wrong places: in great resorts, theatres, gardens, parks, and courts. But this is not a result of materialism. Herbert stresses that it is simply logical: "knowing his great birth," Everyman "Sought him *accordingly*." The Genevan translators recognized the normalcy of such an assumption, claiming in their marginal note to Luke 2:12 that this was the reason the Angel identified the manger and swaddling clothes as a *sign*: to ward off the perfectly normal expectancy of finding the newborn Son of God in one of the regal places of this earth, and the offense and doubt which might attend finding Him in a stable: "Because thei shulde not be offended with Christs poore estate, the Angel preventeth this doute, and sheweth in what sorte they shulde finde him."[6] Arnold Stein recognizes that "the humble petitioner searches in likely places" (p. 185); it is therefore difficult to understand why he several times insists on the "slow-wittedness" of the "protagonist."

Mulder claims that there is no mention of the divine suffering and no feeling of compassion or even surprise in the speaker, who is so mean and self-seeking that he records only the fact which is of interest to himself, that his suit is granted. But once again, a focus on the allegorical nature of the poem changes the emphasis. It is not a materialistic blessing which Everyman has been granted; it is an opportunity to enter into a different sort of relationship with God, a relationship in which, through Christ's merits, a settling of accounts is possible, as opposed to inevitable and frustrating failure. "Christ hath redeemed us from the curse of the law." To focus on the answered prayer is to focus on the grace of God, and for Herbert there is no better focus.

There can be no doubt that "Redemption" is an unusually objective Herbert poem, and the objectivity becomes all the more pronounced by being set within the ordinarily lyrical format of the sonnet. F. E. Hutchinson commented that apart from "The Church-Porch" and "The Church Militant," Herbert's poems are either "colloquies of the soul with God or self-communings as he seeks to bring harmony and order into that complex personality of his."[7] But "Redemption" is neither of these, and we become confused if we expect it to be colloquy either with God or with the self, with all the subjectivity of such communings. The sonnet is objective fiction, an allegorical narrative in the first-person point of view. As in many first-person fictions, the reader gradually comes to identify with the narrator, so that when the speaker finally recognizes Christ among the thieves and murderers on Golgotha, both *his* quest *and ours* comes to a startling, abrupt conclusion. Any expression of the narrator's feeling would interfere with the workings of the reader's emotions: we are left staring at the crucified Christ, grappling with the realization that He has answered our need even before we have had the opportunity to tell Him about it.

The speaker, then, is not mean-spirited and selfishly materialistic, nor is he slow-witted (unless his "wit" is compared to Christ's — hardly a fair standard). He is that part of every man's soul which desires peace with God, crystallized at the historical moment of Christ's incarnation and crucifixion. (In personal histories that moment is replayed whenever the individual becomes aware that he cannot please God by his own virtue, and cries out for vicarious redemption, as in Donne's "Batter my heart, three-person'd God.") The narrator is, strictly speaking, not the protagonist at all. He is simply the searcher; Christ is the protagonist, constantly acting in the background until finally He is picked up by the spotlight for the dazzling conclusion.

As a sonnet, "Redemption" falls into four divisions which are neither Petrarchan nor Shakespearean: two quatrains followed by two tercets (abab, cdcd, eff, egg). The tension mounts through the quatrains and first tercet, and is relieved in the last three lines, with the final emphasis falling on the costliness of redemption: "and died."

The concluding line is a description of "him," of the "rich landlord" whose words from the cross maintain the legal metaphor: "Your suit is granted." At the same time, Christ's words indicate that He is not the price of the tenant's desire for "a new small-rented lease." (In other words, the rent is small for man only because the deficit was paid by God.) Three pauses are strategically located to emphasize (a) the landlord's intuitive understanding of man's plight, (b) His tenderly eager answer to man's unspoken request, and (c) the enormous price to the landlord of making the lease easier for the tenant: "Who straight, (a) *Your suit is granted*, (b) said, (c) and died." Once again, Herbert may have been thinking of the ninth chapter of Hebrews: "where a testament is, there must also of necessity be the death of the testator" (16). It is only the landlord's death which activates his dying testament.

For Herbert's personal emotion concerning the crucifixion, we need only look at the poems which surround "Redemption" in *The Temple*. "Good Friday," which precedes it, laments "How shall I measure out thy blood? / How shall I count what thee befell, / And each grief tell?" And "Sepulchre," which follows it, begins with the sharp emotion of "O Blessed bodie! Whither art thou thrown?" But in his sonnet-account of the redemptive act itself, Herbert places each of his readers among the thieves and murderers at the foot of the cross, writing with laconic objectivity so there will be no interference with our individual reaction to Christ's accomplishment.

GEORGE HERBERT'S "AFFLICTION (I)": THE LIMITS OF REPRESENTATION

Barbara Leah Harman

I

In his haunting essay, "The Voice of the Shuttle," Geoffrey Hartman remarks:

> In human history there are periods of condensation ... where the religious spirit seems to push men up tight against the poles of existence. Middles become suspect; mediations almost impossible. Things move by polarizing or reversing (peripeteia) or collapsing.[1]

Readers of Herbert have frequently observed that many of the poems in *The Temple* end in collapse, reversing the process that has occupied speaker and reader for all but the final few lines. The array of critical opinion on this matter is unusually suggestive; not, of course, simply because Herbert's commentators fail to agree on its import, but because they respond to the discomfort this movement produces by dismissing at least one of its terms — stressing a poem's final collapse at the expense of what precedes it, or diverting attention from collapse in order to credit what precedes it.

Louis Martz, for example, minimized the impact of reversal by pointing out that knowledge of the end was already implicit in the beginning of a meditational sequence. The speaker is "in firm control throughout," already "understands the situation thoroughly," and "knows from the outset how the rebellion must be, and will be, quelled."[2] The purpose of the meditation is still, of course, didactic, but the implication is that the meditator learns a *new* lesson from an *old* experience (thereby arming himself against future occurrences) not that he is still subject to the calamity of the poem's conclusion. Following in Martz's footsteps, William Halewood described suppression of the known ending as a "device" necessitated "by the explicit plan of such a

From *ELH*, 44 (1977), 267-85. © Copyright 1977 by The Johns Hopkins University Press. Reprinted by permission of the author and The Johns Hopkins University Press.

sequence" since "dramatized reconciliation can come only out of dramatized opposition."[3] The purpose of the drama is, again, didactic: the speaker, already master of the experience of the past, must now become master of its lessons.

Rosemond Tuve took early exception to Martz's notion, insisting that there was "something unlike Herbert in the picture of a poet manipulating tensions toward a predetermined end." "They were sins to him," she added, "keeping his savior on the rack."[4] Tuve was not simply reading the poems differently; she was objecting to the suggestion that Herbert's speaker is in control of his subject matter, that he has the kind of distance required to teach himself a lesson, that he has mastery. Designed to illustrate the seriousness of Herbert's method, the Martz position reinvented for Tuve a problem about Herbert's sincerity. She made, instead, this distinction: "truth to an experience which led to an end is not the same as driving conflicting elements with steady hand towards a known end."[5] In Tuve's mind retrospect is not simply a device, but a great manifestation of fidelity: the speaker who reports his experience still suffers from it; he tells the story because he has not overcome it. If Tuve's view has the capacity to restore to us the poem's chronology (it is not, in her view, already "over" when it begins) it cannot, I think, adequately account for the suppression retrospect does impose. While we experience, then, the freedom of the poem's beginning and the humiliating impact of its conclusion, we fail to experience the speaker's difficulty in telling a story whose conclusion he already knows.[6]

When Stanley Fish addressed himself to the collapse of Herbert's poems he treated the reversal strategy with great seriousness. Fish called the poems "self-consuming artifacts" at least in part because their reversing conclusions often render "superfluous the mode of discourse and knowing of which they themselves are examples."[7] If the poem's ending represents a reversal of its own progress, it signals that "undoing" of speaker and poem which the rigor of religious life requires.[8] But if the speaker in Tuve's view attests to the truth of an experience whose calamities he is still subject to, the speaker in Fish's view is, eventually, mastered by experience and claimed by his own account. The emphasis in Fish's view is on the devastation of the poem's conclusion; no longer attesting to its lessons, this speaker is, finally, the disappearing object of them.

In a recent study of *The Temple* Helen Vendler accounted for "abrupt changes of direction" by suggesting that the poems begin with a religious commonplace ("the received idea, the cliché, the devotional triteness") which, by the end of the poem, has been refined and can be discarded, "yielding, finally, a picture of the self wholly itself, individual, unique, and original."[9] The language in which this position is formulated is itself instructive, for it is, clearly, the language of poem as aesthetic object (from the "trite" to the "original") and takes little interest in the religious or psychological costs of the revising and discarding it names. Vendler's work charts a path of retreat out of the desperate situation Fish describes, identifying speaker and poem so completely that a "good" ending redeems not only the reading experience, but the speaker himself. If Fish's view takes reversal in deadly earnest, seeing in it the obliteration of the individual and consumption of the poem, Vendler's view attempts a rescue, preferring to think that it is not Herbert who is lost in God, but God who, by the end of the poem, "now seems *identical to Herbert*."[10]

Critical opinion participates in an important way in the life of Herbert's poetry, for it gives evidence of the enormous difficulty involved in acknowledging contradictory imperatives. Through an examination of one of the more complex instances of reversal and collapse, Herbert's "Affliction (I)," I hope to illustrate the dimensions of the problem. I would like to suggest that: (1) The speaker in Herbert's poems is frequently, as Martz indicated, already in possession of its ending (or one of its endings) and, to the extent that he is, exerts significant control over experience. (2) The control he exerts is, however, problematic, since it contradicts a deep wish that experience were not conclusive. Retrospect is difficult in Herbert both because it recounts an experience that is already over and therefore past remedy, and because the life it describes is no longer available to the speaker who gives the account. Since the retrospective point of view implies difficulties of its own, it is improper to assume in the speaker the kind of mastery over the past which suggests that he no longer suffers from it. (3) There is often an appearance of mastery in a Herbert poem, an illusion which rarely survives the story's end, and which exists only as long as the end is suppressed. That suppression permits the feeling of free movement observed by critics, and accounts for resistance to the idea of control noted in Tuve and others. Even though the illusion does not survive it is a critical one and *must be credited* — especially since it is sustained by the speaker (and often the reader) for the greater part of the poem. (4) If genuine mastery is re-assumed when the narrative's end is acquired, then having mastery is a troublesome and dubious distinction in Herbert, signifying not only conclusiveness, but relinquishment of the illusion of freedom, and acceptance of an often untenable end. Conclusion is achieved at great cost in a Herbert poem and is frequently, as Fish has suggested, a humiliation. (5) There are a number of poems in *The Temple* which resurrect themselves after an illusory "ending," and which require that the speaker relinquish whatever safety closure has to offer. The obligation to survive *beyond the end* is the greatest difficulty these poems impose and is, finally, the true sign of their devotion.[11]

II

The first 54 lines of "Affliction (I)" recount the process of diminishment suffered by a man who, convinced that he lives in a world of possibilities, must learn that he lives in a world of none. But the speaker who tells the story is a man who already knows that he is utterly without means, and knowledge of that end is implicit from the beginning of his retrospective account. So that while in one sense the progress of this poem is towards diminishment, in another sense there is no progress. The retrospective speaker knows that there never were either means or possibilities — only the illusion of them. The present bears down upon the past collapsing it into a mistake awaiting discovery.

The poem presents us, then, with significant difficulties: it offers a chronological account whose presence it promotes (and whose existence we credit) for 54 lines; and yet it hints at, and finally emphasizes, its own despair about the viability of chronological life. When, for example, we read the first line of the poem, "When first thou didst entice to thee my heart,"[12] we can read "entice" as "attract by offer of pleasure or advantage."[13] Read in this way there is nothing essentially duplicitous about the line, especially when we are told, in addition, that this early version of the self "thought the service brave" (2). These lines describe a man with a genuine belief in self-direction who lives in a world where "offers" are made and choice is possible. His words suggest that he could have the service or not have it, choose this position or some other. But we can also hear "entice" as spoken by a man who knows that God has designs upon the heart which the heart, in its innocence, does not see. This speaker also knows that the giving over of the heart is not, and never was, a matter of choice, that the service was neither brave nor not brave: it was simply inescapable.

The world described in the poem's early lines is utterly inhospitable to change, and unaware of its own impending collapse, for the circumstances of the speaker's life seem unqualifiedly good and God's offer unqualifiedly worth accepting:

> So many joyes I writ down for my part,
> Besides what I might have

> Out of my stock of naturall delights,
> Augmented with thy gracious benefits.
>
> (3-6)

By all accounts the terms of the arrangement are excellent. He is a man with an ample "stock of naturall delights" whose riches could only be increased by the association he contemplates. The lines are an illustration of the speaker's confidence, not only in his own resources, but in his command of the world's. In the following lines, God's furniture becomes his furniture and even the stars are "counted mine." He writes down what he imagines his returns will be, he counts his share of the heavens, and well before the contract is sealed his wages are determined and are as good as paid:

> I looked on thy furniture so fine,
>   And made it fine to me:
> Thy glorious houshold-stuffe did me entwine,
>   And 'tice me unto thee.
> Such starres I counted mine: both heav'n and earth
> Payd me my wages in a world of mirth.
>
> (7-12)

Even where conjecture takes the form of a question the question is rhetorical and sounds like a prediction. We can assume that to the question: "What pleasures could I want, whose King I served, / Where joyes my fellows were?" (13-14), the certain self would have answered, clearly, "None!" More to the point, of course, he sees no need to ask the question seriously, for he does not consider a world in which things fail to work out as he desires.

It is tempting to think that the speaker's eventual disillusionment is a product of his early over-confidence. But false confidence is subject to correction, and an unreliable man, appraised of the error of his way, may learn again to rely upon himself — in a world in which learning and reliability are possible. Stanzas 6-9, however, are a lesson in the futility of assuming such a world.

When the speaker discovers, at the end of stanza 5, that he has failed to know what is going on before his eyes and that he has radically misread the terms of relationship with God, the error of the first four stanzas is, by and large, corrected:

> But with my years sorrow did twist and grow,
> And made a partie unawares for wo.
>
> (23-24)

> Sorrow was all my soul; I scarce beleeved,
> Till grief did tell me roundly, that I lived.
>
> (29-30)

He knows that absence and loss are part of experience, that conjecture is subject to error, that he has failed to know himself well and has little knowledge of the world. But stanzas 6-9 illustrate that willingness to see clearly offers no guarantee that life will make sense, that it will be either better or more meaningful than it was before. The speaker's vision, though improved in the following lines, only renders more visible his vulnerable position and the radical unpredictability of his life.

When, in the fifth stanza, the speaker is consumed by sorrow and disease, he thinks his life lost — experiencing the severity of his illness as the closest thing to death he knows. In the sixth stanza he regains health, but again loses his "life / And more" (31-34). He has not, of course, grown ill again. Rather, the definition of life has undergone transformation; it no longer means "health," but the love and comfort of friends. He gains life in stanza 6 only to lose it again on different terms. God's strategy in this stanza is also one of reduction:

> When I got health, thou took'st away my life,
> And more; for my friends die:
> My mirth and edge was lost: a blunted knife
> Was of more use then I.
> Thus thinne and lean without a fence or friend,
> I was blown through with ev'ry storm and winde.
>
> (31-36)

The speaker experiences the loss of usefulness, the loss of joy in that which has no use, the loss of protection, comfort, and aid in the face of loss.

God's second strategy turns the self against its own instincts, so that what one knows is lost and what one gets is foreign:

> Whereas my birth and spirit rather took
> The way that takes the town;
> Thou didst betray me to a lingring book,
> And wrap me in a gown.
>
> (37-40)

If it is difficult to keep pace with God in stanza 6 — he is always capable of inflicting a greater injury than one last thought him capable of — in this stanza man is also in arrears of himself, just coming to know one version when another is forced upon him.

In the eighth stanza the speaker witnesses God's ability to transform completely the very terms of existence. At first he thinks he has reached the end, thinks that paralysis is the final, static point:

> Thou often didst with Academick praise
> Melt and dissolve my rage.
> I took thy sweetned pill, till I came where
> I could not go away, nor persevere.
>
> (45-48)

But he finds that even stasis can be turned around and re-defined:

> Yet lest perchance I should too happie be
> In my unhappinesse,
> Turning my purge to food, thou throwest me
> Into more sicknesses.
>
> (49-52)

In the final lines of stanza 9 we encounter the msot sweeping statement about the nature of God's power with man:

> Thus doth thy power crosse-bias me, not making
> Thine own gift good, yet me from my wayes taking.
>
> (53-54)

God is represented as he who cross-biases the self, but the way in which his "inclination runs athwart or counter to" the self is rather complicated.[14] The problem is not simply that God wants the speaker to be in a gown rather than in town, or that he wants him to be ill rather than well. In fact, even when the speaker resigns his own inclination (happiness, for example) and embraces instead that which he was once inclined to reject (unhappiness), the fact that he does accept becomes, itself, unacceptable. It is called being "too happie . . . In unhappinesse" (49-50).

If God is he who cross-biases the self, it is not because he has specific plans which counter the plans one has for oneself. Rather, God cross-biases by countering every attempt by the self to have plans, to determine who he is, to define the terms of existence. If it is man's inclination to fix, and make peace with, experience, it is God's inclination that he shall not.

III

When, at the 55th line, we arrive at the conclusion of the retrospective account, what we gain, finally, is an accurate perspective, the rectification truth requires. The speaker who says,

> Now I am here, what thou wilt do with me
> None of my books will show,
>
>   (55-56)

has not only been disabused of the notion that all choices are good
choices, that the world is utterly hospitable, that his stock of delights is
ample, God's riches an added abundance. He has been disabused of the
very notion on which the entire beginning of the poem is based. By the
55th line it is clear not only that the terms of the contract were
incorrectly figured, but that it makes no sense to figure the terms of a
contract with God, and that conjecture has no bearing on reality. The
speaker does not, in other words, simply know that he figured poorly,
but knows, rather, that to figure at all is to act where there is no sanction
to act, to participate in a decision where participation has already been
pre-empted and is therefore illusory, to assume the reliability of
judgment where reliability is not only unwarranted but in fact prohibited
under any terms. He has learned, furthermore, that adequate self-
knowledge is unavailable and reliability impossible; that he has the
means neither to make sense of experience, nor to initiate it, nor to
control it; that he is, and has always been, a man without means.

While the 55th line provides us, then, with the rectification truth
requires, it also exacts enormous costs in exchange. For when we gain
the conclusion what we relinquish is nothing less than the speaker's
autobiography — which is, after all, the description of a man at the
beginning of a project, in an indeterminate state of affairs, making
choices, relying on his convictions, and adjusting to changing circumstances. Furthermore, if the implication of the account is that it is a story
written by its narrator, the implication of the conclusion is that the
speaker's story never really was his own. He is not its author because he
was not running his life, and also because he did not know he wasn't
running it.[15] To acquire the end of the narrative account is, then, to
stand corrected. But standing corrected means acknowledging the
inadequacy both of one's former and of one's present life. The speaker
we meet when the story of the past is done (and undone) is not a correct
or even an adequate person. He is, at most, a corrected person who
barely recognizes his own history and whose best news is that he has
learned to say that he does not know what to do. The man who survives
the end of this story does not speak in full knowledge — he speaks in full
knowledge of his ignorance. And the man who arrives at the conclusion
of his autobiographical account has not arrived at the moment of life's
greatest coherence, but at the moment of its most complete collapse.

Of course we do have an experience of the speaker's past. In fact, most of our experience is of his past. Even if we are conscious, from the start, that the speaker is headed toward a "monumental dead end,"[16] we must also acknowledge his effort to prevent error from collapsing the past entirely. Retrospect represents in this poem an effort to sustain the past in order to substitute it for present life at a moment when the latter, if not threatened with extinction, is at least threatened with irrelevance. For past life, though erroneous and illusory, represents a more promising view of experience: the speaker believed he knew who he was, thought he was the agent of his own actions, had not yet witnessed the collapse of possibilities. And present life, though more fully conscious of itself, suffers great deprivation: there is no evidence that meaningful experience is any longer possible.

Life proceeds in "Affliction (I)" as long as the speaker does not know that quest, growth, and freedom are illusions — or as long as the knowledge that they are illusions is postponed or suppressed. Of course, the living the speaker does is thereby rendered defective — not only because it depends on illusory terms, but because it fails to have adequate knowledge of itself. When, on the other hand, consciousness *is* achieved and the defect of life becomes clear, quest and growth become impossible. The poem suggests, in other words, the compatibility of life and impaired consciousness. For life flourishes as long as consciousness fails, and it comes to a dead end when consciousness is achieved: "what thou wilt do with me/None of my books will show."

The shifting emphasis of past and present suggests that the poem lives, and that we read it, on borrowed time. It supports the illusion of life as long as the end which collapses that illusion is suspended. In the broadest sense the illusion is that it makes sense to tell the story at all, and that the terms for life it illustrates have some validity. But, as Walter Benjamin suggests in another context, "It is a dry material on which the burning interest of the reader feeds."[17] For once the story's end is restored (and it always threatens to be restored) it renders visible what was true from the start — it makes no sense to tell the story, the terms for life it illustrates have no validity — and negates the illusion the poem's narrative sustains. Benjamin continues:

"A man who dies at the age of thirty-five," said Moritz Heinmann once, "is at every point of his life a man who dies at the age of thirty-five." Nothing is more dubious than this sentence — but for the sole reason that the tense is wrong. A man — so says the truth that was meant here — who died at the age of thirty-five will appear to *remembrance* at every point in his life as a man who dies at the age of thirty-five. In other words, the statement that makes no sense for real life becomes indisputable for remembered life.[18]

"Real life" in this poem is (or seems) possible only as long as one of its poles is invisible. One gets the story's conclusion at the expense of the story, or one gets the story at the expense of its conclusion.

While in some sense, then, the conclusion of the retrospective account tempts us to think that the past has been rendered "superfluous,"[19] to say so is to utter only half the truth. The poem does tempt us in that direction: it offers a rather long account of the personal past of its speaker only to inform us, at the 55th line, that all of his experiences proceeded out of a basic misconception about the nature of relationship with God. But the dismantling and discarding of the speaker's past is precisely what presents him with a problem. The presence of an autobiographical account suggests a man with an impulse toward having a history and representing it, but that impulse is met by an equally powerful counter lesson which teaches that these things are had only at the expense of consciousness and veracity — and in the end those are expenses which render autobiography suspect. After all, what value can be attached to an incomplete autobiography, a defective narrative account, a misrepresenting representation? At the same time, the mere presence of autobiography — especially in its collapsing frame — represents a wish that things were other than they are. In face of God's lessons the speaker really is at a loss, but knowledge is not immune to the wish that things were otherwise, that life were possible, even when God's lessons to the contrary are executed with the kind of persistence and determination we witness here. The conflict between these contradictory impulses — towards self-representation on the one hand and self-relinquishment on the other — are the defining features of "Affliction (I)" until the 55th line. In a discussion of fictional narrative Edward Said described the conflict in this way:

> In any of the reconstructive techniques, be they history, philoso-phy, or personal narrative ... the objective is both to create alternatives to a confusing reality and to minimize the pain of experience. In other words, the project is an economic one. Yet insofar as it is also a repetetive procedure it has to do with instincts driving the mind over ground already travelled.... The demystifi-cation, or education, of illusions ... then enacts [the character's] increasing molestation by a truer process pushing him to an ending that resembles his beginning out of negation.[20]

IV

I have treated line 55 as a point of significant demarcation, have treated it, in fact, as though it were the poem's final line. I have done so because, although the poem does not of course end here, the autobiographical account does, and the narrative bears characteristics which permit us to identify a complete "story." The 55th line is the point at which the speaker announces himself to be a storyteller: he is no longer a man to whom things happen, he is a man who distinguishes the present from the past and who identifies himself ("Now I am here") as the narrator of a story about his own life. As Hannah Arendt has said:

> Action reveals itself fully only to the storyteller, that is, to the backward glance of the historian, who always knows better what it was all about than the participants.... Even though stories are the inevitable results of action it is not the actor but the storyteller who perceives and "makes" the story.[21]

Much as a storyteller, in Benjamin's words, "borrow[s] his authority from death,"[22] the man in this poem acquires authority from the extinction of his own possibilities. The 55th line is also the point at which the story is complete, its dimensions become clear, and it acquires "transmissable form"[23] — even though its dimensions are problematic for the speaker, outlining as they do a defective past and pre-empted future.

The fiction is, then, that the story is over at the 55th line. If it is true, as Hartman suggests, that "art 'represents' a self which is either insufficiently 'present' or feels itself as not 'presentable,' "[24] the speaker in this account faces a serious dilemma. For the story grants him temporary presence only to render him, at its conclusion, insufficiently present once again. Oddly, what saves the speaker from extinction is that he misrepresents (for he misunderstands) the implication of his story's end. He assumes that its conclusion and his consequent undoing signal the conclusion of his life, while what they really signal is the end of coherence, the end of narrative, the end of representational life. Because the story does collapse when its coherent shape is achieved, it is true that life can no longer be "read" or "told." But life can still proceed — even when its procession lacks coherent form. Unlike the tragic situation in which life folds when its true dimensions are known, in which, for example, "Oedipus, killing his father and marrying his mother, simply elides individual identity and is allowed no being properly his own,"[25] the religious situation demands life's resurrection precisely at the moment when it is least obvious that a revival of any kind is possible or even desireable. The true difficulty this poem imposes, then, is *not* the humiliation of its conclusion but the obligation to revive itself, to continue *beyond* the humiliation of an end.

In lines 57-64 "Affliction (I)" relocates itself as the speaker entertains a series of alternatives all of which are attempts to imagine life in circumstances which fail to make clear that there are alternatives:

> I reade, and sigh, and wish I were a tree
> For sure than I should grow
> To fruit or shade: at least some bird would trust
> Her houshold to me, and I should be just.
>
> Yet, though thou troublest me, I must be meek
> In weaknesse must be stout.
>
> (57-62)

Neither withdrawal "into abstraction"[26] nor the commitment to resolute-ness offers, however, a viable solution to the problem, and the lines which follow test a final, extreme alternative:

> Well, I will change the service, and go seek
> Some other master out.
>
> (63-64)

The alternative tested here is, clearly, a blasphemous one, but not, I think, for the obvious reasons alone. Finding "some other master" is a tempting solution precisely because it is a solution, because it suggests the possibility of obtaining a service whose terms are clear and subject, therefore, to mastery. It represents, in other words, an effort to make life coherent again, to provide it with meaningful closure, to withdraw from its devastating inconclusiveness into the safety of the knowable. For while it is true that the speaker of this poem resists conclusion for the first 55 lines, he does so in order to postpone his own demise: when the only coherent story is the story of one's undoing, endings seem unacceptable, conclusions humiliating. But the lesson imposed at the 55th line — and resisted until the final lines of the poem — is that one is obligated to live on the other side of coherence: beyond representation, beyond the devastation endings impose, beyond the safety closure provides. The speaker of this poem does not want to do that. He wants, as Stanley Cavell has suggested in another context, "to *do* something instead of stopping and seeing. So he goes on doing the very thing which needs making up for."[27] He goes on looking for solutions. Of course the solution he arrives at in the penultimate lines is simply unacceptable. It requires that the speaker live without his "deare God" (65) and he discovers, as he says it, how enormous that loss would be.

"To overcome knowing"[28] is a task which occupies this speaker from the beginning of the poem to the end. Cavell continues:

> But how do we stop? How do we learn that what we need is not more knowledge but the willingness to forgo knowing? For this sounds to us as though we are being asked to abandon reason for irrationality (for we know what these are and we know that these are alternatives).... This is why we think skepticism must mean that we cannot know the world exists, and hence that perhaps there isn't one.... Whereas what skepticism suggests is that since we cannot know the world exists, its presentness to us cannot be a function of knowing. The world is to be accepted; as the presentness of other minds is not to be known, but acknowledged.[29]

The speaker's concern in the final lines of "Affliction (I)" is with the re-establishment of relationship with God, but the relationship is not — and cannot be — stated in positive terms (i.e., Let me love you for now I truly love you). Rather, the possibility of relationship is constituted through a complex negative injunction whose conditions are preventive and forestalling in character:

> Ah my deare God! though I am clean forgot,
> Let me not love thee, if I love thee not.
>
> (65-66)

The speaker declares: Let me not love you (think I love you, act as though I love you, love you partially) if I do not truly love you. And in the event that I only act as though I love you, let me be utterly forgotten, for I would rather be forgotten than be false with you. The double negatives register, at last, the speaker's willingness to avoid generating the conclusion of an experience which is, in fact, not conclusive. They register a resistance to closure, to complete self-representation, to knowledgeable statement — at least insofar as speech can ever exist without insisting on its own presence, or endings can happen without drawing attention to their finality.

In other words, the conclusion of "Affliction (I)" denies its speaker precisely that "substitution of representation for presence" which literature traditionally makes available.[30] While that fact is in itself difficult, it is especially difficult here because access to representation must be resisted at the very moment when self-presence seems least secure. The speaker's willingness to accept a life which guarantees neither adequate presence nor adequate representation is the great manifestation of devotion with which the poem concludes.[31]

V

I have spoken at some length about the motive towards autobiography in "Affliction (I)," suggesting that the poem's speaker tells the story of the past because it is the only story he has and because it has the capacity to represent him. In a remarkable essay on the conditions and limits of autobiography Georges Gusdorf comments:

> The man who goes to the trouble of telling his own story knows that the present differs from the past, and that it won't repeat itself in the future; he has become more sensitive to differences than to resemblances; in the midst of constant change, of the unsettled state of events and of men, he thinks it useful and valuable to fix his own image, thinking without this he might disappear like everything else in the world.[32]

Gusdorf goes on to suggest that the man who tells the story of his own life thinks that story worthy of conservation: "he bears witness to himself; he calls upon others to bear witness to the irreplaceable features of his presence."[33] The dual emphasis in Gusdorf's description — on the threatening features of existence (its capacity to erode individual identity or to see persons as replaceable) and the desire to recover and conserve the self ("to inscribe in nature the mark of [one's] presence")[34] — is appropriate, also, to the situation of Herbert's speaker. The description becomes troubling, however, when we remember the specific nature of autobiographical account in Herbert. For while it is true that the speaker sustains the story of the past as a substitute for the deprivation of life in the present, he does so only temporarily: whatever beliefs we have gathered about the speaker's identity have, by the 55th line, been relinquished, undermining the notion that there *are* stable features of the self or that autobiography, if it has the ability to recover lost time, has the corresponding ability to "fix it forever."[35] If, as Paul Delany suggests, seventeenth century autobiographers "sought ... to commemorate the particular destiny that chance or inclination had given them,"[36] the commemoration we witness here is short-lived and ends by giving testimony to the uncertain nature of the speaker's destiny.

Descriptions of autobiography consistently include the notion that it arranges life's experience into a coherent shape, telling the story from the point of view of a man who, as Scholes and Kellogg point out, "comes to terms with himself, realizes his nature, assumes his vocation."[37] Roy Pascal suggests that autobiography

> imposes a pattern on a life, constructs out of it a coherent story. It establishes certain stages in an individual life, makes links between

them, and defines, implicitly or explicitly, a certain consistency of relationship between the self and the outside world. . . .[38]

Gusdorf calls it a total and "coherent expression of [a man's] entire destiny" and speaks of it as the reconstitution of his "unity."[39] These descriptions hold true for "Affliction (I)" insofar as it offers a complete, chronological account of the significant, shaping events in the life of its speaker, told from the perspective of a man who "realizes his nature." But when the story's shape becomes clear and assumes its coherent form, the word "coherent" suddenly fails to describe the story accurately, becomes paradoxical and disturbing. For when the account comes to a close it simultaneously renders itself suspect: the speaker knows that "choices" once made were not really choices, decisions once contemplated had already been decided by another, understanding once assumed possible never was attainable. When the shaping moment is achieved in "Affliction (I)" it points to the collapse of a coherent view of the self, revealing a speaker estranged from his own history and even from his own account. The pattern of his life is hardly a coherent one — unless we wish to say that coherence is the one thing he is *sure* he does not have.

One of the chief characteristics of autobiography is, as John V. Morris has said, its ordering of experience into a "shape that answers better than mere continuous sequence,"[40] its substitution, in Gusdorf's words, of the "completed fact" for the "fact-in-the-making."[41] The narrator who takes himself as his own subject already knows the order and outcome of events and sees them from a perspective unavailable to the man who lived them. Open ended actions become decisive ones, careless actions take on significance:

> The illusion begins from the moment at which the account *gives meaning* to an event which, when it happened, might have had several meanings and probably had none.[42]

The problem presented to us when we look at "Affliction (I)" from this point of view is that meaning is not given until the conclusion of the account — not because its assignment might alter the sequence of events, but because it would annihilate sequence. Insofar as the meaning of this poem is a lesson in the radical inappropriateness of making meaning, the speaker who reveals his standpoint must acknowledge that all descriptions of experience — including this one — are unreliable, and that experience itself cannot be represented or even read. To acknowledge this from the start is, of course, to *have* no account; to suppress its acknowledgment is to write a defective account; to reveal it in the end is to relinquish the "completed" account. In his role as autobiographer the speaker of "Affliction (I)" both serves and sabotages his own interests.

Analysts of the historical development of autobiography suggest that early accounts were encouraged by Christianity's imperatives: each man, responsible for the state of his soul, was obliged to examine carefully his personal life and conscience, and to confess his sins to the Creator. But the "theological mirror" of the Christian soul in the Middle Ages is, Gusdorf suggests, a "deforming mirror which exploits without kindness the least fault of the moral person. The most elementary law of humility obliges the faithful man to discover everywhere the traces of sin, to suspect, beneath the more or less flattering appearance of his person, the menacing corruption of the flesh. . . ."[43] The disintegration, in the Renaissance, of the dogmatic religious framework which characterizes the Middle Ages frees man to look in a mirror and see himself as he is, "without perversion and without flattery."[44] And yet, while the systematic uncovering of corruption is no longer an imperative in Herbert's time it is also clear that the modern hospitality towards autobiography has not arrived to replace it. As Delany notes:

> Fundamental to the autobiographical urge is a sense of one's importance as an individual; in the twentieth century this is usually taken for granted, but in the seventeenth century it was neither taken for granted — except in so far as men claimed significance because they lived under God's providence — nor supported by a general theory of democratic individualism as it is today.[45]

This brief sketch may suggest to us that the impulse towards self representation — characteristic of all autobiography — does not necessarily achieve sanction when the distorting mirror has been removed. A man may look into a clear mirror and see himself as he is, without having secured the corollary freedom to represent what he sees, give it a shape, assign it a meaning, call an end to it, present it to the world. If the limitations imposed by Medieval imperatives disintegrate in the Renaissance, they do not depart leaving an open field in their place. Herbert's poems have a reference outside of the self to which they owe whatever authority they have. When they temporarily suspend knowledge of their referential nature, autobiography — or lyric, or dream — grows up in the space that suspension provides. But their powers of self-representation are always, in the end, defined and limited by their relationship with the God to whom, ultimately, they are addressed, and to whom they always return. In the case of "Affliction (I)" God's restrictions complicate the shape of autobiographical account — not because they require the speaker to see himself as sinful, but because they threaten the permanence and coherence of the self and frustrate the making of meaning on which autobiography depends. The autobiographical impulse is here; what is not present is the sanction for it.

VII.   LATIN POETRY

THE LATIN POETRY OF GEORGE HERBERT

W. Hilton Kelliher

George Herbert was in his thirty-fifth year when he lost his mother, the most beloved and dominant personal influence of his life. In the first shock of bereavement he composed a series of poems that celebrate her virtues and lament her death, turning for the occasion not to the native instrument of which also he was an assured master, but to Latin and Greek verse. The intimate lyrics and elegies that make up *Memoriae Matris Sacrum* were completed within a few weeks and at his own death in 1633 remained his only mature poems to have achieved print. To reject the vernacular at such a time of crisis argues not only an appreciation of the splendid opportunities offered by the classical languages for memorial verse but also considerable ease and familiarity with them. As a Westminster schoolboy Herbert must have composed Latin verses by the score before ever he tried his hand at English, and like many other poets of the time first appeared in print in the anthologies that the Universities issued to commemorate royal events.[1] His mature Latin work began during the period of his fellowship at Trinity College, Cambridge, and is chiefly comprised in three sequences and a collection of loosely related pieces; *Musae Responsoriae*, his defence of Anglican ritual, was followed by a series of meditations on Christ's Passion and by the gathering together of some miscellaneous moral reflections under the title of *Lucus*. The freedom with which he circulated these and other Latin epigrams contrasts with a marked reticence about his English lyrics, which are not known to survive in any commonplace copies taken during his lifetime; and how much care he took over his non-vernacular compositions appears from the fact that several occasional pieces, written at about this time, are extant in a number of manuscript versions whose variants indicate authorial revision. Moreover *Passio Discerpta* and *Lucus*, copied in his own

Reprinted from *The Latin Poetry of English Poets*, ed. J. W. Binns (London and Boston: Routledge & Kegan Paul Ltd., 1974), pp. 26-57, by permission of the author and publisher.

beautiful hand, are preceded in the Williams manuscript by a scribal transcript of sixty-nine of the poems that were published after his death as *The Temple*, and the collocation suggests that he acknowledged no significant distinction of medium in his poetry.

The sequence of epigrams that Herbert is thought to have circulated earliest bears an inseparable literary and theological aspect, for *Musae Responsoriae*, despite some flattery of King James to whom it is principally dedicated, is a serious venture into religious apologetics. It was provoked by *Anti-Tami-Cami-Categoria*, a long and vigorous Sapphic ode composed by the Scots Presbyterian minister Andrew Melville (1545-1622) in response to the hostile reaction awakened at Oxford and Cambridge by the Puritan Millenary Petition of April 1603. Melville's poem almost certainly remained unpublished until 1620 when another religious exile on the continent, David Calderwood, appended it to a Latin translation of his own tract, *The Perth Assembly*, for two independent replies originating from the Universities are both datable to this later period. Thomas Atkinson, a Fellow of St. John's College, Oxford, dedicated his hendecasyllabic *Melvinus Delirans*[2] to William Laud in terms that set its composition between December 1616 and June 1621. The prefatory epigram that Herbert addressed in *Musae Responsoriae* to the Bishop of Winchester, who may safely be identified as Lancelot Andrewes, must have been written after February 1619, and the very first poem of the sequence proper seems to include a reference to the Latin translation of King James's *Works* that had been presented to Cambridge in May 1620. We may therefore accept as truth the statement made by Walton in the first edition of his *Life of Herbert* that these epigrams were composed 'immediately after Mr. *Herbert* was made *Orator*', in January 1620.

Melville's long ode divides, as Herbert observes in epigram IV, into three principal sections. The first (ll. 1-64) expresses the abhorrence felt by Puritans and Presbyterians for certain ceremonies enjoined by the Anglican Prayer Book; the second (ll. 65-128) claims support for the reforms urged in the Millenary Petition from leading Protestant theologians of the previous century; and the last dwells on the wisdom and majesty of God, contrasted with the senseless pomp and worldly ambition of prelates. Herbert's reply treats chiefly of the first, and it is clear that for him the historical fact of the Millenary Petition was not immediately at issue: in his twelfth epigram he betrays ignorance of its main objectives, misinterpreting Melville's verses and writing as if the petitioners took exception to the churching of women rather than to the custom which permitted a nurse (Melville's *mulier sacerdos*) to administer baptism to infants in danger of death. Mention of *Praesulum fastus*

sets him off on a defence of bishops, though episcopacy as such was not a
target for attack in the Petition. The truth is that he was committed less
to a polemic against Calvinist theology than to an imaginative justification of Anglican ritual. At his best he transcends the particularities of
the *Categoria*, and his satire for all its fireworks and wit tends more to
point out absurdities in the Puritan case than to counter arguments with
venom.

Twelve of the forty epigrams in Herbert's sequence, varying greatly in
tone and working for the most part through metaphor and image,
defend specific points of ceremony challenged by Melville. He complains (XXV) that in stripping the Church of her forms and even her
vestments the Puritans will leave her naked not merely to her enemies
but also before the Lord whose bride she is. Similar metaphors, traced
also in Donne's English poetry, are elaborated in 'The British Church',
and Herbert follows them in *Musae Responsoriae* with some observations on the peculiar fitness of the alb for the Church of Albion (XIV)
and a lively defence of the Romish biretta against the skull-cap (XV).
When Melville rejects the sign of the cross in baptism as not laid down in
Scripture Herbert recalls (X) that Tertullian had likened every Christian
at the font to a fish, adding that the natural position of the body in
swimming is cruciform.[3] In the closing verses he insists that however
much a Puritan may dislike symbolism, the cross — that is, the
Redemption — forms the common heritage of Christians. What would
most irritate an Anglican, however, was Melville's unflattering comparison of a priest's words at baptism to the noise of a screech owl, and of
sacred music to the clash of Phrygian cymbals. This was no gratuitous
insult, but resulted partly from a conviction that to address questions to
inarticulate infants was a superfluous exercise. Herbert's Alcaics *De
Musica Sacra* (XXIII) contain individual stanzas that promise more
than the poem as a whole achieves, but epigram XX makes a neat reply
to Melville's charges against a set liturgy:

> ... Tu perstrepis tamen; utque turgeat carmen
> Tuum tibi, poeta belle, non mystes,
> Magicos rotatus, & perhorridas Striges,
> Dicteriis mordacibus notans, clamas
> Non convenire precibus ista Divinis.
> O saevus hostis! quam ferociter pugnas!
> Nihilne respondebimus tibi? Fatemur.

(Still you raise a clamour, and to fill out your song — fine poet that
you are, though no mystic priest — in bitter phrases you discover
magic wheels and hideous screech owls, crying out that such things

do not suit with divine worship. Fierce adversary, how savagely you fight! Shall we make you no answer? We admit the proposition.)

Herbert valued the ceremonies current in the English Church since the Reformation not because he felt that they enshrined mystical elements or were in themselves essential to salvation, but being grounded in Scripture, rich in Christian symbolism and instinct with holiness they were such, he believed, as no reasonable worshipper could reject. The emphasis that Herbert placed upon 'reasonable service' is borne out by Walton's illustrations of how the parishioners of Bemerton were instructed in the origins and purposes of Anglican ritual.

Herbert's dislike of 'slovenliness' in worship mingles in this sequence with an equally powerful distrust of the religious condition known in his time as 'enthusiasm'. On the whole his derisive treatment of Puritans is familiar enough from popular tradition and the writings of a score of more or less orthodox satirists of his own and the previous age, among whom it was a commonplace to contrast the humble origins and imperfect education of dissenters with their lofty pretensions. In addressing them as *Cathari* (*Katharoi,* 'puritans') Herbert was adopting a term used by and applied to several religious sects of the Middle Ages, amongst whom were numbered the *Tisserants* or *Textores*. In daring to interpret Holy Writ, his weaver is wittily accused (XIX) of pretensions to high academic authority:

De Textore Catharo.
Cum piscatores Textor legit esse vocatos,
 Ut sanctum Domini persequerentur opus;
Ille quoque invadit Divinam Flaminis artem,
 Subtegmen reti dignius esse putans,
Et nunc perlongas Scripturae stamine telas
Torquet, & in Textu Doctor utroque cluet.

(When the weaver reads that fishers were called to carry out the Lord's work he too leaps into the minister's holy office, thinking warp and woof more respectable than nets. Now through the endless yarn of Scripture he weaves his thread and deems himself Doctor both in text and textile.)

A similar technique is found in epigram XI, while the argument of XV turns cleverly on the shape and position of the biretta. The wit and point of such pieces reposes equally in situations imagined or exploited and in pun and word-play, though at times he can poke fairly innocent fun at Melville's Scots accent (XVI, 1. 6) or joke with St Ambrose's name

(XXXIII,1. 20). If to modern tastes his wit seems to be deployed more readily against the Puritans than in the service of Christianity at large, the worst that he has to say concerns their innovations in worship: he nowhere questions the sincerity of their religion, much less denies them hope of salvation. In the mass they are to him merely *seducti innocentes* (XXXVI), while in the fine hendecasyllables of XXXVII he willingly concedes to Melville, although culpable as a leader, the respect due to an older man, a scholar and a poet. This epigram is a minor masterpiece of ironic compliment, but establishes in its opening paragraph a wry good-humour that was rare in contemporary religious debate:

> Atqui te precor unice per ipsam,
> Quae scripsit numeros, manum; per omnes
> Musarum calices, per & beatos
> Sarcasmos quibus artifex triumphas;
> Quin per Presbyteros tuos; per urbem
> Quam curto nequeo referre versu;
> Per charas tibi nobilesque dextras,
> Quas subscriptio neutiquam inquinavit;
> Per quicquid tibi suaviter probatur;
> Ne me carminibus nimis dicacem,
> Aut saevum reputes. Amica nostra est
> Atque edentula Musa, nec veneno
> Splenis perlita contumeliosi.

(So I conjure you most of all by the hand that wrote those verses; by the drinking-cups of the Muses; and by those happy strokes of caustic wit that you excel in. More! by your own Presbyters; by the city that I can't fit into my narrow verses; by those right hands, so noble and dear to you, which the Subscription by no means has stained; or by whatever seems agreeable to you! Don't think me too bitter or satirical in my epigrams. My Muse is a kindly creature, not given to biting, nor dyed in the abusive venom of spleen.)

Behind a playful conjuration that is itself part of the poem's ironic artifice, Herbert's disclaimer remains ingenuous.

Herbert's opening address to Melville (II) is both tactful and assured: he borrows and then restores the elder's years as a duellist returns a defeated adversary's weapon. Yet his confidence that the justice of the cause will make up for his youth and inexperience in debate cannot altogether excuse occasional obfuscation. He fails in epigram XVII to prove that the Puritan dislike of episcopacy was motivated by envy, and his neat conclusion dodges the real issue. In their preference for antitheses and clear-cut situations, controversial poets are prone to exaggeration, and even the central image of epigram VIII, which makes play with a recent invention that Donne had first introduced into English poetry,[4] ultimately leaves its options open:

> Quisquis tuetur perspicillis Belgicis
>   Qua parte tractari solent,
> Res ampliantur, sin per adversam videt,
>   Minora fiunt omnia:
> Tu qui superbos caeteros existimas
>   (Superbius cum te nihil)
> Vertas specillum: nam, prout se res habent,
>   Vitro minus recte uteris.

(If one looks through Dutch telescopes in the normal way objects are magnified, but if in the reverse they are all reduced. You, who think others arrogant — though no one more so than yourself — should turn the glass round: as things stand you are using it incorrectly.)

Herbert was perfectly capable of producing a logically conclusive argument from a similar image in 'The Elixir', and his witty application here argues a humorous awareness of both sides of the case: *solent* is not the same as *debent*. In general the tone of his epigrams is far from being determined by arrogance and obfuscation. The close reasoning, though not the economy of metaphor, to be found in epigrams IX and XII (the latter with its discreet echoes of Scripture) carries over even into the more colourful argument of XXVI. At other times Herbert resorts to popular science and fable (XXII, XXVII) to support or emphasize his contentions, or else commonsensically reminds Melville (XIII) that abuse of ceremonies by some need not render them worthless to all.

Grosart alleged[5] that the two principal faults in the sequence are a lack of charity and too great a concern with the bride at the expense of the bridegroom. A certain amount of satire and witty play is only to be expected in a series of epigrams that sets out to answer point for point a vigorous plea for reform of established practices, and it is inevitable that attention should be focused principally on the temporal church as the immediate ground of contention, rather than on Christianity at large. By the common standards of the day Herbert shows not only restraint but generosity. The language of controversy may sometimes be what passed current in contemporary verse-satire but the prejudices behind it are rooted in a firm personal belief in the aesthetic value of formal worship and its power to edify; while despite Grosart the tone of the discussion is elevated, as in Melville's ode, by the presence of elements that are not polemical or sectarian but affirmative of Christian truths. Scriptural echoes form an indispensable part of the fabric of individual poems throughout the sequence, and a persistent and subtle reply to Melville's rejection of ceremony and set liturgies lies in the traditional Christian metaphors that colour not simply Herbert's language but his thinking too. They may be seen in the opening verses of epigram XVII and, with a more expansive force, in XXII:

> Labeculas maculasque nobis objicis:
> Quid? hoccine est mirum? Viatores sumus.
> Quo sanguis est Christi, nisi ut maculas lavet,
> Quas spargit animae corporis propius lutum?

(You taunt us with our blots and blemishes — why so? Are they so surprising? We are travellers. What is Christ's blood for, if not to wash away the spots that the body's neighbour clay sprinkles on the soul?)

Fusion of these elements occurs in epigram XXV, where the argument is resolved by reference to the 'canons of Holy Writ' from which the imagery of the poem itself derives. In this connection Herbert's adaptation of some verses of Horace to serve as the motto for his final hymn *Ad Deum* is not merely a literary pastiche but parody in the serious sense that was sometimes attached to the term in the early seventeenth century. If to modern tastes the hybrid form and unexpected humour of the opening mar a poem that purports to celebrate divine inspiration the conclusion at least is graceful:

> Quem tu, summe Deus, semel
> Scribentem placido rore beaveris,
>   Illum non labor irritus
> Exercet miserum; non dolor unguium
>   Morsus increpat anxios;
> Non maeret calamus; non queritur caput:
>   Sed faecunda poësews
> Vis, & vena sacris regnat in artubus;
>   Qualis noscius aggerum
> Exundat fluvio Nilus amabili.
>   O dulcissime Spiritus,
> Sanctos qui gemitus mentibus inseris
>   A Te Turture defluos,
> Quod scribo, & placeo, si placeo, tuum est.

(When you, God of all, have blessed a man in his writing with the gentle dew, no fruitless labour employs the wretch's endeavour, no worry cracks his nails with frenzied gnawing: his pen does not grieve nor his head complain. A fertile and masculine vein of poetry reigns in his pious limbs, as the Nile knowing no break-waters overflows with its welcome flood. O sweetest Spirit! The Dove from whom these holy sighs sweep down and steal into men's minds! Whatever I write, however I pleae — if please I do — all is yours.)

The presentation of *Musae Responsoriae* is so managed that various levels of retort to Melville's *Categoria* — witty, discursive, playful, imaginative and satirical — alternate with each other and with more expansive themes. We may fairly claim that Herbert shows the concern of a literary artist to balance the moods of his sequence, for that is partly reflected in the choice and placing of metres. He well knew the various capabilities of the verse-forms perfected by classical epigrammatists (V, ll. 5-6) and it is no accident that except in the case of the staple measure, elegiac couplets. the same metre is never used for two consecutive poems. All this together with the highly personal character of Herbert's defence of Anglicanism make it clear that, despite the formal dress of the sequence, with its flattering dedicatory poems and rather fulsome praise of James in epigram XXXIX, *Musae Responsoriae* was no mere attempt to attract the favourable notice of the Jacobean establishment.

We do not know when the sequence entitled *Passio Discerpta* was composed, though Herbert transcribed it himself into the Williams manuscript, along with the collection of epigrams that he called *Lucus*, not earlier than August 1623. He seems therefore to have regarded them as equal in craftsmanship and character to the English poems which they accompany there. Consequently their omission from the manuscript which he later entrusted to Nicholas Ferrar for publication after his death is probably owing less to a lack of confidence in their merits than to a realization that the reader might not find in them so clear 'a picture of the many spiritual Conflicts that have passed betwixt God and my Soul' as in the vernacular poems that we now know as *The Temple*. The anonymity of neo-Latin sacred epigram is inevitable, while among the moral and theological reflections that make up *Lucus* few poems will compete with the English as a record of Herbert's daily communings with God. Moreover his Latin verses, representing for the most part the outcome of a conflict that has been resolved in God's favour, lack the drama and compulsion that we find in his *Temple* poems. The reason is not far to seek. Most of the epigrams pursue a sacred 'wit' that reflects the paradoxes of Christianity and of faith or points out the correspondences that exist in and between the great books of nature and Holy Writ. Such paradoxes and conjunctions, when explored with the full resources afforded by Latin verse for rhetorical emphasis and verbal nuance, may strike us at first as contrived and chill, but to Herbert, as to Crashaw after him, they fulfilled a spiritual and aesthetic need in a manner that was impossible in English poetry.

Passio Discerpta — the epithet capturing at once the violence of the crucifixion and its analytical dissection in Herbert's verses — is a series of meditations upon Christ's sufferings and death, and for the most part follows closely if selectively the events recorded in the Gospels. Unlike Crashaw's *Epigrammatum Sacrorum Liber* (1634), which owes its existence to academic requirements, Herbert's twenty-one poems appear to represent a spontaneous meditation, and may have been composed as part of his Holy Week devotions. In Lactantius' *Carmen de Passione Domini* contemplation of Christ's suffering and sacrifice is recommended as a stimulus to virtue and a shield against the snares of the enemy, but nothing quite like Herbert's sequence is to be found in Anglo-Latin sacred verse before his time. Singleness of subject marks it out from the miscellanies in which Protestant epigrammatists, chary of striking ingenious conceits from Gospel texts, explored Old Testament themes; and although it is probable that Herbert was acquainted with the work of continental Jesuit poets like Jacob Bidermann, whose *Epigrammatum Libri Tres* (Antwerp, 1620) includes pieces on the events of the Passion,[6] they made no such overwhelming impression on his style as they were to do on Crashaw's. In general Herbert cultivates not so much a dramatic presentation heightened by elaborate verbal techniques as the provocative and witty manner lately introduced into Anglo-Latin verse in Campion's secular *Epigrammatum Libri II* (1619) and John Owen's ten books of epigrams on manners and morals (1615). A certain similarity of style may be traced between the eleventh epigram of Herbert's sequence and Owen's *Christus in cruce*,[7] which revolves around the current adage that 'Virtue is found in the middle':

> In medio Christus latronum quando pependit,
> Aut nunquam, aut Virtus tunc fuit in medio.

(When Christ hung between two thieves, then if ever was virtue in the middle.)

Yet while Owen is here and elsewhere content to rest purely in verbal *pointe* or in wit that is merely surprising, Herbert's epigrams call to mind the deeper meanings of the Redemption.

The nature of *Passio Discerpta* could not be guessed from Christ's long lament in 'The Sacrifice', which figures among the English poems of the Williams manuscript, or from Herbert's observation in his prose treatise that 'The Countrey Parson is generally sad, because hee knows nothing but the Crosse of Christ, his mind being defixed on it with those nailes wherewith his Master was.'[8] Although the prevailing tone of the sequence is deadly earnest the instrument of Herbert's gravest reflections is often, here as in *Lucus*, a wit that consists in making fruitful connections between events recorded in the Bible. The existence of such correspondences is noticed in 'The Holy Scriptures (II)'. Thus in epigram XV he links Christ's plaint that 'the Son of man hath not where to lay his head' with St John's words 'he bowed his head' on the cross:

> Vulpibus antra feris, nidique volucribus adsunt,
>   Quodque suum novit stroma, cubile suum.
> Qui tamen excipiat, Christus caret hospite: tantum
>   In cruce suspendens, unde reclinet, habet.

(Wild 'foxes have holes, and birds of the air have nests'; every creature knows its lair or resting-place. Christ alone lacks a host to take him in; only when hanging on the cross has he anywhere to lay his head.)

Similarly *Lucus* IX suggests that Christ's motive in choosing for his disciple a doctor, St Luke, was to cure the ill effects of the apple that caused the Fall. For Herbert divine providence was inherent not only in the pagan legends that preceded Christ (*Lucus* VIII) but also in the seemingly casual implications of everyday acts, and something more than a love of homely image informs *Passio* VIII:

> Ah! quam caederis hinc & inde palmis!
> Sic unguenta solent manu fricari:
> Sic toti medicaris ipse mundo.

(How they smite you from all sides with their palms! Even thus are ointments rubbed in by the hand: even so do you apply your salve to all the world.)

(It will be seen that Hutchinson is mistaken in tracing a correspondence with the notion that 'Pomanders and wood ... being bruis'd are better sented', from 'The Banquet'.) Like epigram VI, this poem appeals to the awful irony of the Passion, which Herbert sums up with a similar wit in some verses from 'The Thanksgiving': 'Shall thy strokes be my stroking? thorns, my flower? Thy rod, my posie? crosse, my bower?' Elsewhere in the sequence the paradoxes embraced by Herbert's sacred wit include not only familiar topics such as Christ's life-giving death (XVII) but his own characteristic conceit on the earthquake (XVIII) that signalled it.

The metaphors of *Passio Discerpta* bear the stamp of Herbert's character even where they threaten to be most commonplace. His *Pastor* of XIV, ostensibly the biblical Sower or Good Shepherd, turns also into the rustic mower whose fate it is to be mown by his own scythe.[9] In a brief allegory (XVI) the sun is pictured as porter in a household whose master, Christ, must deny his servant what he lacks himself. *Vellum scissum* (XIX), a swift-running poem that accommodates a surprising weight of scriptural detail, opens in mockery of Jewish observances the better to celebrate the Redemption that will substitute glorious realities for the old mystique:

> Excessit tener Orbis ex Ephebis,
> Maturusque suos coquens amores
> Praeflorat sibi nuptias futuras.
> Ubique est Deus, Agnus, Ara, Flamen.

(Our youthful world has come of age, and as adult desires mature savours in anticipation the nuptials yet to come. Everywhere reigns God, Lamb, Altar and Priest.)

The marriage of which Herbert speaks so movingly here expresses in the language of Scripture the intimate bond between Christ and His people which He made by His blood. In the same way the conceits of an epigram *In Coronam spineam* rest partly on Herbert's recollection of St Paul's Epistle to the Ephesians 5:23, 30, and the wit of its two couplets is remarkably complex and allusive. The astonishing assertion of the opening verse seems almost blasphemous until it is recognized as a lament:

> Christe, dolor tibi supplicio, mihi blanda voluptas;
> Tu spina misere pungeris, ipse Rosa.
> Spicula mutemus: capias Tu serta Rosarum,
> Qui Caput es, spinas & tua Membra tuas.

(Your suffering in the sacrifice, Lord, is pure joy to me. Sorely are you pierced by the thorn, but I by the rose. Let us exchange these darts: you, who are the head, take the rose-garlands — we, your members, the thorns.)

Here, as in most sacred epigram, an imagery that is neither visual nor merely emblematic serves as the vehicle for the religious statement.

The passionate appeal made by Herbert in epigrams II and XIII to Christ's redeeming blood reflects perhaps a feature of continental Latin sacred epigram that was well known to English readers from Charles Scribani's poem on the statue of the Virgin and Childe at Halle, which so offended the elder, as it impressed the younger Crashaw. Herbert seems to echo its sentiments in a verse from *Lucus* XXXIV, *Lac cum sanguine posco devolutum*; and his conceits on the sputum (v) or on Christ's side-wound (IV and *Lucus* XXX), in which grim physical details are made a focus for contemplation of the Passion, certainly conform more to the tastes of his own time than ours. A similar tendency is apparent in English poems like 'The Bag', though in the *Temple* poems sanguinary images usually occur as part of a larger, more complex pattern that modifies them considerably. Yet even when the scourge, with its grisly complement of Christ's flesh, is presented (IX) as a stark moral warning we are relieved to learn that in the last resort Herbert sets greater store by individual conscience. The appearance of typically Jesuit aids to devotion in his epigrams is perhaps less remarkable than the economy of his rhetoric on these occasions, for it is only with epigram VII, in which the mocking of Christ is exposed as mummery in its literal sense, or with *Lucus* IV and XXXV, that he approaches the refinement of diction that was favoured by continental practitioners.

Neo-Latin and vernacular poets of the later Renaissance in imitation of Statius' *Silvae* often used the metaphor of a woodland to describe their collections of occasional verse. The trees of Herbert's *Lucus* are planted characteristically in a sacred grove, and show signs of having been gathered together from the nurture of several years. No single theme or clearly definable structure emerges from them, for besides sacred epigrams on New Testament subjects they include many poems of metaphysical speculation or moral reflection — some of which may have begun life as University exercises — and a number of 'character' satires of the sort that Owen and the Jacobean epigrammatists so readily adapted from Martial. Evidence for dating remains scanty. The sixth epigram could not have been written before the outbreak of the Thirty Years'War in 1618, though the full-scale hostilities that give point to its opening couplet did not develop until 1620. Epigram XXV in the Williams manuscript, a series of uncomplimentary anagrams on the name *Roma*, was originally included in *Musae Responsoriae* though it may have been composed at an even earlier date. That it circulated independently of Herbert's replies to Melville is evident from a contemporary copy that survives among Doctor Birch's collections and from the fact that at some time before or during 1620 the epigram reached Cardinal Maffeo Barberini in Italy. Seven elegiac couplets headed *In maledicum, qui in nomen Romae urbis impie lusit* were published in Barberini's *Poemata* of that year; but in a second edition that appeared shortly after his election as Pope Urban VIII in August 1623 the last four couplets were printed correctly as a separate poem.[11] Herbert may have had private notice of these verses, but since he quotes in his manuscript only the first three couplets, and was seemingly acquainted with other poems of Barberini, whom he addresses as Pope, we may assume familiarity with the edition of 1623. Epigram XXVIII, moreover, could not have been composed before Bellarmine's death in September 1621. Herbert's ingenious disposition of the offending anagrams in a single poem yields only to Barberini's apt and economic rejoinder — *Invertis nomen, quid titi dicis? Amor* — and his subsequent replies run from a bitter accusation of priestcraft to a compliment on the literary achievements of the Pope whose family was popularly commemorated in the epigram *quod non fecerunt barbari, fecerunt Barberini*. A further squib (X) turns on the supposed assumption by the Papacy of the motto *Nec Deus Nec Homo*, the true origin of which was in fact a distich[12] composed for inscription on a crucifix by Baudri of Bourgueil (1046-1130):

> Nec deus est, nec homo, praesens quam cernis imago,
> Sed deus est et homo, quem sacra figurat imago.

(The image that you see is neither god nor man, but he whom it depicts is both.)

In several fine epigrams dispersed throughout *Lucus* Herbert explores the relationship between soul and body, and the philosophical problem of knowledge; and while none of them could be commended for novelty of thinking they are nevertheless distinguished by his use of metaphor, in the former case to illuminate a familiar dichotomy. When separated from its native virtue by Adam's sin the human organism hardened like coral torn from the sea-bed (I), but the soul in its prison still experiences divine longings and strives to bore through its casing (II):

> Ut tenuis flammae species caelum usque minatur,
> Igniculos legans, manserit ipsa licet;
> Sic mucronatam reddunt suspiria mentem,
> Votaque scintillae sunt animosa meae....

(As a slender jet of flame still shoots towards heaven, sending up sparks though it remains fixed, so sighs blow heavenwards my spear-sharp soul and my fervent prayers are the sparks.)

A ready parallel for the human condition is found in a sun-dial (XXXI), which for its working combines in equal proportion light and shade as man does spirit and flesh. In such a partnership, however, the soul becomes subject to the body's limitations, and man arrives at knowledge both of himself and of the world around chiefly through the five senses which 'bring grist to the mill'. By contrast Herbert asserts that divine beings (XXIV) have immediate apprehension: angels are their own grist and mill. Man's consolation must lie in the Bible as a source of knowledge that takes precedence even over revelation. In *The Country Parson* Herbert wrote that 'wicked men, however learned, do not know the Scriptures, because they feel them not',[13] and his hendecasyllables *In S. Scripturas* (V) attest that Holy Writ operates on his own system like a physical sensation.

> Heu, quis spiritus, igneusque turbo
> Regnat visceribus, measque versat
> Imo pectore cogitationes?
> Nunquid pro foribus sedendo nuper
> Stellam vespere suxerim volantem,
> Haec autem hospitio latere turpi
> Prorsus nescia, cogitat recessum?
> Nunquid mel comedens, apem comedi
> Ipsa cum domina domum vorando?
> Imo, me nec apes, nec astra pungunt:
> Sacratissima Charta, tu fuisti
> Quae cordis latebras sinusque caecos
> Atque omnes peragrata es angiportus
> Et flexus fugientis appetitus.
> Ah, quam docta perambulare calles
> Maendrosque plicasque, quam perita es!
> Quae vis condidit, ipsa novit aedes.

(Alas, what spirit, what fiery whirlwind reigns within my bowels, turning my thoughts into my inmost heart? Did I, 'as I one evening sat before my cell', swallow a flying star? And is it, all amazed at its lodging in my unworthy breast, seeking a way out? Or did I in tasting honey suck in a bee too, consuming both honeycomb and queen? No; it is neither bee nor star that stings me. Most Holy Scripture, it is you that have penetrated the dark recesses and hiding places of my heart, the retreats of fleeting desire. Ah, how knowing and deft you are at coursing through those meanderings and coils! The power that built the house knows it best!)

As Hutchinson aptly points out, some of the elements in these verses are shared in common with Herbert's English poetry, for *Lucus* is rich in imagery and diction of a strongly personal character. Seldom are

Herbert's moral reflections, even when directly inspired by a passage from Seneca's *Moral Letters* (XXIII), so completely denuded of figurative language as epigram XIII. Rapid alternation of metaphors of the briefest and most diverse kinds marks the iambic trimeters (XX) on vainglory. This habit of composition, owing little or nothing to classical models, is often displayed in Herbert's English poems, and it may well be that the yoking of so many disparate elements is feasible only in the context of a highly associative and dramatic vernacular poem like 'The Collar'. His flair for illuminating religious truths by means of homely pictures receives full play in epigram XV, which evokes Martha's housewifely bustling in preparation to receive Christ.

> Christus adest: crebris aedes percurrite scopis,
> > Excutite aulaea, & luceat igne focus.
> Omnia purgentur, niteat mihi tota supellex,
> > Parcite luminibus, sitque lucerna domus:
> O cessatrices! eccum pulvisculus illic!
> > Corde tuo forsan, caetera munda, SOROR.

('Christ is here! Dash through the house with busy brooms! Shake out the hangings and make up a glowing fire in the hearth! All must be thoroughly scoured, I say, and all the furniture shine. No need of torches — the whole house should be a lamp. Lazybones! There's a speck of dust!' 'In your heart perhaps, sister: all else is clean.')

One wonders to what extent the poem entitled *Amor* that immediately follows is intended as a reply to Mary's rebuke. In his eagerness to read all the signs the subject of the verses is described as one entangled in the tail (*crine*) of a comet like a sheep in briars. Such glimpses of humour are rare in *Lucus*, though a happy exception occurs in the rather unlikely context of some verses *In Simonem Magum* (IV) where Herbert writes of a coin *Si sursum iacias, in caput ipsa ruit* — 'if you toss it in the air it falls on its head', or 'comes down heads'.

Surprisingly enough in a collection of miscellaneous verses that were written over a period of years the metres of *Lucus* are not so varied as those of *Musae Responsoriae*. Hendecasyllabics and imabic trimeters, favoured by Martial, make up a third of the total, while elegiac couplets remain the staple measure. Nevertheless the verse shows no sign of undue constraint as Herbert moves from commonplaces to metaphysical speculation, spirited satire or religious rapture, and his *pièce de résistance* is a hexameter poem in which his bitter opposition to war receives vigorous expression in mock-heroics. The casting of *Triumphus*

Mortis as a prosopopoeia of Death probably represents a hasty adaptation to the purposes of *Lucus* of an earlier version entitled *Inventa Bellica* that is known to have survived in at least two contemporary manuscripts. In its original form the poem may have been intended to complement the *Inventa Adespota* of the Scot Thomas Reid, who served King James as Latin Secretary from 1618 until his death in 1624, for taken together they illustrate Bacon's aphorism from *Novum Organum* (1620) that the inventions of gunpowder, printing and the mariner's compass changed the world. Whether or not Herbert knew Reid personally, as seems most likely, he must have seen his verses in manuscript, for they were first printed in Thomas Farnaby's *He tis Anthologias Anthologia* (1629). In the Chetham Library transcript,[14] where they follow Herbert's own hexameters, they commemorate as in Farnaby's text the inventions of handwriting and printing; but the version published in Scot's *Delitiae Poetarum Scotorum* (1637) concludes with a further section on the mariner's compass. Resemblances between the two poems are underlined by a verbal parallel that links verses 49-50 of *Inventa Bellica* with Reid's *Deerat adhuc, quam nulla satis mirabitur aetas* ... (l. 28).

Herbert's mock-heroic affects to trace the development of warfare from its humble beginnings in a rustic holiday that broke out into a brawl, each man seizing whatever crude weapon came nearest to hand, to its refinement by the *doctus homicida* whose ingenuity devised more efficient ways of murdering his fellow men in hand-to-hand combat or by mass extermination. The centre-piece of the poem, a description of the cannon, bears a close resemblance to certain passages in the sixth book of *Paradise Lost*, which it anticipates by some forty years. In particular, Herbert's verses 66-80 are almost paraphrased in Milton's lines 578-94, where the inflated diction similarly reflects a parodic intent; and a common impulse may have come indirectly from the epic fragments on the Gunpowder Plot that schoolboys and undergraduates were often set to compose during James's reign. The heroic cast of the Latin verses is strengthened by the underworld setting which serves to swell them with classical names, while besides the moral disapproval thus conveyed the seeming grandeur of the surface is everywhere undermined by irony. The cannon-ball, or *glans*, is pointedly dissociated from the acorns that our rude forefathers belched over at their meals, yet 'belches' forth clouds as it flies from the barrel, propelled by the gunpowder which Herbert describes as sugar from the tables of Hell. It is the black-clad herald of Pluto, a lead-sealed summons from the Fates. The ironies and literary parodies of the rustic holiday are even more persistent.

Hic ubi discumbunt per gramina, salsior unus
Omnia suspendit naso, sociosque lacessit:
Non fert Ucalegon, atque amentata retorquet
Dicta ferox: haerent lateri convitia fixo.
Scinditur in partes vulgus ceu compita: telum
Ira facit, mundusque ipse est apotheca furoris.
Liber alit rixas: potantibus omnia bina
Sunt, praeter vitam: saxis hic sternitur, alter
Ambustis sudibus: pars vitam in pocula fundunt,
In patinas alii: furit inconstantia vini
Sanguine, quem dederat, spolians.

(Now as they recline along the sward a scoffer turns everything to jest and libels his fellows. Ucalegon does not brook this but hurls the winged insults back again, and his censure sticks deep in the other's wounded side. The mob divides like the crossroads: rage supplies weapons and earth itself is the arsenal of their fury. Wine feeds the quarrel, as all things grow double to the drinkers but their lives. One is laid low with stones, another with scorched stakes: some pour out their lives into cups, others into trenchers. Wine's treachery flares out, snatching away the life-blood that it gave.)

Ucalegon's wrath recalls Vergil's *iam proximus ardet Ucalegon* (*Aeneid* 2.312) — a metonym that Herbert mischievously twists to his own purposes. The paragraphs that conclude the poem, sombre and unironic by contrast, attribute the invention of gunpowder to a monk and its monstrous abuse in recent times to a Jesuit. Herbert probably knew that Bellarmine, Mariana and Robert Parsons all supported tyrannicide, but at this point surely had in mind the Gunpowder Plot and Father Henry Garnett. The final verses of *Inventa Bellica*, with their grim reminiscences of Vergil's third eclogue and the first murder in Genesis, were replaced in *Triumphus Mortis* by a blander couplet that merely rounds off the prosopopoeia. Yet the lesson was not lost, for into the speech of welcome that Herbert made to Prince Charles on 8 October 1623 he inserted, somewhat boldly in view of the Prince's belligerent designs against Spain, a plea for peace that employs an irony similar to that of *Inventa Bellica*: 'You, a student of philosophy, complain that the bond of body and soul is a hindrance to your meditations: the soldier invades your study and sets you free with his sword.' Herbert's dislike of war and its wastage of lives and creative talents was far from being an academic commonplace: he came after all from a family of warriors, and two of his brothers had died in arms abroad. It is difficult to imagine how, in a poem and a congratulatory address, he might have urged his case more persuasively with equal economy of means.

While the years of Herbert's Fellowship at Trinity saw his three sequences, controversial, meditative and moral, take shape they also witnessed the composition of several Latin poems addressed to older friends. Amongst the epigrams inspired by his admiration for Francis Bacon the most outstanding performance is a set of iambic trimeters composed apparently in the early part of 1621, *post editam ab eo Instaurationem Magnam*, though first printed only in 1637. The fabric of this poem consists of a series of noun-clauses that characterize Bacon's achievements and intellect entirely by means of pithy and sometimes surprising metaphors. This striking technique is also the basis of the English sonnet 'Prayer (I)', but even greater skill was necessary to prevent the Latin verse from degenerating into a monotonous rigmarole. To Herbert in this poem Bacon is — what Epicurus represented to Lucretius — the liberator of mankind from error, who freed the spirit of scientific enquiry and dispelled the Idols of the Tribe. In a bold assertation for one bred under the academic curriculum of those times he proclaims Bacon's complete triumph over Aristotle and scholasticism. If unlike Donne he shows no uneasiness at the new religious doubts created by the advance of natural philosophy it may be because he had accepted, for the purposes of the poem at least, Bacon's own principle of segregation: 'Sacred Theology ought to be derived from the word and oracles of God, and not from the light of nature, or the dictates of reason'.[15] Nevertheless some of the metaphors that occur towards the end of the poem are taken straight from the Bible. Bacon is Noah's dove, finding certainty only in his own powers of reason; while the mustard-seed recalls Christ's parable (Mark 4:30-2) of the grain that grew into a huge tree in which the fowls of the air took shelter, where it symbolizes the Kingdom of Heaven. This introduces a series of associations that is lacking from the overt scheme of disinterested panegyric, and may perhaps be taken as a discreet reminder that all enquiry ends in God.

Herbert's friendship with John Donne is marked by several Latin epigrams on the device that Donne adopted as his seal at about the time of his ordination in January 1615.[16] In the iambic trimeters 'On the sacred anchor of a fisher of men' Christ's cross grown into an anchor becomes not merely a symbol of hope but a mainstay of religious faith, securing the divine presence longer even than Donne's preaching. The concluding conceit, that through his (waxen) seal Donne gives to earth and water a symbol of their own certainty, is rather overworked. In his own elegiacs on the subject Donne wrote that his baptism was sealed (*impressa*) by the sign of the cross, and it may be that Herbert's *sigillum* and *Unda* were intended to recall the 'shining seal' used metaphorically for baptism. The accompanying elegiac distich on the *sancta catena* presented by this device similarly reveals Herbert's preoccupation at this time with neo-Latin sacred epigram. Two Latin triplets whose authorship should surely not be called into question charmingly illustrate Donne's use of the intaglio in sealing letters to his friends, while commemorating, as Walton noted, his gift of such a ring or pendant seal to Herbert 'not long before his death'.

There is no need to trace the origin of Herbert's meditation *In Natales et Pascha Concurrentes*, composed, if Hutchinson is right, on 3 April 1618, to Donne's English poem 'Upon the Annunciation and Passion falling upon one day. 1608'. The incidence of a birthday on Good Friday would naturally impress a pious soul, and more so one who was familiar with the tradition of sacred epigram. Herbert's verses make excellent use of the opportunities for paradox afforded by the subject, but their real climax is the statement, written at a time when he was 'setting foot into Divinity',[17] that only a life like Christ's is worth living. It is tempting to read the final couplet as an epigraph for *Passio Discerpta*, which, were it not for some suspicion of influence from Jesuit verse published later, might also be dated to 1618.

Memoriae Matris Sacrum, the masterpiece of Herbert's Latin poetry, was composed within four or five weeks of his mother's death early in June 1627, probably at his step-father's house adjacent to the Thames and to Chelsea church where she was buried. On 1 July Donne, who had been unable to officiate at the funeral of his friend and patroness of twenty years' standing, preached at Chelsea *A Sermon of Commemoration of the Lady Danvers*, and in the following week it was entered at Stationers' Hall, together with the *other Commemorations* written by her talented youngest son. While like the sermon these highly personal recollections draw a lifelike picture of the virtues, piety and domestic abilities of Magdalen Danvers, they tell us not a little about Herbert himself, whose circumstances are seldom glimpsed in his poetry. We learn (VII) that on his mother's death he was living contentedly in a small house in the country and (XIX) busying himself with the garden, an occupation which he later continued at Bemerton where he 'made a good garden and walkes'. He seems for some time previously to have forsaken poetry, for he says that nothing less than the urge to commemorate his mother had led him back to it: but this was to be his last venture — *semel scribo, perpetuo ut sileam* (XIX). Perhaps he was speaking here primarily of his Latin poetry, and if so it is doubly fitting that her death should inspire the finest, as it is the briefest, lyric (VIII) that he ever published. The metre is that of Horace's 'Beatus ille' epode.

> Parvam piamque dum lubenter semitam
>   Grandi reaeque praefero,
> Carpsit malignum sydus hanc modestiam
>   Vinumque felle miscuit.
> Hinc fremere totus & minari gestio
>   Ipsis severus orbibus;
> Tandem prehensa comiter lacernula
>   Susurrat aure quispiam,
> Haec fuerat olim potio Domini tui.
>   Gusto proboque Dolium.

(While I pursue a humble and religious path in preference to the broad and guilty highway an envious star snatches me from this retiredness, mixing bile with my wine. From this time all my being burns with rage and bluster: I lower against the very heavens. At length someone takes me by the cloak in a friendly way and whispers in my ear: 'this once was your Lord's bitter draught.' I taste and approve the vintage.)

Hutchinson's interpretation that he 'has chosen a humble lot . . . but still finds difficulty in reconciling himself to it'[19] is the exact opposite of Herbert's cry against the fate that will not leave him in peaceful obscurity but visits him with new afflictions. Interlocutors, of course, figure often in his English poems, and in particular this dramatic reversal from acute distress to meek acceptance of God's will at the bidding of an unmistakable *quispiam* finds a parallel in 'The Collar'.

From Walton's biography we know that Magdalen Herbert watched jealously over the moral as well as the formal education of her sons, and in the fine fourth epigram Herbert pays tribute to the example of piety that she set him:

> Per te nascor in hunc globum
> Exemploque tuo nascor in alterum:
>   Bis tu mater eras mihi,
> Ut currat paribus gloria tibiis.

(It was through you that I came into this world, and by your example I am brought into the next. You were twice over a mother to me, and your renown goes in double harness.)

In the previous stanza the turning of his globe is more than a literary metaphor borrowed from Donne and the sixteenth-century cartographers, for it suggests that his true 'sphere' is ceaseless meditation upon his mother's virtues so that he may take stock of his own position from the perspective thus afforded him. We must admire the neatness and clarity of the verses which, by contrast with other pieces in this sequence, speak to the reader without disguise or artifice, for elsewhere in his distress and confusion Herbert sees fit to compare himself, in a popular Renaissance figure, to an inverted tree (XI):[20] his mother's death sentences him, as the fall of Troy Ulysses, to wander in search of a home. Sometimes the sad realities of the situation are conveyed by such transparently literary devices as sickness and dreams. Yet Herbert was sickly, and the fever of epigram VI need not be entirely fictional even if he surmises that his fit of verse was the result of physical prompting — *Mater inest saliente vena.* When he sees a vision of his mother (VII) we may infer that the convenient literary artifice was at least partly inspired by the disruption of his normally delicate state of health by the blow of her death. The Juno, the Astraea with whom he compares the pale spectre of his dream, was the noble lady whose domestic qualities, brilliance of mind and universal charity he feelingly describes in a poem that alone would have sufficed to commend her and display his natural talent for Latin verse (II):

> ... Non illa soles terere comptu lubricos,
> Struices superbas atque turritum caput
> Molita, reliquum deinde garriens diem
> (Nam post Babelem linguae adest confusio)
> Quin post modestam, qualis integras decet,
> Substructionem capitis & nimbum brevem,
> Animam recentem rite curavit sacris
> Adorta numen acri & ignea prece.
> Dein familiam lustrat, & res prandii,
> Horti, colique distributim pensitat.
> Suum cuique tempus & locus datur.
> Inde exiguntur pensa crudo vespere.
> Ratione certa vita constat & domus,
> Prudenter inito quot-diebus calculo.
> Tota renident aede decus & suavitas
> Animo renidentes prius. Sin rarior
> Magnatis appulsu extulit se occasio,
> Surrexit una & illa, seseque extulit:
> Occasione certat, imo & obtinet.
> Proh! quantus imber, quanta labri comitas,
> Lepos severus, Pallas mixta Gratiis;

Loquitur numellas, compedes & retia:
Aut si negotio hora sumenda est, rei
Per angiportus & maeandros labitur,
Ipsos Catones provocans oraculis....

(She did not waste the fleeting hours in efforts to raise a proud structure of towered hair and then — as confusion of tongues followed Babel — chatter idly for the rest of the day. But after arranging her modest tire with a narrow headband, as decent ladies do, she duly refreshed her newly-risen soul with holy rites, addressing God in heartfelt, fervent prayers. She then surveys her household and, each in order, takes stock of the state of kitchen, garden and sewing-parlour. To each duty she allots a proper time and place, and calls for an end to the work in early evening. Her life and her house are ordered by a strict procedure and of both she wisely renders daily account. The grace and sweetness that brighten all her house fill first her soul. Yet if a special event occurs, such as the arrival of some important guest, true to herself she rises with the occasion, meets and masters it. Ah what ease, what affability of conversation she has! A cheerful gravity, wisdom joined with charm! Her words are fetters and nets that take one captive; but when the time comes for business she runs through the intricacies and implications of the matter, rivalling the Catos in their judgments.)

This charming passage from one of the finest memorial poems in Anglo-Latin verse reveals Lady Danvers as the model great lady of her day, who combines the domestic abilities of a country housewife with intellectual resources worthy of a Jacobean society hostess. Herbert emphasizes her restraint in dress and manners by a jibe from Scripture at ladies of fashion. The language of the poem is highly charged with moral values, and in describing his mother's household he never loses sight of how she kept her own soul in order. Though house-proud, she values purity of heart more, unmistakably combining in this Martha and Mary. Her consideration for servants is matched by her appreciation of the needs of great visitors, whom she entertains on equal footing and delights with a flow of good conversation. Walton too wrote of the 'great and harmless wit', the 'cheerful gravity' and 'obliging behaviour' that won her the respect and friendship of eminent men. *Loquitar numellas, compedes & retia*: her words perhaps recall the liquid chains that according to sacred epigrammatists were wept by another Magdalen.[21] While from the very first verse the idiom of the poem is overtly classical its moral tone is set by the presence of Christian values, expressed through echoes of Scripture.

Flowers and gardens take pride of place among the imagery of these commendatory poems. The hint given in epigram IV, that Magdalen Danvers has exchanged her small plot on earth for the Gardens of Paradise, is expanded in the conceits of the succeeding poems, which despite their literary affiliations were surely brought to mind as Herbert walked that June in his step-father's gardens at Chelsea. The summer flowers, condemned here to follow their mistress to a premature grave, are reprieved only long enough to shed a tear at evening, for the poet finds in the flower-beds of Danvers House no garden but a cemetery — the Greek word for a sleeping-chamber — that both 'recalls' and 'lays up' his mother. Sir John Danvers's Italianate gardens were famous in their time. Aubrey describes at length their beds, walks and statuary in his manuscript 'Memoires of naturall remarques in the Countie of Wilts'.[22] For all their formal excellence they retained a domestic character that Lady Danvers loved to foster (II, ll. 18-19), and that is charmingly captured in an anecdote related by Aubrey: 'Sir John was wont in fine mornings in the Summer, to brush his Bever-hatt on the Hysop & Thyme, which did perfume it with its naturall Essence; and would last a morning or longer.' Similarly in Herbert's verses it is not the species or the colours of the blossoms that is significant, but their odours. In the Greek epigram XV his mother in dying draws after her all the sweet garden scents in a single trail which he resolves to follow, trusting to his nose. (He had hoped in epigram III to climb to her by means of a rope of sunbeams reminiscent of the 'silk twist' of divine grace in 'The Pearl'.) The flowers of the fifth epigram are specifically identified with his mother by the pathetic fallacy, and throughout the sequence their odours represent moral virtues in the natural state. Herbert emphasizes the point when he invites (VII) her shade to live with him in his rural retreat:

> Est mihi bis quinis laqueata domuncula tignis
> Rure; brevisque hortus, cuius cum vellere florum
> Luctatur spacium, qualem tamen eligit aequi
> Iudicii dominus, flores ut iunctius halent
> Stipati, rudibusque volis impervius hortus
> Sit quasi fasciculus crescens, & nidus odorum.
> Hic ego tuque erimus, variae suffitibus herbae
> Quotidie pasti: tantum verum indue vultum
> Affectusque mei similem; nec languida misce
> Ora meae memori menti: ne dispare cultu

> Pugnaces, teneros florum turbemus odores,
> Atque inter reliquos horti crescentia foetus
> Nostra etiam paribus marcescant gaudia fatis.

(In the country I have a modest house roofed with ten crossed beams, and a small garden whose plot wrestles with a fleece of flowers. It is just such as its owner has carefully chosen, with flowers compacted so as to breathe a denser fragrance, that the garden itself, untrodden by common feet, may resemble a living nosegay, a nest of odours. Here you and I shall be, nourished daily on the perfumes of the various plants. This only I ask: wear your true aspect, the one which delights me, and do not present this pallid likeness to the mind that still remembers you. For if we differ over ill-matched appearances we may disturb the delicate scent of the blossoms, and our flourishing joys may fade away in equal measure with the other fruits of the garden.)

Together in this Crashavian *nidus odorum* they are to subsist on a diet that would be insubstantial fare even in Arcadia, were it not specifically adapted to the virtuous palate.

The five Greek epigrams of the sequence inevitably share elements in common with the Latin, especially in their appeal to flowers, light and tears. Sun and stars (III and XIV) are the only lodging fit to enshrine Lady Danvers's bright soul, but her children must seek the obscurity of a moonless night to weep at her grave by the Thames (XVIII). In the funerary verse of the age tears were sounded for their secrets until the well of conceit ran dry, and although Herbert's wit is on the whole restrained he could not always avoid lachrymose ingenuity (I) of slight poetic value. His Anacreontics (XVI), almost a drinking-song in reverse, are, however, a modest enough specimen of the genre, while his happiest venture is probably epigram X:

> Nempe huc usque notos tenebricosos
> Et maestum nimio madore Caelum
> Tellurisque Britannicae salivam
> Iniuste satis arguit viator.
> At te commoriente, Magna Mater,
> Recte, quem trahit, aerem repellit
> Cum probro madidum, reumque difflat.
> Nam te nunc Ager, Urbs, & Aula plorant:
> Te nunc Anglia, Scotiaeque binae,
> Quin te Cambria pervetusta deflet,
> Deducens lacrymas prioris aevi

Ne serae meritis tuis venirent.
Non est angulus uspiam serenus,
Nec cingit mare, nunc inundat omnes.

(Until now, it is true, the traveller has censured all too unjustly our
darkening South Winds, our skies heavy with undischarged rain,
and the damps of British soil. But at your death, noble mother, he
is right to expel with a curse the dank air that he breathes, and to
spit out the offender. Country, city, and court bewail you now.
England, the two Gaelic realms and ancient Wales weep for you,
bringing the tears of a former age for fear that they come too late to
answer your deserts. Now not a nook of these islands sees fair
weather, and the sea no more encompasses but rather floods them
all.)

Here Herbert deftly suggests that rain is chiefly the tears of a previous
age held in solution in the sky. When he writes that the English climate is
guilty (*reum*) of his mother's death he is hinting that her constitution had
been, like his own, undermined by 'Rheums and other weaknesses'. But
the traveller who on her account expels the miasmal air with a curse is
also 'voiding his rheum' (*rheuma*). Opinions may differ as to the
propriety of such earthy humour, though elsewhere in the sequence pun
and word-play illuminate the situations that inspire them and add a not
unwelcome salt to these memorial elegies. In the same spirit Herbert
makes the most of his opportunities for indignation (VI) as an artistic
contrast to tears and unstinted eulogy. Stoic ancestry is unflatteringly
traced by puns set in a context (XII) of the Catullan invective for which
he had shown something of a flair since at least *Musae Responsoriae*:
the bones of these callous cynics, says Herbert, are so dry that a ravening
wolfhound could not tear three-farthings' worth of marrow from them.
Elsewhere too his turn of phrase is worthy of the Roman satirists. His
spirited reply to an imaginary critic in epigram II solves the problem of
finding a conclusion that would not be merely anticlimactic, and this
concern with the tone and force of individual poems is reflected equally
in their careful grouping within the sequence, which tends to emphasize
the virtuosity of his performances. There are few purple passages in his
Latin epigrams, as in his English, for the simple reason that each was
conceived as an integral entity. Here also the prevailing metaphors of
dreams, sickness, flowers and tears are brilliantly assimilated to
Herbert's own situation and his mother's character so that they acquire a
real and independent meaning beyond the literary conventions to which
they appeal.

Memoriae Matris Sacrum illustrates by its highly personal tone no less than by the Metaphysical spirit that is evident in individual poems how Herbert's mastery of classical idioms was made to serve his own immediate needs rather than merely to fulfil a literary ideal. Even in his earliest known Latin pieces, those written on the death of Prince Henry and in honour of the Elector Palatine's marriage in 1612 and 1613, he showed some impatience with conventional tributes, while the nature and variety of the images that he so readily employed in all his sequences give his Latin epigrams kinship with contemporary vernacular verse — and in particular with Donne's — rather than with Augustan or Silver Latin poetry. What Hallam wrote of Sannazaro, that the 'unauthorised word, the doubtful idiom, the modern turn of thought, so common in Latin verse, scarce ever appear',[23] could not be said of Herbert. With a few exceptions such as the dedicatory verses of *Musae Responsoriae* the voice of the classical epigrammatists is echoed chiefly in his satire and invective. His wit is recognizably English and Jacobean, but seldom rests in the verbal play upon which so much post-Renaissance epigram depends. Everywhere its perspectives take precedence even over the metaphorical language through which they are expressed, and Hutchinson adds less to our appreciation of lines 23-6 of 'The Church Militant' by likening them on account of their imagery to *Passio* XVIII than if he had pointed out their similarity in conception to XX. A wholly contemporary taste for conceited paradox is as pronounced in *Passio* and *Lucus* as in Herbert's only poem of secular love, *Aethiopissa ambit Cestum Diversi Coloris Virum*, a charming *jeu d'esprit* on the wooing of white by black. What distinguishes Herbert's wit from that of Crashaw in similar situations is the real humour that often shows through the literary game.

In metaphor and imagery Herbert's Latin epigrams compare closely with his own vernacular poetry, and a similar line of development may be traced in each. The language of his earlier sequences reveals the same preoccupation as the English poems of the Williams manuscript with astronomy, household matters, law, commerce and warfare; and in its reliance on medicine and botany *Memoriae Matris Sacrum* approaches the manner of the poems added in the Tanner text of *The Temple*. Among Herbert's many references to flowers in his English verse only the rose and the lily are mentioned by name, while the roses of his Latin flourish not in Lady Danvers's flower-beds but in the crown of *Passio* VI. The application to Christ of such traditional emblems in the line '*Roses* and *Lillies* speak thee', from the very early sonnet to his mother, remains implicit much later in a conceit from 'Dulnesse' — 'Thy bloudy death and undeserv'd, makes thee Pure red and white'. The related images of milk and blood are also to be found in *Passio* and *Lucus*, and taken altogether they show Herbert no less sensitive than the widely read Crashaw to the current fashions in religious poetry, native and foreign.

Yet it is not merely their modern spirit and presentation that distinguish Herbert's Latin epigrams from those of their ultimate literary ancestors. Setting aside irregularities of scansion, which partly resulted from contemporary unawareness of the rules of classical versification, his vocabulary is noticeably broader and less selective than that of the Roman poets. This common feature of neo-Latin verse has been attributed to 'the want of tolerable dictionaries: so that the memory was the only test of classical precedent'[24] at a time when a very heterogeneous Latin was the *lingua franca* of Europe in all areas of learning, letters and diplomacy. We must also bear in mind that Christianity and, more recently, scientific discoveries of many kinds had made available to poets fields of experience not open to the ancients, each with its own developing vocabulary. In these circumstances any extension of the language of poetry need not be viewed merely as a lapse from classical purity. It is no more a serious indictment of modern Latin poems that *stroma, latriam* and *crasis* were not used in Augustan verse than that *blasphemando, Scommata, insultus, Magnas* (noun) and *coemeteria* were drawn from the Vulgate or the early Christian writers, though Herbert might easily have avoided words like *gratitudinem* and *certitudinis*.[25] In his poems, as in the prose that he wrote while Public Orator at Cambridge, the character of his Latin varies but at its best may justly be said to achieve a 'clear Masculine, and apt Expression'.[26]

That the literary careers of such fine vernacular poets as Herbert, Crashaw and Marvell were marked by their habit of turning to Latin for poetry of every description cannot be taken merely as a testimony of the high value that was set upon classical imitation in seventeenth-century Cambridge. In all three cases we may fairly claim that the Latin muse was at least as old as the English, and that well into maturity they invoked either with equal relish and assurance. The poetry that they wrote in these media often shares the same perspectives precisely because so much of their neo-Latin verse owes its name to the idiom rather than to the spirit in which it was conceived. It is poetry first of all.

NOTES

NOTES

ELLRODT, "George Herbert and the Religious Lyric"
1. G. L. Gullickson, 'Order in George Herbert's *The Temple', D. A.* Nov. 1965.
2. This has to be proved at length: see my *Poètes métaphysiques anglais,* i, 313-23.
3. In *The Court of the Gentiles*: see Traherne's 'Commonplace Book', f. 76 r°.

CLEMENTS, "Theme, Tone, and Tradition in George Herbert's Poetry"
1. Work on this paper was supported by a National Endowment for the Humanities Fellowship, for which the author is grateful.
2. George H. Palmer, ed., *The English Works of George Herbert* (London, 1905), I, 74; Margaret Bottrall, *George Herbert* (London, 1954), p. 66; Helen White, *The Metaphysical Poets* (New York, 1936), pp. 165, 174-75, 184-89; Itrat Husain, *The Mystical Element in the Metaphysical Poets of the Seventeenth Century* (London, 1948), pp. 125-58; and Joseph Summers, *George Herbert: His Religion and Art* (Cambridge, Mass., 1954), p. 64. Since the issues of the Dark Night of the Soul and Union will be touched upon later in this essay, it is here noteworthy that Husain, who considers Herbert's poetry to be "rich in mystical content" and illustrative of the mystic stages of Awakening, Purgation, and Illumination, writes that "the higher stages of the Mystic Way, the Dark Night of the Soul, and the Unitive Experience are not to be found in Herbert's poetry" (pp. 158, 126).
3. Louis L. Martz, *The Poetry of Meditation* (New Haven, 1954), p. 20.
4. See, e.g., R. A. Durr, *On the Mystical Poetry of Henry Vaughan* (Cambridge, Mass., 1962) and my *The Mystical Poetry of Thomas Traherne* (Cambridge, Mass., 1969).
5. *The Works of George Herbert,* ed. F. E. Hutchinson (Oxford, 1941), p. 139. All quotations of Herbert's poetry and prose are from this edition.
6. In "Employment" (I), Herbert writes explicitly of this concept:

> I am no link of thy great chain,
> But all my companie is a weed.
> Lord place me in thy consort; give one strain
>   To my poore reed.

7. I am aware of a possible ambiguity in ll. 12-15, particularly l. 14. Rather than stating a conditional argument from which he draws the submissive conclusion of l. 16, Herbert may still be insisting on his own will and way: i.e., "even with blood, I still *do* refuse to wash away my stubborn thought." This reading would see the conflict as continuing right through until the last stanza. However, even though both readings arrive essentially at the same conclusion, I prefer the reading given above in the text for the following reasons: there are no commas before "not" and after "blood" in l. 14; "for" in l. 16 has the force of a

conclusive "therefore"; "ought" in l. 16 is "ought" and not "want" "but" in l. 17 suggests an exception to, not a continuation of, the meaning of the previous lines.

8. See Hutchinson, p. 526, on "shooters." The *OED* defines "artillery" as "engines for discharging missiles"; the heart is such an engine; cf. "Prayer" wherein prayer is called "Engine against th' Almightie . . . Reversed thunder." The *OED* also defines "artillery" as "the science and practice of Gunnery (formerly of Archery)"; hence l. 28, "Shunne not my arrows."

9. Francis Quarles, *Emblems* (London, 1778), pp. 101f. See also Achille Bocchi, *Symbolicarum* . . . (Bologna, 1574), pp. 18, 200; Christopher Harvey, *The School of the Heart* (London, 1778), II, 29; and Mario Praz, *Studies in Seventeenth Century Imagery*, 2nd ed. (Rome, 1964), pp. 94, 97, 103, 105, 107, 111, 150, 152, 155, 229, for additional examples of arrow emblems.

10. *The Poetry of Meditation*, pp. 125-26.

11. Ibid., pp. 126-27; see also 128-35. A readily available modern edition of *Spiritual Combat*, including Scupoli's *Path to Paradise* and with an excellent introduction by H. A. Hodges, is *Unseen Warfare, as edited by Nicodemus . . . and revised by Theophan the Recluse*, trans. E. Kadloubovsky and G. E. H. Palmer (London, 1952).

12. In his commentary, F. E. Hutchinson observes also the "curiously light, bantering tone" which Herbert brings to the "grave subjects" of "Time," "Death," and "Doomsday" (p. 520). On parody in Herbert, see Rosemary Freeman, "Parody as a Literary Form: George Herbert and Wilfred Owen," *Essays in Criticism*, 13 (1963), 307-22.

13. Near the beginning of *A Priest to the Temple*, in discussing "The Parsons Knowledg," Herbert writes that ideally the parson "is full of all knowledg. . . . But the chief and top of his knowledge consists in the book of books . . . the holy Scriptures. There he sucks, and lives." Herbert then describes the four means for understanding what is found in the Bible: "first, a holy Life. . . . The second means is prayer. . . . The third means is a diligent Collation of Scripture with Scripture. . . . The fourth means are Commenters and Fathers." And he adds, "the Countrey Parson hath read the Fathers also, and the Schoolmen, and the later Writers, or a good proportion of all" (pp. 228, 229).

For a fuller discussion of medieval Christian mystical tradition than this essay can present, the reader may consult, e.g., Evelyn Underhill, *Mysticism* (New York, 1955); William R. Inge, *Christian Mysticism*, 3rd ed. (London, 1913); Rufus M. Jones, *Studies in Mystical Religion* (London, 1936); Gerald Bullet, *The English Mystics* (London, 1950); Ray C. Petry, ed., *Late Medieval Mysticism* (Philadelphia, 1957); most of F. C. Happold, *Mysticism* (Baltimore, 1963); and my *The Mystical Poetry of Thomas Traherne*, ch. 1 of which discusses at length the medieval Christian contemplative tradition in relation to Traherne.

14. Julian of Norwich, *Revelations of Divine Love*, trans. Clifton Wolters (Baltimore, 1966), p. 148; Walter Hilton, *The Goad of Love*, ed. Clare Kirchberger (London, 1952), p. 144, in a chapter entitled "How good it is to a man for to be turned into God"; Henri Bremond, *Prayer and Poetry*, trans. Algar Thorold (London, 1927), pp. 108-09.

15. See James Thorpe, "Herbert's 'Love' (III)," *The Explicator*, 24 (1965), item 16.

16. Edgar Daniels, "Herbert's 'The Quip,' l. 23: 'say, I am thine'," *ELN*, 2 (1964), 10-12, argues persuasively for reading the line as a direct quotation.

17. *Revelations of Divine Love*, pp. 86-87.

18. *Mysticism*, p. 395.

19. *The Goad of Love*, p. 144.

20. *Meister Eckhart: A Modern Translation*, trans. R. B. Blakney (New York, 1941), p. 180.

HUGHES, "George Herbert and the Incarnation"

1. George Herbert, "Ungratefulnesse," *The Works of George Herbert*, ed. F. E. Hutchinson, Oxford, 1953, p. 82. All references to Herbert's poetry are drawn from this edition, and page citations will be incorporated into the text of the article.

2. cf. Cyprian Vagaggini, O.S.B., *Theological Dimensions of the Liturgy*, tr. Leonard J. Doyle, Order of Saint Benedict, Minnesota, 1959.

3. Joseph H. Summers, *George Herbert: His Religion and Art*, London, 1954, pp. 76-77.

4. Charles Bigg, *The Christian Platonists of Alexandria*, Oxford, 1886, pp. 14-15.

5. Libellus XI, *Corpus Hermeticum*, ed. Walter Scott, Oxford, 1924, I. 209.

6. It has been suggested that the entire passage from John is a prologue, but written later than the evangelical narrative solely to provide a philosophical basis, rooted in Greek idealism, for the Christian doctrine. cf. J. H. Bernard, *A Critical and Exegetical Commentary on the Gospel According to St. John*, Edinburgh, 1953.

7. cf. Berthold Altaner, *Patrology*, tr. H. C. Graef, Freiburg, 1960.

8. Harry Austryn Wolfson, *The Philosophy of the Church Fathers*, Cambridge, Mass., 1956, I, 178-179.

9. Jean Daniélou, *Origen*, London, 1955, p. 98.

10. Marguerite Harl, *Origène et la Fonction Revélatrice du Verbe Incarné*, Paris, 1959, p. 124.

11. *Ibid.*, p. 129.

12. Johannes Quasten, *Patrology*, Utrecht, 1953, II, 21-22.

13. Clement of Alexandria, *Exhortation to the Greeks*, tr. G. W. Butterworth, London, 1919, p. 11.

14. Rosemond Tuve, *A Reading of George Herbert*, London, 1951, pp. 103-104.

15. cf. R. E. Hughes, "George Herbert's Rhetorical World," *Criticism*, III (Spring, 1961), 86-94.

16. The research for this essay was made possible by a grant from the American Philosophical Society and a Faculty Fellowship award by Boston College.

BELL, " 'Setting Foot into Divinity': George Herbert and the English Reformation"

1. All quotations from Herbert's writings are from *The Works of George Herbert*, ed. F. E. Hutchinson (Oxford, 1941).

2. Vendler, *The Poetry of George Herbert* (Cambridge, Mass., 1975); Martz, *The Poetry of Meditation* (New Haven, 1954); Tuve, *A Reading of George Herbert* (London, 1952).

3. Helen White, *The Metaphysical Poets* (New York, 1936), p. 177.

4. *George Herbert: His Religion and Art* (Cambridge, Mass., and London, 1954); the quotation is from Summers's introduction to *The Selected Poetry of George Herbert* (New York, 1967), p. xxiv. Although William Halewood describes the influence of certain doctrines of grace in *The Poetry of Grace* (New Haven, 1970), his analysis of particular poems is too brief to have greatly altered subsequent readings of *The Temple*.

5. "The Priest," *The Synagogue, or, The Shadow of the Temple* (London, 1640).

6. "The Brittish Church," *The Works of Henry Vaughan*, ed. L. C. Martin, 2nd ed. (Oxford, 1957), p. 410.

7. "A Prefatory View of the Life of Mr. Geo. Herbert," *Herbert's Remains* (London, 1652).

8. See especially Tuve, Martz, Malcolm Ross, *Poetry and Dogma* (New Brunswick, 1954), and Patrick Grant, *The Transformation of Sin* (Amherst, 1974). After this essay was completed, I read Barbara Lewalski's important study of Protestant meditation and

sermons in *Donne's "Anniversaries" and the Poetry of Praise* (Princeton, 1973). Many of her conclusions parallel my own.

9. See *The Sonnets of William Alabaster*, ed. G. M. Story and Helen Gardner (London, 1959). Herbert may have been familiar with, and even influenced by, Alabaster's poems.

10. *The Spiritual Experiences of St. Ignatius of Loyola* (New York, 1948), p. 46.

11. "The Argument of Marvell's 'Garden,' " *EIC*, 2 (1952), 230.

12. These ambiguities may have been more immediately evident to a seventeenth-century reader. Since there were no punctuation marks, readers would have habitually read and re-read lines to determine whether a particular line or phrase was direct quotation.

13. All definitions are taken from *The Compact Edition of the Oxford English Dictionary* (Oxford, 1971).

14. *Seven Types of Ambiguity*, 3rd ed. (New York, 1955), pp. 256-63.

15. All Anglican prayers are quoted from *The Booke of Common Prayer: King James Anno 1604* (London, 1844); the volume is unpaged. This doctrine was legally affirmed by Article 31 of the Thirty-nine Articles.

16. *Certaine Sermons or Homilies Appointed to be Read in Churches in the Time of Queen Elizabeth I*, introd. Mary Ellen Rickey and Thomas B. Stroup (Gainesville, 1968), II, 198. Helen White, "Some Continuing Traditions in English Devotional Literature," *PMLA*, 57 (1942), 966-80, explains that new theological positions on the Virgin, the Passion, and the Eucharist made devotional literature one of the main casualties of the Reformation. In particular, White finds that the Anglican Lord's Supper caused many of the once popular books discussed by Martz to be banned, expurgated, or revised.

17. This is an ancient prayer, but Reformation writings like John Calvin's *Institutes of the Christian Religion* frequently cited it to refute "carnal thinking" of Christ's presence in the Eucharist: "And for the same reason it was established of old that before consecration the people should be told in a loud voice to lift up their hearts. Scripture itself also not only carefully recounts to us the ascension of Christ, by which he withdrew the presence of his body from our sight and company, to shake from us all carnal thinking of him, but also, whenever it recalls him, bids our minds be raised up, and seek him in heaven, seated at the right hand of the Father. According to this rule, we ought rather to have adored him spiritually in heavenly glory than to have devised some dangerous kind of adoration, replete with a carnal and crass conception of God" (ed. John T. McNeill, trans. Ford L. Battles [Philadelphia, 1960], pp. 1412-13).

18. The Injunctions of Elizabeth (1559) bound every church to provide an English Bible and the *Paraphrases* of Erasmus in English for the congregation, and ordered the clergy "to exhort every person to read the same" (*Documents Illustrative of English Church History*, ed. Henry Gee and W. J. Hardy [London, 1896], p. 421). In contrast, St. Ignatius defends the value of images, urging his readers to "praise the building and adornment of churches; and also images, and to venerate them according to what they represent" (p. 176). Moreover, he warns them to place their faith not in a personal interpretation of the Bible but in the Scholastic doctors and the church hierarchy: "To arrive at the truth in all things, we ought always to be ready to believe that what seems to us white is black, if the hierarchical Church so defines it" (p. 177).

19. *George Herbert's Lyrics* (Baltimore, 1968), p. 95.

20. *The Williams Manuscript of George Herbert's Poems: A Facsimile Reproduction*, introd. Amy Charles (Delmar, N.Y., 1977). Charles attributes the Latin poems to 1623, the Williams poems to a period between 1615 and 1617; but the development of Herbert's theological beliefs makes the latter dates implausible.

SUMMERS, "Herbert's Form"

1. See Kenneth B. Murdock's discussion in *Literature & Theology in Colonial New England* (Cambridge, Mass., 1949), pp. 8-29. I owe a great deal to his comments on Herbert, pp. 21-27.

2. *Spiritual Exercises*, ed. Orby Shipley (London, 1870), p. 24.

3. *The Lives*, World's Classics (London, 1927), p. 278.

4. *The Ferrar Papers*, ed. Bernard Blackstone (Cambridge, Eng., 1938), p. 34. For the symbolic design of the chapel at Little Gidding, see p. 28.

5. *Lives*, p. 301.

6. *L'Esthétique de Saint Augustin et ses sources* (Brno, 1933), p. 199. I am reminded of Paul Oskar Kristeller's oral admonition concerning the historical impropriety of the word "aesthetic" in such a context. In their use of the word, however, Svoboda, and Katherine E. Gilbert and Helmut Kuhn in *A History of Esthetics* (New York, 1939), pp. 129-130, 155-160, are conscious of Baumgarten's invention of 1750 and of the fact that "art" meant something quite different to the ancients and the men of the Middle Ages from what it usually means today. Yet thinkers before the Renaissance were immensely concerned with the definition and the meaning of "beauty," and their conceptions of beauty, while never confined to the productions of men's hands, were relevant to such productions. If we clearly understand the modernity of the ideas of an isolated group of "fine arts" and a particular "psychology of the artist," the use of the word "aesthetic" in itself should cause no misconceptions.

7. Augustine, *The Confessions*, tr. Pusey, Book x, Chap. xxxiv.

8. Cf. "Sinne (II)," *The Works of George Herbert*, ed. F. E. Hutchinson, 2nd ed. (Oxford, 1945), p. 63. I refer always to Hutchinson's edition of Herbert's *Works*.

9. *Confessions*, Book x, Chap. xxxiii.

10. *The Anatomy of Melancholy*, ed. Floyd Dell and Paul Jordan-Smith (New York, 1938), p. 95. Burton's "quotation" is hardly fair: in *The Confessions*, Book I, Chap. xvi, Augustine condemned the teaching of erotic pagan poetry to the young.

11. Herbert, "The Pulley," *Works*, p. 160.

12. *Of the Laws of Ecclesiastical Polity*, Book v, Sect. lviii.

13. "George Herbert and the Emblem Books," *RES*, XVII (1941), 151. For a full historical discussion of the form, see Miss Freeman's *English Emblem Books* (London, 1948).

14. See, e.g., the sections of Byrd's "Magnificat" and Morley's "Out of the Deep" printed in Edmund H. Fellowes, *English Cathedral Music from Edward VI to Edward VII* (London, 1941), pp. 77, 84.

15. *Works*, pp. 184-185.

16. Walton, *Lives*, p. 314.

17. Sermon x, 9 April 1615, from *Ninety-Six Sermons, Works* (Oxford, 1841-54), II, 347-348. The entire sermon provides an interesting analogue to Herbert's thought.

18. *The Metaphysical Poets: A Study in Religious Experience* (New York, 1936), pp. 167-168.

19. Hutchinson, *Works*, pp. lv-lvi, summarizes the changes in order: "the first sixteen poems in *W* are in nearly the same order as in *B*, but...after them there are only nine instances of two poems in the same consecutive order in *W* and *B*, until the group of nine *W* poems at the end of *B*. There are no *W* poems in *B* between No. 79 'Obedience' and the final group beginning with No. 156 'The Elixir.'" See Hutchinson's listing of the poems in *W* and his general discussion, pp. liii-lv, lxx-lxxiv.

20. The sequence of poems which I discuss is found in *Works*, pp. 44-61.

21. *Works*, pp. 46-48, 62, 73, 89-90, 97.

22. "George Herbert," *Spectator*, CXLVIII (1932), 360-361.

23. "Mr Herbert's Temple & Church Militant explained and improved by a discourse upon each poem critical & practical," Bodleian MS. Rawlinson D 199. I quote from p. 326 of the MS. copy made in 1904 by A. F. Parker for G. H. Palmer, Houghton Library, Her 2.3.

24. *Works*, p. 67.

25. Herbert, *A Priest to the Temple, Works*, p. 283.

26. See, e.g., "Sepulchre," *Works*, pp. 40-41.

27. *The Metaphysical Poets*, p 183.

28. "The Familie," *Works*, p. 137.

29. "Man," *Works*, p. 92.

30. *Rage for Order: Essays in Criticism* (Chicago, 1948), p. 30.

31. See Herbert's "Grief," *Works*, p. 92.

HUGHES, "George Herbert's Rhetorical World"

1. *The Poems of George Herbert* (Oxford, 1955), p. 45. All references to Herbert's poetry are from this edition; further citations will be made in the text.

MONTGOMERY, "The Province of Allegory in George Herbert's Verse"

1. The most useful writings are: Helen C. White, *The Metaphysical Poets* (New York, 1936), Chap. VII; Rosemary Freeman, *English Emblem Books* (London, 1948), Chap. VI; Rosemund Tuve, *A Reading of George Herbert* (London, 1952); Joseph H. Summers, *George Herbert, His Religion and Art* (Cambridge, Mass., 1954); Louis Martz, *The Poetry of Meditation* (New Haven, 1954), Chaps. I, II, VII, and VIII.

2. *The Poetry of Meditation*, Chaps. VII, VIII; see Part I, *The Art of Meditation*, for a full treatment of the method. Mr. Summers' discussions of Herbert's technique are eclectic. He is, so far as I am aware, the first critic to devote any time at all to Herbert's allegorical method (see *George Herbert*, pp. 171-179), and I am indebted to him for general suggestions.

3. This and other quotations from Herbert are from the standard modern edition of F. E. Hutchinson (Oxford, 1941; repr. 1945).

4. C. S. Lewis, in many ways the most suggestive of the few modern writers on the allegorical method, overstates the role of personification; see *The Allegory of Love* (Oxford, 1936), pp. 42-56.

5. Sunday and the other six days of the week are figured as a man, with Sunday as the face. The analogy is reminiscent of the common Renaissance correspondence between the human body and the structure of society.

6. A succinct discussion of allegorical theory is Edward A. Bloom's "The Allegorical Principle," *English Literary History*, XVIII (1951), 163-190.

7. Harington virtually identifies all poetic fiction as allegory; it is part of his argument for the truth of fiction which must otherwise be condemned as lying; see *A Preface, or rather a Briefe Apologie of Poetrie* in *Elizabethan Critical Essays*, ed. G. Gregory Smith (Oxford, 1904), II, 197-201. Harington is of interest because he stresses allegory as a poetic method, in contrast to the standard rhetorical definition of it as an extended metaphor or inversion.

8. Ellen D. Leyburn, *Satiric Allegory: Mirror of Man* (New Haven, 1956), pp. 5-6.

9. I exclude from the following list those lyrics which are essentially what Mr. Summers (*George Herbert*, p. 123) calls "hieroglyphic" poems, that is, controlled by an exact and detailed correspondence between an object and an idea but lacking a dramatic or narrative development. I retain those items whose fables seem capable of symbolic interpretation.

The order is that of Hutchinson's edition. All poems are from the middle section of *The Temple, The Church*, and the total is thirty-six poems of one hundred and eighty-three (or roughly twenty per cent, including *The Church Porch* and *The Church Militant*): "The Agonie," "Redemption," "Easter," "Affliction" (I), "Faith," "The H. Communion," "Content," "Humilitie," "Avarice," "Christmas," "Ungratefulnesse," "The World," "Affiction" (IV), "Life," "The Quip," "Hope," "Time," "Peace," "Confession," "The Bunch of Grapes," "Love Unknown," "Artillerie," "Church-rents and schismes," "Justice" (II), "The Pilgrimage," "The Discharge," "The Bag," "The Collar," "The Glimpse," "Assurance," "The Pulley," "The Flower," "A Dialogue-Antheme," "The Forerunners," "Death," "Love" (III).

10. *A Reading of George Herbert*, p. 112. She glosses the central image as follows: "It is closely connected with various other symbols or conceits: Christ in the wine-press of the Cross, the saving drink of Blood (Wine), Sion or the Virgin as Vine, Christ as the fruit or as the Vine. These connections are in Herbert as well."

11. *Ibid.*, p. 113.

12. In spite of their freedom, William Empson's suggestions for a multiple reading of this piece are useful for throwing emphasis on the narrative order in which the images occur; see *Seven Types of Ambiguity*, rev. ed. (New York, 1954), pp. 135-136. He further remarks that the plan of alternating long and short lines effects a rhythm nearly meaningful enough to make exact readings unnecessary, but I doubt that we should respond very sensitively to this feature of the poem without having made a clear attempt to establish symbolic meanings for the images. The process of reading such a lyric as "Hope" involves a nearly simultaneous response to rhythmic techniques and implied meaning.

13. *Biographia Literaria* (Everyman ed.), p. 196.

14. *English Emblem Books*, pp. 164, 167. Miss Freeman remarks (p. 164) that "Love Unknown" is Herbert's only poem directly allied to the emblem tradition and method.

15. Louis Martz, *The Poetry of Meditation*, pp. 306-309. He calls it "one of the great nodal poems of the *Temple*," and notes its affinity to passages in *The Imitation of Christ*. The imagery is largely eucharistic, linking the offering of the heart to God with the memory of Christ's sacrifice. Mr. Summers (*George Herbert*, p. 236, n. 3) believes Psalm 51 is "the most important single source," but Herbert, as usual, is eclectic. His imagery derives from a variety of other sources, as Mr. Summers reminds us, and Mr. Martz (p. 308) finds an affinity to a poem of Greene's in *England's Helicon*, while Miss Freeman (*English Emblem Books*, p. 165) suggests a debt to emblems like those in Christopher Harvey's *Schola Cordis*. Harvey's book did not appear until 1647, but see the same plates in his continental model, B. van Haeften, *Schola Cordis*, 2nd ed. (Antwerp, 1635), sigs. O4^v, R5^v, L15^v, for emblems close to Herbert's font, furnace, and thorns.

16. *The Poetry of Meditation*, p. 309.

17. *A Reading of George Herbert*, p. 117.

18. The situation in the poem is perhaps a modification of the early Christian love feast, which was, however, chiefly an occasion for communal fellowship; see the *Oxford Dictionary of the Christian Church*, ed. F. L. Cross (London, 1957), *Agape*, p. 23. Mr. Summers (*George Herbert*, pp. 88-89) finds an echo of Luke 12:37, which tends to confirm his opinion that the poem concerns the soul's final reception into Heaven. The note of humility is also strong in Luke 15:8-11. Louis Martz's suggestion (*The Poetry of Meditation*, p. 318) that Herbert had in mind *The Imitation of Christ*, Book IV, chaps. 1-2, is also likely. These chapters deal with the manner in which the soul should approach the Sacrament, humbly and with a sense of inadequacy, and they stress the "sweetness" of the Lord's words, a tone not found in Luke. Consult the following English translations: R. Whitford's, *The Following of Christ, translated ovt of Latin into Englishe* (1585), and F.

B.'s, *Of the Following of Christ* (1624). F. E. Hutchinson (*Works*, p. 543) sees a structural resemblance between "Love Unknown" and Southwell's *St. Peter's Complaint*; see Louis Martz (p. 197), for a comparison of the relevant passages.

19. William York Tindall, *The Literary Symbol* (Bloomington, 1955), pp. 28-37.

20. *An Apology for Poetry* in *Elizabethan Critical Essays*, I, 156-158, 160-171.

21. *Astrophel and Stella*, Sonnet 28; see also Sonnet 6.

TUVE, "Sacred 'Parody' of Love Poetry, and Herbert"

Prof. William Dinneen of Brown University has given musical assistance to the author, who would like to acknowledge this debt and thank him, without implicating him in the errors or omissions which very probably remain in a field where the writer can claim no special competence. A similar gratitude is due to Miss Nancy Donohue and Dr. F. W. Sternfeld for the helps and suggestions whose incorporation they will recognize.

1. Herbert's model was printed by Grierson among poems attributed to Donne, in *The Poetical Works* (Oxford, 1912), I, 429, with the heading '*Song. Probably by the Earl of Pembroke*'. Herbert's poem begins on p. 183 of F. E. Hutchinson's edition of *The Works* (Oxford, 1941).

2. Chambers thinks it Donne's. No more than did Hutchinson do I venture a sure attribution, not having access to all relevant data, but Chambers' arguments are not of a kind to convince us unless there is a clear case on other grounds for denying the poem to Pembroke. It is printed as Donne's in editions 1635 through 1669 (see Grierson, II, CXXXV), is not in 1633, but is in the important O'Flaherty MS. (see *Divine Poems*, ed. H. Gardner, p. lxxi on the character of *O'F*). Because the Dobell MS. at Harvard (Engl. 966.4) was not used by Grierson, nor, I believe, Engl. 966.7 (formerly Norton 4620*), I examined — without finding 'Soules joy' in any of them — these and other Harvard manuscripts containing or ascribing poems to Donne: Engl. 626F* (formerly Phillipps 13187), Engl. 966 (with Coleridge notes), Engl. 966.2 (eighteenth-century copy from *O'F*), as well as Stephens, Carnaby, the newly acquired Gell Commonplace Book, and Engl. 686, a commonplace book formerly Phillipps 9235. The poem's ascription to Pembroke depends upon Lansdowne 777 and on its appearance (labelled 'P.') in *Poems* by Pembroke and Sir Benjamin Ruddier, ed. by Donne the younger (London, 1660); it appears without ascription in Stowe 962.

3. *Französisches etymologisches Wörterbuch* VII (Basel, 1953). The Pasquier use of the verb is given the date c. 1580 (cited in von Wartburg, Hatzfeld-Darmsteter, *admis* Academy 1718); I used the *1723 Oeuvres*, where the passage — in the long *Lett.* x. 5 — may be found in col. 1422. In *The Optick Glasse of Humors* (London, 1607), p. 35, T. W. clearly intends a travesty when he prefaces Latin lines on the sad effects of surfeit with 'all which in a parode, imitating *Virgil* we may set downe'.

4. Though obviously used in the sixteenth and seventeenth century, the word is not in Cotgrave (1632 or 1673), not in Nicot's *Thresor* (1606), or in Monet's French-Latin *Inventaire* (1636) or in Miège's French-English one (1679), and is not listed in Cayrou's *Français classique*. Incidentally, the Spanish equivalent is not in Covarrubias, 1611 (with add., 1674; ed. Martín de Riquer, Barcelona, 1943).

5. *The Poetry of Meditation* (New Haven, 1954), p. 186 n.; this is a note to the statement that 'Sacred parody of love-poetry plays *an essential part* in much of Herbert's best work' — a preoccupation which points the way to 'a fundamental relation' between him and Southwell (my italics).

6. The extracted and supposedly 'neutral' clause is: 'Verses patched up from great poets, and turned into another sense than their author intended them' (*Essays*, ed. Ker, II, 52). But this contains the same element which prevents all the other definitions from

explaining Herbert's 'neutral' use — that the imitator's eye is primarily fixed on the sense and intent of the original author, upon which his imitation *constitutes a comment*. Travesty, which, it is universally agreed, is not present in Herbert, is but the extreme form of this. The issue is whether Herbert's attention is not otherwise engaged.

7. His brother Edward, baron Herbert of Cherbury bequeathed his lutes and viols to his daughter-in-law, the sister of the Lady of *Comus*; in 1626 this Mary Egerton married Richard (later second Baron of Cherbury), and their son Edward was Lord Edward's favorite; with her sister Alice she received the dedication of Lawes' handsome 1653 publication. The much-travelled Lord Edward also was interested in the Roman liturgy, as remaining books of his show, and on his personal collection (largely in his hand) of lute music and his compositions (now in the Fitzwilliam), see T. Dart, 'Lord Herbert of Cherbury's Lute-book', *Music & Letters XXXVIII (1957), 136-148.*

8. *Treatises of sufficient circulation to find place in musical histories or books on the relations between poetry and music (such as B. Pattison's Music and Poetry of the Renaissance*, London, 1948; C. Ing's *Elizabethan Lyrics*, London, 1951; M. C. Boyd's *Elizabethan Music and Music Criticism*, Philadelphia, 1940). Grove's *Dictionary of Music* (5th ed., ed. E. Blom) treats only *missa parodia*, but Apel in *The Harvard Dictionary of Music* gives both, implying that the simpler use of the term is earlier. The usual definition cited is from Rousseau (1768). There is considerable information to the purpose in F. W. Sternfeld, *Goethe and Music: a List of Parodies* (N. Y., 1954, also in *Bull. N. Y. Publ. Libr.* LIV, 1950; especially p. 108 on derivation, and numerous examples later seen to be pertinent, e.g. no. 9, no. 52, *et al.*).

9. The likeliest ones lack the word *parody*: Cooper, 1578 (thus covering Elyot); Cotgrave, 1632 and 1673; Bullokar, 1641; Blount, 1656; Edward Phillips, 1658 (I give the date of the copy consulted, and omit precise titles, which may be found in Starnes and Noyes, *The English Dictionary from Cawdrey to Johnson*, Chapel Hill, 1946). Only late editions of Rider-Holyoke were seen, but in both 1639 and 1640 *parodia* occurs in the Latin list only, defined as 'a turning of a verse into another signification by altering of some few words'. Yet both *NED* citations and the French dictionaries show the vernacular word to have been in use despite neglect of it by English lexicographers.

Of course country or language makes no difference when it comes to the musical use; what I hope some one will add to this information is precisely when, in any of the used tongues, this meaning of composing new words to a known air (usually employing a few of the original's phrases) could receive a first citation under the term *parody*. Herbert is not given to coinages. To be sure, the link, or the confusion, is all but made by the commonness of the practice itself plus the used term *missa 'parodia'*. G. Reese's first citation of the latter *term* is 1587 (*Music in the Renaissance*, N. Y., 1959, p. 202). The indication by frequent inverted commas that I refer to *practices* by the use of *terms* which may have arisen later becomes so awkward that I must beg the reader to observe my reservations on this point and apply them himself as he reads.

10. *Popular Music of the Olden Time* (London, 1859), I, 215; an earlier tune, printed 1612. In various examples which follow, I do not attempt research into the historical accuracy of matters like 'original tune', 'first setting', and the like — not my affair here, and not relevant to my points so long as chronological limits and possibilities are regarded.

11. This is quite simply not what one hears when one listens. There is no reason to disbelieve the claim that Herbert set songs to music of his own composing, and sang them. This habitual exercise puts a different complexion on his probable interest and pleasure in the musician's form of parodying, as well as his skill and interest in what that requires of the writer of song-texts.

12. See Martz, *op. cit.*, pp. 184-185, and following.

13. It is said by Martz to have 'remained central to Herbert's poetry' from the time of his two sonnets written at 17 (Hutchinson, p. 206) until the time he refers to his grey hair in 'The Forerunners'. I see in the former typically youthful and jejune conceptions of both kinds of love (and both kinds of poetry), which Herbert certainly replaced with profound and humble ideas. I should think he must have turned — much as we do — an eye of mirth upon these fiery and arrogant compositions as he rejected them for his *Temple*.

14. The tunes meanwhile being flatly taken over from the frivolous songs; see O. Douen, *Clément Marot et le psautier huguenot* (Paris, 1878), II, 363 for, e.g., Calvin's preface to Marot's psalter (1543 preface in English in Oliver Strunk, *Source Readings in Music History*, N. Y., 1950, pp. 345-348). The emphasis is less usual in Lutheran materials. Coverdale, in his *Goostly Psalmes and Spirituall Songes*, says to his book: 'Geve them occasyon' to 'thrust under the borde/ All other ballettes of fylthynes', and to the Christian reader: 'would God our minstrels' had nothing else to play and our ploughmen nothing to whistle 'save psalms, hymns, and godly songs' like David's; he adds a sharp reference to women who as they spin can sing nothing but *hey nony nony, hey troly loly*, and more in like vein (*Remains*, Cambridge, 1846, Parker Soc. XIV, pp. 534, 537). On the other hand, it is obvious that such motives did not dictate publication of all the 'pieuses alouettes' and 'rossignols spirituels', using *airs mondains*, which became popular (see Douen, I, 689). The mere practice of 'parody' does not tell us an author's motive.

15. See G. Reese, *Music in the Middle Ages* (N. Y., 1940), p. 218, one example the drinking song set to the Christmas sequence *Laetabundus*; note also his point on p. 219 concerning the importance, to interpretation, of knowing both music and words, and cf. below pp. 274-275. But the volume of 'spiritual' parodies is truly vast; K. Hennig (*Die geistliche Kontrafaktur im Jrh. der Reformation*, Halle, 1909) calls the sixteenth century the *Blütezeit* for the writing of sacred songs on secular models (using both words and tune), throughout Germany, and not only by the reformers. Since his extremely long list of analyzed pairs of examples frequently quotes stanzas of text from each, it is especially easy to find corroboration of points I make later with English materials (especially that touching the transformation of images, p. 264).

16. On these matters of double texts and simultaneous singing see G. Reese, *Music in the Middle Ages* (N. Y., 1940), p. 315 (that motets incorporating bits of original secular motet-words were probably not intended for church services); p. 357 (Pope John's bull, 1324/1325, virtually banning polyphony, but in abeyance before very long; translated in *Oxford History of Music*, 1920, I, 294-296). See very many references in G. Reese, *Music in the Renaissance* (N. Y., 1959), especially p. 55, the motet-chanson as written by Dufay (secular French text for two upper voices and Latin text for lowest part); p. 89, *incipits* of a rondeau by Binchois that survives with both a secular and a sacred text; and *passim*. For the canon of 1562 see pp. 448-449; it is important to have a clear idea of the kind of musical excesses which provoked it.

17. In his edition of *Calvin's First Psalter* [1539] (London, 1932), p. vii; he recalls the popularity in Francis I's court of Marot's psalms set to popular airs, the Huguenot adaptation of known tunes, and the use of Lutheran chorales, of which some of the best were 'originally secular songs', reminding us that equally 'the "popish" origin of a tune' was no obstacle to its use. There are comments in H. C. MacDougall, *Early New England Psalmody* (Brattleboro, Vt., 1940), p. 17, and some corrections of Terry's edition in W. S. Pratt, *Music of the French Psalter of 1562 (N. Y., 1939)*, p. 15 n.

18. Douen, for example, though his massive volumes are a basic piece of research, has both a musical prejudice common at his date ('ce deplorable tonalité gregorienne', II, 364) and a pronounced Protestant bias; he is anxious to claim that the Huguenot psalter introduced no secular melodies 'telles quelles' into its pages, and to answer contemporary

and later accusations concerning its lax and effeminate 'Ionic' and 'Lydian' airs, but he likes at one and the same time to score contemporaries who set German and Flemish and French *Catholic* spiritual songs to secular tunes, and he is very considerably shocked by some kinds of medieval Catholic *contrafactum* and parody masses. See both ch. 22 of I and ch. 24 of II.

19. The Kyrie is Philippe de Monte's, the Beza example is taken from Douen (I, 664-668, 680), where examples abound throughout I, ch. 22 and II, ch. 24. The former chapter gives 30 of the first lines of secular tunes, one per psalm, singled out for use by the 1540 Flemish psalter, and they range from 'J'avais fait choix d'un amant' (for Psalm xii) to 'J'ai perdu la tête' (for Psalm xx; see pp. 682-683); cf. also other examples from the Antwerp psalter of 1541 (p. 712). Secular songs of Marot's own were reused (e.g. for Psalm ciii; see p. 687). Some of the examples most amusing to us with our own more rigid post-nineteenth-century ideas of decorum in religious music come from E. de Beaulieu's volume, *Chrestienne reiouissance*, 1546 — a paternoster set to 'Les Bourguignons ont mis le camp', or the doubtful ingenuity of continuing a love song 'Puisqu' en amours a si beau passe-temps' by adding the clause '...je veuil amer Dieu' (Douen, I, 704 f., 708 ff.) A revealing example is the *quattrocento* Zachara da Teramo's conversion of his own macaronic *ballata* 'enthusiastically' addressed to Pluto into a credo (Reese, *Renaissance*, p. 33). For references to the sources of information on Luther's chorale see the treatments of it indexed in H. Glahn, *Melodistudier til den Lutherske Salmesangs Historic fra 1524 til 1600* (Copenhagen, 1954), especially no. 58, p. 152, and no. 70, p. 181 (in the section 'Verdsligt Melodistof'); this advantageously recent study is helpful because citations and corrections of earlier work on the various tunes are full and convenient, and melodies with variants are transcribed in part II.

20. M. Patrick, *Four Centuries of Scottish Psalmody* (London, 1949), p. 5. Of the book commonly known as *Gude and Godlie Ballatis* (here abbreviated *GGB*) I use the Scottish Text Soc. edition of the 1567 ed., *A Compendious Book of Godly and Spiritual Songs*, ed. A. F. Mitchell, with copious notes and appendices (Edinburgh and London, 1897). In the examples which follow I deliberately keep to a few volumes — Chappell, the *GGB*, Rollins' editions of miscellanies — even though the nineteenth-century editors write without benefit of much information found since, and the character of tunes is sometimes belied in early reprintings. I attempt thus to make it convenient for readers to look at long texts, and at portions of secular originals, or to test out the music — for points about incongruity and the like may not be accepted on the basis of a stanza or two. More up-to-date examples would not affect my points, and unless recent information and research would so do it is not cited. Music for the example next following ('Into a mirthfull...') is found in Forbes' *Cantus* (2d ed., 1666, sig. A2); only the secular words appear.

21. See the present author's *A Reading of George Herbert*, part I, especially pp. 32 ff. The tomb image is probably immediate imitation of thought as well as form, whereas the motifs of 'if there be any sorrow like unto my sorrow', of 'love bought dear', and the testament image, show the kinship with Good Friday complaints. It is quite possible that the secular complaint, composed late, had imitated some other religious poem of this special small 'kind', for the refrain fits best the familiar attitude of Christ in the religious *planctus*.

22. In the notes on p. 289 the editor dates early references, though the secular text quoted is late and there is much controversy about the tune. My points hold no matter what variants of the conventional medieval *aubade* images came directly under the eye of the parodist.

23. I would attach a warning against the idea that what is here noted is 'same *form*, different *content*'. The entrance of figurative meaning is equally a formal element, and

both have altered. What we have yet to devise is ways of distinguishing the differing kinds of contributions made, by formal elements which differ within their sameness, to meaning. We shall thereby arrive at firmer notions of what constitutes *evidence* for claims made on the basis of the true general statement, 'Form is a component of meaning'. I would anticipate that the best route to this is careful historical study of poems, for it is only too easy to claim that some component we hope is there is 'in the form'.

24. See Chappell, I, 60-62, and another appears in *GGB*, p. 174, notes on p. 283. John Thorne's text which I have described was printed by Halliwell, *The Moral Play of Wit and Science* (1848, *Shakespeare Soc.* II).

25. The provision of such an interesting shock often seemed the chief reason for some of the interpretations offered during that decade or so when the Elizabethans were permitted to have no word which simply meant 'die: to expire'.

26. I refer of course to the extreme form of musical double meaning in which abstractions, veritable concepts, are suggested by truly musical means — the riddles and hidden references apparent to a coterie of highly trained musicians. But even the two simpler forms of musical translation of texts — word-painting, and the suiting of pattern to mood — could not have been much attended to by composer, singer, or listener in the really popular borrowings. Only in case we find Pembroke-Herbert music can we examine the possibility of a composer's intended relations to Pembroke's text (of any of these three kinds familiar to musicians), and it would still be difficult to prove that Herbert ironically made capital thereof, *and was so heard*. But I am interested to demonstrate the existence of an interchange between secular and sacred sung texts so habitual and so unself-conscious that we should need just such proof before we should have a right to conclude that Herbert's own imitation of secular lyrics was ambiguously significant. Yet this conclusion is taken for granted in Herbert criticism, and is what makes critics of the whole period think of 'sacred parody' as baroque. On the possibly different situations in other literatures, see E. M. Wilson's article in *Jour. of Ecclesiastical Hist.* IX (1958), 38-53, 'Spanish and English Religious Poetry of the Seventeenth Century'.

27. His *Goostly psalms & spirituall songes*, c. 1543 (STC 5892) was ordered burnt in 1546; see *English Music*, Bodleian exhibit of 1955. For a musical transcription and an examination of the unique copy at Queen's College, Oxford, I owe thanks to my friend James Dalton, fellow of Queen's; 'Be glad now all ye Christen men' occurs at ff. 13^V–15^V (sigg. Di^V–iii^V). Words are given at p. 534 of *Remains of Myles Coverdale*, ed. G. Pearson (1846, Parker Soc. XIV). See n. 19 above; in Thomisson's *Den danske Psalmebog* (ed. of 1569) 'Nu fryder eder' appears on f. 51^V (Glahn's index no. 109, p. 225; see also no. 58, p. 152). For the Wynkyn de Worde song mentioned in this paragraph see a page of music reproduced in App. III of *GGB*, and the sacred text given at p. 271 (compare that on p. 140 from the 1567 *GGB);* the British Museum copy is K.I.e.I, where the song begins on sig. Hi^V and is attributed to John Gwynneth at the end on H4^V.

28. I have not thought it worth while to search beyond the reprinted 'godly ballad' in *GGB*, p. 132, and Chappell, I, 140-142; but for Richard Allison's setting with elaborate variations see Sydney Beck, *The First Book of Consort Lessons* (N. Y., 1959), no. 12, and Reese, *Renaissance*, pp. 874-875 and index. But if we wish to sing it, the godly words are scarcely to be preferred to those well-known ones in the *Knight of the Burning Pestle* III.v: 'Go from my window, love go:| Go from my window my dear,| The wind and the rain will drive you back again,| You cannot be lodged here.| ... Begon, begon my juggy, my puggy, begon my love my dear.| The weather is warm, 'twill do thee no harm, thou canst not be lodged here.'

29. On the ballad and tune 'Where is the life ...', see *A Handful of Pleasant Delights*, p. 88. For all these miscellanies I have used Hyder Rollins' editions, with his helpful notes

and cross references. On the third example, from p. 31, see *Tottell's Miscellany*, II, 283; a 'moralization' of the latter printed by J. P. Collier (*Old Ballads from Early Printed Copies*, 1840, Percy Soc. I, p. 29) treats of the fight against the papists for 'God's Fort'. John Ward treats the 'Music for *A Handefull of Pleasant Delites'* in *Jour. of the Amer. Musicological Soc. X* (1957), 151-180; on 'Lusty Gallant' and 'Fain would I have ...', see pp. 169, 176 — cf. Chappell, I, 92; 16 of the tunes are now recoverable (p. 155).

30. For more careful examinations of such relations and definitions with evidence from the poems, see the present writer's 'George Herbert and *Caritas*', *Jour. of the Warburg and Courtauld Inst.* XXII (1959), 303-331.

31. *Select Musicall Ayres and Dialogues* (1652, 1653, 1655, 1658, 1659, with slight variants in titles); the 1669 *Treasury of Musick* is important for Lawes. Both Lawes brothers' names and Laniere's appear on the title page of the handsome 1653 ed. (the 1652 printings being without Lawes' consent). See the interesting article by E. Fort Hart, 'Introduction to Henry Lawes', in *Music & Letters XXXII (1951), 217-225, 328-344; and on various matters concerning him, Willa Evans, Henry Lawes, Musician and Friend of Poets* (N. Y., 1941). We now have, in the relevant volume (1960) of *Die Musik in Geschichte und Gegenwart*, V. Duckles' article on this composer.

32. Nevertheless, considering the use of airs slightly altered for different sets of words, it seemed wise to look at copies when possible (B. M., Bodleian, Yale) to see if manuscript notes would add information; and for the same reason to look as often as one could at the manuscripts themselves in the case of indexed but unpublished songs. In any 'first-line' index, there are five possible headings for 'Soules joy' (each stanza or half-stanza, and the refrain), the manuscript musical miscellanies especially being content to take tag-lines from any of these places. Hence the request on my first page that musical students looking for other things will keep this text in mind.

33. By Miss M. Crum; to be added, for Bodleian music, is the music index in the Upper Reading Room. Hughes-Hughes' *Catalogue of MS. Music in the British Museum* (1906-1909, and supplements) lists both by composer and first line; the *Catalogue of Music belonging to the Music School* (1854), and Arkwright's *Catalogue of Music in the Library of Christ Church* (1915) cover the most important Oxford collections not in Bodley. Squire's *Catalogue of Printed Music at the Royal College of Music* is by composers, hence that collection and the manuscripts at St. Michael's Tenbury (catalogue in 1924 by Fellowes, but predominantly church music) were inadequately covered. The B. M. Manuscript Students' Room has a recent accessions handlist, and music manuscripts therein were looked at; but any hiatus in the Addit. and Egerton MSS. between the latter and Hughes-Hughes' date is uncovered, since of course no ordinary manuscript catalogue can take care of this type of problem.

34. Laniere's music even for a masque by Jonson (Pembroke's friend), *The Vision of Delight*, has only recently been brought out into view, by J. P. Cutts in *N & Q*. n.s. III (1956), 64-67. It is in MS. Egerton 2013, which says nothing of our song, but I attach this scrap of a 'parody' (in all senses): the famous 'Hence all ye vain delights' (f. 3ᵛ) from Fletcher's *Nice Valour*, with its ending 'Then stretch our bones ... Nothing's so dainty sweet as lovely melancholy' has its attached *L'allegro* on f. 5ᵛ: 'Come all you deare delights ... then stretch your selves upon the Taverne Benches, there's nothinge dainty sweete but wine & wenches'. Images are travestied throughout; musical settings are related but not the same.

35. In which lie, for example, Porter, Peerson, Filmer — I have not seen the last. The F. Sambrooke whom musicologists will connect with the last-named Egerton MS., 3665, and with N. Y. P. L. Drexel 4302, was a chorister, in his forties, at Herbert's funeral (Aubrey); Herbert presumably knew those he went twice weekly to hear.

36. Touching music, the assumption would arise largely because actual experience shows that auditors vary greatly as to their translation of musical elements into this or that mood. This practically necessary neutrality of music (and for similar reasons of many rhetorical effects) must be taken into consideration when we interpret parodic writings, for the incongruities and tensions we care about are those that can be apprehended (in the Herbert example, those that would be inescapably detected by hearers who knew both songs).

37. Only one small facet of this is apparent in the fact that virtually no editor thinks of reprinted music as a necessary part of annotation, though none would dream of editing without providing variant readings. But the first can under certain circumstances present as important a line on the author's original conception as the second. Only one of the sixteenth-seventeenth-century lyrical writers can conveniently be taught by singing him; yet an easy test of the difference this makes to critical response can be made simply by confining all illustrations in a discourse on that one poet — Campion — to *sung* musical quotations.

38. The facts about Herbert's connections with Pembroke and Wiltshire may be found in Hutchinson's admirably succinct presentation in his introduction and his commentary on the letters, supplemented by J. H. Summers' also admirable account. Those on Ruddyard, of whom much more of interest could be told, have here received additions from J. A. Manning, *Memories of Sir Benj. Rudyerd* (London, 1841). Of special interest, in 1628, in connection with alleged similar ideas of Herbert's, is *Sir Benj. Rudierd his Speech in behalfe of the Clergie*, printed at Oxford, arguing vigorously for better-paid livings, and commenting on the shame of the fact that clerics are scorned for their poverty, and churches not maintained in dignity. Herbert's activities in the repair of both Leighton Church and Bemerton are well known; he evidently received £50 help, possibly double that, from Pembroke.

39. His poetic patronage has now been properly studied by Dick Taylor, Jr., in a series of articles, 1955 to 1959; titles may be found in that on 'The Masque and the Lance' in *Tulane Stud. in English* VIII (1958). 'The Third Earl of Pembroke as a Patron of Poetry', in the same *Studies* for 1955, although I had not seen it until my text was written, is especially welcome, gathering together the extremely numerous references to this famous patron and dedicatee of so many poets and dramatists, and confirming our realization that Herbert as poet could not have taken lightly such a kinsman's friendship. Taylor takes no stand on the attribution of 'Soules joy', but see in addition to my previous remarks Summers, *op. cit.*, p. 205.

40. See W. M. Evans, *Henry Lawes*, ch. I, also pp. 30, 37, with dates which support the assumption that Lawes the elder remained at Salisbury quite through Herbert's time. A preface by Henry Lawes in the 1653 *Ayres & Dialogues* shows that he got his texts from their authors directly (one of Pembroke's is included). His pupil and dedicatee Mary Egerton married Herbert's nephew (see n. 7 above).

41. Dowland's song is in Fellowes, *The English School of Lutenist Song Writers*, vol. XII. See on Hume P. Warlock's *English Ayre* (London, 1926). A useful book on the network of connections not present to the memory of a literary student is W. L. Woodfill, *Musicians in English Society* (Princeton, 1953). J. H. Summers' chapter on music is welcome for general connections with Herbert. One's hope that scraps of Herbert's own, or contemporary, settings of his verse might turn up in the manuscript indices I have mentioned is met with disappointing silence, though wordless tunes so often have a just recognizable tag that only scrutiny of the manuscripts is sure proof. When the Christmas anthem in dialogue mentioned in H. Davey's *History of English Music* (London, 1921), pp. 228, 211 as "by Herbert' and set by Ford, is pursued, it turns out to have rather the

words: 'Look shepherds, look!| Why? where?| See you not yonder, there!| ... *The Angel:* Fear not, Shepherds ...' (spelling modernized; from Bodleian MS. Rawlinson poet. 23, f. 151; also in Ashmole 36-7, f. 255 and Harl. 6346, p. 175). As this goes to press, I am grateful to be told by Mr. Vincent Duckles of six three-part polyphonic settings by Jenkins of poems by Herbert (parts of *Christmas, The Dawning, Ephes. iv. 30, The Starre*) in Christ Church MS. 736-730.

42. The derogatory commonplaces are controverted by D. Taylor, Jr., in 'The Earl of Pembroke and the Youth of Shakespeare's Sonnets', *SP* LVI (1959), 26-54, and another essay therein cited. I do not know who was Pembroke's chaplain at this date, not at any rate the one of 1624 whose epitaph adjures us to 'Know! thou that treadst on learned *Smyth* inurn'd' — that man is but an unreversible hour-glass. I quote this from the most trustworthy of the manuscripts containing 'Soules joy', Lansdowne 777, f. 55. Its connections with William Browne would reward inquiry, for Wood and others stress his close association with Wilton from 1625; some doubt of Browne's autograph in it is registered in the B. M. copy of the catalogue. A certain 'T. C.' copied a well-known music manuscript, Addit. 11608, containing much Laniere and Lawes but not our *Song*. Whoever the T. C. of the sermon was, he calls himself, in a phrase oddly like the motto of Bemerton's parson, 'I the least of all the least', minimorum minimus as Bernard speakes'.

43. That the train of requests and persuasions which ended in the Bemerton presentation deed of 16 April was started by William seems likelier than a rapid business assigned all to Philip — initiated, concluded, and officialized within the six days that included his brother's death and burial. Herbert's stature as a poet was known to his friends by 1630, yet no one stresses the fact that congeniality of tastes may have motivated the patron earl as well as the accepting parson; something of this sort probably lies behind Walton's overwritten story. Acceptance must have been at least expected when the deed was dated. Philip was a poor exchange, to any one who had thought the environs of Wilton would be frequently graced by William and by Ruddier.

44. Lans. 777, f. 73, the MS. with the crucial ascription to Pembroke, writes five unindented five-line stanzas in a series, thus completing the text but giving no hint that the seeming third stanza is repeated as a refrain. Actually, if there is music, this is how we copy too; we simply get down all the words. Stowe 962, f. 226, ends with Grierson's line 15, and here also there is no indication that the 'refrain' was felt as other than a third five-line verse. Other texts in this MS. are poor. But as an example of 'parody' in the sense we are not using it, I subjoin one on Jonson's famous lyric: 'Have you seene but a blacke little maggott Come creepinge over a dead dogg| Or an old woeman with a fagott Smotheringe of an hedghogge ... O soe blacke, o soe rough, o soe sower is shee.'

45. It is there presented, however, as a two-stanza piece, labelled 'I' and 'II'. But the indentation is not careful, lines 16-20 are missing entirely, and errors make some lines senseless. Its editor, the younger Donne, either got it from the composers as he says he got many, in his preface, or from a source that was not the one which put it among the Donne materials, and not either MS. mentioned in note 44. Of course he might have taken a longer text from the 1650 Donne which he had had connections with, but this would have included the embarrassment of finding out whether his father wrote it. Copying from music manuscripts would explain some of the vacillation copyists show, about what its stanzaic form is and what place to give to the five lines 'O give ..'. Unlabelled refrains are not visually clear to rapid copyists of song-words from music manuscripts, and there is also some excuse for shuffling a form to make it clear as a read poem.

46. On works by Morley parodying compositions by Croce and others, see J. Kerman, 'Morley and "The Triumphs of Oriana"', *Music & Letters* XXXIV (1953), 185-191, especially p. 188; there is further information in Reese, *Renaissance*, pp. 824 f., with

citations (especially to Kerman's dissertation, to appear). I use without direct citation the following treatments: R. B. Lenaerts, 'The Sixteenth Century Parody Mass in the Netherlands', *Mus. Quar.*, XXXVI (1950), 410-421; J. Schmidt-Goerg, 'Vier Messen aus dem xvi Jhr.' [by Palestrina, Lupus, Clemens, and le Roy, all on one motet by Lupus Hellinck], *Kirchenmusikalisches Jb.*, XXV (1930), 76-93; and P. Pisk, *Das Parodiever-fahren in der Messe des Jac. Gallus* (Wien, 1918, Studien zur Musikwissenschaft). It would be impossible to cite all the relevant information in Reese, and the reader is referred to the rich presentation of pertinent materials throughout that volume.

47. About half of the large number of Palestrina's masses and more of di Lasso's are parody masses, and all names I later include are important representatives of the practice. The four masses analyzed by Schmidt-Goerg were published in 1590, 1532 (Lupus's own), 1570, 1585; others were publishing at later dates, though the parody mass declined during the seventeenth century.

48. Of J. Gallus' 20 masses printed in 1580, 16 are parody masses, and Pisk's analysis indicates no such differentiation in feeling between the 9 based on sacred motets, 3 on German songs, 2 on madrigals, and one with a combined *chanson*-madrigal base.

49. The nature of the distinctions made as this general parallel is forced to take care of divisions into Mannerist, early Mannerist, late Renaissance, Rococo (to give but one example, W. Sypher, *Four Stages of Renaissance Style*, N. Y., 1955, touching Milton), has so far at least seemed unsuitable to the peculiar relation between concept and form in a verbal art like literature. Where distinctions are *by their nature* inadequate to embrace the complexities of that relation criticism has no hope but to remain naive and often totally blind, so that I merely recognize here that many such attempts exist.

50. That men have this freedom will always make it impossible to equate literary works either with 'the history behind them' or the 'the expression of their times'. Yet modern fear of these equations sometimes results in another variant of the confusion between poetry and history. Hence it seems to me the duty of any one dealing even with small examples where all these principles come in question, to proclaim their relation to the ideas which are at stake, and to disregard the risk of overloading a small craft. The tendency to retreat from the intellectual rigors of historical criticism has taken on so many complicated forms during recent years, gaining strength and unexpected forms of adherence across the Atlantic while it weakens somewhat on this side, that one cannot but feel alarm for the future of literary criticism if, as the older forms of rebellious subjectivity fade, we face the growth of an ancient kind of literary pietism, staggered by the problem of relating history to poetry and ready to settle for inner voices (there are many signs of this). It is an evil to substitute knowing the history of something for apprehending it in its living intrinsic essence, and most good historical critics of late have tirelessly pointed out the danger, as they have pointed out the similar abuse of mistaking the irresponsible tracing of 'patterns' of symbolic imagery for the discovery of poets' meanings, and as they have pointed out the manifest impossibility of our somehow through history getting out of our time into another to apprehend first hand an author's true quality in his habit as he lived. These are all forms of shrinking down poetry into history, and all are common. But it is the anti-intellectual and Romantic form of the same evil to let the uniqueness of artistic events obscure all subtler understandings of how authors, and indeed all men, are 'in history' but yet are *not* caught and pinned in their own unique moment of time — in other words produce something that is not only history.

51. Bourgeois, before he quitted Geneva in 1557, had set all but 62 psalms of the Huguenot psalter during the gradual process of its translation by Marot and Beza. Psalm xcvi had been among those sung to a twice-used tune (to cxviii) until the unknown continuator found or wrote melodies for these. The music here given is adapted from

Goudimel's 1565 setting of the Psalter melody for Psalm xcvi; there is no modern reprint of his 1565 settings, but it may be found in a New York Univ. master's thesis by August Ruut, *The Genevan Psalm Melodies set by Claude Goudimel in Chordal Style*, 1956. (There is a modern harmonization of the tune in J. Ver, *Le psautier Huguenot harmonisé*, Réalville, 1918.) W. S. Pratt (*op. cit.* in n. 17), giving in modern notation the tune as in 1562, for text by Beza, notes its secular origin; see Douen, I, 726, 716, where the initial phrase from its supposed original is given. This is found, ascribed to J. Arcadelt, in *Chansons nouuellement composées* ... (*Sixiesme livre*, Paris, Le Roy and Ballard, both 1556 and 1559). The melody was very considerably altered; the secular words begin: 'Le saint serviteur eshonte, Qui abusant de la bonté De sa dame, une autre pourchasse N'ha il merité qu'on le chasse? ...'. Were the scheme of the Pembroke-Herbert stanzas not so extremely rare, I should have found music more capable of enhancing both sets of words, but this is perhaps sufficient to the restricted purpose of demonstration which it here serves.

STEIN, "George Herbert: The Art of Plainness"

1. "The Temper" (II).
2. *City of God*, V, xviii.
3. *Rhetoric*, I, ii (1356ᵃ).
4. *The Christian Doctrine*, IV, vii (15-20).
5. *The Trinity*, XII, 9 (14)—10 (15), trans. Stephen McKenna (The Catholic University of America Press, 1963).
6. These passages are collected in *Coleridge on the Seventeenth Century*, ed. R. F. Brinkley (Duke University Press, 1955), pp. 523, 534.

VENDLER, "The Re-Invented Poem: George Herbert's Alternatives"

1. Valentina Poggi, *George Herbert* (Bologna, 1967), pp. 203 ff.
2. Arnold Stein, *George Herbert's Lyrics* (Baltimore, 1968), pp. 150, 151.
3. When John Wesley rewrote "The Invitation" for hymn-singing, he did far more than adapt the meter. (An adaptation faithful to Herbert's meaning had been made in 1697, reprinted now in *Select Hymns Taken out of Mr. Herbert's Temple* [1697], Augustan Reprint Society No. 98 [Los Angeles, 1962], pp. 31-32). Wesley's adaptation insists on the wickedness and carnality of the sinners, intensifying in every case Herbert's description, and showing none of Herbert's changes of attitude. Wesley's version may be found in the *Collected Poetical Works of John and Charles Wesley*, ed. G. Osborn (London, 1868-69) I, 111-13.
4. *Select Hymns*, p. 13.
5. George Herbert Palmer, ed., *The Works of George Herbert* (Boston, 1905), I, 144.
6. James Montgomery, *The Christian Poet* (Glasgow, 1827), pp. 243-44.
7. William James, *Varieties of Religious Experience* (Boston, 1902), Ch. IV.

FISH, "Catechizing the Reader: Herbert's Socratean Rhetoric"

1. *The Metaphysical Poets* (New York, 1936), p. 185.
2. "The Re-invented Poem: George Herbert's Alternatives," in *Forms of Lyric*, ed. Reuben Brower (New York, 1970), p. 19.
3. *A Reading of George Herbert* (Chicago, 1952), p. 196
4. "The Province of Allegory in George Herbert's Verse," *TSLL* I (1960): 461, 462.
5. "The Unity of George Herbert's *The Temple*: A Reconsideration," *ELH* 35 (1968): 517.
6. *Music for a King* (Baltimore, 1972), p. 194.
7. See Carnes, "The Unity of George Herbert's *The Temple*," p. 519.
8. On this point see Stanley Fish, "Letting Go: The Dialectic of the Self in Herbert's Poetry," in *Self-Consuming Artifacts* (Berkeley, 1972), chap. 3.

9. *The Works of George Herbert*, ed. F. E. Hutchinson (Oxford, 1941), p. 256.

10. Arnold Stein (*George Herbert's Lyrics*, Baltimore, 1968) also relates this chapter of *A Priest To The Temple* to Herbert's poetry (see pp. 182-183), but he views the prose work more as a suggestive analogue than as a source for Herbert's poetic technique, and he is not concerned, as I am, with the implications of Herbert's remarks for the role of the reader. See also Freer, *Music for a King*, pp. 235-36.

11. See Tuve, *A Reading*, pp. 112-33.

12. *Self-Consuming Artifacts*, pp. 173-76.

13. On this point, see Ira Clark's excellent article, " 'Lord, in Thee the *Beauty* Lies in the *Discovery*': 'Love Unknown' and Reading Herbert," *ELH* 39 (1972): 576.

14. *George Herbert: His Religion and Art* (London, 1954), pp. 127-28.

15. From Mirk's *Festival*, quoted by V. A. Kolve, *The Play Called Corpus Christi* (Stanford, 1966), p. 77.

16. John Donne, *Devotions* (Ann Arbor, 1959), p. 127.

17. "The longsuffering of God waited in the days of Noah while the ark was a preparing, wherein few, that is, eight souls were saved by the water. The like figure whereunto even baptism doth also now save us ... by the resurrection of Jesus Christ." (I Peter 3:20-21)

18. "And as Moses lifted up the serpent in the wilderness, even so must the Son of man be lifted up, That whosoever believeth in him shall not perish, but have eternal life." (John 3:14-15) "Your fathers did eat manna in the wilderness, and are dead ... I am the living bread that came down from heaven; if any man eat of this bread, he shall live forever." (John 6:49, 51)

19. Izaak Walton, *The Life of Mr. George Herbert* (London, 1670), p. 74. The authenticity of this report has recently been challenged by J. Max Patrick, "Critical Problems in Editing George Herbert's *The Temple*," in *The Editor As Critic and The Critic as Editor*, ed. Murray Krieger, William Andrews Clark Memorial Library Seminar (Los Angeles, 1973), pp. 3-40.

20. *The Works of Henry Vaughan*, ed. L. C. Martin (Oxford, 1957), p. 391.

21. *"On Mr. G. Herberts booke intituled the Temple of Sacred Poems, sent to a Gentlewoman."* The text is from L. C. Martin's edition (Oxford, 1927), p. 130.

22. "To My Reverend Friend The Author Of The Synagogue," in *The Complete Poems of Christopher Harvey*, ed. A. B. Grosart (Lancashire, 1874), p. 86.

23. In addition to Stein and Freer (cited in note 10), see John R. Mulder's *The Temple of the Mind* (New York, 1969), pp. 106-29. Mulder discusses the echoes in Herbert's poems of Nowell's catechism, but he specifically disclaims any assertion of direct influence (p. 127).

24. *The Living Temple: Herbert and Catechizing*, forthcoming.

FREEMAN, "George Herbert and the Emblem Books"

1. *The Heroicall Devises* of M. Claudius Paradin, translated from Latin into English by P. S. London, 1591; and *The Theatre of Fine Devices*, translated by Thomas Combe. London, 1614. (Entered in *S.R.* 1593.)

2. A full account of the Dutch Emblem Books and the way in which the tradition of Profane Love was modified by the Jesuits for religious purposes is given by Prof. Mario Praz in *Studies in Seventeenth Century Imagery*. Warburg Institute, 1939.

3. Antwerp. 1624. Quarles's other source was *Typus Mundi*, published by the Jesuit College of Rhetoric at Antwerp. 1627. See an article by G. S. Haight, *The Library*, 4th Series, vol. XVI, pp. 188 ff.

4. See E. K. Chambers, *William Shakespeare*. Oxford, 1930. vol. II, p. 153.

5. *Les Amours*. Cf. also *Upon the Priorie Grove*, II, 11-14.

6. *The Temple*, 1633, Oxford University Press, 1913. All quotations are from this text.

7. 1674 and thereafter.

8. *Vertue.*

9. Carleton Brown, *Religious Lyrics of the Fourteenth Century*, No. 5.

10. *The Quip.*

11. *Miserie.*

12. *Even-Song.*

13. *Biographia Literaria*, Bell, 1898, p. 194.

14. See an article by Capt. Acland-Troyte (*Archaeologia* 2nd Series. 1888. i, 188-204), who says there is distinct record of a concordance having been made for Herbert, although no trace of it has survived. Ferrar must obviously have made an extensive collection of engravings, and the same picture occurs in different books. The concordance of the Book of Revelation is in the British Museum. Of course, Herbert might have inspected the collection of engravings while he and Ferrar were rebuilding Leighton Church two miles from Little Gidding.

15. Contrast for tone *Perseverance* in the Williams MS.

> Onely my soule hangs on Thy promisses,
> With face and hands clinging unto Thy brest;
> Clinging and crying, crying without cease,
> "Thou art my Rock, thou art my Rest."

16. iv. *The Parsons Knowledge.*

17. There are two manuscripts of Herbert's poems, the Williams and the Bodleian. The Williams contains fewer poems than the Bodleian, and is thought by Herbert editor, Mr. G. H. Palmer, to be the earlier.

18. *The Quip.*

19. *The Church Militant.*

BOWERS, "Herbert's Sequential Imagery: 'The Temper'"

1. Quotations in *The Temple* are taken from the edition of Bodleian MS Tanner 307, published in 1927 by the Nonesuch Press in London.

2. The idea that the poems in *The Temple* up to "Jordan (I)" form a sequence is nothing new. Joseph H. Summers, in "Herbert's Form," *PMLA*, LXVI (1951), 1065, argued for "a significant order which had little to do with biographical revelation," and thinks of it "as the symbolic record, written by a poet, of a 'typical' Christian life within the Church" p. 1066. His thesis is repeated in his book, *George Herbert: His Religion and Art* (Cambridge, Mass.: Harvard University Press, 1954), pp. 86 ff.

3. Here Rosamund Tuve, *A Reading of George Herbert* (London: Faber & Faber, 1952) is our great authority.

4. *The Works of George Herbert*, ed. F. E. Hutchinson (corrected ed., Oxford at the Clarendon Press, 1945), p. 494.

5. Perhaps there is a pun on the verb *mate*, which means "to equal, rival, to be a match for," or intransitively, "to claim equality with." The *O.E.D.* quotes from Nicholas Rowe in 1702 an appropriate illustration: "Thou ... hast dar'd To lift thy wretched self above the Stars And mate with Power Almighty." The only difficulty with this pun is that it would be man who would be the one to mate with God, whereas Herbert has God meeting arms with man. However, the sense is clearly ironic.

6. This is prefaced by "Man is all weakness; there is no such thing| As Prince or King."

7. "Stone" is bad; hence, Herbert used tempered "steel" (harder than iron) since it is not specifically the hardened sinner, whose stony heart rejects grace, who would melt with pity

here if he could even feel *his part*, what mortal man could feel of divine agony. ("Part" also contains a musical pun.)

8. When God's heat is withdrawn, and cold Sin reigns, the grief that afflicts the soul becomes the measure of the distance that separates it from God, as in "The Search":

> Thy will such a strange distance is,
> As that to it
> East and West touch, the poles doe kisse,
> And parallels meet.
>
> Since then my greife must be as large.
> As is thy space,
> Thy distance from mee; see my charge,
> *Lord*, see my case.

This is the distance mentioned in "The Flowre":

> These are thy wonders, *Lord of Powre*,
> Killing, and quickning, bringing downe to hell,
> And up to heaven in an houre.

And in "Complaining":

> Contract my houre,
> That I may climbe and find releife.

9. J. A. Jungmann, S. J., *The Mass of the Roman Rite* (Benziger, 1951), II, 38-39.

10. This, in fact, I take to be one of the mystic concepts he held about Jordan and its water that so neatly contrasts with the Red Sea as blood. The prefiguration of the New Law held by the Promised Land gave a peculiar significance to the waters of Jordan (see Tuve, *op. cit.*, pp. 187 ff.). That Herbert's tears of repentance under the New Law could be charged with at least imputed salvational efficacy joins with the type of Jordan and the Red Sea as sacramental water in its relation to wine. The mystic passage of the Jordan, therefore, could readily signify to him the passage he was preparing to make from laity to priesthood, paralleled by his dedication to divine poetry — which he regarded as the equivalent of sacerdotal prayer.

11. In Luke 22:44, the only Gospel to mention these drops, the account reads, "and his sweat was as it were great drops of blood falling down to the ground." Unless Herbert's Christ is speaking figuratively, he did not weep blood; but rather sweat fell from his face (and thus resembled tears) like blood in respect to the size of the drops. Nonetheless, Herbert in this passage treats the sweat as if it were actual drops of blood.

12. Since in the Eucharist cup Christ was brought down to earth, the great spaces of eternity (that Herbert had taken as representing the distance between God's will and man) are there contracted in reconciliation within the walls of the cup, and the two are indeed made one.

CHARLES, "George Herbert: Priest, Poet, Musician"

1. George Herbert, *Works*, ed. F. E. Hutchinson (Oxford: Clarendon Press, 1941), p. 289. All references to Herbert's prose and poetry are to this edition and are quoted by permission of the Clarendon Press, Oxford.

2. Izaak Walton, *The Lives of John Donne, Sir Henry Wotton, Richard Hooker, George Herbert, and Robert Sanderson*, ed. S. B. Carter (London: Falcon Educational Books, 1951), p. 241.

574 NOTES TO PAGES 250-258

3. *Ibid.*, p. 243.

4. Jones MS B 62, Dr. Williams' Library, Gordon Square, London.

5. Joseph H. Summers, *George Herbert: His Religion and Art* (London: Chatto and Windus, 1954), p. 160, cites the explanation of Manuel F. Bukofzer, *Music in the Baroque Era* (New York: W. W. Norton, 1947), p. 365, of the correspondence between certain keys and certain affections. This practice of tuning stringed instruments to pitches other than the current a¹ = 440 c.p.s. standard is of particular interest to gambists because it probably accounts for the continuing difference in nomenclature between English and German viols. See the discussion in Appendix B of Nicholas Bessaraboff's *Ancient European Musical Instruments* (Cambridge, Mass.: Harvard University Press, 1941), pp. 357-373. The articles on pitch and on tuning in Grove shed further light.

6. Summers, *op. cit.*, p. 159, citing Edward W. Naylor, "Three Musical Parson-Poets of the xviith Century," *Proceedings of the Musical Association* (Fifty-fourth session; Leeds, 1928), pp. 95-96.

7. Thomas Mace, *Musicks Monument* (London: T. Ratcliffe and N. Thompson, 1676), p. 235. I have used a photostatic copy of the volume in the Huntington Library, in the possession of my colleague, Professor Elizabeth Cowling.

8. Walton, *op. cit.*, p. 258. Walton's life concludes with this note: "*This Lady* Cook, *had preserv'd many of Mr.* Herberts *private Writings, which she intended to make publick; but they, and* Highnam *house, were burnt together, by the late Rebels, and so lost to posterity.*"

9. S. A. Tannenbaum and Dorothy R. Tannenbaum, *George Herbert: A Concise Bibliography* (New York: Tannenbaum, 1946).

10. I omit mention of rhyme schemes as matters of less concern to a composer setting these poems, although the reader interested in such matters might well examine the use of line-length and of rhyme scheme in "The Collar" to see how Herbert employs both to underline the speaker's rebellion from discipline and order. For an excellent discussion of the "hieroglyph form" of this poem, see Summers, *op. cit.*, pp. 90-92.

11. Rosemond Tuve, *A Reading of George Herbert* (Chicago: University of Chicago Press, 1952).

12. John Hollander, *The Untuning of the Sky* (Princeton, New Jersey: Princeton University Press, 1961), p. 288.

13. Walton, *op. cit.*, p. 254.

14. John Aubrey, *Brief Lives*, ed. Oliver L. Dick (Ann Arbor: University of Michigan Press, 1962), p. 137.

SANDLER, "'Solomon vbique regnet': Herbert's Use of the Images of the New Covenant"

1. Mary Ellen Rickey, *Utmost Art: Complexity in the Verse of George Herbert* (Lexington, Ky., 1966), esp. the chapter entitled "The Classical Materials." Rosemond Tuve, *A Reading of George Herbert* (London, 1952). Joseph H. Summers, *George Herbert: His Religion and Art* (London, 1954).

2. Peter Sterry, *The Rise, Race and Royalty of the Kingdom of God in the Soul of Man* (London, 1683), p. 461, quoted by Vivian de Sola Pinto in *Peter Sterry: Platonist and Puritan* (Cambridge, 1934), p. 160. The Hebrew word he has in mind is presumably *hekal*. The full passage runs: "The same word in Hebrew signifieth a Temple, and a Pallace. The name of a Temple in Greek, signifieth a Habitation, or dwelling place. It is a note of a learned Divine, that the Temple had Tables, and a Throne, and a State in it, which was the Golden Mercy Seat called in the Gospel, the Throne of Grace, to signifie that the Temple of God was his Pallace, as he is the great King." Sterry's typological application muddles

his exposition in its overly explicit Trinitarianism. "The Temple of God is filled with the Glory of God. There is a Prophesy in *Malachy*, concerning the times of the Gospel, that he shall come into his Temple. You, O Saints are the Temple, which is here Prophesied of Jesus Christ, as God in the Glory of the Father, in the Third Person, the Holy Ghost, comes into you, into your Bodies also, and fills them with his Glory." Among Puritans, Sterry was, as one might surmise from his title and theme, a professed admirer of Herbert.

3. John David Walker, "The Architectonics of George Herbert's *The Temple*," *ELH* 29 (1962): 289-305. He was answered by Annabel M. Endicott in "The Structure of George Herbert's *Temple:* A Reconsideration," *University of Toronto Quarterly* 24 (1965): 226-37. Endicott is surely correct to read "Sion" as Herbert's *rejection* of the temple of Solomon in favour of the inward temple of the soul; but Walker is also correct when he talks of the fulfillment and the realization of that same model in the Christian soul, for both rejection and fulfillment are implied in the paradoxical relationship between things of the Old Covenant and of the New. However, with regard to Walker's comment that "by absorbing the archetypal Jewish temple, the individual Christian becomes its reality," it should be pointed out, in the interest of precision, that Herbert is dealing with the Hebrew temple not as the archetype but as the scriptural type which is only to be understood in conjunction with its New Testament antitype.

4. All biblical quotations are taken from the King James Version.

5. In support of the reading of the "raise and raze" line as a specific reference to the temple, one might cite the stanza of "The Sacrifice" which runs:

> Some said, that I the Temple to the floore
> In three dayes raz'd, and raised as before.
> Why, he that built the world can do much more:
> > Was ever grief, &c.
> > [ll. 65-68]

In this stanza the reader is intended to recollect the statement made by Jesus in the Fourth Gospel, "Destroy this temple, and in three days I will raise it up," together with the explanation that "he spake of the temple of his body" (John 2: 19-21). Whereas in Mark it is said that certain people falsely accused Jesus of threatening to destroy the temple, in the Fourth Gospel it is assumed that Jesus had indeed spoken about the destruction of the temple, though not as a threat, and that he was thereby instructing his disciples that it would be replaced by the temple of the New Covenant. All quotations from Herbert are taken from *The Works of George Herbert*, ed. F. E. Hutchinson (Oxford, 1941).

6. Compare "The Church Militant," where Herbert traces through history the stages whereby the Empire of Sin has displaced the Church. Here, too, the end can only be "*Justice.*"

7. In *The Latin Poetry of George Herbert: A Bilingual Edition* (Athens, Ohio, 1965). Mark McClosky and Paul R. Murphy translate the poem as follows:

> *The ripped veil*
> You, Jew,
> Huckster of worship, sponger
> Of the Temple, you strut in vain,
> For the ripped veil
> Discloses the hidden God,
> And makes the outer walls, and the sacred
> Inner Temple grounds themselves
> Not one city only, but a world.
> Instead of looking into hearts

As hearts, he looks for altars there,
Till every heart shall seek its maker
And Solomon shall govern everywhere.
New mysteries are opened up;
Phylacteries do not hedge a covered
Worship in a maze. The youthful world
Has departed from its youth,
And making of its ripened love a vintage,
Tastes before its time the fruits of marriage.
And God is everywhere —
The Lamb, the Priest, the Altar too.

8. Today the generally accepted view is that the Epistle to the Hebrews was written by an unknown author, not Paul, despite the decision to that effect by the Council of Trent and the attribution in the King James Version. Herbert may have thought of Paul as the author of the Epistle, or he may have agreed with Luther and Calvin that it was written by another hand. Since the end of the second century A.D., the authorship of this Epistle has been a point of argument.

9.

Ararúmque Hominúmque ortum si mente pererres,
    Cespes viuus, Homo; mortuus, Ara fuit:
Quae diuisa nocent, Christi per foedus, in vnum
    Conueniunt; & Homo viua fit Ara Dei.

McClosky and Murphy in *The Latin Poems of George Herbert* offer the following translation.

If one considers the rise of men and altars,
Earth breathed upon was man, dead earth
An altar. These, which separated
From one another make for harm, through Christ's compacts
Were put together: so man becomes
The living altar of God.

10. Tuve, pp. 18-99.

11. This formula was used in the Book of Common Prayer in Herbert's day and into the twentieth century.

It could be argued that it was from his understanding of the Real Presence of Christ in the Communion elements that Herbert first derived the idea of writing "The Sacrifice" as spoken not merely about Christ on the Cross, but *by* Christ; and that he turned then to the Good Friday Reproaches as being the traditional liturgical form which would best enable him to do this.

12. Louis L. Martz, *The Poetry of Meditation: A Study of English Religious Literature of the Seventeenth Century*, 2d. ed. (New Haven, Conn., 1962), pp. 295-309.

13. "The Church Militant," 1. 174.

14. *Works*, p. 309.

HIGBIE, "Images of Enclosure in George Herbert's *The Temple*"

1. See John David Walker, "The Architectonics of George Herbert's *The Temple*," *ELH*, 29 (1962), 289-305; Joseph H. Summers, *George Herbert: His Religion and His Art* (Cambridge, Mass., 1968), pp. 86-92; and Louis L. Martz, *The Poetry of Meditation: A Study in English Religious Literature of the Seventeenth Century* (New Haven, 1954), pp.

288-320. Fredson Bowers, in "Herbert's Sequential Imagery: 'The Temper,'" *Modern Philology*, 59 (1961-62), 202-213, mentions Herbert's fondness for "container images" (p. 203) and discusses the development of imagery within a sequence of poems; and Jeffrey Hart, in "Herbert's *The Collar* Re-read," *Boston University Studies in English*, 5 (Summer, 1961), 65-73, also deals with the transformation of meaning as Herbert's imagery progresses toward the ideal.

2. George Herbert, *The Works of George Herbert*, ed. F. E. Hutchinson (Oxford, 1941); all quotations of *The Temple* are from this edition.

3. George Herbert, *The Country Parson*, quoted by J. B. Leishman, *The Metaphysical Poets* (New York, 1963), pp. 119-120.

HAYES, "Counterpoint in Herbert"

1. All quotations in this paper are from Palmer's edition (George Herbert, *The English Works*, 3 volumes, edited by G. H. Palmer, Boston and New York, 1905), which I shall hereafter refer to simply by volume and page.

Some of my readers may notice that the statistics here quoted do not agree with Palmer's. Palmer was in most respects the ideal editor, but he was not a mathematician. Certain of his statistics I have been unable to comprehend at all, because he uses a base of 169 poems and I cannot determine which 169 he meant. Accordingly I have made my own statistics, using only the 165 poems printed in *The Temple*. In my tables this figure appears as 167; two poems, "Love" (II, 83) and "Holy Scriptures" (II, 187), consist of two sonnets each and it seemed more convenient, statistically, to regard these as four separate sonnets than as two poems made up of two fourteen-line stanzas.

2. "Jordan" (2), II, 91-93, lines 1-6, 16-18.

3. "Grief," III, 323, lines 13-19.

4. See *Essay on Criticism*, 348-353.

5. So Puttenham; see G. Gregory Smith (editor), *Elizabethan Critical Essays* (Oxford, 1904), II, 70.

6. *Ibid.*, II, 74.

7. *Ibid.*, II, 93.

8. In this respect, Herbert surpassed even those contemporaries who otherwise were most closely related to him. Only 6 of Donne's 49 "Songs and Sonets" hold together; 5 of 37 by Traherne; but 82 out of 127 by Herbert. Moreover, of Herbert's 45 separable stanzas 25 are separable only because of a final couplet — a pattern which Puttenham specifically excepts from his general remarks. Only Vaughan comes anywhere near him, with 45 out of 80, and Vaughan was an admitted disciple.

9. See Chapter XII, "Of Proportion in Figure," *op. cit.*, II, 95-105.

10. *Ibid.*, II, 88.

11. *Ibid.*, II, 93-94.

12. Pierre Legouis, in his excellent monograph, *Donne the Craftsman* (Paris, 1928), estimates 46 out of 49, for he considers the metres of both "The Undertaking" and "Selfe Love" to be 8 6 8 6; to me the normal pattern of the latter, an irregular and incomplete poem, seems 7 6 7 6.

13. *Op. cit.*, p. 18.

14. See footnote 8.

15. *Ibid.*, pp. 29-30.

16. Herbert did borrow one stanza form from Donne, that of "Loves Diet" (*a b a b c c*, 10 10 8 8 10 10), for his "Sion" (III, 265).

17. For the convenience of those who may wish to examine additional poems of each

type in their copies of Herbert, I list the poems of each type by their pages in Palmer's edition:

Type 1: II, 103, 171, 199, 229, 239, 267, 313, 339, 353, 369, 397; III, 15, 19, 29, 97, 101, 111, 155, 205, 219, 253, 273, 277, 289, 321, 325.

Type 2: II, 193, 247, 251, 263, 297, 303, 305, 359, 361, 365; III, 23, 119, 123, 149, 215, 225, 305, 333.

Type 3: II, 15, 91, 97, 119, 201, 225, 319, 389; III, 9, 33, 37, 79, 105, 143, 147, 179, 251, 323, 339.

Type 4: II, 215; III, 59, 117, 133, 153, 193, 229, 231, 255, 259, 263, 267.

Type 5: II, 95, 233, 259, 271, 285, 293, 315, 335, 347, 377, 385; III, 45, 129, 185, 187, 197, 207, 237, 281, 293.

Type 6: II, 87, 99, 123, 157, 163, 301, 311, 373, 381; III, 41, 115, 137, 297, 317, 335.

Type 7: II, 175, 183, 243, 309, 401; III, 11, 27, 49, 53, 109, 125, 151, 157, 265, 269, 271, 331.

If one accepts Palmer's theory that the poems of the second volume were written before Herbert's ordination as priest and those in the third after, one must conclude from this tabulation that Herbert's metrical practice, at least so far as these types are concerned, varied little during the course of his life. However, from the fact that almost all the poems in Type 4 and the majority in Type 7 occur in the third volume, one might guess that Herbert was a more rigid experimenter in his earlier poems; but the evidence is too slight to make it more than a guess. There may be some significance, too, in the fact that 8 of the 13 stanzaic poems in Palmer's Group IX, "Restlessness" (III, 169-240), are in my two contrapuntal types, 4 and 5. Otherwise, the distribution of types is very even throughout Herbert's work.

18. III, 59. As a matter of fact I have simplified here. The quatrain given above alternates with a quatrain in the form of "Mattens," and so the poem should properly be classed as an eight-line stanza of Type 4 — as it is in my tabulations. Even this does not include the full complexity of the poem, for the second halves of the second and fourth eight-line stanzas have a different rime scheme, *a b a b* in place of the *a b b a* in the corresponding halves of the first and third stanzas. Is the poem then composed of two sixteen-line stanzas? It is such intricate schemes as this which make Herbert's versification so difficult to discuss simply.

19. I list herewith all the other poems belonging to Type 5 which I have noted. Undoubtedly others could be found, but not, I think, in significant numbers. It will be observed that none of these except Donne's, and perhaps Lord Herbert's, precede George Herbert.

Bryant, To a Waterfowl: *a b a b*, 6 10 10 6.

Donne, A Jeat Ring Sent: *a a b b*, 8 10 14 10 (couplets).

    Witchcraft by a Picture: *a b a b c c c*, 8 10 10 8 6 8 10.

    Valediction: of my Name in the Window: *a b a b c c*, 6 10 8 8 10 8.

Habington, Nox nocti indicat scientiam (1640): *a b a b*, 6 4 8 8.

Lord Herbert, To her Hair: *a a b c c b*, 10 8 10 10 6 6.

    "How should I love my best?": *a b b a c c a*, 6 10 8 8 10 8 4.

    Ditty, "If you refuse me once": *a a b c c b*, 10 4 10 6 4 8.

    Elegy over a Tomb (1617): *a b b a c c*, 10 8 10 6 10 4.

Herrick, His Poetry His Pillar: *a b a b*, 6 4 4 6.

    To the Yew and Cypress to Grace His Funeral: *a a b b*, 4 6 2 8 (couplets).

    An Ode to Sir Clipsby Crew: *a a b c c b*, 8 4 6 8 2 4.

    The Primrose: *a a b b c c*, 7 8 7 8 7 8 (couplets).

    Upon the Troublesome Times: *a b b a*, 4 4 2 6.

An Ode for Ben Jonson: *a a b b c c d d e e*, 2 4 4 6 4 6 6 8 6 10 (couplets).
Milton, Paraphrase on Psalm III (1653): *a a b c c b*, 8 4 7 4 10 8.
Suckling, Sonnet II (1646): *a a b b c d c d*, 10 6 6 10 10 6 4 8.
Traherne, Speed: *a a b c c b*, 6 8 6 10 8 10.
  The Approach: *a a b b c c*, 8 10 8 10 8 10 (couplets).
  The Only Ill: *a b b c c d d*, 1 6 8 6 8 6 2 (couplets).
Vaughan, The Proffer: *a b b a c c*, 6 4 10 4 10 8.
  The Constellation: *a a b b*, 10 6 10 8 (couplets: same as Herbert III, 185).
  20. W. S. Pratt, *The History of Music* (New York, 1907), p. 212.

OSTRIKER, "Song and Speech in the Metrics of George Herbert"

1. A somewhat outdated, but otherwise very fine, essay is G. H. Palmer's chapter on "Style and Technique" in his edition of the poet's *English Works* (Boston and New York, 1905), I, 123-167. Palmer gives both a nearly-definitive formal analysis of the prosody and a valuable study of how the prosodic means served poetic ends. He errs, however, by stressing Herbert's intellectuality, seeing him as a modified and sweetened Donne, and oversimplifying his poetic temperament. The result for his prosodic analysis is that he fails to show how Herbert often used a complex of conflicting techniques in a single poem, to achieve complex emotional and intellectual effects.

2. Joseph H. Summers, *George Herbert, his Religion and Art* (Cambridge, Mass., 1954), p. 169.

3. Hallett Smith, *Elizabethan Poetry* (Cambridge, Mass., 1952), p. 263.

4. J. Pattison, "Literature and Music," in *The English Renaissance*, Vivian de Sola Pinto (New York, 1950), p. 135.

5. *Elizabethan Critical Essays*, ed. G. G. Smith (Oxford, 1904), II, 89.

6. John C. A. Rathmell, ed., *The Psalms of Sir Philip Sidney and the Countess of Pembroke* (Garden City, N. Y.: Doubleday-Anchor, 1963) points out their concern with variety and with suiting form to meaning (pp. xiv-xix).

7. Passages from Herbert's works are taken from the Hutchinson edition (Oxford, 1940).

8. Helen White, *The Metaphysical Poets* (New York, 1956), pp. 192-194, analyzing the three versions of "The Elixir," establishes the nature of Herbert's insistence upon economy, coherence, and precision of thought, and his "passion for the essential."

9. Palmer, p. 136.

10. Albert McHarg Hayes, "Counterpoint in Herbert," *SP*, XXXV, 43. In the matter of variety, the Sidneys may well have been the decisive influence. Rathmell errs in his statement (p. xvii) that only four pairs of their 172 psalms are metrically identical: 8 and 118, 60 and 119S, 32 and 71, 70 and 144. The latter two pairs are not identical; but 1 and 138; 18 and 71; 21 and 112; 42 and 149; 44 and 93; 45, 80 and 89; 51 and 63; 58 and 68; 78 and 105; 116 and 144, are, except for disparities in the use of feminine rhyme, identically patterned. This still leaves the Sidneys with a higher degree of diversity than Herbert. However, only about one-fifth of their poems, against one-half of Herbert's, use counterpointed rhyme.

11. Hayes, p. 47.

12. Florence Bottrall, *George Herbert* (London, 1954), p. 106.

13. André Malraux, *Les Voix du silence* (Paris, 1951), p. 459.

14. Pierre Legouis, *Donne the Craftsman* (Paris, 1928), p. 16.

15. Legouis, pp. 19, 20.

16. It is impossible to quarrel with the thesis of Wesley Trimpi, *Ben Jonson's Poems: A Study of the Plain Style* (Stanford, 1962), that Jonson derived the critical rationale for his

plain style from his study of Latin authors. However, nobody was more aware than Jonson of the disparity between classical and English prosodic principles. When it came to putting his theories into practice, it is quite unlikely that Jonson would have sought for guidance in classical texts; especially since (although Trimpi fails to mention this) the techniques he needed were already at hand in English dramatic blank verse, of which he was a master.

17. Summers, p. 104.

18. *Works*, ed. Hutchinson, pp. 231-232.

RICKEY, "Herbert's Technical Development"

1. See the principal twentieth-century contributors to an understanding of his craft: George Herbert Palmer, in his well-known introduction to *The Life and Works of George Herbert* (Boston and New York, 1905); Alfred McHarg Hayes, "Counterpoint in Herbert," *SP*, xxxv (1938), 43-60, in which he points out Herbert's counterpointing rhyme correspondences and line lengths; Joseph Summers, *George Herbert: His Religion and Art* (London, 1954), in which he illuminates Herbert's psychology of form. None of them, however, considers the matter of the poet's formal development.

2. For a discussion of this and other *Temple* manuscripts, see F. E. Hutchinson's edition of Herbert's *Works* (Oxford, 1941). pp. lii ff.

3. Hutchinson, p. 66. All further quotations will be designated by their page numbers in this edition.

4. Summers, pp. 124 ff.

5. Summers, p. 92.

STAMBLER, "The Unity of Herbert's 'Temple'"

1. T. S. Eliot, "George Herbert," *The Spectator*, CXLVIII, 12 March, 1932, p. 361.

2. Louis L. Martz, *The Poetry of Meditation*, New Haven (Yale University Press, 1954), pp. 288-320.

3. Joseph Summers, *George Herbert: His Religion and Art*, Cambridge (Harvard University Press, 1954), p. 85.

4. *Ibid.*, p. 87.

5. *Ibid.*, pp. 92-93.

5a. Justification of the words courtier and soldier for Dante's and Petrarch's protagonists in the *Vita Nuova* and *Rime*, as indeed of the concept of a poetic protagonist in those volumes, was the task of earlier chapters of this work. There I argue for the fictive character of the poems' speakers, separable from the personalities of the poets and created within the limits of the volume of poetry. To the role of courtier I attach the protagonists' experience of association with peers at the center of civic life, active in a significant culture, and intensely aware of its issues in science, religion, language, art, and politics. This *engagement* I see as a constant in all the poets of the courtly love tradition from the troubadours to Sidney.

For the protagonist's traditional role as soldier I adduce the concrete references in Sidney and the troubadours, along with all the poets' abundant imagery of physical combat. This imagery always carefully registers the distinctions and nuances among its varied components: the amorous struggle (archetypally Mars' and Venus', perpetuated in Cupid's arrows), feudal contests, the mystical wounding (including that of Jacob). The symbolism of this role is very interesting: it expresses a view of life as a frustrating struggle but one offering human victory; it underlies the ideal Petrarchan contrarieties and also supports the protagonist's career as active man; its finest example, perhaps, is Hamlet's 'Readiness is all.'

6. *The Works of George Herbert*, ed. F. E. Hutchinson (Oxford, 1941), pp. lxv-lxxvii.

7. *Ibid.*, p. xxxvii.

8. Guido Guinizelli, "Of the Gentle Heart," in *Poems and Translations*, Dante Gabriel Rossetti, London and New York, n.d., pp. 168-170. Dante mentions it in *Vita Nuova* xx and xxi.

9. Rosemund Tuve, *A Reading of George Herbert* (University of Chicago Press, 1952), pp. 144-148.

10. *Ibid.*, p. 145.

ENDICOTT-PATTERSON, "The Structure of George Herbert's *Temple*: A Reconsideration"

1. John David Walker, "The Architectonics of George Herbert's *The Temple*," ELH XXIX (1962), 289-305.

2. Walker, 290.

3. Joseph Hall, *Contemplations upon the Principall Passages of the Holy Storie*, in *Works* (London, 1634), II, 1158.

4. John Donne, *The Sermons*, ed. G. R. Potter and E. M. Simpson (Berkeley, 1953-62).

5. Hall, *Contemplations*, 1158.

6. Walker refers in his notes to Clement of Alexandria, Jerome, Origen, Philo, Theodoretus, Theodorus Mopsuestenus, and Josephus. Herbert himself alludes once to Josephus, and once to Tertullian and Chrysostom. All three names appear in Chapter XXXIV of *A Priest to the Temple* (In *Works*, ed. F. E. Hutchinson [Oxford, 1941]) and I have not found any other mention of Church Fathers by name.

7. Hall, *Contemplations*, 773.

8. Lancelot Andrewes, *Apospasmatia Sacra: or A Collection of posthumous and orphan Lectures* (London, 1657). Herbert may have known him as a schoolboy. He also, in his role as Public Orator, wrote to Andrewes in 1618 or 1619 (Epistolae XVIII) and, according to Walton, there was also some private correspondence between them. See Hutchinson, xxiv, 608.

9. Andrewes, *XCVI Sermons* (London, 1629), 484. Joseph Summers drew attention to this sermon in his *George Herbert* (Cambridge, Mass., 1954) in connection with the body-temple analogy, and with the comment that "the entire sermon provides an interesting analogue to Herbert's thought" (220 n.).

10. Andrewes, *XCVI Sermons*, 484.

11. *Ibid.*, 487.

12. Hutchinson, xxxi.

13. Donne, *Sermons*, V, 209. (From *Fifty Sermons*, 1649; preached 1623?)

14. Donne, *Sermons*, VI, 165. (From *LXXX Sermons*, 1640; preached 1625.)

15. Donne, *Sermons*, IV, 300-301. (From *LXXX Sermons*; preached 1622.) See also VII, 318, 324.

16. Joshua Sylvester, *Du Bartas His Divine Weekes and Workes* (London, 1641), 214-215 ("The Magnificence").

17. Walker, 293.

18. Summers, in his appendix on the relationship, formal and informal, between Bacon and Herbert (*Herbert*, 196) remarks that "Herbert followed Bacon's advice in forming his collection of 'wisdom' concerning good morals and good manners, *Outlandish Proverbs*, and he shared the desire of Bacon and the age for a 'practical divinity' which excluded the controversial and the overly speculative." It would be tempting to apply the same comments to the "wisdom" of "The Church Porch."

19. *Catholic Encyclopaedia*, under "Narthex."

20. F. N. Robinson, in his edition of Chaucer's *Works* (Cambridge, Mass., 1957) discusses this custom briefly in connection with the Wife of Bath, and draws attention to G. E. Howard, *A History of Matrimonial Institutions* (Chicago, 1904), I, 291-363.

21. Hall, *Contemplations* 1158: "What the golden Candlesticks, but the illumined understanding, wherein the light of the knowledge of God, and his divine will shineth for ever? What the Tables of Shewbread, but the sanctified memory, which keepeth the bread of life continually?"

22. As a nice example of the ambiguities of the academic process, this poem is used by Walker (299) to prove the opposite, that "by absorbing the archetypal Jewish temple, the individual becomes its reality."

23. Walker, 296, 298.

24. Hutchinson, 543.

25. "The Church Porch," stanza 68.

26. "Passio Discerpta," XIX, *Works*, 408.

STEWART, "Time and *The Temple*"

1. Louis L. Martz, *The Poetry of Meditation* (New Haven, 1954), Ch. 8. Further references to Martz in my text will be to this, the first, edition.

2. John David Walker, "The Architectonics of George Herbert's *The Temple*," *ELH*, XXIX (1962), 289-305.

3. George Herbert, *The Works of George Herbert*, ed. F. E. Hutchinson (Oxford, 1953), p. 26. Further references to *The Temple* in my text will be to this standard edition.

4. Izaak Walton, *The Life of Mr. George Herbert*, bound with *The Lives...* (London, 1950), p. 314.

5. Properly considered, sickness was an occasion for the close scrutiny and humbling of the heart. See William Whately, *The Redemption of Time* (1608), p. 60.

6. Herbert did not think of time in the physical, but in the Augustinian sense, as a mysterious element in human existence. See Book XI of *The Confessions of Saint Augustine*, tr. and ed. Rev. Marcus Dods (Edinburgh, 1876). Roger Matthew's comment may be taken as typical of many seventeenth-century views:

> What saith *David* to our daies? They are saith he, *as a shadow, and thers no abiding.* And what is *Hezekiahs* opinion? As a shepheards tent, of no long stay. A weavers shuttle is of no long race: a pilgrims tabernacle soone flitted.... So is the life in the middest of its fortresse.
>
> How durable is the state of grasse? *We fade away suddenly like the grasse.* What a tales grace? Shortnesse, *Our yeers passe away* as a tale that is told.... Yet, as if these comparisons were yet defective, the Prophet addedth a sleighter manner of similitude, resembling mans life to a dreame, and that when its past.., it was but a thing ... of meere imagination.

The Flight of Time (1634), p. 3. See also Samuel Chew's discussion of time in seventeenth-century literature in *The Pilgrimage of Life* (New Haven, 1962).

7. For a contrary position, see Joseph Summers, *George Herbert: His Religion and Art* (London, 1954), p. 86. Though I am greatly indebted to Professor Summers's analysis of the Temple as the body, I cannot agree that "it was the life of man within [the] Church which formed the principle of organization for Herbert's volume" (p. 87), for it seems to me, rather, that this description applies only to the first two parts of *The Temple*, and especially to "The Church."

8. Cf. "Time" (pp. 122-123) with Aurelian Townshend's "A Dialogue Betwixt Time and a Pilgrim," in *Poems and Masks*, ed. E. K. Chambers (London, 1912), pp. 6-7. For a fine

example of the dial inscriptions to which Herbert's "Time" is related, see Eleanour Rohde, *The Old-World Pleasaunce* (New York, 1925), pp. 33, 172, 179; see also H. Inigo Triggs, *Formal Gardens in England and Scotland* (London, 1902), I, 20: II, 6.

9. For a most helpful analysis of this poem and its background, see Don Cameron Allen, *Image and Meaning* (Baltimore, 1960), Ch. 4.

10. See Frank Manley's "Introduction" to *John Donne: The Anniversaries* (Baltimore, 1963), and Martz, Ch. 6. The Marian theme traced by Allen, Manley, and Martz bears upon the connection between "The Church" and "Church Militant." The Bride who is invited to the Wedding Feast in "Love III" is also described very early in "Church Militant." Mary, the perfect type of the Church, embodied the mystery of the timeless placed in time. Probably Herbert's quinquepartite division of "Church Militant" alludes to the practice of meditating on the mysteries of the Virgin in sequences of five. But "Church Militant" is, rather than a series of meditations on the Virgin, a five-part meditation on the Bride of Christ, the Church:

> Early didst thou arise to plant this vine,
> Which might the more indeare it to be thine.
> Spices come from the East; so did thy Spouse,
> Trimme as the light, sweet as the laden boughs
> Of Noah's shadie vine, chaste as the dove;
> Prepar'd and fitted to receive thy love. (p. 190)

See Martz, pp. 223-226, and Louis Richeome, *The Pilgrime of Loreto*, tr. W. E. (Paris, 1629). Herbert's imagery is drawn from the Song of Songs.

11. *The Psalter of David ... Whereunto is added, Devotions* (1646), p. 285. For an account of the important place reserved for the Psalms at Herbert's beloved Little Gidding, see *The Ferrar Papers*, ed. B. Blackstone (Cambridge, 1938), pp. 12, 33-46, 55-58, 66, 87, 102, esp. pp. 55-58.

12. *The Boke of Psalmes ... With Breife and Apt annotations in the margent* (Geneva, 1559), p. 228.

13. John Calvin, *The Psalmes of Dauid and others, With M. John Caluins Commentaries* (1571), fol. 47ʳ.

14. Calvin, fol. 49.

15. Henry Ainsworth, *Annotations* (1626), p. 180.

16. *The Boke of Psalmes*, p. 357.

CARNES, "The Unity of George Herbert's *The Temple*: A Reconsideration"

1. Rosemond Tuve, *A Reading of George Herbert* (Chicago, 1952).

2. Rosemary Freeman, *English Emblem Books* (London, 1948).

3. Joseph H. Summers, *George Herbert: His Religion and Art* (Cambridge, Mass., 1954).

4. Elizabeth Stambler, "The Unity of Herbert's 'Temple,'" *Cross Currents*, X (1960), 251-66.

5. J. D. Walker, "The Architectonics of George Herbert's *The Temple*," *ELH*, XXIX (1962), 289-307.

6. Thomas Aquinas, *De Veritate*, q. 18, a. i.

7. John Donne, *Devotions Upon Emergent Occasions* (XIX), (Ann Arbor, 1959).

8. Samuel Mather, "To the Reader," in Samuel Stone, *A Congregational Church is a Catholike Visible Church* (London, 1652).

9. George Herbert, *A Priest to the Temple*, ed. F. E. Hutchinson (Oxford, 1941), p. 225.

10. Horace, *Ars Poetica*, Walter Jackson Bate, ed., *Criticism: the Major Texts* (New York, 1952), p. 56.

11. Herbert, *op. cit.*, p. 257.

12. Mary Ellen Rickey, *Utmost Art* (Lexington, 1966), p. 6.

13. Northrop Frye, *The Anatomy of Criticism* (Princeton, 1957), p. 98.

14. *Ibid.*, p. 121.

15. *Ibid.*

16. Quoted in Walker, *op. cit.*, p. 305.

17. Ernst Cassirer, *Language and Myth*, trans. S. Langer (New York, 1946), pp. 32-3.

18. Dietrich Bonhoeffer, *Creation and Fall* (London, 1937), p. 13.

19. Frye, *op. cit.*, p. 121.

ASALS, "The Voice of George Herbert's 'The Church'"

1. Louis Martz, *The Poetry of Meditation* (New Haven, 1962; first published in 1954), p. 273.

2. Both Martz, pp. 273-282, and F. E. Hutchinson in *The Works of George Herbert* (Oxford, 1941) record many of the echoes from the Psalms.

3. *Selections from Ralph Waldo Emerson*, ed. Stephen E. Whicher (Boston, 1960), p. 52.

4. Harold Fisch, *Jerusalem and Albion* (New York, 1964), p. 57.

5. Margaret Bottrall, *George Herbert* (London, 1954), pp. 93-94.

6. Bernard Kneiger, "The Purchase-Sale: Patterns of Business Imagery in the Poetry of George Herbert," *SEL*, VI (1966), 118.

7. *The Prose Works of Sir Philip Sidney*, ed. Albert Feuillerat (Cambridge, 1912), vol. 3, 6-7.

8. George Puttenham, *The Arte of English Poesie*, ed. Gladys Willcock and Alice Walker (Cambridge, 1936), p. 9.

9. Hallett Smith, "English Metrical Psalms in the Sixteenth Century and their Literary Significance," *HLQ*, IX (1946), 255. The quotation is from Lily B. Campbell, *Divine Poetry and Drama in Sixteenth-Century England* (Cambridge, 1959), p. 54. See also Israel Baroway, "The Bible as Poetry in the English Renaissance: An Introduction," *JEGP*, XXXII (1933), 447-480; "The Hebrew Hexameter: A Study in Renaissance Sources and Interpretation," *ELH*, II (1935), 66-91; "'The Lyre of David': A Further Study in Renaissance Interpretation of Biblical Form," *ELH*, VIII (1941), 119-142; and "The Accentual Theory of Hebrew Prosody: A Further Study in Renaissance Interpretation of Biblical Form," *ELH*, XVII (1950), 115-135.

10. George Wither, *A Preparation to the Psalter* (Manchester, 1884), p. 134.

11. Wither, *A Preparation*, p. 140.

12. Ioannis Calvin, *In Librum Psalmorum Commentarius*, ed. A. Tholuck (Berolini, 1836), p. vi.

13. All quotations from Herbert in my text are taken from the standard edition of the *Works*, ed. Hutchinson.

14. *Ennarratio in Psalmum, Pat. Lat.*, vols. 36-37. col. 713.

15. *Pat. Lat.*, col. 167.

16. *Pat. Lat.*, col. 483.

17. *Pat Lat.*, col. 411.

18. *Pat. Lat.*, col. 1804.

19. *Pat. Lat.*, col. 172.

20. *Pat. Lat.*, col. 232.

21. *Pat. Lat.*, col. 219.

22. *Pat. Lat.*, cols. 948-949.

23. *The Sermons of John Donne*, ed. George R. Potter and Evelyn M. Simpson (Berkeley and Los Angeles, 1953), vol. 7, 51.

24. *Pat. Lat.*, col. 409.

25. *Pat. Lat.*, cols. 730-731.

26. *Pat. Lat.*, col 323.

27. Augustine, *Pat. Lat.*, col. 199.

28. *Pat. Lat.*, col. 640.

29. *Pat. Lat.*, col. 713.

30. *Pat. Lat.*, col. 1056.

31. *Pat. Lat.*, col. 1056.

32. *Pat. Lat.*, col. 1085.

33. *Pat. Lat.*, col. 74.

34. Wither, *A Preparation*, pp. 136-137.

35. *Pat Lat.*, col. 38.

36. *Breviarium in Psalmos, Pat. Lat.*, vol. 26, col. 1318.

37. Robert Ellrodt, *Les Poètes Métaphysiques Anglais* (Paris, 1960), vol. 1, 274.

38. *Sermons*, ed. Potter and Simpson, vol. 7, 252.

39. William Chomsky, *Hebrew: The Eternal Language* (Philadelphia, Pa., 1957), pp. 164-165.

40. Chomsky, p. 162.

41. *A Preparation*, p. 117.

42. George Wither, *Psalms of David* (Manchester, 1881), Part I, 14.

43. *Pat. Lat.*, vols. 36-7, col 75.

44. *Sermons*, ed. Potter and Simpson, vol. 6, 39.

45. *Pat Lat.*, col. 123.

46. *Sermons*, ed. Potter and Simpson, vol. 2, 73.

BLAU, "The Poet as Casuist: Herbert's 'Church-Porch'"

An earlier version of this essay was read to the English 1 section of the Midwest M.L.A. at the October 1969 meeting in St. Louis.

1. *Rage for order* (Ann Arbor, 1948), p. 26.

2. For a discussion of the question of Herbert's authorship of this work see F. E. Hutchinson, ed., *The Works of George Herbert* (Oxford, 1945).

3. *The Poetry of Meditation*, 2nd edition (New Haven, 1962), p. 290, and Warren, p. 26.

4. On pp. 290-91 Martz quotes the following passage from the *Imitatio* as a parallel and source for Herbert's intentions in "The Church-Porch":

Weepe and sorowe, that thou art yet so carnall and wordly, so unmortified from thy passions, so full of motions of concupiscences, so unaware, and so evill ordred in thy outward wits, so oft wrapped in vayne phantasies, so muche inclined to outwarde and worldlie thinges, so negligent to inwarde thinges, so redie to laughinge and dissolution, so harde to weepinge and compunction, so readie to easie thinges, and to that that is likinge to the fleshe: so slowe to penance and fervor of spirite, so curious to heare newe thinges, and to see fayre things, so lothe to meeke and abject thinges, so covetous to have muche, so scarse to geve, so glad to holde, so unadvised in speakinge, so incontinent to be still, so evill ordered in maners, so importune in deedes, so greedie upon meat, so deafe to the word of God.

When we look at the full passage in its context in the *Imitatio*, however, we find it beginning with this paragraph:

The priest above all things ought to desire with sovereign reverence and profound meekness of heart, full and firm faith, humble hope and piteous intent to the honour of God to celebrate, take and receive this worthy sacrament, to examine diligently and make clear and open the conscience by true contrition and make confession as far as he hath power, so that thou know nothing that greives thee or bites thy said conscience or lets thee freely to come unto the same daily. [Thomas à Kempis, *Imitation of Christ*, ed. Ernest Rhys (New York, 1910), p. 251.]

5. Martz notes this division of the work. See p. 291.

6. The main differences between Anglican and Roman Catholic casuistry derived from the emphasis in the former on scripture and the individual reason instead of upon authorities, canon law, and the confessional. Anglican casuists also thought of themselves as eminently practical and commonsensical in contrast to their theologically oriented and legalistic Catholic counterparts. For a fuller discussion of their differences see H. R. McAdoo, *The Structure of Caroline Moral Theology* (London, 1949), pp. 79-85.

7. Cited by Walter E. Houghton, *The Formation of Thomas Fuller's Holy and Profane States* (Cambridge, Mass., 1938), pp. 75-76.

8. From "An Advertisement Touching The Controversies of the Church of England," cited by Houghton, p. 72.

9. See I. Breward, "The Significance of William Perkins," *Journal of Religious History*, II (1966), 113-128.

10. See Herbert H. Henson, *Studies in English Religion in The Seventeenth Century* (London, 1903), pp. 171-210.

11. *Works*, p. 230.

12. Ibid., p. 264.

13. Henson, p. 175.

14. Izaak Walton, "The Life of Mr. George Herbert," *The Lives of John Donne, Sir Henry Wotton, Richard Hooker, George Herbert, and Robert Sanderson* (London: Oxford World's Classics, 1927), p. 295.

15. Ibid.

16. *Works*, pp. 232-233.

17. *The First and Second Prayer Books of Edward VI* (London, 1910), p. 390.

CHARLES, "The Williams Manuscript and *The Temple*"

1. The earlier manuscript of Herbert's poems is now preserved at Dr. Williams's Library, Gordon Square, London, where it is catalogued as MS. Jones B 62 — hereafter referred to as W. The Bodleian manuscript, from which the edition of 1633 was probably printed, is catalogued as MS. Tanner 307 — hereafter referred to as *B*. Through the generous cooperation of the authorities of both libraries I have examined the manuscripts at length.

2. *The Metaphysical Poets* (New York, 1936), p. 168.

3. Phyllis Berla Rindler, "George Herbert's *Temple* in the Early Manuscript," (unpubl. diss., Yale, 1960), p. xxxviii.

4. *The Poetry of Meditation* (New Haven, 1954), p. 321.

5. For further discussion of Herbert's use of musical terms, images, and effects, see Joseph H. Summers, *George Herbert: His Religion and Art* (London and New York,

1954); Arnold Stein, *George Herbert's Lyrics* (Baltimore, 1969); and my "George Herbert: Priest, Poet, Musician," *Journal of the Viola da Gamba Society of America*, IV (1967), 27-36.

6. Rindler, pp. 265-267.

7. Summers, p. 89.

8. It need scarcely be added that the copyist, the editor, and the printer effected further changes — whether to suit "house style" or their own vagaries we cannot say. Somewhere in the process the simpler spelling of *W*, closer to Herbert's in his extant English writings, was replaced by the more artificial orthography typical of *B*.

9. Rindler, pp. ix, xxxix.

10. Izaak Walton, *The Life of Mr. George Herbert*, in *The Lives...*, introd. George Saintsbury (London, 1927), p. 315.

11. Walton, p. 314.

12. Bodleian MS. Eng. poet. f. 16, fol. 11. Quoted by permission of the Department of Western Manuscripts.

13. *Enciclopedia della Musica* (Milan, 1964), IV, 23.

14. The interpretation suggested by Gen. 33: 10 is gratitude for a specific crossing achieved with God's help, but with the speaker's sense of unworthiness remaining: "I am not worthy of the least of all thy mercies, which thou hast shewed unto thy servant; for with my staff I passed over this Jordan..." (Herbert's "Posie," "Lesse than the least of all God's mercies," echoes this speech of Jacob before he wrestled with the angel.) Another important crossing of the Jordan is described in Joshua 4.

15. Rindler, pp. 258-268. The Reverend Alexander B. Grosart had no authority for the title he gave these six poems, "Lilies of the Temple," in his edition of the complete works in 1874. Apparently he chose the name as a further variation on *The Temple* to add to those already developed by Christopher Harvey, Richard Crashaw, Henry Vaughan, and Ralph Knevet. The capitals (chapters) of the free-standing brass pillars Jachin and Boaz described in I Kings 7: 13-22 were decorated with pomegranate wreaths surmounted by lilies opening to the heavens, visible therefore not to man, but to God.

16. A most useful study of Herbert's metrics is Albert McHarg Hayes, "Counterpoint in Herbert," *SP*, XXXV (1938), 43-60. See also the more recent work of Mary Ellen Rickey, *Utmost Art* (Lexington, 1966) and of Arnold Stein (mentioned in note 5).

TUVE, "On Herbert's 'Sacrifice'"

1. The present essay was written before the publication of William Empson's "Donne and the Rhetorical Tradition" (this *Review*, Autumn, 1949), in which Mr. Empson takes issue with some of Miss Tuve's interpretations of the Metaphysical poets. — *Editors*.

2. The fact that this poem is related to the *Improperia* is noticed by Rosemary Freeman in a note in her *English Emblem Books*, London, 1948, p. 162. That we had each independently remarked upon this we discovered in a conversation in 1948, when her book was in proof, and a much longer form of this present essay completed in manuscript. In that longer form it will presently make part of a book, treating many more of Herbert's traditional conceits and Christian symbols in this and other poems.

3. From this phrase, the Reproach is often called the *Popule meus*.

4. Empson, p. 294, sees that a medieval tradition in which the Cross was made of the wood of the forbidden tree makes the "joke" "more pointed, and so less odd" — but he does not use what this tradition *meant*, to read the poem with.

5. Empson, p. 282, but less characteristic of the critic who said it than of some others. I wish none of my general strictures laid to his door without my warrant.

HART, "Herbert's *The Collar* Re-Read"

1. Joseph Summers, *George Herbert: His Religion and Art* (London: Chatto & Windus, 1954), p. 90.

2. Summers, p. 91.

3. For these and other examples of Herbert's use of this kind of imagery, see Rosemond Tuve, *A Reading of George Herbert* (Chicago: Univ. of Chicago Press, 1952), pp. 81-87.

4. *The Works of George Herbert*, ed. F. E. Hutchinson (Oxford: Clarendon Press, 1941), p. 531.

5. Helen White, *The Metaphysical Poets* (New York: Macmillan, 1936), p. 183.

6. *The Works of George Herbert*, p. 259.

7. Summers, p. 92.

BROWN and INGOLDSBY, "George Herbert's 'Easter-Wings'"

1. Joan Bennett, *Five Metaphysical Poets* (Cambridge, Eng., 1964), p. 63.

2. J. H. Summers, *George Herbert: His Religion and Art* (London, 1954), pp. 143-145.

3. *Greek Anthology*, in Loeb Classical Library (London, 1919-28), V, 129.

4. Details and copies of pattern poems are found in Margaret Church, "The Pattern Poem," Diss. Radcliffe 1944.

5. Both cherubim and cupids being fair young men; see, e.g., *Annotations upon All the Books of the Old and New Testaments* (2nd ed., 1651), under Ex. xxv.18: "The word Cherub ... is compounded of CHE, that is, AS IT WERE, & RABIN, that is, a boy or young man. Cherubims were figures of appearing Angels, or glorious representations in humane shape, chiefly in the ressemblance of beautiful youth, made with wings."

6. See again *Annotations*, under Mal. iv.2: "And he shall bring in his rays the quickening heat ... health, happiness."

7. Evidently Herbert wanted these two words urgently, for they make one foot too many in his measured line; they are absent in the Williams manuscript.

8. This despite the fact that in the Williams and Bodleian manuscripts the lines are written horizontally. Hutchinson details manuscript variants.

9. Another biblical figure sees Christ riding upon the wings of the cherubim, on the wind, as in Ps. xviii.10; there are also the more complex Chaldean hieroglyphs of Ezek. i and x.

10. Grierson assumed Herbert was referring to the Cambridge Spenserians (*Metaphysical Lyrics and Poems*, Oxford, 1921, p. 230); Hutchinson (p. 495) suggested, equally parochially, the school of Donne. See also R. Tuve, *A Reading of George Herbert* (London, 1952), p. 185.

11. To such a vision Herbert does not pretend, of course, except in the diffident wit of "Love" (III), where part of the irony derives from the fact that he is paraphrasing the Exhortation provided for the priest in the communion service of *BCP* to be read to "the people negligent to come to the holy Communion." In "Love" the pastor submits himself to the rebukes of this Exhortation to his flock.

12. Beside the Greek sense of priestly initiation we must also set the Hebraic rites of purification ("sprinkling") and the protective veil before the *sanctum sanctorum* in the temple; see the sensible discussion of Herbert's use of these figures for Christian baptism in Annabel M. Endicott, "The Structure of George Herbert's *Temple:* A Reconsideration," *UTQ*, XXXIV (1965), 226-237.

13. Bennett, p. 63.

CLARK, " 'Lord in Thee the *Beauty* Lies in the *Discovery*': 'Love Unknown' and Reading Herbert"

1. Chicago, 1952. A brief, lucid history and evaluation of typological exegesis is that of Victor Harris, "Allegory to Analogy in the Interpretation of the Scriptures during the Middle Ages and the Renaissance," *PQ*, 45 (1966), 1-23; an extensive bibliography has been compiled under the direction of Sacvan Bercovitch in supplements to *EAL*, 5, No. 2 (1970), 1-71, and 6, No. 2 (1971), 1-80.

2. See respectively Rosemary Freeman's *English Emblem Books* (London, 1948), especially pp. 164-67 of the Herbert chapter; Louis Martz's *The Poetry of Meditation*, rev. ed. (New Haven, 1962), especially pp. 306-09; Robert L. Montgomery, Jr.'s "The Province of Allegory in George Herbert's Verse," *TSLL*, 1 (1960), 457-72, especially pp. 465-69; both Rosalie L. Colie's *Paradoxia Epidemica* (Princeton, 1966), pp. 190-215, and Valerie Carnes's "The Unity of George Herbert's *The Temple:* A Reconsideration," *ELH*, 35 (1968), 505-26; Helen Vendler's "The Re-invented Poem: George Herbert's Alternatives," in *Forms of Lyric*, ed. Reuben A. Brower (New York, 1970), pp. 19-45; Stanley E. Fish's "Letting Go: The Reader in Herbert's Poetry," *ELH*, 37 (1970), 475-94.

3. My theory differs from Joseph H. Summers' *George Herbert; his Religion and his Art* (Cambridge, Mass., 1954), pp. 80-81, in its emphases on Herbert's central typological pattern, on Herbert's sense of the persona as (not like) a type, and on ironic tensions between the persona's and our readings.

4. Apparently Summers first noticed the parallels, pp. 236-37.

5. I quote *The Works of George Herbert*, ed. F. E. Hutchinson (Oxford, 1941).

6. See Tuve, pp. 113-17; Summers, pp. 126-28; and Mary Ellen Rickey, *Utmost Art* (Lexington, 1966), pp. 156-57. See also related eucharistic poems such as "The H. Communion," "Conscience," "The Collar," "The Invitation," "The Banquet," and "Love (III)."

7. See such acknowledgments as Hutchinson's notes to "Justice (II)" and such examples as the new "sons of Abraham" in "The Jews."

8. *Clavis Bibliorum* (London, 1648), pp. 50, 51.

9. In *George Herbert's Lyrics* (Baltimore, 1968), p. 121, Arnold Stein focusses on the significant personal test and affirmation beyond the typology recognized by Summers, p. 80.

10. See Heather Asals, "The Voice of George Herbert's 'The Church,' " *ELH*, 36 (1969), 511-28.

11. See Martz, pp. 179-93 (his suggestion of Greene appears on p. 308); Elizabeth Stambler, "The Unity of Herbert's 'Temple,' " *Cross Currents*, 10 (1960), 251-66; Rosemary Freeman, "Parody as a Literary Form: George Herbert and Wilfred Owen," *EIC*, 13 (1963), 307-22.

12. Summers first suggested the parallel, p. 236.

13. The handiest guides to Reformation and seventeenth-century Protestant biblical commentators are the compendia gathered in the mid- and latter-seventeenth century by Matthew Poole and John Pearson (I follow Poole's *Synopsis Criticorum*, 5 vols. [London, 1669-76] and Pearson's *Critici Sacri*, 8 vols. [Amsterdam, 1698]); that to Catholic biblical commentators from the fathers is the series compiled by Cornelius à Lapide during the early seventeenth century (I follow the Lyons, 1782 *Commentaria*).

14. I cite the first (London, 1627) edition. To recall widespread use of typology in the period I will usually support my case with commentators and popularizers.

15. See also "The Church-porch" (415-17), "The Church-floore," "Businesse" (4-14), "The Storm," "Artillerie" (19-20), "Praise (III)," and "Grief." The excruciating pain attending such self-purgations is best expressed in the pruning necessary to a bearing tree of life in "Paradise."

16. See Richard Day, *A Booke of Christian Prayers* (London, 1579), p. 16; see also the *Biblia Pauperum* and the Good Friday service.

17. See also 245-47.

18. Such acknowledgments extend from the opening of "Perirrhanterium" through "H. Baptisme (I)" to "Love" in the Williams MS (7-12).

19. Note the similar point of "Longing" (26).

20. See also "The Starre" and the second and third stanzas of "The Priesthood."

21. *Annotations upon All the Books of the Old and New Testament*, 3rd ed. enl., 2 vols. (London, 1657).

22. See "The Sacrifice" (29-31).

23. See also "The Thanksgiving" (13) and "The Collar" (7-9).

24. *Moses Unvailed* (London, 1620), p. 4.

25. Cf. Fredson Bowers, "Herbert's Sequential Imagery: 'The Temper,'" *MP*, 59 (1962), 202-13.

26. See also "Employment (I)" and the first two stanzas of "Perseverance" from the Williams MS.

27. See "The Priesthood."

28. See also "Ungratefulnesse" (25-27), "Gratefulnesse," "Praise (II)" (11-12); note also the offering of "Employment (II)" (21-25).

29. See particularly "The Sinner," "Nature," "The Church-floore," and most, "Jesu."

30. See also the end of "Nature," "Jesu," "The Starre" (5-6), the latter half of "Decay," "Sion," "Praise (II)" (19-20).

31. See "Content" (33-34), "Vanitie (I)" (22-26), "Longing" (8-9) for examples.

32. A similar general point is made by Fish; I cannot agree that Christ's completion and the Christian's reception of grace negate for Herbert the Christian's individuality and ultimately his responsibility.

33. In "Obedience," his most extended and interesting poem posed in contractual terms, Herbert reverses the roles to achieve the same effect; the persona deeds his bleeding heart to God only to find that Christ's previous sacrificial purchase of the heart saves him.

34. See Bernard Knieger's "The Purchase-Sale: Patterns of Business Imagery in the Poetry of George Herbert," *SEL*, 6 (1966), 111-24, and such examples as "The Starre" (6-7), "Dialogue" (9-16), "The Bag" (24), and *Lucus IV* "In Simonem Magnum" (1-4).

35. See R. L. Montgomery, Jr.'s discussion and list of this considerable group, including most of Herbert's best-known poems.

36. See particularly "Submission," "The Crosse," "Love (III)," and the "Affliction" series, as well as Herbert's frequent puns on the combat *topos*, as in "The Temper (I)" (13-14) or the last stanzas of "Artillerie."

37. *The Arte of English Poesie by George Puttenham*, ed. Gladys Doidge Willcock and Alice Walker (Cambridge, 1936), p. 215.

38. See particularly the conclusions of "Redemption," "Jordan (II)," and "The Collar"; see also the opening of "Artillerie."

39. See the frame of "Faith," the last half of "Love. II," "Mattens" (16-20), the opening of "Even-song," the center of "Ungratefulnesse," the whole of "Submission," "The Banquet" (37-48), and the enlightened union concluding "Love (III)."

40. This identification has been suggested before by Martz, p. 309.

ENDE, "George Herbert's 'The Sonne': In Defense of the English Language"

1. Herbert in this poem takes his place among a great number of Englishmen who were at the time deeply interested in and greatly concerned with the English language, its virtues and its inadequacies. For a full account of the interest and concern see Richard Foster Jones, *The Triumph of the English Language: A Survey of Opinions Concerning the Vernacular from the Introduction of Printing to the Restoration* (Stanford, 1953).

2. Father Walter J. Ong, "Tudor Writings on Rhetoric," *Studies in the Renaissance,* XV (1968), 50.

3. Ong, "Writings," p. 50.

4. George Herbert, "The Sonne," *The Works of George Herbert*, ed. F. E. Hutchinson (Oxford, 1953), pp. 167-168.

5. T. S. Eliot, *George Herbert* (London, 1962), p. 13.

6. Harry Levin, "English Literature of the Renaissance," *The Renaissance*, ed. Tinsley Helton (Madison, 1964), p. 146.

7. See Jones, *The Triumph of the Language*, pp. 68-141.

8. Herbert, *Works*, p. 33.

9. William Empson, *Seven Types of Ambiguity* (New York, 1955), pp. 262-263.

10. Rosemond Tuve, *A Reading of George Herbert* (Chicago, 1952), pp. 81-96.

11. Anonymous, *Pearl*, ed. E. V. Gordon (Oxford, 1953), p. 2, ll. 28-32.

12. William Keeling, ed., *Liturgiae Britannicae*, or the Several Editions of The Book of Common Prayer of The Church of England,... Arranged to Shew Their Respective Variations (London, 1851), pp. 104, 106. The text of the passage quoted is that of the Prayer Book authorized by James I in 1604.

MOLLENKOTT, "George Herbert's 'Redemption'"

1. John R. Mulder, *The Temple of the Mind* (New York, 1969), pp. 76-77.

2. Arnold Stein, *George Herbert's Lyrics* (Baltimore, 1968), pp. 123 and 185.

3. F. E. Hutchinson, ed., *The Works of George Herbert* (Oxford, 1941), p. 40.

4. Mulder, p. 77.

5. "Brief Notes on Valdesso's Consideration," in *The Works of George Herbert*, ed., F. E. Hutchinson (Oxford, 1941), p. 308.

6. *The Geneva Bible: A facsimile of the 1560 edition*, Intro., Lloyd E. Berry (Madison, Wis., 1969).

7. F. E. Hutchinson, "George Herbert," *Seventeenth-Century Studies Presented to Sir Herbert Grierson* (Oxford, 1938), p. 156.

HARMAN, "George Herbert's 'Affliction (I)': The Limits of Representation"

1. "The Voice of the Shuttle: Langauge from the Point of View of Literature," in *Beyond Formalism: Literary Essays 1958-1960* (New Haven and London: Yale University Press, 1970), p. 348.

2. *The Poetry of Meditation: A Study of English Religious Literature* (New Haven and London: Yale University Press, 1970), p. 84.

3. *The Poetry of Grace: Reformation Themes and Structures in Seventeenth Century Poetry* (New Haven and London: Yale University Press, 1970), p. 84.

4. "Herbert and Caritas," in *Essays of Rosemond Tuve: Spenser, Herbert, Milton*, ed. Thomas P. Roche (Princeton: Princeton University Press, 1970), p. 181., n. 9.

5. *Ibid.*

6. Though reluctant to posit a consistent formula, Arnold Stein, in a statement akin to Tuve's, suggested that there would indeed be something "inappropriate" in "deliberately

playing aesthetic games with fictions," and added that the concealed "truth which [Herbert] intends to reveal must work its way through natural and personal obstructions." Cf. *George Herbert's Lyrics* (Baltimore: The Johns Hopkins University Press, 1968), p. 12.

7. *Self-Consuming Artifacts: The Experience of Seventeenth-Century Literature* (Berkeley: University of California Press, 1972), p. 158.

8. Cf. Fish, p. 2: "These cleansing powers [of the "good physician"] are also given by God to his minister, who, in the words of Milton, 'beginning at the prime causes and roots of the disease sends in ... divine ingredients of the most cleansing power ... to purge the mind ... a kind of saving by undoing.'"

9. *The Poetry of George Herbert* (Cambridge, Mass. and London: Harvard University Press, 1975), p. 285, n. 13.

10. *Ibid.*, p. 291, n. 4.

11. For other examples of reversal or collapse see "Sinne (I)," "Miserie," "The Reprisall," "The Pearl" "Artillerie," "The Temper (I)." For examples of poems with "resurrected" endings see, especially, "The Collar," "The Holdfast," and "The Pilgrimage."

12. *The Works of George Herbert*, ed. F. E. Hutchinson (London: Oxford University Press, 1941). All citations are to this edition.

13. *OED*, "Entice." The meaning of the word records both innocent and duplicitous intentions.

14. *OED*, "Cross-bias."

15. Cf. M. H. Abrams, *Natural Supernaturalism: Tradition and Revolution in Romantic Literature* (New York: Norton Library, 1973), p. 36: "The plot of history has a hidden author who is also its director and guarantor of things to come. God planned it all before it began, and He controls its details, under the seemingly casual or causal relations of events, by His invisible Providence. The inherent distinction in the Biblical account between the apparent order and connections of things, available to human inspection, and the prepotent but hidden order of Providence, soon emerged in theology as the distinction between secondary causes and the first cause, which is the invisible and immutable working of the purpose of God."

16. Stein, p. 124.

17. "The Storyteller: Reflections on the Works of Nikolai Leskov," in *Illuminations* (New York: Schocken Books, 1973), p. 100.

18. *Ibid.*

19. Fish, p. 158.

20. "Molestation and Authority," in *Aspects of Narrative: Selected Papers from the English Institute*, ed. J. Hillis Miller (London and New York: Columbia University Press, 1971), p. 193.

21. *The Human Condition* (Chicago and London: University of Chicago Press, 1958), p. 193.

22. Benjamin, p. 94.

23. *Ibid.*

24. "I. A. Richards and the Dream of Communication," in *The Fate of Reading & Other Essays* (New Haven and London: Yale University Press, 1975), p. 36.

25. Hartman, "The Voice of the Shuttle," p. 348.

26. Vendler, p. 45.

27. "The Avoidance of Love: A Reading of *King Lear*," in *Must We Mean What We Say?: A Book of Essays* (New York: Charles Schribner's Sons, 1969), p. 284.

28. *Ibid.*, p. 325.

29. *Ibid.*, p. 324.

30. Geoffrey Hartman, "Christopher Smart's *Magnificat:* Towards a Theory of Representation," in *The Fate of Reading*, p. 97.

31. See Robert Scholes & Robert Kellogg, *The Nature of Narrative* (London, Oxford, New York: Oxford University Press, 1966), p. 215: "Inevitably, once an autobiography continues beyond the moment in which the author comes to terms with his vocation, its interest turns outward and its form becomes open ended." This, of course, is precisely what happens from ll. 55-66 of "Affliction (I)." While the obligation to continue beyond the natural resolution is, in Herbert, an obligation imposed by God, it bears a direct relation to the open ended autobiography: both return to life-in-the-making where representation is at best difficult, meanings uncertain, fictional coherence gone.

32. "Conditions et limites de l'autobiographie," in *Formen der Selbstaarstellung: Analakten zu einer Geschichte des literarischen Selbstportraits*, ed. Maurice Boucher (Berlin: Dunker and Humbolt, 1956), p. 107. Translations from the French are mine.

33. *Ibid.*, p. 106.

34. *Ibid.*, p. 107.

35. *Ibid.*, p. 113.

36. *British Autobiography in the Seventeenth Century* (London: Routledge and Kegan Paul; New York: Columbia University Press, 1969), p. 15.

37. Scholes & Kellogg, p. 215.

38. *Design and Truth in Autobiography* (Cambridge, Mass: Harvard University Press, 1960), p. 9.

39. Gusdorf, p. 111.

40. *Versions of the Self: Studies in Autobiography from John Bunyan to John Stuart Mill* (New York & London: Basic Books, 1966), p. 11.

41. Gusdorf, p. 117.

42. *Ibid.*, p. 117.

43. *Ibid.*, p. 110.

44. *Ibid.*, p. 110.

45. Delany, p. 108.

KELLIHER, "The Latin Poetry of George Herbert"

All quotations from Herbert's poetry and prose are taken from Canon F. E. Hutchinson's edition of the *Works of George Herbert*, Oxford, 1941 (henceforth referred to as *Works*). I have, however, followed modern practice as regards *v* and *u*, *j* and *i*, and have dropped diacritical accents. Free-verse renderings of all the Latin and Greek verses printed there are to be found in *The Latin Poetry of George Herbert*, translated by Mark McClosky and Paul R. Murphy, Ohio, 1965. Edmund Blunden has published verse-translations of several epigrams in 'George Herbert's Latin Poems', *Essays and Studies*, XIX (1934), 29-39.

1. Two sets of Latin verses dedicated to Frederick, Elector Palatine were first published by Leicester Bradner in 'New poems by George Herbert: the Cambridge Latin gratulatory anthology of 1613', *Renaissance News*, XV (1962), 208-11.

2. Autograph presentation-copy to Laud, now British Museum MS. Harley 3496, ff. 79-89.

3. Compare Donne's 'The Crosse', l. 19.

4. 'Obsequies to the Lord Harington', ll. 35-8, dating from 1614. The term *perspicillum*, first recorded in 1610, was used by Bacon in *Novum Organum*, 1620, Bk II, 39. See also *Works*, note on p. 602.

5. *The Complete Works of George Herbert*, ed. A. B. Grosart, vol. II, 1875, pp. li-lxiii.

6. See Book I, *passim*. Other collections that Herbert may have known include Bernard van Bauhuysen's *Epigrammatum selectorum libri V*, Antwerp, 1616, and Bauduin Cabilliau's *Epigrammata selecta*, Antwerp, 1620.

7. *Epigrammatum Joannis Owen ... libri decem*, Leipzig, 1615, Bk III, epigram 121.

8. Chapter XXVII (*Works*, p. 267).

9. Compare a later English poem, Marvell's 'Damon the Mower', l. 80.

10. 'Clarus Bonarscius', *Amphitheatrum Honoris*, Antwerp, 1605, pp. 373-4. The poem was translated and its doctrine and diction violently attacked by William Crashaw in *The Jesuites Gospel*, 1610.

11. *Poemata*, Paris, 1620, p. 71: and 2nd edn, Paris, 1623, pp. 60-1. Quotations are taken from the latter.

12. *Les Œuvres Poétique de Baudri de Bourgueil*, ed. Phyllis Abrahams, Paris, 1926, p. 182, no. 187.

13. 'The Country Parson', Chapter IV (*Works*, p. 228).

14. Chetham Library MS. Mun. A.3.48, first printed by G. M. Story, 'George Herbert's *Inventa Bellica*: a new manuscript', *Modern Philology*, LIX (1962), 270-2.

15. *De Augmentis*, Bk IX (*Works of Francis Bacon*, ed. J. Spedding, vol. 1, 1857, p. 830; vol. V, 1858, p. 122).

16. For a full discussion of Herbert's epigrams and Donne's elegiacs on the subject see *The Divine Poems of John Donne*, ed. Helen Gardner, Oxford, 1952, Appendix G, pp. 138-47.

17. Letter III (*Works*, p. 364).

18. John Aubrey's *Brief Lives*, ed. Andrew Clark, Oxford, 1898, vol. 1, p. 309.

19. *Works*, p. xxxiii.

20. See A. B. Chambers, '"I was but an inverted tree": notes toward the history of an idea', *Studies in the Renaissance*, VIII (1961), 291-9.

21. For example Bauduin Cabilliau, *Magdalena*, Antwerp, 1625, *passim*.

22. Bodleian MS. Aubrey 2, ff. 53-9.

23. Henry Hallam, *Introduction to the Literature of Europe in the Fifteenth, Sixteenth and Seventeenth Centuries*, vol. 1, 1837, p. 596.

24. *Ibid.*, p. 268.

25. See *Passio* XV, XIX and *M.M.S.* VI; *Passio* V, VII, XIII, *Lucus* XVII and *M.M.S.* V; *Lucus* XIV and *In Sacram Anchoram*, iambic trimeters.

26. Thomas Tenison, *Baconiana*, 1679, p. 26 (quoted by Joseph Summers, *George Herbert: His Religion and Art*, 1954, p. 97).

THE POETRY OF GEORGE HERBERT:
A SELECTIVE BIBLIOGRAPHY
OF MODERN CRITICISM

For a fully annotated and comprehensive bibliography of modern criticism of Herbert's poetry and prose, the reader is advised to consult John R. Roberts, *George Herbert: An Annotated Bibliography of Modern Criticism, 1905-1974* (Columbia: University of Missouri Press, 1978) which contains eight hundred items. More recent studies are listed in the annual bibliography of the Modern Language Association (*PMLA*).

Additional Bibliographies

Allison, A. F. *Four Metaphysical Poets: George Herbert, Richard Crashaw, Henry Vaughan, Andrew Marvell: A Bibliographical Catalogue of Early Editions of their Poetry and Prose (To the end of the 17th Century).* Pall Mall Bibliographies, No. 3. Folkestone & London: Dawsons of Pall Mall, 1973.
Tannenbaum, Samuel A. and Dorothy R. *George Herbert: A Concise Bibliography.* Elizabethan Bibliographies, No. 35. New York: Samuel A. Tannenbaum, 1946.

Concordance

A Concordance to the Complete Writings of George Herbert, compiled by Mario A. Di Cesare and Rigo Mignani. Ithaca and London: Cornell University Press, 1977.

Major Texts

The Works of George Herbert. Edited with a commentary by F. E. Hutchinson. Oxford: Clarendon Press, 1941. rev. ed., 1945. Reprint, 1964.
The English Poems of George Herbert, ed. C. A. Patrides. London: J. M. Dent & Sons, Ltd., 1974; Totowa, N.J.: Rowman and Littlefield, 1975.

The Latin Poetry of George Herbert: A Bilingual Edition. Translated by
    Mark McCloskey and Paul R. Murphy. Athens, Ohio: Ohio
    University Press, 1965.
The Poems of George Herbert. With an introduction by Helen Gardner.
    The World Classics, No. 109. 2d ed., London, New York,
    Toronto: Oxford University Press, 1961. Reprinted many times.

Biographical Studies

Charles, Amy M. *A Life of George Herbert.* Ithaca and London:
    Cornell University Press, 1977.
Chute, Marchette. *Two Gentle Men: The Lives of George Herbert and
    Robert Herrick.* New York: E. P. Dutton & Co., 1959. Reprint,
    1960.
Hyde, A. G. *George Herbert and His Times.* New York: G. P. Putnam's
    Sons; London: Methuen & Co., 1906.
Novarr, David. *The Making of Walton's Lives.* Cornell Studies in
    English, ed. M. H. Abrams, Francis E. Mineka, and William M.
    Sale, Jr., 41. Ithaca: Cornell University Press, 1958.

Critical Studies

Allen, Don Cameron. *Image and Meaning: Metaphoric Traditions in
    Renaissance Poetry.* Baltimore: John Hopkins University press,
    1960. Revised and enlarged ed., 1968.
Alvarez, A. *The School of Donne.* London: Chatto and Windus, 1961.
Beer, Patricia. *An Introduction to the Metaphysical Poets.* London and
    Basingstoke: The Macmillan Press, Ltd.; Totowa, N.J.: Rowman
    and Littlefield, 1972.
Bennett, Joan. *Five Metaphysical Poets: Donne, Herbert, Vaughan,
    Crashaw, Marvell.* Cambridge: University Press, 1963.
Bottrall, Margaret. *George Herbert.* London: John Murray, 1954.
    Reprint, 1971.
Bradbury, Malcolm and David Palmer, eds. *Metaphysical Poetry.*
    Stratford-Upon-Avon Studies, 11. New York: St. Martin's Press;
    London: Edward Arnold, 1970.
Bradner, Leicester. *Musae Anglicanae: A History of Anglo-Latin Poetry,
    1500-1925.* New York: Modern Language Assn. of America;
    London: Oxford University Press, 1940.
Bush, Douglas. *English Literature in the Earlier Seventeenth Century,
    1600-1660.* Oxford: Clarendon Press, 1945. rev. ed., 1962. (Paper-

back edition without bibliography and chronological charts, 1973).

Carrive, Lucien. *La Poésie religieuse anglaise entre 1625 et 1640: Contributions à l'étude de la sensibilité religieuse à l'âge d'or de l'anglicanisme.* Vol. I. Caen: Assoc. des Pubs. de la Faculté des Lettres et Sciences Humaines de l'Université de Caen, 1972.

Cohen, J. M. *The Baroque Lyric.* London: Hutchinson University Library, 1963.

Colie, Rosalie L. *Paradoxia Epidemica: The Renaissance Tradition of Paradox.* Princeton: Princeton University Press, 1966. Reprint, Hamden, Conn.: The Shoe String Press, Inc., 1976.

―――. "Small Forms: *Multo in Parvo,*" in *The Resources of Kind-Genre Theory in The Renaissance,* ed. Barbara K. Lewalski. Berkeley, Los Angeles, London: University of California Press, 1973.

Cruttwell, Patrick. *The Shakespearean Moment and Its Place in the Poetry of the 17th Century.* London: Chatto and Windus, Ltd., 1954. Reprint, 1960.

Denonain, Jean-Jacques. *Thèmes et formes de la poésie "métaphysique": Étude d'un aspect de la littérature anglaise au dix-septième siècle.* Publication de la faculté des lettres d'Alger, 18. Paris: Presses universitaires de France, 1956.

Duncan, Joseph. *The Revival of Metaphysical Poetry: The History of a Style, 1800 to the Present.* Minneapolis: University of Minnesota Press, 1959.

Ellrodt, Robert. *L'Inspiration personnelle et l'esprit du temps chez les poètes métaphysiques anglais.* Paris: José Corti. 2 parts in 3 vols., 1960. Parts I (vols. 1 & 2): 2d ed. (with new bibliography), 1973.

Eliot, T. S. *George Herbert.* Writers and Their Works, No. 152. London: Longmans, Green and Co., Ltd., 1962. Reprint, American ed., 1964.

Empson, William. *Seven Types of Ambiguity.* London: Chatto and Windus, 1930. 2d ed., 1947; 3rd ed., 1953.

England, Martha Winburn and John Sparrow. *Hymns Unbidden: Donne, Herbert, Blake, Emily Dickinson and the Hymnographers.* New York: New York Public Library, 1966.

Esch, Arno. *Englische Religiöse Lyrik des 17. Jahrhunderts: Studien zu Donne, Herbert, Crashaw, Vaughan.* Buchreihe der Anglia Zeitscrift für englische Philologie, 5. Tübingen: Max Niemeyer, 1955.

Festugière, A. J., O. P. *George Herbert, poète, saint, anglican (1593-1633)*. Études de théologie et d'histoire de la spiritualité, 18. Paris: Librarie philosophique J. Vrin, 1971.

Fisch, Harold. *Jerusalem and Albion: The Hebraic Factor in Seventeenth-Century Literature*. New York: Schocken Books, 1964.

Fish, Stanley E. *The Living Temple: George Herbert and Cathechizing*. Berkeley, Los Angeles, London: University of California Press, 1978.

―――― . *Self-Consuming Artifacts: The Experience of Seventeenth-Century Literature*. Berkeley, Los Angeles, London: University of California Press, 1972.

Ford, Boris, ed. *From Donne to Marvell*. A Guide to English Literature, 3. Pelican Books. London and Baltimore: Penguin Books, 1965. Reprinted several times (with minor revisions).

Freeman, Rosemary. *English Emblem Books*. London: Chatto and Windus, 1948. Reprint, 1967.

Freer, Coburn. *Music for a King: George Herbert's Style and the Metrical Psalms*. Baltimore and London: The John Hopkins University Press, 1972.

Gamberini, Spartaco. *Poeti Metafisici e Cavalieri in Inghilterra*. Biblioteca dell' «Archivium Romanicum»: Serie I: Storia-Letteratura-Paleografia, vol. 60. Florence: Leo S. Olschki, 1959.

Gardner, Helen. *Religion and Literature*. New York: Oxford University Press, 1971.

Gorlier, Claudio. *La Poesia metafisica inglese*. Biblioteca di studi inglesi e americani, 1. Milano: La Goliardica, 1968.

Grant, Patrick. *The Transformation of Sin: Studies in Donne, Herbert, Vaughan, and Traherne*. Montreal and London: McGill-Queen's University Press; Amherst: University of Massachusetts Press, 1974.

Grierson, Herbert J. C., ed. *Metaphysical Lyrics & Poems of The Seventeenth Century: Donne to Butler*. Selected and edited, with an essay by Herbert J. C. Grierson. Oxford: Clarendon Press, 1921. Reprinted many times.

Halewood, William H. *The Poetry of Grace: Reformation Themes and Structures in English Seventeenth-Century Poetry*. New Haven and London: Yale University Press, 1970.

Higgins, Dick. *George Herbert's Pattern Poems in Their Tradition*. West Glover, Vermont and New York: Unpublished Editions, 1977.

Hollander, John. *The Untuning of the Sky: Ideas of Music in English Poetry, 1500-1700*. Princeton: Princeton University Press, 1961. Reprint, 1970.

Hunter, Jim. *The Metaphysical Poets*. Literature in Perspective. London: Evans Brothers Limited, 1965.

Husain, Itrat. *The Mystical Element in the Metaphysical Poets of the Seventeenth Century*. With a Foreword by Evelyn Underhill. Edinburgh and London: Oliver and Boyd, 1948.

Hutchinson, F. E. "George Herbert," in *Seventeenth Century Studies Presented to Sir Herbert Grierson*, pp. 148-60. Oxford: Clarendon Press, 1938. Reprint, 1967.

Jonas, Leah. *The Divine Science: The Aesthetic of Some Representative Seventeenth-Century English Poets*. Columbia University Studies in English and Comparative Literature, No. 151. New York: Columbia University Press, 1940.

Knights, L. C. "George Herbert." *Scrutiny*, 12 (1944), 171-86. Reprinted in *Explorations: Essays in Criticism Mainly on the Literature of the Seventeenth Century*. London: Chatto and Windus, 1946. First Am. ed., 1947.

Leishman, J. B. *The Metaphysical Poets: Donne, Herbert, Vaughan, Traherne*. Oxford: Clarendon Press, 1934. Reprint, 1962, 1963.

Mahood, M. M. *Poetry and Humanism*. New Haven: Yale University Press, 1950. Reprint 1967, 1970.

Martz, Louis L. *The Poetry of Meditation: A Study in English Religious Literature of the Seventeenth Century*. Yale Studies in English, 125. New Haven: Yale University Press, 1954. Rev. ed., 1962.

Miner, Earl, ed. *Illustrious Evidence: Approaches to English Literature of the Early Seventeenth Century*. Berkeley, Los Angeles, London: University of California Press, 1975.

Miner, Earl. *The Metaphysical Mode from Donne to Cowley*. Princeton: Princeton University Press, 1969.

Mourgues, Odette de. *Metaphysical Baroque & Précieux Poetry*. Oxford: Clarendon Press, 1953.

Mulder, John R. *The Temple of the Mind: Education and Literary Taste in Seventeenth-Century England*. Pegasus Backgrounds in English Literature. New York: Pegasus, 1969.

Olivero, Federico. *Lirica Religiosa Inglese*. Turin: S. Lattes & Co., 1936. Rev. ed., 1941.

Peterson, Douglas. *The English Lyric from Wyatt to Donne: A History of the Plain and Eloquent Styles.* Princeton: Princeton University Press, 1967.

Poggi, Valentina. *George Herbert.* Testi e saggi di letterature moderne, 10. Bologna: Casa Editrice Prof. Riccardo Pàtron, 1967.

Rickey, Mary Ellen. *Utmost Art: Complexity in the Verse of George Herbert.* Lexington: University of Kentucky Press, 1966.

Ross, Malcolm Mackenzie. *Poetry and Dogma: The Transformation of Eucharistic Symbols in Seventeenth Century English Poetry.* New Brunswick: Rutgers University Press, 1954.

Stein, Arnold. *George Herbert's Lyrics.* Baltimore: Johns Hopkins University Press, 1968.

Stewart, Stanley. *The Enclosed Garden: The Tradition and the Image in Seventeenth-Century Poetry.* Madison, Milwaukee, London: University of Wisconsin Press, 1966.

Summers, Joseph H. *George Herbert: His Religion and Art.* Cambridge, Mass.: Harvard University Press; London: Chatto and Windus, 1954. Reprint, 1968.

_____ . *The Heirs of Donne and Jonson.* New York and London: Oxford University Press, 1970.

Swardson, H. R. *Poetry and the Fountain of Light: Observations on the Conflict between Christian and Classical Traditions in Seventeenth-Century Poetry.* Columbia: University of Missouri Press; London: G. Allen & Unwin, 1962.

Taylor, Mark. *The Soul in Paraphrase: George Herbert's Poetics.* De Proprietatibus Litterarum: Series Practica, 92. The Hague and Paris: Mouton, 1974.

Thekla, Sister Maria. *George Herbert: Idea and Image.* Buckinghamshire, England: The Greek Orthodox Monastery of the Assumpttion, Filgrave, Newport Pagnell, 1974.

Toliver, Harold E. *Pastoral Forms and Attitudes.* Berkeley, Los Angeles, London: University of California Press, 1971.

Tuve, Rosemond. *Elizabethan and Metaphysical Imagery: Renaissance Poetic and Twentieth-Century Critics.* Chicago: University of Chicago Press, 1947. Reprinted, 1961.

_____ . *Essays by Rosemond Tuve,* ed. Thomas P. Roche, Jr. Princeton: Princeton University Press, 1970.

_____ . *A Reading of George Herbert.* Chicago: University of Chicago Press; London: Faber and Faber; Toronto: W. J. Gage & Co., 1952. Reprint 1965.

Vendler, Helen. *The Poetry of George Herbert.* Cambridge, Mass.: Harvard University Press, 1975.

Wanamaker, Melissa C. *Discordia Concors: The Wit of Metaphysical Poetry*. Port Washington, N.Y.: Kennikat, 1975.

Warnke, Frank J. *European Metaphysical Poetry*. The Elizabethan Club Series, 2. New Haven and London: Yale University Press, 1961.

―――. *Versions of the Baroque: European Literature in the Seventeenth Century*. New Haven and London: Yale University Press, 1972.

Warren, Austin. *Rage for Order: Essays in Criticism*. Chicago: University of Chicago Press, 1948. Reprint 1959.

White, Helen C. *The Metaphysical Poets: A Study in Religious Experience*. New York: Macmillan Co., 1936. Reprint, 1962.

Williamson, George. *The Donne Tradition: A Study in English Poetry from Donne to the Death of Cowley*. Cambridge, Mass.: Harvard University Press, 1930. Reprint, 1958, 1961.

―――. *Six Metaphysical Poets: A Reader's Guide*. New York: Farrar, Straus and Giroux, 1967.